The Presence of Others

Readings for Critical Thinking and Writing

The Presence of Others

Readings for Critical Thinking and Writing

ANDREA A. LUNSFORD
The Ohio State University

JOHN J. RUSZKIEWICZ
The University of Texas at Austin

ST. MARTIN'S PRESS
New York

Key to Cover Photographs:

(From left to right, top to bottom) Andrea Lunsford, John Ruszkiewicz, P. J. O'Rourke, Camille Paglia, Maxine Hong Kingston, Shelby Steele, Virginia Woolf, Zora Neale Hurston, and Martin Luther King, Jr.

Senior Editor Marilyn Moller
Manuscript Editor John Elliott
Project Editor Kristin Bowen
Art Director Sheree Goodman
Text and Cover Design Anna George
Photo Research Barbara Salz
Production Supervisor Alan Fischer
Editorial Assistant Steven Kutz

For information, write:
St. Martin's Press, Inc.
175 Fifth Avenue
New York, NY 10010

ISBN: 0-312-05677x

Acknowledgments

Maya Angelou. "Champion of the World." From *I Know Why the Caged Bird Sings* by Maya Angelou. Copyright © 1969 by Maya Angelou. Reprinted by permission of Random House, Inc.

Acknowledgments and copyrights are continued at the back of the book on pages 633–36, which constitute an extension of the copyright page.

Preface

"For excellence," writes Hannah Arendt, "the presence of others is always required." Not genius, she tells us, not divine inspiration, not even good old-fashioned hard work, but *others*. In choosing a title for this text, we thought of Arendt's statement, because this book aims to lead students toward excellence in reading and writing, toward excellence in thinking through difficult issues, toward excellence in articulating their own positions on issues and providing good reasons to support those positions. If students can achieve such goals, they can achieve excellence throughout their college careers and, we would wager, well beyond their undergraduate days.

Just as important, however, we wish to demonstrate how true excellence is achieved only in and through the presence of others. Put another way, we believe that no one is excellent all alone. Thus our title, *The Presence of Others*, reflects the assumption that critical thinking and writing always occur in relation to other people's thoughts and words.

Indeed, the thoughts, words, and deeds of others set a context for all our thinking, providing the shoulders we can stand on as we try to reach higher and think better than we ever have before. The ideas and actions of others are part of what some call the unending *conversation* of our lives, the ceaseless chorus of language we hear all around us in advertisements, music, television, and other media; in school; and in our everyday exchanges with those we know and love. As the metaphor of the conversation suggests, other people provide varying perspectives on issues, different "takes" that help us to clarify our own assumptions and provide a sounding board for our ideas; they turn our monologues into dialogues or even polylogues. Multiple perspectives thus characterize this anthology; it is a book of strong voices and challenging views.

Two of these voices belong to us, the editors, John Ruszkiewicz and Andrea Lunsford. Friends of some twenty-two years standing, we studied for the Ph.D together at Ohio State, taught together during these years, and graduated together in 1977. We take very different perspectives on most issues—John's views usually conservative and traditional, Andrea's liberal and feminist. Our varying points of view, and many conversations about our differences, inspired this text, and we aim to highlight, not obscure or mute, our own perspectives. Unlike many (perhaps most) composition anthologies, which present their materials as though they were neutral or unaffected by editorial choices and individual agendas, we make our opinions known and try to tell readers directly why we selected particular readings. We invite them, moreover, to question those choices and challenge our points of view, to consider not only what we have included but also what we have excluded—and why.

Our editorial choices and commentaries will quickly suggest that we often disagree. But disagreement, conflict, and agonism are *not* guiding principles of this book. It is not a tennis match of ideas, one that will yield winners and losers. Rather, we are interested in how we all come to know and to take positions on various issues, how to nurture open and realistic exchanges of ideas. Most important, we want to open this exchange to our readers, both students and instructors. This anthology's success will be measured by how actively readers join in conversation with the voices that speak throughout its pages. In short, if this book were a tennis match, it would be one with no spectators sitting on the sidelines. Everyone would be out on the court.

The Presence of Others aims to open and sustain an animated conversation—among the 74 readings in the text, the editors and students whose commentary appears with the readings, and all the teachers and students we hope will enter the discussion. But this text also aims to do something more: to point up the ways in which all these voices speak from particular perspectives, points of view that may not be stated but that are important in understanding what the writers are saying. This highlighting of perspective begins with profiles of the editors and the student commentators. In them, we each try to say a little about our backgrounds and philosophies, likes and dislikes, and to suggest how they have shaped our work on *The Presence of Others*. Understanding varying perspectives, of course, can only be fully realized by the active participation of our readers: they are the ones who we most hope will join the conversation in these pages—to examine the assumptions underpinning the readings and editorial commentary, to examine their own assumptions, and to articulate their own positions on the issues involved. Throughout, *The Presence of Others* attempts to elicit such participation.

These three key terms—*conversation, perspective, participation*—are all fairly abstract, however. To see how they are made concrete in *The Presence of Others,* let us take a brief look at how the book proceeds.

Two introductory chapters provide strategies *on reading and thinking critically* and on moving *from reading to writing.* The first chapter offers guidelines for analytic and critical reading practices. The second reviews the writing process and offers guidelines for the writing assignments in the book as well as tips on using sources and on working effectively with others.

Each *readings chapter* opens with a page of brief, often provocative quotations from the readings, providing a glimpse of what is to come, setting mental wheels turning, and thus opening the conversation of the chapter. *Chapter introductions* announce the issues raised in each chapter, set a context for discussing them, and close with a set of questions that ask readers to begin to articulate their own ideas about the chapter's central issues.

An initial selection, often a piece of sufficient reputation to be regarded as "canonical," opens the intertextual conversation of each chapter. Subsequent readings represent points of view in dialogue with those voiced in the initial reading—and with one another as well. Although the readings are conversationally and thematically related, they represent a wide range of genres—poems, speeches, oral histories, sermons, prayers, short stories, and personal memoirs as well as essays and articles—and they take a wide range of varying and often competing perspectives. In Chapter 3, for instance, on education, John Henry Newman's *The Idea of a University* rubs conversational shoulders with bell hooks's "Keeping Close to Home: Class and Education," Mike Rose's *Lives on the Boundary,* and Gwendolyn Brooks's "We Real Cool"—and it is richly complicated in the process. In another instance, an excerpt from Robert Bly's *Iron John* runs smack into Joe Bob Briggs's parody, "Get in Touch with Your Ancient Spear." Elsewhere, June Jordan defends Anita Hill against her accusers while Naomi Munson questions Hill's credibility. *Cross-references* throughout lead readers back and forth among the readings, helping them to recognize the lines of conversation across the pages. This spirited conversation will, we hope, draw readers into active participation in the discussion.

Headnotes to each reading provide background information about the selection and its relationship to others in the book, and offer explanations for our editorial choices. Because these headnotes also offer our own strong opinions about the selection, each is signed.

Each selection is followed by *questions* that extend the process of careful reading by asking students first to *question the text,* to probe each selection's assumptions (and those in the editors' headnotes as well); to *make connections* with other readings in the text; and to *join the conversation* by responding to the ideas in the reading, and by articulating their own stances. Each reading includes one or two questions designed for small-group work, which we hope will encourage further participation in the intertextual conversation and make concrete the presence of others.

One selection in each chapter includes our own *annotations and reader responses,* and also those of our student commentators. In addition to offering very different "takes" on the readings, these commentaries are intended to disrupt the static nature of the printed page, inserting new voices and points of view, asking questions, talking back to the readings—and to one another. This book has been designed to allow readers to annotate right along with us.

Each chapter concludes with a list of *other readings.* Rather than wrapping the conversation up, this annotated list is intended to open discussion up to the presence of still others.

The accompanying instructor's manual provides detailed advice for teaching this book, including commentary on each selection, sequenced reading and writing assignments, and a selection of essays and articles regarding the current controversies over the college curriculum.

Acknowledgments

This anthology has changed considerably in the three years since we began exploring its possibilities, primarily because of the presence of many, many others whose perspectives and voices echo in these pages. Of great importance throughout the development process have been the extensive support and ongoing spirited conversation we have received from the St. Martin's staff, and particularly from Kristin Bowen, John Elliott, and Steven Kutz. Nor will we soon forget the afternoon of intense discussion we had in Cincinnati with Ed Tiefenthaler and Ira Warshaw; their experience with teachers, their appreciation of students' needs, and their tough questions served as touchstones for us during a critical stage in this project. We have also enjoyed the extraordinary grace of Marilyn Moller's editorial attention for the entire project; her probing questions provided the best and often only means of confronting our own assumptions, particularly those that we ourselves tend not to notice or examine. This book bears the mark of Marilyn's meticulous thought and care on every page.

In addition to these friends at St. Martin's, we are indebted to many colleagues at our home institutions—especially Carrie Shively Leverenz at The Ohio State University and Ed Madden at The University of Texas at Austin. Carrie assisted in the hunt for the best possible readings and prepared the instructor's manual. This manual we believe to be thoroughly informed by contemporary reading theory as well as by Carrie's practical experience from having taught the materials in this book. Ed searched the libraries for selections and also contributed the poem that concludes Chapter 9. We owe sincere thanks as well to Aneil Rallin, Deneen Shepherd, Heather Graves, and Lori Mathis, who helped us chase down obscure bits of information and responded to many of our student exercises; to Murray Beja, who worked patiently to capture a reasonable photograph of Andrea; to Ted Warren, who did the same for John; and to Andrea's secretary, Lorraine Carlat, the calm force that runs an inordinately busy office, who worked her magic on this project as on all others. John, not having a secretary until the last few weeks of the job, muddled through.

We are particularly grateful to the students who agreed to add their voices to this text: Traci McLin and Stephen Wallenfelsz from Ohio State and Geoff Henley and Helen Liu from The University of Texas.

Our thanks, too, to another student, John Brady Woodson, whose poem "The Basketball's Bounce," would have appeared in a chapter on sports, a chapter reluctantly cut for reasons of length. We salute as well the many other students who have taught us over the years how to be better classroom colleagues. In many subtle ways, their voices are everywhere present in this text.

In addition, we have been extremely fortunate to receive support, advice, and criticism from a number of generous and talented folks. Lisa Ede and Beverly Moss raised the kinds of questions perhaps only the best friends can; Gerald Graff took time to help us consider the premises on which this book rests and to challenge us to articulate those premises more clearly and fully throughout. Mike Rose provided a series of smart and sensitive responses to sample chapters and to our table of contents. James Kinneavy and Michael Gagarin assisted with several translations; David Madsen supplied one essential historical allusion; and James Duban offered advice about several headnotes. Thanks, too, to Dusa Gyllensvard and Alan Gribben for helping us to secure an important permission.

Finally, we have been instructed and guided by extraordinarily astute reviewers, with whom we have been in conversation throughout this project. We thank Rise Axelrod, California State University, San Bernardino; Grant Boswell, Brigham Young University; Muriel Davis, San Diego Mesa College; Ann Doyle, University of Washington; William Harrison, Northern Virginia Community College; Dona Hickey, University of Richmond; David Malone, Northern Illinois University; Lisa McClure, Southern Illinois University, Carbondale; Kenneth Miller, American River College; Christina Murphy, Texas Christian University; Mary Rosner, University of Louisville; William Smith, Western Washington University; Sandra Stephen, Youngstown State University; Pat Sullivan, University of New Hampshire; C. Jan Swearingen, University of Texas at Arlington; and Allysen Todd, Community College of Allegheny County. They have consistently joined in and talked back to us, providing a richly textured dialogue we hope these pages reflect.

Profiles of the Editors
and Student Commentators

Andrea A. Lunsford

I was born in Oklahoma and have lived in Maryland, Texas, Washington, Ohio, and British Columbia, yet when I think of "home" I think of the soft rolling foothills of the Smokey Mountains in Eastern Tennessee. The hills there are full of Cunninghams, and my granny, Rosa Mae Iowa Brewer Cunningham, and her husband, William Franklin, seemed to know all of them. Like many people in this region, my mother's folks claimed Scottish descent. When I later travelled to Scotland, I discovered that many of the songs we sang on my grandparents' big porch were Scottish in origin.

The only one of her large family to enjoy post-secondary education, my mom graduated with training in teaching and in French from Maryville College in Tennessee. An uncle helped pay her way to school, and it was on a visit to see him that she met my father, another Scottish descendant, Gordon Grady Abernethy. His college education cut short by World War II and the Great Depression, Dad gave up his goal of following his father into dentistry and instead took examinations to become a Certified Public Accountant. In hard times, he and my mother left Oklahoma and settled near her family, where Dad got a job with a defense contractor at Oak Ridge. Mama taught briefly and then stayed home with me and, later, with my two sisters and brother. I played in a special playhouse I built in the woods, spent weekends with my grandparents and dozens of Cunningham cousins, and alternated attending my grandparents' Baptist Church (where they baptized my cousins by plunging them into a river) and my parents' Presbyterian Church, where baptisms seemed like a snap. On occasional Sundays, I got to visit a sister church whose congregation was all black, where the music was mesmerizing, and where I first began to recognize this country's legacy of segregation and racism. My family, I learned, was proud to have fought for the North, though supporting the Union's cause did not exempt them from that legacy.

We read a lot in Sunday School and at Summer Bible School, and at home as well. There I had the luxury of being read to often: *Gulliver's Travels* as it appeared in *The Book of Knowledge* (our family's one encyclopedia), Joseph and His Coat of Many Colors from Hurlbut's *Stories of the*

Bible, Tigger and Roo and Christopher Robin from A. A. Milne, and poems from *A Child's Garden of Verses* are among my earliest memories of texts that grew, over the years, into an animated chorus of voices I still carry with me. Later, I read all of the Nancy Drew, Hardy Boys, and Cherry Ames Senior Nurse series, to be regularly punished for reading in school when I should have been doing something else. Like many young women, I was often "lost in a book," living in a world of heroines and heroes and happy endings. Only slowly and painfully did I come to question the master plot most of these stories reproduced, to realize that endings are never altogether happy and that the roles I play in my own story have been in some important senses scripted by systems beyond my control.

My father wanted me to begin secretarial work after high school, but when I won a small scholarship and got a student job, he and my mother agreed to help me attend our state school, the University of Florida. I graduated with honors but was encouraged by my (male) adviser not to pursue graduate school but rather to "go home and have babies." Instead, I became a teacher, a reasonable job for a woman to aspire to in 1966. Only seven years later did I gather my courage to apply to graduate school after all—and to pursue my Ph.D. Teaching in high school, at a two-year college (Hillsborough Community College in Tampa), and as a graduate assistant helped me reaffirm my commitment to a career in education and introduced me to the concerns that have occupied my professional life ever since: What can I know of myself through my relationships with others? How do people develop as readers and writers? What is the connection between teaching and learning? What does it mean, as the twentieth century draws to a close, to be fully literate?

I pursued these questions in graduate school and beyond, all the while trying to live through two marriages and the loss of my granny, of both my parents, and of my younger brother. Such experiences have led me to think hard not only about the burdens every human life entails but also about the privileges my status as a white, relatively middle-class woman has afforded me. These privileges are considerable, and I do not wish to forget them. In addition, I have enjoyed the support of a vital network of women friends and colleagues. Thanks in large measure to them, I am now a professor in a large research university, and I savor the time I can spend with those I love (especially Lisa Ede, my sisters, their children, and my friend and partner William), and I am somewhat able to indulge my desire to experience as much of the world as possible. I even have season tickets to Ohio State basketball games (no mean feat in the state of Ohio), which I attend regularly with my colleague and friend Beverly Moss. These relationships—and my very special relationship with my students—have added to the chorus of animated voices I carry with me always.

These and other formative relationships and experiences have helped me learn a lesson that informs my teaching, my life, and my work on this book:

that where you stand influences in great measure what you can see. My college adviser, standing as he did in an all–white male professoriate, couldn't quite "see" a young woman joining this elite group, even as a student. My parents, standing as they did in a lower middle class, single-income family with vivid memories of the Depression, couldn't easily "see" beyond the desire for their oldest daughter to get a good, steady secretarial job as soon as possible. And I, standing where *I* do now, am not able to "see" through my students' eyes, to experience the world as they experience it.

Keeping this point in mind leads me to two acts that are by now habitual with me: examining where I stand, with all that implies about inevitably partial vision and perspective; and asking myself where others stand as well. So I came to this textbook project with at least one specific agenda item: to look as carefully and respectfully as I could at John's perspective, at where he stands, and to do the same thing for myself and for every voice included in this text. Such acts are necessary, I believe, before I can say that my opinions are fully considered. My view will always be heavily informed by where I stand. But insofar as I am able to entertain other points of view, I have a chance to understand my own better and to broaden my point of view as well.

John J. Ruszkiewicz

My grandparents never spoke much about their reasons for emigrating from Eastern Europe earlier this century; their grounds for starting new lives in the United States must have seemed self-evident. Moreover, they did abandon those "old countries." Only rarely did I hear them talk nostalgically about the lands they left behind. So I'm a second-generation American with roots in, but no strong ties to, Slovakia, Poland, and Ukraine.

My father and mother were both born in rural Pennsylvania, my dad with five brothers and sisters, my mom with seven—eight if you count the infant who died of measles. Both of my grandfathers and several uncles mined coal in western Pennsylvania, a dangerous and difficult living. After World War II, my parents moved to Cleveland, where jobs were more plentiful, and my dad began a thirty-year stretch at Carling's Brewery. I did my share of manual labor too, for a short time working in a tool-and-die factory, even paying dues to the Teamsters.

But my blue-collar stints were merely summer jobs between college semesters. Education would be my generation's ticket to the American dream. My parents never allowed my brother (who became a physician) or me to consider that we had any choice but college. We attended parochial schools, where headstrong nuns and priests introduced us to learning, moral responsibility, and culture. (By the eighth grade, students at St. Benedict's elementary school could sing three high Masses and two Requiems, one of those services in Gregorian chant. We understood what most of the Latin words meant too.) As grade schoolers, we had homework every night, hours of it. High school was the same, only tougher. I didn't have a free period in high school until the semester I graduated—and I'm still thankful for that discipline.

The ethnic neighborhood in Cleveland where I grew up in the 1950s is now considered inner-city. It was very much *in the city* when I lived there too, but a nine- or ten-year-old could safely trudge to church alone at 6:00 AM to serve Mass or ride the rapid transit downtown to see a baseball game. I did so, often. In the long, hot summer of 1966, however, Cleveland erupted in riots. From my front porch, I could see the fires.

Politically, I come from a family of Democrats—my gregarious mother, far more interested in people than issues, a party worker in Cleveland's 29th Ward. One of my first political memories is watching John F. Kennedy parade down Euclid Avenue in 1960 during his presidential campaign. But frankly, I was more interested in the new Chrysler convertible ferrying the portly Governor of Ohio. I have retained my fondness for old Chryslers—and just about anything with four wheels.

The first President I voted for was George McGovern, but what could you expect from a kid who spent high school listening to Bob Dylan and who attended college in the sixties? In fact, it was during an anti-war rally at St. Vincent College in Latrobe, Pennsylvania, where my drift to the political right began. I had read enough about the history of Vietnam to know that the communist Viet Cong were no angels, but the people at that demonstration believed they were. A professor of physics delivered an impassioned anti-American speech filled with what I knew to be distortions, but no one seemed to care. That moment resonates, after all these years.

Despite the activist times, my college days remained focused on academic subjects—philosophy, history, literature, and cinema. St. Vincent's was small enough to nurture easy commerce between disciplines. I knew faculty from every field, and my roommates were all science majors with views of the world quite different from my own. Debate was lively, frequent, and good-natured. Emotionally I leaned left, but intellectually I found, time and again, that conservative writers described the world more accurately for me. They still do.

Politics didn't matter much in graduate school at Ohio State in the mid 1970s—though I was the only Ph.D. candidate in English who would admit to voting for Gerald Ford. My interests then were *Beowulf,* Shakespeare, and rhetoric. I first met my co-editor, Andrea Lunsford, the first term at Ohio State in an Old English class; we graduated on the same day five years later.

Today, I consider myself an academic and political conservative. Where I work, that makes me a member of the counter-culture, a role I now frankly enjoy. Unfortunately there aren't many conservatives among humanities professors in American universities, which is a shame. The academy would be a richer place were it more diverse. Politically and intellectually, I find myself in much greater sympathy with Jefferson, Madison, and Burke (Edmund, not Kenneth) than with Rousseau, Marx, Freud, or Foucault. I voted twice for Ronald Reagan and in my office hangs a poster of Margaret Thatcher given to me by a student. It scares the daylights out of some colleagues. My professional friends are mainly Democrats or worse, but I respect them. They sometimes say that they are surprised to find me so reasonable and pleasant, being a Republican and all. I tell them they need to meet—and hire—more Republicans.

Like any good conservative, I prefer to keep my life simple—I could be content with a good car, a sensible dog, and a capable racquetball partner. But for the past fifteen years, I've been teaching at the University of Texas at Austin where life is rarely so simple. I've had a front row seat for many of the recent controversies over political correctness on college campuses. I've even been on stage a few times and have met many of the people who make leftists apoplectic—Lynne Cheney, William Bennett, Dinesh D'Souza, Ed Meese, Christina Sommers, David Horowitz—and have been a fellow of the Heritage Foundation. Yet when I taught a course on the automobile in American culture, I was accused in the local press of teaching a leftist "cultural studies" course. ("What next, guns and ammo?" one amused colleague asked.)

While my politics differ from Andrea's on almost every issue, from abortion to higher taxes on productive people, we agree completely about one thing—the importance of teaching undergraduates how to write. So when I proposed an anthology for writing classes that would broaden the range of readings available to students and make the political persuasion of the editors a part of the package, Andrea agreed to the project. She said it embodied the feminist concept of "situated knowledge." Well, sure, if that makes her happy. I'm no theorist. I was just glad to have the privilege and pleasure of working with my good friend and political *other*.

Geoff Henley

When I met David Horowitz, the editor of the underground newspaper *Heterodoxy*, he said immediately, "You're a real Texan." I don't live on a ranch, but I was born in Dallas, stand six-two, wear boots, and have wrecked a truck. I did my undergraduate work at the University of Texas at Austin and plan to earn a master's degree from the Columbia School of Journalism before going to law school and pursuing a career in media law.

To finance my education, I've held a variety of jobs, everything from working as a reporter for the *Houston Post* during the 1992 Republican convention to selling cars at a Ford dealership in Mesquite. But my greatest responsibility and personal achievement was serving for a year as editor of *The Daily Texan,* the student newspaper at the University of Texas at Austin.

As one of the few conservative editors-in-chief in that paper's recent history, I took pride in managing to restore objectivity to the news pages, reserving opinions for the editorial pages. But my right-wing views upset more than a few liberals, accustomed as they were to controlling the student newspaper. Forty left-wing English professors once found my commentary so outrageous that they spent more than a hundred dollars of their own money on an advertisement attacking me. And though George Bush turned out to be a weak-kneed disappointment, I take pride in having been the first editor there *ever* to endorse a Republican presidential candidate.

As a reporter for the *Texan* and the *Post,* I covered the likes of Bill Clinton, Louis Sullivan, Camille Paglia, Dan Quayle, and the American Gladiators. With the exception of the Gladiators, I covered them all with equal fairness.

Newspapers have played an important role in my life. From fifth to eighth grade my mother patiently split two *Dallas Morning News* routes with me. As a single mother with four kids (I have two brothers and a sister), she helped me learn the value of work and money. For that I'm grateful.

I hope one day to own a chain of newspapers—where I will continue to work at keeping the rest of the media elite honest.

Helen Liu

For as long as I can remember, I've always wanted to be a teacher. I've never really known what or even whom I wanted to teach, just that I wanted to help others learn. I am a senior at the University of Texas at Austin majoring in journalism. After graduation, I will attend Stanford Law School. I will practice law afterward, but eventually I would like to become a professor. I guess I'm taking the indirect route to teaching, but I'm trying to experience everything I can on the way.

I was born in Virginia but grew up in Texas. My family moved five times beginning from when I was in kindergarten to when I started the fourth grade. We finally settled in Arlington, Texas, where my parents still live. I have a younger brother and a cat.

The past two summers, I have written for the national political trade journal, *Campaigns & Elections,* and interned at the U.S. House of Representatives for the Committee on Ways and Means. On campus, I have worked as a graphic designer for the magazine *Tejas* and have chaired a committee sponsoring recreational events for university students. I have also played intramural softball.

Traci McLin

··

As a native of suburban Cleveland and one of thirty-plus grandchildren, I have always been considered the "proper" one in my family. "She talks funny" or "you sound just like my mom" were frequent comments. Eventually I came to realize that the chuckles were in response to my attempt to sound as articulate and elegant as my mother did. Today this trait plays a big part in my aspiration to become a spokesperson for a major corporation.

Born in 1973 as the first daughter of Dale and Myra McLin, and now the big sister of Summer McLin, I turned to reading early in my childhood in order to find some type of entertainment. Though I was an usher at the Greater Mt. Zion Baptist Church and participated in other activities away from home, the five-year difference between my sister and me often left me with few alternatives around the house. If I was bored, my parents always suggested reading a book. At first, this seemed unlikely to turn me on, but then I discovered Dr. Seuss and Judy Blume. Their books seemed to tap a volcano of energy inside me.

In grade school, Maurice Sendak's movielike pictures in "Where The Wild Things Are" frightened me; in high school, Toni Morrison's lesson that history repeats itself, "The Bluest Eye," saddened me—and more recently, Terry McMillan's "Waiting To Exhale" seemed like it was written just for me. This book will be required reading for any man I date seriously. Language fascinates me. But I tend to be extremely critical about what I read. My responses are strong, for they express my emotions. I would be lost without the opportunity to express my thoughts in writing.

I consider myself a Democrat and like Bill Clinton. Unlike Ronald Reagan or George Bush, he seems to be for the people. But I don't agree with everything Clinton is doing. I haven't been voting long, though, and am more interested in my major at Ohio State: interpersonal and organizational communications. My capstone area is marketing, and I intern in the Marketing Department at Ohio State during my summers. Just recently I completed my eighth year studying French, the language of romance. When I am not reading or writing, for class or for personal enjoyment, I enjoy public speaking and playing the flute. I would be at an emotional standstill without the ability to express my ideas completely. I release everything inside me with the scroll of the pen!

Stephen Wallenfelsz

··

When I was born in Columbus in 1969, the last child and only son of Richard and Judith Wallenfelsz, there was a seven-year gap between me and my nearest sibling. The only stories I know of my three older sisters and me playing together come from other people, old snapshots, and badly lit home movies. By the time my own memories begin, my sisters were already in high and junior high school, much too busy to deal with their younger brother except for occasionally taking charge of him. Much of my time at home, therefore, was spent by myself or sometime later hanging around Ohio State, where my sisters went to school. I remember belonging briefly to the Cub Scouts, but getting kicked out for acting up. In retrospect, I don't think they had enough activities to keep me busy.

The first book I owned was by Dr. Seuss, though I can't remember which one. I was probably more enthralled at the time by the detailed pictures and the bright colors than by the text; I can still remember the intricate cars and roads, and the characters that flowed from page to page, making me want to go faster and faster through the book, and back again. But the texts were even more wonderful when I learned to read them. Reading was an activity I could do happily alone, or quietly when my father was at home. He was not at all tolerant of young children at play, and a desire to stay out of his sight fostered a dependency on the world I found in books, one that allowed me to be anyone and go anyplace, whenever I wanted. This passion continued even after my parents were divorced and I had made more friends in school and the neighborhood. Although I kept busy outside, I always found time to read, devouring the Hardy Boys, the Three Investigators, and, when I had ran out of the others, all of my sisters' Bobbsey Twins collection.

At the Catholic schools I attended, my reading paid off when I placed in advanced reading groups; twice I skipped a grade ahead. Although I did all right in school, I saved my real enthusiasm for pleasure reading. In English classes, I often turned in my projects late, much to the consternation of my teachers, who seemed to favor only repetitious spelling exercises and lengthy book reports. I often felt that these activities distracted me from the real prize in reading, the pleasure of discovering new worlds. With so much to be explored and experienced, who had time for nagging little details?

In high school I had less time for pleasure reading—and more insistent demands placed on me by teachers. But when I did find time to read, the books were often titles I had heard of in classes at school. I struggled through Dante's *Divine Comedy* after a referral in a social studies class, the legends of King Arthur because of their mention in history, science fiction after reading a few short stories in English.

Most importantly, I started to look closely at the writing in the books, not just the subjects they were written about. By the time I started college I had realized that what was *not* written in the books I was reading was as important as what *was* written in them, maybe even more so. This discovery has had a definite impact on how I view my classes and on what I get out of them. I still read for pleasure on subjects which I find important, maybe more than is helpful with all my college work.

I am currently pursuing dual degrees in writing and rhetoric and in international business management, and I hope to attend law school after graduation. In spite of my interest in these subjects, I don't think of myself as political—though I can recall campaigning actively for Jimmy Carter when I was in second grade! I believe that part of what has encouraged me and enabled me to maintain my interest in ideas has been reading and the critical perspective I bring to everything I read.

Contents

"If then a practical end must be assigned to a University course, I say it is that of training good members of society."

"A deprecating, silvery, kindly gentleman . . . regretted in a low voice as he waved me back that ladies are only admitted to the library if accompanied by a Fellow of the College. . . ."

....

PART TWO   WHAT WE BELIEVE   *149*

4.   Faith: One Nation, Under God   *151*

The Presence of Others

Readings for Critical Thinking and Writing

PART ONE

How We Learn

On Reading and Thinking Critically

Introduction

THIS IS A BOOK for and about reading. Its pages contain a number of voices joined in conversation and debate over issues of importance to all of us: What, how, and under what circumstances should we go about learning and becoming educated? Who are we as individuals and as members of various groups and cultures? What do we believe? How do we choose to live? In the conversations surrounding these and other issues, the editors of this book have joined in, and you will find our explanations for choosing particular selections and our thoughts about these selections running throughout this text. Its primary aim, however, is to invite *you* to join in this conversation, to add your voice to the discussion ongoing in these pages. Doing so invites you to assume the perspective of a critical reader.

• • •

WHAT IS CRITICAL READING?

If you've been wondering what we mean by critical reading, you're already demonstrating one of the hallmarks of a critical reader: a questioning attitude, one that probes for definitions, explanations, proofs, assumptions, and so on. Perhaps we can further clarify what we mean by critical reading by focusing on two everyday uses of the word *critical*. In its most common usage, *critical* means acting like a critic, as in "many voters have been highly critical of Clinton's economic policies," or "some members of the African American community have been critical of what they see as Spike Lee's appropriation of Malcolm X." In this sense of the word, *critical* suggests that you have explored an issue (like an economic policy or a particular movie) and are ready to evaluate it, to see whether and how it meets your standards. But *critical* is also used to denote something of singular importance, as in "critical care unit" or a "critical point in negotiations." In this sense of the word, *critical* suggests that you attach importance to what you are examining and to your own critical responses to it. For the purposes of this text, then, critical readers are those who bring all their powers to bear on understanding, analyzing, and evaluating some important question, issue, or perspective contained in a piece of writing. Critical readers, in other words, do not accept things blindly or "at face value," but instead look at them from a variety of perspectives, saying both yes *and* no to them until they are ready to take their own stance on the issues at hand.

Saying Yes, No, and Maybe

The chapters of this text will allow you many chances to practice saying yes and no—and sometimes *maybe*—to ideas. As you read the selections in Chapter 3, Education, for example, you will encounter many widely varying perspectives on who and what higher education is for as well as what its content should be. When you read Virginia Woolf's "A Room of One's Own," arguing for women's right to higher education, her position may seem perfectly reasonable to you; you find you can understand her point of view and say yes to her ideas. But then you being to wonder about them and to say, well, maybe, or even to say no. Are Woolf's ideas really applicable to conditions today? Although she is speaking for women, would she speak equally for other groups who have been excluded from higher education? Are the charges she brings fair and accurate? All of these acts—saying yes, maybe, and/or no—are necessary for critical reading, for the kind of reading that is truly open to new ideas but that insists on thinking them through from every perspective, every angle available to you.

Thus, critical reading is the kind of reading you do when you need to understand the terms of a contract you are about to sign, decide which of several automobile financing plans will be best for you, master the material necessary to shine on an important examination, evaluate the arguments for or against a political proposal or candidate, or compare doctors' opinions about whether you should or should not undergo surgery. It is the kind of reading Mortimer Adler is talking about when he says, "When [people] are in love and are reading a love letter, they read for all they are worth. They read every word three ways; they read between the lines and in the margins; they read the whole in terms of the parts, and each part in terms of the whole."

WHY BECOME A CRITICAL READER?

Given our definition of critical reading, the answer to this question is probably already obvious to you. Critical readers are "in on" the conversation surrounding any issue. They resist ready-made or hand-me-down opinions whenever they can. Much in our society makes such critical reading difficult; we are, after all, inundated with ready-made opinions on television and in other mass media as well as in educational, religious, political, and even family institutions. In fact, so many forces are at work to make up our minds for us that there are many who question whether people aren't fooling themselves to think that they can control and use language at all, rather than the other way around.

You can probably think of a number of instances in your own life to support this view. The insistent bombardment of commercials at the movies, for example, serves to make you buy popcorn and Coca-Cola. Or you may be aware of the extent to which educational labels like "honors" or "remedial" have dramatically affected your life. Many studies suggest that we tend to live up (or down) to such labels—for better or worse. This fact of modern life led one theorist of language to say that the words we try to use or control are already "half-way in someone else's mouth," meaning that the words we use are already so weighed down with the meanings our society and institutions have given them that it is very hard to do anything other than simply accept those meanings. It's hard, that is, for any one person to resist the lure of advertising or to reject the power of educational or social labels.

To some extent, this theory clearly rings true: we are not absolutely in control of the language we use or read. But the end result of such a position is to give in, to give up striving to get in on the conversation, to give up trying to make your voice heard, to bring about any change. Why become a critical reader, then? In order to resist being controlled by other people's language, to exert some control of your own, to test your wits against and with the wits of others, to define for yourself your own perspective on any issue, to contribute to the thoughts and actions related to those issues. You become a critical reader, in short, **to get involved in the conversation and to make your voice count.**

ARE YOU A CRITICAL READER?

Our guess is that when you really need to be, you are already a critical reader. You may want to take stock of your general reading habits, however, by answering the following questions. As a general rule, when you are reading material you want or need to understand—such as an important chapter in one of your textbooks—do you

1. Read carefully, either with or without skimming first?
2. "Talk back" to what you are reading, noting what does or doesn't make sense, what seems right or wrong?
3. Ask questions as you read?
4. Take notes in the margins or on a separate sheet of paper?

5. Ask yourself why the writer takes the position he or she does?
6. Think about the writer's perspective—what his or her interests are in writing the piece?
7. Ask what larger social, economic, political, or other conditions may have influenced the creation of this piece of writing?
8. Consider what in your experience and background leads you to agree with or like, or to disagree with or dislike, the piece of writing?
9. Imagine other ways of looking at the subjects or ideas presented?
10. Summarize the gist of what you have read?
11. Compare what you're reading with other things you have read about the subject?

If you've answered "yes" to most of these questions, you are already reading with a critical eye, and you will understand what we mean when we say reading is really a partnership: the text in front of you has words set down, but you are the one who realizes the ideas in those words, tests them against what you know, and puts them to use in your own life.

Examining Your Reading Habits   Take five or ten minutes to write a description of yourself as a reader. How do you usually approach a text that you want or need to understand? Do you usually practice critical reading habits? Why, or why not? Bring your description to class for discussion. Compare your description to those of two or three other students in your class. Note the ways in which your reading strategies are similar and/or different.

HOW CAN YOU BECOME A MORE CRITICAL READER?

If you have compared your notes on how you typically read with those of friends or classmates, you will probably have noted some differences. Indeed, reading practices vary widely, and even highly skilled readers may differ dramatically in the approaches they take. The most effective and satisfying critical reading strategies for you may be quite different than those for your friends. In particular, your reading strategies are undoubtedly related to who you are, to your gender, age, cultural background, life experiences, prior reading experiences, even your eyesight. In addition, strategies for reading vary widely depending on purpose and situation: you might skim the ingredients listed on a food package just to check that it doesn't contain something you are allergic to, or you might pore slowly over the directions for connecting a modem to make sure that you don't make a mistake.

Thus part of your job as a critical reader is to get to know your own preferred strategies, your own strengths and weaknesses, and to build on your strengths. While we can't know exactly what will be most effective for any one individual reader, then, we can offer some general guidelines you can experiment with. From them you should be able to design your individual blueprint for reading. We hope that these guidelines will be particularly helpful for you when you have to tackle difficult reading material or material for which you have almost no background. In the annotated essays in chapters 3 through 10 of this book there are examples of most of these guidelines, written in the margins and responses to those essays.

Previewing

- Determine your purpose for reading—to gather information for a writing assignment? to determine whether a source will be useful for a research project? to study for an examination? to prepare for class discussion? to determine your own stance toward the topic—and what in your experience and background leads you to take that stance?
- Consider the title. What does it tell you about what is to come?
- Think about what you already know about the subject. What opinions do you hold on this subject? What major topics do you anticipate? What do you hope to learn? What other things about this topic have you read?
- What do you know about the author? What expertise does he or she have in the subject? What particular perspective on the subject might he or she hold?
- Look at how the text is structured. Are there subdivisions? Read over any headings. Skim the opening sentences of each paragraph.
- Decide what you think the main point or theme of the text will be.

Annotating

- Read carefully, marking places that are confusing or that you want to reread.
- Identify key points or arguments, important terms, recurring images, and interesting ideas, either by underlining them in the text or by making notes in the margin.
- Note any statements you question or disagree with and any counter-evidence or counterarguments that occur to you.
- Note any sources used in the text.

Summarizing

- Summarize the main points. Do they match your expectations?
- Jot down any points you want to remember, questions you want to raise, and ideas for how you may use this material.

Analyzing

- Identify evidence that supports the main argument or illustrates the main point. Is it sufficient to convince you? Is there any evidence that seems to contradict the author's point?
- Identify the writer's underlying assumptions about the subject, where he or she is "coming from" on this issue.
- Ask what may have led the author to this position.
- Question the sources used. Ask yourself whether the source is timely, whether it has sufficient expertise, and whether its perspective or position on the subject is different from yours or from others you know and respect. If so, why?
- Think of other points of view on this topic, perhaps from other things you have read or seen. Is the author's perspective the most persuasive— and why?

Rereading

- Reread quickly to be sure you have understood the reading.
- Identify the author's purpose(s). Were those purposes accomplished?
- Determine whether the questions you had during the first reading have been answered.

Responding

- What one question would you like to ask the writer? How do you think the writer might respond?
- Think about the reading as a whole. What did you like best about it? What puzzled or irritated you? What caused you to like or dislike the piece? Were your expectations met? If not, why not? What more would you like to know about the subject?
- Note what you have learned about effective writing from this reading.

If you keep a reading log, record these notes there. (For three example reading log entries turn to p. 545.)

WHAT DOES READING HAVE TO DO WITH WRITING?

In one sense, critical reading *is* writing. That is, as you read carefully, asking questions and talking back to a text, you inevitably create your own version of that text. And even if that interpretation is not literally written down on paper, it is "written" in your mind, composed and put into words you can understand and remember. And if you add some of your own ideas—or those you and classmates develop together—to what you read, you can build toward a new text altogether, one you may later write down.

As our society makes increasing use of electronic texts, in fact, reading and writing will almost certainly become even more inextricably intertwined. The "reader" of interactive fiction or a hypertext, for instance, writes part of the text. Those on electronic bulletin boards or conferences may write their own ideas and responses into what they are reading on the screen, something first written by another reader.

But critical reading is also closely related to your own writing, because it enables you to assess what you have written, to say yes *and* no *and* maybe to your own ideas—to evaluate the logic of your prose, the effectiveness of your word choice, the degree to which you have gotten your points across. In short, you can apply these very same reading strategies to your own writing, to see your own words with a clear, critical eye. Thus reading critically and writing effectively become reciprocal activities, strengthening each other as you become more powerful in your use of language.

Because we are convinced that reading and writing are very closely related, we want this text to offer you many opportunities for moving back and forth from reading to writing to reading . . . and so on. We will, in fact, be inviting you to experiment with a number of kinds of writing as you read your way into the conversations taking place in the chapters that follow. We turn now, therefore, to Chapter 2, From Reading to Writing, for an overview of the writing practices this book invites you to experience.

2

From Reading to Writing

Introduction

IN SPITE OF ALL the social forces that influence and shape your reading practices, no one can predict precisely how you will respond to what you read. A pamphlet arriving in the mail may persuade you to vote for or against a ballot proposition; a slick brochure might convince you to buy a health insurance policy or to complain about false advertising to a state regulatory agency. A dull book could provide exercise for your throwing arm. A great book might change your life. Clearly, reading can lead to action.

One action that evolves naturally from reading is writing. When you react to something you read by writing something of your own, you preserve and extend ideas. You enter a conversation someone else has started and invite still other readers to join you. Sometimes the connections you'll make between your reading and yourself will be close and personal. At other times, you'll be bridging much wider gaps, linking remote historical epochs, examining works from different cultures, or reconciling positions that at first seem incompatible.

• • •

WRITING TO LEARN

You will have many occasions in college to write. Almost every class requires some written work, though some tasks may seem so routine you may not even think of them as "writing." Yet even the most routine forms of writing can help fix ideas in your mind or suggest relationships you hadn't considered before. Here are some types of writing common to college work, writing that can help you be a more effective student: class notes, lab notes, reading notes and annotations, comments on other students' work, reading or writing log entries, abstracts of articles, summaries, outlines, and essay examinations. These writings, if you are systematic and careful about them, can help you learn course material—and to retain what you learn.

LEARNING TO WRITE EFFECTIVELY

Many of your college courses will ask you to prepare formal essays or other extended pieces of writing related to what you read, hear, or learn. The following guidelines are designed to help you respond effectively to such assignments.

Considering the Assignment

You should always find out as much as you can about an assignment before starting to write.

- Analyze a writing project carefully. Look for key words in the assignment, terms such as *analyze, summarize, compare, contrast, illustrate, argue, defend, refute, persuade,* and so on.
- If you don't understand an assignment or any of its terms, ask your instructor for a clarification.
- Pay attention to limits on length and time. The length of an assignment will surely influence the focus and thesis of any paper. In general, the shorter the piece, the narrower its focus will need to be.
- Plan your time to allow for all necessary reading, thinking, drafting, revising, reading more, revising more, writing more, editing, and polishing.

Considering Purpose and Audience

Beyond what the assignment itself dictates, consider the larger purpose of the writing. A piece that is largely informative (such as a report) will be somewhat different from one that takes an aggressively argumentative stance (such as an editorial). What does the writing have to accomplish to be successful? Your responses to that question will help determine the form, organization, tone, style, and length of your writing. Here are some other questions to help you think about purpose:

- Does the assignment itself specify a purpose?
- What does your instructor expect you to do in this assignment? What do you need to do to meet those expectations?
- How do you want readers to react to your writing? Do you want them to be entertained? Should they learn something? Should they be moved to action?
- Where might you like to have this piece published?

Consider also who will read your piece. The primary audience for your college writing may be your instructors, but *they* may have in mind some other specific audience—your classmates, for example, or the general public.

Following are some questions that can help identify key characteristics of your audience:

- Do your readers belong to some identifiable group: college students, Democrats, women, parents, sociologists?

- How would you characterize your readers? What values and principles do you hold in common with them? What differences are there between you?

- Are your readers likely to know more or less than you do about your subject? What background information do you need to provide?

- Are your readers likely to be engaged by your subject, or do you have to win their attention?

- Are your readers likely to be favorable, neutral, or hostile to your positions?

- Should you use simple, general, or technical language?

- Are you addressing more than one audience? If so, do any of these audiences seem incompatible?

Generating Ideas and Making Plans

You don't necessarily need to know what you are going to say before you begin writing. Many experienced writers, in fact, report that their best ideas emerge *during* writing, and others say they make elaborate plans only to see them go awry as they write. Even so, all writers must start somewhere to generate ideas. You may find some of the following techniques helpful in discovering ideas:

- Read any assigned material carefully, annotating key information, summarizing main points, and noting connections among readings.

- Try specific techniques for developing ideas, such as freewriting, brainstorming, or journal writing.

- Get more information—from the library, from data banks, from professional organizations, from friends or instructors, and so on.

- Do field research. Conduct a survey or some interviews.

- Get involved in discussions about your subject. Talk to people. Listen to their ideas and opinions.

- Draw on your personal experiences, especially when dealing with social, cultural, and political issues. *Your* experience counts.

Once you have ideas, sketch out a plan, a scheme to make a project manageable. Here are some ways of working out a plan:

- Fix on a tentative thesis statement or main point you want to prove, defend, or illustrate. Think of it as a promise to your readers of what you intend to do.
- Prepare a scratch outline by listing the major ideas you want to cover and then arranging them in an order that makes sense to you.
- Construct a phrase or sentence outline if you find such formal devices useful.
- Try a "zero draft"—a quick, discardable version of a paper to help you focus on the major issues.

Drafting

Drafting is the point in the writing process when words are put down on the page or up on the screen. The cold swimming hole approach works best for some writers: just plunge in. After all, you can't do much as a writer until you produce some words. In case you don't much like cold water, however, here's some other advice for getting started on a first draft:

- Control your expectations. No one expects a first draft to be perfect. In fact, no one expects a final draft to be the last word on any subject. So take it easy.
- Skip the introduction if you find yourself stuck on the opening sentences. Start somewhere else, perhaps with an idea you are especially eager to develop. Then write another portion of the essay, and then another. You can put all the parts together later; if you are working on a computer, you'll need only a few keystrokes.
- Set some reasonable production goals, especially for longer projects. Commit yourself to writing one or two pages before getting up from your desk, and try to stop at a point where you feel confident about what comes next. That way, beginning again will be easier. Reward yourself when you meet your goal.
- Try a quick draft: sketch out the full paper without stopping.

Getting—and Giving—Feedback

Seek responses from other readers. Within whatever guidelines your instructor establishes, ask classmates, friends, or any potential readers for their reactions to your drafts. Here are some guidelines you can ask your readers to use in reviewing your draft:

- Begin by describing objectively what you think the draft is saying. That description might prove enlightening to the author.

- Point out anything that is confusing or unclear.

- What is the writer's attitude toward the topic? How do you know?

- Describe what is most memorable.

- Focus initially on big issues: What is its intended purpose? Who is its desired audience? How is it organized? What are its arguments? Its examples and illustrations?

- List the strengths of the draft. How can they be enhanced?

- List the weaknesses. How might they be eliminated or minimized?

- Suggest necessary revisions. Be specific: What more do you as one reader want or need to know? Which other arguments or ideas should be considered?

Revising

Respond to comments on a first draft by looking at the entire project anew. Reshape the project as much as necessary to serve your purpose, your subject matter, and your readers. Here are some specific suggestions for revising:

- To gain perspective, put the draft aside for a day or two.

- Be as tough-minded as you can about the condition of a draft. Discard whole paragraphs or pages when they simply don't work. Don't just tinker or look for the easiest way of salvaging weak material. You may need a new thesis or a completely different structure.

- Consider any response you've gotten very carefully.

- Consider alternative plans for organization. Be flexible.

- Consider the overall strategy of the essay. Might a different point of view or tone make it more effective?

- Review your thesis or main idea. Does it achieve the purpose you had in mind? Is the thesis fully explained and supported?

- Reconsider whether you know enough about your subject to write about it with authority. If not, go back to your sources or do more reading.

- Pay attention to transitions. You can often fortify an entire essay with a few careful phrases that point to where you're going—or where you've been.

Editing

Once you've revised your draft, it's time to edit your work by attending carefully to the structure of paragraphs, the shape of sentences, the choice of words, and the conventions of punctuation and mechanics.

- Reconsider openings and closings. In academic writing, openings should capture the reader's attention and identify key points while conclusions should summarize ideas and draw implications.
- Read your draft aloud, paying attention to the length, variety, rhythm, and coherence of sentences.
- Look for wordiness. Stylistically, nothing hurts a paper more than empty phrases.
- Consider your vocabulary for appropriateness. Is it appropriate to use contractions or slang or dialect? Do any technical terms need defining?
- Check any documentation of sources for the correct form. Reconsider also the way you incorporate sources—do you quote, paraphrase, and summarize appropriately? Do you weave quotations smoothly into your own text?
- Check for problems of grammar and usage, particularly any that have caused you problems in the past.
- For detailed examples and answers to questions of grammar, usage, and style, check a handbook.
- Find a suitable title. For most academic work, titles should provide clear descriptions of the contents.

Preparing the Final Copy

Now is the time to assemble and check your final copy.

- Review the assignment to be sure you have met all requirements of form. Does your instructor want a title page? An outline? Must the paper be typed?
- Be sure your name is on the paper in the proper place(s).
- Paginate, and clip the pages together. (Do not staple them.)
- Proofread one last time for typographical errors, spelling errors, and

other slips. If you have a spell checker, run it for a final check. If need be, make minor last-minute corrections by hand.

- Make sure the paper is neatly written, typed, or printed.

AN ALPHABETICAL CATALOGUE OF THE WRITING ASSIGNMENTS IN THIS BOOK

Throughout *The Presence of Others* we invite you to respond to the readings we've selected, to join in conversation with all the people who've collaborated to write this book—writers, editors, reviewers, and students. Following is an alphabetical catalogue of guidelines to the writing assignments you may be asked to do as you use this book.

Analyzing

Analytical writing puts ideas under scrutiny. To analyze a reading, you examine its ideas systematically, questioning the validity of arguments, the accuracy of facts, the logical relationship of ideas, the fairness of conclusions, and the assumptions underlying them.

- To begin, identify exactly what you want to analyze, from a paragraph to a full work.
- Note any preconceptions or assumptions you bring to the topic of your analysis. Think about how these may affect your analysis.
- Mark the text you are analyzing thoroughly. Annotate its margins, highlight key quotations, and circle terms you think are especially important.
- Divide the text into its main ideas, and look at each one carefully. What support exists for each idea?
- Identify the author's attitude toward the topic. How does that attitude color his or her arguments? What social, political, economic, or other conditions may have shaped his or her attitudes and arguments?
- Look for connections between ideas. Are these connections clear and logical to you?
- Try to think of opposing points of view or alternative perspectives on the topic. Has the writer considered them fairly?
- Study the evidence, draw conclusions, and then present the findings of your analysis.

For examples of analysis, see the essays by Adrienne Rich (p. 56) and Jay Overocker (p. 528).

Arguing

Among a writer's toughest jobs is making a persuasive argument, one that moves readers to reaffirm a commitment—or to consider changing their minds or taking action. Almost all the readings in this book contain arguments. As you work at reading these pieces, you may want to construct arguments of your own. Here are some suggestions for writing an effective academic argument:

- Develop a clear, carefully limited thesis to defend. This thesis will often evolve gradually as you learn more about your subject.

- Find various good reasons for someone to agree with the thesis. Support all statements with specific and appropriate evidence.

- Show that any evidence you have gathered is fair, appropriate, and accurate; that your various arguments support one another; and that they outweigh possible counterarguments.

- When building an argument from something you've read, regard that text and everything connected with it as potential evidence. This would include the language and style of the writer, his or her background and reputation, the time and place of publication, the reputation of the publisher, and so on.

- Quote from the piece carefully to demonstrate the points you are making. Bring the writer's voice into your side of the conversation.

- Appeal to the readers you are trying to convince by connecting your argument to things they are likely to know and care about. An effective argument stimulates thinking and conversation. It doesn't close off discussion or create instant enemies.

For examples of effective arguments, see the essays by Virginia Woolf (p. 43) and David Reiff (p. 406).

Brainstorming

Brainstorming is an activity that can help start you thinking, record thoughts and impressions, and stockpile material for more formal kinds of writing. Basically, it consists of putting down ideas—about a reading, a writing topic, a problem to solve, whatever—as they come to mind.

You can certainly brainstorm alone, though it probably works better in a group. If you are working with a group, assign one person to jot down notes. You can brainstorm either as you read or immediately afterward. Here are some specific tips for brainstorming:

- List your thoughts as they occur to you. Put down whatever comes to mind; let your ideas flow. Prune and reorder ideas *later.*

- Try to include examples from your reading to develop your thoughts.

- Don't judge the quality of your brainstorming prematurely. Record your intuitions. Give yourself slack to explore ideas—even silly or outlandish ones.

- Once you've got all your thoughts down, look for connections among them. What conclusions can you draw about your position on the subject by looking at these connections?

Comparing and Contrasting

Strictly speaking, when you compare things, you are looking for similarities; when you contrast them, you are pointing out differences. Here are some suggestions for comparing and contrasting:

- Break your subject into parts or aspects that can be studied profitably. As the old saying goes, you don't want to compare apples and oranges.

- Pursue your analysis systematically, point by point. Group the comparisons or contrasts purposefully so that they make or support a point about your subject.

- Use appropriate transitional words and phrases. Readers can easily get lost if a writer jumps from one point of comparison or contrast to another without providing the necessary bridges.

- Be fair. Even when you are inclined to favor one side over another, be sure to consider the other side fairly.

The selections by Shelby Steele (p. 102) and Serena (p. 549) both provide examples of comparing and contrasting.

Defining

When asked to define a word or concept in a paragraph, you're usually expected to write an extended explanation of the term, accompanied by illustrations and examples. Terms can also be defined through descriptions of their components, descriptions of processes (how something works), or any appropriate combination of these methods. Here are some suggestions for defining:

- To define a term, place it within a larger category and then list features or characteristics that distinguish it from other items in that category: "A skyscraper is a building of unusual height."

- Then expand the simple definition by providing additional distinguishing details: "A skyscraper is a building of unusual height, most often supported by a steel skeleton and having many stories. The earliest skyscrapers appeared in American cities, especially Chicago and New York, late in the nineteenth century. The height of buildings was confined at first by construction techniques that required massive masonry walls and by the limits of elevator technology. The invention of steel skeletons that supported both floors and walls and the development of high-speed elevators made much taller buildings possible. Among the most famous skyscrapers are the Empire State Building in New York and the Sears Tower in Chicago."

- In most cases, try to keep the tone of a definition factual and impersonal.

Differences of definition often give rise to the disagreements people have about important political and social issues. That's why you should always be sensitive to the key words in a text. Quite often, you will find that while you and other readers agree upon the core meanings of such important terms (their denotations), you may not share the feelings, images, and associations that these words evoke (their connotations). For examples of definition, see the essays by Peggy Orenstein (p. 251) and Hector St. Jean De Crèvecoeur (p. 380).

Describing

Descriptions provide a snapshot of an object—explaining what it looks like at a particular moment.

- Consider your perspective on the object. From what angle are you observing it? Share this point of view with readers.

- Record the most distinctive features and details, those that will enable readers to visualize what you are describing. In most types of writing, your goal is to convey an accurate *impression* of what you have seen, be it person, thing, or even idea.

- Descriptions depend heavily on modifiers—words that specify shape, size, color, smell, and so on. Modifiers should be chosen very deliberately—and used sparingly.

For effective examples of description, see the selections by Virginia Woolf (p. 43) and Steven Spence (p. 584).

Writing a Dialogue

A dialogue is a conversation between two or more people—as in an interview, where ideas and opinions are exchanged, or in fiction or nonfiction writing, where a conversation is reproduced or imagined. To write such a conversation, you need to know something about the way the participants think, how they view the world, even the way they speak. Writing a fictional dialogue thus requires—and allows—imaginative role playing. Here are some suggestions for creating one:

- Try to put yourself within the minds of the characters and consider how they might respond to each other. Look closely at the typical attitudes, interests, habits, and expressions used by your characters. Try to reproduce them.

- It's not enough just to have characters "talk"; you have to figure out a subject for them to talk about. The liveliest dialogues usually feature some exchange of ideas or opinions.

- Set the dialogue in a particular place and time.

- A dialogue can be a stimulating way to respond to a reading. Imagine a dialogue among yourself and some friends on the reading—or place yourself in conversation with the writer. What would you like to say to Mary Shelley, bell hooks, or Allan Bloom? What might they say to you?

For a brief example of dialogue, see J.R.'s introduction to the Terry Eastland essay on p. 492.

Evaluating

Writing an evaluation involves making and justifying judgments. First of all, you need to determine the appropriate criteria for the evaluation. Obviously, you wouldn't use the same standards in evaluating an elementary school play that you would in reviewing a Broadway production. In most cases, it is best to take a clear position in a review. Don't make your evaluation so subtle that no one can tell what your stance is. Here are some suggestions for writing an evaluation:

- Determine the appropriate criteria for the evaluation. Sometimes these standards will be obvious or given. In other cases, you will have to establish and define them. Readers will want to know why you are applying certain measures so that they can determine whether to trust your opinions.

- Measure your subject according to these standards.

- Base your evaluation on clear and sufficient evidence. A good evaluation is based on tangible facts and compelling arguments.
- Let readers see how you arrived at your judgment. For example, if you raise doubts about the competence of an author, make clear what led you to that conclusion.
- Arrange your arguments in logical order—perhaps in order of increasing importance. Sometimes you can bolster your argument by comparing and contrasting your subject with objects or ideas already familiar to your readers.

For an example of evaluation, see the essay by P. J. O'Rourke (p. 506).

Exploring

The point of exploratory writing is to examine subjects imaginatively, so such essays are often more tentative than reports or more purely argumentative writing. Exploratory pieces allow you to take risks, to jump into controversies too complex to be resolved easily. So when you want to explore some issue in writing, try to go beyond predictable and safe positions. Following are some strategies for doing so:

- Read a series of provocative articles from various perspectives. Talk with friends or colleagues. Reach for dialogue, discussion, and debate.
- Be prepared for multiple drafts. Your best ideas are likely to emerge during the composing process.
- Be open to alternative views and marginalized voices. Bring other writers into the discussion.
- As the piece evolves, show it to interested readers and ask for their frank response. Incorporate questions, debates, or other material into the discussion. Dialogue can be a particularly stimulating technique for exploration.
- Don't expect to wrap up this kind of writing with a neat bow. Be prepared for gaps. Exploratory writing often produces more questions than answers.

For examples of exploratory writing, see the essays by Lewis Thomas (p. 233) and Zora Neale Hurston (p. 386).

Freewriting

Freewriting is a technique for generating ideas. When you freewrite about something, you follow ideas to see where they lead. Freewriting in response to reading might be prompted by particular words, phrases, or passages that you have highlighted while reading. It can also be useful for exploring connections between two or three different selections. Here are some specific tips for freewriting:

- One way to get started is by answering a question—for instance, "This topic makes me think of . . ." or "When I think of this topic, I feel . . ."

- Write nonstop for a fixed period of time—five or ten minutes, perhaps. Don't stop during that time; the idea is to generate as much material as you can.

- If you can't think of anything to write, put down a nonsense phrase or repeat a key word just to keep your pen or cursor moving.

- Don't stop to question or correct your work while freewriting. Forget about style and correctness. Get the intellectual juices flowing.

- After freewriting, read the words you have produced to recover the ideas you may have generated. If you have come up with observations worthy of more exploration, make those ideas the focus of more freewriting.

Interviewing

We routinely ask people questions to satisfy our curiosity, so we all have had some experience with interviews. But to turn a conversation with an interesting and knowledgeable person into a useful interview, you need to do your homework. The first step is to decide who you wish to interview—and you don't have to limit yourself to experts only. Friends and colleagues have knowledge and opinions you might tap by interviewing them. Think of an interview as a high-powered conversation, a new way to learn. Here are some suggestions for arranging, conducting, and recording an interview:

- Call or write ahead for an appointment.

- Prepare your questions in advance, perhaps brainstorming a preliminary list, then augmenting it with who-what-where-when-why-how items. Arrange your queries in a sensible order, perhaps beginning with more factual questions and then moving to more complex questions of opinion.

- Prepare some open-ended questions—the kind that can't be answered in a word or phrase. Give yourself leeway to take the conversation down any paths that open up.

- Record your subject's responses carefully, double-checking with him or her later any direct quotations you might want to use. Use a tape recorder if your subject approves.

- Record time, date, place, and other pertinent information about the conversation for your records.

- After an interview, summarize the information briefly in your own words.

This book includes excerpts from a published interview with Rosa Parks (p. 460).

Writing a Letter to the Editor

A familiar kind of persuasive writing is the letter to the editor, in which writers explain why they agree or disagree with something they've read. Such letters are typically composed in response to positions taken by newspapers, magazines, or journals. In most cases, letters to the editor are spirited arguments, somewhat personal, and carefully targeted.

Letters to the editor follow the conventions of business letters and should be dated and signed. Here are some suggestions for writing one:

- Think about who reads the periodical to which the letter will be sent. Because such a letter is intended for publication, it is usually written more to win the support of other readers than to influence editors or publishers.

- Identify your target article within the first line or two. Let readers know exactly what piece provoked your ire or admiration.

- Make your case quickly. Since space for letters is very limited in most publications, expect to make only one or two points. Execute them powerfully and memorably, using the best examples and reasons you can.

- When appropriate, use irony, satire, or humor.

For an example, see the letter to the editor written by Susan Rubin Suleiman (p. 491).

Narrating

Whereas descriptions usually refer to stationary objects, narratives depict motion, whether it be the action of a single person or the unfurling of a complex historical event, such as a war or social movement. When you narrate, you usually tell a story of some kind. But narratives may also explain *how something occurred* (analyzing a process) or *why something happened* (tracing cause and effect). Here are some suggestions for narrating:

- Place the events you are discussing in a meaningful order, usually chronological—first this happened, then this, then this, and so on.
- Provide necessary background information by answering the questions who, what, where, when, why, and how the events occurred.
- Most narrative calls for some description. Flesh out any characters and describe any scenic details necessary to the narrative.
- Use transitional phrases (*then, next, on the following day*) and sequences (*in the spring, during the summer, later in the year*) to keep the sequence of the narrative clear. Remember, however, that the sequence doesn't always have to be chronological (you've certainly seen flashbacks in movies).

For examples of narration, see the selections by Mary Shelley (p. 213) and Maxine Hong Kingston (p. 319).

Parodying

Your appreciation of a written work can't be tested better than by parody. A parody is an imitation, either of an author or of a work, written with a critical and usually humorous edge. Parody succeeds when readers recognize both your target and your criticism; they should laugh at the wit in your mimicking something they too have read.

When you write a parody, you are in certain ways collaborating with another writer. You will necessarily learn much about the way he or she thinks and uses language. Here are some suggestions for writing a parody:

- Choose a distinctive piece to parody. The more recognizable or famous a work is, the easier it is to imitate. But even the most vapid work can be mocked for its dullness.
- Look for an author's favorite subjects, motifs, or opinions, and distort them enough to be funny but not so much that the original work becomes unrecognizable.
- When parodying a well-known work or writer, try shifting from a serious theme to a frivolous one; for example, imagine a pompous opera critic reviewing Janet Jackson's latest video or a dour news commentator interviewing the ghost of Elvis.
- Pinpoint your subject's habits of language—typical sentence openers, preferred words and phrases, distinctive patterns of repetition, favorite sentence patterns, unusual punctuation. Then exaggerate those habits, making sure that your readers see the resemblance.

- Don't make your parody too long. Parody is a form of wit, and brevity is its soul.
- Above all, have fun. When a parody ceases being funny, it becomes simply bad imitation.

For an example of parody, see the selection by Joe Bob Briggs (p. 368).

Writing a Position Paper

A position paper is a short (often one-page) argument that can sometimes be exploratory. In it, you will usually present a thesis—a statement that needs to be proved or defended. But such a paper is often assigned to jump-start discussions or to get various points of view on the table, so you should feel free to take risks and examine new approaches. A position paper need not have the gloss of a polished argument, and its language can be livelier than that of more formal academic arguments. It should stimulate your readers—often your classmates—to respond actively to your ideas. Here are some suggestions for writing a position paper:

- Begin by taking a stand on a subject. Find a statement you can defend reasonably well.
- Support your thesis with various kinds of evidence—arguments, examples, statistics, illustrations, expert opinions, and so on.
- If the position paper is very brief, suggest the direction a fuller argument might take.
- Write an open-ended conclusion, qualifying your original thesis or pointing to avenues for further study.

For two papers that take different positions on the same topic, see the selections by Naomi Munson (p. 348) and June Jordan (p. 354).

Proposing Solutions

Proposals identify a problem and suggest action that will remedy the problem. You need to convince readers first that a problem exists and is serious, then that your solution is a feasible remedy. Often you will try as well to inspire your readers to take some action.

- To demonstrate that the problem exists, give examples and cite evidence such as statistics or the testimony of experts.
- To convince readers to accept your solution, you need to show that it is feasible—and that it is better than other solutions that might reasonably be proposed.

- Consider your audience. Are they likely to be aware of the problem? Try to connect the problem to concerns they might have.

For examples of writing that proposes solutions, see the essays by Adrienne Rich (p. 56) and Allan Bloom (p. 75).

Keeping a Reading Log

Many writers use reading logs to record their feelings and detailed impressions about what they're reading and thinking. Your instructor may ask you to keep one and turn it in as part of your work for a course. Here are some suggestions for keeping a reading log:

- If you want to remember what you've read, take time to summarize or list its main ideas.
- Then write out your immediate reactions to the reading. These may include memorable images, things that made you angry, sad, puzzled, or delighted, or things that you want to know more about. Later, in a more extended comment, summarize your thoughts about the reading. Reflect on what in the reading and in your experience may have shaped your reactions.
- Make some notes about the author's perspective, where he or she seems to be coming from, noting places in the reading that provide clues to the perspective.
- Write in an informal, exploratory style, almost as if you were talking to yourself.
- Date your entries, and be sure to identify the reading.
- Look at your commentary in the context of your notes on other readings. Do you see any useful or interesting connections?

For examples of reading log entries, see the editors' responses to Anthony Brandt's essay, p. 180.

Reporting

Doing a report is one of the most common academic assignments. Reports are explanations that transfer information from writers to readers. That information may come directly from the writers' minds or from other sources of information—from traditional libraries to field research to computer networks.

- Focus a report around a thesis, a clear statement of purpose. The thesis is the *point* or *controlling idea* of a piece. A thesis statement makes a promise to readers, telling them what to expect, and it limits the subject matter and scope of your report.

- Acknowledge any sources you use.
- Define any terms your readers may not know.
- Arrange information according to a plan your readers can easily follow. For example, a report on the major events of the Cold War could follow a chronological organization: first, second, third. A report on the Cold War policies of Joseph Stalin and Harry Truman might use a structure comparing and contrasting the two leaders.
- Conclude by summarizing your work and exploring its implications.
- Give the report a concise, factual, and descriptive title.

For examples of reports, see the selections by William Rathje and Cullen Murphy (p. 268) and by Marianne Moore (p. 622).

WORKING WITH SOURCES

Much of the college writing you will do will involve the use of source materials. Here are some guidelines for quoting, paraphrasing, and summarizing sources.

Quoting

Quoting involves noting down a source's *exact words*. You will have many occasions in working with the readings in this book to use direct quotation. Many of the headnotes that introduce each reading show examples of direct quotation.

- Copy quotations *carefully,* with original punctuation, capitalization, and spelling exactly as in the original.
- Bracket any words of your own you need to add to the quotation.
- Use ellipses to indicate any omitted words.
- Enclose the quotation in quotation marks.

Paraphrasing

A paraphrase accurately states all the relevant information from a passage *in your own words and phrasing,* without any additional comment or elaboration. Use paraphrases when you want to cite ideas from a source but have no need to quote exact words.

- Include the main points and some important details from the original, in the same order in which they were presented.
- Use your own words and sentence structures. If you want to include especially memorable language from the original, enclose it in quotation marks.
- Leave out your own comments and reactions.
- Recheck the paraphrase against the original to be sure that the words and structures are your own and that they express the author's meaning accurately.

Summarizing

A summary concisely restates key ideas *in your own words*. Sometimes you may need to summarize something in a sentence or two: "P. J. O'Rourke's 'The Death of Communism' describes the euphoria he feels the moment he realizes that the West has won the Cold War." Often a more detailed synopsis is necessary. Preparing such a summary takes some planning. Here are some suggestions:

- Outline the text you are summarizing. Identify its main points, subpoints, and key bits of supporting evidence.
- Flesh out the outline with necessary details, taking care to show the connections between key ideas.
- Check that your concise version of a longer work can stand on its own. Remember that your readers may not have access to the original piece, so all references need to be clear.
- Double-check against the piece you are summarizing to make sure the wording in your summary is your own.

For an example of summary, see portions of Norman Podhoretz's essay (p. 331).

Deciding Whether to Quote, Paraphrase, or Summarize

- *Quote*
  Wording that is so memorable or expresses a point so perfectly that you cannot improve or shorten it without weakening the meaning you need
  Authors' opinions you wish to emphasize

Respected authorities whose opinions support your own ideas

Authors whose opinions challenge or vary from others in the field

- *Paraphrase*

Passages that you do not wish to quote but whose details you wish to note *fully*

- *Summarize*

Long passages whose *main points* you wish to record *selectively*

Incorporating Sources

Incorporate quotations, paraphrases, and summaries into your own writing carefully, often by using a signal phrase ("he said" or "she remarks"). Choose the verbs you use to introduce source material carefully; be sure they express your thoughts accurately. Notice, for instance, the difference between saying someone "said," "claimed," or "asserted." For effective incorporation of sources, see the many quotations in Adrienne Rich's essay (p. 56).

Acknowledging Sources

When quoting, paraphrasing, or summarizing sources in formal essays, reports, or research projects, be sure to acknowledge all sources according to the conventions required by your field or instructor.

WORKING WITH OTHERS

The title for this text recalls a remark by philosopher Hannah Arendt that "for excellence, the presence of others is always required." Nowhere is Arendt's observation more accurate than in the college community. Your college coursework will call on you to read, write, and research a vast amount of material. But you will not—or need not—do all that reading, writing, and researching alone. Far from it. Instead, you can be part of a broad conversation that includes all the texts you read; all the writing you produce; all the discussions you have with teachers, friends, family members, and classmates; all the observations and interviews you conduct. Throughout this book, we draw on Arendt's concept, from our title to the way we group readings in conversation with one another to the many assignments that ask you to work with others.

Collaboration can play an important part in all the writing you do, first if you talk with others about your topic and your plans for approaching it, then if you seek responses to your draft and gather suggestions for improving it. In much the same way, reading can be done "with others"—first by entering into mental conversation with the author and with the social and historical forces at work shaping the author's text, then by comparing your understanding of the text with that of other readers and using points of agreement or disagreement as the basis for further analysis.

As you read this book, the most immediate and valuable of your collaborators may be the members of your class. Indeed, you can learn a great deal by listening carefully to your instructor and your classmates. You can profit even more by talking over issues with them, by comparing notes and ideas with them, and by using them as a first and very important audience for your writing. They will inevitably offer you new perspectives, new ways of seeing and knowing.

- Once you establish a group, trade phone numbers and schedules, and set a time to meet.

- Set an agenda for each meeting. If you intend to study or compare certain readings, be sure everyone knows in advance and brings the essay or book to the meeting. Perhaps begin by brainstorming major questions you have about the reading.

- Use the group to work through difficult readings. If a reading is especially long, have each member take one section to explain and "teach" to the others.

- If there is something you need to prepare as a group, decide on a fair and effective means of dividing the task. Assign each group member specific duties. Arrange for a time to meet when those individual duties will have been accomplished. At the meeting, work to review the various parts and put them together.

- If a project involves a group presentation or report, figure out what each member will contribute. Plan all the work that is to be done and schedule any necessary meetings. For the presentation, make sure every group member is involved in some way. Decide on any visual aids or handouts in advance and prepare them carefully. Finally, *practice the presentation.* Everyone will benefit from a "dress rehearsal."

- Most important, listen to every member of the group carefully and respectfully; everyone's ideas must be taken into consideration. If conflict arises—and in any lively and healthy collaboration, it will—explore all areas of the conflict openly and fairly before seeking resolution.

- Take time each meeting to assess the effectiveness of the group. Consider these questions: What has the group accomplished so far? With what has it been most helpful? With what has it been least helpful? What have you contributed? What has each of the others contributed? How can you all make the group more effective?

Education:
The Idea of a University

*If then a practical end must be assigned to a University course, I say it
is that of training good members of society.*
JOHN HENRY NEWMAN, *The Idea of a University*

*A deprecating, silvery, kindly gentleman . . . regretted in a low voice
as he waved me back that ladies are only admitted to the library if accompanied
by a Fellow of the College. . . .*
VIRGINIA WOOLF, *A Room of One's Own*

*The university is above all a hierarchy. At the top is a small cluster of
highly paid and prestigious persons, chiefly men, whose careers entail the
services of a very large base of ill-paid or unpaid persons, chiefly women.*
ADRIENNE RICH, *Toward a Woman-Centered University*

The university has to stand for something.
ALLAN BLOOM, *The Student and the University*

*If the canon itself is the answer to our educational inequities, why has it
historically invited few and denied many?*
MIKE ROSE, *Lives on the Boundary*

What has emerged on campus in recent years . . . is a politics *of difference, a troubling, volatile politics in which each group justifies itself, its sense
of worth and its pursuit of power, through difference alone.*
SHELBY STEELE, *The Recoloring of Campus Life*

*Studying at Stanford, I began to think seriously about class differences.
To be materially underprivileged at a university where most folks . . . are
materially privileged provokes such thought.*
BELL HOOKS, *Keeping Close to Home: Class and Education*

*Today there is a potentially fatal idea in circulation. It is the idea that
there should not be . . . any core culture passed on from generation to
generation.*
GEORGE WILL, *Commencement at Duke*

We real cool. We left school.
GWENDOLYN BROOKS, *We Real Cool*

I n t r o d u c t i o n

YOU MAY BE SURPRISED to learn that until fairly recently in the United States most people either did not have the resources to attend college or were excluded from the majority of colleges for other reasons (such as race or gender). Today, on the other hand, nearly half of all high school graduates extend their education at a two-year or four-year college or university. And many older individuals who had never pursued higher education or had left college for some reason are now returning to the classroom. But if it seems that more and more people are attending college these days, what kind of education are they receiving?

In fact, questions of the purpose of education have been under scrutiny at least since Socrates was put on trial in 399 B.C.E. on charges of corrupting the youth of Athens by his teaching of philosophy. But no one seems to agree these days in the United States, any more than in ancient Greece, about what the role of higher education should be. Who should be allowed to attend colleges and universities—and who should not be? Should education be a mechanism for advancing the welfare of the nation—augmenting its productivity, management skills, and technology and preserving the quality of its work force? Should it be an instrument of social change—teaching ideas of social justice, adjusting to new demographics in the population it serves, and providing the rationale for radical reforms of the economic order? Should it exist primarily to stimulate the intellect and the imagination of their students? Or should schooling serve other or multiple purposes?

In this chapter, we have selected readings that bring different perspectives—and offer very different answers—to these central questions about the purposes of higher education. We hope these readings will lead you to consider such questions yourself, to think hard and long about what higher education is for and what it *should* be for in the future. Before you begin reading, however, you may want to think over some of the issues raised in this chapter. Here are some questions to get you started thinking:

1. What are your reasons for coming to college? Do you think your reasons correspond to your college's or university's goals for its students?
2. In what ways was your decision to attend college shaped or influenced by factors outside your control?
3. What should be the goals of higher education? If you were president of your college or university, what would you list as the school's aims? What would be your top priorities?

4. Have you ever felt excluded in any way from school? Have you ever experienced anything that discouraged you from going to school? On the other hand, what particular encouragement have you had to go to school?

5. What metaphor, simile, or analogy seems to you most appropriate for college? To get started, complete the following sentence: College is like a _____.

6. What role should a college or university play in any of the following areas: shaping students' moral character? providing students with intellectual stimulation and satisfaction? preparing people for jobs? preparing citizens to participate in a democracy? preparing workers to compete in a global economy? preparing people to advance the frontiers of scientific research? You may find it interesting to discuss with a few classmates which of these goals they consider most important.

• • •

JOHN HENRY NEWMAN
The Idea of a University

THE IDEA OF A UNIVERSITY *is among the most famous attempts to define a liberal arts education. Originally written in 1852 in response to a papal proposal for a Roman Catholic University in Ireland,* The Idea of a University *served as an intellectual manifesto for Catholics, who had long been an oppressed minority in the British Isles. Full emancipation occurred for them only in 1829; prior to that date, Catholics had been denied political rights in England and Ireland as well as admission to the great British universities, Oxford and Cambridge.*

John Henry Newman (1801–90), a well-known Anglican priest who had converted to the Roman church, wrote The Idea of a University *to explore what a Catholic university would be like—how it might merge religious and secular concerns. He was also responding to a world growing ever more secular in its interests, more scientific in its methods, more utilitarian in its philosophy. Revolutions in technology and industrial organization seemed to be reshaping every human endeavor, including the academy.*

Newman had reservations about these changes, many of which we take for granted today, such as the division of universities into various "schools" (arts, sciences, professional schools), the selection by students of their own programs of study, and the establishment of areas of specialization (what we would call "majors"). His aim is to defend the value of learning for its own sake.

The Idea of a University *is an example of deliberative rhetoric: Newman is both recommending and defending the proposal for a Catholic university. He faces both an entrenched Anglican tradition and a scholarly community leaning in the direction of what is today called "secular humanism." The following excerpts from this book-length work do not focus on religious issues, however. Instead, they explain some of Newman's goals for the liberal arts university.* *— J.R.*

DISCOURSE V
KNOWLEDGE ITS OWN END

1

I have said that all branches of knowledge are connected together, because the subject-matter of knowledge is intimately united in itself, as being the acts and the work of the Creator. Hence it is that the Sciences, into which our knowledge may be said to be cast, have multiplied bearings one on another, and an internal sympathy, and admit, or rather demand, comparison and adjustment. They complete, correct, balance each other. This consideration, if well-founded, must be taken into account, not only as regards the attainment of truth, which is their common end, but as regards the influence which they exercise upon those whose education consists in the study of them. I have said already, that to give undue prominence to one is to be unjust to another; to neglect or supersede these is to divert those from their proper object. It is to unsettle the boundary lines between science and science, to disturb their action, to destroy the harmony which binds them together. Such a proceeding will have a corresponding effect when introduced into a place of education. There is no science but tells a different tale, when viewed as a portion of a whole, from what it is likely to suggest when taken by itself, without the safeguard, as I may call it, of others.

Let me make use of an illustration. In the combination of colours, very different effects are produced by a difference in their selection and juxta-position; red, green, and white, change their shades, according to the contrast to which they are submitted. And, in like manner, the drift and meaning of a branch of knowledge varies with the company in which it is introduced to the student. If his reading is confined simply to one subject, however such division of labour may favour the advancement of a particular pursuit, a point into which I do not here enter, certainly it has a tendency to contract his mind. If it is incorporated with others, it depends on those others as to the kind of influence which it exerts upon him. Thus the Classics, which in England are the means of refining the taste, have in France subserved the spread of revolutionary and deistical doctrines. In Metaphysics, again, Butler's Analogy of Religion,* which has had so much to do with the conversion to the Catholic faith of members of the University of Oxford, appeared to Pitt* and others, who had received a different training, to operate only in the direction of infidelity. And so again, Watson, Bishop of Llandaff,* as I think he tells us in the narrative of his life, felt the science of Mathematics to indispose the mind to religious belief, while others see in its investigations the best parallel, and thereby defence, of the Christian Mysteries. In like manner, I suppose, Arcesilas* would not have handled logic as Aristotle, nor Aristotle have criticized poets as Plato; yet reasoning and poetry are subject to scientific rules.

It is a great point then to enlarge the range of studies which a University

---

Butler's Analogy of Religion: a defense of Christian revelation (1736) by Joseph Butler (1692–1752)

Pitt: William Pitt (1708–78), British parliamentarian and orator

Watson, Bishop of Llandaff: Richard Watson (1737–1816), a professor of chemistry and divinity

Arcesilas: Greek philosopher (c. 316–241 B.C.E.) who advocated rational skepticism

professes, even for the sake of the students; and, though they cannot pursue every subject which is open to them, they will be the gainers by living among those and under those who represent the whole circle. This I conceive to be the advantage of a seat of universal learning, considered as a place of education. An assemblage of learned men, zealous for their own sciences, and rivals of each other, are brought, by familiar intercourse and for the sake of intellectual peace, to adjust together the claims and relations of their respective subjects of investigation. They learn to respect, to consult, to aid each other. Thus is created a pure and clear atmosphere of thought, which the student also breathes, though in his own case he only pursues a few sciences out of the multitude. He profits by an intellectual tradition, which is independent of particular teachers, which guides him in his choice of subjects, and duly interprets for him those which he chooses. He apprehends the great outlines of knowledge, the principles on which it rests, the scale of its parts, its lights and its shades, its great points and its little, as he otherwise cannot apprehend them. Hence it is that his education is called "Liberal." A habit of mind is formed which lasts through life, of which the attributes are, freedom, equitableness, calmness, moderation, and wisdom; or what in a former Discourse I have ventured to call a philosophical habit. This then I would assign as the special fruit of the education furnished at a University, as contrasted with other places of teaching or modes of teaching. This is the main purpose of a University in its treatment of its students.

And now the question is asked me, What is the *use* of it? and my answer will constitute the main subject of the Discourses which are to follow.

DISCOURSE VI
KNOWLEDGE VIEWED IN RELATION TO LEARNING

5

Now from these instances, to which many more might be added, it   5
is plain, first, that the communication of knowledge certainly is either a condition or the means of that sense of enlargement or enlightenment, of which at this day we hear so much in certain quarters: this cannot be denied; but next, it is equally plain, that such communication is not the whole of the process. The enlargement consists, not merely in the passive reception into the mind of a number of ideas hitherto unknown to it, but in the mind's energetic and simultaneous action upon and towards and among those new ideas, which are rushing in upon it. It is the action of a formative power, reducing to order and meaning the matter of our acquirements; it is a making

the objects of our knowledge subjectively our own, or, to use a familiar word, it is a digestion of what we receive, into the substance of our previous state of thought; and without this no enlargement is said to follow. There is no enlargement, unless there be a comparison of ideas one with another, as they come before the mind, and a systematizing of them. We feel our minds to be growing and expanding *then,* when we not only learn, but refer what we learn to what we know already. It is not the mere addition to our knowledge that is the illumination; but the locomotion, the movement onwards, of that mental centre, to which both what we know, and what we are learning, the accumulating mass of our acquirements, gravitates. And therefore a truly great intellect, and recognized to be such by the common opinion of mankind, such as the intellect of Aristotle, or of St. Thomas,* or of Newton, or of Goethe, (I purposely take instances within and without the Catholic pale, when I would speak of the intellect as such,) is one which takes a connected view of old and new, past and present, far and near, and which has an insight into the influence of all these one on another; without which there is no whole, and no centre. It possesses the knowledge, not only of things, but also of their mutual and true relations; knowledge, not merely considered as acquirement, but as philosophy.

Accordingly, when this analytical, distributive, harmonizing process is away, the mind experiences no enlargement, and is not reckoned as enlightened or comprehensive, whatever it may add to its knowledge. For instance, a great memory, as I have already said, does not make a philosopher, any more than a dictionary can be called a grammar. There are men who embrace in their minds a vast multitude of ideas, but with little sensibility about their real relations towards each other. These may be antiquarians, annalists, naturalists; they may be learned in the law; they may be versed in statistics; they are most useful in their own place; I should shrink from speaking disrespectfully of them; still, there is nothing in such attainments to guarantee the absence of narrowness of mind. If they are nothing more than well-read men, or men of information, they have not what specially deserves the name of culture of mind, or fulfils the type of Liberal Education.

In like manner, we sometimes fall in with persons who have seen much of the world, and of the men who, in their day, have played a conspicuous part in it, but who generalize nothing, and have no observation, in the true sense of the word. They abound in information in detail, curious and entertaining, about men and things; and, having lived under the influence of no very clear or settled principles, religious or political, they speak of every one and every thing, only as so many phenomena, which are complete in themselves, and lead to nothing, not discussing them, or teach-

---

St. Thomas: Thomas Aquinas (c. 1225–74), Christian philosopher

ing any truth, or instructing the hearer, but simply talking. No one would say that these persons, well informed as they are, had attained to any great culture of intellect or to philosophy.

The case is the same still more strikingly where the persons in question are beyond dispute men of inferior powers and deficient education. Perhaps they have been much in foreign countries, and they receive, in a passive, otiose, unfruitful way, the various facts which are forced upon them there. Seafaring men, for example, range from one end of the earth to the other; but the multiplicity of external objects, which they have encountered, forms no symmetrical and consistent picture upon their imagination; they see the tapestry of human life, as it were on the wrong side, and it tells no story. They sleep, and they rise up, and they find themselves, now in Europe, now in Asia; they see visions of great cities, and wild regions; they are in the marts of commerce, or amid the islands of the South; they gaze on Pompey's Pillar,* or on the Andes; and nothing which meets them carries them forward or backward, to any idea beyond itself. Nothing has a drift or relation; nothing has a history or a promise. Every thing stands by itself, and comes and goes in its turn, like the shifting scenes of a show, which leave the spectator where he was. Perhaps you are near such a man on a particular occasion, and expect him to be shocked or perplexed at something which occurs; but one thing is much the same to him as another, or, if he is perplexed, it is as not knowing what to say, whether it is right to admire, or to ridicule, or to disapprove, while conscious that some expression of opinion is expected from him; for in fact he has no standard of judgment at all, and no landmarks to guide him to a conclusion. Such is mere acquisition, and, I repeat, no one would dream of calling it philosophy.

6

Instances, such as these, confirm, by the contrast, the conclusion I have already drawn from those which preceded them. That only is true enlargement of mind which is the power of viewing many things at once as one whole, of referring them severally to their true place in the universal system, of understanding their respective values, and determining their mutual dependence. Thus is that form of Universal Knowledge, of which I have on a former occasion spoken, set up in the individual intellect, and constitutes its perfection. Possessed of this real illumination, the mind never views any part of the extended subject-matter of Knowledge without recollecting that it is but a part, or without the associations which spring from this recollection. It makes every thing in some sort lead to every thing else; it would communicate the image of the whole to every separate portion,

---

Pompey's Pillar: a red granite column erected at Alexandria, Egypt, in 302 C.E. to honor the Emperor Diocletian

till that whole becomes in imagination like a spirit, every where pervading and penetrating its component parts, and giving them one definite meaning. Just as our bodily organs, when mentioned, recall their function in the body, as the word "creation" suggests the Creator, and "subjects" a sovereign, so, in the mind of the Philosopher, as we are abstractedly conceiving of him, the elements of the physical and moral world, sciences, arts, pursuits, ranks, offices, events, opinions, individualities, are all viewed as one, with correlative functions, and as gradually by successive combinations converging, one and all, to the true centre.

To have even a portion of this illuminative reason and true philosophy is the highest state to which nature can aspire, in the way of intellect; it puts the mind above the influences of chance and necessity, above anxiety, suspense, unsettlement, and superstition, which is the lot of the many. Men, whose minds are possessed with some one object, take exaggerated views of its importance, are feverish in the pursuit of it, make it the measure of things which are utterly foreign to it, and are startled and despond if it happens to fail them. They are ever in alarm or in transport. Those on the other hand who have no object or principle whatever to hold by, lose their way, every step they take. They are thrown out, and do not know what to think or say, at every fresh juncture; they have no view of persons, or occurrences, or facts, which come suddenly upon them, and they hang upon the opinion of others, for want of internal resources. But the intellect, which has been disciplined to the perfection of its powers, which knows, and thinks while it knows, which has learned to leaven the dense mass of facts and events with the elastic force of reason, such an intellect cannot be partial, cannot be exclusive, cannot be impetuous, cannot be at a loss, cannot but be patient, collected, and majestically calm, because it discerns the end in every beginning, the origin in every end, the law in every interruption, the limit in each delay; because it ever knows where it stands, and how its path lies from one point to another. It is the τετράγωνος* of the Peripatetic, and has the "nil admirari"* of the Stoic,—

> Felix qui potuit rerum cognoscere causas,
> Atque metus omnes, et inexorabile fatum
> Subjecit pedibus, strepitumque Acherontis avari.*

There are men who, when in difficulties, originate at the moment vast ideas or dazzling projects; who, under the influence of excitement, are able to

---

τετράγωνος: a Greek word—*tetragonos*—denoting a figure with four angles, a Stoic representation of completeness and perfection

nil admirari: Latin for "Be astonished by nothing."

Felix . . . avari.: A quotation from the Roman poet Vergil, *Georgics* II, lines 409–92. Harold Arnold Hedges translates the lines in this way: "Felicitous is he who recognizes causes/ and fear of all and inexorable Fate/and noisy Acheron has subjected to his feet."

cast a light, almost as if from inspiration, on a subject or course of action which comes before them; who have a sudden presence of mind equal to any emergency, rising with the occasion, and an undaunted magnanimous bearing, and an energy and keenness which is but made intense by opposition. This is genius, this is heroism; it is the exhibition of a natural gift, which no culture can teach, at which no Institution can aim; here, on the contrary, we are concerned, not with mere nature, but with training and teaching. That perfection of the Intellect, which is the result of Education, and its *beau ideal,* to be imparted to individuals in their respective measures, is the clear, calm, accurate vision and comprehension of all things, as far as the finite mind can embrace them, each in its place, and with its own characteristics upon it. It is almost prophetic from its knowledge of history; it is almost heart-searching from its knowledge of human nature; it has almost supernatural charity from its freedom from littleness and prejudice; it has almost the repose of faith, because nothing can startle it; it has almost the beauty and harmony of heavenly contemplation, so intimate is it with the eternal order of things and the music of the spheres.*

Discourse VII
Knowledge Viewed in Relation to Professional Skill

10

But I must bring these extracts to an end. To-day I have confined myself to saying that that training of the intellect, which is best for the individual himself, best enables him to discharge his duties to society. The Philosopher, indeed, and the man of the world differ in their very notion, but the methods, by which they are respectively formed, are pretty much the same. The Philosopher has the same command of matters of thought, which the true citizen and gentleman has of matters of business and conduct. If then a practical end must be assigned to a University course, I say it is that of training good members of society. Its art is the art of social life, and its end is fitness for the world. It neither confines its views to particular professions on the one hand, nor creates heroes or inspires genius on the other. Works indeed of genius fall under no art; heroic minds come under no rule; a University is not a birthplace of poets or of immortal authors, of founders of schools, leaders of colonies, or conquerors of nations. It does not promise a generation of Aristotles or Newtons, of Napoleons or Washingtons, of Raphaels or Shakespeares, though such miracles of nature

---

music of the spheres: in Ptolemaic cosmology, the sound made by the turning of the crystalline orbs that carried the sun, moon, and planets

it has before now contained within its precincts. Nor is it content on the other hand with forming the critic or the experimentalist, the economist or the engineer, though such too it includes within its scope. But a University training is the great ordinary means to a great but ordinary end; it aims at raising the intellectual tone of society, at cultivating the public mind, at purifying the national taste, at supplying true principles to popular enthusiasm and fixed aims to popular aspiration, at giving enlargement and sobriety to the ideas of the age, at facilitating the exercise of political power, and refining the intercourse of private life. It is the education which gives a man a clear conscious view of his own opinions and judgments, a truth in developing them, an eloquence in expressing them, and a force in urging them. It teaches him to see things as they are, to go right to the point, to disentangle a skein of thought, to detect what is sophistical, and to discard what is irrelevant. It prepares him to fill any post with credit, and to master any subject with facility. It shows him how to accommodate himself to others, how to throw himself into their state of mind, how to bring before them his own, how to influence them, how to come to an understanding with them, how to bear with them. He is at home in any society, he has common ground with every class; he knows when to speak and when to be silent; he is able to converse, he is able to listen; he can ask a question pertinently, and gain a lesson seasonably, when he has nothing to impart himself; he is ever ready, yet never in the way; he is a pleasant companion, and a comrade you can depend upon; he knows when to be serious and when to trifle, and he has a sure tact which enables him to trifle with gracefulness and to be serious with effect. He has the repose of a mind which lives in itself, while it lives in the world, and which has resources for its happiness at home when it cannot go abroad. He has a gift which serves him in public, and supports him in retirement, without which good fortune is but vulgar, and with which failure and disappointment have a charm. The art which tends to make a man all this, is in the object which it pursues as useful as the art of wealth or the art of health, though it is less susceptible of method, and less tangible, less certain, less complete in its result.

QUESTIONING THE TEXT

1. Newman suggests that students gain a perspective on different kinds of knowledge by living among scholars from many fields. Is this a practical ideal on campuses today? Can a part-time or day student benefit from a liberal arts education as Newman understands it? What assumptions does he seem to make about the time, place, age, sex, and status of those able to receive a liberal education?
2. Examine the goals Newman explicitly provides for the university in

the passage from Discourse VII. Do these goals still seem relevant today? Why, or why not? If you keep a reading log, record your response there.

3. As you re-read Newman's essay, record your reactions to his style in the margins. Does it feel stuffy or solemn? Does it move you or impress you? When you are finished, draw some conclusions from your comments.

MAKING CONNECTIONS

4. Would Mike Rose or the students he describes in the reading starting on p. 87 fit into the university Newman describes? Write a two- or three-page essay exploring this issue.

5. One of the major complaints made against contemporary universities by Allan Bloom (p. 75) is that they fragment knowledge into many separate disciplines and then give students no guidance through or sense of connection among them. Discuss the underlying principle in Newman and Bloom that a good liberal education approaches knowledge as a whole, not as a collection of separate courses, fields, or career paths.

JOINING THE CONVERSATION

6. Can Newman's concept of "liberal arts" survive in our world today? Does it deserve to? Why, or why not? Write a position paper on this subject.

7. For a national news magazine, write an evaluation of American higher education as you imagine Newman might regard it if he were living today. What might he admire? What would he criticize?

8. With a group of classmates, discuss the "usefulness" of the education you have had in high school and college. Which courses of study seem to have the most direct application to daily life? Which (if any) seem designed primarily as learning for its own sake?

VIRGINIA WOOLF
A Room of One's Own

BORN IN 1882 *into an affluent British family, Virginia Woolf was educated not at Oxford or Cambridge, from which she was, as a woman, excluded, but at home by her parents. She pursued her own education avidly, determined to acquire the kind of learning that was readily available to males of her social class and to explore the differences between the lives of young women and those of young men. At twenty-four, she wrote her first novel,* The Voyage Out, *and she continued to write novels and essays until her death in 1941.*

In one of her most famous essays, Woolf asks a deceptively simple question—what if Shakespeare had had a sister?—and goes on to meditate on what this imaginary sister's life would have been like. What kind of education would have been available to her? Woolf explores these issues further in her long essay "A Room of One's Own," the first chapter of which is excerpted below. Originally given as lectures on "women and fiction" at Cambridge's women's colleges in 1928, the essay argues that to write fiction a woman must have "money and a room of her own." To support this claim, she recounts her experiences at an imaginary university, "Oxbridge." This narrative allows her to advance her argument while illuminating not only what it feels like to be locked out of such an educational establishment but also exactly in what those "locked into" the institution are enclosed.

Many selections in this chapter give explicit definitions of a university's goals: to establish a philosophical habit of mind (John Henry Newman), to prepare thinkers to seek a "unified view of nature and man's place in it" (Allan Bloom), and so on. Woolf does not make such an explicit argument. Instead, she evokes the flavor, the emotional and intellectual climate, of a particular kind of university—one that excludes women. In doing so, she challenges not only the traditional idea of an exclusively male university but also traditional notions of how arguments should be constructed.

I chose this selection because it presents an implicit rather than an explicit argument, evoking rather than attacking women's exclusion from higher education, and because of the musical, lyrical quality of Woolf's descriptions. In addition, the context for the original presentation of these remarks appeals to my imagination: I can just picture Virginia Woolf, tall and full of presence, rising to address the subject of women and fiction. As this essay reveals, she quickly realized she could not really talk about women and literature without discussing the larger issue of women's lack of control over the conditions of their lives—and in particular their education. – A.L.

But, you may say, we asked you to speak about women and fiction—what has that got to do with a room of one's own? I will try to explain. When you asked me to speak about women and fiction I sat down on the banks of a river and began to wonder what the words meant. They might mean simply a few remarks about Fanny Burney; a few more about Jane Austen; a tribute to the Brontës and a sketch of Haworth Parsonage under snow; some witticisms if possible about Miss Mitford; a respectful allusion to George Eliot; a reference to Mrs. Gaskell and one would have done. But at second sight the words seemed not so simple. The title women and fiction might mean, and you may have meant it to mean, women and what they are like; or it might mean women and the fiction that they write; or it might mean women and the fiction that is written about them; or it might mean that somehow all three are inextricably mixed together and you want me to consider them in that light. But when I began to consider the subject in this last way, which seemed the most interesting, I soon saw that it had one fatal drawback. I should never be able to come to a conclusion. I should never be able to fulfil what is, I understand, the first duty of a lecturer—to hand you after an hour's discourse a nugget of pure truth to wrap up between the pages of your notebooks and keep on the mantelpiece for ever. All I could do was to offer you an opinion upon one minor point—a woman must have money and a room of her own if she is to write fiction; and that, as you will see, leaves the great problem of the true nature of woman and the true nature of fiction unsolved. I have shirked the duty of coming to a conclusion upon these two questions—women and fiction remain, so far as I am concerned, unsolved problems. But in order to make some amends I am going to do what I can to show you how I arrived at this opinion about the room and the money. I am going to develop in your presence as fully and freely as I can the train of thought which led me to think this. Perhaps if I lay bare the ideas, the prejudices, that lie behind this statement you will find that they have some bearing upon women and some upon fiction. At any rate, when a subject is highly controversial—and any question about sex is that—one cannot hope to tell the truth. One can only show how one came to hold whatever opinion one does hold. One can only give one's audience the chance of drawing their own conclusions as they observe the limitations, the prejudices, the idiosyncrasies of the speaker. Fiction here is likely to contain more truth than fact. Therefore I propose, making use of all the liberties and licences of a novelist, to tell you the story of the two days that preceded my coming here—how, bowed down by the weight of the subject which you have laid upon my shoulders, I pondered it, and made it work in and out of my daily life. I need not say that what I am about to describe has no existence; Oxbridge is an invention; so is Fernham; "I" is only a convenient term for somebody who has no real being. Lies will flow from my lips, but there may perhaps be some truth mixed up with them; it is for you to seek out this truth and to decide whether any part of it is worth keeping. If not, you will of course throw the whole of it into the wastepaper basket and forget all about it.

Here then was I (call me Mary Beton, Mary Seton, Mary Carmichael or by any name you please—it is not a matter of any importance) sitting on the banks of a river a week or two ago in fine October weather, lost in thought. That collar I have spoken of, women and fiction, the need of coming to some conclusion on a subject that raises all sorts of prejudices and passions, bowed my head to the ground. To the right and left bushes of some sort, golden and crimson, glowed with the colour, even it seemed burnt with the heat, of fire. On the further bank the willows wept in perpetual lamentation, their hair about their shoulders. The river reflected whatever it chose of sky and bridge and burning tree, and when the undergraduate had oared his boat through the reflections they closed again, completely, as if he had never been. There one might have sat the clock round lost in thought. Thought—to call it by a prouder name than it deserved—had let its line down into the stream. It swayed, minute after minute, hither and thither among the reflections and the weeds, letting the water lift it and sink it, until—you know the little tug—the sudden conglomeration of an idea at the end of one's line: and then the cautious hauling of it in, and the careful laying of it out? Alas, laid on the grass how small, how insignificant this thought of mine looked; the sort of fish that a good fisherman puts back into the water so that it may grow fatter and be one day worth cooking and eating. I will not trouble you with that thought now, though if you look carefully you may find it for yourselves in the course of what I am going to say.

But however small it was, it had, nevertheless, the mysterious property of its kind—put back into the mind, it became at once very exciting, and important; and as it darted and sank, and flashed hither and thither, set up such a wash and tumult of ideas that it was impossible to sit still. It was thus that I found myself walking with extreme rapidity across a grass plot. Instantly a man's figure rose to intercept me. Nor did I at first understand that the gesticulations of a curious-looking object, in a cut-away coat and evening shirt, were aimed at me. His face expressed horror and indignation. Instinct rather than reason came to my help; he was a Beadle;* I was a woman. This was the turf; there was the path. Only the Fellows* and Scholars* are allowed here; the gravel is the place for me. Such thoughts were the work of a moment. As I regained the path the arms of the Beadle sank, his face assumed its usual repose, and though turf is better walking than gravel, no very great harm was done. The only charge I could bring against the Fellows and Scholars of whatever the college might happen to

---

Beadle: an officer of the college
Fellows: senior members of the college with special privileges
Scholars: students of the college

be was that in protection of their turf, which has been rolled for 300 years in succession, they had sent my little fish into hiding.

What idea it had been that had sent me so audaciously trespassing I could not now remember. The spirit of peace descended like a cloud from heaven, for if the spirit of peace dwells anywhere, it is in the courts and quadrangles of Oxbridge on a fine October morning. Strolling through those colleges past those ancient halls the roughness of the present seemed smoothed away; the body seemed contained in a miraculous glass cabinet through which no sound could penetrate, and the mind, freed from any contact with facts (unless one trespassed on the turf again), was at liberty to settle down upon whatever meditation was in harmony with the moment. As chance would have it, some stray memory of some old essay about revisiting Oxbridge in the long vacation brought Charles Lamb to mind— Saint Charles, said Thackeray, putting a letter of Lamb's to his forehead. Indeed, among all the dead (I give you my thoughts as they came to me), Lamb is one of the most congenial; one to whom one would have liked to say, Tell me then how you wrote your essays? For his essays are superior even to Max Beerbohm's, I thought, with all their perfection, because of that wild flash of imagination, that lightning crack of genius in the middle of them which leaves them flawed and imperfect, but starred with poetry. Lamb then came to Oxbridge perhaps a hundred years ago. Certainly he wrote an essay—the name escapes me—about the manuscript of one of Milton's poems which he saw here. It was *Lycidas* perhaps, and Lamb wrote how it shocked him to think it possible that any word in *Lycidas* could have been different from what it is. To think of Milton changing the words in that poem seemed to him a sort of sacrilege. This led me to remember what I could of *Lycidas* and to amuse myself with guessing which word it could have been that Milton had altered, and why. It then occurred to me that the very manuscript itself which Lamb had looked at was only a few hundred yards away, so that one could follow Lamb's footsteps across the quadrangle to that famous library where the treasure is kept. Moreover, I recollected, as I put this plan into execution, it is in this famous library that the manuscript of Thackeray's *Esmond* is also preserved. The critics often say that *Esmond* is Thackeray's most perfect novel. But the affectation of the style, with its imitation of the eighteenth century, hampers one, so far as I remember; unless indeed the eighteenth-century style was natural to Thackeray—a fact that one might prove by looking at the manuscript and seeing whether the alterations were for the benefit of the style or of the sense. But then one would have to decide what is style and what is meaning, a question which— but here I was actually at the door which leads into the library itself. I must have opened it, for instantly there issued, like a guardian angel barring the way with a flutter of black gown instead of white wings, a deprecating, silvery, kindly gentleman, who regretted in a low voice as he waved me

back that ladies are only admitted to the library if accompanied by a Fellow
of the College or furnished with a letter of introduction.

That a famous library has been cursed by a woman is a matter of   5
complete indifference to a famous library. Venerable and calm, with all its
treasures safe locked within its breast, it sleeps complacently and will, so
far as I am concerned, so sleep for ever. Never will I wake those echoes,
never will I ask for that hospitality again, I vowed as I descended the steps
in anger. Still an hour remained before luncheon, and what was one to do?
Stroll on the meadows? sit by the river? Certainly it was a lovely autumn
morning; the leaves were fluttering red to the ground; there was no great
hardship in doing either. But the sound of music reached my ear. Some
service or celebration was going forward. The organ complained magnifi-
cently as I passed the chapel door. Even the sorrow of Christianity sounded
in that serene air more like the recollection of sorrow than sorrow itself;
even the groanings of the ancient organ seemed lapped in peace. I had no
wish to enter had I the right, and this time the verger might have stopped
me, demanding perhaps my baptismal certificate, or a letter of introduction
from the Dean. But the outside of these magnificent buildings is often as
beautiful as the inside. Moreover, it was amusing enough to watch the
congregation assembling, coming in and going out again, busying themselves at the door of the Chapel like bees at the mouth of a hive. Many
were in cap and gown; some had tufts of fur on their shoulders; others were
wheeled in bath-chairs; others, though not past middle age, seemed creased
and crushed into shapes so singular that one was reminded of those giant
crabs and crayfish who heave with difficulty across the sand of an aquarium.
As I leant against the wall the University indeed seemed a sanctuary in
which are preserved rare types which would soon be obsolete if left to fight
for existence on the pavement of the Strand.* . . . The clock struck. It
was time to find one's way to luncheon.

It is a curious fact that novelists have a way of making us believe that
luncheon parties are invariably memorable for something very witty that
was said, or for something very wise that was done. But they seldom spare
a word for what was eaten. It is part of the novelist's convention not to
mention soup and salmon and ducklings, as if soup and salmon and ducklings
were of no importance whatsoever, as if nobody ever smoked a cigar or
drank a glass of wine. Here, however, I shall take the liberty to defy that
convention and to tell you that the lunch on this occasion began with soles,
sunk in a deep dish, over which the college cook had spread a counterpane
of the whitest cream, save that it was branded here and there with brown
spots like the spots on the flanks of a doe. After that came the partridges,

---

Strand: a commercial street in London

but if this suggests a couple of bald, brown birds on a plate you are mistaken. The partridges, many and various, came with all their retinue of sauces and salads, the sharp and the sweet, each in its order; their potatoes, thin as coins but not so hard; their sprouts, foliated as rosebuds but more succulent. And no sooner had the roast and its retinue been done with than the silent serving-man, the Beadle himself perhaps in a milder manifestation, set before us, wreathed in napkins, a confection which rose all sugar from the waves. To call it pudding and so relate it to rice and tapioca would be an insult. Meanwhile the wineglasses had flushed yellow and flushed crimson; had been emptied; had been filled. And thus by degrees was lit, halfway down the spine, which is the seat of the soul, not that hard little electric light which we call brilliance, as it pops in and out upon our lips, but the more profound, subtle and subterranean glow, which is the rich yellow flame of rational intercourse. No need to hurry. No need to sparkle. No need to be anybody but oneself. We are all going to heaven and Vandyck is of the company—in other words, how good life seemed, how sweet its rewards, how trivial this grudge or that grievance, how admirable friendship and the society of one's kind, as, lighting a good cigarette, one sunk among the cushions in the window-seat. . . .

This [lunch party], thanks to the hospitality of the host, had lasted far into the afternoon. The beautiful October day was fading and the leaves were falling from the trees in the avenue as I walked through it. Gate after gate seemed so close with gentle finality behind me. Innumerable beadles were fitting innumerable keys into well-oiled locks; the treasure-house was being made secure for another night. After the avenue one comes out upon a road—I forget its name—which leads you, if you take the right turning, along to Fernham. But there was plenty of time. Dinner was not till half-past seven. One could almost do without dinner after such a luncheon. . . .

As I have said already that it was an October day, I dare not forfeit your respect and imperil the fair name of fiction by changing the season and describing lilacs hanging over garden walls, crocuses, tulips and other flowers of spring. Fiction must stick to facts, and the truer the facts the better the fiction—so we are told. Therefore it was still autumn and the leaves were still yellow and falling, if anything, a little faster than before, because it was now evening (seven twenty-three to be precise) and a breeze (from the south-west to be exact) had risen. . . . The gardens of Fernham lay before me in the spring twilight, wild and open, and in the long grass, sprinkled and carelessly flung, were daffodils and bluebells, not orderly perhaps at the best of times, and now wind-blown and waving as they tugged at their roots. The windows of the building, curved like ships' windows among generous waves of red brick, changed from lemon to silver under the flight of the quick spring clouds. Somebody was in a hammock, somebody, but in this light they were phantoms only, half guessed, half seen, raced across the grass—would no one stop her?—and then on the terrace, as if popping out to breathe the air, to glance at the garden, came a bent figure, formidable yet humble, with her great forehead and her shabby dress—could it be the famous scholar, could it be J—— H—— herself? All was dim, yet intense too, as if the scarf which the dusk had flung over the garden were torn asunder by star or sword—the flash of some terrible reality leaping, as its way is, out of the heart of the spring. For youth——

Here was my soup. Dinner was being served in the great dining-hall. Far from being spring it was in fact an evening in October. Everybody was assembled in the big dining-room. Dinner was ready. Here was the soup. It was a plain gravy soup. There was nothing to stir the fancy in that. One could have seen through the transparent liquid any pattern that there might have been on the plate itself. But there was no pattern. The plate was plain. Next came beef with its attendant greens and potatoes—a homely trinity, suggesting the rumps of cattle in a muddy market, and sprouts curled and yellowed at the edge, and bargaining and cheapening, and women with string bags on Monday morning. There was no reason to complain of human nature's daily food, seeing that the supply was sufficient and coal miners doubtless were sitting down to less. Prunes and custard followed. And if any one complains that prunes, even when mitigated by custard, are an uncharitable vegetable (fruit they are not), stringy as a miser's heart and exuding a fluid such as might run in misers' veins who have denied themselves wine and warmth for eighty years and yet not given to the poor, he should reflect that there are people whose charity embraces even the prune. Biscuits and cheese came next, and here the water-jug was liberally passed round, for it is the nature of biscuits to be dry, and these were biscuits to the core. That was all. The meal was over. Everybody scraped their chairs back; the swing-doors swung violently to and fro; soon the hall was emptied of every sign of food and made ready no doubt for breakfast next morning. Down corridors and up staircases the youth of England went banging and singing. And was it for a guest, a stranger (for I had no more right here in Fernham than in Trinity or Somerville or Girton or Newnham or Christchurch*), to say, "The dinner was not good," or to say (we were now, Mary Seton and I, in her sitting-room), "Could we not have dined up here alone?" for if I had said anything of the kind I should have been prying and searching into the secret economies of a house which to the stranger wears so fine a front of gaiety and courage. No, one could say nothing of the sort. Indeed, conversation for a moment flagged. The human frame being what it is, heart, body and brain all mixed together, and not contained in separate compartments as they will be no doubt in another

---

Trinity . . . Christchurch: colleges that are part of Oxford and Cambridge universities

million years, a good dinner is of great importance to good talk. One cannot think well, love well, sleep well, if one has not dined well. The lamp in the spine does not light on beef and prunes. We are all *probably* going to heaven, and Vandyck is, we *hope,* to meet us round the next corner—that is the dubious and qualifying state of mind that beef and prunes at the end of the day's work breed between them. Happily my friend, who taught science, had a cupboard where there was a squat bottle and little glasses— (but there should have been sole and partridge to begin with)—so that we were able to draw up to the fire and repair some of the damages of the day's living. In a minute or so we were slipping freely in and out among all those objects of curiosity and interest which form in the mind in the absence of a particular person, and are naturally to be discussed on coming together again—how somebody has married, another has not; one thinks this, another that; one has improved out of all knowledge, the other most amazingly gone to the bad—with all those speculations upon human nature and the character of the amazing world we live in which spring naturally from such beginnings. While these things were being said, however, I became shamefacedly aware of a current setting in of its own accord and carrying everything forward to an end of its own. One might be talking of Spain or Portugal, of book or racehorse, but the real interest of whatever was said was none of those things, but a scene of masons on a high roof some five centuries ago. Kings and nobles brought treasure in huge sacks and poured it under the earth. This scene was for ever coming alive in my mind and placing itself by another of lean cows and a muddy market and withered greens and the stringy hearts of old men—these two pictures, disjointed and disconnected and nonsensical as they were, were for ever coming together and combating each other and had me entirely at their mercy. The best course, unless the whole talk was to be distorted, was to expose what was in my mind to the air, when with good luck it would fade and crumble like the head of the dead king when they opened the coffin at Windsor. Briefly, then, I told Miss Seton about the masons who had been all those years on the roof of the chapel, and about the kings and queens and nobles bearing sacks of gold and silver on their shoulders, which they shovelled into the earth; and then how the great financial magnates of our own time came and laid cheques and bonds, I suppose, where the others had laid ingots and rough lumps of gold. All that lies beneath the colleges down there, I said; but this college, where we are now sitting, what lies beneath its gallant red brick and the wild unkempt grasses of the garden? What force is behind that plain china off which we dined, and (here it popped out of my mouth before I could stop it) the beef, the custard and the prunes?

Well, said Mary Seton, about the year 1860—Oh, but you know the story, she said, bored, I suppose, by the recital. And she told me—rooms were hired. Committees met. Envelopes were addressed. Circulars were drawn up. Meetings were held; letters were read out; so-and-so has promised so much; on the contrary, Mr. —— won't give a penny. The *Saturday Review* has been very rude. How can we raise a fund to pay for offices? Shall we hold a bazaar? Can't we find a pretty girl to sit in the front row? Let us look up what John Stuart Mill* said on the subject. Can any one persuade the editor of the —— to print a letter? Can we get Lady —— to sign it? Lady —— is out of town. That was the way it was done, presumably, sixty years ago, and it was a prodigious effort, and a great deal of time was spent on it. And it was only after a long struggle and with the utmost difficulty that they got thirty thousand pounds together.[1] So obviously we cannot have wine and partridges and servants carrying tin dishes on their heads, she said. We cannot have sofas and separate rooms. "The amenities," she said, quoting from some book or other, "will have to wait."[2]

At the thought of all those women working year after year and finding it hard to get two thousand pounds together, and as much as they could do to get thirty thousand pounds, we burst out in scorn at the reprehensible poverty of our sex. What had our mothers been doing then that they had no wealth to leave us? Powdering their noses? Looking in at shop windows? Flaunting in the sun at Monte Carlo? There were some photographs on the mantelpiece. Mary's mother—if that was her picture—may have been a wastrel in her spare time (she had thirteen children by a minister of the church), but if so her gay and dissipated life had left too few traces of its pleasures on her face. She was a homely body; an old lady in a plaid shawl which was fastened by a large cameo; and she sat in a basket-chair, encouraging a spaniel to look at the camera, with the amused, yet strained expression of one who is sure that the dog will move directly the bulb is pressed. Now if she had gone into business; had become a manufacturer of artificial silk or a magnate on the Stock Exchange; if she had left two or three hundred thousand pounds to Fernham, we could have been sitting at our ease tonight and the subject of our talk might have been archaeology, botany, anthropology, physics, the nature of the atom, mathematics, astronomy, relativity, geography. If only Mrs. Seton and her mother and her mother before her had learnt the great art of making money and had left their money, like their fathers and their grandfathers before them, to found

---

John Stuart Mill: English economist, philosopher, political theorist, and proponent of women's rights (1806–73)

[1] "We are told that we ought to ask for £30,000 at least. . . . It is not a large sum, considering that there is to be but one college of this sort for Great Britain, Ireland and the Colonies, and considering how easy it is to raise immense sums for boys' schools. But considering how few people really wish women to be educated, it is a good deal."—Lady Stephen, *Life of Miss Emily Davies.*

[2] Every penny which could be scraped together was set aside for building, and the amenities had to be postponed.—R. Strachey, *The Cause.*

fellowships and lectureships and prizes and scholarships appropriated to the use of their own sex, we might have dined very tolerably up here alone off a bird and a bottle of wine; we might have looked forward without undue confidence to a pleasant and honourable lifetime spent in the shelter of one of the liberally endowed professions. We might have been exploring or writing; mooning about the venerable places of the earth; sitting contemplative on the steps of the Parthenon, or going at ten to an office and coming home comfortably at half-past four to write a little poetry.* Only, if Mrs. Seton and her like had gone into business at the age of fifteen, there would have been—that was the snag in the argument—no Mary. What, I asked, did Mary think of that? There between the curtains was the October night, calm and lovely, with a star or two caught in the yellowing trees. Was she ready to resign her share of it and her memories (for they had been a happy family, though a large one) of games and quarrels up in Scotland, which she is never tired of praising for the fineness of its air and the quality of its cakes, in order that Fernham might have been endowed with fifty thousand pounds or so by a stroke of the pen? For, to endow a college would necessitate the suppression of families altogether. Making a fortune and bearing thirteen children—no human being could stand it. Consider the facts, we said. First there are nine months before the baby is born. Then the baby is born. Then there are three or four months spent in feeding the baby. After the baby is fed there are certainly five years spent in playing with the baby. You cannot, it seems, let children run about the streets. People who have seen them running wild in Russia say that the sight is not a pleasant one. People say, too, that human nature takes its shape in the years between one and five. If Mrs. Seton, I said, had been making money, what sort of memories would you have had of games and quarrels? What would you have known of Scotland, and its fine air and cakes and all the rest of it? But it is useless to ask these questions, because you would never have come into existence at all.* Moreover, it is equally useless to ask what might have happened if Mrs. Seton and her mother and her mother before her had amassed great wealth and laid it under the foundations of college and library, because, in the first place, to earn money was impossible for them, and in the second, had it been possible, the law denied them the right to possess what money they earned. It is only for the last forty-eight years that Mrs. Seton has had a penny of her own. For all the centuries before that it would have been her husband's property—a thought which, perhaps, may have had its share in keeping Mrs. Seton and her mothers off the Stock Exchange. Every

---

We might have . . . a little poetry: For a different view of the working world, see Naomi Munson, "Harassment Blues," p. 348.

Making a fortune . . . come into existence: For a discussion of the difficulties that childcare poses to women *within* the university, see Adrienne Rich, "Toward a Woman-Centered University," p. 56.

penny I earn, they may have said, will be taken from me and disposed of according to my husband's wisdom—perhaps to found a scholarship or to endow a fellowship in Balliol or Kings,* so that to earn money, even if I could earn money, is not a matter that interests me very greatly. I had better leave it to my husband.

At any rate, whether or not the blame rested on the old lady who was looking at the spaniel, there could be no doubt that for some reason or other our mothers had mismanaged their affairs very gravely. Not a penny could be spared for "amenities"; for partridges and wine, beadles and turf, books and cigars, libraries and leisure. To raise bare walls out of the bare earth was the utmost they could do.

So we talked standing at the window and looking, as so many thousands look every night, down on the domes and towers of the famous city beneath us. It was very beautiful, very mysterious in the autumn moonlight. The old stone looked very white and venerable. One thought of all the books that were assembled down there; of the pictures of old prelates and worthies hanging in the panelled rooms; of the painted windows that would be throwing strange globes and crescents on the pavement; of the tablets and memorials and inscriptions; of the fountains and the grass; of the quiet rooms looking across the quiet quadrangles. And (pardon me the thought) I thought, too, of the admirable smoke and drink and the deep armchairs and the pleasant carpets: of the urbanity, the geniality, the dignity which are the offspring of luxury and privacy and space. Certainly our mothers had not provided us with anything comparable to all this—our mothers who found it difficult to scrape together thirty thousand pounds, our mothers who bore thirteen children to ministers of religion at St. Andrews.

So I went back to my inn, and as I walked through the dark streets I pondered this and that, as one does at the end of the day's work. I pondered why it was that Mrs. Seton had no money to leave us; and what effect poverty has on the mind; and what effect wealth has on the mind; and I thought of the queer old gentlemen I had seen that morning with tufts of fur upon their shoulders; and I remembered how if one whistled one of them ran; and I thought of the organ booming in the chapel and of the shut doors of the library; and I thought how unpleasant it is to be locked out; and I thought how it is worse perhaps to be locked in; and, thinking of the safety and prosperity of the one sex and of the poverty and insecurity of the other and of the effect of tradition and of the lack of tradition upon the mind of a writer, I thought at last that it was time to roll up the crumpled skin of the day, with its arguments and its impressions and its anger and its laughter, and cast it into the hedge. A thousand stars were flashing across the blue wastes of the sky. One seemed alone with an inscrutable society.

Balliol or Kings: colleges of Oxford and Cambridge, respectively

All human beings were laid asleep—prone, horizontal, dumb. Nobody seemed stirring in the streets of Oxbridge. Even the door of the hotel sprang open at the touch of an invisible hand—not a boots was sitting up to light me to bed, it was so late.

QUESTIONING THE TEXT

1. How would you describe Woolf's tone—her attitude toward her subject—in this essay? Specifically, what is her attitude toward the fictional Oxbridge? Pick out a few sentences that especially illustrate this tone.
2. Woolf muses that "the University indeed seemed a sanctuary in which are preserved rare types which would soon be obsolete if left to fight for existence on the pavement of the Strand." To what extent do you think colleges and universities serve to protect those things that have little value in the world outside? Explain.
3. The introduction to this reading says that Woolf's implicit argument challenges "traditional notions of how arguments should be constructed." What *is* the "thesis" of her argument? How do you know? Are you sympathetic to or persuaded by the argument? Why, or why not?

MAKING CONNECTIONS

4. Woolf and Adrienne Rich, the author of the next reading, are both concerned with the position of women within a university. How do their views compare? What are your ideas on the subject? If you are keeping a reading log, record your responses to these questions there.
5. Look back to the way John Henry Newman defines a university in the previous reading. Take a few minutes to review Newman's argument and to write a brief (two- or three-sentence) summary of what he sees as an ideal university. Would Woolf accept such a view of the university? List several points from her essay that you could cite as support for your conclusion regarding her views.

JOINING THE CONVERSATION

6. Although universities are ostensibly open to women, are there still ways in which women are shut out or excluded? Write a page or two in which you explore this question.
7. Woolf describes the stifling effect that being told she didn't belong at the university had upon her ability to think. Describe a time when

someone told you that you didn't belong or that you weren't capable of doing something you were trying to do. What effects did this incident have on you?

8. Spend some time brainstorming with two or three members of your class about ways in which your own college or university may be most like "Oxbridge." Then compile a list of the four or five most notable characteristics and bring them to class for discussion.

ADRIENNE RICH
Toward a Woman-Centered University

*A*DRIENNE *R*ICH *(b. 1929) has been a writer and a teacher all her life. Winner of the Yale Series of Younger Poets Award in 1951 for her first volume of poems,* A Change of World, *and of the National Book Award for Poetry in 1974 (for* Diving into the Wreck*), she has also written novels, plays, and essays, including the one you are about to read.*

If John Henry Newman describes the university as "an assemblage of learned men" and Virginia Woolf paints a word picture of a university to which women are admitted only at the discretion of men and endure distinctly inferior conditions, Rich offers an alternative vision, a "woman-centered university." If that phrase sounds "outrageous, biased, or improbable," she says, "we need only try the sound of its opposite. . . . What we have at present is a man-centered university, a breeding ground . . . of masculine privilege."

This essay was originally written for Women and the Power to Change *(1975), a volume sponsored by the Carnegie Commission on Higher Education. In it Rich articulates a position that has been a persistent theme in her work: the intense need to take women's experiences and existence seriously. This intensity also characterizes her commitment as a teacher at a number of universities, including the City University of New York, Cornell, and Stanford.*

I chose this selection because it has been important in explaining my own experience in higher education. When I went to college in the 1960s, I never had a woman professor and I read hardly any works by women. I came away from that experience thinking that all truly important thinkers were men. Rich (and writers like her) have helped me re-examine my own education and challenge the ways in which I may inadvertently pass on such a one-sided education to my own students. — A.L.

Early in my thinking about this essay, it had two titles. The first stands at the head of this page. The second grew out of a passage in Mary Beard's *Woman as Force in History,* where she describes the conditions of thought and education at the time of the Renaissance, prior to discussing the role played by women in intellectual life.

> In the promotion of the new learning, two tasks had to be carried out. The first included the recovery of additional classical works, the preparation of critical editions, the re-issue of the best . . . and critical study of the new texts. The second was the dissemination of the knowledge obtained from this critical study.

> In the dissemination of the new learning . . . five methods were widely and intensively employed: tutoring and self-directed study in families, education in schools, humanist lecturing, conversations in small private groups and larger coteries, and correspondence.[1]

I had just been reading the syllabi of women's studies programs and courses all over the country, and it was natural to translate Beard's description into terms of this new curriculum, as well as of the feminist study groups, conferences, periodicals, and "conversations in small private groups and larger coteries" that have become legion over the past few years. And so for a while the working title of this essay was "Notes toward a Feminist Renaissance." It is by now clear that a feminist renaissance is under way, that in the struggle to discover women and our buried or misread history, feminists are doing two things: questioning and reexploring the past, and demanding a humanization of intellectual interests and public measures in the present. In the course of this work, we are recovering lost sources of knowledge and of spiritual vitality, while familiar texts are receiving a fresh critical appraisal, and the whole process is powered by a shift in perspective far more extraordinary and influential than the shift from theology to humanism of the European Renaissance. Much of this research, discussion, and analysis is already being carried on in the university, but even more is taking place outside it, in precisely the kind of unofficial, self-created groups described by Mary Beard. It could be said that a women's university-without-walls exists already in America, in the shape of women reading and writing with a new purposefulness, and the growth of feminist bookstores, presses, bibliographic services, women's centers, medical clinics, libraries, art galleries, and workshops, all with a truly educational mission; and that the members of this university are working and studying out of intense concern for the quality of human life as distinct from the ego-bound achievement of individual success. With the help of the duplicating machine, documents, essays, poems, statistical tables are moving from hand to hand, passing through the mails; the "dissemination of the knowledge obtained from this study" is not accountable in terms of the sales of a single edition or even dependent solely on commercial publication.

I returned to my original title—less elegant, more blunt, some might say more provocative—because immense forces in the university, as in the whole patriarchal society, are intrinsically opposed to anything resembling an actual feminist renaissance, wherever that process appears to be a serious undertaking and not merely a piece of decorative reformism. If the phrase "woman-centered university" sounds outrageous, biased, or improbable, we need only try the sound of its opposite, the "man-centered university"—

---

[1]Mary Beard, *Woman as Force in History* (New York: Collier/Macmillan, 1971), p. 260; first published 1945.

not forgetting that grammar reveals the truth and that "man," the central figure of that earlier renaissance, was indeed the male, as he still is. Or, as the catalog of one "coeducational" institution has it:

> Brandeis University has set itself to develop the whole man, the sensitive, cultured, open-minded citizen who grounds his thinking in facts, who is intellectually and spiritually aware, who believes that life is significant, and who is concerned with society and the role he will play in it.[2]

This is no semantic game or trivial accent of language. What we have at present is a man-centered university, a breeding ground not of humanism, but of masculine privilege. As women have gradually and reluctantly been admitted into the mainstream of higher education, they have been made participants in a system that prepares men to take up roles of power in a man-centered society, that asks questions and teaches "facts" generated by a male intellectual tradition, and that both subtly and openly confirms men as the leaders and shapers of human destiny both within and outside academia. The exceptional women who have emerged from this system and who hold distinguished positions in it are just that: the required exceptions used by every system to justify and maintain itself. That all this is somehow "natural" and reasonable is still an unconscious assumption even of many who grant that women's role in society is changing, and that it needs to change.

Since this condition reflects the unspoken—and outspoken—assumptions of man-centered society, it would be naive to imagine that the university can of itself be a vanguard for change. It is probable that the unrecognized, unofficial university-without-walls I have described will prove a far more important agent in reshaping the foundations on which human life is now organized. The orthodox university is still a vital spot, however, if only because it is a place where people can find each other and begin to hear each other. (It is also a source of certain kinds of power.[3])   5

Women in the university therefore need to address themselves—against the opprobrium and obstruction they do and will encounter—to changing the center of gravity of the institution as far as possible; to work toward a woman-centered university because only if that center of gravity can be shifted will women really be free to learn, to teach, to share strength, to explore, to criticize, and to convert knowledge to power. It will be objected that this is merely "reverse chauvinism." But given the intensive training all women go through in every society to place our own long-term and collective interests second or last and to value altruism at the expense of independence

---

[2]Brandeis University Bulletin, 1972–1973, p. 11.
[3]See A. Leffler, D. Gillespie, E. Ratner, "Academic Feminists and the Women's Movement," *Ain't I a Woman?*, vol. 4, no. 1, 1973, p. 7.

and wholeness—and given the degree to which the university reinforces that training in its every aspect—the most urgent need at present is for women to recognize, and act on, the priority of recreating ourselves and each other, after our centuries of intellectual and spiritual blockading. . . .

The university is above all a hierarchy. At the top is a small cluster of highly paid and prestigious persons, chiefly men, whose careers entail the services of a very large base of ill-paid or unpaid persons, chiefly women: wives, research assistants, secretaries, teaching assistants, cleaning women, waitresses in the faculty club, lower-echelon administrators, and women students who are used in various ways to gratify the ego. Each of these groups of women sees itself as distinct from the others, as having different interests and a different destiny. The student may become a research assistant, mistress, or even wife; the wife may act as secretary or personal typist for her husband, or take a job as lecturer or minor administrator; the graduate student may, if she demonstrates unusual brilliance and carefully follows the rules, rise higher into the pyramid, where she loses her identification with teaching fellows, as the wife forgets her identification with the student or secretary she may once have been. The waitress or cleaning woman has no such mobility, and it is rare for other women in the university, beyond a few socially aware or feminist students, to support her if she is on strike or unjustly fired.* Each woman in the university is defined by her relationship to the men in power instead of her relationship to other women up and down the scale.

Now, this fragmentation among women is merely a replication of the fragmentation from each other that we undergo in the society outside; in accepting the premise that advancement and security—even the chance to do one's best work—lie in propitiating and identifying with men who have some power, we have always found ourselves in competition with each other and blinded to our common struggles. This fragmentation and the invisible demoralization it generates work constantly against the intellectual and emotional energies of the woman student.

The hidden assumptions on which the university is built comprise more than simply a class system. In a curious and insidious way the "work" of a few men—especially in the more scholarly and prestigious institutions—becomes a sacred value in whose name emotional and economic exploitation of women is taken for granted. The distinguished professor may understandably like comfort and even luxury and his ego requires not merely a wife and secretary but an au pair girl, teaching assistant, programmer, and student mistress; but the justification for all this service is the almost religious concept of "his work." (Those few women who rise to the top of their

---

Each of these groups . . . unjustly fired: For other reflections on the relationship between women in the "academic" and "maintenance" parts of the university, see bell hooks, "Keeping Close to Home: Class and Education," starting on p. 124.

professions seem in general to get along with less, to get their work done along with the cooking, personal laundry, and mending without the support of a retinue.) In other words, the structure of the man-centered university constantly reaffirms *the use of women as means* to the end of male "work"— meaning male careers and professional success. Professors of Kantian ethics or Marxist criticism are no more exempt from this exploitation of women than are professors of military science or behavioral psychology. In its very structure, then, the university encourages women to continue perceiving themselves as means and not as ends—as indeed their whole socialization has done.

It is sometimes pointed out that because the majority of women work-   10
ing in the university are in lower-status positions, the woman student has few if any "role models" she can identify with in the form of women professors or even high-ranking administrators. She therefore can conceive of her own future only in terms of limited ambitions. But it should be one of the goals of a woman-centered university to do away with the pyramid itself, insofar as it is based on sex, age, color, class, and other irrelevant distinctions. I will take this up again further on. . . .

V

I have tried to show that the androcentric* university not only under-mines and exploits women but forces men who wish to succeed in it further into the cul-de-sac of one-sided masculinity. In this it is simply a microcosm of society. Virginia Woolf was a forerunner of contemporary feminist ana-lysts in criticizing the drive for goals without consideration of means and process, the glorification of competition, the confusion between human beings and objects as products of this one-sided masculinity of culture; and in this century we have seen culture brought low and discredited because of them. Without pretending that we can in our present stage of understand-ing and of mystification through language define crisply and forever what is "masculine" and what is "feminine," we *can* at least say that the above corruptions and confusions are products of a male-dominated history.

The world as a whole is rapidly becoming Westernized. In no culture more than in Western culture is the failure of ideas like "industrialization" and "development" more evident; for without famine, without authentic scarcity, without the naked struggle to stay alive, and with the apparent "freedom" of unveiled and literate women, the condition of woman has remained that of a nonadult, a person whose exploitation—physical, eco-nomic, or psychic—is accepted *no matter to what class she belongs*. A society

---

androcentric: male-centered

that treats any group of adults as nonadult—that is, unfit to assume utmost responsibility in society and unfit for doing the work of their choice—will end by treating most of its citizens as patriarchal society has treated children—that is, lying to them and using force, overt or manipulative, to control them.

I want to suggest two categories of women's needs that would, if genuinely met, change the nature of the university and to some extent the community outside the university, and I am suggesting further that these needs of women are congruent with the humanizing of the community-at-large. The first category includes both the content of education and the style in which it is treated. The second includes institutionalized obstacles that effectively screen out large numbers of able women from full or partial engagement in higher education.

First, as to curriculum: As the hitherto "invisible" and marginal agent in culture, whose native culture has been effectively denied, women need a reorganization of knowledge, of perspectives and analytical tools that can help us know our foremothers, evaluate our present historical, political, and personal situation, and take ourselves seriously as agents in the creation of a more balanced culture. Some feminists foresee this culture as based on female primacy, others as "androgynous"; whatever it is to become, women will have the primary hand in its shaping. This does not and need not mean that the entire apparatus of masculine intellectual achievement should be scrapped, or that women should simply turn the whole apparatus inside out and substitute "she" for "he." Some of the structures will be seen as unhealthy for human occupation even while their grandeur in [their] own day can be appreciated; like old and condemned buildings, we may want to photograph these for posterity and tear them down; some may be reconstructed along different lines; some we may continue to live [with] and use. But a radical reinvention of subject, lines of inquiry, and method will be required. As Mary Daly has written:

> The tyranny of methodolatry hinders new discoveries. It prevents us from raising questions never asked before and from being illumined by ideas that do not fit into pre-established boxes and forms. . . . Under patriarchy, Method has wiped out women's questions so totally that even women have not been able to hear and formulate our own questions to meet our own experiences.

Daly also calls for "breaking down the barriers between technical knowledge and that deep realm of intuitive knowledge which some theologians call ontological reason."[4] In fact, it is in the realm of the apparently unimpeachable sciences that the greatest modifications and revaluations will undoubtedly occur. It may well be in this domain that has proved least hospitable

---

[4]Mary Daly, *Beyond God the Father* (Boston: Beacon, 1973), pp. 11–12, 39.

or attractive to women—theoretical science—that the impact of feminism and of woman-centered culture will have the most revolutionary impact. It was a woman, Simone Weil, who wrote, in the early thirties:

> . . . the technicians are ignorant of the theoretical basis of the knowledge which they employ. The scientists in their turn not only remain out of touch with technical problems but in addition are cut off from that over-all vision which is the very essence of theoretical culture. One could count on one's fingers the number of scientists in the entire world who have a general idea of the history and development of their own particular science; there is not one who is really competent as regards sciences other than his own . . .[5]

A more recent writer points out the historical origins for the scientist's   15 claim to neutrality, his [*sic*] assertion of normative freedom, and his "conscious rejection and ignorance of the subjective and the a-rational in human activity."[6] He suggests that every attempt to bring public and social sanctions to bear on the scientist's designs has hitherto met with defeat and that every attempt to extend the boundaries of accepted epistemology, including psychoanalysis, has been labeled "pseudoscience." (He fails, however, to mention the healing and midwifery of wisewomen that were even more violently driven underground. Mendelsohn's article, in fact, though it is concerned with the return of science to the service of human needs, and though it was delivered as a lecture to a Radcliffe Institute symposium on women, never touches on the connection between the masculinization of the sciences and their elitism, indifference to values, and rigidity of method.) He ends, however, by calling for certain kinds of change in the procedures and priorities of the science that can be applied by extension to the entire body of knowledge and method that the university has adopted for its province:

> A reconstructed science would value truth, but also compassion. It would have an inbuilt ethic that would defend both being and living; that is, knowledge that would be non-violent, non-coercive, non-exploitative, non-manipulative . . . that would renounce finally the Faustian quest to achieve the limits of the universe or total knowledge, that would work to construct models that would be more explanatory and more inclusive—science practiced among and derived from the public. What if we were to say that we would not undertake to develop what could not be understood and publicly absorbed, that we were intent on building a science not confined to academies and institutions.[7]

---

[5]Richard Rees, *Simone Weil: A Sketch for a Portrait* (London: Oxford, 1966), pp. 20–21.
[6]Everett Mendelsohn, "A Human Reconstruction of Science," prepared for "Women: Recourse for a Changing World," Radcliffe Institute Symposium, 1972; *Boston University Journal*, vol. 21, no. 2, Spring 1973, p. 48.
[7]Ibid., p. 52.

Certainly a major change will be along the lines already seen in women's studies: a breakdown of traditional departments and "disciplines," of that fragmentation of knowledge that weakens thought and permits the secure ignorance of the specialist to protect him from responsibility for the applications of his theories. It is difficult to imagine a woman-centered curriculum where quantitative method and technical reason would continue to be allowed to become means for the reduction of human lives, and where specialization would continue to be used as an escape from wholeness.[8]

It has been almost a given of women's courses that style and content are inseparable. A style has evolved in the classroom, more dialogic, more exploratory, less given to pseudo-objectivity, than the traditional mode. A couple of examples of the feminist approach are quoted below. The first comes from a description of an applied psychology course on discrimination against women, taught at the University of Wales in Cardiff:

> A "personal style" was adopted. By this I mean a style of communication which avoided such constructions as "it is said," "it is thought," "it is considered." In short, I acknowledged the subjective element by not avoiding the use of the personal pronoun. This style is more appropriate to a non-exploitative, non-patriarchal interaction between students and teacher. It is conducive to a greater degree of academic rigour. . . . It seems to me that the form of many communications in academia, both written and verbal, is such as to not only obscure the influence of the personal or subjective but also to give the impression of divine origin— a mystification composed of sybilline statements—from beings supposedly emptied of the "dross" of self. Additionally I believe that a "personal style" probably encourages greater creativeness. Further, it seems to me, that, when teaching, such a style encourages the active involvement of all concerned. It is opposed to any form of alienation. It seems particularly appropriate that women's studies should counteract the misleading tendency in academe to camouflage the influence of the subject.*

The second example comes from the actual syllabus handed to students in a course, "The Education of Women in Historical Perspective."

---

[8]Mina P. Shaughnessy has written of the failures of measurement to account for actual events in the teaching process: "In how many countless and unconscious ways do we capitulate to the demand for numbers? . . . In how many ways has the need for numbers forced us to violate the language itself, ripping it from the web of discourse in order to count those things that can be caught in the net of numbers?" ("Open Admissions and the Disadvantaged Teacher," keynote speech at the Conference on College Composition and Communication, New Orleans, April 1973 [unpublished]).

A "personal style" . . . in academe: For another woman's account of adopting a more "personal" style in academic speaking, in her case for overcoming what she sees as class barriers, see bell hooks, "Keeping Close to Home: Class and Education," p. 124. For a man's critique of scientific practices, see Freeman J. Dyson, "Engineers' Dreams," p. 222.

I am teaching this course because I believe that education is the key to social change. Despite the generally conservative role that formal institutions play in society, philosophers, statesmen and parents have looked to schools for improving the *status quo*. Access to schools has been used as a method of social control, as have curriculum and teaching methods. The schools can become vehicles for indoctrination, for oppression, as well as for healthy stimulation of individual and societal freedom; the line between "education" and indoctrination is difficult to define, but essential to look for.

. . . I look at issues historically; that has been my training, and my primary interest. I have trouble with the twentieth century, far preferring the puzzle of the nineteenth. In women's education, this was when the biggest changes took place, when education for women was a revolutionary question. However, we may be in the midst of another revolutionary time, and an understanding of the past is essential for appreciation of the contemporary scene. History can be a delightful escape into a world where there is a finite number of questions. . . . This course is my attempt to escape from my ostrich tendencies, to understand my own role in the present movement.

I want to stress this problem of bias because scholarship is supposed to be as bias-free as possible. We will look at all questions and issues from as many sides as we can think of; but I am inescapably a feminist. . . . You must question my assumptions, my sources, my information; that is part of learning to learn. You should also question your own assumptions. Skepticism about oneself is essential to continued growth and a balanced perspective.[9]

The underlying mode of the feminist teaching style is thus by nature antihierarchical.

VI

I have described the university as a hierarchy built on exploitation. To become truly educated and self-aware, against the current of patriarchal education, a woman must be able to discover and explore her root connection with *all women*. Her previous education has taught her only of her prescribed relationships with men, or "Women beware women." Any genuine attempt to fill this need would become a force for the dehierarchizing of the university. For it would have to involve all women in the institution, simultaneously, as students and as teachers, besides drawing on the special experience of nonacademic women, both within and outside the university—the grand-

---

[9]Deborah Rosenfelt, ed., *Female Studies,* vol. 7 (Old Westbury, N.Y.: Feminist Press, 1973), pp. 10, 187.

mothers, the high-school dropouts, the professionals, the artists, the political women, the housewives. And it would involve them at an organic level, not as interesting exhibits or specimens.

There is one crucial hub around which all the above revolves—one need that is primary if women are to assume any real equality in the academic world, one challenge that the university today, like the society around it, evades with every trick in its possession. This is the issue of childcare. The welfare mother badgered to get out and work, the cafeteria worker whose child wears a latchkey, the student or assistant professor constantly uncertain about the source and quality of the next baby-sitter, all have this at stake; all are constantly forced to improvise or to give up in the struggle to fill this social vacuum. Full-time mothering is a peculiar and late-arrived social phenomenon and is assumed to be the "normal" mode of childrearing in the United States; but full-time mothering, even by choice, is not an option for the majority of women. There is no improvisation of childcare—even if it be the child's own father who "generously" agrees to share the chores— that can begin to substitute for an excellent, dependable, nonsexist, imaginative system of care, cheap enough for all, and extending identical opportunities to the children of the poorest and the highest-paid women on the campus.

Alice Rossi has described some of the possibilities and practical solutions to this question in her "Equality between the Sexes: An Immodest Proposal,"[10] and much of what I am going to say here will merely develop what she earlier sketched out. Perhaps I shall say it with a greater sense of urgency, because even in the years since her essay was written, the struggle over childcare and the need for it have become more clear-cut. Attention to how children are to be cared for and socialized can be seen as a kind of test of the "humanism" of the university, which has hitherto been so responsive to the masters of war. In the past the university has *used* children, in its special kindergartens and laboratory schools, as guinea pigs for tests and new methods, just as it has used the community around it for such purposes.

The degree to which patriarchal society has neglected the problem of childcare is in some ways reflective of its need to restrict the lives of women. Even in "revolutionary" socialist societies, where women are a needed sector of the labor force, and where state-supported collective childcare exists, the centers are staffed by women and women bear the ultimate responsibility for children. This may not in itself be undesirable; but the relegation of this responsibility to women reflects a reactionary thinking about sexual roles rather than a conscious decision made in the light of a feminist analysis. In both China and the Soviet Union the grandmother is an important adjunct

20

---

[10]In Robert J. Lifton, ed., *The Woman in America* (Boston: Beacon, 1968), pp. 121–24.

to collective day care; the grandfather goes unmentioned in this role.[11] In the United States, the rapid increase in single-parent families and female heads of households does not alter the fact that, as of today, the fantasy of the family as consisting of a breadwinning father, a homemaking mother, and children is the model on which most social constructs are based. School holidays and lunch and coming-home hours, for example, often reflect the assumption that there is a nonworking mother whose major responsibility is to be there when the children come home. Even within the women's movement, childcare for women who wish to be politically or culturally active is sometimes a neglected priority in the arranging of conferences and workshops.

It is difficult to imagine, unless one has lived it, the personal division, endless improvising, and creative and intellectual holding back that for most women accompany the attempt to combine the emotional and physical demands of parenthood and the challenges of work. To assume one can naturally combine these has been a male privilege everywhere in the world. For women, the energy expended in both the conflict and the improvisation has held many back from starting a professional career and has been a heavy liability to careers once begun. The few exceptions in this country have been personal solutions; for the majority of mothers no such options exist.

Since this essay is concerned, not with an ideal future but with some paths toward it, I am assuming that within the foreseeable future few if any adequate community children's centers will be available, certainly on the scale and of the excellence we need. Until such exist in every community, it will be necessary for any university concerned with shifting its androcentric imbalance to provide them. But again, they cannot be merely token custodial units, or testing grounds run by the university for its own experimental ends. The kind of childcare I am going to describe would be designed first of all in the interests of the children and mothers it serves.

1. Childcare would be available for children of all students, staff, and faculty, with additional places for community children, at a subsidized rate that would make it effectively open to all. This is an absolutely necessary, though not sufficient, condition for the kinds of change we envision.
2. Childcare would be of the highest quality; no merely custodial center would be tolerated. The early nurture and education of the children

---

[11]Ruth Sidel (*Women and Child-Care in China* [New York: Hill & Wang, 1972], p. 25) reports of China: "All nursery and kindergarten teachers are women. There seems to be no effort to recruit men into fields in which they would be working with small children. And there seems to be no concern for breaking down the traditional sex roles in professions such as teaching and nursing, both of which are virtually all female." See also Toni Blanken, "Preschool Collectives in the Soviet Union," in Pamela Roby, ed., *Child Care: Who Cares?* (New York: Basic Books, 1973), pp. 386–97.

would be as flexible and imaginative as possible. There would be a conscious counterthrust against the sex-role programming of patriarchal society.

3. The centers would be staffed, under experienced and qualified directorship, by women and men who have chosen and been trained for this kind of work. They would be assisted by several kinds of people:
   a. College students, female and male, who want experience in early education or just want to spend time with children. (Several experienced baby-sitters could work with several times the number of children they ordinarily "sit" with in private homes, and with more expert supervision.)
   b. High-school students similar to the college students in a.
   c. Older women and men from the community—"grandparents" with special qualifications, informal or formal.
   d. Parents who want to share their children's lives on a part-time basis during the working day.
   e. Apprentices from graduate programs in education, pediatrics, psychology, the arts, etc.

The children would thus be in contact with a wide range of women and men, of different ages, as "nurturant" figures from an early age. The core staff of the centers should be as sexually balanced and as permanent as possible.

I am aware that some feminists, including some lesbian mothers, might prefer to see the nurture and acculturation of young children entirely in the hands of women—not as an acting out of traditional roles, but as a cultural and political choice. I tend, however, to agree with Michelle Rosaldo when she writes:

> . . . American society is . . . organized in a way that creates and exploits a radical distance between private and public, domestic and social, female and male . . . this conflict is at the core of the contemporary rethinking of sex roles. . . . If the public world is to open its doors to more than an elite among women, the nature of work itself will have to be altered, and the asymmetry between work and the home reduced. For this we must . . . bring men into the sphere of domestic concerns and responsibilities.[12]

4. There should be flexibility enough to allow parents to, say, take their children to the university museum or for lunch in the cafeteria if they so desire. Nursing mothers should be able to come and feed their babies.

---

[12]In M. Rosaldo and L. Lamphere, eds., *Woman, Culture and Society* (Stanford, Calif.: Stanford University, 1974), p. 42.

5. A well-baby clinic, with both medical and dental care, should be regularly provided for all the children as a service of the centers. A referral service for mothers with physical or psychic problems should be available.
6. There should be opportunities for staff and parents of the centers to discuss, in small groups, ideas of childrearing, criticisms of the running of the center, and ways in which it can better serve its clients.

While excellent universal early childhood care should be a major priority in any reasonably humane society, the primary and moving impulse behind the children's center would be to help equalize the position of women.[13]

VII

The notion of the "full-time" student has penalized both women and the poor. The student with a full-time job and a full-time academic program is obviously more handicapped than the student who can afford to go to college without working. Many women—married, divorced, or single mothers—have the equivalent of an unpaid full-time job at home and are discouraged from considering advanced study. Until universal and excellent childcare is developed these women are handicapped in undertaking a full-time program. Sometimes only a year or so of part-time study would make the difference between continuing their education and dropping out, or between real achievement and a frantic attempt to muddle through.[14]

But in a university not dedicated primarily to reduplicating the old pyramid, two other groups will need the availability of part-time study. Women faculty should make it one of their special concerns that staff and community women be brought into the educational process. All staff—women and men—should have paid time off for auditing or taking courses

---

[13]See Simmons and Chayes, "University Day Care," and Hagen, "Child Care and Women's Liberation," in Roby, op. cit. Obviously, day care is both an educational and a political issue and can evoke different ideas of goal and quality from different groups. For example, the heterosexual mother and the lesbian mother may each see quite different objectives for the kind of center in which she would want to place her child. (See *Ain't I a Woman,* double issue on childcare, spring 1973.) These differences will undoubtedly emerge and have to be worked through, sometimes painfully; but I agree with Gross and MacEwen (in Roby, p. 295) that it must be the parents (I would say particularly the mothers) who establish goals for the center and that the university should be seen purely as a provider of space and funding.

[14]K. Patricia Cross ("The Woman Student," in *Women in Higher Education,* Washington D.C.: American Council on Education, 1972, p. 49 ff) observes furthermore that "mature women constitute a significant segment of the [new student] population" and asserts the need for a recognition of American mobility (in which the wife is uprooted by the husband's career) through systems of transferable credits and credit-by-examination.

for credit, as well as access to libraries and to academic counseling. Community women must be taken seriously as potential users of the university. Many of these women have suffered from the burdens of both race and sex; tracked into the nonacademic stream in high school, carrying the responsibilities of early marriages and large families, they have worked hard both within and outside the home and yet have often been dismissed in the most offhand stereotyping both by the radical male left and by male "liberals."

Whether invisible as scrubwomen or cafeteria workers, or vaguely   30
perceived as shoppers in the local supermarket or mothers pushing prams in the community, these women are also becoming increasingly awake to expectations they have been denied.[15] The working women employed by the university and the women of its local community both have claims upon the resources it so jealously guards. They should be able to look to a nonelitist university for several kinds of resources: a women's health center, with birth-control and abortion counseling, Pap tests, pamphlets and talks on women's health problems; a rape crisis center; an adult education program in which women at first too shy or uncertain to enroll for college classes might test their interests and abilities (this might include remedial reading and writing, math, women's history, basic economics, current events, community organizing workshops, poetry and art workshops, etc.); a woman-staffed women's psychological counseling center with both group and individual counseling; a law clinic. A large university should be prepared to integrate services contributed to such centers with the other academic commitments of any faculty member willing and qualified to work in them. And, undoubtedly, a great deal of reciprocal education would be going on as women of very different backgrounds and shades of opinion began to meet, hold discussions, and discover their common ground.

I can anticipate one response to these recommendations, partly because it has been leveled at me in conversation, partly because I have leveled it at myself. The university cannot, it may be argued, become all to each; it cannot serve the education of young adults, train future specialists, provide a conduit for research and scholarship, and do all these other things you are suggesting. I have, I confess, thought long and hard on that side of the question. Part of my final resolution comes from the fact that we are talking

---

[15]A *New York Times Magazine* article carried a series of transcribed conversations with middle-aged, mostly blue-collar, second-generation Italian and Jewish women in East Flatbush, all in their forties and members of a consciousness-raising group, all concerned with changing and expanding their lives now that their children are grown up. One recalls "how hard I fought for my girls to go to college." The author comments that "two main concerns spurred their interest in feminism: the feeling that society in general, and their husbands in particular, no longer viewed them as sexually interesting . . . and the realization that they were 'out of a job' in the same sense as a middle-aged man who is fired by his employer of 20 years" (Susan Jacoby, "What Do I Do for the Next Twenty Years?" *New York Times Magazine,* June 17, 1973).

about a process involving simultaneous changes both in society "out there" and in the university, and that when the local or national community becomes able to develop strong and responsive centers such as I have been describing for all its citizens, the burden would not have to fall on the university. Ideally, I imagine a very indistinct line between "university" and "community" instead of the familiar city-on-a-hill frowning down on its neighbors, or the wrought-iron gates by which town and gown have traditionally defined their relationship. For centuries women were by definition people of the town, not of the gown; and still, there are many more of us "down there."

Moreover, the university in contemporary America has not been at such pains to refrain from providing services to *certain* communities: consulting for industry and government, conducting classified military research, acting as a recruitment center for the military-industrial and intelligence communities. What I am really suggesting is that it change its focus but still continue its involvement outside the ivy—or graffiti—covered walls. Instead of serving such distant and faceless masters as the "challenge of Sputnik," Cold War "channeling," or the Air Force, a university responsive to women's needs would serve the needs of the human, visible community in which it sits—the neighborhood, the city, the rural county, its true environment. In a sense the solution I am proposing is anarchistic: that the university should address itself to the microcosms of national problems and issues that exist locally, and that it should do so with the greatest possible sense that it will not simply be giving, but be receiving, because academe has a great deal to learn from women and from other unprivileged people.

I have described the kinds of ad hoc teaching that might take place under university auspices. As a research institution, it should organize its resources around problems specific to its community; for example, adult literacy; public health; safer, cheaper, and simpler birth control; drug addiction; community action; geriatrics and the sociology and psychology of aging and death; the history and problems of women and those of people in nonwhite, non–middle-class cultures; urban (or rural) adolescence; public architecture; child development and pediatrics; urban engineering with the advice and consent of the engineered; folk medicine; the psychology, architecture, economics, and diet of prisons; union history; the economics of the small farmer—the possibilities would vary from place to place. The "community" is probably a misleading term. In fact, most large urban universities have many communities. The "community" around Columbia University, for example, is not simply black and Puerto Rican, but white middle-class, poor and aged, Jewish, Japanese, Cuban, etc. A sympathetic and concerned relationship with all these groups would involve members of the university in an extremely rich cluster of problems. And the nature of much research (and its usefulness) might be improved if it were conceived as research *for,* rather than *on,* human beings.

VIII

I have been trying to think of a celebrated literary utopia written by a woman. The few contenders would be contemporary: Monique Wittig's *Les Guerillères,* but that is really a vision of epic struggle, or Elizabeth Gould Davis's early chapters in *The First Sex,* but those are largely based on Bachofen. Shulamith Firestone noted the absence of a female utopia in *The Dialectic of Sex* and proceeded, in the last chapter, to invent her own. These thoughts occur because any vision of things-other-than-as-they-are tends to meet with the charge of "utopianism," so much power has the way-things-are to denude and impoverish the imagination. Even minds practiced in criticism of the status quo resist a vision so apparently unnerving as that which foresees an end to male privilege and a changed relationship between the sexes. The university I have been trying to imagine does not seem to me utopian, though the problems and contradictions to be faced in its actual transformation are of course real and severe. For a long time, academic feminists, like all feminists, are going to have to take personal risks—of confronting their own realities, of speaking their minds, of being fired or ignored when they do so, of becoming stereotyped as "man-haters" when they evince a primary loyalty to women. They will also encounter opposition from successful women who have been the token "exceptions." This opposition—this female misogyny—is a leftover of a very ancient competitiveness and self-hatred forced on women by patriarchal culture. What is now required of the fortunate exceptional women are the modesty and courage to see why and how they have been fortunate at the expense of other women, and to begin to acknowledge their community with them. As one of them has written:

> The first responsibility of a "liberated" woman is to lead the fullest, freest and most imaginative life she can. The second responsibility is her solidarity with other women. She may live and work and make love with men. But she has no right to represent her situation as simpler, or less suspect, or less full of compromises than it really is. Her good relations with men must not be bought at the price of betraying her sisters.[16]

To this I would add that from a truly feminist point of view these two responsibilities are inseparable.

I am curious to see what corresponding risks and self-confrontations   35 men of intelligence and goodwill will be ready to undergo on behalf of women. It is one thing to have a single "exceptional" woman as your wife, daughter, friend, or protégée, or to long for a humanization of society by

---

[16]Susan Sontag, "The Third World of Women," *Partisan Review,* vol. 40, no. 2, 1973, p. 206.

women; another to face each feminist issue—academic, social, personal—as it appears and to evade none. Many women have felt publicly betrayed time and again by men on whose good faith and comradeship they had been relying on account of private conversations. I know that academic men are now hard-pressed for jobs and must fear the competition of women entering the university in greater numbers and with greater self-confidence. But masculine resistance to women's claims for full humanity is far more ancient, deeply rooted, and irrational than this year's job market. Misogyny should itself become a central subject of inquiry rather than continue as a desperate clinging to old, destructive fears and privileges. It will be interesting to see how many men are prepared to give more than rhetorical support today to the sex from which they have, for centuries, demanded and accepted so much.

If a truly universal and excellent network of childcare can begin to develop, if women in sufficient numbers pervade the university at all levels—from community programs through college and professional schools to all ranks of teaching and administration—if older, more established faculty women begin to get in touch with their (always, I am convinced) latent feminism, if even a few men come forward willing to think through and support feminist issues beyond their own immediate self-interest, there is a strong chance that in our own time we would begin to see some true "universality" of values emerging from the inadequate and distorted corpus of patriarchal knowledge. This will mean not a renaissance but a *nascence,* partaking of some inheritances from the past but working imaginatively far beyond them.

It is likely that in the immediate future various alternatives will be explored. Women's studies programs, where they are staffed by feminists, will serve as a focus for feminist values even in a patriarchal context. Even where staffed largely by tokenists, their very existence will make possible some rising consciousness in students. Already, alternate feminist institutes are arising to challenge the curriculum of established institutions.[17] Feminists may use the man-centered university as a base and resource while doing research and writing books and articles whose influence will be felt far beyond the academy. Consciously woman-centered universities—in which women shape the philosophy and the decision making though men may choose to study and teach there—may evolve from existing institutions. Whatever the forms it may take, the process of women's repossession of ourselves is irreversible. Within and without academe, the rise in women's expectations has gone far beyond the middle class and has released an incalcu-

---

[17]*Commenting in 1978, Adrienne Rich writes:* For example, the Feminist Studio Workshop in Los Angeles, the Sagaris Institute, Maiden Rock Institute in Minnesota, the projected Feminist Art Institute in New York.

lable new energy—not merely for changing institutions but for human redefinition; not merely for equal rights but for a new kind of being.

QUESTIONING THE TEXT

1. Rich argues that what we need is a "woman-centered" university, since what we have is a "man-centered" university. What does she mean by those two terms? If you are keeping a reading log, include your discussion of these definitions there.
2. To support her argument, Rich quotes from a wide range of outside sources. What perspective do these sources take toward Rich's argument? Do they support her position, and if so, how? What is the effect of these quotations on you as a reader? Which one or two did you find most effective? least effective? Why?

MAKING CONNECTIONS

3. Do you agree with Rich that women have different educational needs than do men? Why, or why not? In the reading starting on p. 34, John Henry Newman seems to suggest that all students have the *same* basic needs. How might Rich respond to him on this point?
4. Rich and Virginia Woolf grew up in different contexts and very different times. Yet they have certain attitudes and experiences in common. Read Woolf's essay (starting on p. 43), and write a brief (one-page) dialogue between the two women on the subject of "the ideal university."
5. How might George Will respond to Rich? Read his Duke commencement speech on p. 137, and imagine one or two questions or comments he might have.

JOINING THE CONVERSATION

6. Rich argues that the structure of most educational institutions mirrors that of the culture at large, noting specifically that the man-centered university is just a mirror of a man-centered society. In what ways does the structure of your college or university mirror contemporary American society? You may want to consider such things as admission standards, grading policies, course requirements, and classroom organization.
7. What, if any, changes has your school made in the last ten years to accommodate the needs of women students? Consider investigating

such things as increased hiring of women faculty, the opening of a women's center, the starting of a women's studies program, invitations to speakers on women's issues, and improvements in campus safety. Write a brief editorial intended for your campus newspaper in which you evaluate the extent to which your school is woman-centered. Feel free to propose changes that would make it a more hospitable place for women students—or for all students.

8. Working with two or three other students in your class, interview at least three women faculty members about their experiences in the colleges and universities where they received their education and the ones where they have taught. Each of you should interview one of the women. Afterward, compare the responses each of you obtained, and write a brief joint report to your class summarizing what the women said and drawing conclusions, if possible, about the ways they feel about your college or university.

ALLAN BLOOM
The Student and the University

IN THE LAST DECADE, *perhaps no book on the academy has been more widely read, debated, and attacked than* The Closing of the American Mind *(1987) by Allan Bloom (1930–92), who taught at the University of Chicago as Professor in the Committee on Social Thought and the College. Bloom recommended the same sort of visionary liberal education that John Henry Newman had championed more than a century earlier in* The Idea of a University. *His book, a wide-ranging assault on many modern assumptions about education, calls for a return—at least at the schools he considers "first-rank"—to a traditional curriculum centered on Great Books deeply read and understood.*

Newman wrote The Idea of a University *in the midst of a debate similar to that initiated by Bloom's book in the United States; both authors argue against those who would reshape education along more utilitarian lines. Yet while they have much in common, I am struck by their differences in tone. Newman portrays his version of liberal education as a true engine of progress, the best way of achieving a better world. Bloom, on the other hand, seems more pessimistic, offering his Great Books curriculum as a slim hope for recapturing a paradise already quite lost, an academic garden where dedicated faculty and serious students might ponder enduring philosophical questions.*

I've included a section from The Closing of the American Mind *entitled "Liberal Education" partly because Bloom's work remains so controversial and partly because I think he was right in arguing that a college degree these days often certifies little more than that a student has sat through a specified number of unrelated courses. The university has become a supermarket stuffed with trendy subjects and majors. Like shoppers grabbing fast foods and seduced by slick advertising and eye-catching displays, too many students choose classes for all the wrong reasons—to get their fifteen hours, to meet a core requirement, to accommodate their work schedules.*

Surely, we can do better.

The line I remember best from Bloom is the one I've highlighted in the opening to this chapter: "The university has to stand for something." Need I add, besides football? — J.R.

LIBERAL EDUCATION

What image does a first-rank college or university present today to a teen-ager leaving home for the first time, off to the adventure of a liberal education? He has four years of freedom to discover himself—a space between the intellectual wasteland he has left behind* and the inevitable dreary professional training that awaits him after the baccalaureate. In this short time he must learn that there is a great world beyond the little one he knows, experience the exhilaration of it and digest enough of it to sustain himself in the intellectual deserts he is destined to traverse. He must do this, that is, if he is to have any hope of a higher life. These are the charmed years when he can, if he so chooses, become anything he wishes and when he has the opportunity to survey his alternatives, not merely those current in his time or provided by careers, but those available to him as a human being. The importance of these years for an American cannot be overestimated. They are civilization's only chance to get to him.

In looking at him we are forced to reflect on what he should learn if he is to be called educated; we must speculate on what the human potential to be fulfilled is. In the specialties we can avoid such speculation, and the avoidance of them is one of specialization's charms. But here it is a simple duty. What are we to teach this person? The answer may not be evident, but to attempt to answer the question is already to philosophize and to begin to educate. Such a concern in itself poses the question of the unity of man and the unity of the sciences. It is childishness to say, as some do, that everyone must be allowed to develop freely, that it is authoritarian to impose a point of view on the student. In that case, why have a university? If the response is "to provide an atmosphere for learning," we come back to our original questions at the second remove. Which atmosphere? Choices and reflection on the reasons for those choices are unavoidable. The university has to stand for something. The practical effects of unwillingness to think positively about the contents of a liberal education are, on the one hand, to ensure that all the vulgarities of the world outside the university will flourish within it, and, on the other, to impose a much harsher and more illiberal necessity on the student—the one given by the imperial and imperious demands of the specialized disciplines unfiltered by unifying thought.

The university now offers no distinctive visage to the young person. He finds a democracy of the disciplines—which are there either because they are autochthonous or because they wandered in recently to perform

---

four years of . . . intellectual wasteland: For a different perspective on what a student brings to his or her undergraduate experience, see bell hooks, "Keeping Close to Home: Class and Education," p. 124.

some job that was demanded of the university. This democracy is really an anarchy, because there are no recognized rules for citizenship and no legitimate titles to rule. In short there is no vision, nor is there a set of competing visions, of what an educated human being is. The question has disappeared, for to pose it would be a threat to the peace. There is no organization of the sciences, no tree of knowledge. Out of chaos emerges dispiritedness, because it is impossible to make a reasonable choice. Better to give up on liberal education and get on with a specialty in which there is at least a prescribed curriculum and a prospective career. On the way the student can pick up in elective courses a little of whatever is thought to make one cultured. The student gets no intimation that great mysteries might be revealed to him, that new and higher motives of action might be discovered within him, that a different and more human way of life can be harmoniously constructed by what he is going to learn.

Simply, the university is not distinctive. Equality for us seems to culminate in the unwillingness and incapacity to make claims of superiority, particularly in the domains in which such claims have always been made—art, religion and philosophy. When Weber* found that he could not choose between certain high opposites—reason vs. revelation, Buddha vs. Jesus—he did not conclude that all things are equally good, that the distinction between high and low disappears. As a matter of fact he intended to revitalize the consideration of these great alternatives in showing the gravity and danger involved in choosing among them; they were to be heightened in contrast to the trivial considerations of modern life that threatened to overgrow and render indistinguishable the profound problems the confrontation with which makes the bow of the soul taut. The serious intellectual life was for him the battleground of the great decisions, all of which are spiritual or "value" choices. One can no longer present this or that particular view of the educated or civilized man as authoritative; therefore one must say that education consists in knowing, really knowing, the small number of such views in their integrity. This distinction between profound and superficial—which takes the place of good and bad, true and false—provided a focus for serious study, but it hardly held out against the naturally relaxed democratic tendency to say, "Oh, what's the use?" The first university disruptions at Berkeley were explicitly directed against the multiversity smorgasbord and, I must confess, momentarily and partially engaged my sympathies. It may have even been the case that there was some small element of longing for an education in the motivation of those students. But nothing was done to guide or inform their energy, and the result was merely to add multilife-styles to multidisciplines, the diversity of perversity

---

Weber: Max Weber (1864–1920), German social scientist and author of *The Protestant Ethic and the Spirit of Capitalism*

to the diversity of specialization. What we see so often happening in general happened here too; the insistent demand for greater community ended in greater isolation. Old agreements, old habits, old traditions were not so easily replaced.*

Thus, when a student arrives at the university, he finds a bewildering   5
variety of departments and a bewildering variety of courses. And there is no official guidance, no university-wide agreement, about what he *should* study. Nor does he usually find readily available examples, either among students or professors, of a unified use of the university's resources. It is easiest simply to make a career choice and go about getting prepared for that career. The programs designed for those having made such a choice render their students immune to charms that might lead them out of the conventionally respectable. The sirens sing *sotto voce* these days, and the young already have enough wax in their ears* to pass them by without danger. These specialties can provide enough courses to take up most of their time for four years in preparation for the inevitable graduate study. With the few remaining courses they can do what they please, taking a bit of this and a bit of that. No public career these days—not doctor nor lawyer nor politician nor journalist nor businessman nor entertainer—has much to do with humane learning. An education, other than purely professional or technical, can even seem to be an impediment. That is why a countervailing atmosphere in the university would be necessary for the students to gain a taste for intellectual pleasures and learn that they are viable.

The real problem is those students who come hoping to find out what career they want to have, or are simply looking for an adventure with themselves. There are plenty of things for them to do—courses and disciplines enough to spend many a lifetime on. Each department or great division of the university makes a pitch for itself, and each offers a course of study that will make the student an initiate. But how to choose among them? How do they relate to one another? The fact is they do not address one another. They are competing and contradictory, without being aware of it. The problem of the whole is urgently indicated by the very existence of the specialties, but it is never systematically posed. The net effect of the student's encounter with the college catalogue is bewilderment and very often demoralization. It is just a matter of chance whether he finds one or two professors who can give him an insight into one of the great visions of education that have been the distinguishing part of every civilized nation. Most professors are specialists, concerned only with their own fields, interested in the advancement of those fields in their own terms, or in their own

---

multidisciplines . . . easily replaced: Contrast Bloom here with Adrienne Rich's call for a totally reconstituted university in "Toward a Woman-Centered University," p. 56.

wax in their ears: an allusion to Homer's *Odyssey,* in which the hero, Odysseus, orders his sailors to put wax in their ears to escape the seductive song of the Sirens

personal advancement in a world where all the rewards are on the side of professional distinction. They have been entirely emancipated from the old structure of the university, which at least helped to indicate that they are incomplete, only parts of an unexamined and undiscovered whole. So the student must navigate among a collection of carnival barkers, each trying to lure him into a particular sideshow. This undecided student is an embarrassment to most universities, because he seems to be saying, "I am a whole human being. Help me to form myself in my wholeness and let me develop my real potential," and he is the one to whom they have nothing to say.

Cornell was, as in so many other things, in advance of its time on this issue. The six-year Ph.D. program, richly supported by the Ford Foundation, was directed specifically to high school students who had already made "a firm career choice" and was intended to rush them through to the start of those careers. A sop was given to desolate humanists in the form of money to fund seminars that these young careerists could take on their way through the College of Arts and Sciences. For the rest, the educators could devote their energies to arranging and packaging the program without having to provide it with any substance. That kept them busy enough to avoid thinking about the nothingness of their endeavor. This has been the preferred mode of not looking the Beast in the Jungle in the face—structure, not content. The Cornell plan for dealing with the problem of liberal education was to suppress the students' longing for liberal education by encouraging their professionalism and their avarice, providing money and all the prestige the university had available to make careerism the centerpiece of the university.

The Cornell plan dared not state the radical truth, a well-kept secret: the colleges do not have enough to teach their students, not enough to justify keeping them four years, probably not even three years. If the focus is careers, there is hardly one specialty, outside the hardest of the hard natural sciences, which requires more than two years of preparatory training prior to graduate studies. The rest is just wasted time, or a period of ripening until the students are old enough for graduate studies. For many graduate careers, even less is really necessary. It is amazing how many undergraduates are poking around for courses to take, without any plan or question to ask, just filling up their college years. In fact, with rare exceptions, the courses are parts of specialties and not designed for general cultivation, or to investigate questions important for human beings as such. The so-called knowledge explosion and increasing specialization have not filled up the college years but emptied them. Those years are impediments; one wants to get beyond them. And in general the persons one finds in the professions need not have gone to college, if one is to judge by their tastes, their fund of learning or their interests. They might as well have spent their college years in the Peace Corps or the like. These great universities—which can split the atom, find cures for the most terrible diseases, conduct surveys of whole populations and produce massive dictionaries of lost languages—cannot generate a modest program of general education for undergraduate students. This is a parable for our times.

There are attempts to fill the vacuum painlessly with various kinds of fancy packaging of what is already there—study abroad options, individualized majors, etc. Then there are Black Studies and Women's or Gender Studies, along with Learn Another Culture. Peace Studies are on their way to a similar prevalence. All this is designed to show that the university is with it and has something in addition to its traditional specialties. The latest item is computer literacy, the full cheapness of which is evident only to those who think a bit about what literacy might mean. It would make some sense to promote literacy literacy, inasmuch as most high school graduates nowadays have difficulty reading and writing. And some institutions are quietly undertaking this worthwhile task. But they do not trumpet the fact, because this is merely a high school function that our current sad state of educational affairs has thrust upon them, about which they are not inclined to boast.

Now that the distractions of the sixties are over, and undergraduate   10
education has become more important again (because the graduate departments, aside from the professional schools, are in trouble due to the shortage of academic jobs), university officials have had somehow to deal with the undeniable fact that the students who enter are uncivilized, and that the universities have some responsibility for civilizing them. If one were to give a base interpretation of the schools' motives, one could allege that their concern stems from shame and self-interest. It is becoming all too evident that liberal education—which is what the small band of prestigious institutions are supposed to provide, in contrast to the big state schools, which are thought simply to prepare specialists to meet the practical demands of a complex society—has no content, that a certain kind of fraud is being perpetrated. For a time the great moral consciousness alleged to have been fostered in students by the great universities, especially their vocation as gladiators who fight war and racism, seemed to fulfill the demands of the collective university conscience. They were doing something other than offering preliminary training for doctors and lawyers. Concern and compassion were thought to be the indefinable X that pervaded all the parts of the Arts and Sciences campus. But when that evanescent mist dissipated during the seventies, and the faculties found themselves face to face with ill-educated young people with no intellectual tastes—unaware that there even are such things, obsessed with getting on with their careers before having looked at life—and the universities offered no counterpoise, no alternative goals, a reaction set in.

Liberal education—since it has for so long been ill-defined, has none of the crisp clarity or institutionalized prestige of the professions, but nevertheless perseveres and has money and respectability connected with it—has always been a battleground for those who are somewhat eccentric in relation to the specialties. It is in something like the condition of churches as opposed to, say, hospitals. Nobody is quite certain of what the religious institutions are supposed to do anymore, but they do have some kind of role either responding to a real human need or as the vestige of what was once a need, and they invite the exploitation of quacks, adventurers, cranks and fanatics. But they also solicit the warmest and most valiant efforts of persons of peculiar gravity and depth. In liberal education, too, the worst and the best fight it out, fakers vs. authentics, sophists vs. philosophers, for the favor of public opinion and for control over the study of man in our times. The most conspicuous participants in the struggle are administrators who are formally responsible for presenting some kind of public image of the education their colleges offer, persons with a political agenda or vulgarizers of what the specialties know, and real teachers of the humane disciplines who actually see their relation to the whole and urgently wish to preserve the awareness of it in their students' consciousness.

So, just as in the sixties universities were devoted to removing requirements, in the eighties they are busy with attempts to put them back in, a much more difficult task. The word of the day is "core." It is generally agreed that "we went a bit far in the sixties," and that a little fine-tuning has now become clearly necessary.

There are two typical responses to the problem. The easiest and most administratively satisfying solution is to make use of what is already there in the autonomous departments and simply force the students to cover the fields, i.e., take one or more courses in each of the general divisions of the university: natural science, social science and the humanities. The reigning ideology here is *breadth,* as was *openness* in the age of laxity. The courses are almost always the already existing introductory courses, which are of least interest to the major professors and merely assume the worth and reality of that which is to be studied. It is general education, in the sense in which a jack-of-all-trades is a generalist. He knows a bit of everything and is inferior to the specialist in each area. Students may wish to sample a variety of fields, and it may be good to encourage them to look around and see if there is something that attracts them in one of which they have no experience. But this is not a liberal education and does not satisfy any longing they have for one. It just teaches that there is no high-level generalism, and that what they are doing is preliminary to the real stuff and part of the childhood they are leaving behind. Thus they desire to get it over with and get on with what their professors do seriously. Without recognition of important questions of common concern, there cannot be serious liberal education, and attempts to establish it will be but failed gestures.

It is a more or less precise awareness of the inadequacy of this approach to core curricula that motivates the second approach, which consists of what one might call composite courses. There are constructions developed especially for general-education purposes and usually require collaboration of professors drawn from several departments. These courses have titles like "Man in Nature," "War and Moral Responsibility," "The Arts and Creativity," "Culture and the Individual." Everything, of course, depends upon who plans them and who teaches them. They have the clear advantage of requiring some reflection on the general needs of students and force specialized professors to broaden their perspectives, at least for a moment. The dangers are trendiness, mere popularization and lack of substantive rigor. In general, the natural scientists do not collaborate in such endeavors, and hence these courses tend to be unbalanced. In short, they do not point beyond themselves and do not provide the student with independent means to pursue permanent questions independently, as, for example, the study of Aristotle or Kant as wholes once did. They tend to be bits of this and that. Liberal education should give the student the sense that learning must and can be both synoptic and precise. For this, a very small, detailed problem can be the best way, if it is framed so as to open out on the whole. Unless the course has the specific intention to lead to the permanent questions, to make the student aware of them and give him some competence in the important works that treat of them, it tends to be a pleasant diversion and a dead end—because it has nothing to do with any program of further study he can imagine. If such programs engage the best energies of the best people in the university, they can be beneficial and provide some of the missing intellectual excitement for both professors and students. But they rarely do, and they are too cut off from the top, from what the various faculties see as their real business. Where the power is determines the life of the whole body. And the intellectual problems unresolved at the top cannot be resolved administratively below. The problem is the lack of any unity of the sciences and the loss of the will or the means even to discuss the issue. The illness above is the cause of the illness below, to which all the good-willed efforts of honest liberal educationists can at best be palliatives.

Of course, the only serious solution is the one that is almost universally rejected: the good old Great Books approach, in which a liberal education means reading certain generally recognized classic texts, just reading them, letting them dictate what the questions are and the method of approaching them—not forcing them into categories we make up, not treating them as historical products, but trying to read them as their authors wished them to be read. I am perfectly well aware of, and actually agree with, the objections to the Great Books cult. It is amateurish; it encourages an autodidact's self-assurance without competence; one cannot read all of the Great Books carefully; if one only reads Great Books, one can never know what a great, as opposed to an ordinary, book is; there is no way of determining who is to decide what a Great Book or what the canon is; books are made the ends and not the means; the whole movement has a certain coarse evangelistic tone that is the opposite of good taste; it engenders a spurious

15

intimacy with greatness; and so forth. But one thing is certain: wherever the Great Books make up a central part of the curriculum, the students are excited and satisfied, feel they are doing something that is independent and fulfilling, getting something from the university they cannot get elsewhere. The very fact of this special experience, which leads nowhere beyond itself, provides them with a new alternative and a respect for study itself. The advantage they get is an awareness of the classic—particularly important for our innocents; an acquaintance with what big questions were when there were still big questions; models, at the very least, of how to go about answering them; and, perhaps most important of all, a fund of shared experiences and thoughts on which to ground their friendships with one another. Programs based upon judicious use of great texts provide the royal road to students' hearts. Their gratitude at learning of Achilles or the categorical imperative is boundless. Alexandre Koyré, the late historian of science, told me that his appreciation for America was great when—in the first course he taught at the University of Chicago, in 1940 at the beginning of his exile—a student spoke in his paper of Mr. Aristotle, unaware that he was not a contemporary. Koyré said that only an American could have the naive profundity to take Aristotle as living thought, unthinkable for most scholars. A good program of liberal education feeds the student's love of truth and passion to live a good life. It is the easiest thing in the world to devise courses of study, adapted to the particular conditions of each university, which thrill those who take them. The difficulty is in getting them accepted by the faculty.

None of the three great parts of the contemporary university is enthusiastic about the Great Books approach to education. The natural scientists are benevolent toward other fields and toward liberal education, if it does not steal away their students and does not take too much time from their preparatory studies. But they themselves are interested primarily in the solution of the questions now important in their disciplines and are not particularly concerned with discussions of their foundations, inasmuch as they are so evidently successful. They are indifferent to Newton's conception of time or his disputes with Leibniz about calculus; Aristotle's teleology is an absurdity beneath consideration. Scientific progress, they believe, no longer depends on the kind of comprehensive reflection given to the nature of science by men like Bacon,* Descartes, Hume, Kant and Marx. This is merely historical study, and for a long time now, even the greatest scientists have given up thinking about Galileo and Newton. Progress is undoubted. The difficulties about the truth of science raised by positivism, and those about the goodness of science raised by Rousseau and Nietzsche, have not

---

The natural scientists . . . men like Bacon: For a different assessment of the "comprehensive reflection given to the nature of science by men like Bacon," see Evelyn Fox Keller, p. 241.

really penetrated to the center of scientific consciousness. Hence, no Great Books, but incremental progress, is the theme for them.

Social scientists are in general hostile, because the classic texts tend to deal with the human things the social sciences deal with, and they are very proud of having freed themselves from the shackles of such earlier thought to become truly scientific. And, unlike the natural scientists, they are insecure enough about their achievement to feel threatened by the works of earlier thinkers, perhaps a bit afraid that students will be seduced and fall back into the bad old ways. Moreover, with the possible exception of Weber and Freud, there are no social science books that can be said to be classic. This may be interpreted favorably to the social sciences by comparing them to the natural sciences, which can be said to be a living organism developing by the addition of little cells, a veritable body of knowledge proving itself to be such by the very fact of this almost unconscious growth, with thousands of parts oblivious to the whole, nevertheless contributing to it. This is in opposition to a work of imagination or of philosophy, where a single creator makes and surveys an artificial whole. But whether one interprets the absence of the classic in the social sciences in ways flattering or unflattering to them, the fact causes social scientists discomfort. I remember the professor who taught the introductory graduate courses in social science methodology, a famous historian, responding scornfully and angrily to a question I naively put to him about Thucydides with "Thucydides was a fool!"

More difficult to explain is the tepid reaction of humanists to Great Books education, inasmuch as these books now belong almost exclusively to what are called the humanities. One would think that high esteem for the classic would reinforce the spiritual power of the humanities, at a time when their temporal power is at its lowest. And it is true that the most active proponents of liberal education and the study of classic texts are indeed usually humanists. But there is division among them. Some humanities disciplines are just crusty specialties that, although they depend on the status of classic books for their existence, are not really interested in them in their natural state—much philology, for example, is concerned with the languages but not what is said in them—and will and can do nothing to support their own infrastructure. Some humanities disciplines are eager to join the real sciences and transcend their roots in the now overcome mythic past. Some humanists make the legitimate complaints about lack of competence in the teaching and learning of Great Books, although their criticism is frequently undermined by the fact that they are only defending recent scholarly interpretation of the classics rather than a vital, authentic understanding. In their reaction there is a strong element of specialist's jealousy and narrowness. Finally, a large part of the story is just the general debilitation of the humanities, which is both symptom and cause of our present condition.

To repeat, the crisis of liberal education is a reflection of a crisis at the peaks of learning, an incoherence and incompatibility among the first principles with which we interpret the world, an intellectual crisis of the greatest magnitude, which constitutes the crisis of our civilization. But perhaps it would be true to say that the crisis consists not so much in this incoherence but in our incapacity to discuss or even recognize it. Liberal education flourished when it prepared the way for the discussion of a unified view of nature and man's place in it, which the best minds debated on the highest level. It decayed when what lay beyond it were only specialties, the premises of which do not lead to any such vision. The highest is the partial intellect; there is no synopsis.

QUESTIONING THE TEXT

1. How would you characterize Bloom's tone, especially at the beginning of the essay? What does he assume about the quality of a person's life both before and after the college experience? Cite examples from the essay to support your response. If you keep a reading log, record your thoughts there.
2. Bloom distinguishes between prestigious private liberal arts colleges and state universities. What mission does he ascribe to each? How do you react to that distinction? What are its implications?
3. Explore Bloom's analogy that likens liberal arts colleges to churches. What are the strengths of the analogy? The weaknesses? After exploring the comparison, try to suggest an analogy of your own.
4. Do you agree or disagree with J.R.'s rationale for including this reading in this chapter? Explain your reasoning.

MAKING CONNECTIONS

5. Imagine that you are Allan Bloom. Now annotate the margins of the next reading, by Mike Rose (especially his comments on the Great Books). How did assuming Bloom's perspective affect your reading of Rose? If you keep a reading log, note your response there.
6. Bloom finally suggests that the best approach to a liberal arts education is "the good old Great Books approach." Who else in this chapter might support Bloom? Why?

JOINING THE CONVERSATION

7. Bloom claims that a liberal arts education should give a student the feeling that learning can be both *synoptic* and *precise*. Examine the meaning of those terms in a dictionary, and then explore in writing

why it is that Bloom believes that a smattering of introductory college courses in different disciplines provides an inadequate perspective on learning.

8. Are you satisfied with your own education? Write an essay exploring this important question. Where do you think Bloom hits the mark in his criticisms? Do any groups seem to be excluded from his program of study? Do any aspects of life seem neglected?

9. Working together with some classmates, list works you have individually read that you believe should be on a list of Great Books. Then discuss what makes a book "great." Can people in a culture as diverse as that in the United States agree on a core of Great Books? If so, explain the criteria you would use to determine such a list.

MIKE ROSE
Lives on the Boundary

As a child, *Mike Rose (b. 1944) never thought of going to college. The son of Italian immigrants, he was placed in the "vocational track" in school (through a clerical error, as it turns out) and, as he says, "lived down to expectations beautifully." He was one of those who might well have been, in Virginia Woolf's words, "locked out" of the university. In his prize-winning volume* Lives on the Boundary *(1989), Rose recalls those circumstances that opened up the university to him, and he argues forcefully that education in a democracy must be truly open to all.*

In the excerpt from Lives *that follows, Rose describes several students he has known, considering the ways in which the "idea of a university" either includes or excludes them. In an extended discussion of what he calls the "canonical curriculum," he concludes that "books can spark dreams," but "appeals to elevated texts can also divert attention from the conditions that keep a population from realizing its dreams."*

I wanted to include this passage from Rose's book because he explicitly addresses the call made by Allan Bloom and others for a university curriculum based on "Great Books," books that by definition exclude the experiences of the students Rose describes. In addition, I chose this selection because Rose is a graceful prose stylist, a gifted scholar, and a much-valued friend.

The associate director of writing programs at UCLA, Rose is also a truly extraordinary teacher. His own story, and the stories of those students whose lives he has touched, attest to the transformational power of the kind of educational experience he advocates. To "have any prayer of success" at making such experiences possible, Rose says, "we'll need many . . . blessings." We'll also need many more teachers and writers like Mike Rose. – A.L.

I have a vivid memory of sitting on the edge of my bed—I was twelve or thirteen maybe—listening with unease to a minute or so of classical music. I don't know if I found it as I was turning the dial, searching for the Johnny Otis Show or the live broadcast from Scribner's Drive-In, or if the tuner had simply drifted into another station's signal. Whatever happened, the music caught me in a disturbing way, and I sat there, letting it play. It sounded like the music I heard in church, weighted, funereal. Eerie chords echoing from another world. I leaned over, my fingers on the tuner, and, in what I remember as almost a twitch, I turned the knob away from the melody of these strange instruments. My reaction to the other high culture I encountered—*The Iliad* and Shakespeare and some schoolbook

poems by Longfellow and Lowell—was similar, though less a visceral rejection and more a rejecting disinterest, a sense of irrelevance. The few Shakespearean scenes I did know—saw on television, or read or heard in grammar
school—seemed snooty and put-on, kind of dumb. Not the way I wanted
to talk. Not interesting to me.

There were few books in our house: a couple of thin stories read to
me as a child in Pennsylvania (*The Little Boy Who Ran Away,* an *Uncle
Remus* sampler), the *M* volume of the *World Book Encyclopedia* (which I
found one day in the trash behind the secondhand store), and the Hollywood
tabloids my mother would bring home from work. I started buying lots
of Superman and Batman comic books because I loved the heroes' virtuous
omnipotence—comic books, our teachers said, were bad for us—and, once
I discovered them, I began checking out science fiction novels from my
grammar school library. Other reading material appeared: the instructions
to my chemistry set, which I half understood and only half followed, and,
eventually, my astronomy books, which seemed to me to be magical rather
than discursive texts. So it was that my early intrigue with literacy—my
lifts and escapes with language and rhythm—came from comic books and
science fiction, from the personal, nonscientific worlds I created with bits
and pieces of laboratory and telescopic technology, came, as well, from the
Italian stories I heard my uncles and parents tell. It came, too, from the
music my radio brought me: music that wove in and out of my days, lyrics
I'd repeat and repeat—"gone, gone, gone, jumpin' like a catfish on a pole"—
wanting to catch that sound, seeking other emotional frontiers, other places
to go. Like rocker Joe Ely, I picked up Chicago on my transistor radio.

Except for school exercises and occasional cards my mother made me
write to my uncles and aunts, I wrote very little during my childhood; it
wasn't until my last year in high school that Jack MacFarland* sparked an
interest in writing. And though I developed into a good reader, I performed
from moderately well to terribly on other sorts of school literacy tasks.
From my reading I knew vocabulary words, and I did okay on spelling
tests—though I never lasted all that long in spelling bees—but I got C's and
D's on the ever-present requests to diagram sentences and label parts of
speech. The more an assignment was related to real reading, the better I
did; the more analytic, self-contained, and divorced from context, the lousier
I performed. Today some teachers would say I was a concrete thinker. To
be sure, the development of my ability to decode words and read sentences
took place in school, but my orientation to reading—the way I conceived
of it, my purpose for doing it—occurred within the tight and untraditional
confines of my home. The quirks and textures of my immediate environ-

---

Jack MacFarland: a teacher, currently at a California community college, whom Rose
calls "the teacher who saved [my] life"

ment combined with my escapist fantasies to draw me to books. "It is what we are excited about that educates us," writes social historian Elizabeth Ewen. It is what taps our curiosity and dreams. Eventually, the books that seemed so distant, those Great Books, would work their way into my curiosity, would influence the way I framed problems and the way I wrote. But that would come much later—first with Jack MacFarland (mixed with his avant-garde countertradition), then with my teachers at Loyola and UCLA—an excitement and curiosity shaped by others and connected to others, a cultural and linguistic heritage received not from some pristine conduit, but exchanged through the heat of human relation.

A friend of mine recently suggested that education is one culture embracing another. It's interesting to think of the very different ways that metaphor plays out. Education can be a desperate, smothering embrace, an embrace that denies the needs of the other. But education can also be an encouraging, communal embrace—at its best an invitation, an opening. Several years ago, I was sitting in on a workshop conducted by the Brazilian educator Paulo Freire. It was the first hour or so and Freire, in his sophisticated, accented English, was establishing the theoretical base of his literacy pedagogy—heady stuff, a blend of Marxism, phenomenology, and European existentialism. I was two seats away from Freire; in front of me and next to him was a younger man, who, puzzled, finally interrupted the speaker to ask a question. Freire acknowledged the question and, as he began answering, he turned and quickly touched the man's forearm. Not patronizing, not mushy, a look and a tap as if to say: "You and me right now, let's go through this together." Embrace. With Jack MacFarland it was an embrace: no-nonsense and cerebral, but a relationship in which the terms of endearment were the image in a poem, a play's dialogue, the winding narrative journey of a novel.

More often than we admit, a failed education is social more than intellectual in origin. And the challenge that has always faced American education, that it has sometimes denied and sometimes doggedly pursued, is how to create both the social and cognitive means to enable a diverse citizenry to develop their ability. It is an astounding challenge: the complex and wrenching struggle to actualize the potential not only of the privileged but, too, of those who have lived here for a long time generating a culture outside the mainstream and those who, like my mother's parents and my father, immigrated with cultural traditions of their own. This painful but generative mix of language and story can result in clash and dislocation in our communities, but it also gives rise to new speech, new stories, and once we appreciate the richness of it, new invitations to literacy.

Pico Boulevard, named for the last Mexican governor of California, runs an immense stretch west to east: from the wealth of the Santa Monica beaches to blighted Central Avenue, deep in Los Angeles. Union Street is comparatively brief, running north to south, roughly from Adams to Temple, pretty bad off all the way. Union intersects Pico east of Vermont Avenue and too far to the southwest to be touched by the big-money development that is turning downtown Los Angeles into a whirring postmodernist dreamscape. The Pico-Union District is very poor, some of its housing as unsafe as that on Skid Row, dilapidated, overcrowded, rat-infested. It used to be a working-class Mexican neighborhood, but for about ten years now it has become the concentrated locale of those fleeing the political and economic horror in Central America. Most come from El Salvador and Guatemala. One observer calls the area a gigantic refugee camp.

As you move concentrically outward from Pico-Union, you'll encounter a number of other immigrant communities: Little Tokyo and Chinatown to the northeast, Afro-Caribbean to the southwest, Koreatown to the west. Moving west, you'll find Thai and Vietnamese restaurants tucked here and there in storefronts. Filipinos, Southeast Asians, Armenians, and Iranians work in the gas stations, the shoe-repair stores, the minimarts. A lawn-mower repair shop posts its sign in Korean, Spanish, and English. A Korean church announces "Jesus Loves You" in the same three languages. "The magnitude and diversity of immigration to Los Angeles since 1960," notes a report from UCLA's Graduate School of Architecture and Urban Planning, "is comparable only to the New York–bound wave of migrants around the turn of the century." It is not at all uncommon for English composition teachers at UCLA, Cal-State L.A., Long Beach State—the big urban universities and colleges—to have, in a class of twenty-five, students representing a dozen or more linguistic backgrounds: from Spanish and Cantonese and Farsi to Hindi, Portuguese, and Tagalog. Los Angeles, the new Ellis Island.

On a drive down the Santa Monica Freeway, you exit on Vermont and pass Rick's Mexican Cuisine, Hawaii Discount Furniture, The Restaurant Ecuatoriano, Froggy's Children's Wear, Seoul Autobody, and the Bar Omaha. Turn east on Pico, and as you approach Union, taking a side street here and there, you'll start seeing the murals: The Virgin of Guadalupe, Steve McQueen, a scene resembling Siqueiros's heroic workers, the Statue of Liberty, Garfield the Cat. Graffiti are everywhere. The dreaded Eighteenth Street gang—an established Mexican gang—has marked its turf in Arabic as well as Roman numerals. Newer gangs, a Salvadoran gang among them, are emerging by the violent logic of territory and migration; they have Xed out the Eighteenth Street *placas* and written their own threatening insignias in place. Statues of the Blessed Mother rest amid potted plants in overgrown front yards. There is a rich sweep of small commerce: restaurants, markets, bakeries, legal services ("Income Tax y Amnestia"), beauty salons ("Lolita's Magic Touch—Salon de Belleza—Unisex"). A Salvadoran restaurant sells teriyaki burgers. A "Discoteca Latina" advertises "great rap hits." A clothing store has a Dick Tracy sweatshirt on a half mannequin;

a boy walks out wearing a blue t-shirt that announces "Life's a Beach." Culture in a Waring blender.

There are private telegram and postal services: messages sent straight to "domicilio a CentroAmerica." A video store advertises a comedy about immigration: *Ni de Aqui/Ni de Alla,* "Neither from Here nor from There." The poster displays a Central American Indian caught on a wild freeway ride: a Mexican in a sombrero is pulling one of the Indian's pigtails, Uncle Sam pulls the other, a border guard looks on, ominously suspended in air. You see a lot of street vending, from oranges and melons to deco sunglasses: rhinestones and plastic swans and lenses shaped like a heart. Posters are slapped on posters: one has rows of faces of the disappeared. Santa Claus stands on a truck bumper and waves drivers into a ninety-nine cent outlet.

Families are out shopping, men loiter outside a cafe, a group of young girls collectively count out their change. You notice, even in the kaleidoscope you pick out his figure, you notice a dark-skinned boy, perhaps Guatemalan, walking down Pico with a cape across his shoulders. His hair is piled in a four-inch rockabilly pompadour. He passes a dingy apartment building, a *pupuseria,* a body shop with no name, and turns into a storefront social services center. There is one other person in the sparse waiting room. She is thin, her gray hair pulled back in a tight bun, her black dress buttoned to her neck. She will tell you, if you ask her in Spanish, that she is waiting for her English class to begin. She might also tell you that the people here are helping her locate her son—lost in Salvadoran resettlement camps—and she thinks that if she can learn a little English, it will help her bring him to America.

The boy is here for different reasons. He has been causing trouble in school, and arrangements are being made for him to see a bilingual counselor. His name is Mario, and he immigrated with his older sister two years ago. His English is halting, unsure; he seems simultaneously rebellious and scared. His caseworker tells me that he still has flashbacks of Guatemalan terror: his older brother taken in the night by death squads, strangled, and hacked apart on the road by his house. Then she shows me his drawings, and our conversation stops. Crayon and pen on cheap paper: blue and orange cityscapes, eyes on billboards, in the windshields of cars, a severed hand at the bus stop. There are punks, beggars, piñatas walking the streets—upright cows and donkeys—skeletal homeboys, corseted girls carrying sharpened bones. "He will talk to you about these," the caseworker tells me. "They're scary, aren't they? The school doesn't know what the hell to do with him. I don't think he really knows what to do with all that's in him either."

In another part of the state, farther to the north, also rich in immigration, a teacher in a basic reading and writing program asks his students to interview one another and write a report, a capsule of a classmate's life. Caroline, a black woman in her late forties, chooses Thuy Anh, a Vietnamese woman many years her junior. Caroline asks only five questions—Thuy Anh's English is still difficult to understand—simple questions: What is your name? Where were you born? What is your education? Thuy Anh talks about her childhood in South Vietnam and her current plans in America. She is the oldest of nine children, and she received a very limited Vietnamese education, for she had to spend much of her childhood caring for her brothers and sisters. She married a serviceman, came to America, and now spends virtually all of her time pursuing a high school equivalency, struggling with textbook descriptions of the American political process, frantically trying to improve her computational skills. She is not doing very well at this. As one of her classmates observed, she might be trying too hard.

Caroline is supposed to take notes while Thuy Anh responds to her questions, and then use the notes to write her profile, maybe something like a reporter would do. But Caroline is moved to do something different. She's taken by Thuy Anh's account of watching over babies. "Mother's little helper," she thinks. And that stirs her, this woman who has never been a mother. Maybe, too, Thuy Anh's desire to do well in school, her driven eagerness, the desperation that occasionally flits across her face, maybe that moves Caroline as well. Over the next two days, Caroline strays from the assignment and writes a two-and-a-half page fiction that builds to a prose poem. She recasts Thuy Anh's childhood into an American television fantasy.

Thuy Anh is "Mother's little helper." Her five younger sisters "are happy and full of laughter . . . their little faces are bright with eyes sparkling." The little girls' names are "Hellen, Ellen, Lottie, Alice, and Olie"— American names—and they "cook and sew and make pretty doll dresses for their dolls to wear." Though the family is Buddhist, they exchange gifts at Christmas and "gather in the large living room to sing Christmas carols." Thuy Anh "went to school every day she could and studied very hard." One day, Thuy Anh was "asked to wright a poem and to recite it to her classmates." And, here, Caroline embeds within her story a prose poem— which she attributes to Thuy Anh:

> My name is Thuy Anh I live near the Ocean. I see the waves boisterous and impudent bursting and splashing against the huge rocks. I see the white boats out on the blue sea. I see the fisher men rapped in heavy coats to keep their bodys warm while bringing in large fishes to sell to the merchants, Look! I see a larg white bird going on its merry way. Then I think of how great God is for he made this great sea for me to see and yet I stand on dry land and see the green and hillie side with flowers rising to the sky. How sweet and beautiful for God to have made Thuy Anh and the sea.

I interview Caroline. When she was a little girl in Arkansas, she "would   15
get off into a room by myself and read the Scripture." The "poems in King

Solomon" were her favorites. She went to a segregated school and "used to write quite a bit" at home. But she "got away from it" and some years later dropped out of high school to come west to earn a living. She's worked in a convalescent hospital for twenty years, never married, wishes she had, comes, now, back to school and is finding again her love of words. "I get lost . . . I'm right in there with my writing, and I forget all my surroundings." She is classified as a basic student—no diploma, low-level employment, poor test scores—had been taught by her grandmother that she would have to earn her living "by the sweat of my brow."

Her work in the writing course had been good up to the point of Thuy Anh's interview, better than that of many classmates, adequate, fairly free of error, pretty well organized. But the interview triggered a different level of performance. Caroline's early engagement with language reemerged in a lyrical burst: an evocation of an imagined childhood, a curious overlay of one culture's fantasy over another's harsh reality. Caroline's longing reshaped a Vietnamese girlhood, creating a life neither she nor Thuy Anh ever had, an intersection of biblical rhythms and *Father Knows Best.*

Over Chin's bent head arches a trellis packed tight with dried honeysuckle and chrysanthemum, sea moss, mushrooms, and ginseng. His elbow rests on the cash register—quiet now that the customers have left. He shifts on the stool, concentrating on the writing before him: "A young children," he scribbles, and pauses. "Young children," that doesn't sound good, he thinks. He crosses out "children" and sits back. A few seconds pass. He can't think of the right way to say it, so he writes "children" again and continues: "a young children with his grandma smail . . ." "Smail." He pulls a Chinese-English dictionary from under the counter.

In front of the counter and extending down the aisle are boxes of dried fish: shark fins, mackerel, pollock. They give off a musky smell. Behind Chin are rows of cans and jars: pickled garlic, pickled ginger, sesame paste. By the door, comic books and Chinese weeklies lean dog-eared out over the thin retaining wire of a dusty wooden display. Chin has found his word: It's not *smail,* it's *smile.* "A young children with his grandma smile . . ." He reaches in the pocket of his jeans jacket, pulls out a piece of paper, and unfolds it. There's a word copied on it he has been wanting to use. A little bell over the door jingles. An old man comes in, and Chin moves his yellow pad aside.

Chin remembers his teacher in elementary school telling him that his writing was poor, that he didn't know many words. He went to middle school for a few years but quit before completing it. Very basic English—the ABCs and simple vocabulary—was, at one point, part of his curriculum, but he lived in a little farming community, so he figured he would never use it. He did, though, pick up some letters and a few words. He immigrated to America when he was seventeen, and for the two years since has been living with his uncle in Chinatown. His uncle signed him up for English classes at the community center. He didn't like them. He did, however, start hanging out in the recreation room, playing pool and watching TV. The English on TV intrigued him. And it was then that he turned to writing. He would "try to learn to speak something" by writing it down. That was about six months ago. Now he's enrolled in a community college literacy program and has been making strong progress. He is especially taken with one tutor, a woman in her mid-thirties who encourages him to write. So he writes for her. He writes stories about his childhood in China. He sneaks time when no one is in the store or when customers are poking around, writing because he likes to bring her things, writing, too, because "sometime I think writing make my English better."

The old man puts on the counter a box of tea guaranteed to help you   20 stop smoking. Chin rings it up and thanks him. The door jingles and Chin returns to his writing, copying the word from his folded piece of paper, a word he found in *People* magazine: "A young children with his grandma smile *gleefully*."

Frank Marell, born Meraglio, my oldest uncle, learned his English as Chin is learning his. He came to America with his mother and three sisters in September 1921. They came to join my grandfather who had immigrated long before. They joined, as well, the millions of Italian peasants who had flowed through Customs with their cloth-and-paper suitcases, their strange gestural language, and their dark, empty pockets. Frank was about to turn eight when he immigrated, so he has faint memories of Calabria. They lived in a one-room stone house. In the winter, the family's scrawny milk cow was brought inside. By the door there was a small hole for a rifle barrel. Wolves came out of the hills. He remembers the frost and burrs stinging his feet as he foraged the countryside for berries and twigs and fresh grass for the cow. *Chi esce riesce,* the saying went—"he who leaves succeeds"—and so it was that my grandfather left when he did, eventually finding work amid the metal and steam of the Pennsylvania Railroad.

My uncle remembers someone giving him bread on the steamship. He remembers being very sick. Once in America, he and his family moved into the company housing projects across from the stockyard. The house was dirty and had gouges in the wood. Each morning his mother had to sweep the soot from in front of the door. He remembers rats. He slept huddled with his father and mother and sisters in the living room, for his parents had to rent out the other rooms in order to buy clothes and shoes and food. Frank never attended school in Italy. He was eight now and would enter school in America. America, where eugenicists were attesting, scientifically, to the feeblemindedness of his race, where the popular press ran articles about the immorality of these swarthy exotics. Frank would enter school here. In many ways, you could lay his life like a template over a current life in the Bronx, in Houston, in Pico-Union.

He remembers the embarrassment of not understanding the teacher, of not being able to read or write. Funny clothes, oversize shoes, his hair slicked down and parted in the middle. He would lean forward—his assigned seat, fortunately, was in the back—and ask other Italian kids, ones with some English, to tell him what for the love of God was going on. He had big, sad eyes, thick hands, skin dark enough to yield the nickname Blacky. Frank remembers other boys—Carmen Santino, a kid named Hump, Bruno Tucci—who couldn't catch on to this new language and quit coming to school. Within six months of his arrival, Frank would be going after class to the back room of Pete Mastis's Dry Cleaners and Shoeshine Parlor. He cleaned and shined shoes, learned to operate a steam press, ran deliveries. He listened to the radio, trying to mimic the harsh complexities of English. He spread Pete Mastis's racing forms out before him, copying words onto the margins of newsprint. He tried talking to the people whose shoes he was shining, exchanging tentative English with the broken English of Germans and Poles and other Italians.

Eventually, Frank taught his mother to sign her name. By the time he was in his teens, he was reading flyers and announcements of sales and legal documents to her. He was also her scribe, doing whatever writing she needed to have done. Frank found himself immersed in the circumstance of literacy.

With the lives of Mario and Caroline and Chin and Frank Marell as   25
a backdrop, I want to consider a current, very powerful set of proposals about literacy and culture.

There is a strong impulse in American education—curious in a country with such an ornery streak of antitraditionalism—to define achievement and excellence in terms of the acquisition of a historically validated body of knowledge, an authoritative list of books and allusions, a canon. We seek a certification of our national intelligence, indeed, our national virtue, in how diligently our children can display this central corpus of information. This need for certification tends to emerge most dramatically in our educational policy debates during times of real or imagined threat: economic hard times, political crises, sudden increases in immigration. Now is such a time, and it is reflected in a number of influential books and commission reports. E. D. Hirsch* argues that a core national vocabulary, one oriented toward the English literate tradition—Alice in Wonderland to zeitgeist—will build a knowledge base that will foster the literacy of all Americans. Diane Ravitch* and Chester Finn* call for a return to a traditional historical and literary

---

E. D. Hirsch: author of *Cultural Literacy: What Every American Needs to Know,* which argues for a standard national public school curriculum that would ensure that all Americans share a common cultural vocabulary

Diane Ravitch: author of *Developing National Standards in Education* and an Education Department official in the Reagan administration

Chester Finn: undersecretary of education in the Reagan administration

curriculum: the valorous historical figures and the classical literature of the once-elite course of study. Allan Bloom, Secretary of Education William Bennett, Mortimer Adler* and the Paideia Group, and a number of others have affirmed, each in their very different ways, the necessity of the Great Books: Plato and Aristotle and Sophocles, Dante and Shakespeare and Locke, Dickens and Mann and Faulkner. We can call this orientation to educational achievement the canonical orientation.

At times in our past, the call for a shoring up of or return to a canonical curriculum was explicitly elitist, was driven by a fear that the education of the select was being compromised. Today, though, the majority of the calls are provocatively framed in the language of democracy. They assail the mediocre and grinding curriculum frequently found in remedial and voca-tional education. They are disdainful of the patronizing perceptions of stu-dent ability that further restrict the already restricted academic life of disadvantaged youngsters. They point out that the canon—its language, conventions, and allusions—is central to the discourse of power, and to keep it from poor kids is to assure their disenfranchisement all the more. The books of the canon, claim the proposals, the Great Books, are a window onto a common core of experience and civic ideals. There is, then, a spiritual, civic, and cognitive heritage here, and *all* our children should receive it. If we are sincere in our desire to bring Mario, Chin, the younger versions of Caroline, current incarnations of Frank Marell, and so many others who populate this book—if we truly want to bring them into our society—then we should provide them with this stable and common core. This is a forceful call. It promises a still center in a turning world.

I see great value in being challenged to think of the curriculum of the many in the terms we have traditionally reserved for the few; it is refreshing to have common assumptions about the capacities of underprepared students so boldly challenged. Many of the people we have encountered in these pages have displayed the ability to engage books and ideas thought to be beyond their grasp. There were the veterans: Willie Oates* writing, in prison, ornate sentences drawn from *The Mill on the Floss.** Sergeant Gonza-lez* coming to understand poetic ambiguity in "Butch Weldy."* There was the parole aide Olga who no longer felt walled off from *Macbeth*. There were the EOP* students at UCLA, like Lucia who unpackaged *The Myth of Mental Illness* once she had an orientation and overview. And there was

---

Mortimer Adler: educator and philosopher, author of many books, including three vol-umes on the Paideia Proposal, an educational framework based on ancient Greek concepts
Willie Oates, Sergeant Gonzalez: students in a veterans' program Rose worked in
The Mill on the Floss: a novel (1860) by George Eliot (1819–80)
"Butch Weldy": a poem in *Spoon River Anthology* (1915) by Edgar Lee Masters (1869–1950)
EOP: Equal Opportunity Program

Frank Marell who, later in his life, would be talking excitedly to his nephew about this guy Edgar Allan Poe. Too many people are kept from the books of the canon, the Great Books, because of misjudgments about their potential. Those books eventually proved important to me, and, as best I know how, I invite my students to engage them. But once we grant the desirability of equal curricular treatment and begin to consider what this equally distributed curriculum would contain, problems arise: If the canon itself is the answer to our educational inequities, why has it historically invited few and denied many? Would the canonical orientation provide adequate guidance as to how a democratic curriculum should be constructed and how it should be taught? Would it guide us in opening up to Olga that "fancy talk" that so alienated her?

Those who study the way literature becomes canonized, how linguistic creations are included or excluded from a tradition, claim that the canonical curriculum students would most likely receive would not, as is claimed, offer a common core of American experience. Caroline would not find her life represented in it, nor would Mario. The canon has tended to push to the margin much of the literature of our nation: from American Indian songs and chants to immigrant fiction to working-class narratives. The institutional messages that students receive in the books they're issued and the classes they take are powerful and, as I've witnessed since my Voc. Ed. days, quickly internalized. And to revise these messages and redress past wrongs would involve more than adding some new books to the existing canon—the very reasons for linguistic and cultural exclusion would have to become a focus of study in order to make the canon act as a democratizing force. Unless this happens, the democratic intent of the reformers will be undercut by the content of the curriculum they propose.

And if we move beyond content to consider basic assumptions about $\quad$ 30 teaching and learning, a further problem arises, one that involves the very nature of the canonical orientation itself. The canonical orientation encourages a narrowing of focus from learning to that which must be learned: It simplifies the dynamic tension between student and text and reduces the psychological and social dimensions of instruction. The student's personal history recedes as the what of the classroom is valorized over the how. Thus it is that the encounter of student and text is often portrayed by canonists as a transmission. Information, wisdom, virtue will pass from the book to the student if the student gives the book the time it merits, carefully traces its argument or narrative or lyrical progression. Intellectual, even spiritual, growth will *necessarily* result from an encounter with Roman mythology, *Othello,* and "I heard a Fly buzz—when I died—,"* with biographies and historical sagas and patriotic lore. Learning is stripped of confusion

---

"*I heard a Fly buzz—when I died—*": poem by Emily Dickinson (1830–86)

and discord. It is stripped, as well, of strong human connection. My own initiators to the canon—Jack MacFarland, Dr. Carothers, and the rest—knew there was more to their work than their mastery of a tradition. What mattered most, I see now, were the relationships they established with me, the guidance they provided when I felt inadequate or threatened. This mentoring was part of my entry into that solemn library of Western thought—and even with such support, there were still times of confusion, anger, and fear. It is telling, I think, that once that rich social network slid away, once I was in graduate school in intense, solitary encounter with that tradition, I abandoned it for other sources of nurturance and knowledge.

The model of learning implicit in the canonical orientation seems, at times, more religious than cognitive or social: Truth resides in the printed texts, and if they are presented by someone who knows them well and respects them, that truth will be revealed.* Of all the advocates of the canon, Mortimer Adler has given most attention to pedagogy—and his Paideia books contain valuable discussions of instruction, coaching, and questioning. But even here, and this is doubly true in the other manifestos, there is little acknowledgment that the material in the canon can be not only difficult but foreign, alienating, overwhelming.

We need an orientation to instruction that provides guidance on how to determine and honor the beliefs and stories, enthusiasms, and apprehensions that students reveal. How to build on them, and when they clash with our curriculum—as I saw so often in the Tutorial Center at UCLA—when they clash, how to encourage a discussion that will lead to reflection on what students bring and what they're currently confronting. Canonical lists imply canonical answers, but the manifestos offer little discussion of what to do when students fail. If students have been exposed to at least some elements of the canon before—as many have—why didn't it take? If they're encountering it for the first time and they're lost, how can we determine where they're located—and what do we do then?

Each member of a teacher's class, poor *or* advantaged, gives rise to endless decisions, day-to-day determinations about a child's reading and writing: decisions on how to tap strength, plumb confusion, foster growth. The richer your conception of learning and your understanding of its social and psychological dimensions, the more insightful and effective your judgments will be. Consider the sources of literacy we saw among the children in El Monte: shopkeepers' signs, song lyrics, auto manuals, the conventions of the Western, family stories and tales, and more. Consider Chin's sources—television and *People* magazine—and Caroline's oddly generative mix of the Bible and an American media illusion. Then there's the jarring

---

model of learning . . . truth will be revealed: For another comparison of education to religion, see Allan Bloom, "The Student and the University," p. 75.

confluence of personal horror and pop cultural flotsam that surfaces in Mario's drawings, drawings that would be a rich, if volatile, point of departure for language instruction. How would these myriad sources and manifestations be perceived and evaluated if viewed within the framework of a canonical tradition, and what guidance would the tradition provide on how to understand and develop them? The great books and central texts of the canon could quickly become a benchmark against which the expressions of student literacy would be negatively measured, a limiting band of excellence that, ironically, could have a dispiriting effect on the very thing the current proposals intend: the fostering of mass literacy.

To understand the nature and development of literacy we need to consider the social context in which it occurs—the political, economic, and cultural forces that encourage or inhibit it. The canonical orientation discourages deep analysis of the way these forces may be affecting performance. The canonists ask that schools transmit a coherent traditional knowledge to an ever-changing, frequently uprooted community. This discordance between message and audience is seldom examined. Although a ghetto child can rise on the lilt of a Homeric line—books *can* spark dreams—appeals to elevated texts can also divert attention from the conditions that keep a population from realizing its dreams. The literacy curriculum is being asked to do what our politics and our economics have failed to do: diminish differences in achievement, narrow our gaps, bring us together. Instead of analysis of the complex web of causes of poor performance, we are offered a faith in the unifying power of a body of knowledge, whose infusion will bring the rich and the poor, the longtime disaffected and the uprooted newcomers into cultural unanimity. If this vision is democratic, it is simplistically so, reductive, not an invitation for people truly to engage each other at the point where cultures and classes intersect.

I worry about the effects a canonical approach to education could have on cultural dialogue and transaction—on the involvement of an abandoned underclass and on the movement of immigrants like Mario and Chin into our nation. A canonical uniformity promotes rigor and quality control; it can also squelch new thinking, diffuse the generative tension between the old and the new. It is significant that the canonical orientation is voiced with most force during times of challenge and uncertainty, for it promises the authority of tradition, the seeming stability of the past. But the authority is fictive, gained from a misreading of American cultural history. No period of that history was harmoniously stable; the invocation of a golden age is a mythologizing act. Democratic culture is, by definition, vibrant and dynamic, discomforting and unpredictable. It gives rise to apprehension; freedom is not always calming. And, yes, it can yield fragmentation, though often as not the source of fragmentation is intolerant misunderstanding of diverse traditions rather than the desire of members of those traditions to remain hermetically separate. A truly democratic vision of knowledge and social structure would honor this complexity. The vision might not be soothing, but it would provide guidance as to how to live and teach in a country made up of many cultural traditions.

We are in the middle of an extraordinary social experiment: the attempt to provide education for all members of a vast pluralistic democracy. To have any prayer of success, we'll need many conceptual blessings: A philosophy of language and literacy that affirms the diverse sources of linguistic competence and deepens our understanding of the ways class and culture blind us to the richness of those sources. A perspective on failure that lays open the logic of error. An orientation toward the interaction of poverty and ability that undercuts simple polarities, that enables us to see simultaneously the constraints poverty places on the play of mind* and the actual mind at play within those constraints. We'll need a pedagogy that encourages us to step back and consider the threat of the standard classroom and that shows us, having stepped back, how to step forward to invite a student across the boundaries of that powerful room. Finally, we'll need a revised store of images of educational excellence, ones closer to egalitarian ideals—ones that embody the reward and turmoil of education in a democracy, that celebrate the plural, messy human reality of it. At heart, we'll need a guiding set of principles that do not encourage us to retreat from, but move us closer to, an understanding of the rich mix of speech and ritual and story that is America.

QUESTIONING THE TEXT

1. What do you think Rose means when he says that "a failed education is social more than intellectual in origin"? Look back to A.L.'s profile on p. xi. Does anything there suggest a time when her education failed for social—or intellectual—reasons? Describe a time when your education failed—or succeeded—largely because of social reasons. If you are keeping a reading log, record your answers there.
2. Rose quotes a friend who says that education can be thought of as "one culture embracing another." Give a few examples from his essay that illustrate this embrace, and then give an example from your own educational experience.
3. Why do you think Rose includes the stories of Mario, Caroline, Chin, and Frank Marell as a backdrop for his discussion about current concepts of literacy in America? What do their stories have in common? What kinds of students does he leave unmentioned?

---

constraints . . . on the play of mind: For another reflection on the effect of poverty—and of wealth—on the mind, see Virginia Woolf, "A Room of One's Own," p. 43.

MAKING CONNECTIONS

4. Imagine Rose responding to Allan Bloom's arguments (starting on p. 75) about what a university should teach the students he's concerned with. What would Rose and Bloom agree on? Where would they disagree—and why?
5. Spend some time thinking about one of the students Rose describes. Then write a brief poem (using Gwendolyn Brooks as a model, perhaps; see p. 146) that would characterize that student's attitude toward school.

JOINING THE CONVERSATION

6. Try to remember a time when your relationship with someone (teacher, parent, coach, religious leader) made it easier (or harder) for you to learn what that person was trying to teach you. Write a brief description of this event for your class, concluding by summarizing those things about another person that most *help* you to learn from him or her.
7. Rose remembers that his earliest interest in literacy came from "comic books and science fiction, from the personal, nonscientific worlds I created with bits and pieces of laboratory and telescopic technology, came, as well, from the Italian stories I heard my uncles and parents tell." Brainstorm with two or three other students about your earliest out-of-school experiences with reading and writing. How were they like or unlike your experiences of reading and writing in school?

SHELBY STEELE
The Recoloring of Campus Life

*T*HE TITLE OF *Shelby Steele's book on race relations in the United States,*
The Content of Our Character *(1990), comes from Martin Luther King,
Jr.'s "I Have a Dream" speech, delivered at a civil rights demonstration in
Washington, D.C., in 1963. In that address, King called for the eradication
of racial prejudices: "I have a dream my four little children will one day live
in a nation where they will not be judged by the color of their skin but by the
content of their character." A generation later, Steele (b. 1946) poses the painful
question of whether the civil rights establishment has abandoned King's dream.
Has the goal of desegregation, he asks, been supplanted by ethnic and racial
separation? Has the ideal of equal opportunity been tainted by quotas?*

    *The lengthy chapter of the book reprinted here examines the sensitive
subject of race relations on campus frankly and openly. Steele, a professor of
English at San Jose State University in California, is a controversial figure, a
black man whose views, like those of Clarence Thomas and the economist
Thomas Sowell, challenge the agenda of many civil rights organizations. Steele
confronts the anxieties of both blacks and whites with uncommon directness. It
is a measure of the national discomfort we feel in talking about race and racism
that some people regard views like Steele's as politically "incorrect." Judge for
yourself whether he is raising issues that ought not to be matters of debate.*   — J.R.

---

*The U.S. has
about 3,000 col-
leges and univer-
sities. Do 80
incidents a
year—most in-
volving ethnic
"insensitivity"
—really consti-
tute an increase
in racial ten-
sions? Was there
a time when such
incidents were
fewer?*   — J.R.

    In the past few years, we have witnessed what
the National Institute Against Prejudice and Violence calls a "proliferation" of racial incidents on
college campuses around the country. Incidents of
on-campus "intergroup conflict" have occurred at
more than 160 colleges in the last two years, according to the institute. The nature of these incidents has ranged from open racial violence—most
notoriously, the October 1986 beating of a black
student at the University of Massachusetts at Amherst after an argument about the World Series
turned into a racial bashing, with a crowd of up
to three thousand whites chasing twenty blacks—
to the harassment of minority students and acts of
racial or ethnic insensitivity, with by far the greatest number of episodes falling in the last two categories. At Yale last year, a swastika and the words

*What is this insti-
tute—and what
is its agenda?*
— A.L.

"white power" were painted on the university's Afro-American cultural center. Racist jokes were aired not long ago on a campus radio station at the University of Michigan. And at the University of Wisconsin at Madison, members of the Zeta Beta Tau fraternity held a mock slave auction in which pledges painted their faces black and wore Afro wigs. Two weeks after the president of Stanford University informed the incoming freshman class last fall that "bigotry is out, and I mean it," two freshmen defaced a poster of Beethoven—gave the image thick lips—and hung it on a black student's door.

These examples make me think of racist acts on my own campus—but also of attempts to counter those acts with acts of respect and generosity for all people.
— A.L.

Why do racial incidents proliferate on campuses usually regarded as "progressive"— Stanford, Berkeley, Wisconsin, U Mass? — J.R.

In response, black students around the country have rediscovered the militant protest strategies of the sixties. At the University of Massachusetts at Amherst, Williams College, Penn State University, University of California–Berkeley, UCLA, Stanford University, and countless other campuses, black students have sat in, marched, and rallied. But much of what they were marching and rallying about seemed less a response to specific racial incidents than a call for broader action on the part of the colleges and universities they were attending. Black students have demanded everything from more black faculty members and new courses on racism to the addition of "ethnic" foods in the cafeteria. There is the sense in these demands that racism runs deep. Is the campus becoming the battleground for a renewed war between the races? I don't think so, not really. But if it is not a war, the problem of campus racism does represent a new and surprising hardening of racial lines within the most traditionally liberal and tolerant of America's institutions—its universities.

After specific acts of fraternity racism in 1990 at UT-Austin, several groups pressured the administration for African American studies throughout the curriculum.
— G.H.

Is he suggesting that racism doesn't run deep? If so, I'll need a lot of evidence to be convinced.
— A.L.

As a black who has spent his entire adult life on predominantly white campuses, I found it hard to believe that the problem of campus racism was as dramatic as some of the incidents seemed to make it. The incidents I read or heard about often seemed prankish and adolescent, though not necessarily harmless. There is a meanness in them but not much menace; no one is proposing to reinstitute Jim Crow on campus. On the California campus

Interesting that he presents his own perspective ("not much menace") as the only one. Other

where I now teach, there have been few signs of racial tension.

And, of course, universities are not where racial problems tend to arise. When I went to college in the mid-sixties, colleges were oases of calm and understanding in a racially tense society; campus life—with its traditions of tolerance and fairness, its very distance from the "real" world—imposed a degree of broad-mindedness on even the most provincial students. If I met whites who were not anxious to be friends with blacks, most were at least vaguely friendly to the cause of our freedom. In any case, there was no guerrilla activity against our presence, no "mine field of racism" (as one black student at Berkeley recently put it to me) to negotiate. I wouldn't say that the phrase "campus racism" is a contradiction in terms, but until recently it certainly seemed an incongruence.

But a greater incongruence is the generational timing of this new problem on the campuses. Today's undergraduates were born after the passage of the 1964 Civil Rights Act. They grew up in an age when racial equality was for the first time enforceable by law. This too was a time when blacks suddenly appeared on television, as mayors of big cities, as icons of popular culture, as teachers, and in some cases even as neighbors. Today's black and white college students, veterans of "Sesame Street" and often of integrated grammar and high schools, have had more opportunities to know each other than any previous generation in American history. Not enough opportunities, perhaps, but enough to make the notion of racial tension on campus something of a mystery, at least to me.

To look at this mystery, I left my own campus with its burden of familiarity and talked with black and white students at California schools where racial incidents had occurred: Stanford, UCLA, and Berkeley. I spoke with black and white students— not with Asians and Hispanics—because, as always, blacks and whites represent the deepest lines of division, and because I hesitate to wander onto the complex territory of other minority groups. A phrase by William H. Gass—"the hidden inter-

African Americans may not have this perspective at all.
– A.L.

I was in college at this same time and this does not describe my experience on a very racist and often hostile campus.
– A.L.

He's now assuming it's a "new" problem, but he hasn't proven it. – A.L.

I don't follow him here. What does he mean by "hidden internality"?
— A.L.

nality of things"—describes, with maybe a little too much grandeur, what I hoped to find. But it is what I wanted to find, for this is the kind of problem that makes a black person nervous, which is not to say that it doesn't unnerve whites as well. Once every six months or so someone yells "nigger" at me from a passing car. I don't like to think that these solo artists might soon make up a chorus, or worse, that this chorus might one day soon sing to me from the paths of my own campus.

I have been called "white boy" in anger maybe 2 or 3 times in the 23 years of my life. But I would assume that the sting I felt was negligible compared to Steele's.
— G.H.

I have long believed that the trouble between the races is seldom what it appears to be. It was not hard to see after my first talks with students that racial tension on campus is a problem that misrepresents itself. It has the same look, the archetypal pattern, of America's timeless racial conflict—white racism and black protest. And I think part of our concern over it comes from the fact that it has the feel of a relapse, illness gone and come again. But if we are seeing the same symptoms, I don't believe we are dealing with the same illness. For one thing, I think racial tension on campus is more the result of racial equality than inequality.

Maybe this is what he means—the old appearance/ reality binary.
— A.L.

How to live with racial difference has been America's profound social problem. For the first hundred years or so following emancipation it was controlled by a legally sanctioned inequality that kept the races from each other. No longer is this the case. On campuses today, as throughout society, blacks enjoy equality under the law—a profound social advancement. No student may be kept out of a class or a dormitory or an extracurricular activity because of his or her race. But there is a paradox here: on a campus where members of all races are gathered, mixed together in the classroom as well as socially, differences are more exposed than ever. And this is where the trouble starts. For members of each race—young adults coming into their own, often away from home for the first time—bring to this site of freedom, exploration, and (now, today) equality, very deep fears, anxieties, inchoate feelings of racial shame, anger, and guilt. These feelings could lie dormant in the home, in familiar neighborhoods, in simpler days of childhood. But

Is this the main point he is arguing?
— A.L.

He's right: higher education challenges the comfortable assumptions most students bring to campus. — J.R.

the college campus, with its structures of interaction and adult-level competition—the big exam, the dorm, the mixer—is another matter. I think campus racism is born of the rub between racial difference and a setting, the campus itself, devoted to interaction and equality. On our campuses, such concentrated micro-societies, all that remains unresolved between blacks and whites, all the old wounds and shames that have never been addressed, present themselves for attention—and present our youth with pressures they cannot always handle.

I have mentioned one paradox: racial fears and anxieties among blacks and whites, bubbling up in an era of racial equality under the law, in settings that are among the freest and fairest in society. But there is another, related paradox, stemming from the notion of—and practice of—affirmative action. Under the provisions of the Equal Employment Opportunity Act of 1972, all state governments and institutions (including universities) were forced to initiate plans to increase the proportion of minority and women employees and, in the case of universities, of students too. Affirmative action plans that establish racial quotas were ruled unconstitutional more than ten years ago in *University of California* v. *Bakke,* but such plans are still thought by some to secretly exist, and lawsuits having to do with alleged quotas are still very much with us. But quotas are only the most controversial aspect of affirmative action; the principle of affirmative action is reflected in various university programs aimed at redressing and overcoming past patterns of discrimination. Of course, to be conscious of past patterns of discrimination—the fact, say, that public schools in the black inner cities are more crowded and employ fewer top-notch teachers than a white suburban public school, and that this is a factor in student performance—is only reasonable. But in doing this we also call attention quite obviously to difference: in the case of blacks and whites, racial difference. What has emerged on campus in recent years—as a result of the new equality and of affirmative action and, in a sense,

This idealistic view of a university as "free and fair" would be contested by many. – A.L.

Since the mid-1980s, the UT law school has had separate admissions standards for blacks, Mexican Americans, and whites. In 1992, white plaintiffs sued the school over this policy. – G.H.

The beneficiaries of affirmative action are usually middle-class students—not poor minority youth from inner cities. Do middle-class whites resent that fact? – J.R.

*I will never for-
get how disap-
pointed I was to
realize that many
factions within
the university
cared nothing
about truths
common to all,
but only about
preferential
rewards.*
— G.H.

as a result of progress—is a *politics of difference,* a troubling, volatile politics in which each group justifies itself, its sense of worth and its pursuit of power, through difference alone.

In this context, racial, ethnic, and gender differences become forms of sovereignty, campuses become balkanized, and each group fights with whatever means are available. No doubt there are many factors that have contributed to the rise of racial tension on campus: What has been the role of fraternities, which have returned to campus with their inclusions and exclusions? What role has the heightened notion of college as some first step to personal, financial success played in increasing competition, and thus tension? But mostly, what I sense is that in interactive settings, fighting the fights of "difference," old ghosts are stirred and haunt again. Black and white Americans simply have the power to make each other feel shame and guilt. In most situations, we may be able to deny these feelings, keep them at bay. But these feelings are likely to surface on college campuses, where young people are groping for identity and power, and where difference is made to matter so greatly. In a way, racial tension on campus in the eighties might have been inevitable.

*Identity politics
(I get my iden-
tity solely and
only through
one characteris-
tic, such as race)
to me is different
from politics of dif-
ference, which
seek to honor
differences among
all people while
not ignoring
commonalities.*
— A.L.

*Black shame and
white guilt?
Steele's analysis
looks simplistic.
Can he sustain
it?* — J.R.

I would like, first, to discuss black students, their anxieties and vulnerabilities. The accusation black Americans have always lived with is that they are inferior—inferior simply because they are black. And this accusation has been too uniform, too ingrained in cultural imagery, too enforced by law, custom, and every form of power not to have left a mark. Black inferiority was a precept accepted by the founders of this nation; it was a principle of social organization that relegated blacks to the sidelines of American life. So when young black students find themselves on white campuses surrounded by those who have historically claimed superiority, they are also surrounded by the myth of their inferiority.

Of course, it is true that many young people come to college with some anxiety about not being good enough. But only blacks come wearing a

*When he uses
"of course" I al-
ways wonder*

color that is still, in the minds of some, a sign of inferiority. Poles, Jews, Hispanics, and other groups also endure degrading stereotypes. But two things make the myth of black inferiority a far heavier burden—the broadness of its scope and its incarnation in color. There are not only more stereotypes of blacks than of other groups, but these stereotypes are also more dehumanizing, more focused on the most despised human traits: stupidity, laziness, sexual immorality, dirtiness, and so on. In America's racial and ethnic hierarchy, blacks have clearly been relegated to the lowest level—have been burdened with an ambiguous, animalistic humanity. Moreover, this is made unavoidable for blacks by sheer visibility of black skin, a skin that evokes the myth of inferiority on sight. Today this myth is sadly reinforced for many black students by affirmative action programs, under which blacks may often enter college with lower test scores and high school grade point averages than whites. "They see me as an affirmative action case," one black student told me at UCLA. This reinforces the myth of inferiority by implying that blacks are not good enough to make it into college on their own.

whether I'll agree with what comes next! – A.L.

Test scores reflect biased test designs, and grades can too. I don't buy this argument. – A.L.

So when a black student enters college, the myth of inferiority compounds the normal anxiousness over whether he or she will be good enough. This anxiety is not only personal but also racial. The families of these students will have pounded into them the fact that blacks are not inferior. And probably more than anything it is this pounding that finally leaves the mark. If I am not inferior, why the need to say so?

This myth of inferiority constitutes a very sharp and ongoing anxiety for young blacks, the nature of which is very precise: it is the terror that somehow, through one's actions or by virtue of some "proof" (a poor grade, a flubbed response in class), one's fear of inferiority—inculcated in ways large and small by society—will be confirmed as real. On a university campus where intelligence itself is the ultimate measure, this anxiety is bound to be triggered.

A black student I met at UCLA was disturbed a little when I asked him if he ever felt vulnerable—anxious about "black inferiority"—as a black student. But after a long pause, he finally said, "I think I do." The example he gave was of a large lecture class he'd taken with over three hundred students. Fifty or so black students sat in the back of the lecture hall and "acted out every stereotype in the book." They were loud, ate food, came in late—and generally got lower grades than whites in the class. "I knew I would be seen like them, and I didn't like it. I never sat by them." Seen like what, I asked, though we both knew the answer. "As lazy, ignorant, and stupid," he said sadly.

Or smart but bored? – A.L.

Had the group at the back been white fraternity brothers, they would not have been seen as dumb whites, of course. And a frat brother who worried about his grades would not worry that he [had] been seen "like them." The terror in this situation for the black student I spoke with was that his own deeply buried anxiety would be given credence, that the myth would be verified, and that he would feel shame and humiliation not because of who he was but simply because he was black. In this lecture hall his race, quite apart from his performance, might subject him to four unendurable feelings—diminishment, accountability to the preconceptions of whites, a powerlessness to change those preconceptions, and finally, shame. These are the feelings that make up his racial anxiety, and that of all blacks on any campus. On a white campus a black is never far from these feelings, and even his unconscious knowledge that he is subject to them can undermine his self-esteem. There are blacks on any campus who are not up to doing good college-level work. Certain black students may not be happy or motivated or in the appropriate field of study—*just like whites.* (Let us not forget that many white students get poor grades, fail, drop out.) Moreover, many more blacks than whites are not quite prepared for college, may have to catch up, owing to factors beyond their control: poor previous schooling, for example. But the white who has to catch up will not be anxious that

Steele makes a convincing distinction here. Growing up, I heard Polish jokes and slurs, but not often enough to think that society really believed the stereotype. That makes a difference.
– J.R.

I'm irritated by his continued attempts to speak for all African Americans.
– A.L.

Do Asian American students feel similarly pressured by a stereotype that marks them all as diligent, hardworking, and extraordinarily smart? – J.R.

his being behind is a matter of his whiteness, of his being racially inferior. The black student may well have such a fear.

This, I believe, is one reason why black colleges in America turn out 37 percent of all black college graduates though they enroll only 16 percent of black college students. Without whites around on campus, the myth of inferiority is in abeyance and, along with it, a great reservoir of culturally imposed self-doubt. On black campuses, feelings of inferiority are personal; on campuses with a white majority, a black's problems have a way of becoming a "black" problem.

But this feeling of vulnerability a black may feel, in itself, is not as serious a problem as what he or she does with it. To admit that one is made anxious in integrated situations about the myth of racial inferiority is difficult for young blacks. It seems like admitting that one is racially inferior. And so, most often, the student will deny harboring the feelings. This is where some of the pangs of racial tension begin, because denial always involves distortion.

In order to deny a problem we must tell ourselves that the problem is something different from what it really is. A black student at Berkeley told me that he felt defensive every time he walked into a classroom of white faces. When I asked why, he said, "Because I know they're all racists. They think blacks are stupid." Of course it may be true that some whites feel this way, but the singular focus on white racism allows this student to obscure his own underlying racial anxiety. He can now say that his problem—facing a classroom of white faces, *fearing* that they think he is dumb—is entirely the result of certifiable white racism and has nothing to do with his own anxieties, or even that this particular academic subject may not be his best. Now all the terror of his anxiety, its powerful energy, is devoted to simply *seeing* racism. Whatever evidence of racism he finds—and looking this hard, he will no doubt find some—can be brought in to buttress his distorted view of the problem while his actual deep-seated anxiety goes unseen.

This helps explain the dilemma of many black students on mainly white campuses. – J.R.

Affirmative action admissions policies often result in low minority retention. – G.H.

As a student, I have seen a similar anxiety in female instructors, particularly during discussions regarding women's roles in history. The anxiety gets worse when they face hostile questions requiring them to justify the need to study gender issues. – G.H.

This seems a kind of false either/or argument to me. Either the problem is all external (white racists) or all internal (deep-seated anxieties). – A.L.

Denial, and the distortion that results, places the problem *outside* the self and in the world. It is not that I have any inferiority anxiety because of my race; it is that I am going to school with people who don't like blacks. This is the shift in thinking that allows black students to reenact the protest pattern of the sixties. *Denied racial anxiety–distortion–reenactment* is the process by which feelings of inferiority are transformed into an exaggerated white menace—which is then protested against with the techniques of the past. Under the sway of this process, black students believe that history is repeating itself, that it's just like the sixties, or fifties. In fact, it is not-yet-healed wounds from the past, rather than the inequality that created the wounds, that is the real problem.

Excessive attention to race can breed racist feelings. That's one reason I'm uneasy with multicultural curriculums that emphasize difference.
— J.R.

This process generates an unconscious need to exaggerate the level of racism on campus—to make it a matter of the system, not just a handful of students. Racism is the avenue away from the true inner anxiety. How many students demonstrating for black theme dorms—demonstrating in the style of the sixties, when the battle was to win for blacks a place on campus—might be better off spending their time reading and studying? Black students have the highest dropout rate and the lowest grade point average of any group in American universities. This need not be so. And it is not the result of not having black theme dorms.

People said the same thing to the '60s civil rights protesters.
— A.L.

It was my very good fortune to go to college in 1964, when the question of black "inferiority" was openly talked about among blacks. The summer before I left for college, I heard Martin Luther King speak in Chicago, and he laid it on the line for black students everywhere: "When you are behind in a footrace, the only way to get ahead is to run faster than the man in front of you. So when your white roommate says he's tired and goes to sleep, you stay up and burn the midnight oil." His statement that we were "behind in a footrace" acknowledged that, because of history, of few opportunities, of racism, we were, in a sense, "inferior." But this had to do with what had been done to our parents and their parents, not with inherent inferiority. And because it was acknowledged, it was presented to us as a challenge rather than a mark of shame.

Of the eighteen black students (in a student body of one thousand) who were on campus in my freshman year, all graduated, though a number of us were not from the middle class. At the university where I currently teach, the dropout rate for black students is 72 percent, despite the presence of several academic support programs, a counseling center with black counselors, an Afro-American studies department, black faculty, administrators, and staff, a general education curriculum that emphasizes "cultural pluralism," an Educational Opportunities Program, a mentor program, a black faculty and staff association, and an administration and faculty that often announce the need to do more for black students.

At my university, these programs are tiny and underfunded. At Ohio State, only 3.2% of faculty are African American.
– A.L.

It may be unfair to compare my generation with the current one. Parents do this compulsively and to little end but self-congratulation. But I don't congratulate my generation. I think we were advantaged. We came along at a time when racial integration was held in high esteem. And integration was a very challenging social concept for both blacks and whites. We were remaking ourselves— that's what one did at college—and making history. We had something to prove. This was a profound advantage; it gave us clarity and a challenge. Achievement in the American mainstream was the goal of integration, and the best thing about this challenge was its secondary message—that we *could* achieve.

Integration is a goal rarely mentioned in campus discussions of racial problems these days.
– J.R.

Is "achievement in the American mainstream" another way of saying "being like white people"?
– A.L.

There is much irony in the fact that black power would come along in the late sixties and change all this. Black power was a movement of uplift and pride, and yet it also delivered the weight of pride—a weight that would burden black students from then on. Black power "nationalized" the black identity, made blackness itself an object of celebration, an allegiance. But if it transformed a mark of shame into a mark of pride, it also, in the name of pride, required the denial of racial anxiety. Without a frank account of one's anxieties, there

This may be true, but it's another one of those either/or argu-

is no clear direction, no concrete challenge. Black students today do not get as clear a message from their racial identity as my generation got. They are not filled with the same urgency to prove themselves because black pride has said, *You're already proven, already equal, as good as anybody.*

The "black identity" shaped by black power most forcefully contributes to racial tensions on campuses by basing entitlement more on race than on constitutional rights and standards of merit. With integration, black entitlement derived from constitutional principles of fairness. Black power changed this by skewing the formula from rights to color—if you were black, you were entitled. Thus the United Coalition Against Racism (UCAR) at the University of Michigan could "demand" two years ago that all black professors be given immediate tenure, that there [be] a special pay incentive for black professors, and that money be provided for an all-black student union. In this formula, black becomes the very color of entitlement, an extra right in itself, and a very dangerous grandiosity is promoted in which blackness amounts to specialness.

Race is, by any standard, an unprincipled source of power. And on campuses the use of racial power by one group makes racial, ethnic, or gender difference a currency of power for all groups. When I make my *difference* into power, other groups must seize upon their difference to contain my power and maintain their position relative to me. Very quickly a kind of politics of difference emerges in which racial, ethnic, and gender groups are forced to assert their entitlement and vie for power based on the single quality that makes them different from one another.

On many campuses today academic departments and programs are established on the basis of difference—black studies, women's studies, Asian studies, and so on—despite the fact that there is nothing in these "difference" departments that cannot be studied within traditional academic disciplines. If their rationale is truly past exclusion from the mainstream curriculum, shouldn't the

ments I'm always leery of. – A.L.

I agree. Balkanization can present a danger, but that doesn't mean we should reject difference. – A.L.

goal now be complete inclusion rather than separateness? I think this logic is overlooked because those groups are too interested in the power their difference can bring, and they insist on separate departments and programs as tribute to that power.

This politics of difference makes everyone on campus a member of a minority group. It also makes racial tension inevitable. To highlight one's difference as a source of advantage is also, indirectly, to inspire the enemies of that difference. When blackness (and femaleness) become power, then white maleness is also sanctioned as power. A white male student I spoke with at Stanford said, "One of my friends said the other day that we should get together and start up a white student union and come up with a list of demands."

It is certainly true that white maleness has long been an unfair source of power. But the sin of white male power is precisely its use of race and gender as a source of entitlement. When minorities and women use their race, ethnicity, and gender in the same way, they not only commit the same sin but also, indirectly, sanction the very form of power that oppressed them in the first place. The politics of difference is based on a tit-for-tat sort of logic in which every victory only calls one's enemies to arms.

This elevation of difference undermines the communal impulse by making each group foreign and inaccessible to others. When difference is celebrated rather than remarked, people must think in terms of difference, they must find meaning in difference, and this meaning comes from an endless process of contrasting one's group with other groups. Blacks use whites to define themselves as different, women use men, Hispanics use whites and blacks, and on it goes. And in the process each group mythologizes and mystifies its difference, puts it beyond the full comprehension of outsiders. Difference becomes inaccessible preciousness toward which outsiders are expected to be simply

Another either/ or. I don't accept the notion that we must honor only one or the other— difference or community.
– A.L.

and uncomprehendingly reverential.* But beware: in this world, even the insulated world of the college campus, preciousness is a balloon asking for a needle. At Smith College graffiti appears: "Niggers, spics, and chinks. Quit complaining or get out."

I think that those who run our colleges and universities are every bit as responsible for the politics of difference as are minority students. To correct the exclusions once caused by race and gender, universities—under the banner of affirmative action—have relied too heavily on race and gender as criteria. So rather than break the link between difference and power, they have reinforced it. On most campuses today, a well-to-do black student with two professional parents is qualified by his race for scholarship monies that are not available to a lower-middle-class white student. A white female with a private school education and every form of cultural advantage comes under the affirmative action umbrella. This kind of inequity is an invitation to backlash.

These generalizations simply are not true. Affirmative action at my school does nothing to advantage the students described here. — A.L.

What universities are quite rightly trying to do is compensate people for past discrimination and the deprivations that followed from it. But race and gender alone offer only the grossest measure of this. And the failure of universities has been their backing away from the challenge of identifying principles of fairness and merit that make finer and more equitable distinctions. The real challenge is not simply to include a certain number of blacks, but to end discrimination against all blacks and to offer special help to those with talent who have also been economically deprived.

I agree. — A.L.

With regard to black students, affirmative action has led universities to correlate color with poverty and disadvantage in so absolute a way as to encourage the politics of difference. But why have they gone along with this? My belief is that it is due to

---

Difference becomes . . . reverential: For another critical look at "elevation of difference," see David Rieff, "The Case Against Sensitivity," p. 406.

the specific form of racial anxiety to which whites are most subject.

Most of the white students I talked with spoke as if from under a faint cloud of accusation. There was always a ring of defensiveness in their complaints about blacks. A white student I spoke to at UCLA told me: "Most white students on this campus think the black student leadership here is made up of oversensitive crybabies who spend all their time looking for things to kick up a ruckus about." A white student at Stanford said, "Blacks do nothing but complain and ask for sympathy when everyone really knows that they don't do well because they don't try. If they worked harder, they could do as well as everyone else."

That these students felt accused was most obvious in their compulsion to assure me that they were not racist. Oblique versions of some-of-my-best-friends-are stories came ritualistically before or after critiques of black students. Some said flatly, "I am not a racist, but . . ." Of course, we all deny being racist, but we only do this compulsively, I think, when we are working against an accusation of bias. I think it was the color of my skin itself that accused them.

This was the meta-message that surrounded these conversations like an aura, and it is, I believe, the core of white American racial anxiety. My skin not only accused them; it judged them. And this judgment was a sad gift of history that brought them to account whether they deserved such accountability or not. It said that wherever and whenever blacks were concerned, they had reason to feel guilt. And whether it was earned or unearned, I think it was guilt that set off the compulsion in these students to disclaim. I believe it is true that, in America, black people make white people feel guilty.

Guilt is the essence of white anxiety just as inferiority is the essence of black anxiety. And the terror that it carries for whites is the terror of discovering that one has reason to feel guilt where blacks are concerned—not so much because of what blacks might think but because of what guilt can say about oneself. If the darkest fear of blacks is inferiority, the darkest fear of whites is that their better lot in life is at least partially the result of their capacity for evil—their capacity to dehumanize an entire people for their own benefit and then to be indifferent to the devastation their dehumanization has wrought on successive generations of their victims. This is the terror that whites are vulnerable to regarding blacks. And the mere fact of being white is sufficient to feel it, since even whites with hearts clean of racism benefit from being white—benefit at the expense of blacks. This is a conditional guilt having nothing to do with individual intentions or actions. And it makes for a very powerful anxiety because it threatens whites with a view of themselves as inhuman, just as inferiority threatens blacks with a similar view of themselves. At the dark core of both anxieties is a suspicion of incomplete humanity.

So, the white students I met were not just meeting me; they were also meeting the possibility of their own inhumanity. And this, I think, is what explains how some young white college students in the late eighties could so frankly take part in racially insensitive and outright racist acts. They were expected to be cleaner of racism than any previous generation—they were born into the Great Society. But this expectation overlooks the fact that, for them, color is still an accusation and judgment. In black faces there is a discomforting reflection of white collective shame. Blacks remind them that their racial innocence is questionable, that they are the beneficiaries of past and present racism, and the sins of the father may well have been visited on the children.

And yet young whites tell themselves that they had nothing to do with the oppression of black people. They have a stronger belief in their racial innocence than any previous generation of whites and a natural hostility toward anyone who would challenge that innocence. So (with a great deal of individual variation) they can end up in the paradoxical position of being hostile to blacks as a way of defending their own racial innocence.

I think this is what the young white editors of the *Dartmouth Review* were doing when they harassed black music professor William Cole. Weren't they saying, in effect, I am so free of racial guilt that I can afford to attack blacks ruthlessly and still be racially innocent? The ruthlessness of these attacks was a form of denial, a badge of innocence. The more they were charged with racism, the more ugly and confrontational their harassment became (an escalation unexplained even by the serious charges against Professor Cole). Racism became a means of rejecting racial guilt, a way of showing that they were not, ultimately, racists.

The politics of difference sets up a struggle for innocence among all groups. When difference is the currency of power, each group must fight for the innocence that entitles it to power. To gain this innocence, blacks sting whites with guilt, remind them of their racial past, accuse them of new and more subtle forms of racism. One way whites retrieve their innocence is to discredit blacks and deny their difficulties, for in this denial is the denial of their own guilt. To blacks this denial looks like racism, a racism that feeds black innocence and encourages them to throw more guilt at whites. And so the cycle continues. The politics of difference leads each group to pick at the vulnerabilities of the other.

Men and women who run universities—whites, mostly—participate in the politics of difference because they handle their guilt differently than do many of their students. They don't deny it, but still they don't want to *feel* it. And to avoid this feeling of guilt they have tended to go along with whatever blacks put on the table rather than work with them to assess their real needs. University administrators have too often been afraid of guilt and have relied on negotiation and capitulation more to appease their own guilt than to help blacks and other minorities. Administrators would never give white students a racial theme dorm where they could be "more comfortable with people of their own kind," yet more and more universities are doing this for black students, thus fostering a

This is undoubtedly often true. — A.L.

kind of voluntary segregation. To avoid the anxieties of integrated situations blacks ask for theme dorms; to avoid guilt, white administrators give theme dorms.

When everyone is on the run from their anxieties about race, race relations on campus can be reduced to the negotiation of avoidances. A pattern of demand and concession develops in which both sides use the other to escape themselves. Black studies departments, black deans of student affairs, black counseling programs, Afro houses, black theme dorms, black homecoming dances and graduation ceremonies—black students and white administrators have slowly engineered a machinery of separatism that, in the name of sacred difference, redraws the ugly lines of segregation.

Black students have not sufficiently helped themselves, and universities, despite all their concessions, have not really done much for blacks. If both faced their anxieties, I think they would see the same thing: academic parity with all other groups should be the overriding mission of black students, and it should also be the first goal that universities have for their black students. Blacks can only *know* they are as good as others when they are, in fact, as good—when their grades are higher and their dropout rate lower. Nothing under the sun will substitute for this, and no amount of concessions will bring it about.

Universities can never be free of guilt until they truly help black students, which means leading and challenging them rather than negotiating and capitulating. It means inspiring them to achieve academic parity, nothing less, and helping them to see their own weaknesses as their greatest challenge. It also means dismantling the machinery of separatism, breaking the link between difference and power, and skewing the formula for entitlement away from race and gender and back to constitutional rights.

As for the young white students who have rediscovered swastikas and the word "nigger," I think that they suffer from an exaggerated sense of their own innocence, as if they were incapable of evil

And university administrators—who are often under pressure from minority caucuses in the legislature—are more than happy to make such concessions.
— G.H.

White professors who make comparable observations are sometimes charged with racism. What does such an accusation reveal about the advocates of a campus "politics of difference"?
— J.R.

White administrators and faculty suffer the double guilt of enjoying the benefits of past discriminatory practices while they themselves scrap academic merit and sacrifice white students to affirmative action in the name of equity. — G.H.

Not an exaggerated sense of their own importance and power? — A.L.

and beyond the reach of guilt. But it is also true
that the politics of difference creates an environment that threatens their innocence and makes
them defensive. White students are not invited to
the negotiating table from which they see blacks
and others walk away with concessions. The presumption is that they do not deserve to be there
because they are white. So they can only be defensive, and the less mature among them will be aggressive. Guerrilla activity will ensue. Of course
this is wrong, but it is also a reflection of an environment where difference carries power and where
whites have the wrong "difference."

I think universities should emphasize commonality as a higher value than "diversity" and "pluralism"—buzzwords for the politics of difference.
Difference that does not rest on a clearly delineated
foundation of commonality is not only inaccessible
to those who are not part of the ethnic or racial
group, but also antagonistic to them. Difference
can enrich only the common ground.

Integration has become an abstract term today,
having to do with little more than numbers and racial balances. But it once stood for a high and admirable set of values. It made difference second to
commonality, and it asked members of all races to
face whatever fears they inspired in each other. I
doubt the word will have a new vogue, but the values, under whatever name, are worth working for.

Afterwords

The most striking line to me in this selection is Steele's almost casual
observation that "every six months or so someone yells 'nigger' at me from
a passing car." I admire the courageous way he reacts to such racist acts.
Unlike some of the activists I've observed on my own campus—people who
seem to build careers by exploiting "difference"—Steele refuses to dwell upon
the pain and insult he must certainly feel. Taking no pleasure in the
convincing evidence he has that racism endures in the United States, Steele
patiently searches for solutions to the problem, exempting no one from
scrutiny, treating no one with contempt. That search is what "The Recoloring
of Campus Life" is all about.

It has been my experience, unfortunately, that many campus activists today *lack the humanity and patience of a Shelby Steele. They seem almost to enjoy the ranting speeches and pious posturing that follow in the aftermath of a perceived campus outrage—whether it be the insensitivity of a student, the imprudent remark of a faculty member, or the gaffe of a politician. Confirmed in grace by their opponents' fall, they exploit the incident for political purposes and quickly lose the support of many who would otherwise stand with them. Barriers go up, groups are divided by race and ethnicity, and the content of character becomes irrelevant.*

The activists' answers to racism and sexism typically involve more stereotyping, more sensitivity seminars, and still more separation (ethnic dorms, minority student unions, multicultural courses). As Steele suggests, such solutions only make honesty in racial relationships that much harder to achieve. — J.R.

I am puzzled, J.R., by your shift from considering Steele's argument to what I take to be an attack on "activists." Ironically, it seems to me that you stereotype "activists" even as you accuse them of "more stereotyping."

While I agree with many individual points Steele makes (all students should be challenged to achieve their full potential; commonalities among us are important and should be nurtured), I came away disappointed in this article for several reasons. First, Steele seems too glib in his dismissal of affirmative action, which for all its flaws helped him to achieve and to prosper. In addition, his tendency to locate the source of racial tension in individual anxieties—inferiority for African Americans, guilt for Caucasians—tends to put the blame for problems on campus onto individuals or on "a handful of students." In doing so, Steele ignores the degree to which the system of higher education and much else in American society—with its hypercompetition, rank-ordering, and glorification of the kind of extreme individualism that breeds alienation—work to fuel racism that ends up harming all students. Finally, I find that Steele thinks, ironically, in black-and-white terms: either commonality or *difference; either affirmative action* or *equality for all; either black studies, women's studies, and so on,* or *a fair and "common" core. My own experience tells me that such polarized thinking is usually oversimplified and that "both/and" is preferable to "either/ or." I want to celebrate and value and understand differences among people* and *those common ties that bind us together. I want to know and appreciate what makes me unique, as well as what makes me like other folks, including Shelby Steele. The college campus, I believe, is just the place to enact such a "both/ and" philosophy. That's why I like being there. And that's why I have a more hopeful reading of "the recoloring of campus life" than does Steele.* — A.L.

It's tempting to characterize any generalizations we dislike as stereotypes. You will note, A.L., that I aim my barbs chiefly at activists who exploit racial and ethnic differences. I wish such people were so rare on college campuses that one couldn't generalize about their tactics and behavior. But that's not been my experience. — J.R.

The issue of race rubs emotions raw. Steele's steady candor should make readers feel more comfortable with their own thoughts, and there certainly is a need to hear opinions like his. Dinesh D'Souza, a native of India who has also criticized affirmative action quotas, admits that he can do so chiefly because of his minority status. Regrettably, one has to wonder whether honesty about racial issues can come only from minorities.

Preferential treatment programs for minorities abound at universities. For example, minority candidates with grade point averages below a 3.0 and LSAT scores below the 50th percentile have been admitted to the University of Texas School of Law. Whites must have GPAs above 3.5 and LSAT scores near or above the 90th percentile. But with so few minority critics and so many white advocates, it's unlikely such affirmative action programs will end, as Steele hopes. And as evidenced by the growing number of political and academic appointments being made in the name of "racial diversity," the likelihood of change in the situation he describes seems remote.   – G.H.

QUESTIONING THE TEXT

1. "The Recoloring of Campus Life" contains a great number of "cause and effect" analyses. Identify one example of an effect that Steele traces to its root causes, and then write a paragraph assessing the persuasiveness of his reasoning.
2. Steele notes that about once every six months, someone yells a racial epithet at him from a passing car. Freewrite about such an incident, perhaps describing a similar experience and/or considering how it would feel to be a victim of one.
3. Look at the use of quotation marks in the annotations next to Steele's text. Which ones are used to mark direct quotations, and which ones are used for some other purpose? What other purposes do A.L., G.H., and J.R. have for placing certain words in quotes?

MAKING CONNECTIONS

4. Compare the perspectives on education offered by bell hooks (starting on p. 124) and Shelby Steele and the language they use to make their cases. How do they differ in tone and language? What audience do you believe each is trying to reach? Do you find one author more successful than the other? Why, or why not?
5. Would John Henry Newman's concept of the university, as described starting on p. 34, be able to accommodate the kinds of problems with "difference" that Steele describes? Explore the question in a brief essay.

JOINING THE CONVERSATION

6. Steele seems to blame affirmative action programs for many of the racial problems on campuses. Talk to officials on your campus or use the library to augment your understanding of such programs. How do they operate? What is their relationship to the sensitive issue of quotas? Bring your findings to class for discussion.

7. Steele inveighs against the establishment of black "theme" dorms. In a brief column such as might appear in a student newspaper, argue for or against the establishment of dormitories, student unions, or campus cultural programs designed to serve particular ethnic or racial groups.

8. Steele deliberately does not explore the status of other minorities on campus—notably Hispanic and Asian students. With a group of classmates, discuss the problems faced by these groups or others on your campus, such as women, homosexuals, older students, men, Christians, Jews, and so on. Then write a report applying what Steele observes about black-white relationships to the relationship between one of these groups and other students.

BELL HOOKS
Keeping Close to Home: Class and Education

*V*IRGINIA WOOLF, *Adrienne Rich, and Mike Rose give us ways to know what it means to see education as the practice of exclusion. In her book* Talking Back: Thinking Feminist, Thinking Black, *bell hooks (b. 1952) says that "[g]enerations of black people have known what it means to see education as the practice of freedom." Her own education was both difficult and hard-won. As she says, "To a southern black girl from a working-class background who had never been on a city bus, who had never stepped on an escalator, who had never travelled by plane, leaving the comfortable confines of a small town Kentucky life to attend Stanford University was not just frightening; it was utterly painful."*

In fact, hooks drafted her first book, Ain't I a Woman: black women and feminism, *when she was a Stanford undergraduate. She has since written several other volumes:* Feminist Theory: from margin to center *(1984);* Talking Back *(1989), from which the following selection is taken; and* Yearning: Race, Gender, and Cultural Politics *(1990). In "Keeping Close to Home," hooks talks about her experiences as an undergraduate and offers an implicit argument for the role a university should play in the life of a nation. She also offers an implicit response to Shelby Steele by explaining why she wanted to acquire the "mainstream" education Stanford had to offer and to retain her own separate background and values as well. "Both/and," hooks says, in response to Steele's "either/or."*

A few years ago I heard hooks speak about her experiences as a teacher in largely white universities. I was struck by how open and responsive hooks was to her again almost all white audience, and I particularly noted a gesture that she made. In signaling to one questioner after another, hooks never once pointed her finger. Instead, she extended an open palm, issuing an invitation rather than a command (or an accusation). I've never forgotten that gesture, or her passion as she spoke about her own need for an education and her determination to gain that education without giving up her own voice and style. Thus I jumped at a chance to include her voice in these pages. — A.L.

We are both awake in the almost dark of 5 a.m. Everyone else is sound asleep. Mama asks the usual questions. Telling me to look around, make sure I have everything, scolding me because I am uncertain about the actual time the bus arrives. By 5:30 we are waiting outside the closed station.

Alone together, we have a chance to really talk. Mama begins. Angry with her children, especially the ones who whisper behind her back, she says bitterly, "Your childhood could not have been that bad. You were fed and clothed. You did not have to do without—that's more than a lot of folks have and I just can't stand the way y'all go on." The hurt in her voice saddens me. I have always wanted to protect mama from hurt, to ease her burdens. Now I am part of what troubles. Confronting me, she says accusingly, "It's not just the other children. You talk too much about the past. You don't just listen." And I do talk. Worse, I write about it.

Mama has always come to each of her children seeking different responses. With me she expresses the disappointment, hurt, and anger of betrayal: anger that her children are so critical, that we can't even have the sense to like the presents she sends. She says, "From now on there will be no presents. I'll just stick some money in a little envelope the way the rest of you do. Nobody wants criticism. Everybody can criticize me but I am supposed to say nothing." When I try to talk, my voice sounds like a twelve year old. When I try to talk, she speaks louder, interrupting me, even though she has said repeatedly, "Explain it to me, this talk about the past." I struggle to return to my thirty-five year old self so that she will know by the sound of my voice that we are two women talking together. It is only when I state firmly in my very adult voice, "Mama, you are not listening," that she becomes quiet. She waits. Now that I have her attention, I fear that my explanations will be lame, inadequate. "Mama," I begin, "people usually go to therapy because they feel hurt inside, because they have pain that will not stop, like a wound that continually breaks open, that does not heal. And often these hurts, that pain has to do with things that have happened in the past, sometimes in childhood, often in childhood, or things that we believe happened." She wants to know, "What hurts, what hurts are you talking about?" "Mom, I can't answer that. I can't speak for all of us, the hurts are different for everybody. But the point is you try to make the hurt better, to heal it, by understanding how it came to be. And I know you feel mad when we say something happened or hurt that you don't remember being that way, but the past isn't like that, we don't have the same memory of it. We remember things differently. You know that. And sometimes folk feel hurt about stuff and you just don't know or didn't realize it, and they need to talk about it. Surely you understand the need to talk about it."

Our conversation is interrupted by the sight of my uncle walking across the park toward us. We stop to watch him. He is on his way to work dressed in a familiar blue suit. They look alike, these two who rarely discuss the past. This interruption makes me think about life in a small town. You always see someone you know. Interruptions, intrusions are part of daily life. Privacy is difficult to maintain. We leave our private space in the car to greet him. After the hug and kiss he has given me every year since I was born, they talk about the day's funerals. In the distance the bus approaches.

He walks away knowing that they will see each other later. Just before I board the bus I turn, staring into my mother's face. I am momentarily back in time, seeing myself eighteen years ago, at this same bus stop, staring into my mother's face, continually turning back, waving farewell as I returned to college—that experience which first took me away from our town, from family. Departing was as painful then as it is now. Each movement away makes return harder. Each separation intensifies distance, both physical and emotional. *

To a southern black girl from a working-class background who had never been on a city bus, who had never stepped on an escalator, who had never travelled by plane, leaving the comfortable confines of a small town Kentucky life to attend Stanford University was not just frightening; it was utterly painful. My parents had not been delighted that I had been accepted and adamantly opposed my going so far from home. At the time, I did not see their opposition as an expression of their fear that they would lose me forever. Like many working-class folks, they feared what college education might do to their children's minds even as they unenthusiastically acknowledged its importance. They did not understand why I could not attend a college nearby, an all-black college. To them, any college would do. I would graduate, become a school teacher, make a decent living and a good marriage. And even though they reluctantly and skeptically supported my educational endeavors, they also subjected them to constant harsh and bitter critique. It is difficult for me to talk about my parents and their impact on me because they have always felt wary, ambivalent, mistrusting of my intellectual aspirations even as they have been caring and supportive. I want to speak about these contradictions because sorting through them, seeking resolution and reconciliation has been important to me both as it affects my development as a writer, my effort to be fully self-realized, and my longing to remain close to the family and community that provided the groundwork for much of my thinking, writing, and being.

Studying at Stanford, I began to think seriously about class differences.   5 To be materially underprivileged at a university where most folks (with the exception of workers) are materially privileged provokes such thought. Class differences were boundaries no one wanted to face or talk about. It was easier to downplay them, to act as though we were all from privileged backgrounds, to work around them, to confront them privately in the solitude of one's room, or to pretend that just being chosen to study at such an institution meant that those of us who did not come from privilege were already in transition toward privilege. To not long for such transition marked one as rebellious, as unlikely to succeed. It was a kind of treason

---

Departing was . . . physical and emotional: For another account of the emotions stirred by revisiting one's family, see Joan Didion, "On Going Home," p. 519.

not to believe that it was better to be identified with the world of material privilege than with the world of the working class, the poor.* No wonder our working-class parents from poor backgrounds feared our entry into such a world, intuiting perhaps that we might learn to be ashamed of where we had come from, that we might never return home, or come back only to lord it over them.

Though I hung with students who were supposedly radical and chic, we did not discuss class. I talked to no one about the sources of my shame, how it hurt me to witness the contempt shown the brown-skinned Filipina maids who cleaned our rooms, or later my concern about the $100 a month I paid for a room off-campus which was more than half of what my parents paid for rent. I talked to no one about my efforts to save money, to send a little something home. Yet these class realities separated me from fellow students. We were moving in different directions. I did not intend to forget my class background or alter my class allegiance. And even though I received an education designed to provide me with a bourgeois sensibility, passive acquiescence was not my only option. I knew that I could resist. I could rebel. I could shape the direction and focus of the various forms of knowledge available to me. Even though I sometimes envied and longed for greater material advantages (particularly at vacation times when I would be one of few if any students remaining in the dormitory because there was no money for travel), I did not share the sensibility and values of my peers. That was important—class was not just about money; it was about values which showed and determined behavior. While I often needed more money, I never needed a new set of beliefs and values. For example, I was profoundly shocked and disturbed when peers would talk about their parents without respect, or would even say that they hated their parents. This was especially troubling to me when it seemed that these parents were caring and concerned. It was often explained to me that such hatred was "healthy and normal." To my white, middle-class California roommate, I explained the way we were taught to value our parents and their care, to understand that they were not obligated to give us care. She would always shake her head, laughing all the while, and say, "Missy, you will learn that it's different here, that we think differently." She was right. Soon, I lived alone, like the one Mormon student who kept to himself as he made a concentrated effort to remain true to his religious beliefs and values. Later in graduate school I found that classmates believed "lower class" people had no beliefs and values. I was silent in such discussions, disgusted by their ignorance.

Carol Stack's anthropological study, *All Our Kin,* was one of the first books I read which confirmed my experiential understanding that within

---

better to be identified with . . . material privilege: For the view of someone who *does* believe this, see Virginia Woolf, "A Room of One's Own," p. 43.

black culture (especially among the working class and poor, particularly in southern states), a value system emerged that was counter-hegemonic, that challenged notions of individualism and private property so important to the maintenance of white-supremacist, capitalist patriarchy. Black folk created in marginal spaces a world of community and collectivity where resources were shared. In the preface to *Feminist Theory: from margin to center,* I talked about how the point of difference, this marginality can be the space for the formation of an oppositional world view. That world view must be articulated, named if it is to provide a sustained blueprint for change. Unfortunately, there has existed no consistent framework for such naming. Consequently both the experience of this difference and documentation of it (when it occurs) gradually loses presence and meaning.

Much of what Stack documented about the "culture of poverty," for example, would not describe interactions among most black poor today irrespective of geographical setting. Since the black people she described did not acknowledge (if they recognized it in theoretical terms) the oppositional value of their world view, apparently seeing it more as a survival strategy determined less by conscious efforts to oppose oppressive race and class biases than by circumstance, they did not attempt to establish a framework to transmit their beliefs and values from generation to generation. When circumstances changed, values altered. Efforts to assimilate the values and beliefs of privileged white people, presented through media like television, undermine and destroy potential structures of opposition.

Increasingly, young black people are encouraged by the dominant culture (and by those black people who internalize the values of this hegemony) to believe that assimilation is the only possible way to survive, to succeed. Without the framework of an organized civil rights or black resistance struggle, individual and collective efforts at black liberation that focus on the primacy of self-definition and self-determination often go unrecognized. It is crucial that those among us who resist and rebel, who survive and succeed, speak openly and honestly about our lives and the nature of our personal struggles, the means by which we resolve and reconcile contradictions. This is no easy task. Within the educational institutions where we learn to develop and strengthen our writing and analytical skills, we also learn to think, write, and talk in a manner that shifts attention away from personal experience. Yet if we are to reach our people and all people, if we are to remain connected (especially those of us whose familial backgrounds are poor and working-class), we must understand that the telling of one's personal story provides a meaningful example, a way for folks to identify and connect.

Combining personal with critical analysis and theoretical perspectives   10 can engage listeners who might otherwise feel estranged, alienated. To speak simply with language that is accessible to as many folks as possible is also important. Speaking about one's personal experience or speaking with simple language is often considered by academics and/or intellectuals (irre-spective of their political inclinations) to be a sign of intellectual weakness or even anti-intellectualism. Lately, when I speak, I do not stand in place—reading my paper, making little or no eye contact with audiences—but instead make eye contact, talk extemporaneously, digress, and address the audience directly. I have been told that people assume I am not prepared, that I am anti-intellectual, unprofessional (a concept that has everything to do with class as it determines actions and behavior), or that I am reinforcing the stereotype of black people as non-theoretical and gutsy.

Such criticism was raised recently by fellow feminist scholars after a talk I gave at Northwestern University at a conference on "Gender, Culture, Politics" to an audience that was mainly students and academics. I deliber-ately chose to speak in a very basic way, thinking especially about the few community folks who had come to hear me. Weeks later, KumKum Sangari, a fellow participant who shared with me what was said when I was no longer present, and I engaged in quite rigorous critical dialogue about the way my presentation had been perceived primarily by privileged white female academics. She was concerned that I not mask my knowledge of theory, that I not appear anti-intellectual. Her critique compelled me to articulate concerns that I am often silent about with colleagues. I spoke about class allegiance and revolutionary commitments, explaining that it was disturbing to me that intellectual radicals who speak about transforming society, ending the domination of race, sex, class, cannot break with behav-ior patterns that reinforce and perpetuate domination, or continue to use as their sole reference point how we might be or are perceived by those who dominate, whether or not we gain their acceptance and approval.

This is a primary contradiction which raises the issue of whether or not the academic setting is a place where one can be truly radical or subversive. Concurrently, the use of a language and style of presentation that alienates most folks who are not also academically trained reinforces the notion that the academic world is separate from real life, that everyday world where we constantly adjust our language and behavior to meet diverse needs. The academic setting is separate only when we work to make it so. It is a false dichotomy which suggests that academics and/or intellectuals can only speak to one another, that we cannot hope to speak with the masses. What is true is that we make choices, that we choose our audiences, that we choose voices to hear and voices to silence. If I do not speak in a language that can be understood, then there is little chance for dialogue. This issue of language and behavior is a central contradiction all radical intellectuals, particularly those who are members of oppressed groups, must continually confront and work to resolve. One of the clear and present dangers that exists when we move outside our class of origin, our collective ethnic experience, and enter hierarchical institutions which daily reinforce domination by race, sex, and class, is that we gradually assume a mindset similar to those who dominate and oppress, that we lose critical consciousness because it is not reinforced or affirmed by the environment. We must be ever vigilant. It is important that we know who we are speaking to, who we most want to hear us, who we most long to move, motivate, and touch with our words.

When I first came to New Haven to teach at Yale, I was truly surprised by the marked class divisions between black folks—students and professors—who identify with Yale and those black folks who work at Yale or in surrounding communities. Style of dress and self-presentation are most often the central markers of one's position. I soon learned that the black folks who spoke on the street were likely to be part of the black community and those who carefully shifted their glance were likely to be associated with Yale. Walking with a black female colleague one day, I spoke to practically every black person in sight (a gesture which reflects my upbringing), an action which disturbed my companion. Since I addressed black folk who were clearly not associated with Yale, she wanted to know whether or not I knew them. That was funny to me. "Of course not," I answered. Yet when I thought about it seriously, I realized that in a deep way, I knew them for they, and not my companion or most of my colleagues at Yale, resemble my family. Later that year, in a black women's support group I started for undergraduates, students from poor backgrounds spoke about the shame they sometimes feel when faced with the reality of their connection to working-class and poor black people. One student confessed that her father is a street person, addicted to drugs, someone who begs from passersby. She, like other Yale students, turns away from street people often, sometimes showing anger or contempt; she hasn't wanted anyone to know that she was related to this kind of person. She struggles with this, wanting to find a way to acknowledge and affirm this reality, to claim this connection. The group asked me and one another what we [should] do to remain connected, to honor the bonds we have with working-class and poor people even as our class experience alters.

Maintaining connections with family and community across class boundaries demands more than just summary recall of where one's roots are, where one comes from. It requires knowing, naming, and being ever-mindful of those aspects of one's past that have enabled and do enable one's self-development in the present, that sustain and support, that enrich. One must also honestly confront barriers that do exist, aspects of that past that do diminish. My parents' ambivalence about my love for reading led to intense conflict. They (especially my mother) would work to ensure that I had access to books, but would threaten to burn the books or throw them away if I did not conform to other expectations. Or they would insist that reading too much would drive me insane. Their ambivalence nurtured in me a like uncertainty about the value and significance of intellectual endeavor which took years for me to unlearn. While this aspect of our class reality was one that wounded and diminished, their vigilant insistence that being smart did not make me a "better" or "superior" person (which often got on my nerves because I think I wanted to have that sense that it did indeed set me apart, make me better) made a profound impression. From them I learned to value and respect various skills and talents folk might have, not just to value people who read books and talk about ideas. They and my grandparents might say about somebody, "Now he don't read nor write a lick, but he can tell a story," or as my grandmother would say, "call out the hell in words."

Empty romanticization of poor or working-class backgrounds under- 15
mines the possibility of true connection. Such connection is based on under-standing difference in experience and perspective and working to mediate and negotiate these terrains. Language is a crucial issue for folk whose movement outside the boundaries of poor and working-class backgrounds changes the nature and direction of their speech. Coming to Stanford with my own version of a Kentucky accent, which I think of always as a strong sound quite different from Tennessee or Georgia speech, I learned to speak differently while maintaining the speech of my region, the sound of my family and community. This was of course much easier to keep up when I returned home to stay often. In recent years, I have endeavored to use various speaking styles in the classroom as a teacher and find it disconcerts those who feel that the use of a particular patois excludes them as listeners, even if there is translation into the usual, acceptable mode of speech. Learning to listen to different voices, hearing different speech challenges the notion that we must all assimilate—share a single, similar talk—in educational institutions. Language reflects the culture from which we emerge. To deny ourselves daily use of speech patterns that are common and familiar, that embody the unique and distinctive aspect of our self is one of the ways we become estranged and alienated from our past. It is important for us to have as many languages on hand as we can know or learn. It is important for those of us who are black, who speak in particular patois as well as standard English, to express ourselves in both ways.

Often I tell students from poor and working-class backgrounds that if you believe what you have learned and are learning in schools and universities separates you from your past, this is precisely what will happen. It is important to stand firm in the conviction that nothing can truly separate us from our pasts when we nurture and cherish that connection. An important strategy for maintaining contact is ongoing acknowledgement of the primacy of one's past, of one's background, affirming the reality that such bonds are not severed automatically solely because one enters a new environment or moves toward a different class experience.

Again, I do not wish to romanticize this effort, to dismiss the reality of conflict and contradiction. During my time at Stanford, I did go through a period of more than a year when I did not return home. That period was one where I felt that it was simply too difficult to mesh my profoundly disparate realities. Critical reflection about the choice I was making, particularly about why I felt a choice had to be made, pulled me through this difficult time. Luckily I recognized that the insistence on choosing between the world of family and community and the new world of privileged white people and privileged ways of knowing was imposed upon me by the outside. It is as though a mythical contract had been signed somewhere which demanded of us black folks that once we entered these spheres we would immediately give up all vestiges of our underprivileged past. It was my responsibility to formulate a way of being that would allow me to participate fully in my new environment while integrating and maintaining aspects of the old.*

One of the most tragic manifestations of the pressure black people feel to assimilate is expressed in the internalization of racist perspectives. I was shocked and saddened when I first heard black professors at Stanford downgrade and express contempt for black students, expecting us to do poorly, refusing to establish nurturing bonds. At every university I have attended as a student or worked at as a teacher, I have heard similar attitudes expressed with little or no understanding of factors that might prevent brilliant black students from performing to their full capability. Within universities, there are few educational and social spaces where students who wish to affirm positive ties to ethnicity—to blackness, to working-class backgrounds—can receive affirmation and support. Ideologically, the message is clear—assimilation is the way to gain acceptance and approval from those in power.

Many white people enthusiastically supported Richard Rodriguez's vehement contention in his autobiography, *Hunger of Memory,* that attempts to maintain ties with his Chicano background impeded his progress, that he had to sever ties with community and kin to succeed at Stanford and in the larger world, that family language, in his case Spanish, had to be made secondary or discarded. If the terms of success as defined by the standards of ruling groups within white-supremacist, capitalist patriarchy are the only standards that exist, then assimilation is indeed necessary. But they are not. Even in the face of powerful structures of domination, it remains possible for each of us, especially those of us who are members of oppressed and/ or exploited groups as well as those radical visionaries who may have race, class, and sex privilege, to define and determine alternative standards, to decide on the nature and extent of compromise. Standards by which one's success is measured, whether student or professor, are quite different from those of us who wish to resist reinforcing the domination of race, sex, and class, who work to maintain and strengthen our ties with the oppressed,

---

too difficult to mesh . . . new environment: For a perspective on assimilation in Latino communities, see Linda Chavez, "Toward a New Politics of Hispanic Assimilation," p. 426.

with those who lack material privilege, with our families who are poor and working-class.

When I wrote my first book, *Ain't I a Woman: black women and feminism,* the issue of class and its relationship to who one's reading audience might be came up for me around my decision not to use footnotes, for which I have been sharply criticized. I told people that my concern was that footnotes set class boundaries for readers, determining who a book is for. I was shocked that many academic folks scoffed at this idea. I shared that I went into working-class black communities as well as talked with family and friends to survey whether or not they ever read books with footnotes and found that they did not. A few did not know what they were, but most folks saw them as indicating that a book was for college-educated people. These responses influenced my decision. When some of my more radical, college-educated friends freaked out about the absence of footnotes, I seriously questioned how we could ever imagine revolutionary transformation of society if such a small shift in direction could be viewed as threatening. Of course, many folks warned that the absence of footnotes would make the work less credible in academic circles. This information also highlighted the way in which class informs our choices. Certainly I did feel that choosing to use simple language, absence of footnotes, etc. would mean I was jeopardizing the possibility of being taken seriously in academic circles but then this was a political matter and a political decision. It utterly delights me that this has proven not to be the case and that the book is read by many academics as well as by people who are not college-educated.

Always our first response when we are motivated to conform or compromise within structures that reinforce domination must be to engage in critical reflection. Only by challenging ourselves to push against oppressive boundaries do we make the radical alternative possible, expanding the realm and scope of critical inquiry. Unless we share radical strategies, ways of rethinking and revisioning with students, with kin and community, with a larger audience, we risk perpetuating the stereotype that we succeed because we are the exception, different from the rest of our people. Since I left home and entered college, I am often asked, usually by white people, if my sisters and brothers are also high achievers. At the root of this question is the longing for reinforcement of the belief in "the exception" which enables race, sex, and class biases to remain intact. I am careful to separate what it means to be exceptional from a notion of "the exception."

Frequently I hear smart black folks, from poor and working-class backgrounds, stressing their frustration that at times family and community do not recognize that they are exceptional. Absence of positive affirmation clearly diminishes the longing to excel in academic endeavors. Yet it is important to distinguish between the absence of basic positive affirmation and the longing for continued reinforcement that we are special. Usually liberal white folks will willingly offer continual reinforcement of us as exceptions—as special. This can be both patronizing and very seductive. Since we often work in situations where we are isolated from other black folks, we can easily begin to feel that encouragement from white people is the primary or only source of support and recognition. Given the internalization of racism, it is easy to view this support as more validating and legitimizing than similar support from black people. Still, nothing takes the place of being valued and appreciated by one's own, by one's family and community. We share a mutual and reciprocal responsibility for affirming one another's successes. Sometimes we have to talk to our folks about the fact that we need their ongoing support and affirmation, that it is unique and special to us. In some cases we may never receive desired recognition and acknowledgement of specific achievements from kin. Rather than seeing this as a basis for estrangement, for severing connection, it is useful to explore other sources of nourishment and support.

I do not know that my mother's mother ever acknowledged my college education except to ask me once, "How can you live so far away from your people?" Yet she gave me sources of affirmation and nourishment, sharing the legacy of her quilt-making, of family history, of her incredible way with words. Recently, when our father retired after more than thirty years of work as a janitor, I wanted to pay tribute to this experience, to identify links between his work and my own as writer and teacher. Reflecting on our family past, I recalled ways he had been an impressive example of diligence and hard work, approaching tasks with a seriousness of concentration I work to mirror and develop, with a discipline I struggle to maintain. Sharing these thoughts with him keeps us connected, nurtures our respect for each other, maintaining a space, however large or small, where we can talk.

Open, honest communication is the most important way we maintain relationships with kin and community as our class experience and backgrounds change. It is as vital as the sharing of resources. Often financial assistance is given in circumstances where there is no meaningful contact. However helpful, this can also be an expression of estrangement and alienation. Communication between black folks from various experiences of material privilege was much easier when we were all in segregated communities sharing common experiences in relation to social institutions. Without this grounding, we must work to maintain ties, connection. We must assume greater responsibility for making and maintaining contact, connections that can shape our intellectual visions and inform our radical commitments.

The most powerful resource any of us can have as we study and teach   25
in university settings is full understanding and appreciation of the richness, beauty, and primacy of our familial and community backgrounds. Maintaining awareness of class differences, nurturing ties with the poor and working-class people who are our most intimate kin, our comrades in struggle, transforms and enriches our intellectual experience. Education as

the practice of freedom becomes not a force which fragments or separates, but one that brings us closer, expanding our definitions of home and community.

QUESTIONING THE TEXT

1. Hooks contends that "[w]ithin universities, there are few educational and social spaces where students who wish to affirm positive ties to ethnicity—to blackness, to working-class backgrounds—can receive affirmation and support. Ideologically, the message is clear—assimilation is the way to gain acceptance and approval from those in power." What is hooks's attitude toward assimilation? What in the text reveals that attitude? Freewrite for 10 or 15 minutes on how your own school is leading you to assimilate to some things, such as academic language, grading standards, or ways of behaving—both in and out of class.

2. In this essay, hooks describes several occasions when she was accused of writing or speaking in ways that were unacceptable according to academic standards. Does this essay meet the criteria for academic writing as you understand it? Give examples to illustrate what you find "academic" about this essay.

MAKING CONNECTIONS

3. A.L. chose both this reading and the one by Mike Rose (starting on p. 87). What do these pieces have in common that might have appealed to A.L.? What, on the other hand, might hooks and Rose be expected to disagree on?

4. In the previous reading, Shelby Steele represents African American students as affected by a "myth of inferiority." Would hooks agree? Why, or why not?

JOINING THE CONVERSATION

5. Hooks says that after arriving at college a person may find it difficult to stay connected to her or his home community, especially if that community is quite different from the academic community. Do you agree? Has coming to college changed your relationship with your family and/or home community? If you keep a reading log, record your answers there.

6. Hooks suggests that her experiences with people who were different from her—her white, middle-class roommate, for example—strength-

ened her sense of herself as a black, working-class person. How has your involvement with people who are different from you affected your sense of who you are? Write a paragraph or two about some memorable character who has shaped your sense of self.

7. Working with two or three classmates, come up with a list of characteristics of an "academic" style of speaking or writing. What kinds of language use does your group think the university would consider unacceptable? What arguments would you make for—or against—such academic writing? Together prepare a brief letter to incoming students explaining how the university defines "academic writing."

GEORGE F. WILL
Commencement at Duke

GEORGE F. WILL *(b. 1941) is a Pulitzer Prize–winning writer whose columns appear regularly in* Newsweek *and in almost five hundred newspapers. He is a familiar figure on ABC-TV's Sunday morning news program, where he provides a conservative perspective, often jousting with liberal Sam Donaldson. Will has also written a number of books, including the best-seller* Men at Work: The Craft of Baseball *(1990).*

With bow tie and wire-rim glasses, Will looks and often talks like a scholar, so perhaps it isn't surprising that he has kept close tabs on trends in American universities. He has written repeatedly against the politicization of college campuses by "multiculturalists," including columns about a change in the freshman English curriculum proposed by my own department at the University of Texas.

A major premise of multiculturalism is that education in American schools is "Eurocentric"—that is, it has been too exclusively shaped by the attitudes of Americans of European descent. As a result, the proponents of multiculturalism argue, the perspectives of women, racial and ethnic minorities, homosexuals, and the poor have been deliberately and systematically excluded from the literary, philosophical, and political works making up the Western canon of Great Books. In the crudest version of the multiculturalist indictment, Western culture is the racist, sexist, and homophobic product of dead European white males. And colleges and universities only perpetuate oppression if they teach that traditional canon without drawing attention to its inherently repressive political nature.

Will challenges these assumptions in a commencement address he delivered at Duke University at the end of the very academic year (1990–91) that multiculturalism and "political correctness" exploded as controversial issues on many campuses, including Duke's.

Choosing a commencement speech for a collection like this seems especially appropriate. Such speeches represent one of the few occasions in the United States when eminent people are encouraged to speak at length about the values and principles of our society. Will's tone in addressing this divisive subject is muted and hopeful, as might be expected on a graduation day. Still, there's no question that he regards debates about the college curriculum today as a good deal more than "academic." — J.R.

Commencement speakers often say, somberly, that graduates are bidding good-bye to campus tranquillity and entering the real world's turbulence. But lately some of society's stresses have come to campuses, including this one. Duke's Class of 1991 can be forgiven for feeling that, in recent years, the ivory tower has been topped by battlements. So deservedly great is Duke's stature, its disputes resonate far beyond its broad lawns. Indeed, there is, in several senses, a national interest in the great debate, in which Duke partakes, concerning academic policies.

So today I want to tread, gingerly, onto that dark and bloody ground. I do so respectfully. I am a former professor, and the son of one. I am respectful of this magnificent institution, which has earned its eminence. And I am respectful of the complexity of the academic disputes that have, of late, enlivened life at Duke and elsewhere.

The adjective *academic* is often used as a dismissive synonym for *inconsequential,* as in the phrase "the point is of only academic interest." And it is often said that the bitterness of academic politics is inversely proportional to the stakes—that what happens on campuses does not much matter "out there" in the "real" world. But history is the history of mind; you are what you read; ideas have consequences—indeed, only ideas have lasting consequences. Therefore, the quality of our national life reflects, after a short lag, the quality of thinking on campuses.

Conditions on some campuses call to mind the tombstone in a rural English churchyard, which contains the simple six-word epitaph: "I told you I was sick." Duke is not sick. The vigor of its arguments suggests not anemia but robustness. Indeed, it has been your good fortune, you of the class of 1991, to be present here for arguments that clarify the nature not only of the academic enterprise but also of the American experiment.

Every sermonette, such as mine here, should pick some cogent thought   5
to construe. My text today comes from a great giver of advice, the poet Robert Frost, who once said: "Don't join too many gangs. Join few if any. Join the United States and join the family—but not much in between unless a college."

That advice, like the man who proffered it, is quintessentially American. It is very American in its general injunction in favor of individualism and against excessive joining—against defining oneself too much by group affiliations. But it also is especially American in its inclusion of an institution of higher education, along with family and nation, in a trinity of essential allegiances.

Why did Frost do that? Because universities are entrusted with nothing less than a task central to America's identity and success. Theirs is the task of transmitting the best of the West—the culture of our civilization—to successive generations who will lead America, which is the most successful expression of that civilization.

We are, as Lincoln said at Gettysburg, a nation "dedicated to a proposi-

tion." There is a high idea-content to American citizenship. It is a complicated business, being an American. We are all like Jay Gatsby*—made up,
by ourselves. But we are not made up of randomly aggregated moral and
intellectual materials. Rather, we are made up of moral and intellectual
resources that have been winnowed by time and must be husbanded by
universities.

By decisions about what schools should do—about what we should
study and read—we define our polity. This is why America's primary
and secondary schools have always been cockpits of religious and ethnic
conflicts.

What is now occurring on campuses is an episode in the unending   10
American drama of adjusting the rights of the individual and the rights of
the community. Individuals have a broad right to study and teach what
they wish—up to a point. (I shall return to that four-word phrase—"up to
a point.") That point is set, in part, by the community's right to perpetuate
itself.

Lincoln said: "A house divided against itself cannot stand." It is equally
true that a society unaware of itself—with no consensus about its premises
and purposes—cannot endure. In Lincoln's day, a collision of two clear and
diametrically opposed premises nearly proved fatal to America. Today there
is a potentially fatal idea in circulation. It is the idea that there should not
be in this pluralistic society any core culture passed on from generation to
generation.

To those who say we are threatened by a suffocating "hegemony" of
Western civilization's classic works, I say: If only that were the problem!
The real danger is not cultural hegemony but cultural amnesia, and the
concomitant Balkanization of the life of the mind.

I just used a verb derived from a proper noun, the verb "to Balkanize."
That verb was born of the sorrows of the Balkan nations in that unhappy
European region where, it was said, more history was produced than could
be consumed locally. The First World War, and hence most of this century's
horrors, began in the Balkans, where fragmentation was contagious.

Today there is ample evidence of the Balkanization of America's intellectual life. This Balkanization begins with the assertion that any syllabus
composed of traditional classics of Western civilization will "underrepre-
sent" certain groups—racial, sexual, ethnic, or class-based groups.

Well, are the great works of Western civilization primarily products   15
of social elites? Yes, of course—for many reasons, including the fact that
these works come to us from centuries where literacy itself was an elite

---

Jay Gatsby: the central character in *The Great Gatsby* (1925), a novel by F. Scott Fitzgerald
(1896–1940), who tells fantastic stories about his past to conceal the humble origins from
which he has risen to great wealth

attainment. But it is fallacious to argue that therefore these works perpetuate an oppressiveness that allegedly is the essence of Western civilization.

Some people who fancy themselves intellectually emancipated—who think themselves liberated from what they call a stultifying cultural inheritance—are, in fact, far from free. They actually reside in "the clean, well-lit prison of one idea." Today's imprisoning idea is philosophically primitive and empirically insupportable. It is that any humanities text merely "reflects" its social context and thus should be read as a political document.

Too often the meaning of the crucial word *reflects* disappears in a mist of imprecision. Usually the assertion that a text "reflects" its context is either trivially true or flagrantly false. It is trivially true if it means only that the text, like its author, stands in some relation to the setting in which the author wrote. But it is false if it means that any text should be construed politically, with politics understood crudely as mere power relations of domination and subordination in the era in which the author wrote.

Such thinking causes the study of literature to become a subdivision of political history and to be studied as sociology. This reduction of the arts to social sciences is reverse alchemy—turning gold into lead.*

This is the result of the imprisoning idea that the nature of everything, from intellectual works to political acts, is determined by race, gender, and class. Alas, any single idea purporting to be a universal explanation, a comprehensive simplifier of social complexities, requires its adherents to be simple, and makes them so. Today's dubious idea also makes its adherents condescending—and worse.

It is condescending and deeply anti-democratic when intellectuals consign blacks, or women, or ethnics, or the working class, or whomever, to confining categories, asserting that they can be fully understood as mere "reflections" of their race, sex, or class, and that members of those groups have the limited "consciousness" supposedly characteristic of those groups.   20

The root of this mischief is the assertion—the semantic fiat—that everything is political. If the word *political* is promiscuously used to describe any choice or judgment involving values, then *political* becomes a classification that does not classify. One cannot say it too emphatically: Not all value judgments are political judgments.

It is not a political judgment that certain works have contributed mightily to the making of our civilization and hence must be known if we are to know ourselves. It is not a political judgment that certain books have demonstrated the power, down the generations, to instruct us in history, irony, wit, tragedy, pathos, and delight. Education is an apprenticeship in those civilized—and civilizing—passions and understandings, and not all texts are equal as teachers.

---

text should be construed politically . . . *turning gold into lead:* For another view, see the selection from Mike Rose's, *Lives on the Boundary,* p. 87.

We must husband our highest praise, as Karl Marx did. Marx celebrated the art of Greek antiquity, not because it had a proletarian origin—
it did not—but because it met—indeed, set—standards that transcend any
particular class or culture.

The legacy of Western thought is a mind capable of comprehending
and valuing other cultures while avoiding the nihilism that says all cultures
are incommensurable and hence all of equal merit.

Sensible people rejoice at any chance to study another culture's   25
Rousseau or Cervantes or Dickens. But education is too serious a matter
to become a game of let's pretend, a ritual of pretending that enduring
works of the humanities are evenly distributed throughout the world's
cultures.

We want to be able imaginatively to enter, and to empathize with,
other cultures. But we must live in our own. And our own is being injured
by some academic developments that impede understanding.

We see on campuses the baneful habit of joining what Robert Frost
would have considered too many gangs—and the wrong sorts of gangs.
We see the spread of intellectual gerrymandering, carving up curricula into
protected enclaves for racial, sexual, and ethnic groups. Often this is done
on the condescending premise that members of these groups have only a
watery individuality—that they have only derivative identities, derived from
membership in victim groups.

The premise of this analysis is that Western civilization has a disreputa-
ble record consisting primarily of oppression and exploitation—that Western
civilization has been prolific only at producing victims.

That idea leads, in turn, to the patronizing notion that members of a
victim group are disadvantaged unless taught by members of their own
group and unless they study works by group members. Otherwise (or so
the theory goes) members of the group will lack self-esteem, an attribute
which is presumed to be a precondition for, not a result of, achievement.
This sort of thinking promotes envy, resentment, suspicion, aggression,
self-absorption, and, ultimately, separatism.

It is a crashing non sequitur to say that because America is becoming   30
more diverse, university curricula must be Balkanized. Actually, America's
increasing diversity increases the importance of universities as transmitters
of the cultural legacy that defines and preserves national unity.

Some policies advanced today in the name of "diversity" might better
be associated with a less agreeable word—"fragmentation."

Some policies instituted in the name of "multiculturalism" are not
celebrations of the pluralism from which American unity is woven. Some
of these policies are capitulations: they involve withdrawal from the challenge of finding, and teaching, common ground on which Americans can
stand together—not the little patches of fenced-off turf for irritable groups,
but the common ground of citizenship in the nation, which is one of the
good gangs of which Robert Frost spoke.

Many of today's Balkanizing policies are products of a desire to show sensitivity to the feelings of particular groups. Sensitivity is a good thing. But, remember: the four most important words in political discourse are "up to a point." Armies, police, taxation, even freedom and equality are good only "up to a point."

In the context of today's campus disputes, sensitivity, too, is good—up to a point. What is not good is the notion that sensitivity about one's own opinions generates for oneself an entitlement not to be disagreed with or otherwise offended. Or that the only way to prove one's sensitivity is by subscribing to a particular political agenda.*

Some critics complain that a traditional curriculum built around the canon of great works of the Western mind necessarily reinforces authority and docile acceptance of existing arrangements. But these critics, some of whom fancy themselves radicals, could take lessons in real radicalism from many of the writers of those classic works.

Virtually every subsequent radicalism was anticipated in Plato's inquiries. No person more radical than Machiavelli ever put pen to paper—Machiavelli, whose *The Prince* became the handbook for modern masterless men and women who are obedient only to rules they write for themselves.

Four years after *The Prince* was written, Martin Luther nailed his 95 theses to a church door, asserting the primacy of private judgment—conscience. There is a golden thread of magnificent radicalism connecting that white German theologian to his namesake, the black American minister—a thread connecting Luther's 95 theses and Dr. King's "Letter from Birmingham Jail."

Do not try to tell the deposed tyrants of Eastern Europe that the study of the central figures of American civilization inculcates subordination to the status quo. Europe's recent revolutions against tyranny were fueled by the words of American presidents, particularly the third and sixteenth, Jefferson and Lincoln.

There is today a warmhearted idea that every academic activity must contribute to the reforming of society by assuaging this or that group's grievances. This idea leads to fracturing the community into antagonistic groups; to the drowning of individuality in group thinking; to the competitive cultivation of group grievances; to the subordination of education to political indoctrination. In short, some good intentions produce bad educations.

Today's complacent judgment that American education is healthier than it seems is akin to Mark Twain's jest that Wagner's music is better than it sounds. Eight years ago a national commission stated, "For the first time in the history of our country, the education skills of one generation will not surpass, will not equal, will not even approach those of their parents." This disaster is, I think, partly a result of too much educational energy being invested in the pursuit of social goals, which, though arguably worthy, are undoubtedly peripheral to the main mission of schools.

Fortunately, we need not deplore the education that has been given to the portion of this generation that is privileged to be graduating from Duke. Embarrassing though the fact may be, it is a fact that you, the Class of '91, who may consider the word *elitist* an epithet, are, this day, certifiably of the elite. But let me assuage any uneasiness you may feel. Elitism— meaning a disproportionate role in government and society by small groups—is inevitable. The question for any society is not whether elites shall rule, but which elites shall rule. The problem for any democracy is to achieve consent to rule by suitable elites.

To produce suitable elites, universities need leaders with the confidence of Benjamin Jowett, who for many years was head of Oxford's Balliol College. Once when Jowett submitted a matter to a vote of Balliol's dons and was displeased with the result, he announced, "The vote is 22-to-2. I see we are deadlocked."

Jowett, like many great university statesmen, understood that a university cannot be a democracy, all sail and no anchor, blown about by gusts of opinion and fashion. It must be anchored in the convictions of intellectual leaders who are confident of their authority because they know they stand on the shoulders of giants—those great thinkers of whose legacy today's teachers are custodians and transmitters.

On March 4, 1861, with the fabric of America unraveling around him, Lincoln delivered his First Inaugural Address. In one of the most felicitous phrases in American rhetoric, he held out the hope that Americans would be summoned back to friendship by "the mystic chords of memory."

It is always thus: America is always dependent on its collective mem- 45 ory. And universities are keepers of that flame. Arguments about university curricula are not narrowly, crudely political, but they are, in an important sense, constitutional arguments: they concern how the American mind shall be constituted. And in a democracy, mind is all that ultimately matters, because everything rests on the shiftable sands of opinion.

That is why democracies are in permanent danger; and why it is prudent to be pessimistic—not fatalistic, not resigned to the worst, but pessimistic, alert to the dangers.

I subscribe to the "Ohio in 1895 Theory of History," so named, by me, for the obscure but illuminating fact that in 1895, in Ohio, there were just two automobiles—and they collided. The moral of the human story is that things go wrong more often than they go right because there are so many more ways to go wrong. Truths increase arithmetically; but errors increase exponentially. Most new ideas are false; hence most "improvements" make matters worse. That is why wise people are wary of intellectual fads and are respectful of the received greatness which, in academic context, is called the canon.

The nice part about being a pessimist is that you are constantly being either proven right or pleasantly surprised. Duke is one of life's pleasant surprises. As you have been passing through Duke, Duke has been passing through a fiery furnace of debate, and it, like you, is, like steel, stronger for having been tempered by the heat. That is why I predict special success for the class of 1991 and continued greatness for Duke.

My life around politics has taught me the hazards of making predictions. When I was at Oxford thirty years ago, the university press published volume three of Isaac Deutscher's biography of Trotsky, and the student Marxist Association had for Deutscher a party, which I infiltrated. There I heard Deutscher say—quite solemnly—this about Trotsky: "Proof of Trotsky's farsightedness is that none of his predictions have come true yet." Recurring predictions about the final ruin of America's universities have not come true yet and, I wager, never will.

QUESTIONING THE TEXT

1. Will points out that Karl Marx had great respect for ancient Greek culture. Why do you think this well-known conservative writer would cite Marx as an example on his side of the argument?
2. Do you think J.R. depicts multiculturalism fairly in his introduction? Cite examples from his words in support of your answer. If you keep a reading log, put your response there.

MAKING CONNECTIONS

3. In the previous reading, bell hooks claims that her education at Stanford was "designed to provide [her] with a bourgeois sensibility." How might Will respond to her assertion? Write a brief dialogue between these two writers about this issue.
4. Will suggests that American education is in decline in part because it is distracted by the pursuit of worthy but peripheral social goals. Explore this idea by reviewing the aims of education sketched out by John Henry Newman starting on p. 34. Then discuss with classmates what role (if any) American colleges and universities should play in improving social conditions.

JOINING THE CONVERSATION

5. With your classmates, discuss Will's assertion that "[t]he question for any society is not whether elites shall rule, but which elites shall rule." Do you feel like a member of an elite group? Can forms of elitism be compatible with democratic ideals? Following the discussion, write a position paper on this issue.

6. In an essay, explore the metaphor of "Balkanization" Will uses in this speech. Is he justified in calling for a more unified curriculum precisely because American students now come from so many different groups? Or is there virtue in emphasizing the differences between racial, sexual, and ethnic groups on campus?

GWENDOLYN BROOKS
We Real Cool

When Gwendolyn Brooks (b. 1917) was a little girl, her mother challenged her to be "the first lady Paul Lawrence Dunbar," a powerful and well-known black poet. Brooks met her mother's challenge and then some, becoming the first African American writer to win the Pulitzer Prize for poetry (for Annie Allen *in 1950) and the first African American woman to be elected to the National Institute of Arts and Letters or to serve as Consultant in Poetry to the Library of Congress. A 1936 graduate of Chicago's Wilson Junior College, Brooks has received more than four dozen honorary degrees.*

In her most distinguished career, Brooks has drawn on the traditions of African American sermons and musical forms—especially the blues, jazz, and the spiritual—to explore the American condition and, in particular, the realities of African American life. Her brief poem "We Real Cool/The Pool Players./ Seven at the Golden Shovel." depicts a group of young people who have rejected—or been rejected by—their schools. This is the first poem by Brooks I ever read, and it inspired me to seek out her other poetry and prose and to be a lifelong fan of her work. It also made me think about what my life would have been like if I had "left school." — A.L.

The Pool Players.
Seven at the Golden Shovel.

We real cool. We
Left school. We

Lurk late. We
Strike straight. We

Sing sin. We
Thin gin. We

Jazz June. We
Die soon.

IN RESPONSE

1. What message do you take away from Brooks's poem? In what ways does it speak personally to you? If you are keeping a reading log, record your response there.
2. How do you think the students in the reading by Mike Rose (starting on p. 87) might respond to the poem?
3. Brooks's poem was written in 1960, and it refers to and uses the style of an even earlier jazz tradition. Write your own 1990s version of "We Real Cool," calling on contemporary music and culture to do so.

OTHER READINGS

Bennett, William J. "The Great University Debates." *The De-valuing of America*. New York: Summit, 1992. 152–77. A former Secretary of Education decries the state of our universities.

Bok, Derek. "The Demise and Rebirth of Moral Education." *Universities and the Future of America*. Durham: Duke UP, 1990. 55–78. Suggests that universities have a responsibility to teach morality.

Cheney, Lynne. *Telling the Truth*. Washington: National Endowment for the Humanities, 1992. Argues that politics is corrupting American colleges and universities.

DuBois, W. E. B. "Of the Training of Black Men." *The Souls of Black Folk*. Chicago: A. C. McClurg & Co., 1920. Argues for the importance of a liberal arts education.

D'Souza, Dinesh. *Illiberal Education: The Politics of Race and Sex on Campus*. New York: Free Press, 1991. Argues that the barbarians are running the academy today.

Graff, Gerald. *Beyond the Culture Wars: How Teaching the Conflicts Can Revitalize American Education*. New York: Norton, 1993. Proposes a curriculum that examines difference.

Hill, Patrick J. "Multiculturalism: The Crucial Philosophical and Organizational Issues." *Change* July–Aug. 1991. Lays out a rationale for multicultural education.

Hook, Sidney. "In Defense of the Humanities." *Convictions*. Buffalo: Prometheus, 1990. Argues that no apologies are needed for Western values.

Howe, Florence. *Myths of Coeducation: Selected Essays 1964–1983*. Bloomington: Indiana UP, 1984. Argues in favor of women's studies programs.

Johnson, Julie. "Are Black Colleges Worth Saving?" *Time* 11 Nov. 1990: 81–83. Reports on the pros and cons of all African-American colleges.

Kimball, Roger. *Tenured Radicals*. New York: Harper, 1990. Argues that radicals from the sixties are reshaping American universities.

Pelikan, Jaroslav. *The Idea of the University: A Re-examination*. New Haven: Yale, 1992. Examines higher education today in "dialogue" with John Henry Newman's book.

Pratt, Mary Louise. "Humanities for the Future: Reflections on the Western Culture Debate at Stanford." *The South Atlantic Quarterly*, Winter 1990, vol. 89, no. 1, pp. 7–25. On revising the Stanford humanities course to include more on cultural diversity.

PART TWO

What We Believe

Faith: One Nation, Under God

At times we may feel that we do not need God, but on the days when the storms of disappointment rage, the winds of disaster blow, and the tidal waves of grief beat against our lives, if we do not have a deep and patient faith our emotional lives will be ripped to shreds.
MARTIN LUTHER KING, JR., *Our God Is Able*

The American Way of Life is a middle-class way, just as the American people in their entire outlook and feeling are a middle-class people.
WILL HERBERG, *This American Way of Life*

College graduates are no less likely than other groups to believe in an afterlife.
GEORGE GALLUP, JR., and JIM CASTELLI, *An American Faith*

"Maybe there is a heaven," I said, "and that's where they are." Yeah, maybe. And maybe not.
ANTHONY BRANDT, *Do Kids Need Religion?*

"Tonight I can give you ten reasons why I'm a monk. Tomorrow I might see ten new ones. I don't have a single unchanging answer. Hope that doesn't disappoint you."
WILLIAM LEAST HEAT MOON, *Conversation with a Trappist Monk in Georgia*

No one has better appreciated the Earth than the Native American. . . . [E]verything to the Indian was a relative. Everything was a human being.
ALICE WALKER, *Everything Is a Human Being*

The Church of England did not provide me with any spiritual awakening, nor any intimacy with God, but it anointed me with language; yea, verily, it steeped me in it.
ROBERT MACNEIL, *Wordstruck*

The breath of every living thing shall bless thy name, O Lord our God. . . .
THE *NISHMAT* PRAYER

Rainbow is your sister, / she loves you. The winds are your brothers, / they sing to you.
LESLIE MARMON SILKO, *Lullaby*

Introduction

ABOUT FAITH, humans have had perhaps the longest and most intense of ongoing conversations, for every people in the world, every culture we know of, enjoys some form(s) of faith or religion, beliefs that are often carried in the myths, stories, or key texts of those cultures. If you take a moment to think of some of the world's great religions, you may list Buddhism, Christianity, Islam, Judaism, Shinto, or the pantheisms of Native Americans. All these religions—and many others—are practiced today in the United States. Thus our religious landscape, like our ethnic and linguistic heritages, reflects the rich variety of peoples who are part of American culture.

Yet faith goes well beyond organized religion, beyond church, temple, or ritual. People in this country have, if we're lucky, faith in ourselves. More subtly, perhaps, we have faith in what rhetorician Richard Weaver called "God terms," those values that guide our lives, even if we are not fully aware of them. Weaver argued that in the middle of the twentieth century, the supreme American God term was "progress," that we as a people had faith in and even might be said to have "worshiped" progress. Others have suggested "democracy," "health," or "financial security" as God terms for Americans, ideas or ideals we tend to put great faith in.

Thus, whether or not you belong to or practice an organized religion, we are guessing that you have faith—perhaps a number of faiths. This chapter invites you to begin examining how you have developed such faith, how you have accepted, rejected, or challenged religions, religious creeds, or other cultural values. To do so, we have chosen articles that take very different perspectives on the subject of faith. Is Christianity, for instance, a wellspring of salvation for all? Or is it a system that inevitably oppresses and excludes some? Is all life on earth sacred? Or is human life somehow privileged over other forms? Do Americans of whatever creed hold any faiths in common?

We hope the selections in this chapter will prompt you to join the age-old conversation these questions are part of. Following are some questions you may want to ponder as you read this chapter.

1. What are the three things you *most* believe in? What makes these things important to you?

2. What makes a particular belief "religious"? What do the terms "religion" and "God" mean to you? To people with religious views different from yours?

3. Where did you get your major beliefs? From family? From friends? From an institution such as a church or school?

4. How are people shaped by what they believe? Does religion make for a better society?

5. How important is religion to Americans? Have we become a secular society? What, in addition to (or instead of) God, do you think some Americans tend to "worship" or have great faith in? Why, do you think, do they do so? You may want to discuss these issues with a group of classmates.

• • •

MARTIN LUTHER KING, JR.
Our God Is Able

THE REVEREND MARTIN LUTHER KING, JR. (1929–68), is remembered to-day for many things: his leadership of the movement for civil rights for African Americans in the 1950s and 1960s, his advocacy of nonviolent resistance to oppressive systems, his influential writings (such as the "Letter from Birmingham Jail"), his powerful and moving speeches, and his Christian ministry. In King, all these elements came together in a figure who changed the face of American public life and reframed the questions any society striving for justice must seek to address. When he was assassinated in Memphis on April 4, 1968, the world lost a major spokesperson for the power religious faith can exert in people's lives. Shortly before his death, in fact, King spoke of the extreme strife in Memphis, of the challenges facing both black and white communities there, and he called on all people of goodwill to keep the faith. Of his own faith, King seemed secure and sure. In a speech delivered the night before his assassination, he said,

> Well, I don't know what will happen now. We've got some difficult days ahead. But it doesn't matter with me now. Because I've been to the mountaintop. And I don't mind. Like anybody, I would like to live a long life. Longevity has its place. But I'm not concerned about that now. I just want to do God's will. And He's allowed me to go up to the mountain. And I've looked over. And I've seen the promised land. I may not get there with you. But I want you to know tonight, that we, as a people will get to the promised land. And I'm happy tonight. I'm not worried about anything. I'm not fearing any man. Mine eyes have seen the glory of the coming of the Lord.

The following sermon was published in the collection Strength to Love *in 1963, the year that King joined other civil rights leaders in the "March on Washington." There at the foot of the Lincoln Memorial he delivered one of his most memorable and moving speeches, "I Have a Dream," to some 250,000 people, the largest protest demonstration in American history up to that time. In "Our God Is Able," King speaks of another kind of dream, one that shows us the challenges that evil in a variety of forms presents to Christianity. Warning that all our greatest strengths in science, technology, or other human endeavors are useless or even destructive unless guided by a divine spirit, King urges all to "remember that there is a great benign Power in the universe whose name is God, and he is able to make a way out of no way, and transform dark yesterdays into bright tomorrows." Faith, he tells us, has seen him through the dark days of bigotry and prejudice, through the Montgomery bus boycott Rosa Parks talks about in Chapter 8, through personal threats and attacks on him, his family, and his home. His advice and his*

154

experience are well worth attending to, whatever your religious affiliation or beliefs. — A.L.

Now unto him that is able to keep you from falling.
                              Jude 24

At the center of the Christian faith is the conviction that in the universe there is a God of power who is able to do exceedingly abundant things in nature and in history. This conviction is stressed over and over in the Old and the New Testaments. Theologically, this affirmation is expressed in the doctrine of the omnipotence of God. The God whom we worship is not a weak and incompetent God. He is able to beat back gigantic waves of opposition and to bring low prodigious mountains of evil. The ringing testimony of the Christian faith is that God is able.

There are those who seek to convince us that only man is able. Their attempt to substitute a man-centered universe for a God-centered universe is not new. It had its modern beginnings in the Renaissance and subsequently in the Age of Reason, when some men gradually came to feel that God was an unnecessary item on the agenda of life. In these periods and later in the industrial revolution in England, others questioned whether God was any longer relevant. The laboratory began to replace the church, and the scientist became a substitute for the prophet. Not a few joined Swinburne in singing a new anthem: "Glory to Man in the highest! for Man is the master of things."

The devotees of the new man-centered religion point to the spectacular advances of modern science as justification for their faith. Science and technology have enlarged man's body. The telescope and television have enlarged his eyes. The telephone, radio, and microphone have strengthened his voice and ears. The automobile and airplane have lengthened his legs. The wonder drugs have prolonged his life. Have not these amazing achievements assured us that man is able?

But alas! something has shaken the faith of those who have made the laboratory "the new cathedral of men's hopes." The instruments which yesterday were worshiped today contain cosmic death, threatening to plunge all of us into the abyss of annihilation. Man is not able to save himself or the world. Unless he is guided by God's spirit, his new-found scientific power will become a devastating Frankenstein monster that will bring to ashes his earthly life.

At times other forces cause us to question the ableness of God. The stark and colossal reality of evil in the world—what Keats calls "the giant agony of the world"; ruthless floods and tornadoes that wipe away people as though they were weeds in an open field; ills like insanity plaguing some individuals from birth and reducing their days to tragic cycles of meaninglessness; the madness of war and the barbarity of man's inhumanity to man—why, we ask, do these things occur if God is able to prevent them? This problem, namely, the problem of evil, has always plagued the mind of man. I would limit my response to an assertion that much of the evil which we experience is caused by man's folly and ignorance and also by the misuse of his freedom. Beyond this, I can say only that there is and always will be a penumbra of mystery surrounding God. What appears at the moment to be evil may have a purpose that our finite minds are incapable of comprehending. So in spite of the presence of evil and the doubts that lurk in our minds, we shall wish not to surrender the conviction that our God is able.

I

Let us notice, first, that God is able to sustain the vast scope of the physical universe. Here again, we are tempted to feel that man is the true master of the physical universe. Man-made jet planes compress into minutes distances that formerly required weeks of tortuous effort. Man-made space ships carry cosmonauts through outer space at fantastic speeds. Is not God being replaced in the mastery of the cosmic order?

But before we are consumed too greatly by our man-centered arrogance, let us take a broader look at the universe. Will we not soon discover that our man-made instruments seem barely to be moving in comparison to the movement of the God-created solar system? Think about the fact, for instance, that the earth is circling the sun so fast that the fastest jet would be left sixty-six thousand miles behind in the first hour of a space race. In the past seven minutes we have been hurtled more than eight thousand miles through space. Or consider the sun which scientists tell us is the center of the solar system. Our earth revolves around this cosmic ball of fire once each year, traveling 584,000,000 miles at the rate of 66,700 miles per hour or 1,600,000 miles per day. By this time tomorrow we shall be 1,600,000 miles from where we are at this hundredth of a second. The sun, which seems to be remarkably near, is 93,000,000 miles from the earth. Six months from now we shall be on the other side of the sun—93,000,000 miles beyond it—and in a year from now we shall have been swung completely around it and back to where we are right now. So when we behold the illimitable expanse of space, in which we are compelled to measure stellar distance in light years and in which heavenly bodies travel at incredible speeds, we are forced to look beyond man and affirm anew that God is able.

II

Let us notice also that God is able to subdue all the powers of evil. In affirming that God is able to conquer evil we admit the reality of evil.

Christianity has never dismissed evil as illusory, or an error of the mortal mind. It reckons with evil as a force that has objective reality. But Christianity contends that evil contains the seed of its own destruction. History is the story of evil forces that advance with seemingly irresistible power only to be crushed by the battling rams of the forces of justice. There is a law in the moral world—a silent, invisible imperative, akin to the laws in the physical world—which reminds us that life will work only in a certain way. The Hitlers and the Mussolinis have their day, and for a period they may wield great power, spreading themselves like a green bay tree, but soon they are cut down like the grass and wither as the green herb.

In his graphic account of the Battle of Waterloo in *Les Misérables,* Victor Hugo wrote:

> Was it possible that Napoleon should win this battle? We answer no. Why? Because of Wellington? Because of Blücher? No. Because of God. . . . Napoleon had been impeached before the Infinite, and his fall was decreed. He vexed God. Waterloo is not a battle; it is the change of front of the universe.

In a real sense, Waterloo symbolizes the doom of every Napoleon and   10 is an eternal reminder to a generation drunk with military power that in the long run of history might does not make right and the power of the sword cannot conquer the power of the spirit.

An evil system, known as colonialism, swept across Africa and Asia. But then the quiet invisible law began to operate. Prime Minister Macmillan* said, "The wind of change began to blow." The powerful colonial empires began to disintegrate like stacks of cards, and new, independent nations began to emerge like refreshing oases in deserts sweltering under the heat of injustice. In less than fifteen years independence has swept through Asia and Africa like an irresistible tidal wave, releasing more than 1,500,000 people from the crippling manacles of colonialism.

In our own nation another unjust and evil system, known as segregation, for nearly one hundred years inflicted the Negro with a sense of inferiority, deprived him of his personhood, and denied him his birthright of life, liberty, and the pursuit of happiness. Segregation has been the Negroes' burden and America's shame. But as on the world scale, so in our nation, the wind of change began to blow. One event has followed another to bring a gradual end to the system of segregation. Today we know with certainty that segregation is dead. The only question remaining is how costly will be the funeral.

These great changes are not mere political and sociological shifts. They represent the passing of systems that were born in injustice, nurtured in inequality, and reared in exploitation. They represent the inevitable decay of any system based on principles that are not in harmony with the moral

---

Prime Minister Macmillan: Harold Macmillan, British prime minister from 1957 to 1963

laws of the universe. When in future generations men look back upon these turbulent, tension-packed days through which we are passing, they will see God working through history for the salvation of man. They will know that God was working through those men who had the vision to perceive that no nation could survive half slave and half free.

God is able to conquer the evils of history. His control is never usurped. If at times we despair because of the relatively slow progress being made in ending racial discrimination and if we become disappointed because of the undue cautiousness of the federal government, let us gain new heart in the fact that God is able. In our sometimes difficult and often lonesome walk up freedom's road, we do not walk alone. God walks with us. He has placed within the very structure of this universe certain absolute moral laws. We can neither defy nor break them. If we disobey them, they will break us. The forces of evil may temporarily conquer truth, but truth will ultimately conquer its conqueror. Our God is able. James Russell Lowell was right:

> Truth forever on the scaffold, Wrong forever on the throne,—
> Yet that scaffold sways the future, and, behind the dim unknown,
> Standeth God within the shadow, keeping watch above his own.

III

Let us notice, finally, that God is able to give us interior resources to   15
confront the trials and difficulties of life. Each of us faces circumstances in life which compel us to carry heavy burdens of sorrow. Adversity assails us with hurricane force. Glowing sunrises are transformed into darkest nights. Our highest hopes are blasted and our noblest dreams are shattered.

Christianity has never overlooked these experiences. They come inevitably. Like the rhythmic alternation in the natural order, life has the glittering sunlight of its summers and the piercing chill of its winters. Days of unutterable joy are followed by days of overwhelming sorrow. Life brings periods of flooding and periods of drought. When these dark hours of life emerge, many cry out with Paul Laurence Dunbar:

> A crust of bread and a corner to sleep in,
> A minute to smile and an hour to weep in,
> A pint of joy to a peck of trouble,
> And never a laugh but the moans come double;
>   And that is life!

Admitting the weighty problems and staggering disappointments, Christianity affirms that God is able to give us the power to meet them. He is able to give us the inner equilibrium to stand tall amid the trials and burdens of life. He is able to provide inner peace amid outer storms. This inner stability of the man of faith is Christ's chief legacy to his disciples. He offers neither material resources nor a magical formula that exempts us from suffering and persecution, but he brings an imperishable gift: "Peace I leave with thee." This is that peace which passeth all understanding.

At times we may feel that we do not need God, but on the day when the storms of disappointment rage, the winds of disaster blow, and the tidal waves of grief beat against our lives, if we do not have a deep and patient faith our emotional lives will be ripped to shreds. There is so much frustration in the world because we have relied on gods rather than God. We have genuflected before the god of science only to find that it has given us the atomic bomb, producing fears and anxieties that science can never mitigate. We have worshiped the god of pleasure only to discover that thrills play out and sensations are short-lived. We have bowed before the god of money only to learn that there are such things as love and friendship that money cannot buy and that in a world of possible depressions, stock market crashes, and bad business investments, money is a rather uncertain deity. These transitory gods are not able to save us or bring happiness to the human heart.

Only God is able. It is faith in him that we must rediscover. With this faith we can transform bleak and desolate valleys into sunlit paths of joy and bring new light into the dark caverns of pessimism. Is someone here moving toward the twilight of life and fearful of that which we call death? Why be afraid? God is able. Is someone here on the brink of despair because of the death of a loved one, the breaking of a marriage, or the waywardness of a child? Why despair? God is able to give you the power to endure that which cannot be changed. Is someone here anxious because of bad health? Why be anxious? Come what may, God is able.

As I come to the conclusion of my message, I would wish you to permit a personal experience. The first twenty-four years of my life were years packed with fulfillment. I had no basic problems or burdens. Because of concerned and loving parents who provided for my every need, I sallied through high school, college, theological school, and graduate school without interruption. It was not until I became a part of the leadership of the Montgomery bus protest that I was actually confronted with the trials of life. Almost immediately after the protest had been undertaken, we began to receive threatening telephone calls and letters in our home. Sporadic in the beginning, they increased day after day. At first I took them in stride, feeling that they were the work of a few hotheads who would become discouraged after they discovered that we would not fight back. But as the weeks passed, I realized that many of the threats were in earnest. I felt myself faltering and growing in fear.

After a particularly strenuous day, I settled in bed at a late hour. My wife had already fallen asleep and I was about to doze off when the telephone rang. An angry voice said, "Listen, nigger, we've taken all we want from you. Before next week you'll be sorry you ever came to Montgomery." I hung up, but I could not sleep. It seemed that all of my fears had come down on me at once. I had reached the saturation point.

I got out of bed and began to walk the floor. Finally, I went to the kitchen and heated a pot of coffee. I was ready to give up. I tried to think of a way to move out of the picture without appearing to be a coward. In this state of exhaustion, when my courage had almost gone, I determined to take my problem to God. My head in my hands, I bowed over the kitchen table and prayed aloud. The words I spoke to God that midnight are still vivid in my memory. "I am here taking a stand for what I believe is right. But now I am afraid. The people are looking to me for leadership, and if I stand before them without strength and courage, they too will falter. I am at the end of my powers. I have nothing left. I've come to the point where I can't face it alone."

At that moment I experienced the presence of the Divine as I had never before experienced him. It seemed as though I could hear the quiet assurance of an inner voice, saying, "Stand up for righteousness, stand up for truth. God will be at your side forever." Almost at once my fears began to pass from me. My uncertainty disappeared. I was ready to face anything. The outer situation remained the same, but God had given me inner calm.

Three nights later, our home was bombed. Strangely enough, I accepted the word of the bombing calmly. My experience with God had given me a new strength and trust. I know now that God is able to give us the interior resources to face the storms and problems of life.

Let this affirmation be our ringing cry. It will give us courage to face   25
the uncertainties of the future. It will give our tired feet new strength as we continue our forward stride toward the city of freedom. When our days become dreary with low-hovering clouds and our nights become darker than a thousand midnights, let us remember that there is a great benign Power in the universe whose name is God, and he is able to make a way out of no way, and transform dark yesterdays into bright tomorrows. This is our hope for becoming better men. This is our mandate for seeking to make a better world.

QUESTIONING THE TEXT

1. King argues that God is able to overcome evil, to "beat back gigantic waves of opposition." What examples or reasons or proof can you offer to support *or* to refute King's claim?
2. Paraphrase the verse from Paul Laurence Dunbar on p. 158. Do you agree with this assessment of life? Why, or why not?
3. A.L.'s introduction to this speech presents King in a very positive light. Yet some have criticized him for his advocacy of nonviolence

as well as for other perceived failings. What do you know about King? Does your own knowledge support the introduction's perspective? What other perspectives might be possible? Spend five minutes jotting down notes in response to these questions, and bring them to class for discussion.

MAKING CONNECTIONS

4. King links what he calls a "man-centered religion" to a Frankenstein monster. Does the monster represented in the excerpt from Mary Shelley's novel beginning on p. 213 seem to be a product of a "man-centered religion"? Why, or why not? How compelling do you find King's analogy of science without God to a "Frankenstein monster"? Explain your answers to the questions in a paragraph or two.
5. In the next selection, Will Herberg argues that middle-class values constitute a common religion in America. Would King agree? Who is likely to be left out of such a "common religion"—and why?

JOINING THE CONVERSATION

6. King says that in those times of dark despair and disappointment, if we do not have faith our "emotional lives will be ripped to shreds." Does your own experience bear out King's assertion? Explore this question in writing—in a reading log, if you keep one.
7. Do you see evidence of a "man-centered religion" in the United States today? In a one- or two-page letter to members of your class, explain your reasons for answering this question as you have.
8. Writing in the early 1960s, King uses "man" to refer to human beings in general and masculine pronouns (*he*, *his*, etc.) to refer to God and to individual humans. Working with one or two classmates, look carefully through this essay, noting any uses of language that might be criticized today for excluding women. Then write a brief report to your class describing any exclusionary language and recommending ways to revise it if you believe revision is necessary.

WILL HERBERG
This American Way of Life

WILL HERBERG'S Protestant—Catholic—Jew: An Essay in American
Religious Sociology *is regarded as something of a classic. Although the book
was published in 1955, its descriptions of American faith and religion still
illuminate essential aspects of our national character. We are not the same people
we were when Herberg (1902–77) wrote, yet we are not so different either.*

At first glance, the following excerpt from Protestant—Catholic—Jew
*may seem to have little to do with religion. But the "American Way of Life"
that Herberg sketches out tentatively here is a set of beliefs powerful enough to
forge a national identity that transcends differences of culture, race, and creed.
Americans' religious convictions are shaped, in part, by a secular faith in democracy and individualism. So we can talk sensibly about American* Protestants,
American *Jews, and American* Catholics, *knowing that we are describing
people with a strong bond of shared beliefs despite their deep religious differences.
I think that bond is worth exploring again at a time when many Americans
seem more inclined to explore diversity.* – J.R.

What is this American Way of Life that we have said constitutes
the "common religion" of American society? An adequate description and
analysis of what is implied in this phrase still remains to be attempted, and
certainly it will not be ventured here; but some indications may not be out
of place.

The American Way of Life is the symbol by which Americans define
themselves and establish their unity. German unity, it would seem, is felt
to be largely racial-folkish, French unity largely cultural; but neither of these
ways is open to the American people, the most diverse in racial and cultural
origins of any in the world. As American unity has emerged, it has emerged
more and more clearly as a unity embodied in, and symbolized by, the
complex structure known as the American Way of Life.

If the American Way of Life had to be defined in one word,
"democracy" would undoubtedly be the word, but democracy in a
peculiarly American sense. On its political side it means the Constitution;
on its economic side, "free enterprise"; on its social side, an equalitarianism
which is not only compatible with but indeed actually implies vigorous
economic competition and high mobility. Spiritually, the American Way
of Life is best expressed in a certain kind of "idealism" which has come
to be recognized as characteristically American. It is a faith that has its

symbols and its rituals, its holidays and its liturgy, its saints and its sancta; and it is a faith that every American, to the degree that he is an American, knows and understands.

The American Way of Life is individualistic, dynamic, pragmatic. It affirms the supreme value and dignity of the individual; it stresses incessant activity on his part, for he is never to rest but is always to be striving to "get ahead"; it defines an ethic of self-reliance, merit, and character, and judges by achievement: "deeds, not creeds" are what count. The American Way of Life is humanitarian, "forward looking," optimistic. Americans are easily the most generous and philanthropic people in the world, in terms of their ready and unstinting response to suffering anywhere on the globe. The American believes in progress, in self-improvement, and quite fanatically in education. But above all, the American is idealistic.* Americans cannot go on making money or achieving worldly success simply on its own merits; such "materialistic" things must, in the American mind, be justified in "higher" terms, in terms of "service" or "stewardship" or "general welfare." Because Americans are so idealistic, they tend to confuse espousing an ideal with fulfilling it and are always tempted to regard themselves as good as the ideals they entertain: hence the amazingly high valuation most Americans quite sincerely place on their own virtue. And because they are so idealistic, Americans tend to be moralistic: they are inclined to see all issues as plain and simple, black and white, issues of morality. Every struggle in which they are seriously engaged becomes a "crusade." To Mr. Eisenhower, who in many ways exemplifies American religion in a particularly representative way, the second world war was a "crusade" (as was the first to Woodrow Wilson); so was his campaign for the presidency ("I am engaged in a crusade . . . to substitute good government for what we most earnestly believe has been bad government"); and so is his administration—a "battle for the republic" against "godless Communism" abroad and against "corruption and materialism" at home. It was Woodrow Wilson who once said, "Sometimes people call me an idealist. Well, that is the way I know I'm an American: America is the most idealistic nation in the world"; Eisenhower was but saying the same thing when he solemnly affirmed: "The things that make us proud to be Americans are of the soul and of the spirit."

The American Way of Life is, of course, anchored in the American's   5
vision of America. The Puritan's dream of a new "Israel" and a new "Promised Land" in the New World, the *"novus ordo seclorum"** on the Great Seal of the United States reflect the perennial American conviction that in the New World a new beginning has been made, a new order of things estab-

---

The American Way of Life . . . is idealistic: For a decidedly different perspective on American character, see Alice Walker's essay, "Everything Is a Human Being," p. 189.

novus ordo seclorum: Latin for "a new order of the ages"

lished, vastly different from and superior to the decadent institutions of the Old World. This conviction, emerging out of the earliest reality of American history, was continuously nourished through the many decades of immigration into the present century by the residual hopes and expectations of the immigrants, for whom the New World had to be really something new if it was to be anything at all. And this conviction still remains pervasive in American life, hardly shaken by the new shape of the world and the challenge of the "new orders" of the twentieth century, Nazism and Communism. It is the secret of what outsiders must take to be the incredible self-righteousness of the American people, who tend to see the world divided into an innocent, virtuous America confronted with a corrupt, devious, and guileful Europe and Asia. The self-righteousness, however, if self-righteousness it be, is by no means simple, if only because virtually all Americans are themselves derived from the foreign parts they so distrust. In any case, this feeling about America as really and truly the "new order" of things at last established is the heart of the outlook defined by the American Way of Life.

In her *Vermont Tradition,* Dorothy Canfield Fisher lists as that tradition's principal ingredients: individual freedom, personal independence, human dignity, community responsibility, social and political democracy, sincerity, restraint in outward conduct, and thrift. With some amplification—particularly emphasis on the uniqueness of the American "order" and the great importance assigned to religion—this may be taken as a pretty fair summary of some of the "values" embodied in the American Way of Life. It will not escape the reader that this account is essentially an idealized description of the middle-class ethos. And, indeed, that is just what it is. The American Way of Life is a middle-class way, just as the American people in their entire outlook and feeling are a middle-class people. But the American Way of Life as it has come down to us is not merely middle-class; it is emphatically inner-directed. Indeed, it is probably one of the best expressions of inner-direction in history. As such, it now seems to be undergoing some degree of modification—perhaps at certain points disintegration—under the impact of the spread of other-direction in our society. For the foreseeable future, however, we may with some confidence expect the continuance in strength of the American Way of Life as both the tradition and the "common faith" of the American people.

QUESTIONING THE TEXT

1. How does Herberg define democracy? Do we abide by the same definition today?
2. Identify five to ten key words that Herberg uses to characterize the American way of life—terms like *democracy* and *individualism*. Then

explain whether those terms make sense in defining the American experience as you have known it.

3. Underline three or four specific sentences that Herberg would likely rewrite were his book being published today instead of in 1955. Then rewrite them, entering the rewritten versions in your reading log if you keep one.

MAKING CONNECTIONS

4. Where might the secular values Herberg describes in his essay conflict with the religious principles articulated in the previous selection, Martin Luther King, Jr.'s, "Our God Is Able"?

5. Write an essay arguing for or against this statement: The version of American life described by Herberg in the 1950s indicates that the American people were, in most respects, better off in the Eisenhower era than they are today. Be sure to back up your arguments with specific examples and illustrations.

JOINING THE CONVERSATION

6. Write a brief response to "This American Way of Life," reflecting upon how well you fit into the description today.

7. In the way that Herberg has written an essay defining the "American Way of Life," write an equally serious analysis of a class of American experience with which you are personally knowledgeable: the Italian-American way of life, the evangelical way of life, the Southern California way of life, the suburban way of life, and so on.

8. Herberg insists that Americans typically see themselves as different from the rest of world, a more idealistic people not tainted by the corruption and guile of Europe and Asia. Be prepared to discuss whether this is still a representative view. What events since 1955 might have confirmed Americans in this opinion or altered it?

GEORGE GALLUP, JR., and JIM CASTELLI
An American Faith

You could not tell it from what appears on primetime television or what gets taught in public schools, but the United States is, by no small margin, the most religious nation in the industrialized world. Startling (by European standards) percentages of Americans claim to believe in God and to attend church regularly. But churchgoing does not always determine behavior; we are a materialistic people too, fond of sin and extravagance and inclined to equate prosperity with divine favor. Surely, if we have two cars and a condo in Fort Lauderdale, it's because God wants it that way.

Many students encounter the first serious challenges to their faith in college, where the academic environment (though not always professors and instructors themselves) can seem defiantly secular, even sometimes openly hostile to religion. The enthusiasm for "difference" on campuses today rarely extends to students with strong religious convictions. They are usually required to check their belief in God at the classroom door and to consider a world view where all knowledge is assumed to be of human origin. The "absolute moral laws" Martin Luther King, Jr., describes in "Our God Is Able" now seem to belong to another age.

So I include this portion of George Gallup, Jr., and Jim Castelli's book-length study of America's religious attitudes to remind those of us in academic settings how powerfully religion still shapes our nation's attitudes. The People's Religion: American Faith in the 90's *(1989) helps to explain why Americans argue so passionately over issues like abortion, sexual ethics, mercy killing, and prayer in public schools. George Gallup, Jr. (b. 1930), bears a name synonymous with opinion polling in the United States; Jim Castelli writes about religion in the United States.* — J.R.

RELIGION AND EDUCATION

The United States is unique because it combines a high degree of education with a high level of religious faith. On many measures of religious belief, commitment decreases as the education level increases. Nevertheless, the level of faith among college-educated Americans remains quite high, and in some key areas—including belief in God and church membership and attendance—there are no significant differences among Americans on the basis of educational background.

Overall, 19 percent of Americans are college graduates and another 25 percent have either attended college or a technical school; 33 percent have graduated from high school but not gone on for further education, while 23 percent of Americans have not graduated from high school.

There are a number of areas in which increased education correlates with decreased religious activity or belief:

- The importance of religion declines with education. Table 1 shows the importance Americans place on religion in their lives, by educational level.

- While 40 percent of those with less than a high school education read the Bible at least once a week, only 28 percent of those with education beyond high school do so.

- While 45 percent of those with less than a high school education believe the Bible is the literal word of God, only 11 percent of college graduates hold this view; only 11 percent of those with less than a high school degree believe the Bible is not even inspired by God, while 33 percent of college graduates hold that view.

- 90 percent of those with a high school degree or less and 83 percent of those with some college, but only 66 percent of college graduates, believe Jesus is God or the Son of God.

- 68 percent of those with less than a high school degree, but 84 percent of college graduates, believe it is possible to be a good Christian or Jew without going to church or synagogue; 77 percent of those with educational levels in between hold this view.

- 40 percent of those with less than a high school education, 35 percent of high school graduates, 31 percent of those with some college or technical school and 22 percent of college graduates describe themselves as Born-Again Christians.

Despite these differences, there are important religious issues on which there is no significant difference by educational level, and some on which college graduates are more active:

- 91 percent of college graduates, 93 percent of those with some college, 96 percent of high school graduates and 93 percent of those with

Table 1   Importance of religion, by education

	College Graduate	Some College/ Tech. School	High School Graduate	Less Than H.S. Grad.
Very Important	50%	50%	52%	63%
Fairly Important	29	32	36	27
Not at All Important	19	18	11	9

less than a high school education believe in God. College graduates, however, are more likely to believe in an impersonal God.

- College graduates (74 percent) are more likely than those with less education to be church members; 67 percent of those with some college and 69 percent of those with high school degrees or less are members.

- Similarly, 46 percent of college graduates attend church in a given week, while 38 percent of those with some college, 39 percent of high school graduates and 37 percent of those who did not graduate from high school attend weekly.

- College graduates are as likely as other Americans to regard themselves as "a religious person."

- College graduates are no less likely than other groups to believe in an afterlife.

- College graduates are no less likely than others to say they want religious training for their children, and are more likely to actually provide such training.

- Those with at least some college education are more likely than others to take part in Bible study or prayer groups outside of church.

AMERICANS' ATTITUDES TOWARD THEIR CHURCHES

Americans have become more critical of their churches and synagogues   5
over the past decade. A large majority believes the churches are too concerned with internal organizational issues and not sufficiently concerned with spiritual matters. A plurality believes the churches are not concerned enough about social justice. And a growing minority—one American in three—believes that the morality being taught by the churches is too restrictive.

At the same time, Americans give churches high marks for being warm and accepting places and for being effective in helping people find meaning in their lives. They give them lower marks for having a clear sense of the spiritual.

In general, Catholics are less critical of the churches than are Protestants. Since church members are more likely to express their attitudes toward their own denominations than toward churches in general, this suggests that American Catholics are more satisfied than American Protestants with their churches. These findings come from "Unchurched Americans—1988," a Gallup study conducted for Congress '88, a coalition of twenty-two religious groups.

In 1978, 51 percent of Americans said the churches were too concerned with organizational issues, while 27 percent disagreed; the rest were uncertain. Ten years later, however, 59 percent said the churches were too concerned with organizational issues, while only 16 percent disagreed. This

may partly reflect the widespread publicity over the past decade of develop-
ments such as the struggle between fundamentalists and moderates for control of the Southern Baptist Convention and tensions between American
Catholics and the Vatican.

Protestants criticized the churches' concern with organizational matters
by 62 to 16 percent, while Catholics were less critical, with 54 percent
saying the churches were too concerned with organizational matters and 22
percent saying they were not.

A decade ago, Americans were evenly divided, with 35 percent agree-   10
ing that the churches were not concerned enough about social justice and
another 35 percent disagreeing with that statement. In 1988, however, 41
percent said the churches were not concerned enough about social justice,
while 29 percent said they were.

Catholics, again, were slightly less critical than Protestants. Among
Protestants, 42 percent said the churches were not concerned enough about
social justice, while 27 percent disagreed. Among Catholics, the margin
was 37 to 35 percent. This may reflect the fact that Catholic leaders have
been highly visible on peace and justice issues over the past decade; the U.S.
Catholic bishops have issued lengthy, well-publicized pastoral letters on
peace and economic justice.

Blacks were considerably more critical of the churches on social justice
issues than were whites or Hispanics: 51 percent of blacks and 40 percent
each of whites and Hispanics said the churches were not concerned enough
about social justice; 23 percent of blacks, 28 percent of Hispanics and 30
percent of whites disagreed.

In 1978, Americans rejected by 52 to 27 percent the statement that
"the rules about morality preached by the churches and synagogues today
are too restrictive." In 1988, that margin fell to 46 to 32 percent.

A larger number of Catholics than Protestants were uncertain in their
responses. Catholics (28 percent) were as likely as Protestants (26 percent)
to say the morality was too restrictive, but they were less likely—by 41
percent to 55 percent—to disagree.

Those under 50 were more likely than those over 50 to view the   15
churches' morality as too restrictive: 34 percent of those under 30, 36 percent
of those 30–49 and 25 percent of those over 50 held this view.

In only two groups did a plurality say the churches' morality was too
restrictive: Hispanics (by 39 to 33 percent) and single people (by 37 to 34
percent).

In other findings:

- 64 percent of Americans agree that "most churches and synagogues
  today are warm and accepting of outsiders"; only 17 percent disagreed.

- 67 percent of Americans agreed that "most churches and synagogues
  today are effective in helping people find meaning in life"; 15 percent
  disagreed.

- 48 percent of Americans agreed that "most churches and synagogues today have a clear sense of the real spiritual nature of religion"; 31 percent disagreed.

CONCLUSIONS

This survey of Americans' beliefs about important religious issues paints a picture of the faith of both the "typical" American and individual groups of Americans. It certainly shows that Americans are unique for the way they combine high levels of religious belief with high levels of education. Their education may change that faith, but it doesn't necessarily weaken it. As Americans become more educated, their faith tends to become more intellectual—or at least they look for more intellectual ways to confront it—and their religious practices may change; but their faith does not disappear.

Americans do, however, take a very independent approach to religion. Their faith must make sense to them, and it must reflect the values of freedom that they assume in their daily social and political lives. The pattern is clear:

- While Americans value church membership and religious activity, they do not believe that formal institutional ties are necessary for faith.

- They welcome changes in their own faith lives and feel strengthened by the challenges of questioning their faith—and, in so doing, show a great deal of confidence in their faith.

- While they believe in God, and most believe in a personal God, they look to themselves to make the critical moral decisions in their lives; they see ambiguity in moral questions, particularly regarding sex, and want to make up their own minds.

- They have a clear sense of what they want from their churches—and, in fact, they tend to view their churches less as sources of faith than as resources for their personal and family religious and spiritual needs. Earlier, we saw that Americans' religious practice does not fall off when they lose confidence, even temporarily, in their religious institutions. Now, we see that their faith itself does not weaken when they become increasingly critical of their churches' activities.

Given this strong, typically American independent streak, the degree 20 of religious orthodoxy found among Americans is simply amazing. A country in which such large proportions of the population believe in a personal God who will call them to Judgment Day to determine how they spend the afterlife; in which so many believe that God has a plan for their lives and communicates with them; in which one-third report intense, life-changing religious experiences; in which so many worship Jesus Christ—such a nation cannot by any stretch of the imagination be described as secular in its core beliefs.

Not all Americans, however, match up to this "typical" profile. It would be inaccurate, and unfair, to categorize groups of people as more or less "religious" on the basis of their religious practices and beliefs; we would need to know both their behavior and what we mean by "religious." But, in terms of attitudes toward basic religious beliefs, we can draw conclusions about group behavior because some patterns recur too often to be meaningless.

For example, we have seen the religious "gender gap" again and again, with women considerably more likely than men to hold traditional religious beliefs. Similarly, belief in traditional religious views consistently increases with age; those over 50 are the most traditional in their views, those under 30 the least traditional. By most measures, blacks are more "religious" than whites. Those with less education are far more traditional in their beliefs than those with more education, although, as we have seen, college graduates have their own brand of religion. Protestants and Catholics hold similar views of basic beliefs; Protestants rely more on the Bible and emotional experience, while Catholics are more independent in their approach to religion. Evangelicals consistently score the highest on levels of traditional belief.

One of the most fascinating insights survey data provide is the relationship between significant changes in life situations and faith. We saw that young adults, forming their own identities as they break away from their families and begin their careers, have the least interest in religion and the least traditional beliefs. But religious interest and belief increase with age, more so for women. When a person marries, interest in religion increases; divorce leads to decreased religious activity, though not necessarily decreased religious belief, while widowhood intensifies both. Traumatic events like abortion weaken faith. Understanding this deceptively simple pattern is crucial to understanding the present and future status of religious life in America.

QUESTIONING THE TEXT

1. What is the most surprising fact you encountered in the reading? Are you inclined to believe it? Why, or why not?
2. Are the differences in attitudes toward religion between college-educated people and those with less formal education either greater or smaller than you would have expected? What might account for these differences?
3. Do you agree with J.R.'s contention in his introduction that the academic environment is often hostile to religion? Why, or why not?

MAKING CONNECTIONS

4. Is the faith described in Martin Luther King, Jr.'s, "Our God Is Able" (p. 154) that of the "typical" American Gallup and Castelli describe on p. 170? Why, or why not?
5. Early in "Do Kids Need Religion?" (starting on p. 173), Anthony Brandt claims that "we are a thoroughly secularized society." Do the statistics Gallup and Castelli quote undermine Brandt's claim? Why, or why not?

JOINING THE CONVERSATION

6. In a small group, discuss what obligations, if any, a college has to respect the religious beliefs of students. In what courses or situations are conflicts with religion likely to arise? Have you had to deal with them? If so, how have you responded?
7. How much attention was given to religion in your high school education—in your history or literature classes, for example? Write a short evaluation of whether the treatment of religion was fair and adequate.
8. Should campus codes discouraging comments offensive to women or ethnic and sexual minorities also extend to specific religious groups? Write a position paper on the topic.

ANTHONY BRANDT
Do Kids Need Religion?

ANTHONY BRANDT, a contributing editor at Parenting *magazine, focuses on the relationship of children to religious faith. Whereas Robert MacNeil approaches the question through his own experience as a child in church, Brandt speaks as a parent, one concerned about how best to help his children face the losses and traumas life always brings. In this essay, published in 1991 in the progressive* Utne Reader, *he describes himself as a "run-of-the-mill modern skeptic," without faith or belief, and asks us to consider the uses of religion in what he terms a largely secular society. Might religion serve as a unifying cultural force, even for people who don't "believe"? Even more important, Brandt asks, "What sort of meaning does a secular society offer a child?" These questions suggest that Brandt is searching for a basis on which he can make some very hard choices about how he will (and should) raise his children.*

I admire Brandt's straightforward approach here, his willingness to consider various options, and his refusal to argue that his *way to spirituality is the only or even the best way. In addition, I find that Brandt finally establishes some common ground for* all *people, regardless of differences in religious faith or creed, when he says, "The longing for meaning is something we all share. . . ."* — A.L.

This happened nearly 20 years ago, so I may not have all the details right. As I remember, my daughter was about 10 years old. She had spent the weekend with her grandparents, and while she was gone, a house down the road from ours burned to the ground. Three children died in the fire. One was a houseguest. The other two were my daughter's closest friends.

My wife went to see the bereaved parents. They were devout Catholics and they took their loss amazingly well. They talked to her about their two girls being angels in heaven now, and they really believed it. At the funeral, they were strong and brave, braver than many others there, including myself.

My tears were bitter. I didn't think their children were angels, I thought they were dead. I had little confidence in any sort of existence beyond that. I

I'm not sure what Brandt's intention is in describing himself as a "run-of-the-mill modern skeptic." It strikes me as an easy way to discount the viewpoint.
— S.W.

was not a devout Catholic or a devout anything. I was your run-of-the-mill modern skeptic who long before had stopped going to church, thought most religious doctrine absurd, and was resolved to live without the illusions of belief.

What does your run-of-the-mill modern skeptic tell his 10-year-old daughter when her closest friends have just died in a fire? My wife and I told her what had happened when she got home from her grandparents' house. I was crying and so was my wife, but my daughter just sat there, stunned, in shock. I wanted so much to console her, to find something to say that would explain, would justify these deaths and give them meaning. But I didn't think these deaths had any meaning. All I could come up with was something I didn't believe. "Maybe there is a heaven," I said, "and that's where they are." Yeah, maybe. And maybe not.

It's natural to want to comfort children in this situation, but is it good to do it by offering them a viewpoint in which you don't believe?
— S.W.

Doesn't Brandt underestimate the influence of religion in the USA here?
— J.R.

I'm old enough to know now that there's no living without illusions of some sort, that we all need to find or generate some kind of meaning for our lives if life is not to become unbearable. But what kind? It goes without saying that we are no longer a religious society in the conventional sense of the word.* Religion no longer stands at the center of our culture as it did a hundred or so years ago. Rather, we are a thoroughly secularized society. The miracles we marvel at are the miracles of technology. For the answers to our questions about the meaning of things, we look not to the elders of a church, but to science.

An event like the cruel and pointless death of three little girls, however, presents a fundamental challenge. What sort of meaning does a secular society offer a child? What do parents with no religious beliefs do when their children start asking those difficult questions about where Grandpa has gone, Grandpa having just died, or why Jesus was crucified, and why people are so mean, and what will happen to them when they die?

I'm thinking of children I know who have experienced the death of a loved one "up close and personal." Our society holds death so much at arm's length and tries to deny it in so many ways that we don't in any way prepare children (or ourselves) for its reality. — A.L.

Is Brandt saying that meaning is always in some sense an illusion? I don't think I would use the word illusion here. A construct, perhaps, but not an illusion.
— A.L.

We're not so "thoroughly secularized." Many people live their lives in accord with their religious beliefs.
— S.W.

It goes without saying . . . religious society: For a different point of view, see George Gallup, Jr., and Jim Castelli, "An American Faith," p. 166.

For some parents, to be sure, questions like these present no problem. Either they have religious beliefs and are confident they can transmit them to their kids, or they have no religious beliefs at all and see no reason to raise their children to have any. I asked one father what he had done about his kids' religious education and he said, "Nothing whatsoever." Well, I went on, how did he answer their questions about God and things like that? He didn't remember there being any. And even if there are questions, a parent can say, "Go ask your mother" or "I'm no expert on that" or simply "I don't know," and let it go at that. Western culture is so secularized that parents can evade or dismiss "religious" questions without feeling that they're merely getting themselves off the hook. No one is surprised anymore by this kind of religious indifference.

Why don't these parents offer what they believe to be the truth? His real question seems to be "What do parents who don't believe in an afterlife or salvation tell their children to shield them from those harsh realities?"
— S.W.

For believers, too, the problem doesn't exist. Secure in their own faith, they can confidently answer the questions of a child.

Surprised? No. But what are the consequences?
— J.R.

Another mother and father, not so secure in their faith, say it was actually their children who brought them back to religion. They had both been raised Roman Catholic; each had children from a previous marriage; both had lapsed from the church. But they were sending their kids to a Protestant Sunday school. One night at dinner the oldest child said, "Don't you think we should pray for this food?" This was something of a shock. It was even more so when the child said, in prayer, "And thank you, God, for bringing our whole family together." The following Sunday the parents went to church. They have been actively involved (in a Protestant congregation) ever since. "Children come up with some really interesting questions," the mother told me, "and we still have to do a lot of explaining. But we have faith. We don't feel that we're alone with these questions."

For those of us without faith it's not so easy. Do we send our kids to Sunday school when we ourselves never go to church? Do we have them baptized even though we have no intention of rais-

This isn't at all clear to me. Faith in what? And how does this faith have to do with not "being alone" with these questions?
— A.L.

The author seems earnest. Why do I feel uneasy as a reader? — J.R.

ing them to be religious? I argued against having my son baptized. It's a meaningless ritual, I said. I didn't think he had been "born in sin," so why wash him free of it, even symbolically? Why bow to convention simply for convention's sake? I gave in, but only to keep peace in the family.

For me religious education raised the issue of honesty. I thought it would be hypocritical to make my kids attend Sunday school when I not only didn't go to church but also didn't have any religious beliefs. My parents had sent me to Sunday school when neither of them was in the least religious, and under the circumstances I came to think Sunday school was a joke. I learned a few Bible stories, but that was all. I believed I should spare my children that kind of charade. My wife took them to church from time to time, but only once or twice did they attend a Sunday school class.

Are there reasons for sending children to Sunday school that go beyond religious beliefs? — A.L.

I'm still wondering whether we did the right thing. In *Childhood and Society* the renowned psychoanalyst Erik Erikson makes the unsettling remark that "many are proud to be without religion whose children cannot afford their being without it." Children may not need a religious upbringing, but, says Erikson, they do need a sense of "basic trust," a feeling not only that their fundamental bodily needs will be met and that their parents love them and will take care of them, but also that they have not been abandoned to the empty haphazardness of existence.

I can't see offhand why religion is the only thing that could fulfill this need not to feel abandoned. — A.L.

Erikson relates this sense of trust to the psychosocial origins of religious life. "The parental faith which supports the trust emerging in the newborn," he writes, "has throughout history sought its institutional safeguard . . . in organized religion." The trust of the infant in the parents, in other words, finds its parallel—and takes its mature form—in the parents' trust in God. The implication is that if trust has no institutional reinforcement, it will tend to wither. Basic trust will become basic mistrust, and there will be more work for mental health experts such as Erikson.

Since he claims we live in a secular society, has this withering already happened? — S.W.

The institutional form that trust has taken in America has historically remained within the Judeo-Christian tradition, and the decision to deny that tradition to a child ought at the very least to be well thought out. Children will become aware of the tradition with or without parental teaching; they'll bring it home from school or the playground, wanting to know why their friend Jimmy says they'll go to hell if they don't go to church, or why Alice is getting a beautiful white confirmation dress and they're not. A psychoanalyst, Ana-Marie Rizzuto, once pointed out that no matter what parents teach their children, "religious symbols and language are so widely present in this society that virtually no child reaches school age without having constructed—with or without religious instruction—an image or images of God."

Brandt equates religion with objects and symbols, not beliefs and moral choices. I'm disappointed that all he's worried about is that his children won't fit into a Judeo-Christian culture. — J.R.

I broached the subject with one couple who have a three-year-old daughter. The father, Pete, was raised in a fundamentalist family and rebelled against it; religion holds a kind of perverse fascination for him, but he is not what you would call a believer. His wife, Valerie, has no religious beliefs to speak of. Yet they both want their daughter to go to Sunday school. "I don't want her to grow up in a religious vacuum," says Pete. He thinks that if they don't give her a religious background they will be depriving her of a choice later on. If she has the background, she can always reject it when she gets older, he says; if she doesn't, there will be nothing to reject but nothing to affirm, either. He doesn't think she would be likely to come to that crossroads on her own. Valerie agrees with this reasoning: "I want her to know the Bible stories, the mythology," she says. "It's a major part of our culture. And I want her to have a sense of mystery, of awe." A sense, says Pete, that in our society has largely been lost.

Did these parents want their daughter to have faith or to know about faith? There's a difference in the comfort you receive from a belief you just acknowledge and from one you accept. — S.W.

If this approach seems paradoxical coming from parents who are not themselves believers, it also makes a certain amount of sense. No matter what we believe in, our society's Judeo-Christian tradition retains a good deal of its power. I reject organized religion, yet I cannot listen to Mozart's *Requiem Mass* without being moved. Perhaps nonpracticing Jews feel the same when they hear Hebrew prayers sung. Much of Western culture springs from religious feeling; we are secular but our heritage is not, and there is no true identification with a culture without some feel for its past. To raise children in a culture without at least exposing them to its religious traditions, even if you yourself have abandoned the beliefs on which they are based, may be doing them a disservice. The children will be exposed to those traditions in any case, so why not give them some real instruction?

Pete and Valerie are not alone; among the nonbelieving parents I talked to, theirs was a common rationale for sending their children to Sunday school, and the most common solution to the problem. Several other parents, however, admitted to qualms. "Kids pick up on your real feelings about things pretty fast," one father said. "If you're making them do something you yourself don't believe in, they're going to figure it out." And a mother told me, "I think you can transmit values to your kids, but belief is different. Values—respect for other people, respect for life, not taking what doesn't belong to you, things like that—they're universal, they're everywhere. But belief is a special thing. You have to come to it on your own; nobody can impose it on you."

Too, it is impossible to predict with any confidence what effect a religious education will have on children. It can be more than a little uncomfortable when your children take religious teaching more seriously than you do. It is unsettling to think that they might need religion when you have decided you do not. Do kids in fact need religion? They need "basic trust," as Erikson says, but beyond that, nobody has conclusive answers. We used to think that without religious beliefs, social behavior would come unglued. "If God is dead," wrote Dostoyevski, "then everything is permitted." It hasn't happened.

Morality can survive without religion, it appears; children can be taught the importance of

What Brandt wants for his children is "religious appreciation," not religion. No hard choices here—religion as art. — J.R.

How typical of our times to regard "values" as universal and belief as contingent. We'd better hope there is no God! — J.R.

There's a big difference between introducing children to the religious traditions of our culture (which are quite diverse) and training them into one set of religious beliefs as absolutely the truth and the one way. — A.L.

Well, yes, or any other training, for that matter. Some of the most horrible characters in our history, for instance, were thoroughly trained in religions and/or other traditions. — A.L.

*Wrong. What—
besides racism
and sexism—is
regarded as sin-
ful these days?
Adultery? Por-
nography? Idol-
atry? Abortion?
Covetousness?*
— J.R.

right versus wrong without benefit of religious training. Jean Piaget and Lawrence Kohlberg* have shown that moral understanding is acquired in stages, that it is a developmental process that unfolds, to some extent, as naturally as intelligence itself.

My daughter, now age 27, who was exposed to little more than my own deep skepticism, is studying Buddhism. As I write, in fact, she is in Tibet, on a journey that I'm sure is at least partly spiritual. I have made spiritual journeys during my adult life, all of them outside the sphere of Christianity that I was raised in. I continue to distrust and dislike organized religion but find it hard, as I grow older, to live with only my vague faith that life must have some kind of meaning, even if I don't know what it is.

To believe is to be connected, and those of us who don't believe cannot help but miss the feelings that come with belonging to something larger than ourselves. I hope my children find a straighter road than I've found. "I very much wish I had had some religion, for my kids' sake," one father told me. "My son's into tarot cards now. There's not much comfort in tarot cards."

The longing for meaning is something we all share, parent and child alike. But it may be that this is an area where a parent can't help a child much. Meaning may be something all of us have to find in our own way. I don't know. I am loath to give advice. Robert Coles* quotes a black woman who worked as a servant for a wealthy white Southern family: "My momma told me: Remember that you're put here only for a few seconds of God's time, and he's testing you. He doesn't want answers, though. He wants you to know how to ask the right questions." Teaching our kids how to ask the right questions may be the best we can do.

If he equates believing in something with a belief in religion, I disagree. We can feel connectedness outside of a religious system. I think we'd all like to find a straighter road to travel, but I'm not at all sure that it's paved with religion.
— S.W.

This is a safe and predictable conclusion. No strong position is taken. I'm disappointed.
— J.R.

This is an interesting definition of belief—"to be connected." I'll have to think about this; I'm not sure I agree.
— A.L.

I end up wondering where Brandt stands on his original question. I'll need to reread this to decide whether his answer is yes, no, or maybe.
— A.L.

Jean Piaget (1896–1980) *and* Lawrence Kohlberg (1927–87): psychologists who studied the mental and moral development of children and young adults

Robert Coles: an educational psychologist (b. 1929) whose work on the ethical life of children has been widely influential

A f t e r w o r d s

I agree that human beings seek meaning, that we yearn for meaning so strongly that we will make meaning(s) at all cost. Further, I consider this yearning to be a function related to our being inside a world of languages— which is why the philosopher Kenneth Burke defines people as "symbol-using, symbol-abusing animals." Language allows us to assign meaning, and if this capacity is by definition human, *then it makes perfect sense that we would need to assign meaning,* demand *to make meaning.*

That said, I'm willing to follow in Brandt's steps as he explores the central question of his essay, which I would rephrase as "Will religion help kids make or find meaning?" Put this way, my answer would be conditional; organized religion can help people make *meaning, and it can do so largely by way of its own language, its symbolicity. But I'd also say that organized religion won't* automatically *help kids or anyone else find meaning.*

Brandt claims not to have religion, but rather "spirituality." What seems to give meaning to him and his life is his connection to others, particularly his family, and his commitment to intellectual inquiry, to continued probing of important issues, including those of religion and meaning. In this regard, I am most sympathetic to him. I find meaning in my own life in relationship to someone else, either in person (as with my friends, my family, and especially my students) or in words (with persons I know only through books). Meaning, it strikes me, isn't ever in us or indeed in any one thing; rather, meaning arises out of connections and relations. For me, these are the pathways to spirituality, ones I'd like to share with "kids" of all ages. — A.L.

One reason I am not now particularly religious is that I am unmoved by "soft" notions of religion such as put forth by Brandt and to some extent by A.L. Raised in a strict Catholic tradition, I take little solace or intellectual satisfaction in faith represented chiefly as a quest for meaning or selfhood. Religion makes more sense to me if it also deals with timeless, if evolving, truths.

To offer religion to children as an alternative to harsh reality—as a way of explaining to a ten-year-old why her best friends died in a fire, to use Brandt's example—turns religion into a booster club. That a nonbelieving parent like Brandt might expose his children to organized religion because he wants them to know the tradition behind Mozart's Requiem *is to treat faith with secular contempt, rendering it as worthless as sunshine patriotism. Religion is about hard choices, not easy ones; about truths, not feelings. Questions of faith compel individuals to face the abyss and to confront the responsibility we have for our own souls. Religion defines meaning not in terms of historical and cultural artifacts, but in terms of God. At some point, this faith requires a difficult, uncompromising, and final credo.*

I am not able to speak that word yet, but when and if I do, I don't expect my life to be any easier. — J.R.

Brandt seems to claim that we now live in a thoroughly secularized society, and that because of this children no longer have anything to believe and trust in. He sums this point up when he says "those of us who don't believe cannot help but miss the feelings that come with belonging to something larger than ourselves."

He is right in saying that sometimes, without a religious system to guide us, it is hard to make sense of the tragic and seemingly arbitrary events life can throw at us. This is especially true for children, and religion goes a long way toward helping them deal with these matters. But Brandt tends to discount the idea of finding any meaning or connectedness outside of organized religion, which is where I would disagree with him.

In looking for a straighter road to answers for his own children, he wonders if it might be through religion. I hesitate to think it is. With the multitude of religions that exist, which single one should we choose for our children? Are they all equally able to give meaning to children's lives? And why must our beliefs and feelings of connectedness come to us through a religion? Isn't it possible to find answers ourselves, rather than just accept those of others? Why can't we give our children connectedness through family, or community, or friendship, or any of a host of other ways? Brandt makes it too black and white; you accept religion, and therefore meaning, or you don't. That doesn't work for me.

I like the concept that we are not here necessarily to find all the answers, but to ask the right questions. Whatever a person's beliefs are, they should be well reasoned before they are handed on to children. To offer children a religion that will answer their questions simply so that they do not have to find meaning for themselves is to do them, and ourselves, a disservice. — S.W.

QUESTIONING THE TEXT

1. Brandt quotes a psychoanalyst as saying "religious symbols and language are so widely present in this society that virtually no child reaches school age without having constructed . . . an image or images of God." Does your experience bear out this claim? If so, how did you construct such an image or images? What are your friends' experiences? Do you know some who have *not* constructed some image of God? If so, how did they avoid doing so?

2. What is Brandt's answer to his title question, "Do kids need religion?" What in the essay most clearly tells you what the answer is? Record your answers to these questions in your reading log, if you keep one.

3. Look at the questions A.L., J.R., and S.W. pose in their marginal

commentary on this piece. Choose several of their questions and decide what functions each question serves. Can you see any differences in the kinds of questions each reader tends to ask?

MAKING CONNECTIONS

4. Judging from the selection by him in this chapter (starting on p. 154), what advice would Martin Luther King, Jr. likely give Brandt about children and religion? What advice might Robert MacNeil give (the selection by him starts on p. 200)? Imagine that you are either King or MacNeil, and write a letter to Brandt offering such advice.
5. In what ways might Brandt's spiritual quest resemble Alice Walker's in "Everything Is a Human Being" (starting on p. 189)? How do Brandt and Walker differ in their relationship to belief/faith?

JOINING THE CONVERSATION

6. Like several other authors in this chapter, Brandt seems to distinguish between spirituality or spiritual quest and religion. Try your hand at comparing and contrasting these terms in writing, and bring your definitions to class for discussion.
7. Working with two or three classmates, answer Brandt's question, "Do kids need religion?" Then together draw up a list of reasons, examples, or other evidence to support your answer. Finally, on your own, draft a one-page position paper, beginning either with "Kids need religion" or "Kids don't need religion."

WILLIAM LEAST HEAT MOON
Conversation with a Trappist Monk in Georgia

*W*HEN *W*ILLIAM *L*EAST *H*EAT *M*OON *(b. 1939) lost his job teaching English, he decided to hit the road "in search of places where change did not mean ruin and where time and men and deeds connected." His intention was to travel the circumference of the continental United States on its smaller roads, the ones colored blue on old highway maps. His adventures and discoveries are recorded in* Blue Highways *(1982), a book rich in characters and descriptions.*

Living out of the back of a 1975 Ford Econoline van he named "Ghost Dancing," Least Heat Moon, part Native American and part Anglo, found much that was appealing in small-town America, in places like Conyers, Georgia, for instance, where he stopped at a Trappist monastery, shared a meatless meal with sixty-five monks, joined them in a chapel service, and then interviewed one of them. In the selection from Blue Highways *reprinted here, he opens his interview with Brother Patrick with the question many of us would pose: "Tell me why a man becomes a Trappist monk."*

The Trappists (or Reformed Cistercians) are an order of Roman Catholic monks founded in the seventeenth century and renowned for their austerity, hard work, and isolation from the world. They live in self-supporting communities, producing their own food, building their own buildings, following a rule that reveres silence and demands poverty, chastity, and obedience to their superiors within the order. Quite obviously, a Trappist community is not much like the rest of America today.

I chose this passage from Blue Highways *because it shows how two men living different lives can pursue a similar quest for meaning, Least Heat Moon on the road, Brother Patrick behind the wall of his monastery.* – J.R.

He used to be Patrolman Patrick Duffy. Now he was usually just Brother Patrick. A name didn't count for much anyway. Angular, sinewy, red beard, shaved head, white tunic. Distinctly medieval in spite of the waffle-soled hiking boots. About him was an unacademic, unpietistic energy—the kind that the men who made Christianity must have possessed. Quite capable of driving snakes out of Ireland,* or anywhere else for that matter.

---

driving snakes out of Ireland: An allusion to St. Patrick (c. 390–461?), who according to tradition drove the snakes from Ireland. For a different religious perspective on snakes, see the reading by Alice Walker, "Everything Is a Human Being," starting on p. 189.

"I hear you have questions," he said. None of the usual feeling out before a conversation on a sensitive topic begins. A frontal assault man.

I picked it up. "Tell me why a man becomes a Trappist monk. Answers I heard today sounded like catechism recited a thousand times."

"It isn't an easy question—or at least the answer isn't easy."

"Tell me how it happened to you. How you got here."   5

"I've been here five years. I was a policeman in Brooklyn—Bedford-Stuyvesant. On my way to becoming a ghetto cop. Did it for seven years. Before that, I was an Army medic. Attended St. Francis College part-time and worked in the Brooklyn Public Library. And education has come in other ways too. I hitched around the country in nineteen fifty-seven and again in 'fifty-eight. Went to Central America on the second trip and spent time in Honduras."

"Jack Kerouac? *On the Road?*"*

"Something like that. I came back to New York and worked as a sandhog digging subway tunnels in Manhattan. Then I got seaman's papers to go into the merchant marine—listen, papers are hard to come by. I had to scramble to get them, then I never used them."

"Why not?"

"Got interested in police work, but I was still unsettled and afraid of   10
getting stuck on a ship. Afraid of drudgery. I like changes."

"Changes? In here? Of all you could find here, I'd think change would be the least likely."

"I mean growth and a change of pace. I work four hours as an electrician's assistant. Watch out, this is going to be philosophical, but you could make some kind of analogy between being an electrician and a monk—the flow of energy from a greater source to smaller outlets. Still, the electrical work is different from the spiritual work, even if I try to merge them."

"Two things don't seem like much change."

"I'm also what you might describe as the monastery forest ranger. They call me Smokey the Monk. I oversee the wooded part of the grounds. Try to keep the forest healthy. Just for fun, I've been cataloging all the wildflowers here. We've identified about two hundred species, not counting the blue unknowns and pink mysteries. Working on shrubs now. And I've taken to bird-watching since I came. I spend a lot of time in the woods reading, thinking. That's when real changes can happen."

"What do you read?"   15

"In the woods, some natural history, some Thoreau. Always scripture and theology. Reading about the charismatic movement* now." He was silent a moment. "Does any of this explain why I'm here?"

Jack Kerouac: An American writer (1922–69) whose novel *On the Road* (1957) chronicles the rootlessness of post–World War II American youth. An excerpt appears in Chapter 10, p. 574.

charismatic movement: a grassroots Christian movement emphasizing the Holy Spirit

"It all must be part of an answer."

"For years I've been fascinated by intense spiritual experiences of one kind and another. When I was seventeen—I'm forty-two now—I thought about becoming a monk. I'm not sure why, other than to say I felt an incompleteness in myself. But after a while, the desire seemed to disappear. That's when I started traveling. I learned to travel, then traveled to learn. Later, when I was riding a radio car in Brooklyn, I began to want a life— and morality—based not so much on constraint but on aspiration toward a deeper spiritual life. Damn, that was unsettling. I thought about seeing a psychiatrist, but after a couple of months, I just stopped worrying whether I was crazy."

"What happened?"

"I'm not sure. Maybe I got cured when I started working part-time   20 with the Franciscans in New York. They do a lot of community work at the street level, and that gave me a chance to look into this 'monkey business,' as a friend calls it. I joined the Franciscans Third Order* for two years, to test whether I really wanted to enter a monastery, although their work is secular rather than monastic. Then I worked with the Little Brothers of the Gospel. They live communally, in stark simplicity, in the Bowery. That helped make up my mind. I liked what I could see of a religious life. I began to see my problem was not trusting myself—being afraid of what I really wanted."

He pulled up his tunic and scratched his leg. "Understand, there was nothing wrong with riding a radio car, although I got tired of the bleeding and the shot and cut people I was bandaging up. Seemed I was a medic again. And delivering babies in police car backseats. Thirteen of those. The poor tend to wait to the last minute, then they call the police." He stopped. "Forgot what I was talking about."

"Trusting yourself."

"Better to say a lack of self-trust. As a kid, I was always searching for something beyond myself, something to bring harmony and make sense of things. Whatever my understanding of that something is, I think it began in the cop work and even more when I was assisting the friars in New York. I was moving away from things and myself, toward concerns bigger than me and my problems, but I didn't really find a harmony until I came here. I don't mean to imply I have total and everlasting harmony; I'm just saying I feel it more here than in other places."

He was quiet for some time. "Tonight I can give you ten reasons why I'm a monk. Tomorrow I might see ten new ones. I don't have a single unchanging answer. Hope that doesn't disappoint you."

"Try it in terms of what you like about the life here."   25

Franciscans Third Order: a group of lay people who follow a version of the Franciscan monastic rule

"I've always been attracted to hermitic living—I didn't say 'hermetic living'—but only for short periods. I go off in the woods alone, but I come back. Here, nobody asks, 'What happened to you? You off the beam again?' Living behind that front wall—it doesn't surround us, by the way—living here doesn't mean getting sealed off. This is no vacuum. We had a new kid come in. He left before he took his vows because he couldn't find so-called stability—stability meaning 'no change.' I told him this place was alive. People grow here. The brothers are likely to start sprouting leaves and blossoms. This is no place to escape from what you are because you're still yourself. In fact, personal problems are prone to get bigger here. Our close community and reflective life tend to magnify them."

"How did you finally make the decision to 'come aside'?"

"A friend's father told me, 'If you don't do what you want when you're young, you'll never do it.' So I quit waiting for certainty to come."

"A five-year experiment. Was it the right thing?"

"Right? It's *one* of the right things. The *best* right thing. I believe in   30
it enough I'm taking my permanent vows in October."

"You don't have second thoughts?"

"Second, third, fourth. I go with as much as I can understand. And I've gotten little signs. Like listening to Beethoven. I loved Beethoven. Been here two years, and one day I just went over and turned the stereo off. Beethoven was too complex, I guess, for me. My tastes have developed toward simpler things. Merton* calls it 'the grace of simplicity.' Haven't broken myself of Vivaldi though."

I wanted to ask a question, but it seemed out of bounds. I decided to anyway. "I'd like to know something, partly out of curiosity and partly out of trying to imagine myself a monk." He didn't laugh but I did. "My question, let's see, I guess I want to know how you endure without women."

"I don't 'endure' it. I choose it." He was silent again. "Sometimes, when I'm doing my Smokey duties, I come across a couple picnicking, fooling around. Whenever that happens, when I'm reminded where I've been, I sink a little. I feel an emptiness. Not for a woman so much as for a child—I would like to have had a son. That's the emptiness."

"What do you do?"   35

His answers were coming slowly. "I try to take desires and memories of companionship—destructive ones—and let them run their course. Wait it out. Don't panic. That's when the emptiness is intense."

"And that's it?"

"That's the beginning. Then I turn the pain of absence into an offering to God. Sometimes that's all I have to offer."

Merton: Thomas Merton (1915–68), Catholic monk and author of *The Seven-Storey Mountain* (1948), a best-selling spiritual autobiography

"You mean what you've given up?"

"Does it seem like I'm giving nothing?"   40

"It seems like a gift of giving up a gift. For he so loved God he gave up his only unbegotten son."

Brother Patrick smiled. "Just say I try to turn the potential for destructiveness into a useful force. In that way, the attraction of the outside reinforces. It's another way to come closer to God."

"Someone else today used that phrase about coming closer to God. It sounds like the Hindus who renounce the world and move away from things, including their own desires, so they can get closer to their god."

"Simplicity reveals the universals we all live under. Material goods can blunt your perception of greater things. Here, the effort is to free yourself from blindness, arrogance, selfishness."

The bells rang for compline.* It was so dark I heard Duffy more than   45
I saw him. He said, "I begin with this broken truth that I am. I start from the entire broken man—entire but whole. Then I work to become empty. And whole. In looking for ways to God, I find parts of myself coming together. In that union, I find a regeneration."

"Sounds like spiritual biology."

"Why not?" After a pause he said, "Coming here is following a call to be quiet. When I go quiet I stop hearing myself and start hearing the world outside me. Then I hear something very great."

QUESTIONING THE TEXT

1. How effective do you find William Least Heat Moon as an interviewer? What other questions would you have liked him to ask?

2. Brother Patrick makes a point of distinguishing between the words *hermitic* and *hermetic* (see page 186). Look these words up in the dictionary, consider them in the context of Patrick's other remarks, and then suggest what the point is that he may be making.

MAKING CONNECTIONS

3. When Brother Patrick mentions the time he spent on the road, Least Heat Moon asks, "Jack Kerouac? *On the Road*?" Read the excerpt from *On the Road* starting on page 574, and then explain the point of Least Heat Moon's allusion.

4. Compare Brother Patrick's religious life with the experience of God

---

compline: the final hour in a priest's or monk's daily schedule of prayer

Martin Luther King, Jr., describes himself as having had after a telephone threat (on p. 154). Freewrite for 10 or 15 minutes about the differences between the religious experiences of these men.

JOINING THE CONVERSATION

5. Can you imagine any circumstances under which a life of silence and seclusion would appeal to you? In a paragraph or two, either describe those circumstances or explain why you would never make Brother Patrick's choice.
6. Interview someone whose way of life puzzles or intrigues you. Then write up the interview as Least Heat Moon does, taking care not only to report what your interviewee says, but also to describe him or her.
7. In a group, discuss why a religious order might demand chastity from its members. What is gained by a life of chastity? What is lost? Then, on your own, write a short exploratory essay about the subject, pursuing it from any angle that interests you.

ALICE WALKER
Everything Is a Human Being

$P_{ERHAPS\ BEST\ KNOWN}$ *for her award-winning 1982 novel* The Color Purple, *Alice Walker (b. 1944) is a writer of distinction in many areas, including other novels (*The Third Life of Grange Copeland, *1970;* The Temple of My Familiar, *1989), poetry (*Revolutionary Petunias, *1973;* Horses Make a Landscape Look More Beautiful, *1984), short stories (*In Love and Trouble, *1973), and essays (*In Search of Our Mothers' Gardens, *1983). The themes of her works often grow out of her experiences as one of eight children of Georgia sharecroppers. Walker attended Spelman College and graduated from Sarah Lawrence College in 1965. In 1967 she moved to Mississippi and taught at Jackson State College while working as a civil rights activist during one of the most harrowing times in our nation's history. Her personal courage during those years is reflected in the actions of many of her fictional characters, as is her commitment to celebrating the lives and achievements of African American women.*

In the essay that follows (from Living by the Word, *1988), Walker celebrates the life of the earth and all its creatures. Written in honor of the birth of Martin Luther King, Jr., and delivered as an address at the University of California at Davis on January 15, 1983, "Everything Is a Human Being" argues that the sacred spirit exists in every life form. In making a connection between the inhumane and degrading treatment of people and the inhumane and degrading treatment of nature, Walker creates a link between the spiritual beliefs of African Americans like King and that of Native Americans like Leslie Marmon Silko (whose poem appears at the end of this chapter). She argues that the Indians are the parents of the land that is now the United States and tells us "we must get to know these parents 'from our mother's [Earth's] side' before it is too late. It has been proved that the land can exist without the country—and be better for it; it has not been proved . . . that the country can exist without the land. And the land is being killed." Thus Walker asks us to consider the ways in which we pollute, rape, and devour the land that could and would support us, the Mother Earth that nurtures people of all faiths. Throughout, her implicit question is just this: Can guardianship of our planet, our literally shared land, provide symbolic common ground on which all—of whatever religious creed or conviction—can stand?*

I chose this essay because it is one I have puzzled over many times, asking myself whether it is possible that people in this country can learn to value and protect the earth. Most of the time it seems completely impossible to me. But then I think of the alternative, the death of the earth, and I come back to Walker's essay once more. — A.L.

. . . There are people who think that only people have emotions like pride, fear, and joy, but those who know will tell you all things are alive, perhaps not in the same way we are alive, but each in its own way, as should be, for we are not all the same. And though different from us in shape and life span, different in Time and Knowing, yet are trees alive. And rocks. And water. And all know emotion.

ANNE CAMERON, *Daughters of Copper Woman*[1]

Some years ago a friend and I walked out into the countryside to listen to what the Earth was saying, and to better hear our own thoughts. We had prepared ourselves to experience what in the old days would have been called a vision, and what today probably has no name that is not found somewhat amusing by many. Because there is no longer countryside that is not owned by someone, we stopped at the entrance to a large park, many miles distant from the city. By the time we had walked a hundred yards, I felt I could go no farther and lay myself down where I was, across the path in a grove of trees. For several hours I lay there, and other people entering the park had to walk around me. But I was hardly aware of them. I was in intense dialogue with the trees.*

As I was lying there, really across their feet, I felt or "heard" with my feelings the distinct request from them that I remove myself. But these are not feet, I thought, peering at them closely, but roots. Roots do not tell you to go away. It was then that I looked up and around me into the "faces." These "faces" were all middle-aged to old conifers, and they were all suffering from some kind of disease, the most obvious sign of which was a light green fungus, resembling moss and lichen, that nearly covered them, giving them—in spite of the bright spring sunlight—an eerie, fantastical aspect. Beneath this greenish envelopment, the limbs of the trees, the "arms," were bent in hundreds of shapes in a profusion of deformity. Indeed, the trees reminded me of nothing so much as badly rheumatoid elderly people, as I began to realize how difficult, given their bent shapes, it would be for their limbs to move freely in the breeze. Clearly these were sick people, or trees; irritable, angry, and growing old in pain. And they did not want me lying on their gnarled and no doubt aching feet.

Looking again at their feet, or roots—which stuck up all over the ground and directly beneath my cheek—I saw that the ground from which they emerged was gray and dead-looking, as if it had been poisoned. Aha, I thought, this is obviously a place where chemicals were dumped. The soil has been poisoned, the trees afflicted, slowly dying, and they do not like it. I hastily communicated this deduction to the trees and asked that they understand it

---

[1]Vancouver: Press Gang, 1981.

a vision . . . with the trees: For another encounter with the woods, see Joe Bob Briggs, "Get in Touch with Your Ancient Spear," p. 368.

was not *I* who had done this. I just moved to this part of the country, I said. But they were not appeased. Get up. Go away, they replied. But I refused to move. Nor could I. I needed to make them agree to my innocence.

The summer before this encounter I lived in the northern hills of California, where much logging is done. Each day on the highway, as I went to buy groceries or to the river to swim, I saw the loggers' trucks, like enormous hearses, carrying the battered bodies of the old sisters and brothers, as I thought of them, down to the lumberyards in the valley. In fact, this sight, in an otherwise peaceful setting, distressed me—as if I lived in a beautiful neighborhood that daily lost hundreds of its finest members, while I sat mournful but impotent beside the avenue that carried them away.

It was of this endless funeral procession that I thought as I lay across   5
the feet of the sick old relatives whose "safe" existence in a public park (away from the logging trucks) had not kept them safe at all.

I *love* trees, I said.

Human, *please,* they replied.

But I do not cut you down in the prime of life. I do not haul your mutilated and stripped bodies shamelessly down the highway. It is the lumber companies, I said.

Just go away, said the trees.

All my life you have meant a lot to me, I said. I love your grace, your   10
dignity, your serenity, your generosity . . .

Well, said the trees, before I actually finished this list, we find you without grace, without dignity, without serenity, and there is no generosity in you either—just ask any tree. You butcher us, you burn us, you grow us only to destroy us. Even when we grow ourselves, you kill us, or cut off our limbs. That we are alive and have feelings means nothing to you.

But *I,* as an individual, am innocent, I said. Though it did occur to me that I live in a wood house, I eat on a wood table, I sleep on a wood bed.

My uses of wood are modest, I said, and always tailored to my needs. I do not slash through whole forests, destroying hundreds of trees in the process of "harvesting" a few.

But finally, after much discourse, I understood what the trees were telling me: Being an individual doesn't matter. Just as human beings perceive all trees as one (didn't a U.S. official say recently that "when you've seen one tree, you've seen 'em all"?), all human beings, to the trees, are one. We are judged by our worst collective behavior, since it is so vast; not by our singular best. The Earth holds us responsible for our crimes against it, not as individuals, but as a species—this was the message of the trees. I found it to be a terrifying thought. For I had assumed that the Earth, the spirit of the Earth, noticed exceptions—those who wantonly damage it and those who do not. But the Earth is wise. It has given itself into the keeping of all, and all are therefore accountable.

And how hard it will be to change our worst behavior!   15

Last spring I moved even deeper into the country, and went eagerly up the hill from my cabin to start a new garden. As I was patting the soil around the root of a new tomato plant, I awakened a small garden snake who lived in the tomato bed. Though panicked and not knowing at the time what kind of snake it was, I tried calmly to direct it out of the garden, now that I, a human being, had arrived to take possession of it. It went. The next day, however, because the tomato bed *was* its home, the snake came back. Once more I directed it away. The third time it came back, I called a friend—who thought I was badly frightened, from my nervous behavior—and he killed it. It looked very small and harmless, hanging from the end of his hoe.

Everything I was ever taught about snakes—that they are dangerous, frightful, repulsive, sinister—went into the murder of this snake person, who was only, after all, trying to remain in his or her home, perhaps the only home he or she had ever known. Even my ladylike "nervousness" in its presence was learned behavior. I knew at once that killing the snake was not the first act that should have occurred in my new garden, and I grieved that I had apparently learned nothing, as a human being, since the days of Adam and Eve.

Even on a practical level, killing this small, no doubt bewildered and disoriented creature made poor sense, because throughout the summer snakes just like it regularly visited the garden (and deer, by the way, ate all the tomatoes), so that it appeared to me that the little snake I killed was always with me. Occasionally a very large mama or papa snake wandered into the cabin yard, as if to let me know its child had been murdered, and it knew who was responsible for it.

These garden snakes, said my neighbors, are harmless; they eat mice and other pests that invade the garden. In this respect, they are even helpful to humans. And yet, I am still afraid of them, because that is how I was taught to be. Deep in the psyche of most of us there is this fear—and long ago, I do not doubt, in the psyche of ancient peoples, there was a similar fear of trees. And of course a fear of other human beings, for that is where all fear of natural things leads us: to fear of ourselves, fear of each other, and fear even of the spirit of the Universe, because out of fear we often greet its outrageousness with murder.

That fall, they say, the last of the bison herds was slaughtered by the Wasichus.[2] I can remember when the bison were so many that they

---

[2]Wasichu was a term used by the Oglala Sioux to designate the white man, but it had no reference to the color of his skin. It means: He who takes the fat. It is possible to be white and not a Wasichu or to be a Wasichu and not white. In the United States, historically speaking, Wasichus of color have usually been in the employ of the military, which is the essence of Wasichu.

could not be counted, but more and more Wasichus came to kill them until there were only heaps of bones scattered where they used to be. The Wasichus did not kill them to eat; they killed them for the metal that makes them crazy, and they took only the hides to sell. Sometimes they did not even take the hides, only the tongues; and I have heard that fire-boats came down the Missouri River loaded with dried bison tongues. You can see that the men who did this were crazy. Sometimes they did not even take the tongues; they just killed and killed because they liked to do that. When we hunted bison, we killed only what we needed. And when there was nothing left but heaps of bones, the Wasichus came and gathered up even the bones and sold them.

Black Elk Speaks[3]

In this way, the Wasichus starved the Indians into submission, and   20
forced them to live on impoverished "reservations" in their own land. Like the little snake in my garden, many of the Indians returned again and again to their ancient homes and hunting grounds, only to be driven off with greater and greater brutality until they were broken or killed.

The Wasichus in Washington who ordered the slaughter of bison and Indian and those on the prairies who did the deed are frequently thought of, by some of us, as "fathers of our country," along with the Indian killers and slave owners Washington and Jefferson and the like.

Yet what "father" would needlessly exterminate any of his children?

Are not the "fathers," rather, those Native Americans, those "wild Indians" like Black Elk, who said, "It is the story of all life that is holy and is good to tell, and of us two-leggeds sharing in it with the four-leggeds and the wings of the air and all green things; for these are children of one mother and their father is one Spirit"?

Indeed, America, the country, acts so badly, so much like a spoiled adolescent boy, because it has never acknowledged the "fathers" that existed before the "fathers" of its own creation. It has been led instead—in every period of its brief and troubled history—by someone who might be called Younger Brother (after the character in E. L. Doctorow's novel *Ragtime*, set in turn-of-the-century America), who occasionally blunders into good and useful deeds, but on the whole never escapes from the white Victorian house of racist and sexist repression, puritanism, and greed.

The Wasichu speaks, in all his U.S. history books, of "opening up   25
virgin lands." Yet there were people living here, on "Turtle Island," as the Indians called it, for thousands of years; but living so gently on the land that to Wasichu eyes it looked untouched. Yes, it was "still," as they wrote over and over again, with lust, "virginal." If it were a bride, the Wasichus would have permitted it to wear a white dress. For centuries on end Native Americans lived on the land, making love to it through worship and praise,

[3]By John G. Neihardt (New York: William Morrow, 1932).

without once raping or defiling it. The Wasichus—who might have chosen to imitate the Indians, but didn't because to them the *Indians* were savages—have been raping and defiling it since the day they came. It is ironic to think that if the Indians who were here then "discovered" America as it is now, they would find little reason to want to stay. This is a fabulous *land,* not because it is a country, but because it is soaked in so many years of love. And though the Native Americans fought as much as any other people among themselves (much to their loss!), never did they fight against the earth, which they correctly perceived as their mother, or against their father, the sky,* now thought of mainly as "outer space," where primarily bigger and "better" wars have a projected future.

The Wasichus may be fathers of the country, but the Native Americans, the Indians, are the parents ("guardians," as they've always said they are) of the land.[4] And, in my opinion, as Earthling above all, we must get to know these parents "from our mother's side" before it is too late. It has been proved that the land can exist without the country—and be better for it; it has not been proved (though some space enthusiasts appear to think so) that the country can exist without the land. And the land is being killed.

Sometimes when I teach, I try to help my students understand what it must feel like to be a slave. Not many of them can go to South Africa and ask the black people enslaved by the Wasichus there, or visit the migrant-labor camps kept hidden from their neighborhoods, so we talk about slavery as it existed in America, a little over a hundred years ago. One day I asked if any of them felt they had been treated "like dirt." No; many of them felt they had been treated badly at some time in their lives (they were largely middle class and white) but no one felt he or she had been treated like dirt. Yet what pollution you breathe, I pointed out, which the atmosphere also breathes; what a vast number of poisons you eat with your food, which the Earth has eaten just before you. How unexpectedly many of you will fall ill and die from cancer because the very ground on which you build your homes will be carcinogenic. As the Earth is treated "like dirt"—its dignity demeaned by wanton dumpings of lethal materials all across its proud face and in its crystal seas—so are we all treated.*

Native Americans lived on the land . . . their mother: For an expression of this Native American perception of nature, see the lullaby by Leslie Marmon Silko on p. 208.

[4]Though much of what we know of our Indian ancestors concerns the male, it is good to remember who produced him; that women in some tribes were shamans, could vote, and among the Onondaga still elect the men who lead the tribe. And, inasmuch as "women's work" has always involved cleaning up after the young, as well as teaching them principles by which to live, we have our Indian female parent to thank for her care of Turtle Island, as well as the better documented male who took her instructions so utterly to heart.

pollution . . . so are we all treated: For a less apocalyptic view of the environmental situation, see William Rathje and Cullen Murphy, "Five Major Myths about Garbage, and Why They're Wrong," p. 268.

Some of us have become used to thinking that woman is the nigger of the world, that a person of color is the nigger of the world, that a poor person is the nigger of the world. But, in truth, Earth itself has become the nigger of the world. It is perceived, ironically, as other, alien, evil, and threatening by those who are finding they cannot draw a healthful breath without its cooperation. While the Earth is poisoned, everything it supports is poisoned. While the Earth is enslaved, none of us is free. While the Earth is "a nigger," it has no choice but to think of us all as Wasichus. While it is "treated like dirt," so are we.

In this time, when human life—because of human greed, avarice, ignorance, and fear—hangs by a thread, it is of disarmament that every thoughtful person thinks; for regardless of whether we all agree that we deserve to live, or not, as a species, most of us have the desire. But disarmament must also occur in the heart and in the spirit. We must absolutely reject the way of the Wasichu that we are so disastrously traveling, the way that respects most (above nature, obviously above life itself, above even the spirit of the Universe) the "metal that makes men crazy." The United States, the country, has no doubt damned its soul because of how it has treated others, and if it is true that we reap what we sow, as a country we have only to recognize the poison inside us as the poison we forced others to drink. But the land is innocent. It is still Turtle Island, and more connected to the rest of the Universe than to the United States government. It is beginning to throw up the poisons it has been forced to drink, and we must help it by letting go of our own; for until it is healthy and well, we cannot be.

Our primary connection is to the Earth, our mother and father; regard- 30 less of who "owns" pieces and parts, we, as sister and brother beings to the "four-leggeds (and the fishes) and the wings of the air," share the whole. No one should be permitted to buy a part of our Earth to dump poisons in, just as we would not sell one of our legs to be used as a trash can.

Many of us are afraid to abandon the way of the Wasichu because we have become addicted to his way of death. The Wasichu has promised us so many good things, and has actually delivered several. But "progress," once claimed by the present chief of the Wasichus to be their "most important product," has meant hunger, misery, enslavement, unemployment, and worse to millions of people on the globe. The many time-saving devices we have become addicted to, because of our "progress," have freed us to watch endless reruns of commercials, sitcoms, and murders. *

Our thoughts must be on how to restore to the Earth its dignity as a living being; how to stop raping and plundering it as a matter of course.

---

hunger, misery . . . sitcoms, and murders: For another skeptical view of "progress," see the reading by Daniel Grossman, "Neo-Luddites: Don't Just Say Yes to Technology," on p. 261.

We must begin to develop the consciousness that everything has equal rights because existence itself is equal. In other words, we are all here: trees, people, snakes, alike. We must realize that even tiny insects in the South American jungle know how to make plastic, for instance; they have simply chosen not to cover the Earth with it. The Wasichu's uniqueness is not his ability to "think" and "invent"—from the evidence, almost everything does this in some fashion or other—it is his profound unnaturalness. His lack of harmony with other peoples and places, and with the very environment to which he owes his life.

In James Mooney's *Myths of the Cherokee and Sacred Formulas of the Cherokees,* collected between 1887 and 1890, he relates many interesting practices of the original inhabitants of this land, among them the custom of asking pardon of slain or offended animals. And in writing about the needless murder of the snake who inhabited our garden—the snake's and mine—I ask its pardon and, in the telling of its death, hope to save the lives of many of its kin.

> The missionary Washburn [says Mooney] tells how among the Chero-
> kees of Arkansas, he was once riding along, accompanied by an Indian
> on foot, when they discovered a poisonous snake coiled beside the path.
> "I observed Blanket turned aside to avoid the serpent, but made no
> sign of attack, and I requested the interpreter to get down and kill it.
> He did so, and I then inquired of Blanket why he did not kill the serpent.
> He answered, 'I never kill snakes and so snakes never kill me.' "
>   The trader Henry [Mooney observes elsewhere] tells of similar behav-
> ior among the Objibwa of Lake Superior in 1764. While gathering wood
> he was startled by a sudden rattle . . . "I no sooner saw the snake,
> than I hastened to the canoe, in order to procure my gun; but, the
> Indians observing what I was doing, inquired the occasion, and being
> informed, begged me to desist. At the same time, they followed me to
> the spot, with their pipes and tobacco pouches in their hands. On
> returning, I found the snake still coiled.
>   "The Indians, on their part, surrounded it, all addressing it by turns,
> and calling it their *grandfather;* but yet keeping at some distance. During
> this part of the ceremony, they filled their pipes; and now each blew
> the smoke toward the snake, who, as it appeared to me, really received
> it with pleasure. In a word, after remaining coiled, and receiving incense,
> for the space of half an hour, it stretched itself along the ground, in
> visible good humor. Its length was between four and five feet. Having
> remained outstretched for some time, at last it moved slowly away, the
> Indians following it, and still addressing it by the title of grandfather,
> beseeching it to take care of their families during their absence, and to
> be pleased to open the heart of Sir William Johnson (the British Indian
> Agent, whom they were about to visit) so that he might *show them
> charity,* and fill their canoe with rum. One of the chiefs added a petition,
> that the snake would take no notice of the insult which had been offered

by the Englishman, who would even have put him to death, but for the interference of the Indians, to whom it was hoped he would impute no part of the offense. They further requested, that he would remain, and inhabit their country, and not return among the English. . . ."

What makes this remarkable tale more so is that the "bite" of the Englishman's rum was to afflict the Indians far more severely than the bite of any tremendous number of poisonous snakes.

That the Indians were often sexist, prone to war, humanly flawed, I do not dispute. It is their light step upon the Earth that I admire and would have us emulate. The new way to exist on the Earth may well be the ancient way of the steadfast lovers of this particular land. No one has better appreciated Earth than the Native American. Whereas to the Wasichus only the white male attains full human status, everything to the Indian was a relative. Everything was a human being.

As I finish writing this, I notice a large spider sleeping underneath my desk. It does not look like me. It is a different size. But that it loves life as I do, I have no doubt. It is something to think about as I study its many strange but oddly beautiful dozen or so legs, its glowing coral-and-amber coloring, its thick web, whose intricate pattern I would never be able to duplicate. Imagine building your house from your own spit!

In its modesty, its fine artistry and self-respecting competency, is it not like some gay, independent person many of us have known? Perhaps a rule for permissible murder should be that beyond feeding and clothing and sheltering ourselves, even abundantly, we should be allowed to destroy only what we ourselves can re-create. We cannot re-create this world. We cannot re-create "wilderness." We cannot even, truly, re-create ourselves. Only our behavior can we re-create, or create anew.

> Hear me, four quarters of the world—a relative I am! Give me the strength to walk the soft earth, a relative to all that is! Give me the eyes to see and the strength to understand, that I may be like you. . . .
>
> Great Spirit, Great Spirit, my Grandfather, all over the earth the faces of living things are all alike. With tenderness have these come up out of the ground. Look upon these faces of children without number and with children in their arms, that they may face the winds and walk the good road to the day of quiet.
>
> *Black Elk Speaks*

NOTE

The Onondagas are the "Keepers of the Fire" of the Six Nation Confederacy in New York state. The Confederacy (originally composed of five nations) is perhaps the oldest democratic union of nations in the Western world, dating back roughly to the time of the Magna Carta. It is governed under an ancient set of principles known as the "Gayaneshakgowa," or Great Law of Peace, which in written form is the constitution of the Six Nation Confederacy.

This remarkable document contains what well may have been the first detailed pronouncements on democratic popular elections, the consent of the governed, the need to monitor and approve the behavior of governmental leaders, the importance of public opinion, the rights of women, guarantees of free speech and religion, and the equitable distribution of wealth.

Benjamin Franklin and Thomas Jefferson acknowledged in the mid- 40 18th century that their own ideas for a democratic confederacy were based largely on what they had learned from the Six Nations. A century later Friedrich Engels paid a similar tribute to the Great Law of Peace while making his contribution to the theory of Marxism.

JON STEWART, *Pacific News Service*

QUESTIONING THE TEXT

1. Walker says "the United States . . . has no doubt damned its soul because of how it has treated others, and if it is true that we reap what we sow, as a country we have only to recognize the poison inside us as the poison we forced others to drink." What main examples does Walker offer to support this statement? What additional examples can you offer to support it? Can you think of examples to *refute* her claim?

2. What is Walker's view of the Wasichus? How do you know what she thinks of them? With your answers to these questions in mind, reread A.L.'s introduction to this essay. Does A.L. share Walker's view? Does she make some effort to appear neutral? What evidence helps you answer these questions?

3. What does Walker learn from the trees she discourses with? Do you think you would have learned the same lesson? Why, or why not?

MAKING CONNECTIONS

4. In the selection starting on p. 162, Will Herberg argues that the American "way" is one of individualism. What would Walker say about this characteristic value? Would she approve or disapprove of the middle-class ethic Herberg describes? Why?

5. Why do you think Walker wrote this address in honor of Martin Luther King, Jr.'s birth? What in it reminds you of King and the beliefs he expresses in "Our God Is Able" (p. 154)? If you keep a reading log, put your answer there.

JOINING THE CONVERSATION

6. List all the reasons you can think of for agreeing with Walker's position. Then list reasons for not agreeing with her position. Finally, prepare a short statement for your class entitled "Where I Stand on 'Everything Is a Human Being.' "

7. Working with two or three classmates, prepare an introduction to Alice Walker. Assign one person to gather biographical information, perhaps, while another reads two or three other essays in *Living by the Word* and another finds out all he or she can about Walker's novels. Pool your information, and select from it material for a 15-minute class presentation—"Introducing Alice Walker: Why She Believes Everything Is a Human Being."

ROBERT MacNEIL
Wordstruck

*FOR SOME, faith is deeply personal, interior, and solitary—a special commerce
with God. For others, it is bound up with community, a way of experiencing
the larger world as a sacred fellowship. For others still, especially people raised
in religious traditions, faith can be remarkably routine, a means of marking the
seasons, acknowledging life's passages, legislating one's choices.*

Of course, faith can also encompass all these qualities.

*How deeply religious practices can shape our lives is the subject of the
following selection from journalist Robert MacNeil's autobiography,* Wordstruck *(1989). MacNeil (b. 1931), the co-host of public television's* MacNeil-
Lehrer Newshour, *recalls how the prayers and songs of his Anglican church
in Halifax, Nova Scotia, introduced him as a young man to the richest cadences
of the English language. Though irreverent at times, MacNeil helps us to
understand the experiences that molded his life and, I think, he moves attentive
readers to think about their own. — J.R.*

We were Anglicans, my mother fervently, my father ceremoniously,
and the Cathedral of All Saints on Tower Road was one of the hubs of my
young life. The Church of England did not provide me with any spiritual
awakening, nor any intimacy with God, but it anointed me with language;
yea, verily, it steeped me in it. We attended once every Sunday until I joined
the choir, and then it was twice, occasionally three times, not to mention
choir practice one evening a week.

All Saints was not a rich church. Its front was unfinished for lack of
funds, the omission masked for many years by a grey wooden façade. The
simple Gothic interior was stained by many water leaks from ill-fitting
leaded windows. These chalky streaks gave the stuccoed walls and the
carved stone columns a patina of false antiquity. Otherwise it was very plain,
with little ornamentation, because too few generations of Haligonians* had
passed on to be commemorated and too few sinners had cluttered the place
with benefactions in hope of purchasing redemption.

That also meant that the cathedral was unusually bright, because it
could not afford stained glass in the windows of the transept. They carried
a substitute glazing with a faint green or pink cast, suggesting reverence-
in-waiting. That admitted lots of God's sunshine, and especially on bright

---

Haligonians: residents of Halifax, Nova Scotia

winter days with light reflected from the snow, the whole cathedral flushed out the shadowy spirituality of the Old World with the honest clarity of the New.

Until, as a member of the choir, I became an actor in the drama I loathed going to church. The service seemed endless and meaningless; I never knew why or where it was going. My knees ached from the hard prayer benches. And I hated, on a non-school day, having to put on suit, collar, and tie and shine my black shoes. Several times I solved the problem by fainting and forcing my mother to leave.

I could sense it coming on. The air would become thick and un-   5 breathable; the space in front of my eyes would dissolve into a grey-green mist that turned objects increasingly fuzzy. My stomach would feel as if I were about to be sick and—then—I would be crumpling up on the floor, causing a stir, being fanned and helped outside. Once out in the fresh air, I instantly recovered. Like Tom Sawyer's Aunt Polly, my mother thought I was faking, but I wasn't, and it happened often enough that I could use it as a threat. "If you make me go to church today, I'll faint! You know I will." Occasionally it worked.

All Saints was not, to my mother's regret, High Church enough to burn incense, but it had a mélange of smells that became the odour of sanctity* for me. The chancel was perfumed with beeswax candles and strongly scented flowers. There was the smell of the varnish of the pew backs against which I pressed my face while pretending to pray; the starched smell of the freshly laundered surplices of ministers and choir against the mustier odour of the less often cleaned cassocks; and the bouquet of many soaps and scents of worshippers newly bathed for their devotions.

There was also a waft of stale body odour noticeable when the School for the Blind occupied the usual block of seats in the nave. Their smell of neglect, their chopped hair and motley clothing repelled yet saddened me, reminding me of my clean home and the Sunday roast then cooking. They were what I imagined the inmates of David Copperfield's school or the workhouse in *Oliver Twist* to be like: kept by the principle that creatures deprived in one sense wouldn't notice deprivation in most others. Since these blind youngsters couldn't notice what they looked like, the institution didn't. They sat at the front of the church, touching each other to know when to rise or kneel. They were like medieval carvings, holding their heads at awkward angles and making strange grimaces as they lifted clouded eyes towards the beams of light from the transept windows. They compelled me to stare and to be ashamed of staring at their misfortune.

If there was an odour of sanctity, there was also its sound. Forced

---

odour of sanctity: the fragrance said to be put forth by the bodies of saints, before or after death

attendance meant that I was compelled for years to listen to and to utter some of the most glorious prose in the language. In print it meant nothing to me at first, and I'm not sure that it meant anything aurally for a long time, but the words, spoken, chanted, or sung, resonant and important, sank in.

The diction of the Anglican Church in Canada in those days was crisply English, with vowels arched to reverberate in Gothic spaces and consonants bitten out so that they clicked back from the stone walls. It was highly theatrical speech, a professional voice like that adopted by Shakespearean actors in Canada and the United States. The rounded tones lost clarity but gained drama in the confused acoustics of All Saints, further scrambled by a weak amplification system.

There was poured into the porches of this child's mind a rich, echoing   10
soup of sound which made literal sense only when recollected years later. If scientists could examine my brain, as they do the contents of murder victims' stomachs, they would find that I had gorged myself when young on plum puddings and fruitcakes of this seventeenth-century prose; each word simple in itself, the combination rich and fruity, loved for the taste on the tongue, though years in the digesting; words for their own sake. That was particularly true of the often-repeated passages from the Book of Common Prayer, paraphrases of biblical verses that constitute English worship since the sixteenth century.

> Lighten our darkness, we beseech thee, O Lord; and by thy great mercy defend us from all perils and dangers of this night.
> The Lord bless thee, and keep thee.
> The Lord make his face shine upon thee and be gracious unto thee:
> The Lord lift up his countenance upon thee, and give thee peace.
> Let the words of my mouth, and the meditation of my heart, be acceptable in thy sight, O Lord, my strength and my redeemer.
>
> Forgive us our trespasses as we forgive those who trespass against us. And lead us not into temptation, but deliver us from evil: For thine is the kingdom, and the power, and the glory, for ever and ever. Amen.

Incantations absently said hundreds of times in hundreds of moods, the needle playing the same groove again and again until the phrases have a hypnotic, even narcotic effect, independent of meaning.

Those were the early words, which I said and sang as a member of the cathedral choir. I took great pleasure in the singing. It was fun when there were settings with descants, as at Christmas and Easter, with the entire congregation as well as the choir singing and the great organ thundering away, to come in over the top of it all with our treble voices hitting the highest notes.

There were moments when the thrill was greater. During the processional hymns, when the choir paraded around the whole church, it was gratifying to hear our loud, trained voices alongside the puny efforts of the ordinary members of the congregation. If one of them—insufficiently awed—presumed to compete with us, we sang even louder, to drown the upstart out. On one of those occasions, I heard a woman say to another as the boys' section of the choir passed by, "Aren't they sweet!" We did not feel "sweet." We felt powerful and important. But she made me realise the theatrical effect we were having: our twelve-year-old scruffiness hidden under newly-starched ruffs and surplices, our hair clean and combed, beams of light from the high windows of the nave striking us picturesquely, as our clear voices soared out vigorously—more or less in tune.

Vanity of vanities, saith the preacher, all is vanity. Perhaps that is why the adults in the choir kept coming back year after year, and put up with our snickering, our telling dirty jokes behind our music sheets, as we hunched down in the choir stalls laughing at some big-bosomed lady of the choir; our parking gum behind the carved angels or rattling marbles in our pockets; our not knowing the place, or missing our cue, or singing off tune, or being late for practice. We boys got paid ten cents a service, triple during festivals. The adults got nothing.

Before my voice changed, it grew sure enough to carry a little solo   15 work with school choirs, which terrified me but added to the gratification.

None of this made me religious, but it had the side effect of making me much more conscious of the sound of words. Disciplined singing demanded not only musical training but exercise in diction. Singing the phrase *Lord, now lettest thou thy servant depart in peace, according to thy word* requires that the words be stretched out to fit the musical setting. You cannot expand a word like *peace,* as rock singers do now, by splintering it into many syllables, *pee-ee-ee-ees,* with a little grunt of air on each. You have to ride the one syllable smoothly and elastically for a bar or more of the music.

I came to understand the value of the vowels and wanted, when speaking or reading them, not singing, to give them full measure. It was the same with the consonants in singing. If the piece was a quiet setting for a psalm, we learned to give the terminal *d*'s and *t*'s enough notice with our tongue and teeth so they would carry, without at the same time exaggerating them.

Also, we became thoroughly familiar with all the anachronistic verb forms, like the second person singular, *When thou doest alms, let not thy left hand know,* and the third person, *what thy right hand doeth.* Such phrases do not come trippingly off the tongue if the mind still trips on them. Repeated use made the idiom perfectly familiar. Twisters for twentieth-century tongues like

> And why beholdest thou the mote that is in thy brother's eye, but
> considerest not the beam that is in thine own eye?

heard or said often enough become part of the pattern of one's thinking; in effect, another language learned in childhood. Hitting the English poets, from Elizabethans onwards, a few years later, was like parachuting into friendly territory, my basic Berlitz course* already memorised. And, as with music, affection grows with familiarity.

All this exposure to the King James Bible, the Book of Common Prayer, and the hymns seasoned me with the words and the forms that had launched British navies and armies into battle and imperial civil servants on their missions; the words that had christened the babies, married the daughters, and buried the dead of the Empire:

> Naked came I out of my mother's womb, and naked shall I return thither: the Lord gave, and the Lord hath taken away; blessed be the name of the Lord

were still being pronounced over my generation of Canadians. It was like the tannin of English tea staining our souls for life. You do not lose it ever.

> Far called, our navies melt away;
> On dune and headland sinks the fire:
> Lo, all our pomp of yesterday
> Is one with Nineveh and Tyre!
> Lord God of hosts, be with us yet
> Lest we forget, lest we forget.

We sang with lusty pride the great hymns of an empire, in the 1940s   20
still largely intact.

> Land of Hope and Glory, Mother of the Free,
> How shall we extol thee, who are born of thee?
> Wider still and wider shall thy bounds be set;
> God, who made thee mighty, make thee mightier yet.

And Blake's thrilling poem, somehow appropriated by muscular, industrial, martial Christianity,*

> And did those feet in ancient time
> Walk upon England's mountains green?
> And was the holy Lamb of God
> On England's pleasant pastures seen?

> I will not cease from mental fight,
> Nor shall my sword sleep in my hand
> Till we have built Jerusalem
> In England's green and pleasant land.

At the very beginning of the Second World War, in the spring of 1940, all the school children of Halifax, dressed in white, were massed on

---

Berlitz course: a program of foreign language instruction
muscular . . . Christianity: muscular Christianity was a movement in Victorian England linking vigorous physical activity to the practice of virtue

the Wanderer's Ground.* We filled the bleachers and sang in our thousands of little voices the songs of the First World War:

> We're the soldiers of the Queen, my lads . . .
>
> There's a long, long trail a-winding . . .
>
> Keep the home fires burning . . .
>
> It's a long way to Tipperary . . .

And when the songs of the Second World War came along, we sang them with stirring hearts, as though they were hymns:

> There'll always be an England
> And England shall be free . . .
>
> There'll be bluebirds over
> The white cliffs of Dover . . .

The war took on a kind of religious meaning; singing stirring songs about the defence of England was on the same level as singing hymns praising God and praying for victory, except that the songs were more appealing. Gracie Fields* singing "wish me luck as you wave me goodbye" moved me so much when played at a friend's summer cottage that I became acutely homesick and had to be sent home.

Every day before classes at Tower Road School we sang a hymn, and it was often

> O, hear us when we cry to Thee
> For those in peril on the sea!

which I sang with burning eyes but full of pride. Psalm 107 had the same effect on me:

> They that go down to the sea in ships,
> That do business in great waters.

QUESTIONING THE TEXT

1. MacNeil's selection has many descriptive passages. Analyze one of the paragraphs especially heavy with sights, smells, textures, and sounds. List the details that stand out.
2. MacNeil describes the "theatrical effect" the boys' section of the choir

---

Wanderer's Ground: probably the sports field of an amateur athletic association founded in Halifax in 1882

Gracie Fields: a popular English music hall performer (1898–1979), who also appeared in films

has on a woman in the congregation. Where else in the selection does he describe rituals or activities that have a similar effect?

MAKING CONNECTIONS

3. Reread the selection from *Wordstruck* along with Anthony Brandt's "Do Kids Need Religion?" (starting on p. 173). Do the essays illuminate each other? After reading MacNeil, how would you answer Brandt's question? Give it a try in a short essay.
4. Compare Martin Luther King, Jr.'s discussion of military power and God (p. 154) to what MacNeil observes about the relationship he experienced between religion and war.

JOINING THE CONVERSATION

5. MacNeil's years in the church choir did not make him religious. Yet he clearly enjoyed those times. With a group of classmates, discuss the role a church, synagogue, mosque, or other place of worship can play as a cultural and social institution.
6. With a group of classmates, discuss any relationships or differences you perceive between religious and patriotic feelings and between the purposes served by religious and national rituals. Then write an exploratory essay on the subject suitable for use as an opinion column in a news magazine.

The Nishmat *Prayer*

In "Our God Is Able," Martin Luther King, Jr., explains how, in a moment of personal crisis, he resolves his dilemma by taking his problem to God: "My head in my hands, I bowed over the kitchen table and prayed aloud." Such recourse to prayer in times of trouble seems almost instinctual, a human trait as distinctive as tears or smiles. Indeed, the rabbi Herbert M. Baumgard defines prayer as "the yearning of the divine spark within man to join itself to more of itself."

To represent that conversation with God we call prayer, I've selected a brief portion of the Jewish Sabbath morning service as recorded in the Siddur, *the Hebrew prayer book. Transcribed into Roman characters, the prayer begins Nishmat Kol Hai.* — J.R.

The breath of every living being shall bless thy name, O Lord our God, and the spirit of all flesh shall continually glorify and exalt thy memorial, O our King; from everlasting to everlasting thou art God; and beside thee we have no King who redeemeth and saveth, setteth free and delivereth, who supporteth and hath mercy in all times of trouble and distress; yea, we have no King but thee.

He is God of the first and of the last, the God of all creatures, the Lord of all generations, who is extolled with many praises, and guideth his world with lovingkindness and his creatures with tender mercies. The Lord slumbereth not, nor sleepeth; he arouseth the sleepers and awakeneth the slumberers; he maketh the dumb to speak, loseth the bound, supporteth the falling, and raiseth up the bowed.

To thee alone we give thanks.

IN RESPONSE

1. In what relationship does God stand to his creatures in the *Nishmat* prayer? Which authors in this chapter would likely find the prayer affirming? Which authors might find it incompatible with their beliefs?
2. Does the secular world have its equivalents of prayer—rituals, songs, readings not directed to a deity that nonetheless generate something akin to religious feelings? Write a short paper exploring this question.
3. What occasions or circumstances evoke prayer? Have you ever had a experience with prayer like that Martin Luther King, Jr., describes in "Our God is Able"? If so, narrate it—perhaps in your reading log, if you are keeping one.

LESLIE MARMON SILKO
Lullaby

Growing up next door to her great-grandmother on New Mexico's Laguna Pueblo Reservation, Leslie Marmon Silko (b. 1948) learned the history, culture, and traditions of the Laguna people. She has used that knowledge to powerful effect in poems, stories, and novels since 1974, when her collection of poems Laguna Woman *was published. Since then Silko has given readers* Ceremony *(1977), now recognized as the first full-length work of fiction by a Native American woman to be published, and a collection of short fiction,* Storyteller, *from which the following poem is taken.*

The poem is a song, a lullaby, sung by Ayah, the elderly grandmother at the center of the story "Lullaby." In singing it, Ayah reaffirms the interconnectedness of all life, the indissoluble ties between people and nature. More important, she offers comfort, solace, and hope beyond the devastation of Native American lands and cultures that Silko's story reveals and that Alice Walker's essay laments. For years, I have carried a copy of this lullaby around with me, and I refer to it often. It reminds me of songs my own granny sang to me—and of the importance of the oral tradition in passing on what is really important in life. I chose this lullaby for these reasons, then, as well as for the fact that in its simple but profound theme, it speaks to me of a spirituality that runs deeper than words. — A.L.

The earth is your mother,
    she holds you.
The sky is your father,
    he protects you.
Sleep,
sleep.

Rainbow is your sister,
    she loves you.
The winds are your brothers,
    they sing to you.
Sleep,
sleep.

We are together always
We are together always
There never was a time
when this
was not so.

IN RESPONSE

1. What lullabies or songs do you remember from your childhood? Choose one and spend a few minutes jotting down what you remember of its words and of how hearing it made you feel. Then write a brief description of it, trying to express its major theme(s) and what it represented to you. Bring your description to class for discussion and comparison.

2. Think for a while about your own spiritual and/or religious beliefs—or about your secular beliefs. Then try your hand at writing a lullaby that would capture the essence of those beliefs, keeping it as brief as possible. Then try to set your lullaby to a tune you know.

OTHER READINGS

Balmer, Randall. "Phoenix Prophet." *Mine Eyes Have Seen the Glory: A Journey into the Evangelical Subculture in America*. New York: Oxford, 1989. 71–91. Describes a faith healer.

Bennett, William J. "The Great Cultural Divide: Religion in American Political Life." *The De-Valuing of America*. New York: Summit, 1992. 203–24. Explores the complex politics of religion in America.

Berman, Philip L. *The Search for Meaning: Americans Talk about What They Believe and Why*. New York: Ballantine, 1990. Contains short pieces by a variety of Americans discussing their beliefs.

Crow Dog, Mary, and Richard Erdoes. "Crying for a Dream." *Lakota Woman*. New York: Harper-Perennial, 1990. Examines the religious role of peyote.

Fritz, Leah. "An Atheist Speaks Her Mind." *Utne Reader* Jan.-Feb. 1991. Makes a case against formal religion.

Gibbs, Nancy. "America's Holy War." *Time* 9 Dec. 1991: 61–65. Asks whether separation of church and state has gone too far.

King, Martin Luther, Jr. *Strength to Love*. New York: Harper, 1963. Includes a collection of his sermons.

Lewis, Bernard. "State and Society Under Islam." *The Best of* The Wilson Quarterly: *A Reader*. Washington: Woodrow Wilson International Center for Scholars, n.d. 26–35. Looks at a religious tradition of growing importance in the United States.

McCarthy, Mary. *Memories of a Catholic Girlhood*. New York: Harcourt, 1957. Traces the effects of a Catholic upbringing on a distinguished novelist and social critic.

Phillips, Andrew. "The 'Satanic' Furor." *Macleans* 27 Feb. 1989: 16–19. Discusses Ayatollah Khomeini's death threat against British novelist Salman Rushdie.

Soto, Gary. "The Confession." *A Summer Life*. Hanover, NH: UP of New England, n.d. 47–49. Describes a first confession in the Roman Catholic tradition.

Winter, Miriam Therese. "The Women-Church Movement." *Christian Century* 8 Mar. 1989: 258–60. Describes an interdenominational movement of women seeking freedom from the limits of traditional church structures.

Woodward, Kenneth L. "Talking to God." *Newsweek* 6 Jan. 1992: 39–44. Explores how Americans pray.

Science: O Brave New World   5

Learn from me . . . how dangerous is the acquirement of knowledge and how much happier that man is who believes his native town to be the world, than he who aspires to become greater than his nature will allow.
                                    MARY SHELLEY, *Frankenstein*

There are two ways to predict the progress of technology. One way is economic forecasting, the other way is science fiction.
                                    FREEMAN J. DYSON, *Engineers' Dreams*

Should we stop short of learning about some things, for fear of what we, or someone, will do with the knowledge?
                                    LEWIS THOMAS, *The Hazards of Science*

To put it quite bluntly, I laughed. Laws of nature are universal—how could they possibly depend on the sex of their discoverers?
                                    EVELYN FOX KELLER, *From Working Scientist to Feminist Critic*

I came to Cyberthon curious, but terribly smug (indeed superior) in my neoluddism. By daybreak, though, I was convinced that people who care about media, art, and education shouldn't just pass this off as the latest trend among techno-weenies with weird hair.
                                    PEGGY ORENSTEIN, *Get a Cyberlife*

The unwanted social consequences that accompany today's technological innovations . . . may far outweigh any benefits.
                                    DANIEL GROSSMAN, *Neo-Luddites: Don't Just Say Yes to Technology*

. . . garbage isn't mathematics. To understand garbage you have to touch it, to feel it, to sort it, to smell it.
                                    WILLIAM RATHJE and CULLEN MURPHY, *Five Major Myths about Garbage, and Why They're Wrong*

We will never forget them, nor the last time we saw them—this morning, as they prepared for their journey, and waved good-bye, and "slipped the surly bonds of earth" to "touch the face of God."
                                    RONALD REAGAN, *Tribute to the* Challenger *Astronauts*

But Microscopes *are prudent / In an Emergency.*
                                    EMILY DICKINSON, *"Faith" Is a Fine Invention*

Introduction

TIME AND AGAIN in the twentieth century, we have found our industrial society—like the hero of Mary Shelley's *Frankenstein* (1818)—creating and using technologies that drive it beyond the limits of moral, legal, and ethical precedents. Indeed, there seem to be no boundaries to what the human imagination can first contemplate and then achieve. Scientists have already mapped out the genes that control life, performed surgery in the womb, extracted the secrets of the atom, and planned colonies in outer space. Occasionally, experiments escape our control and we watch them poison our landscapes or explode before our eyes. But the quest for knowledge continues.

Julius Caesar, a military genius and a shrewd politician, observed once that "it is better to have expanded the frontiers of the mind than to have pushed back the boundaries of the empire." As Caesar doubtless understood, the two are often the same thing, the powers of mind enabling one people or nation to dominate others, to cast itself in the role of a god and its neighbors as servants or slaves.

This chapter is designed to explore the resonances of *Frankenstein,* the many questions it raises, and the ways it makes us think about science, progress, and alienation. In our mythologies, ancient and modern, we show a fondness for rebels like Victor Frankenstein, who would steal the fire of the gods and, with their new knowledge, shake the foundations of empires. Yet we cannot entirely identify with such figures either. They remain a threat to us too, a reminder that humanity finally lacks the wisdom to play God.

Your own thinking about these issues may be stimulated by considering the following questions:

1. Why do contemporary readers (and moviegoers) continue to find *Frankenstein* fascinating?
2. What makes the intellectual dreamer or rebel an attractive figure?
3. Why does a society usually react with suspicion toward people who, like Victor Frankenstein's monster, seem different? How do we define the outsider? How does the outsider act as a result?
4. What motivates people to explore what is unknown and possibly dangerous?
5. Does scientific progress always entail some loss or disruptive change? You might want to discuss this issue with a group of classmates.

• • •

MARY SHELLEY
Frankenstein

*W*ITH FRANKENSTEIN, *Mary Shelley (1797–1851) created a myth as power-ful, complex, and frightening as the monster in the novel itself. The book intrigues us today as a narrative with many dimensions and interpretations. It works as the story of a scientist whose ambitions exceed his understanding, as an account of a scientific project that begins with great promise but leads to disaster, as the lament of an alien creature spurned by his maker, as the tract of an outsider besieged by his sense of difference, as the protest of a rebel striking out against a conventional and restrictive society.*

The daughter of early feminist Mary Wollstonecraft and political theorist William Godwin and the wife of Percy Bysshe Shelley, Mary Shelley began Frankenstein; or, The Modern Prometheus, *to use its full title, in the summer of 1816 after the poet Byron invited his friends at a lake resort in Switzerland to "each write a ghost story." The short piece she composed eventu-ally grew through several revisions (1818, 1823, 1831) into the novel we know today.*

The protagonist of her work, Victor Frankenstein, is an ambitious young scholar who discovers how to bestow "animation upon lifeless matter," assembles a grotesque manlike creature, and then, horrified by what he has done, abandons it the moment he brings it to life. The monster, endowed with perceptions and passions but no knowledge of its own, wanders the Alps until he learns to speak and read by spying on the residents of an isolated cottage—blind Mr. De Lacey, his daughter Agatha, his son Felix, and Felix's wife, Safie, an Arabian refugee. With knowledge comes a deepening sense of deprivation and loneliness as the creature realizes he dwells in an alien and hostile world. The following selection from the novel begins the day after the monster inadvertently terrifies the De Laceys in an attempt to communicate with them. Attacked by Felix, the monster flees the cottage where he had hoped to find friendship and kindness, complaining to Victor about the condition of his existence. – J.R.

CHAPTER 16

'Cursed, cursed creator! Why did I live? Why, in that instant, did I not extinguish the spark of existence which you had so wantonly bestowed? I know not; despair had not yet taken possession of me; my feelings were those of rage and revenge. I could with pleasure have destroyed the cottage and its inhabitants and have glutted myself with their shrieks and misery.

213

'When night came I quitted my retreat and wandered in the wood; and now, no longer restrained by the fear of discovery, I gave vent to my anguish in fearful howlings. I was like a wild beast that had broken the toils, destroying the objects that obstructed me and ranging through the wood with a staglike swiftness. Oh! What a miserable night I passed! The cold stars shone in mockery, and the bare trees waved their branches above me; now and then the sweet voice of a bird burst forth amidst the universal stillness. All, save I, were at rest or in enjoyment; I, like the arch-fiend, bore a hell within me, and finding myself unsympathized with, wished to tear up the trees, spread havoc and destruction around me, and then to have sat down and enjoyed the ruin.

'But this was a luxury of sensation that could not endure; I became fatigued with excess of bodily exertion and sank on the damp grass in the sick impotence of despair. There was none among the myriads of men that existed who would pity or assist me; and should I feel kindness towards my enemies? No; from that moment I declared ever-lasting war against the species, and more than all, against him who had formed me and sent me forth to this insupportable misery.

'The sun rose; I heard the voices of men and knew that it was impossible to return to my retreat during that day. Accordingly I hid myself in some thick underwood, determining to devote the ensuing hours to reflection on my situation.

'The pleasant sunshine and the pure air of day restored me to some   5 degree of tranquillity; and when I considered what had passed at the cottage, I could not help believing that I had been too hasty in my conclusions. I had certainly acted imprudently. It was apparent that my conversation had interested the father in my behalf, and I was a fool in having exposed my person to the horror of his children. I ought to have familiarized the old De Lacey to me, and by degrees to have discovered myself to the rest of his family, when they should have been prepared for my approach. But I did not believe my errors to be irretrievable, and after much consideration I resolved to return to the cottage, seek the old man, and by my representations win him to my party.

'These thoughts calmed me, and in the afternoon I sank into a profound sleep; but the fever of my blood did not allow me to be visited by peaceful dreams. The horrible scene of the preceding day was forever acting before my eyes; the females were flying and the enraged Felix tearing me from his father's feet. I awoke exhausted, and finding that it was already night, I crept forth from my hiding-place, and went in search of food.

'When my hunger was appeased, I directed my steps towards the well-known path that conducted to the cottage. All there was at peace. I crept into my hovel and remained in silent expectation of the accustomed hour when the family arose. That hour passed, the sun mounted high in the heavens, but the cottagers did not appear. I trembled violently, apprehending some dreadful misfortune. The inside of the cottage was dark, and I heard no motion; I cannot describe the agony of this suspense.

'Presently two countrymen passed by, but pausing near the cottage, they entered into conversation, using violent gesticulations; but I did not understand what they said, as they spoke the language of the country, which differed from that of my protectors. Soon after, however, Felix approached with another man; I was surprized, as I knew that he had not quitted the cottage that morning, and waited anxiously to discover from his discourse the meaning of these unusual appearances.

' "Do you consider," said his companion to him, "that you will be obliged to pay three months' rent and to lose the produce of your garden? I do not wish to take any unfair advantage, and I beg therefore that you will take some days to consider of your determination."

' "It is utterly useless," replied Felix; "we can never again inhabit your cottage. The life of my father is in the greatest danger, owing to the dreadful circumstance that I have related. My wife and my sister will never recover from their horror. I intreat you not to reason with me any more. Take possession of your tenement and let me fly from this place."

'Felix trembled violently as he said this. He and his companion entered the cottage, in which they remained for a few minutes, and then departed. I never saw any of the family of De Lacey more.

'I continued for the remainder of the day in my hovel in a state of utter and stupid despair. My protectors had departed and had broken the only link that held me to the world. For the first time the feelings of revenge and hatred filled my bosom, and I did not strive to control them, but allowing myself to be borne away by the stream, I bent my mind towards injury and death. When I thought of my friends, of the mild voice of De Lacey, the gentle eyes of Agatha, and the exquisite beauty of the Arabian, these thoughts vanished and a gush of tears somewhat soothed me. But again when I reflected that they had spurned and deserted me, anger returned, a rage of anger, and unable to injure anything human, I turned my fury towards inanimate objects. As night advanced I placed a variety of combustibles around the cottage, and after having destroyed every vestige of cultivation in the garden, I waited with forced impatience until the moon had sunk to commence my operations.

'As the night advanced, a fierce wind arose from the woods and quickly dispersed the clouds that had loitered in the heavens; the blast tore along like a mighty avalanche and produced a kind of insanity in my spirits that burst all bounds of reason and reflection. I lighted the dry branch of a tree and danced with fury around the devoted cottage, my eyes still fixed on the western horizon, the edge of which the moon nearly touched. A part of its orb was at length hid, and I waved my brand; it sank, and with a loud scream I fired the straw, and heath, and bushes, which I had collected. The wind fanned the fire, and the cottage was quickly enveloped by the flames, which clung to it and licked it with their forked and destroying tongues.

'As soon as I was convinced that no assistance could save any part of the habitation, I quitted the scene and sought for refuge in the woods.

'And now, with the world before me, whither should I bend my steps?   15 I resolved to fly far from the scene of my misfortunes; but to me, hated and despised, every country must be equally horrible. At length the thought of you crossed my mind. I learned from your papers that you were my father, my creator; and to whom could I apply with more fitness than to him who had given me life? Among the lessons that Felix had bestowed upon Safie, geography had not been omitted; I had learned from these the relative situations of the different countries of the earth. You had mentioned Geneva as the name of your native town, and towards this place I resolved to proceed.

'But how was I to direct myself? I knew that I must travel in a southwesterly direction to reach my destination, but the sun was my only guide. I did not know the names of the towns that I was to pass through, nor could I ask information from a single human being; but I did not despair. From you only could I hope for succour, although towards you I felt no sentiment but that of hatred. Unfeeling, heartless creator! You had endowed me with perceptions and passions and then cast me abroad an object for the scorn and horror of mankind. But on you only had I any claim for pity and redress, and from you I determined to seek that justice which I vainly attempted to gain from any other being that wore the human form.

'My travels were long and the sufferings I endured intense. It was late in autumn when I quitted the district where I had so long resided. I travelled only at night, fearful of encountering the visage of a human being. Nature decayed around me, and the sun became heatless; rain and snow poured around me; mighty rivers were frozen; the surface of the earth was hard and chill, and bare, and I found no shelter. Oh, earth! How often did I imprecate curses on the cause of my being! The mildness of my nature had fled, and all within me was turned to gall and bitterness. The nearer I approached to your habitation, the more deeply did I feel the spirit of revenge enkindled in my heart. Snow fell, and the waters were hardened, but I rested not. A few incidents now and then directed me, and I possessed a map of the country; but I often wandered wide from my path. The agony of my feelings allowed me no respite; no incident occurred from which my rage and misery could not extract its food; but a circumstance that happened when I arrived on the confines of Switzerland, when the sun had recovered its warmth and the earth again began to look green, confirmed in an especial manner the bitterness and horror of my feelings.

'I generally rested during the day and travelled only when I was secured by night from the view of man. One morning, however, finding that my path lay through a deep wood, I ventured to continue my journey after the sun had risen; the day, which was one of the first of spring, cheered even me by the loveliness of its sunshine and the balminess of the air. I felt emotions of gentleness and pleasure, that had long appeared dead, revive within me. Half surprized by the novelty of these sensations, I allowed myself to be borne away by them, and forgetting my solitude and deformity, dared to be happy. Soft tears again bedewed my cheeks, and I even raised my humid eyes with thankfulness towards the blessed sun, which bestowed such joy upon me.

'I continued to wind among the paths of the wood, until I came to its boundary which was skirted by a deep and rapid river, into which many of the trees bent their branches, now budding with the fresh spring. Here I paused, not exactly knowing what path to pursue, when I heard the sound of voices, that induced me to conceal myself under the shade of a cypress. I was scarcely hid when a young girl came running towards the spot where I was concealed, laughing, as if she ran from some one in sport. She continued her course along the precipitous sides of the river, when suddenly her foot slipped, and she fell into the rapid stream. I rushed from my hiding-place and with extreme labour from the force of the current, saved her and dragged her to shore. She was senseless, and I endeavoured by every means in my power to restore animation, when I was suddenly interrupted by the approach of a rustic, who was probably the person from whom she had playfully fled. On seeing me, he darted towards me, and tearing the girl from my arms, hastened towards the deeper parts of the wood. I followed speedily, I hardly knew why; but when the man saw me draw near, he aimed a gun, which he carried, at my body, and fired. I sank to the ground, and my injurer, with increased swiftness, escaped into the wood.

'This was then the reward of my benevolence! I had saved a human being from destruction, and as a recompense I now writhed under the miserable pain of a wound which shattered the flesh and bone. The feelings of kindness and gentleness which I had entertained but a few moments before gave place to hellish rage and gnashing of teeth. Inflamed by pain, I vowed eternal hatred and vengeance to all mankind. But the agony of my wound overcame me; my pulses paused, and I fainted.

'For some weeks I led a miserable life in the woods, endeavouring to cure the wound which I had received. The ball had entered my shoulder, and I knew not whether it had remained there or passed through; at any rate I had no means of extracting it. My sufferings were augmented also by the oppressive sense of the injustice and ingratitude of their infliction. My daily vows rose for revenge—a deep and deadly revenge, such as would alone compensate for the outrages and anguish I had endured.

'After some weeks my wound healed, and I continued my journey. The labours I endured were no longer to be alleviated by the bright sun or gentle breezes of spring; all joy was but a mockery which insulted my desolate state and made me feel more painfully that I was not made for the enjoyment of pleasure.

'But my toils now drew near a close, and in two months from this time I reached the environs of Geneva.

'It was evening when I arrived, and I retired to a hiding-place among the fields that surround it to meditate in what manner I should apply to you. I was oppressed by fatigue and hunger and far too unhappy to enjoy the gentle breezes of evening or the prospect of the sun setting behind the stupendous mountains of Jura.

'At this time a slight sleep relieved me from the pain of reflection,   25 which was disturbed by the approach of a beautiful child, who came running into the recess I had chosen, with all the sportiveness of infancy. Suddenly, as I gazed on him, an idea seized me that this little creature was unprejudiced and had lived too short a time to have imbibed a horror of deformity. If, therefore, I could seize him and educate him as my companion and friend, I should not be so desolate in this peopled earth.

'Urged by this impulse, I seized on the boy as he passed and drew him towards me. As soon as he beheld my form, he placed his hands before his eyes and uttered a shrill scream; I drew his hand forcibly from his face and said, "Child, what is the meaning of this? I do not intend to hurt you; listen to me."

'He struggled violently. "Let me go," he cried; "monster! Ugly wretch! You wish to eat me and tear me to pieces. You are an ogre. Let me go, or I will tell my papa."

' "Boy, you will never see your father again; you must come with me."

' "Hideous monster! Let me go. My papa is a syndic—he is M. Frankenstein—he will punish you. You dare not keep me."

' "Frankenstein! You belong then to my enemy—to him towards   30 whom I have sworn eternal revenge; you shall be my first victim."

'The child still struggled and loaded me with epithets which carried despair to my heart; I grasped his throat to silence him, and in a moment he lay dead at my feet.

'I gazed on my victim, and my heart swelled with exultation and hellish triumph; clapping my hands, I exclaimed, "I too can create desolation; my enemy is not invulnerable; this death will carry despair to him, and a thousand other miseries shall torment and destroy him."

'As I fixed my eyes on the child, I saw something glittering on his breast. I took it; it was a portrait of a most lovely woman. In spite of my malignity, it softened and attracted me. For a few moments I gazed with delight on her dark eyes, fringed by deep lashes, and her lovely lips; but presently my rage returned; I remembered that I was forever deprived of the delights that such beautiful creatures could bestow and that she whose resemblance I contemplated would, in regarding me, have changed that air of divine benignity to one expressive of disgust and affright.

'Can you wonder that such thoughts transported me with rage? I only wonder that at that moment, instead of venting my sensations in exclamations and agony, I did not rush among mankind and perish in the attempt to destroy them.

'While I was overcome by these feelings, I left the spot where I had committed the murder, and seeking a more secluded hiding-place, I entered a barn which had appeared to me to be empty. A woman was sleeping on some straw; she was young, not indeed so beautiful as her whose portrait I held, but of an agreeable aspect and blooming in the loveliness of youth and health. Here, I thought, is one of those whose joy-imparting smiles are bestowed on all but me. And then I bent over her and whispered, "Awake, fairest, thy lover is near—he who would give his life but to obtain one look of affection from thine eyes; my beloved, awake!"

'The sleeper stirred; a thrill of terror ran through me. Should she indeed awake, and see me, and curse me, and denounce the murderer? Thus would she assuredly act if her darkened eyes opened and she beheld me. The thought was madness; it stirred the fiend within me—not I, but she, shall suffer; the murder I have committed because I am forever robbed of all that she could give me, she shall atone. The crime had its source in her; be hers the punishment! Thanks to the lessons of Felix and the sanguinary laws of man, I had learned now to work mischief. I bent over her and placed the portrait securely in one of the folds of her dress. She moved again, and I fled.

'For some days I haunted the spot where these scenes had taken place, sometimes wishing to see you, sometimes resolved to quit the world and its miseries forever. At length I wandered towards these mountains, and have ranged through their immense recesses, consumed by a burning passion which you alone can gratify. We may not part until you have promised to comply with my requisition. I am alone and miserable; man will not associate with me; but one as deformed and horrible as myself would not deny herself to me. My companion must be of the same species and have the same defects. This being you must create.'

CHAPTER 17

The being finished speaking and fixed his looks upon me in the expectation of a reply. But I was bewildered, perplexed, and unable to arrange my ideas sufficiently to understand the full extent of his proposition. He continued, 'You must create a female for me with whom I can live in the interchange of those sympathies necessary for my being. This you alone can do, and I demand it of you as a right which you must not refuse to concede.'

The latter part of his tale had kindled anew in me the anger that had died away while he narrated his peaceful life among the cottagers, and as he said this I could no longer suppress the rage that burned within me.

'I do refuse it,' I replied; 'and no torture shall ever extort a consent from me. You may render me the most miserable of men, but you shall never make me base in my own eyes. Shall I create another like yourself, whose joint wickedness might desolate the world? Begone! I have answered you; you may torture me, but I will never consent.'

'You are in the wrong,' replied the fiend; 'and instead of threatening, I am content to reason with you. I am malicious because I am miserable. Am I not shunned and hated by all mankind? You, my creator, would tear me to pieces and triumph; remember that, and tell me why I should pity man more than he pities me? You would not call it murder if you could precipitate me into one of those ice-rifts and destroy my frame, the work of your own hands. Shall I respect man when he condemns me? Let him live with me in the interchange of kindness, and instead of injury I would bestow every benefit upon him with tears of gratitude at his acceptance. But that cannot be; the human senses are insurmountable barriers to our union. Yet mine shall not be the submission of abject slavery. I will revenge my injuries; if I cannot inspire love, I will cause fear, and chiefly towards you my arch-enemy, because my creator, do I swear inextinguishable hatred. Have a care; I will work at your destruction, nor finish until I desolate your heart, so that you shall curse the hour of your birth.'

A fiendish rage animated him as he said this; his face was wrinkled into   5
contortions too horrible for human eyes to behold; but presently he calmed himself and proceeded, 'I intended to reason. This passion is detrimental to me, for you do not reflect that *you* are the cause of its excess. If any being felt emotions of benevolence towards me, I should return them a hundred and a hundredfold; for that one creature's sake I would make peace with the whole kind! But I now indulge in dreams of bliss that cannot be realized. What I ask of you is reasonable and moderate; I demand a creature of another sex, but as hideous as myself; the gratification is small, but it is all that I can receive, and it shall content me. It is true, we shall be monsters, cut off from all the world; but on that account we shall be more attached to one another. Our lives will not be happy, but they will be harmless and free from the misery I now feel. Oh! My creator, make me happy; let me feel gratitude towards you for one benefit! Let me see that I excite the sympathy of some existing thing; do not deny me my request!'

I was moved.

QUESTIONING THE TEXT

1. What role does nature play in these chapters? How does the natural environment affect the monster?
2. What rationale does the monster offer for killing a child and implicating a young woman in the murder?

MAKING CONNECTIONS

3. Does Frankenstein's fear of creating a female companion for his monster relate in any way to the fears of the neo-Luddites described in Daniel Grossman's article (starting on p. 261)?
4. At an earlier point in the novel, Victor Frankenstein warns that knowledge is dangerous: "how much happier that man is who believes his native town to be the world, than he who aspires to become greater than his nature will allow."' Freewrite upon this idea after reading the essays in this chapter by Freeman J. Dyson (p. 222) and Lewis Thomas (p. 233).

JOINING THE CONVERSATION

5. With a group of classmates, discuss the monster's feeling of alienation. Does it make sense to compare his situation to that of other individuals or groups considered "different" in society? Then write a brief position paper about Frankenstein's monster as a symbol of what it means to be different. Is the comparison convincing? Why?
6. Write a report about a technology, a product, or even a law that has had effects (not necessarily harmful ones) different from those originally anticipated. Describe in detail both the expectations and the actual results. Then try to account for those differences.
7. Annotate the margins of the selection to highlight those places that examine the responsibilities Frankenstein bears to and for his creation. Then write an exploratory essay on the obligations—if any—that inventors of new technologies have to society in general.
8. Some critics suggest that *Frankenstein* reflects an early view of industrialization as a monstrous creation out of control. Use the library to discover what changes the industrial revolution was imposing on the landscape of England during the nineteenth century. Try also to determine how favorably people regarded the changes they were seeing, such as the building of factories and railroads. This subject is complex enough to support a full-scale research paper. Give it a try.

FREEMAN J. DYSON
Engineers' Dreams

NOT ALL SCIENTISTS and engineers are Dr. Frankensteins. Nor are all failures of technology the threat we see in Mary Shelley's novel or in some interpretations drawn from it.

In the following reading Freeman J. Dyson (b. 1923), a distinguished physicist and philosopher who teaches at Princeton University, writes about the virtual impossibility of predicting the directions of technological progress. Even the greatest minds and shrewdest organizations sometimes cannot see beyond not-so-distant horizons. Dyson gives us interesting perspectives on two familiar technological achievements of our time, the computer and space travel.

"Engineers' Dreams" is a chapter from Dyson's book Infinite in All Directions (1989) and was originally a lecture given in Scotland in 1985. I chose this selection as a counterpoint to Frankenstein, that is, as a less gloomy assessment of human possibilities. Dyson, as you see, remains critical of some technologies, but traces failures to predictable human behaviors—not to monsters haunting our imaginations.   – J.R.

There are two ways to predict the progress of technology. One way is economic forecasting, the other way is science fiction. Economic forecasting makes predictions by extrapolating curves of growth from the past into the future. Science fiction makes a wild guess and leaves the judgment of its plausibility to the reader. Economic forecasting is useful for predicting the future up to about ten years ahead. Beyond ten years it rapidly becomes meaningless. Beyond ten years the quantitative changes which the forecast assesses are usually sidetracked or made irrelevant by qualitative changes in the rules of the game. Qualitative changes are produced by human clever-ness, the invention of pocket calculators destroying the market for slide rules, or by human stupidity, the mistakes of a few people at Three Mile Island destroying the market for nuclear power stations. Neither cleverness nor stupidity is predictable. For the future beyond ten years ahead, science fiction is a more useful guide than forecasting. But science fiction does not pretend to predict. It tells us only what might happen, not what will happen. It deals in possibilities, not in probabilities. And the most important develop-ments of the future are usually missed both by the forecasters and by the fiction writers. Economic forecasting misses the real future because it has too short a range; fiction misses the future because it has too little imagination.

I took the title of this chapter from one of my favorite books, *Engineers' Dreams* by Willy Ley. Ley's book is concerned with the dreams of the 1930s, the time when Ley was a young man. Ley was a frustrated rocket engineer who later became a successful writer. The dreams which are recorded in his book are mostly projects of civil engineering, enormous dams, tunnels, bridges, artificial lakes and artificial islands. The interesting thing about them is that they are today totally dead. Nobody would want to build them today even if we could afford it. They are too grandiose, too inflexible, too slow. The rules of the political game have changed three or four times in the decades since Willy Ley wrote his book. History passed these dreams by. We do not any longer find it reasonable to think of flooding half of the forests of Zaire in order to provide water for irrigating the deserts of Chad. Instead of huge dams and power stations, soft drinks and machine guns became the hot items in the commerce of Central Africa. Instead of traveling in ships on inland seaways, the people of Africa and South America find it more convenient to use airstrips and light aircraft.

Perhaps it is possible to discern a persistent pattern in the rise and fall of engineering technologies. The pattern resembles in some ways the rise and fall of species in the evolution of plants and animals. A technology during its phase of rapid growth and spectacular success is usually small, quick and agile. As it grows mature it becomes settled and conservative, prevented by the inertia of size from reacting quickly to sudden shocks. When a technology has grown so big and sluggish that it can no longer bend with the winds of change, it is ripe for extinction. Extinction may be long delayed or avoided in sheltered corners, but an overripe technology cannot regain its lost youth. New small and quick alternatives will be waiting to occupy the ecological niche left vacant by the decline of the old. This rhythm, which repeats itself in the evolution of species over periods of millions of years, seems to run about a hundred thousand times faster in the evolution of human technology.

The technology of computers is a particularly clear example of the evolutionary pattern. I am old enough to have been present almost at the creation of computer technology. I was in Princeton in the late 1940s and early 1950s when John von Neumann was building our famous JOHNNIAC computer. Von Neumann was a great mathematician and had the reputation at that time of being the cleverest man in the world. He was supposed to be the intellectual force driving the whole development of computers. He was a great thinker and a great entrepreneur. And yet he totally misjudged the role that computers were to play in human affairs.

I remember a talk that Von Neumann gave at Princeton around 1950, 5 describing the glorious future which he then saw for his computers. Most of the people that he hired for his computer project in the early days were meteorologists. Meteorology was the big thing on his horizon. He said, as soon as we have good computers, we shall be able to divide the phenomena of meteorology cleanly into two categories, the stable and the unstable. The unstable phenomena are those which are upset by small disturbances, the stable phenomena are those which are resilient to small disturbances. He said, as soon as we have some large computers working, the problems of meteorology will be solved. All processes that are stable we shall predict. All processes that are unstable we shall control. He imagined that we needed only to identify the points in space and time at which unstable processes originated, and then a few airplanes carrying smoke generators could fly to those points and introduce the appropriate small disturbances to make the unstable processes flip into the desired directions. A central committee of computer experts and meteorologists would tell the airplanes where to go in order to make sure that no rain would fall on the Fourth of July picnic. This was John von Neumann's dream. This, and the hydrogen bomb, were the main practical benefits which he saw arising from the development of computers.

The meteorologists who came to work with Von Neumann knew better. They did not believe in the dream. They only wanted to understand the weather, not to control it. They had a hard enough time trying to understand it. They tried especially hard to predict a particular hurricane which came up from the Gulf of Mexico and passed close by Princeton in the fall of 1949. Again and again they set the initial conditions in the Gulf of Mexico and tried to predict the hurricane for several years after it happened. So far as I remember, they never did succeed in getting the hurricane on the computer to end up anywhere near Princeton. Now another thirty-five years have gone by, and we have built four more generations of computers, and still we are not doing very well with the prediction of hurricanes. Nobody any longer believes seriously in the possibility of controlling the weather.

What went wrong? Why was Von Neumann's dream such a total failure? The dream was based on a fundamental misunderstanding of the nature of fluid motions. It is not true that we can divide fluid motions cleanly into those that are predictable and those that are controllable. Nature is as usual more imaginative than we are. There is a large class of classical dynamical systems, including non-linear electrical circuits as well as fluids, which easily fall into a mode of behavior that is described by the word "chaotic." A chaotic motion is generally neither predictable nor controllable. It is unpredictable because a small disturbance will produce exponentially growing perturbation of the motion. It is uncontrollable because small disturbances lead only to other chaotic motions and not to any stable and predictable alternative. Von Neumann's mistake was to imagine that every unstable motion could be nudged into a stable motion by small pushes and pulls applied at the right places. The same mistake is still frequently made by economists and social planners, not to mention Marxist historians.

But the misunderstanding of fluid dynamics was not Von Neumann's worst mistake. He not only guessed wrong about the problems to which computers could be usefully applied. He also guessed wrong about the evolution of the computer itself. Right up to the end of his life, he was thinking of computers as big, expensive and rare, to be cared for by teams of experts and owned by prestigious institutions like Princeton and Los Alamos. He missed totally the real wave of the future which started to roll when outfits like Texas Instruments and Hewlett Packard got into the game. The real wave of the future was to make computers small, cheap and widely available. Nowhere in Von Neumann's writings does one find the shadow of a hint that computers might be sold for a few hundred dollars and be owned by teenagers and housewives. Never did he imagine the flexibility and versatility that computers could achieve once they became small and cheap. He did not dream of the computer-toy industry, the chess-playing machine that fits inside a chessboard and plays a tolerably expert game, the endless varieties of computer-simulated pinball and Dungeons and Dragons. He failed altogether to foresee the rise of the software industry, the buying and selling of computer programs which would help the housewife to organize her recipes and help the teenager to correct the spelling of her homework.

I have a friend, a young American physicist, who spent a year doing theoretical physics in the Soviet Union. He likes to go to the Soviet Union, not because it is a good place to do physics, but because it is a good place to observe the human comedy. When he went back to Leningrad recently for a shorter visit, he received a proposal of marriage and was called in twice for questioning by the KGB, all within the first week. He speaks fluent Russian, and the KGB people find it difficult to believe he is not a spy. He tells me that there is now a flourishing black market in software in the Soviet Union. Designer blue jeans and tape recorders are passé; the new symbols of status among the trendy youth are floppy disks. But there is a shortage of hardware to go with the software. It is not so easy to pick up an IBM PC from a smuggler hanging around a street corner on the Nevskii Prospekt. My friend considers that we in the West are missing a great opportunity to disrupt the economy of the Evil Empire. He says we ought to be flooding the Soviet Union with personal computers and software. This would give a boost to all kinds of private and semi-legal enterprises with which the official state enterprises could not easily compete. The official economy is still living in the Von Neumann era, with big expensive computers under central control. My friend believes that small-computer technology would flow around the apparatus of the state-controlled economy. He finds it more plausible to dream of drowning the Soviet party apparatchiki in a flood of Macintoshes than to dream of starving them into submission with a technological blockade. Small modern computers and software are good tools for eroding the machinery of totalitarian government. That is another engineer's dream which may or may not come true.

I now leave the subject of computers and move to an area with which I am more familiar, the exploration of space. In January 1986 I had the great   10 joy of sitting with the space engineers at the Jet Propulsion Laboratory (JPL) in California while they watched the pictures come in from the Voyager spacecraft encountering Uranus. That was not only a great day for science but a masterpiece of good engineering. The most impressive aspect of the operation was that not everything went smoothly. Several times the engineers had serious problems. Every time there was a problem, they were prepared for it. They had thought ahead. They had Plan B ready as soon as Plan A ran into trouble. At a tense moment at the beginning of the Uranus encounter, an urgent call for help arrived from the Europeans tracking their Giotto spacecraft on its way to Halley's Comet. The Giotto spacecraft had slipped. Its high-gain antenna beam was no longer pointing at Earth. The Europeans had lost contact with it. There was serious danger that the whole Giotto mission would be lost if they could not quickly regain contact. So they telephoned JPL.

JPL runs the Deep Space Net with the three most sensitive receivers in the world, the only receivers capable of picking up the Voyager signals from Uranus. As it happened, the Deep Space Net dish at Goldstone in California was the only one that could point at the Giotto spacecraft at that moment, and it was also the only one that could point at Uranus. So the JPL engineers changed their schedule so as to hand Voyager over as soon as possible to the Deep Space Net dish in Australia, and then pointed the Goldstone dish at Giotto. Goldstone picked up the feeble signal from Giotto's omnidirectional antenna and transmitted the order to Giotto to reorient the high-gain antenna to the direction of Earth. Within half an hour the high-gain signal from Giotto came in loud and clear, and the control was handed back to Europe. Plan B was immediately put into effect. The Voyager encounter sequence was reprogrammed so as to compensate for the Giotto interruption without losing any scientific data.

The JPL engineers managed to perform another new trick at Uranus which they had not done at Jupiter and Saturn. After passing by Uranus, the spacecraft went behind the planet as seen from the Earth. It was behind Uranus for eighty-three minutes before it reappeared on the other side. During the whole of this hour-long eclipse, the Voyager high-gain antenna was kept accurately pointed at the edge of Uranus, so that the transmitted signal might be refracted around Uranus within the Uranus atmosphere and from there continue on its way to Earth. The signal coming from Voyager to Earth, after creeping around the planet through the Uranus atmosphere, was detected from beginning to end of the eclipse. As a result, we now have precise knowledge of the structure of the Uranus atmosphere down to a pressure of three Earth atmospheres. This at a distance of 2 billion miles with a spacecraft which was launched nine years ago. All of us who were there in the room at JPL were deeply impressed. That was an engineer's dream which came true. We agreed to meet again at JPL on August 25, 1989, for the encounter with Neptune.

Three days after the Uranus encounter, I was flying home to Princeton on a commercial jet with a news program on the television screen and saw the Shuttle blow up. What a sad contrast! The Voyager team at JPL with their superb competence and their triumphant success; the Shuttle, stumbling from one misfortune to another until in the end this last disaster did not come as a surprise. Immediately I thought of the two explorers, the Norwegian Amundsen and the British Scott, who went to the South Pole in the summer of 1911 to 1912. Another of my favorite books is *The Worst Journey in the World,* by Apsley Cherry-Garrard, one of the survivors of the Scott expedition. Cherry-Garrard ends his book with an overall assessment of the expedition in which he had struggled and suffered ten years earlier. Here is his verdict:

> In the broad perspective opened up by ten years' distance, I see not one journey to the pole, but two, in startling contrast one to another. On the one hand, Amundsen going straight there, getting there first, and returning without the loss of a single man, and without having put any greater strain on himself and his men than was all in the day's work of polar exploration. Nothing more businesslike could be imagined. On the other hand, our expedition, running appalling risks, performing prodigies of superhuman endurance, achieving immortal renown, commemorated in august cathedral sermons and by public statues, yet reaching the pole only to find our terrible journey superfluous, and leaving our best men dead on the ice. . . . Any rather conservative whaling captain might have refused to make Scott's experiment with motor transport, ponies and man-hauling, and stuck to the dogs; and it was this quite commonplace choice that sent Amundsen so gaily to the pole and back, with no abnormal strain on men or dogs, and no great hardship either. He never pulled a mile from start to finish.

That is, in a few words, the story of Amundsen and Scott, Amundsen the explorer who knew his business, and Scott the tragic hero who didn't. Almost every word of Cherry-Garrard's verdict applies equally well to Voyager and Shuttle. It is important to remember that there was not one expedition but two. The British in 1913 made Scott into a national hero and ignored Amundsen. The Americans now are making the seven astronauts into national heroes and are ignoring Voyager. Amundsen's dog-sleds in 1911 took him gaily to the pole, just as the Titan-Centaur launcher in 1977 sent Voyager gaily on its way to Uranus. Nobody said in England in 1913, "Wasn't it stupid of Scott not to use dog-sleds?" and nobody in the official board of inquiry into the Shuttle accident said, "Wasn't it stupid of NASA not to use Titan-Centaur?" Most of the payloads which the Shuttle is supposed to carry into orbit could have been launched more conveniently by Titan-Centaur without risking any lives. But NASA decided, after Voyager was on its way, to shut down the production of Titan-Centaur. Scott happened to dislike dogs and NASA happened to dislike Titan-Centaur. Titans occasionally blow up too, but when they blow up it is not a major tragedy.

There are some missions which have human activity in space as a   15 primary purpose. For these the Shuttle was an appropriate vehicle. But many missions, and the fatal Challenger mission in particular, carried payloads having nothing to do with human activity. If you want to launch a military or commercial communications satellite, it is much more convenient not to have people on board the launcher. You need to put communications satellites or scientific spacecraft into a variety of orbits, but the exigencies of landing with a human crew restrict the orbit that the Shuttle can reach. When you carry people, you lose flexibility in the choice of orbit as well as in the time of launching.

What should we be learning from the misfortunes of the Shuttle? I hope the American public will not be led to believe that the misfortunes arose merely from poorly designed O-rings. The lessons we ought to be learning are similar to the lessons we have learned from the failure of Von Neumann's dreams of weather control. It was stupid of Von Neumann to push his computers toward one grandiose objective and ignore the tremendous diversity of more modest applications to which computers would naturally adapt themselves. We have learned that the right way to develop a computer industry is to find out first what the customers need and then design the machines to do it. The customers want many kinds of things, so we build many kinds of computers. Most of the customers have modest needs, and therefore most of the computers are small and cheap. These lessons are just as valid in space as they are here on the ground. Customers' needs should drive the industry, not engineers' dreams. The Shuttle was an engineer's dream.

The fundamental mistake of the Shuttle program was the dogmatic insistence of NASA that this single launch system was to take care of all the customers regardless of their needs. Few of the customers wanted the Shuttle. The space-science community hated the Shuttle because it deprived us of the frequent and flexible launch opportunities that science requires. The military hated the Shuttle for similar reasons. The industrial customers, who need the Shuttle mostly for launching communication satellites, hated it less, but they too would have preferred a choice between several launch systems with more flexible schedules. The insistence that [the] Shuttle be the sole launch system was directly responsible for the disaster of January 1986. If alternative launch systems had been available for launching unmanned satellites, there would have been no strong pressure to keep the Shuttle on schedule and no strong reason to fly the Shuttle in bad weather. If the Shuttle had been used only for the missions for which human passengers were essential, it could have waited for good weather and the crew of the Challenger would still be alive and well.

It is interesting to try to imagine what kind of space program we would have today if the program had been driven by customers' needs rather than by engineers' dreams. First of all, we would have kept the passenger business and the freight business separate. The railroads learned long ago that it does not pay to carry passengers on a freight train or to carry coal on a passenger train. If passengers and coal were forced to travel together, the railroads would be in even worse shape than the Shuttle. The launch systems existing in the 1970s, the Scout, Delta and Titan with a variety of upper stages, were well suited to the variety of customers requiring freight transportation in space. We could have satisfied the customers' needs in the freight business merely by keeping these systems in operation. A customer-driven freight business in space would not need any new kinds of launcher. The customers have learned to increase the profitability of space operations by applying new technology to the payloads, not to the launchers. It is far more profitable to use technology to increase the value per pound of the payload rather than to try to decrease the cost per pound of the launch. A customer-driven space program, so far as the freight business is concerned, would still be using the old Scout, Delta and Titan launchers, with the possible addition of a new ultra-light system designed to orbit small payloads as cheaply as possible.

The more difficult and controversial question is, what would a customer-driven manned space program look like? What are the customers' needs for passenger transportation in space? The customers in this case are the astronauts. What kind of a vehicle do the astronauts really need? Here we can again learn a useful lesson from the past. I am so old that I can remember the days when the *Queen Mary* and the *Queen Elizabeth* were carrying passengers in large numbers across the Atlantic and making large profits for the Cunard-White Star steamship company. At that time the two *Queens* were the largest and fastest ships and held the speed record for Atlantic crossings. The British public was proud of its steamships and believed that the *Queens* were profitable because they were the biggest and the fastest ships afloat. But Lord Cunard, the chairman of the steamship line, said that this belief was the opposite of the truth. Lord Cunard said that his steamship line had never intended to build the biggest and fastest ships afloat. The *Queens* were in fact designed to be the smallest and slowest ships that could do what the customers needed, namely, to provide with two ships a reliable weekly service across the Atlantic. They were profitable because they were the slowest and smallest ships that could do the job. The fact that they incidentally broke speed records had nothing to do with it. And the Boeing 707 eventually drove them out of business because it was smaller and could do the job better.

A customer-driven Shuttle would be like the *Queen Mary* and the *Queen Elizabeth*. It would be the smallest and cheapest vehicle that could provide the astronauts with a flexible and reliable service into orbit. It would not need to carry freight. It would not need to carry a crew of seven. It would not need to be heavy. It would not need to strain the limits of rocket and engine technology. On the other hand, it should be in some respects more capable than the existing Shuttle. It should be able to stay in space with its crew for a month. It should possess a larger margin of performance, so that it could reach a greater variety of orbits. And it should be capable of rendezvous and docking with other spacecraft in orbit. A Shuttle with these characteristics is what the astronauts need, and it could probably have been provided more quickly and more cheaply than the existing Shuttle. Above all, what the astronauts need is flexibility. Nobody can predict what they will want to do ten or twenty years ahead. To give them flexibility, the Shuttle should be like a high-performance two-seater airplane, small and light and carrying a big reserve of fuel, capable of jumping to take advantage of unexpected opportunities.

We saw in the operation of the Voyager fly-by at Uranus what flexibility means. The conditions for taking pictures of the moons of Uranus were far less favorable than the conditions which Voyager enjoyed at the encounter with Saturn five years earlier. Sunlight at Uranus is four times dimmer than at Saturn. Longer exposures were required in order to collect the same amount of light. The radio signals received at Earth from Voyager were four times fainter. The instruments on board Voyager were the same at Uranus as they were at Saturn, only five years older. Nevertheless, the pictures of the Uranus moons achieved an angular resolution twice as good as the pictures of the moons of Saturn.

How was this possible? How could the angular resolution be improved by a factor of two without changing a single detail of the hardware? The improvement was possible because the Voyager operation was controlled by on-board software which was almost completely reprogrammable. The software could be, and was, reprogrammed by the JPL engineers at a distance of 2 billion miles. The JPL engineers had five years between Saturn and Uranus to think of improvements and to redesign the software. The new software allowed Voyager to compensate more accurately for the motion of the spacecraft during the taking of the pictures, and the better compensation resulted in better angular resolution. Flexibility means being able to teach an old spacecraft new tricks. When we were sitting at JPL on January 25, 1986, watching the raw unprocessed pictures of Uranus' moon Miranda come in, as sharp and as beautiful as pictures published in *National Geographic,* we knew that flexibility had paid off. It was appropriate that this moon of Uranus happened to be named after the young heroine of Shakespeare's play, *The Tempest.* In the play, Miranda is the one who exclaims: "O brave new world, That has such creatures in it!" And we were sitting there, seeing her Brave New World for the first time.

When we pay our respect to the dead and build our public monuments to the crew of the Challenger,* we should not forget Voyager and the

_____

respect to . . . Challenger: For President Ronald Reagan's speech about the *Challenger* disaster, see p. 280.

engineers who built her. It is good that we give honor to the brave victims of our stupidity, just as we gave honor to Robert Scott. But we should also give honor to those who were clever and survived, to Roald Amundsen and his dog team, to the JPL engineers who used their brains and reprogrammed the Voyager software 2 billion miles away to give us our first glimpse of a new world.

QUESTIONING THE TEXT

1. Dyson mentions a number of grandiose engineering projects that never reached the construction stage. Can you recall reading about any such projects that fired the imagination but that never became reality? Can you think of any technological projects currently on the drawing board that may not be built?

2. Dyson sketches out the evolutionary process of a technology as follows: a phase of rapid growth, a mature phase, and a sluggish phase where technological mass and lethargy lead to extinction. Can you apply this model to any familiar piece of technology or even to non-technological movements? Record your response in a reading log if you keep one.

3. Were you surprised by the harshness of Dyson's criticism of the space shuttle? Had you heard such criticisms before? Do you think it is possible for the public to make intelligent assessments of such technology, which they pay for through their taxes?

MAKING CONNECTIONS

4. If Dyson is correct that failed adventures like the *Challenger* disaster receive more attention than successful exploits like the *Voyager* space probe, what are the implications for public support of scientific inquiries? Are we in danger of believing too readily in the more dramatic versions of technological failure (Frankenstein's monster, the ecologists' nuclear winter) and too little in the more mundane but substantial contributions that science makes to our lives? Explore this question in an essay, taking time first to read and compare the essays by Lewis Thomas and Daniel Grossman (starting on pp. 233 and 261, respectively).

5. Read Peggy Orenstein's "Get a Cyberlife" (starting on p. 251), and then describe some of the applications of Virtual Reality that might be operating twenty-five years from now. Compare your predictions with those made by others in your class.

JOINING THE CONVERSATION

6. To Victor Frankenstein, scientific discovery provides "continual food for wonder and awe." Describe your reaction to some memorable encounter with an engineer's dream made real.

7. Dyson's essay, written just before the dissolution of the Soviet empire, contains a suggestion from a young physicist that flooding totalitarian regimes with small computers would effectively destroy the central control that these governments had. In light of subsequent events, the prediction seems a perceptive insight into the inability of political systems to control channels of information in an electronic age. In what ways can technology itself be politically subversive? Write a short exploratory essay on this theme.

8. With a group of classmates, discuss how Dyson's analysis of the space shuttle's excessive size, complexity, and inflexibility might apply to other technologies or institutions that you believe don't work very well. Then write a brief report detailing such failings and how they might be corrected.

AFTER GRADUATING from Princeton University and Harvard Medical School, Lewis Thomas (b. 1913) served on the staff of many important hospitals and medical schools, as dean of medicine at Newfoundland University, and as president of the Sloane-Kettering Cancer Institute in New York City. At the invitation of a journal editor, he began writing the essays for a wide-ranging audience that have been collected in Lives of a Cell, *winner of a National Book Award, and several other volumes, including* The Medusa and the Snail; Etcetera, Etcetera; *and* The Youngest Science. *In the following essay, Thomas opens by considering the question of hubris, that overreaching pride that leads humans to start "doing things reserved for the gods." This pride is, of course, central to Victor Frankenstein's quest—and to his fall. Thomas puts a different spin on the word* hubris, *however, and in doing so offers a complex answer to the question "are there some kinds of information . . . human beings are really better off not having?"*

I chose Thomas's piece because he raises the specter of Frankensteinian destruction in the opening paragraph, because his argument is so clear and succinct, and because he allows us to challenge and question science without rejecting it. Most of all, I admire the way Thomas makes his work accessible to nonscientists like me—and thus allows me in on some of the conversation animating science today. — A.L.

The code word for criticism of science and scientists these days is "hubris." Once you've said that word, you've said it all; it sums up, in a word, all of today's apprehensions and misgivings in the public mind—not just about what is perceived as the insufferable attitude of the scientists themselves but, enclosed in the same word, what science and technology are perceived to be doing to make this century, this near to its ending, turn out so wrong.

"Hubris" is a powerful word, containing layers of powerful meaning, derived from a very old world, but with a new life of its own, growing way beyond the limits of its original meaning. Today, it is strong enough to carry the full weight of disapproval for the cast of mind that thought up atomic fusion and fission as ways of first blowing up and later heating cities as well as the attitudes which led to strip-mining, offshore oil wells, Kepone, food additives, SSTs, and the tiny spherical particles of plastic recently discovered clogging the waters of the Sargasso Sea.

The biomedical sciences are now caught up with physical science and technology in the same kind of critical judgment, with the same pejorative word. Hubris is responsible, it is said, for the whole biological revolution. It is hubris that has given us the prospects of behavior control, psychosurgery, fetal research, heart transplants, the cloning of prominent politicians from bits of their own eminent tissue, iatrogenic disease, overpopulation, and recombinant DNA. This last, the new technology that permits the stitching of one creature's genes into the DNA of another, to make hybrids, is currently cited as the ultimate example of hubris. It is hubris for man to manufacture a hybrid on his own.

So now we are back to the first word again, from "hybrid" to "hubris," and the hidden meaning of two beings joined unnaturally together by man is somehow retained. Today's joining is straight out of Greek mythology: it is the combining of man's capacity with the special prerogative of the gods, and it is really in this sense of outrage that the word "hubris" is being used today. That is what the word has grown into, a warning, a code word, a shorthand signal from the language itself: if man starts doing things reserved for the gods, deifying himself, the outcome will be something worse for him, symbolically, than the litters of wild boars and domestic sows were for the ancient Romans.

To be charged with hubris is therefore an extremely serious matter, and not to be dealt with by murmuring things about antiscience and antiintellectualism, which is what many of us engaged in science tend to do these days. The doubts about our enterprise have their origin in the most profound kind of human anxiety. If we are right and the critics are wrong, then it has to be that the word "hubris" is being mistakenly employed, that this is not what we are up to, that there is, for the time being anyway, a fundamental misunderstanding of science.

I suppose there is one central question to be dealt with, and I am not at all sure how to deal with it, although I am quite certain about my own answer to it. It is this: are there some kinds of information leading to some sorts of knowledge that human beings are really better off not having? Is there a limit to scientific inquiry not set by what is knowable but by what we *ought* to be knowing? Should we stop short of learning about some things, for fear of what we, or someone, will do with the knowledge? My own answer is a flat no, but I must confess that this is an intuitive response and I am neither inclined nor trained to reason my way through it.

There has been some effort, in and out of scientific quarters, to make recombinant DNA into the issue on which to settle this argument. Proponents of this line of research are accused of pure hubris, of assuming the rights of gods, of arrogance and outrage; what is more, they confess themselves to be in the business of making live hybrids with their own hands. The mayor of Cambridge and the attorney general of New York have both been advised to put a stop to it, forthwith.

5

It is not quite the same sort of argument, however, as the one about limiting knowledge, although this is surely part of it. The knowledge is already here, and the rage of the argument is about its application in technology. Should DNA for making certain useful or interesting proteins be incorporated into *E. coli* plasmids or not? Is there a risk of inserting the wrong sort of toxins or hazardous viruses, and then having the new hybrid organisms spread beyond the laboratory? Is this a technology for creating new varieties of pathogens, and should it be stopped because of this?

If the argument is held to this level, I can see no reason why it cannot be settled, by reasonable people. We have learned a great deal about the handling of dangerous microbes in the last century, although I must say that the opponents of recombinant-DNA research tend to downgrade this huge body of information. At one time or another, agents as hazardous as those of rabies, psittacosis, plague, and typhus have been dealt with by investigators in secure laboratories, with only rare instances of self-infection of the investigators themselves, and no instances at all of epidemics. It takes some high imagining to postulate the creation of brand-new pathogens so wild and voracious as to spread from equally secure laboratories to endanger human life at large, as some of the arguers are now maintaining.

But this is precisely the trouble with the recombinant-DNA problem: 10
it has become an emotional issue, with too many irretrievably lost tempers on both sides. It has lost the sound of a discussion of technological safety, and begins now to sound like something else, almost like a religious controversy, and here it is moving toward the central issue: are there some things in science we should not be learning about?

There is an inevitably long list of hard questions to follow this one, beginning with the one which asks whether the mayor of Cambridge should be the one to decide, first off.

Maybe we'd be wiser, all of us, to back off before the recombinant-DNA issue becomes too large to cope with. If we're gong to have a fight about it, let it be confined to the immediate issue of safety and security, of the recombinants now under consideration, and let us by all means have regulations and guidelines to assure the public safety wherever these are indicated or even suggested. But if it is possible let us stay off that question about limiting human knowledge. It is too loaded, and we'll simply not be able to cope with it.

By this time it will have become clear that I have already taken sides in the matter, and my point of view is entirely prejudiced. This is true, but with a qualification. I am not so much in favor of recombinant-DNA research as I am opposed to the opposition to this line of inquiry. As a longtime student of infectious-disease agents I do not take kindly the declarations that we do not know how to keep from catching things in laboratories, much less how to keep them from spreading beyond the laboratory walls. I believe we learned a lot about this sort of thing, long ago. Moreover, I regard it as a form of hubris-in-reverse to claim that man can make deadly pathogenic microorganisms so easily. In my view, it takes a long time and a great deal of interliving before a microbe can become a successful pathogen. Pathogenicity is, in a sense, a highly skilled trade, and only a tiny minority of all the numberless tons of microbes on the earth has ever been involved itself in it; most bacteria are busy with their own business, browsing and recycling the rest of life. Indeed, pathogenicity often seems to me a sort of biological accident in which signals are misdirected by the microbe or misinterpreted by the host, as in the case of endotoxin, or in which the intimacy between host and microbe is of such long standing that a form of molecular mimicry becomes possible, as in the case of diphtheria toxin. I do not believe that by simply putting together new combinations of genes one can create creatures as highly skilled and adapted for dependence as a pathogen must be, any more than I have ever believed that microbial life from the moon or Mars could possibly make a living on this planet.

But, as I said, I'm not at all sure this is what the argument is really about. Behind it is that other discussion, which I wish we would not have to become enmeshed in.

I cannot speak for the physical sciences, which have moved an immense distance in this century by any standard, but it does seem to me that in the biological and medical sciences we are still far too ignorant to begin making judgments about what sorts of things we should be learning or not learning. To the contrary, we ought to be grateful for whatever snatches we can get hold of, and we ought to be out there on a much larger scale than today's, looking for more.

We should be very careful with that word "hubris," and make sure it is not used when not warranted. There is a great danger in applying it to the search for knowledge. The application of knowledge is another matter, and there is hubris in plenty in our technology, but I do not believe that looking for new information about nature, at whatever level, can possibly be called unnatural. Indeed, if there is any single attribute of human beings, apart from language, which distinguishes them from all other creatures on earth, it is their insatiable, uncontrollable drive to learn things and then to exchange the information with others of the species. Learning is what we do, when you think about it. I cannot think of a human impulse more difficult to govern.

But I can imagine lots of reasons for trying to govern it. New information about nature is very likely, at the outset, to be upsetting to someone or other. The recombinant-DNA line of research is already upsetting, not because of the dangers now being argued about but because it is disturbing, in a fundamental way, to face the fact that the genetic machinery in control of the planet's life can be fooled around with so easily. We do not like the idea that anything so fixed and stable as a species line can be changed. The notion that genes can be taken out of one genome and inserted in another is unnerving. Classical mythology is peopled with mixed beings—part man, part animal or plant—and most of them are associated with tragic stories. Recombinant DNA is a reminder of bad dreams.

The easiest decision for society to make in matters of this kind is to appoint an agency, or a commission, or a subcommittee within an agency to look into the problem and provide advice. And the easiest course for a committee to take, when confronted by any process that appears to be disturbing people or making them uncomfortable, is to recommend that it be stopped, at least for the time being.

I can easily imagine such a committee, composed of unimpeachable public figures, arriving at the decision that the time is not quite ripe for further exploration of the transplantation of genes, that we should put this off for a while, maybe until next century, and get on with other affairs that make us less discomfited. Why not do science on something more popular, say, how to get solar energy more cheaply? Or mental health?

The trouble is, it would be very hard to stop once this line was begun. 20 There are, after all, all sorts of scientific inquiry that are not much liked by one constituency or another, and we might soon find ourselves with crowded rosters, panels, standing committees, set up in Washington for the appraisal, and then the regulation, of research. Not on grounds of the possible value and usefulness of the new knowledge, mind you, but for guarding society against scientific hubris, against the kinds of knowledge we're better off without.

It would be absolutely irresistible as a way of spending time, and people would form long queues for membership. Almost anything would be fair game, certainly anything to do with genetics, anything relating to population control, or, on the other side, research on aging. Very few fields would get by, except perhaps for some, like mental health, in which nobody really expects anything much to happen, surely nothing new or disturbing.

The research areas in the greatest trouble would be those already containing a sense of bewilderment and surprise, with discernible prospects of upheaving present dogmas.

It is hard to predict how science is going to turn out, and if it is really good science it is impossible to predict. This is in the nature of the enterprise. If the things to be found are actually new, they are by definition unknown in advance, and there is no way of telling in advance where a really new line of inquiry will lead. You cannot make choices in this matter, selecting things you think you're going to like and shutting off the lines that make for discomfort. You either have science or you don't, and if you have it you are obliged to accept the surprising and disturbing pieces of information, even the overwhelming and upheaving ones, along with the neat and promptly useful bits. It is like that.*

The only solid piece of scientific truth about which I feel totally confident is that we are profoundly ignorant about nature. Indeed, I regard this as the major discovery of the past hundred years of biology. It is, in its way, an illuminating piece of news. It would have amazed the brightest minds of the eighteenth-century Enlightenment to be told by any of us how little we know, and how bewildering seems the way ahead. It is this sudden confrontation with the depth and scope of ignorance that represents the most significant contribution of twentieth-century science to the human intellect. We are, at last, facing up to it. In earlier times, we either pretended to understand how things worked or ignored the problem, or simply made up stories to fill the gaps. Now that we have begun exploring in earnest, doing serious science, we are getting glimpses of how huge the questions are, and how far from being answered. Because of this, these are hard times for the human intellect, and it is no wonder that we are depressed. It is not so bad being ignorant if you are totally ignorant; the hard thing is knowing in some detail the reality of ignorance, the worst spots and here and there the not-so-bad spots, but no true light at the end of any tunnel nor even any tunnels that can yet be trusted. Hard times, indeed.

But we are making a beginning, and there ought to be some satisfaction, even exhilaration, in that. The method works. There are probably no questions we can think up that can't be answered, sooner or later, including even the matter of consciousness. To be sure, there may well be questions we can't think up, ever, and therefore limits to the reach of human intellect which we will never know about, but that is another matter. Within our limits, we should be able to work our way through to all our answers, if we keep at it long enough, and pay attention.   25

I am putting it this way, with all the presumption and confidence that I can summon, in order to raise another, last question. Is this hubris? Is there something fundamentally unnatural, or intrinsically wrong, or hazardous for the species in the ambition that drives us all to reach a comprehensive understanding of nature, including ourselves? I cannot believe it. It would seem to me a more unnatural thing, and more of an offense against nature, for us to come on the same scene endowed as we are with curiosity, filled to overbrimming as we are with questions, and naturally talented as we are for the asking of clear questions, and then for us to do nothing about it or, worse, to try to suppress the questions. This is the greater danger for our species, to try to pretend that we are another kind of animal, that we do

---

You cannot make choices . . . like that: For a somewhat different view of scientific objectivity, see Evelyn Fox Keller, "From Working Scientist to Feminist Critic," p. 241.

not need to satisfy our curiosity, that we can get along somehow without inquiry and exploration and experimentation, and that the human mind can rise above its ignorance by simply asserting that there are things it has no need to know. This, to my way of thinking, is the real hubris, and it carries danger for us all.

QUESTIONING THE TEXT

1. What is hubris? Why does Thomas begin his essay with a discussion of that term?
2. Thomas suggests that the question of what to do with certain kinds of scientific knowledge—about recombinant DNA, for example—should not be treated as "an emotional issue" or "a religious controversy." Do you agree? Why, or why not?
3. What is A.L.'s attitude toward Thomas and his argument? What words, phrases, or sentences in her headnote to this essay reveal her attitude to you?

MAKING CONNECTIONS

4. In the next selection, Evelyn Fox Keller speaks of the belief that scientific objectivity has been synonymous with "thinking like a man." In what ways does Thomas's discussion of hubris support (or refute) Keller's statement?
5. If Thomas were charged with the task of writing an evaluation of Victor Frankenstein's work, what do you think he would say? Try your hand at such an evaluation.
6. "New information about nature," Thomas says, "is very likely, at the outset, to be upsetting to someone or other." Would Peggy Orenstein, the author of "Get a Cyberlife" (p. 251), agree? Why, or why not?

JOINING THE CONVERSATION

7. With two or three classmates, spend some time brainstorming about and then discussing what Thomas identifies as "the central question" of his essay: "are there some kinds of information leading to some sorts of knowledge that human beings are really better off not having?" Then record your own answer to this question in your reading log, if you are keeping one.

8. Thomas defends scientific inquiry by noting, "I do not believe that looking for new information about nature, at whatever level, can possibly be called unnatural. Indeed, if there is any single attribute of human beings, apart from language, which distinguishes them from all other creatures on earth, it is their insatiable, uncontrollable drive to learn things and then to exchange the information with others of the species." Do you agree? Write a brief position paper in which you argue for or against the accuracy of Thomas's claim.

EVELYN FOX KELLER
From Working Scientist to Feminist Critic

IN A 1990 INTERVIEW with Bill Moyers, Evelyn Fox Keller mused about Mary Shelley's Frankenstein, *calling it an "archetypal story" of man's attempt to take for himself the procreative powers of women. That myth, says Keller, results not in the secret of life but in "a monster who becomes the secret of death" and in some ways the epitome of man's attempts to control nature. This attempt at controlling the natural world Keller sees as one of mankind's deepest desires— a desire she says too often operates as if it had no consequences. "To what end" is this knowledge and this control, Keller asks over and over again in her work. To what end?*

Keller comes to this question from years of considering the ways in which the "ends" of science, its goals as well as its means and methods, have traditionally been masculine ones. These questions reverberate throughout Keller's work, from Reflections on Gender and Science *(1985) to the collection of essays from which the following excerpt is taken,* Secrets of Life, Secrets of Death: Essays on Language, Gender, and Science *(1992).*

In much of this work, Keller traces the exclusion of women from science and the link between masculinity, rationality, and scientific endeavors. She sees a science whose very structures and ways of talking about nature are masculine, with scientific "objectivity" regarded as a masculine quality and, moreover, as a highly valued quality by Western society.

In the selection that follows, Keller speaks first of the impact this link between scientific objectivity and masculinity has had on her own life and career. She then turns to another link that troubles her, that between science and nature. Against those who believe that science holds a mirror up to nature and captures a faithful and neutral reflection, Keller argues that science can give us only descriptions of nature, not nature itself. And these descriptions, which must be conveyed through language, will always be presented from some particular perspective. It becomes the task of those who seek to understand science, therefore, to examine its perspectives, its points of view, and especially its language. Doing so, Keller argues, will help us attend not only to the knowledge science yields but also to the purposes to which such knowledge will be put, to the implications such knowledge will have for women and men everywhere.

As someone who has studied the history and theory of rhetoric for most of my adult life, I am particularly interested in Keller's questioning "to what ends" our knowledge will be put. Moreover, I am concerned to study the way our manner of talking about things inevitably shapes how we can know (and not

*know) those things. In addition, I want to support Keller's efforts to examine
the gendered nature of the language of science and the ways in which that
language still too often excludes women from pursuing scientific careers.* — A.L.

I begin with three vignettes, all drawn from memory.

1965. In my first few years out of graduate school, I held quite conventional beliefs about science. I believed not only in the possibility of clear and certain knowledge of the world, but also in the uniquely privileged access to this knowledge provided by science in general, and by physics in particular. I believed in the accessibility of an underlying (and unifying) "truth" about the world we live in, and I believed that the laws of physics gave us the closest possible approximation of this truth. In short, I was well trained in both the traditional realist worldviews assumed by virtually all scientists and in the conventional epistemological ordering of the sciences. I had, after all, been trained, first, by theoretical physicists, and later, by molecular biologists. This is not to say that I lived my life according to the teachings of physics (or molecular biology), only that when it came to questions about what "really is," I knew where, and how, to look. Although I had serious conflicts about my own ability to be part of this venture, I fully accepted science, and scientists, as arbiters of truth. Physics (and physicists) were, of course, the highest arbiters.

Somewhere around this time, I came across the proceedings of the first major conference held in the United States on "Women and the Scientific Professions" (Mattfield and Van Aiken 1965)—a subject of inevitable interest to me. I recall reading in those proceedings an argument for more women in science, made by both Erik Erikson and Bruno Bettelheim, based on the invaluable contributions a "specifically female genius" could make to science. Although earlier in their contributions both Erikson and Bettelheim had each made a number of eminently reasonable observations and recommen-

As a college student, I never thought to question the "truths" or objectivity of science. — A.L.

She describes the way most people think of the world. — J.R.

I looked up arbiter—it's defined as "a person with full power to judge." Are scientists less discoverers or presenters of truth than simply people making subjective decisions? — H.L.

dations, I flew to these concluding remarks as if waiting for them, indeed forgetting everything else they had said. From the vantage point I then occupied, my reaction was predictable: To put it quite bluntly, I laughed. Laws of nature are universal—how could they possibly depend on the sex of their discoverers? Obviously, I snickered, these psychoanalysts know little enough about science (and by implication, about truth).

1969. I was living in a suburban California house and found myself with time to think seriously about my own mounting conflicts (as well as those of virtually all my female cohorts) about being a scientist. I had taken a leave to accompany my husband on his sabbatical, remaining at home to care for our two small children. Weekly, I would talk to the colleague I had left back in New York and hear his growing enthusiasm as he reported the spectacular successes he was having in presenting our joint work. In between, I would try to understand why my own enthusiasm was not only not growing, but actually diminishing. How I went about seeking such an understanding is worth noting: What I did was to go to the library to gather data about the fate of women scientists in general—more truthfully, to document my own growing disenchantment (even in the face of manifest success) as part of a more general phenomenon reflecting an underlying misfit between women and science. And I wrote to Erik Erikson for further comment on the alarming (yet somehow satisfying) attrition data I was collecting. In short, only a few years after ridiculing his thoughts on the subject, I was ready to at least entertain if not embrace an argument about women in, or out of, science based on "women's nature." Not once during that entire year did it occur to me that at least part of my disenchantment might be related to the fact that I was in fact not sharing in the *kudos* my colleague was reaping for our joint work.

1974. I had not dropped out of science, but I had moved into interdisciplinary, undergraduate

How can she assume to know the conflicts of almost all her female colleagues?
— H.L.

I find myself as skeptical of Keller as she was of Erikson and Bettelheim.
— J.R.

I know scientists who believe they are simply reporting "the facts." They don't agree that the "facts" they choose to report are always selected from among many and that their statements about them are inevitably interpretations as well. — A.L.

The data on women in science are truly alarming. At Ohio State, hardly any women are professors in the sciences; those who do get hired are subjected to innumerable pressures because of their sex. — A.L.

teaching. And I had just finished teaching my first women's studies course when I received an invitation to give a series of "Distinguished Lectures" on my work in mathematical biology at the University of Maryland. It was a great honor, and I wanted to do it, but I had a problem. In my women's studies course, I had yielded to the pressure of my students and colleagues to talk openly about what it had been like, as a woman, to become a scientist. In other words, I had been persuaded to publicly air the exceedingly painful story of the struggle that had actually been—a story I had previously only talked about in private, if at all. The effect of doing this was that I actually came to *see* that story as public, that is, of political significance, rather than as simply private, of merely personal significance. As a result, the prospect of continuing to present myself as a disembodied scientist, of talking about my work as if it had been done in a vacuum, as if the fact of my being a woman was entirely irrelevant, had come to feel actually dishonest.

I resolved the conflict by deciding to present in my last lecture a demographic model of women in science—an excuse to devote the bulk of that lecture to a review of the many barriers that worked against the survival of women as scientists, and to a discussion of possible solutions. I concluded my review with the observation that perhaps the most important barrier to success for women in science derived from the pervasive belief in the intrinsic masculinity of scientific thought. Where, I asked, does such a belief come from? What is it doing in science, reputedly the most objective, neutral, and abstract endeavor we know? And what consequences does that belief have for the actual doing of science?

In 1974 "women in science" was not a proper subject for academic or scientific discussion; I was aware of violating professional protocol. Having given the lecture—having "carried it off"—I felt profoundly liberated. I had passed an essential milestone.

I "dropped out" of science in high school, after a series of teachers bored me to tears. – A.L.

Women hit a "glass ceiling" in most careers. – H.L.

The "masculinity of scientific thought"—that's the point I would have to understand better before agreeing with Keller. – J.R.

Although I did not know it then, and wouldn't recognize it for another two years, this lecture marked the beginning of my work as a feminist critic of science. In it I raised three of the central questions that were to mark my research and writing over the next decade. I can now see that, with the concluding remarks of that lecture, I had also completed the basic shift in mind-set that made it possible to begin such a venture. Even though my views about gender, science, knowledge, and truth were to evolve considerably over the years to come, I had already made the two most essential steps: I had shifted attention from the question of male and female nature to that of *beliefs about* male and female nature, that is, to gender ideology. And I had admitted the possibility that such beliefs could affect science itself.

In hindsight, these two moves may seem simple enough, but when I reflect on my own history, as well as that of other women scientists, I can see that they were not. Indeed, from my earlier vantage point, they were unthinkable. In that mind-set, there was room neither for a distinction between sexual identity and beliefs about sexual identity (not even for the prior distinction between sex and gender upon which it depends), nor for the possibility that beliefs could affect science—a possibility that requires a distinction analogous to that between sex and gender, only now between nature and science. I was, of course, able to accommodate a distinction between belief and reality, but only in the sense of "false" beliefs—that is, mere illusion, or mere prejudice; "true" beliefs I took to be synonymous with the "real."

It seems to me that in that mind-set, beliefs per se were not seen as having any real force—neither the force to shape the development of men and women, nor the force to shape the development of science. Some people may "misperceive" nature, human or otherwise, but properly seen, men and women simply *are,* faithful reflections of male and female biology—just as science simply *is,* a faithful reflection of nature.

When beliefs affect scientific results, can the results still be considered scientific? Doesn't the scientist properly seek to minimize the intrusion of distorting prejudices? – J.R.

Her emphasis on "beliefs" makes me wonder if she thinks that differences in male and female nature are only perceived? – H.L.

So even science's notions of maleness and femaleness are grounded in beliefs about nature, not in nature itself. – A.L.

Gravity has (or is) a force, DNA has force, but beliefs do not. In other words, as scientists, we are trained to see the locus of real force in the world as physical, not mental.

There is of course a sense in which they are right: Beliefs per se cannot exert force on the world. But the people who carry such beliefs can. Furthermore, the language in which their beliefs are encoded has the force to shape what others—as men, as women, and as scientists—think, believe, and, in turn, actually do. It may have taken the lens of feminist theory to reveal the popular association of science, objectivity, and masculinity as a statement about the social rather than natural (or biological) world, referring not to the bodily and mental capacities of individual men and women, but to a collective consciousness; that is, as a set of beliefs given existence by language rather than by bodies, and by that language, granted the force to shape what individual men and women might (or might not) do. But to see how such culturally laden language could contribute to the shaping of science takes a different kind of lens. That requires, first and foremost, a recognition of the social character (and force) of the enterprise we call "science," a recognition quite separable from—and in fact, historically independent of—the insights of contemporary feminism.

Here's the old metaphor of science as a mirror of nature: science holds up a mirror and what we see in it is nature itself. Keller says no: we see our perceptions of nature, mediated by the language we use to describe them. – A.L.

I get the impression that Keller thinks it is possible and even easy to separate the "social" from the "natural." I disagree. – H.L.

Afterwords

At the end of this brief excerpt, Keller raises an issue that seems increasingly important to me. As science comes closer and closer to identifying the "secrets of life," the need to understand what Keller calls the "culturally laden language" of science becomes critical. In short, whatever these secrets of life may be, we can know them only through the language science puts them in. Those who would understand the full implications of new scientific knowledge, therefore, must learn to study its language. As Keller suggests, the very structures and language of science have traditionally reflected masculine assumptions about knowledge and about the relationship between humans and nature. Such value-laden structures are inevitable in language use, and so she doesn't seem to be assigning blame. Rather, she is exploring ways in which the language of science has led us to focus on some questions while ignoring others.

I agree with the spirit of Keller's argument. Every thinker or investigator must stand somewhere. The idea that scientists are somehow "above" stances seems patently false. And where you stand, of course, significantly affects what you will or even can see. Since science has stood in a masculinist place for a very, very long time in the Western world, it is only sensible to acknowledge how that place has affected what science has seen or even attempted to see. To make this statement is not to condemn science. Far from it. It is rather to seek to broaden the number of places where science can stand, and thus to see ever more and different things. Increased vision and perspective should be goals we can all agree on, goals that remain true to the ideals of science.

Indeed, I find that today, at the age of fifty, I am a fan of science; I read books on the history of science and on figures in science, and I try to read popular scientific magazines. But coming to this position has not been easy. As a child, I was expected not to like science (or math), was discouraged in subtle but clear ways from participating in "unladylike" things like science. As a student, I never had a single science teacher (all, of course, were men) who showed me that science had anything even vaguely to do with people or what I thought of as the "big questions" of life; for me, science was disengaged and boring, one long list of "facts" to memorize or meaningless experiments to perform. I wondered occasionally why some of the men I knew liked science.

Now I think I know why, and that "why" has a lot to do with the language and structures of science. I lost a great deal by not learning to participate in the conversations of science until my middle years. But it seems to me science may also have lost by excluding people like me who don't easily fit the traditional objectivist molds of thought. Evelyn Fox Keller made it, albeit with difficulty, into the ranks of scientists. How many women, and the powerful insights they might have brought with them, have been excluded? As I write these words, I am thinking particularly of J.R. and of how he will respond to this piece. I wonder why I think I already know?   – A.L.

Just before composing this response to Evelyn Fox Keller and A.L., I read an article by Jeffrey Salmon explaining how, for political and personal reasons, some scientists may have overstated the dangers of global warming. In the conclusion of "Greenhouse Anxiety" (Commentary, *July 1993: 25–28), Salmon warns that "undoing the harm this has done to the credibility of the scientific community may be the work of generations." It concerns me that in advocating more attention to the social character of science, Evelyn Fox Keller could be inadvertently nurturing similar violations of scientific method. Might it not prove tempting for scientists to distort, slant, or selectively report evidence when they think they are acting for a higher societal good—protecting the environment, for example, or seeking more funding for* AIDS *research? Does*

*anyone recall how neatly the now discredited nuclear winter scenario coincided
with the politics of the scientists advancing it? Good science doesn't follow scripts
penned by activists or politicians. It looks beyond social factors, including the
race, class, religion, nationality, politics, and yes, gender of its practitioners.*

*At any given moment, scientific studies might reflect the societal biases of
an age or of individual investigators, but the results of such work would, over
time, be recognized as distortions of proper scientific method, and consequently,
in need of correction. For this reason, I think it is unwise to conceive of science
in gendered or particularistic terms—to think of its method as "masculinist,"
"feminist," or even "Western" or "European" because such characterizations
merely describe a limited and disfigured pursuit of knowledge.*

*Even if the West invented the scientific method, it does not belong to the
West; if men have been the major practitioners of science, it is not their birthright.
If scientists who happen to be women direct their attention to new areas of study,
they are merely expanding the horizons of science, not feminizing its method
of inquiry. And they will (I hope) pursue truths separate from any special
interests so that the results they report will be the same for women and men and
Kenyans and Fiji Islanders.*

*It is fashionable to assert, as A.L. does in her response, that where you
stand alters what you see, but that notion itself is so ancient that science can be
regarded as the refreshing attempt to pursue what we can know separate from
particularities of time, place, and prejudice. Galileo may have been compelled
to recant his belief that the earth moves because the situated knowledge of his
inquisitors did not permit them to see beyond their noses, but as Galileo himself
asserted, "E pur si muovo"—nevertheless, it does move. The motions of the
universe are a good deal grander than our sexual differences. And so is science.*

*Unlike A.L., I was drawn to science as a youngster—and my elementary
school science teachers were all women, nuns even. I loved science fiction and
I was captivated by the space race, in full progress during my adolescence. I
read everything I could about the* Mercury, Gemini, *and* Apollo *programs
and thought long and hard about a career in science. I could blame my failure
to follow a career in science on the neo-Luddite attitudes of my college professors
in the sixties. But the fact is I wasn't cut out for science: I lack the mathematical
skill, the proper turn of mind, and the special patience that science requires. I
remain a fan of science, but that's a very different thing from being a
scientist.   – J.R.*

*Unlike A.L. and J.R., this piece strikes me more as a feminist cry than a
discussion of gender biases in science. My reaction may be due in part to the
fact that I found Keller's arguments easily applicable to fields other than science.
Men dominate almost all career fields. On average, women executives earn only
sixty-five cents for every dollar their male counterparts earn. And those fields
that women do dominate—teaching and nursing, for example—are considered
less prestigious than others.*

Reading A.L.'s response, however, made me feel a bit ashamed of those initial thoughts. Instead of accepting and trying to fit into a male-dominated world, A.L. made me feel as if I should challenge it. My feelings weren't quite as strong as A.L.'s, though. It may simply be that I'm younger and less experienced in the "real" world, but I've never felt oppressed by male dominance. My parents have always encouraged me to study whatever I wanted, and I've never felt intimidated from pursuing a certain career path simply due to a lack of women role models.

Although I agree with J.R. that the scientific process basically works, I never felt, as he appears to have, that Keller was attacking the scientific process. To me, she was merely making some observations with which I could easily agree. When I was young, my parents actually encouraged me to study science, but I could never quite grasp the concepts; perhaps the language bias accounts for some of my difficulty. J.R.'s comments make me curious as to how other male readers will react to this excerpt. I wonder if men really do not see such biases as readily—or if they simply won't. I think that those in positions of power—in this case, men—often ignore or refuse to accept the existence of such biases in order to protect the status quo. – H.L.

QUESTIONING THE TEXT

1. Keller writes about the masculine ways of science. Can you think of other fields that are dominated by males or females?

2. In A.L.'s introduction to this selection, were you at all surprised by Keller's assertion that *Frankenstein* is a "story of dispensing with female procreativity"? Freewrite for 10 minutes on your response to her claim.

3. How does the language A.L. and J.R. use affect your reading of their commentary? In paragraph 2 of A.L.'s response to Keller, for example, notice her assertion "it is only sensible;" in paragraph 2 of J.R.'s response, notice his use of "merely." How do these words affect your own conclusions about Keller's argument?

MAKING CONNECTIONS

4. Keller clearly does not see the truths that science has produced as unmixed blessings. Which other authors in this chapter might agree with her? Which ones might disagree?

5. How might Keller respond to Peggy Orenstein's description of the Cyberthon (in the reading on p. 251)? What in Orenstein's essay supports Keller's claim that science is primarily a masculine realm?

JOINING THE CONVERSATION

6. Keller describes her experience of having to learn the language of science. Brainstorm for a short while on your own experiences learning the language of a particular field or job. Take 10–15 minutes writing about the challenges you faced.
7. Working with two classmates, consider H.L.'s question "as to how other male readers will react" to Keller's assertions about language bias in science. Compile your notes and bring them to class for discussion.

PEGGY ORENSTEIN
Get a Cyberlife

IF THOUGHTS OF strip-mining and ecological disaster lead Lewis Thomas to contemplate "The Hazards of Science," these same thoughts direct Peggy Orenstein, a former managing editor of the progressive magazine Mother Jones, to escapist fantasies and Virtual Reality, "the newest, fringiest, most talked about technological boom since artificial intelligence went bust." In this essay, published in 1991, Orenstein reports on her visit to Cyberthon, a conference demonstration of Virtual Reality technology. Along the way, she confronts an issue that is at the heart of Frankenstein and the conversation in this chapter: When is man-made "reality" or science-made reality more real than nature—and how can we distinguish between the two? Finally, what laws of ethics will govern the "virtually" real?

This selection is of special interest to me because I believe electronic literacy and new technologies will change not only what science can do but also how we think about science—and, indeed, how we think at all. In addition, I am drawn to Orenstein's wit and to her breezy, slightly irreverent style. — A.L.

I've never been wed to reality. I've never even been engaged to it. I'll fling myself wholeheartedly into anything that can help me forget, at least momentarily, the thrum of war, toxic waste, ecological disaster, nuclear annihilation, poverty, destitution, or the fact that the tremendous amount of effort I just put into redecorating my apartment may be for naught if the entire city that I live in shakes, rattles, and rolls into the sea. There are times when I've looked at the world's problems and wished that I could just go find another world, one I would populate only with people I like. Sometimes I'm not so sure about them. There are people out there in California's Silicon Valley, at the University of Washington in Seattle, and at the University of North Carolina who are responding to such escapist fantasies. They're using computers to generate three-dimensional alternative environments—of, say, Tahiti to the inside of the human brain or Mars—that, at least some day, will be as photographically "real" as the room you're sitting in right now. This winter I got a preview of that future at Cyberthon, a twenty-four-hour marathon conference and demonstration of Virtual Reality, the newest, fringiest, most talked about technological boom since artificial intelligence went bust.

Standard VR gear consists of heavy, computerized, blacked-out goggles and a Lycra glove. When you move your goggled head, the computer responds by changing your perspective on the scene around you, just like in "real" reality. If you grab an image with your gloved hand, the computer notes that too and moves the image accordingly.

Some architects are using VR (also called "cyberspace," a term coined by writer William Gibson, who dreamed up VR in his novel *Neuromancer*) to show clients what a structure will look like before it's built. Doctors are using it to practice surgery without making a single cut. A cyberpunk counterculture, spearheaded by people like Brian Eno and director George Coates, is creating a whole new technology-driven spectrum of post-postmodern, nihilistic art. And, of course, NASA and the Defense Department (which hopes to replace jet pilots with VR screens) have been following—and funding—VR since its inception.

Cyberthon took place at a soundstage at the edge of San Francisco, in a specially built maze designed with a calculated irreverence toward day, night, right, left, and the entire history of empiricist philosophy. The exhibits within these virtual walls were mostly technological pupae: visual, tactile, and aural bits and bytes, which, their inventors believe, will someday achieve the sum of their parts and blossom into something revolutionary.

In the nethermost reaches of the maze I found Sense8. Among the big three VR companies (the others being VR granddaddy Virtual Programming Languages Research [VPL] and Autodesk, Inc., which caters primarily to architects), Sense8 is the cheap seats, either the lowest tech or the most practical, depending on your perspective. Whereas VPL uses two computers to generate its virtual world, Sense8 and Autodesk use only a single computer. The difference in quality is significant, and so is the difference in price: about $15,000 a pop as opposed to VPL's $250,000. (In fact, VPL declined to haul its more complex, high-wattage gear down to San Francisco for a demo.) 5

I waited in line impatiently for my turn at the Cyberhood, a long, View-Master–like contraption, which focuses your eyes on a computer-generated 3-D image; you manipulate yourself, or "fly," by gripping a ball to the left of the machine. The ball, Sense8 president Eric Gullichsen kept repeating to the users, is like your head, think of it as your head. The trouble with that notion is that most people don't yank, twist, twirl, and push their heads, so most people were having trouble with the image: flipping it upside down, pulling their "head" back so far that the image became tiny and distant, hitting the floor with their wide-open eyeballs.

The man in front of me, a shortish, plump guy in a blue shirt and jeans, was muttering to himself as he yanked at his "head." Finally he gave in and straightened up. He turned out to be Robin Williams, but no one paid much attention in this crowd—the machines were the celebrities.

I asked him what it was like.

"Try it," he said, then dropped his voice to a Bela Lugosi whisper. "Don't be scared."

Was it fun?   10
"Yeah," he said, unconvincingly. "In a vertigo kind of way."

In the Cyberhood I saw a room with a purple-and-chartreuse linoleum
floor. There was a red chair, a brown desk, preternaturally blue walls, a
book, a lamp, a painting on the wall. None of it looked particularly "real."
It looked flat and cartoonish—I've heard it compared to Toontown, a sort
of two-dimensional three-dimensionality, if you can grok that.

I yanked my "head" and moved in on the chair. Suddenly the purple-
and-green floor cracked me in the "face." I pulled back and the whole thing
flipped over. I took a deep breath and steadied myself. I'm not very good
at Nintendo either. To my right (my real right, not my virtual right) there
was a joystick. I hit the button and a red-and-white-checked missile flew
down from the ceiling and bounced on the floor. A woman's rude laugh
followed. Gullichsen explained that you're supposed to move the joystick
to make the missiles hit the target. I tried again; this time a yellow airplane
came out and I manipulated it toward the chair. It hit and exploded with
a crash of broken glass.

I'd had enough.

Back in the real room, Gullichsen introduced me to Alison Kennedy,   15
a.k.a. Queen Mu, the "domineditrix"* of the sporadically published cyberpunk rag *Mondo2000* as well as the anthropologist who first explained that
licking a certain genus of toad can induce a hallucinogenic experience. Genuinely pleased to initiate a sister-in-publishing into the VR scene, she broke
into a wide, ethereal grin and invited me to visit her house in the Berkeley
hills once she returned from a Druid festival in Graz. Queen Mu and her
stunning smile seem to have many of the VR boys wrapped like the gold
bracelet around her upper arm. The new cyberians all publish in *M2,* which
is as hot hot hot as Mickey Rourke and Jerry Lewis in France and Japan.

She was chatting with Stephen Beck about his Virtual Light exhibit,
which wasn't working (and never did). Virtual Light? I asked. Don't we
already have that? Isn't it called the light bulb?

"I guess you could think of it that way," Beck answered thoughtfully.
"But no, the light bulb is artificial light. This is Virtual Light. You can see
it with your eyes closed."

"I can see electric light with my eyes closed."

At this, Beck launched into a long explanation of Virtual Light, the
only word of which I recognized was "photon." And I'm not quite sure
what that means.

"domineditrix": a blend of *dominatrix* and *editor*

By now I was hungry, so I strolled over to the virtual eating exhibit   20
that a group of local art students had set up. I didn't know what to expect—
perhaps it could make me feel virtually full. Perhaps no calories would be
involved. There was a reservation book graced with a real red rose outside
the closed-off room. I wrote my name down. There was a ten- to fifteen-
minute wait for a table. Just like real life, I thought. I wondered where I
could get a virtual Stoli* while I waited.

I told the man in front of me in line, a guy with a stringy ponytail
down to the center of his back, that I had done Virtual Reality. He asked
how it was. I told him the most exciting thing about it was that Robin
Williams was next to me.

"You mean you were virtually with Robin Williams? That's great!"

No, I tried to explain, he was really next to me.

"You mean virtually really, or really really?"

I began to get a headache.   25

"Robin Williams was actually next to me, in line, waiting for a turn
on the machine."

Mr. Ponytail looked crestfallen. "Well, did he say anything funny?"
he asked, perking up some.

Virtual eating turned out to be a bunch of 3-D video images of food,
projected onto a plate-shaped screen. A well-rounded meal, yes, but
inedible.

Since I was already experiencing a taste of the third dimension, I
hustled over to something called a Flying Mouse. If you've ever used an
Apple computer, you know that you move the cursor with something that
does not resemble but is nevertheless called a mouse. You move the mouse
up and down to make the cursor move up and down, left and right to move
the cursor back and forth. If you're feeling really crazy, you can spin the
mouse in a circle, but that's about the most exciting effect you could achieve.
Up until now.

The Flying Mouse is shaped like a manta ray and operates in 3-D.   30
Simgraphics president Steve Tice called up a double image of Gumby's twin
sister on screen and handed me a pair of LCD glasses. The lenses blink so
rapidly—sixty times a second—that the eye can't perceive it. Suddenly, the
two images on the screen merged into one three-dimensional figure. I could
move her back and forth and up and down the conventional way, but, by
lifting the mouse up off the table, I could also pull her out toward my face,
push her back deep into the screen, or make her legs and arms kick and
twist in agony. And when I "selected" a body part, I felt a tingly pressure

---

Stoli: Stolichnaya, a brand of vodka

on my index finger—tactile feedback! It didn't reflect notions of hard or soft or round or sharp, but I definitely felt like I'd touched something.

Habitat, an interactive, two-dimensional, animated program originally designed for Commodore computers, touched something in me, too. Like a raw nerve. To its users, Habitat is clearly much more than a computer game: it's truly an alternative universe, a mythical place where cartoon figures representing users throughout the country travel about, talk via typed overhead balloons, earn "money" through entrepreneurial ventures to purchase various luxury items, and observe strict codes of etiquette (if someone talks to you, it's rude not to talk back). Habitat users, programmer Randy Farmer explained to me, can go to a head shop and trade in their heads and bodies for new ones. Farmer himself had a large, blue dragon head. On screen, that is. In real life, he conformed to the stereotype of a hacker: shaggy hair, scruffy clothes, glasses, bad skin, paunchy.

And self-aware: "A lot of these people," he told me, "buy Marilyn Monroe heads, or Robert Redford heads, or some other gorgeous head-body combination. But the truth is, the kind of people who stare into a computer screen for hours and hours a day probably aren't the most beautiful people. On the outside, anyway. They're beautiful on the inside. So sometimes you meet one of these people who've represented themselves with these beautiful faces, and you're disappointed. You think, 'Oh, she doesn't look like Marilyn Monroe at all.'* I figure, if I have a monster head and someone meets me someday, I come out ahead. The way I really look won't seem so bad."

As he talked, two figures appeared on the screen, a "man" with a nondescript head and body (all the men's bodies are nondescript, all the women's bodies have huge breasts and wasp waists. Guess which gender designed Habitat?) who said he was from Nebraska, and a headless female with major mamambas from North Carolina.

The man reached out and grabbed the woman's breasts. "Nice boobs," he said.

Randy told me the gesture was bad form, but then again, so was 35 walking around without a head. In the meantime, the woman had begun to talk.

"I'm a man, you idiot," she said.

"What's with the boobs, then?" typed man number one, in consternation.

"They're muscles. Now get off 'em."

Let's talk about the birds and the cyberbees. Everyone I told about Cyberthon (including the editors of *Mother Jones*) asked if virtual sex was

---

beautiful on the inside . . . doesn't look like Marilyn: For another perspective on Marilyn Monroe, see "The Marilyn Monroe Poem" on p. 511.

possible. At first I thought maybe that was just the kind of lowlife I hang around with, but during a question-and-answer session later that night, Jaron Lanier—the thirty-one-year-old founder of VPL, who is renowned for his spherical belly and the light-brown, lichen-like dreadlocks that sprout from his visionary skull—rolled his eyes when he was asked what he calls "the sex question."

But "the sex question" is really a misnomer. These guys, the bedrock   40
of this new technology, didn't, and don't, really ask "the sex question"; they ask "the porn question": they don't want to know how to enhance intimacy with a partner; they want to know if they can make that Habitat babe 3-D and then spend all day feeling her virtual breasts.

There's even a word for VR sex: "dildonics." Note the emphasis here. It's not ovanics, or clitonics, or even cybersex. Dildonics. And Lanier, who has struggled to keep his Virtual Reality squeaky-clean, denied that people will want to use his machine for dildonic ends. "VR won't be used success-fully as a porn media," he insisted. "Porn is cinema and photography that leaves something to the imagination. Completely knowing makes you deal with what's really on your plate. The reality here, the virtual reality, is that you'd have a girl made of polygons. And no one wants to have sex with a bunch of polygons."

Lanier went on to tout VR as a great equalizer. "Virtual Reality is the ultimate lack of class or race distinctions or any other form of pretense, since all form is variable," he said. In VR, said Lanier, gender, race, age—all become invention. You can be who or even what you want. If you can choose your form, you don't have to make it a human one: you can appear as a cat, a table, a piano.* He told the crowd that, because VR is interactive, it can be community-enhancing, like the telephone or the light bulb, rather than reinforcing the numbing alienation of the television. "We live in this very weird time in history where we're passive recipients of a very immature, noninteractive broadcast media," he said. "Mission number one is to kill TV."

Someone commented that Nintendo is interactive, but it doesn't seem like a stride toward establishing an authentic electronic community.

"Nintendo is a little interactive," Lanier corrected. "You're being guided down a narrow set of predetermined possibilities, like a rat in a maze. VR is an endless range. If we're going to call Nintendo interactive, then I want a different word for VR."

Throughout Cyberthon, William Gibson played Darth Vader to La-   45
nier's Luke Skywalker. His vision of Virtual Reality, as articulated in *Neuro-mancer,* was a bleak one, in which those unfortunate enough to be mired in

---

form is variable . . . appear as a cat, a table: Compare Virtual Reality's "lack of . . . distinctions" to Alice Walker's point of view in "Everything Is a Human Being," p. 189.

the physical world were called "meat" by those who roamed the cyber-range. When someone subsequently asked *him* whether he believed VR could be an electronic utopia, he shot back, "I think it could be lethal, like freebasing American TV." Disheveled, hunched over, looking like he'd rather be out back smoking, Gibson leaned into the microphone. "I don't think that anyone who read my book seems to have understood it," he said in his adenoidal twang. "It was supposed to be ironic. The book was really a metaphor about how I felt about the media. I didn't expect anyone to actually go out and build one of these things."

You want VR? Try staying among black-walled mazes for eighteen hours straight. Try making a Jif peanut butter and generic white bread sandwich in "Mom's Kitchen," assuming Mom was just thawed after being cryonically frozen in 1932 (and, given this crowd, that's a pretty fair assumption). Walk into a big room at 3 A.M. and have Timothy Leary* tell you all reality is virtual. Believe him.

At six in the morning, Kit Galloway, the ponytailed artist whose "Electronic Cafe" provides communal video-telephone hookups in public places, free of charge, got up to speak. He suggested that cyber-elitism could be avoided by using the technology we already have. "To get into computer-shared electronic space, you need to be rich," he said to a bleary-eyed but attentive audience. "The telephone has all kinds of potential. There are gridlocks in the cities, and people can't run around the country in jet planes, punching holes in the ozone, for an ecology conference in Chicago—it doesn't make sense. Why not telecommute or teleconference by video-phone? Telephones are the only thing that will get cheaper—they're our magic, our epitaph."

Galloway said that the new technology we need to achieve VR's grand claims could be found in the least likely places, and, just before breakfast, I discovered he was right. Chris Hardman, whose Antenna Theater produces taped tours that re-create the pivotal events of historical sites like Dallas's School Book Depository,* was exhibiting his virtual jump off the Golden Gate Bridge.

I strapped on a Walkman and stood by a waist-high cadmium-red–painted wooden fence overlooking a blue plastic ocean. Voices came from all sides—a soft, seductive man's voice telling me: "Tense your shoulders, clench your fists. Relax your shoulders. Don't look down. Don't look down . . . look down. Put one foot on the rail. Feel the rail. . . ." A

Timothy Leary: a Harvard University professor (b. 1920) who became, in the 1960s, an outspoken advocate of the use of LSD and other hallucinogens

Dallas's School Book Depository: the building from which President John F. Kennedy was assassinated in 1963

nasal, Brooklyn-accented woman's voice relating the story of her averted suicide: "So he said: 'You're gonna jump? So jump. I haven't got all day.' And I said: 'You shit! I'm going to kill myself, and you're not going to stay here and talk to me?' " A young, angry woman, out for a walk on the bridge to get some air. . . . "Don't look down. Look down." The voices rising like so many waves, swirling together, repeating themselves, urging me up and over the rail. . . .

". . . Everyone jumps off the east side. Why? They face the city.   50
You jump off the west side, you face nothing as you go down. . . ."

". . . What keeps you from doing it is, what if you changed your mind halfway down? That would be horrible."

". . . Don't look down. Look down."

". . . If you don't do it, it's okay. Because after that, everything is a gift. Everything in life that comes after is a gift. . . ."

As I listened, the fog rolled out of machines; the plastic ocean covering a soft mattress beckoned.

Some of the people around me climbed the wooden railing.   55
Some people jumped.

I did not, although I'm not sure why. Shyness, perhaps. Or maybe the spell was broken by the sound of bodies crunching on plastic instead of being swallowed silently by waves. Or maybe the whole thing was, finally, just too real.

I came to Cyberthon curious, but terribly smug (indeed superior) in my neoluddism.* By daybreak, though, I was convinced that people who care about media, art, and education shouldn't just pass this off as the latest trend among techno-weenies with weird hair. This time, we have the chance to enter the debate about the direction of a revolutionary technology, before that debate has been decided for us.

How to do that is, of course, hard to say, if you're the kind of person who still hasn't mastered all ten function keys on your PC. During a panel on the social implications of VR, a woman who identified herself as an artist and educator stepped up to the microphone and announced, "Who gets to use this should be part of the design."

It was a nice idea, and everyone agreed, but the discussion went no   60
further. How could it? You can't prevent technology from being abused. There will be those who use VR rudely, stupidly, dangerously—just as they do the telephone or the computer. Like the telephone and the modem, its popular rise will also eliminate the need for certain fundamental kinds of human contact, even as it enhances our ability to communicate. That's

---

neoluddism: opposition to new technology. For an explanation of the origin of the term, see the introduction to the next reading (p. 261).

not comforting, but it is inevitable, and worth noting. At the very least, Cyberthon, where nontechnicians—teachers, artists, and writers—were included in the discourse, gave me hope that if we all are plugged into VR someday, there's a possibility that more than just one hand will control the switch.

Before I left Cyberthon, I watched the crowd around Atari's Hard Drivin' computer game. Drivers were surrounded on three sides by screens, which projected various racecourse scenes. They drove as fast as they could around curves (watch those cows!), through loops (accelerate . . . now!), along straightaways (gun it, man, gun it!). When they crashed, the computer showed an instant replay from the third-person perspective. As it turns out, it's a lot more fun (not to mention boffo yucks) to watch devastation from the outside. I watched the game for half an hour, then walked into the bright light of what I still perceive as the real world and hopped into my car.

As I rode down the freeway, I found myself going a little faster than usual, edging my curves a little sharper, coming a little closer than was really comfortable to the truck merging in the lane ahead of me. Maybe I was just tired. It had been a long night. But maybe it just doesn't take the mind that long to grab onto the new and make it real. Even when you don't want it to.

QUESTIONING THE TEXT

1. What is Virtual Reality? What is Orenstein's attitude toward it? What in her essay reveals her attitude?

2. What are some of the ways in which Virtual Reality as a technology could benefit society? What are some of the ways in which it could be harmful?

3. At the end of her essay, Orenstein suggests that her experiences at Cyberthon have changed the way she views "reality." What do you think she means when she says that "maybe it just doesn't take the mind that long to grab onto the new and make it real. Even when you don't want it to"?

MAKING CONNECTIONS

4. Freewrite about the ways in which the creators of Virtual Reality are similar to and/or different from Victor Frankenstein. If you've seen some Frankenstein or other horror movies, you might try to sketch out a plot for a horror movie about Virtual Reality.

5. After reading Ronald Reagan's speech on the *Challenger* disaster (p. 280), return to Orenstein's essay. Might anything she says about Virtual Reality suggest ways in which this new technology could have averted the disaster?

JOINING THE CONVERSATION

6. Write a letter to a friend in which you analyze how being introduced to a different kind of "reality"—perhaps through an education or work experience or exposure to a different culture—changed the way you viewed your everyday life.
7. New technologies are often seen as both exciting and threatening. With a group of two or three classmates, discuss your own attraction to and fear of specific new technologies. Then record your feelings in your reading log, if you are keeping one.

DANIEL GROSSMAN
Neo-Luddites:
Don't Just Say Yes to Technology

*T*HE TITLE OF ESSAYIST *Daniel Grossman's article yokes two very different allusions. The first is to the Luddites, a group of nineteenth-century British workers who sabotaged the machinery in textile mills as a means of protesting the mechanization of labor and the resulting unemployment and reduction in wages. Grossman also links the idea of criticism of new scientific technologies with an allusion to Nancy Reagan's "Just Say No to Drugs," which became a catch phrase of conservatives during the 1980s. The new Luddites he describes, however, resist blanket condemnation of technology ("just say no") and instead warn us, "Don't just say yes."*

Written especially for the Utne Reader, *a magazine that reprints the best articles from progressive publications, this article was part of a 1990 theme issue on recent advances in science and technology. I chose it because it puts in contemporary terms a lesson that writers as different as Plato, Mary Shelley, and Carl Sagan have tried to teach: science ignores ethics to the ultimate peril of all of us. We have only to look out our windows to see the ways in which technology has lowered air quality or turn on our faucets to be reminded of the hazards of drinking locally treated water. Similarly, many of our cities are drowning in the waste created by high technology. Grossman asks us to think of these and other examples, and to think about them hard. In asking that we consider the human and ethical dimensions of any new technology, he thus enters the conversation initiated in this chapter's opening selection from* Frankenstein. – A.L.

Americans are in love with technology, says Daniel Boorstin, librarian emeritus of Congress and a prominent historian. Every day, he exclaims, "we receive invitations to try something new. And we still give the traditional, exuberant American answer: 'Why not!' "

Yet in the face of ever-more sophisticated technologies—with ever greater potential for disrupting our lives—this traditional American enthusiasm may be diminishing. More and more people are looking skeptically at technologies that threaten their ways of life. Whether it is growing resistance to new technologies, such as opposition in the farm belt to a growth-prompting drug for livestock that could put small dairy farmers out of business, or a campaign to prevent a pay telephone from being installed on the pastoral town green of New Milford, Connecticut, widespread misgivings about technology are being expressed almost everywhere. A 1987 survey conducted by the National Science Foundation, for example, found that 41 percent of all Americans believe that science and technology will have a negative effect on "people's moral values," and the U.S. Office of Technology Assessment discovered that 42 percent of the public believes technological development must be restrained to "protect the overall safety of our society."

In some instances, opposition takes the form of a personal protest. Poet and philosopher Wendell Berry, for example, prefers a pencil and paper and his 1956 Royal standard typewriter to a personal computer. . . . Computers are not, he writes, "bring[ing] us one step nearer" to what really matters: "peace, economic justice, ecological health, political honesty, family and community stability, good work."* In other cases, successful resistance to technology requires collective action because, once introduced, use of the technology in question will become mandatory. In a groundbreaking court case, 15 California farm workers and a rural-advocacy group sued the University of California for failing to consider the full effects of how their research developing mechanized farm equipment would affect the lives of agricultural laborers. Although they lead different kinds of lives in different places, the Kentucky poet and the California farm workers share a similar view of technology: They evaluate an innovation by its effects on their lives. Like an increasing number of other North Americans, they prefer to say no to changes that threaten valued traditions, customs, and institutions. This grass-roots phenomenon is taking the shape of a new political movement whose adherents are sometimes called Neo-Luddites. And, increasingly, they are beginning to achieve many of their goals.

Anyone willing to oppose the introduction of a new technology is sooner or later bound to be stamped a Luddite. When the farm workers brought suit against the University of California, an editorial in *The Los Angeles Times* compared the plaintiffs to "the pathetic Luddites." That label refers to Ned Ludd and other skilled laborers in early 19th century Britain who responded to the advent of the industrial revolution by literally smashing factory machinery. Historians have long noted that mechanization benefited business owners more than labor. To many skilled workers the introduction of labor-saving machinery was not an improvement but a threat to their dignity and livelihood. Between 1811 and 1816, under the leadership of the mythical "General Ludd," textile workers across the English Midlands rebelled against these changes by destroying machines responsible for lost jobs and wage cuts.

Computers are not . . . good work: For a somewhat different spin on computers, see Freeman J. Dyson, "Engineers' Dreams," p. 222.

The year 1830 saw an equally widespread uprising among English farm workers against the recently introduced threshing machine. This time, under the banner of "Captain Swing," workers destroyed hundreds of threshers and dozens of other agricultural machines throughout southern England. According to British historian Eric Hobsbawn, farm owners introduced labor-saving threshing machines during the boom years of the Napoleonic Wars. But after these wars, the machines made little economic sense: Troops returning home flooded an already swollen agricultural labor market. With no alternative other than deepening impoverishment, the workers struck out against the machines they held responsible for their predicament. The rebellion lasted only a few months, but it destroyed virtually every threshing machine in the area.

Throughout the 20th century, these Luddites have been looked on as hapless peasants, destined to fail: By attacking threshing machines, shearing frames, and other mechanized innovations, they opposed what we think of today as the inevitable march of progress. Today, the term "Luddite" is used with derision to dismiss any critics of modern technology. The work of several historians, however, has called into doubt this view of the early Luddites as ineffective. First, as Hobsbawn points out, the Luddites did not fail. On their own terms, they did achieve limited success. Farm laborers, for instance, kept threshing machines at bay for more than a generation— earning them plenty of time to accommodate the changes brought about by this technology, notes historian David Noble. More important, Hobsbawn and others have shown that the Luddites were opposed to neither progress nor technology in general. What they fought were changes that prevented them from living decent, healthy lives.

This re-examination of the 19th century machine busters throws a   5
new light on 20th century critics of technology. With some of the negative connotations of the term stripped away by Noble's and Hobsbawn's research, modern-day critics of industrial automation, nuclear technology, pesticides, genetic engineering, and other dubious technologies proudly wear the label of "Neo-Luddites." Indeed, the 19th century Luddites, who demonstrated the ability of ordinary people to critically assess the value of new technologies, offer a source of inspiration for today's Neo-Luddites.

It would be difficult to find a thoughtful person today willing to accept any new technology without some reservations. "People have become much more circumspect about the impacts of new technologies," says anti-nuclear activist and author Harvey Wasserman. The environmental destruction caused by DDT and the tragic deformities and illnesses caused by thalidomide and diethylstilbestrol (DES) have curbed the public's appetite for miracle chemical solutions to all problems. The toxic plumes of Union Carbide's chemical plant in Bhopal, India, and the Soviet Union's nuclear power plant in Chernobyl have clouded the cheerful technological optimism we saw in the 1950s and '60s. The toxic disasters that turned Times Beach, Missouri, and the Love Canal neighborhood of Niagara Falls, New York, into ghost towns have brought the issue home for many Americans.

Since the 1970s, widespread concerns about the harmful effects of various technologies have spawned a growing regulatory wing of federal, state, and local governments charged with environmental protection, highway safety, occupational health, and the like. Regulators equipped with economic studies, risk analyses, and technology assessments have been assigned to guard against technology's unintended impacts. But what distinguishes the Neo-Luddites from these cautious bureaucrats, however, is their willingness to just say no to risky innovations. Furthermore, Neo-Luddites judge the acceptability of a technology not merely by its impact on human health and the environment but also by its effects on human dignity and traditions of society. When they oppose nuclear power, for instance, they note not only the threat of radioactive contamination but also the threats to democratic institutions that could result from a power supply directly linked to the most awful tools of destruction ever created. The lethal potential of radioactive material as a weapon means that nuclear plants must be constantly kept under armed guard. As another example, some feminists in Europe are challenging the use of a whole range of new medical engineering techniques, such as in vitro fertilization and surrogate motherhood, arguing that they are an attack on women's emancipation.

Unlike their 19th century forebears, today's Neo-Luddites most often choose not to break machinery to accomplish their goals; they generally prefer legal methods such as political organizing and court challenges. But like the earlier displaced farm and factory workers, Neo-Luddites are unwilling to accept disruptive technological forces as the inevitable cost of progress.

American farmers have a long tradition of skepticism and, in many instances, opposition to disruptive technologies. In 1927, inhabitants of California's Owens Valley blew up portions of an aqueduct that was diverting their water to faraway Los Angeles. In 1978, after exhausting legal avenues of opposition to a 400-mile-long high-voltage transmission line crossing their land, Minnesota farmers began toppling power line towers. The embittered farmers worried about the health risks of living beneath the massive power lines and saw the towers as a symbol of powerful forces of technological change over which they had little control.

Today, in the heart of rural Wisconsin, John Kinsman, a small dairy   10
farmer, is upholding this tradition—albeit without resorting to violence. He is opposing agribusiness corporations' plans to boost milk production by injecting cows with a synthesized growth regulator. Bovine somatotropin, also known as bovine growth hormone (BGH), was first synthesized by biotechnologists in the early 1980s. Pending approval from the Food and Drug Administration, a group of chemical and pharmaceutical giants, including Monsanto, Upjohn, Eli Lilly, and American Cyanamid, are now

poised to introduce the technology to the dairy industry. They estimate that it might become a $100-million- to $500-million-a-year business. Since Wisconsin is the nation's leading milk producer, BGH's future could well depend on the response in this state. Kinsman questions the safety of consuming dairy products from cows injected with the synthetic compound, and the damage to cows themselves after milk production is increased up to 25 percent per animal. He is also concerned that the commercial introduction of BGH will spell the end of family operated dairy farms in the Midwest and New England. Four years ago Kinsman and other local farmers formed the Wisconsin Family Farm Defense Fund to oppose the hormone. It's "a useless product," says Kinsman. While no sentimentalist, Kinsman says that working a family farm is "a satisfying way of life." He is determined not to let this lifestyle disappear.

By all accounts, the number of farms in the United States has been declining steadily since it peaked at 6.8 million in 1935. A 1986 report on the effects of technological advances on agriculture conducted by the U.S. Office of Technology Assessment predicted that by the year 2000, a mere 50,000 farms will supply three quarters of the nation's food. Mechanization in agriculture is largely responsible for this (along with government policies that favor corporate farms) because big farmers can afford to use new technologies and chemicals that boost production. The same would be true for BGH, which would favor corporate farm dairies in southwestern and western states, where the average herd is many times larger than in Wisconsin. According to the Office of Technology Assessment report, the result will be a "massive exodus of small to moderate dairy farms" over the coming decade. The victims will be not only farmers but also the rural communities they support.

BGH not only threatens rural life but defies economic logic. The Department of Agriculture estimated that last year 147 billion pounds of milk would be produced in the United States—7 billion more than would be consumed. To prevent the market from bottoming out, putting farmers out of business, the government buys whatever can't be sold on the market. Unless taxpayers are willing to pay for the additional surpluses promised by BGH, the government may have to lower price supports, bankrupting many dairy families and increasing the need for government services to deal with dislocated farmers. Testifying to the Agricultural Committee of the U.S. House of Representatives, Jeremy Rifkin, the nation's most well-known Neo-Luddite, called BGH "a good example of a product where the economic, environmental, and social costs may well exceed any benefits." [Rifkin's organization, the Foundation on Economic Trends, has been active in opposing BGH and tests of genetically altered substances in the open environment.]

The Wisconsin Family Farm Defense Fund's strategy has been to rally like-minded farmers and activists and to gain support in state government. Organized opposition is necessary because isolated farmers refusing to adopt an otherwise widely accepted technology for increasing yield can only guarantee their own financial ruin. The political heat of the fund's supporters is already being felt. In April 1989 the group brought together a broad coalition—called the Coalition for Responsible Technology—of environmental, labor, animal rights, farmer, and church organizations opposed to BGH.

The Wisconsin Legislature, in response, is currently considering a bill that would require products from BGH-treated cows to be labeled. Although that bill is not as strong as he would like, Danny Caneff, director of the Wisconsin Rural Development Center, says, "In effect it would be a ban," since consumers would be wary of milk with new additives. Its chances of passage are very good, he says. Last spring Wisconsin Agricultural Secretary Howard C. Richards endorsed a moratorium on commercial sale of the drug until its effect on the state's economy can be assessed.

Meanwhile, firms across the country—including food giants such as   15
Kraft and Borden as well as five of the nation's largest supermarket corporations—have announced that they will not accept milk from herds treated with the drug. Last summer Ben and Jerry's, the popular Vermont ice cream firm, announced that its products would not accept such milk and would bear labels proclaiming "Save Family Farms." The battle lines are drawn for what promises to be a major test of the political strength of this Neo-Luddite movement.

Langdon Winner, an insightful critic of technological change, compares our traditional eagerness to adopt new technologies with the blind rambles of a somnambulist. It's a "puzzle of our times," he writes in the book *The Whale and the Reactor* (University of Chicago Press, 1986), that we so willingly "sleepwalk through the process of reconstituting the conditions of human existence." Neo-Luddites such as Kinsman are desperately trying to awaken us. The unwanted social consequences that accompany today's technological innovations, they insist, may far outweigh any benefits. Like the 19th century machine smashers, these Neo-Luddites are not against technology per se. Rather, they have decided, based on personal and community circumstances, that *particular* technologies are of no use—or worse, represent a threat.

Historian David Noble suggests a provisional list of three criteria for judging technologies. "Technologies might be opposed," he writes, "if they degrade people and diminish their freedom and control without any apparent economic or other compensating benefit; if their technical and economic viability is ambiguous, but they pose serious social problems; or if they are clearly viable in the narrow technical or economic sense but are nonetheless destructive for society as a whole." Right now, the biggest project of the emerging Neo-Luddite movement is to develop yardsticks to measure the ill effects of technologies—both new and old. Rather than responding exuberantly "Why not!" to every invitation offered by a new technology,

Americans can, with the help of these new measures, in some cases confidently explain *why* not.

QUESTIONING THE TEXT

1. Attempt a definition of the term "Neo-Luddite." Bring your definition to class and compare it with the definitions prepared by your classmates. Where do your definitions differ—and why?
2. Is Grossman sympathetic to the Neo-Luddites? How do you know? Locate places in his text that reveal his attitude.
3. From what she says in the headnotes to the Orenstein (p. 251) and Grossman articles, do you think A.L. is a Neo-Luddite? Why might she be (or not be) sympathetic to their cause?

MAKING CONNECTIONS

4. Might Victor Frankenstein be described as a Neo-Luddite? Or is he more like Grossman's description of Americans—hopelessly attracted to the "new"? Prepare a list of reasons to support one of these claims.
5. Freeman J. Dyson concludes his essay (on p. 231) by reminding us that we should "give honor to the brave victims of our stupidity." Would Grossman agree? Why, or why not? And if so, what "victims of our stupidity" would he wish to honor?

JOINING THE CONVERSATION

6. Freewrite for 15 minutes or so about a time when you felt that your way of life was being threatened by a new way of doing things. How did you respond?
7. Investigate the actions of some group that is currently protesting against some technological change—the opening of a nuclear power plant, for instance, or legalization of the day-after abortion pill. Write a brief position paper in which you argue that the actions are justified or unjustified.
8. With two or three classmates, brainstorm a list of cutting-edge technologies. As a group, decide whether any one is potentially the most harmful, and then work together to make a list of at least six or seven good reasons for resisting it. Finally, prepare a brief summary of your reasons to present to your class.

WILLIAM RATHJE and
CULLEN MURPHY
Five Major Myths about Garbage, and Why They're Wrong

THIS CHAPTER *is so full of far-out notions of science—animated monsters, Neo-Luddites, Virtual Reality, exploding space shuttles—that I thought it needed a piece on a more mundane subject, one perhaps closer to all our lives. And so I selected William Rathje and Cullen Murphy's article about America's garbage problem, a 1992 report published in* Smithsonian *magazine that summarizes a twenty-year study of waste dumps. It is exactly the kind of lively and astute piece one expects to find in the handsome journal affiliated with our national museums, a periodical aimed at people curious in a nonprofessional way about everything, from dinosaur tracks in New Mexico to the architecture of Moorish Spain.*

Smithsonian, it is worth noting, is stuffed with ads for luxury cars and exotic vacations. So why would its upscale audience be interested in garbage? Because it seems that everyone *is concerned about what science, technology, and industrialization have done to our natural environment, an evangelically "green" press having convinced many Americans that the country is about to be toxified by acid rain, toasted through a tear in the ozone layer, and inundated by nonbiodegradable plastics and disposable diapers. On this small and fragile planet, mankind and his science (and I am using masculine references deliberately) have made a mess of things on a scale that makes Victor Frankenstein's monster seem like small potatoes. Or so one side of the environmental debate goes.*

Fortunately, we are beginning to hear from policy makers staking out a middle ground between developers who would bulldoze the Grand Canyon to build a shopping mall and those who'd turn New York City into a nature preserve, preferably without people. Environmentalists have often been strident and apocalyptic, too quick to draw conclusions and to push agendas many see as hostile to property rights and free-market enterprise. Yet both the natural environment and the prosperity of industrialized nations with the wealth to protect it are too fragile to entrust to foolhardy and nonscientific speculation. That's why an article like "Five Major Myths about Garbage" comes as a breath of fresh air to chasten us for our bad environmental practices, but also to reassure us that the sky isn't falling quite yet. The article was adapted from Rathje and Murphy's book Rubbish! The Archaeology of Garbage. — J.R.

Would that it were possible to study garbage in the abstract. But, alas, garbage isn't mathematics. To understand garbage you have to touch it, to feel it, to sort it, to smell it. You have to pick through hundreds of tons of it, counting and weighing all the daily newspapers, the telephone books, the soiled diapers, the foam clamshells that once briefly held hamburgers, the lipstick cylinders coated with grease, the medicine vials still encasing brightly colored pills, the empty Scotch bottles, the half-full cans of paint and muddy turpentine, the forsaken toys, the cigarette butts. You have to sort and weigh and measure the volume of all the organic matter, the discards from thousands of plates: the noodles and the Cheerios and the tortillas; the pet food that made its own gravy; the hardened jelly doughnuts, bleeding from their side wounds; the half-eaten bananas, mostly still within their peels, black and incomparably sweet in the embrace of final decay.

You have to confront sticky green mountains of yard waste, and slippery brown hills of potato peels, and ossuaries of brittle chicken bones and T-bones. And then, finally, there are the "fines," the vast connecting mixture of tiny bits of paper, metal, glass, plastic, dirt, grit and former nutrients that suffuses every landfill like a kind of grainy lymph. To understand garbage you need thick gloves and a mask and some booster shots. But the yield in knowledge offsets the grim working conditions.

To an archaeologist, ancient garbage pits, which usually can be located within a short distance of any ruin, are among the happiest of finds. Every archaeologist dreams of discovering spectacular objects—the Mask of Agamemnon,* the Ark of the Covenant—but the bread-and-butter work of archaeology involves the most common and routine kinds of discards. It is not entirely fanciful to define archaeology as the discipline that tries to learn from old garbage.

The Garbage Project, conceived in 1971 and officially established at the University of Arizona in 1973, was an attempt to apply archaeological principles to a modern society: ours. Over the years some 750 people working for the project have processed more than 250,000 pounds of garbage— 14 tons of it excavated from landfills (*Smithsonian,* April 1990), the rest obtained fresh from the truck or the curb. Sorted, weighed, coded and catalogued, it has produced a unique database that yields all sorts of insights and questions about American life. Most notably the question of whether there is a garbage crisis at all.

Americans certainly do produce lots of garbage, and we have achieved   5
no consensus about what to do with it. That *is* a big problem. But the work of the Garbage Project underscores a second problem, one that helps explain why we have been unable to deal with the first problem: much conventional

---

Mask of Agamemnon: a gold mask dated 1580–1550 B.C.E., found in Mycenae, Greece, by the archaeologist Heinrich Schliemann (1822–90)

wisdom about garbage and its disposal consists of myths and assertions that turn out, upon investigation, to be misleading—or dead wrong.

Myth Number One.   Fast-food packaging, polystyrene foam and disposable diapers are major constituents of American garbage.

Over the years, Garbage Project researchers have asked people who have never seen the inside of a landfill to estimate what percentage of a landfill's contents is made up of fast-food packaging, expanded polystyrene foam and disposable diapers. In September of 1989 this very question was asked of a group attending the biennial meeting of the National Audubon Society, and the results were generally consistent with those obtained from surveys at universities, business meetings, and conferences of state and local government officials.

Estimates of the volume of fast-food packaging fell mainly between 20 and 30 percent of a typical landfill's contents; of expanded polystyrene foam, between 25 and 40 percent; of disposable diapers, between 25 and 45 percent. The overall estimate, then, of the proportion of a landfill's contents taken up by the three types of garbage together ranged from a suspiciously high 70 percent to an obviously impossible 115 percent.

The physical reality inside a landfill is, in fact, quite different. Of the 14 tons of garbage from nine municipal landfills that the Garbage Project has excavated and sorted in the past five years, there was less than a hundred pounds of fast-food packaging—that is, containers or wrappers for hamburgers, pizzas, chicken, fish and convenience-store sandwiches, as well as the accessories most of us deplore, such as cups, lids, straws, sauce containers, and so on.

In other words, less than one-half of 1 percent of the weight of the   10
materials excavated from landfills consisted of fast-food packaging. As for the amount of space that fast-food packaging takes up—a more important consideration than weight—the Garbage Project estimate is that fast-food packages account for no more than one-third of 1 percent of the total volume of the average landfill's contents.

What about expanded polystyrene foam? The stuff is, of course, used for many things. But only about 10 percent of all foam plastics manufactured during the past decade was used for fast-food packaging. Most foam was (and is) blown into egg cartons, meat trays, coffee cups, lightweight "peanuts" for packing delicate things, and the intriguing molded forms that keep electronic appliances safe in their shipping cases. Judging from the results of detailed landfill excavations, all the expanded polystyrene foam that is thrown away in the United States every year accounts for no more than 1 percent of the volume of landfilled garbage.

Expanded polystyrene foam, nevertheless, has been the focus of many vocal campaigns to ban it outright. It is worth remembering that if such foam were banned, the relatively small amount of space that it takes up in landfills would not be saved. Eggs, hamburgers, coffee and stereos must still be put in something.

When it comes to disposable diapers, some startling numbers do get bandied about. In 1987 the Portland *Oregonian* reported that disposable diapers made up one-quarter of the contents of local landfills. According to another estimate used by government agencies in recent years, disposable diapers constitute about 12 percent of total trash. These numbers are not, in fact, correct. The Garbage Project has consistently found that, on average, disposable diapers make up no more than 1 percent by weight of a typical landfill's total solid-waste content—and no more than 1.4 percent by volume.

Fast-food packaging, foam and disposable diapers have acquired high visibility because they are so noticeable among casual litter, and people think the components of everyday litter are the same as landfilled garbage. As a result, these items have become powerful symbolic targets. But if they disappeared tomorrow, landfill operators would hardly notice.

Myth Number Two. Plastic is also a big problem.   15

For the record, it should be noted that the item most frequently encountered in landfills is plain old paper—it accounts for more than 40 percent of a landfill's contents; this proportion has held steady for decades and in some landfills has actually risen. Newspapers alone may take up as much as 13 percent of the space in American landfills. A year's worth of copies of the *New York Times* has been estimated to be equivalent in volume to 18,660 crushed aluminum cans or 14,969 flattened Big Mac clamshells.

There was a lot of talk some years ago about how technology, computers in particular, would bring about a "paperless office"—a risky prediction given the already apparent increase caused by the photocopy machine. Today there are 59 million personal computers in the United States with printers attached. Where the creation of paper waste is concerned, technology is proving to be not so much a contraceptive as a fertility drug.

That said, what is the situation with respect to plastic? In landfill after landfill excavated by the Garbage Project, the volume of all plastics—foam, film and rigid; toys, utensils and packages—amounted to between 20 and 24 percent of all garbage, as sorted; when compacted along with everything else, as it is in landfills, the volume of plastics fell to only about 16 percent.

Even if plastics' share of total garbage is, at the moment, fairly low, isn't it true that plastics take up a larger and larger proportion of landfill space with every passing year? Unquestionably, a larger number of physical objects are made of plastic today than were in 1970, or 1950. But a curious phenomenon becomes apparent when garbage deposits from our own time are compared with those from landfill strata characteristic of, say, the 1970s. While the *number* of individual plastic objects to be found in a deposit of garbage of a given size has increased considerably in the course of a decade and a half—more than doubling—the *proportion* of landfill space taken up by those plastics has not changed; at some landfills the proportion of space taken up by plastics was actually a little less in the 1980s than in the '70s.

The explanation appears to be the result of what is known in the   20 plastics industry as "light-weighting"—making objects in such a way that the object retains all the necessary functional characteristics but requires the use of less resin. The concept of light-weighting is not limited to the making of plastics; the makers of glass bottles have been light-weighting their wares for decades, with the result that bottles today are 25 percent lighter than they were in 1984.

Using fewer raw materials for a product that is lighter and therefore cheaper to transport usually translates into a competitive edge, and companies that rely heavily on plastics have been light-weighting ever since plastics were introduced. Soda bottles made of polyethylene terephthalate (PET) weighed 67 grams in 1974; today they weigh 48 grams. In the mid-'60s high-density polyethylene milk jugs weighed about 120 grams; today the number is 65. Plastic grocery bags had a thickness of 30 microns in 1976; the thickness today is at most 18 microns. Even the plastic in disposable diapers has been light-weighted, although the superabsorbent material that was added at the same time (1986) ensures that while diapers may enter the house lighter, they will leave it heavier than ever. In most cases, when plastic gets lighter, it also gets thinner and more crushable. The result is that many more plastic items can be squeezed into a given volume of landfill space today than could fit 10 or 20 years ago.

Myth Number Three.   A lot of biodegradation takes place in modern landfills.

Plastic is the Great Satan of garbage: gaudy, cheap, a convenient scapegoat for people who claim we waste and consume too much. Although it is paper more than anything else that is filling up landfills, in paper's defense one frequently hears: Well, at least paper biodegrades; plastic remains inert and will take up space in a landfill until the end of time.

Not really.

Misconceptions about the interior life of landfills are profound—not   25 surprisingly, since so very few people can (or would want to) venture inside one. There is a popular notion that in the depths of a typical municipal landfill lies a roiling caldron of fermentation—intense chemical and biological activity. That perception is accompanied by a certain ambivalence. Landfills are seen, on the one hand, as places where organic matter is rapidly breaking down—biodegrading—into a sort of rich, moist brown humus, returning at last to the bosom of Mother Nature. In this view, biodegradation is something devoutly to be wished, an environmentally correct outcome of the first magnitude. On the other hand, coexisting with the romance of biodegradation, there is the view of landfills as environments from which a toxic broth of chemicals leaches into the surrounding soil, polluting groundwater and nearby lakes and streams. What both views have in common is the assumption that a great deal of biodegradation is taking place.

Well, some biodegradation *is* taking place—otherwise landfills would produce none of the large amounts of methane and trace amounts of other gases that they do in fact produce. In reality, however, the dynamics of a modern landfill are very nearly the opposite of what most people think. Biologically and chemically, a landfill is much more static than we commonly suppose. For some kinds of organic garbage, biodegradation goes on for a while and then slows to a virtual standstill. For other kinds, biodegradation never gets under way at all.

Biodegradation was the target of a major Garbage Project research program. The first question observers set out to answer was: After a period of 10 or 15 years, is there much identifiable paper and other organic debris remaining in a typical landfill? Or has it mostly been transformed into methane and humus? Landfills vary, of course, but when the paper items are combined with food waste, yard waste and wood (mostly lumber used in construction), the overall volume of old organic material recovered largely intact from the landfills excavated by the Garbage Project turned out to be astonishingly high.

For example, at the Mallard North Landfill, outside Chicago, organics represented 50.6 percent of the 10-to-15-year-old garbage excavated. Some 40 percent of 25-year-old garbage at Sunnyvale Landfill, near San Francisco, was organic. And at the Rio Salado Landfill, near Phoenix, organics totaled nearly 50 percent of the excavated garbage that dated back to the 1950s.

Almost all this material remained readily identifiable: pages from coloring books were still clearly that; onion parings were onion parings, carrot tops were carrot tops. In the course of every excavation the Garbage Project has done, whole hot dogs have been found, some of them in strata suggesting an age upwards of several decades. From the newspapers in America's landfills you could relive the New Deal.

The picture of biodegradation that emerges from these and other 30 Garbage Project investigations is something like the following. Under normal landfill conditions—in which garbage is covered with dirt after being dumped, and the landfill is kept relatively dry—the only types of garbage that truly decompose are certain kinds of food and yard waste. And these obligingly biodegradable items account for less than 10 percent of the average landfill's contents. Even after two decades, a third to a half of supposedly vulnerable organics remain in recognizable condition. This portion may continue to experience biodegradation, but at a snail's pace.

That finding accords with what is known of the typical life cycle of a field of methane wells, which are drilled to draw gas out of landfills. For 15 or 20 years after a landfill has stopped accepting garbage, the wells vent methane in fairly substantial amounts. Then methane production drops off rapidly, indicating that the landfill has stabilized. Henceforth, it would seem, whatever is in the landfill won't be changing very much.

Well-designed and well-managed landfills, in particular, seem to be far more apt to preserve their contents for posterity than to transform them into humus or mulch. They are not vast composters; rather, they are vast mummifiers. But no need to panic. This may be a good thing. For while there are advantages to biodegradation, it is unquestionably true that the more things decompose in a landfill, the more opportunities there will be for a landfill's noxious contents to come back and haunt us.

Myth Number Four.   America is running out of safe places to put landfills.

There can be no disputing the fact that there is, for the time being, an acute shortage of landfills that are still available for deposits, especially in the Northeastern United States. Since 1978, according to the Environmental Protection Agency, some 14,000 landfills have been shut down nationwide (leaving some 6,000 in operation). Still, as the University of Pennsylvania's waste-management expert, Iraj Zandi, has shown, these figures somewhat overstate the problem. Many of the shut-down "landfills" were actually open dumps being closed for environmental reasons. And whatever the nature of the sites, they have tended to be relatively small, whereas those that remain open are quite large.

In 1988, for example, 70 percent of the country's landfills—the smaller ones—handled less than 5 percent of the municipal solid waste that was landfilled nationwide; that same year, fewer than 500 landfills, or about 8 percent of the total—the bigger ones—handled nearly 75 percent of our landfilled garbage. "It appears," Zandi writes, "that the trend is toward operating fewer but larger landfills. This phenomenon coincides with the trend in the rest of the industrialized world." As of 1990, some 42 percent of all landfills were under 10 acres in size, 51 percent were between 10 and 100 acres, and 6 percent were larger than 100 acres. Regionally, of course, the situation is in many cases dire. In New Jersey (pop. 7.7 million), the number of landfills has dropped from more than 300 to about a dozen during the past 15 years.

The customary formulation of the problem that we face is that within the next five years 50 percent of the landfills now in use will close down. Describing the situation this way makes it seem as if Americans have somehow speeded up the throwaway society. As it happens, it has always been the case that half of all landfills in use at any given time will close within five years. It was true back in 1970 and in 1960, too, because the waste-management industry has never seen the need to maintain excess capacity beyond a certain level. In the past, however, new landfill capacity was rarely hard to obtain. The difference today is not that we're filling up landfills at a rapidly increasing pace, but that in many places used-up capacity is simply not being replaced.

Why aren't more permits being granted? The reasons usually have nothing to do with the claim most frequently offered: We are running out of room for landfills. Yes, it is sometimes the case that a community or a state has run out of room. In the congested Northeast there is not all that much space left for landfills, at least not safe ones. In the nation as a whole, however, there is room aplenty. The United States is a big country, heavily urbanized but with enormous tracts of empty countryside.

In a study published by the Washington-based think tank Resources for the Future, economist A. Clark Wiseman has calculated that at the current rate of waste generation, all of America's garbage for the next 1,000 years would fit into a single landfill space only 120 feet deep and 44 miles square—a patch of land about the size of three Oklahoma Citys.

So vast a landfill is, for any number of reasons, completely impractical, of course. The point here is simply that the total amount of space necessary will not be all that large. Few nations are as substantially endowed with uncongested territory as ours is, and there is appropriate land available even in some relatively populous areas. Recently, Browning-Ferris Industries, one of the nation's two biggest full-service garbage disposal companies, commissioned an environmental survey of eastern New York State with the express aim of determining where landfills might safely be located. The survey pinpointed sites that represented 200 square miles of territory— which constituted only 1 percent of the region's land area. Yet with all this available land, the state has, since 1982, closed down 349 landfills and opened only 6.

The obstacles to new sanitary landfills these days are to some extent 40
monetary—landfills are indeed expensive. But more important, the obstacles are psychological and political. Nobody wants a garbage dump in his or her backyard. It is ironic. We have convinced ourselves that our big flaw is that we are wasteful and profligate, while a much more serious flaw goes unnoticed: as a nation, on the subject of garbage, at least, we have become politically impotent.

Myth Number Five.   On a per-capita basis, Americans are producing garbage at a rapidly accelerating rate.

Not much comparable data is available on garbage-generation rates during different periods of time, but what little there is does not support the view that per-capita rates have steadily accelerated. Garbage Project sortings of large amounts of household garbage in Milwaukee during the late seventies found that households there threw out garbage at a rate of about a pound and a half per person per day. Fortuitously, data exists for

Milwaukee from a period 20 years earlier—1959, specifically. A study done at the time for a doctoral dissertation in environmental engineering by John Bell of Purdue University found that Milwaukee households were throwing away slightly more garbage than were their 1970s counterparts: about 1.9 pounds per person per day. Admittedly, this estimate involved only household waste, not the larger category of municipal solid waste. But household waste is by far the largest contributor to municipal solid waste, and the Milwaukee comparison at least deserves a place in the evidence pile.

Looking at the matter another way, let us assume that the Environmental Protection Agency is right when it estimates that the average American throws out about 1,500 pounds of garbage a year. That certainly seems like a lot. History reminds us, though, that many former components of American garbage no longer exist—major components whose absence does not even register in the collective memory. Thus, we do not see the 1,200 pounds per year of coal ash that the average American generated from home stoves and furnaces at the turn of the century—and usually dumped on the poor side of town. We do not see the more than 20 pounds of manure that each of the more than three million horses living in cities produced every day at the turn of the century, or the hundreds of thousands of dead horses that cities had to dispose of every year. We do not see all the food that households once wasted willy-nilly because refrigeration and sophisticated packaging were not yet widespread.

It is undeniable that Americans as a whole are producing more municipal solid waste than they did 50 or 100 years ago. But this is largely because there are more Americans than there were 100 or even 50 years ago (63 million in 1890, 132 million in 1940, 248 million now).

These days, debates swirl about the fine points of per-capita garbage-generation rates and whether they've been going up slightly year by year in recent decades, and by how much. Certainly, wars, recessions and social innovation (for example, the advent of curbside recycling) cause yearly variations in the solid-waste stream, though in ways that economists and social scientists cannot yet accurately describe. But a long view of America's municipal solid waste would suggest that, on a per-capita basis, the nation's record is hardly one of unrestrained excess. Indeed, the word that best describes the situation with respect to overall volume may be "stability." 45

If the work of the Garbage Project seems somewhat reassuring, the reassurance is an unsatisfying kind: it suggests that we may not be quite as bad as we thought, that our problems are perhaps not quite as terrible as we believed. But the disposal of garbage remains a matter in need of serious attention. And the most critical part of the garbage problem in America may be that our notions about the creation and disposal of garbage are riddled with misconceptions. We go after glamorous symbolic targets rather than the serious but mundane ones. Impelled by a sense of crisis, we make hasty decisions when nothing about the situation warrants anything but calm. We castigate ourselves for certain imperfections but not for the ones that really matter.

And we lose sight of fundamentals. The solid-waste stream has not suddenly become a raging torrent. The means we have for disposing of garbage—in landfills, through incineration, through recycling—have never been safer or more technically advanced. And since the late 19th century, America's record with respect to garbage disposal has been one of gradual improvement. It remains to be seen whether this record can be sustained in the face of not-in-my-backyard outrage that has led to political impasse on solid-waste issues all over the country.

What should be done? To a certain extent, that depends on where you are. Conditions vary. In the future, a congested place like New York City, hemmed in by suburbs, will have to burn its garbage, whereas a place like Tucson, in open country, will probably be able to rely on landfills forever.

Whatever the disposal means that are selected, we should be willing to pay prorated fees for the collection and disposal of nonrecyclable garbage. Charging a fee for nonrecyclable garbage thrown away, while not charging for recyclable refuse, has precisely the effect economic theory would predict: recycling rates improve, and the overall volume of nonrecyclable garbage diminishes. This system, tried in cities like Seattle, works. Adopted on a broad scale, the impact will ripple backward, encouraging manufacturers to use less packaging and to make products with ease of recycling in mind.

We should buy goods and packaging with a high recycled content. 50 The biggest problem faced by recycling is not the technological process of turning one thing into another. Anything can be recycled—and would be if demand for what it could be recycled into were great enough. The key, then, is demand, and demand for many recyclables is often soft. Consumers can increase demand by buying wisely. But to do so they will have to become garbage literate, because labels can be deceptive. For example, the word "recycled" on a package generally means not that a product has been made, at least in part, out of something that a consumer once bought and then turned in for recycling, but rather that it has been made in part with scrap left over from the normal manufacturing process—business as usual in any well-run factory. The label one needs to look for is "post-consumer recycled," and ideally the label will include a percentage, as in "30 percent post-consumer recycled." Anything above 10 percent is worthwhile.

Finally, the garbage problems that the United States has experienced will have had an unexpected welcome outcome if they drive home a lesson relevant to multiple public policy issues: namely, that public and political *notions* of our situation and what our situation really *is* do not match. In many cases they do not even closely approximate each other. This conclusion has emerged time and again from Garbage Project studies. Disdained commodity though it is, garbage offers a useful, if ironic, reminder of one of the fundamentals of critical self-knowledge—that we do not necessarily know many things that we think we know. That is not the usual starting point of most discussions in America, especially political ones. But it is not a bad starting point at all.

QUESTIONING THE TEXT

1. The beginning of this article is heavily descriptive. Point out the most graphic passages and assess the effectiveness of the authors' technique. Does the introduction get you involved in the subject?
2. Does the article have a sentence that functions as a thesis? Which sentence(s) would you say come(s) closest to stating the point of this report?
3. How did you react to J.R.'s introduction to this reading? Pay special attention to his language—what does it tell you about his assumptions? Does his language make his introduction more or less persuasive? Cite examples in your answer.

MAKING CONNECTIONS

4. In the selection starting on p. 222, Freeman J. Dyson describes the difficulties in predicting the direction technology will take. How might his warning apply to environmental issues and problems? What qualifications might you place upon Rathje and Murphy's suggestion that we likely have more than enough space in the United States to handle our waste products for the next thousand years?

JOINING THE CONVERSATION

5. Respond to Rathje and Murphy's assertion that "on the subject of garbage, at least, we have become politically impotent." What do they mean by "politically impotent"? To what other cultural and social matters might this description be applied? If you keep a reading log, put your response there.
6. With two or three classmates, discuss Rathje and Murphy's warning at the end of their article: "we do not necessarily know many things that we think we know." About which important subjects might the general public not be well enough informed to make intelligent

decisions? Choose one such subject and write a position paper, in the form of an opinion column that might appear on the last page of a popular news magazine, arguing that the public either can or cannot make a knowledgeable decision about it.

RONALD REAGAN
Tribute to the Challenger *Astronauts*

Scheduled to deliver a State of the Union speech on the evening of January 28, 1986, President Ronald Reagan instead had to address a nation stunned earlier in the day by the destruction of the space shuttle Challenger. *The vehicle had exploded only moments after rising from its launch pad in Florida, killing the entire crew, including Christa McAuliffe, the first teacher selected for a mission in space. Millions of American schoolchildren had been watching from their classrooms.*

I chose Reagan's address, composed in haste by his speechwriter Peggy Noonan, because it puts many of the themes explored in this chapter in painfully human terms. Like many scientists and explorers before them, the men and women of Challenger *gave their lives extending the frontiers of knowledge.* – J.R.

Ladies and gentlemen, I had planned to speak to you tonight to report on the State of the Union, but the events of earlier today have led me to change those plans. Today is a day for mourning and remembering.

Nancy and I are pained to the core by the tragedy of the shuttle *Challenger.* We know we share this pain with all of the people of our country. This is truly a national loss.

Nineteen years ago almost to the day, we lost three astronauts in a terrible accident on the ground. But we have never lost an astronaut in flight. We have never had a tragedy like this. And perhaps we have forgotten the courage it took for the crew of the shuttle. But they, the *Challenger* Seven, were aware of the dangers—and overcame them, and did their jobs brilliantly.

We mourn seven heroes—Michael Smith, Dick Scobee, Judith Resnik, Ronald McNair, Ellison Onizuka, Gregory Jarvis, and Christa McAuliffe. We mourn their loss as a nation, together.

To the families of the Seven: We cannot bear, as you do, the full impact of this tragedy—but we feel the loss, and we are thinking about you so very much. Your loved ones were daring and brave and they had that special grace, that special spirit that says Give me a challenge and I'll meet it with joy. They had a hunger to explore the universe and discover its truths. They wished to serve and they did—they served us all.

And I want to say something to the schoolchildren of America who were watching the live coverage of the shuttle's takeoff. I know it's hard to understand, but sometimes painful things like this happen—it's all part of the process of exploration and discovery—it's all part of taking a chance and expanding man's horizons. The future doesn't belong to the fainthearted, it belongs to the brave. The *Challenger* crew was pulling us into the future—and we'll continue to follow them.

I've always had great faith in and respect for our space program—and what happened today does nothing to diminish it. We don't hide our space program, we don't keep secrets and cover things up, we do it all up front and in public. That's the way freedom is, and we wouldn't change it for a minute.

We'll continue our quest in space. There will be more shuttle flights and more shuttle crews and, yes, more volunteers, more civilians, more teachers in space. Nothing ends here—our hopes and our journeys continue.

I want to add that I wish I could talk to every man and woman who works for NASA or who worked on this mission and tell them: Your dedication and professionalism have moved and impressed us for decades, and we know of your anguish. We share it.

There's a coincidence today. On this day 390 years ago the great   10 explorer Sir Francis Drake died aboard ship off the coast of Panama. In his lifetime the great frontiers were the oceans. And a historian later said, "He lived by the sea, died on it, and was buried in it." Today we can say of the *Challenger* crew: Their dedication was, like Drake's, complete.

The crew of the space shuttle *Challenger* honored us by the manner in which they lived their lives. We will never forget them, nor the last time we saw them—this morning, as they prepared for their journey, and waved good-bye, and "slipped the surly bonds of earth" to "touch the face of God."*

IN RESPONSE

1. What specific values does Reagan affirm in the face of a national disaster? Why the allusion to Sir Francis Drake?
2. In his essay starting on p. 222, Freeman J. Dyson describes the *Challenger* astronauts as "the brave victims of our stupidity" because, he argues, NASA had built the shuttle to serve engineers' dreams, not the needs of scientists or potential customers in the military or industry. Should men and women explore space, or should that task be left to cheaper, more efficient robotic spacecraft? Write a letter to the editor (or to a member of Congress) on the subject.
3. Consider the contrast between Reagan's confidence after the shuttle's destruction ("Nothing ends here") and Victor Frankenstein's doubts about the monster he has created. Why does Reagan say the shuttle program will go forward? Why must Frankenstein's experiments end?

"slipped the surly bonds of earth" to "touch the face of God": from "High Flight" (1941), a poem by John Gillespie Magee, Jr. (1922–41)

EMILY DICKINSON
"Faith" Is a Fine Invention

EMILY DICKINSON (1830–86), who lived all her life in Amherst, Massachusetts, wrote her poetry during a time in which industrial and scientific progress was revolutionizing the U.S. economy and, in turn, our entire society. An astute and passionate observer of both the natural and the spiritual worlds, Dickinson was also interested in the ways in which questions of nature and the spirit were addressed by science. In this four-line poem, first published in 1891, Dickinson offers one of her characteristic witty insights, playing with the notion of faith as an invention (a scientific invention?) and playing on the word see.

I chose this selection because of its lighthearted and slightly mischievous tone and because it captures so well—and in so few words—the dilemma of those who would link moral and spiritual concerns with the quests of science. What faith, we might ask, did Victor Frankenstein have? How much could he "see"? — A.L.

"Faith" is a fine invention
When Gentlemen can *see*—
But *Microscopes* are prudent
In an Emergency.

IN RESPONSE

1. What does Dickinson mean by the word *"faith"*? How does her assertion that it is an "invention" complicate traditional definitions of religious faith?
2. Are you a person who depends primarily on "faith" or on "microscopes" when you need to make a decision? Explain.
3. Compare Dickinson's view of science with the view expressed by one of the scientists represented in this chapter—Victor Frankenstein (p. 213), Freeman J. Dyson (p. 222), or Lewis Thomas (p. 233), perhaps. Bring your list of similarities or dissimilarities to class for discussion.
4. Try your hand at a four- or six-line poem about "faith" or "science."

OTHER READINGS

Brennan, Richard P. *Levitating Trains and Kamikaze Genes: Technical Literacy for the 1990s.* New York: Wiley, 1990. Explains his view of what Americans need to know about science.

Diamond, Irene, and Gloria Feman Orenstein, eds. *Reweaving the World: The Emergence of Ecofeminism.* San Francisco: Sierra Club Books, 1990. Critiques science and technology from a feminist perspective.

Goldberg, Steven. "Feminism Against Science." *National Review* 18 Nov. 1991: 30–33. Attacks the notion of "gendered" science.

Krugg, Edward. "Fish Story: The Great Acid Rain Flimflam." *Policy Review* Spring 1990: 44–48. Provides surprising facts about acidic lakes in the American Northeast.

Oppenheimer, Robert. "Speech to the Association of Los Alamos Scientists, November 2, 1945." *Robert Oppenheimer: Letters and Recollections.* Eds. Alice Kimball Smith and Charles Weiner. 315–25. Defends and critiques the atomic bomb, which Oppenheimer helped to create.

Rigden, John S., and Sheila Tobias. "Tune In, Turn Off, Drop Out: Why So Many College Students Abandon Science After the Introductory Courses." *The Sciences* Jan./Feb. 1991: 16–20. Suggests how we might teach science more effectively.

Sagan, Carl. *Broca's Brain.* New York: Random, 1976. Explores the romance of science.

Toulmin, Stephen. *The Return of Cosmology: Postmodern Science and the Theology of Nature.* Berkeley: U of California P, 1982. Traces the debate about cosmology—the theory of the universe—as it has changed from 1945 to the present.

Tudor, Andrew. *Monsters and Mad Scientists: A Cultural History of the Horror Movie.* Oxford: Blackwell, 1989. Studies some of our favorite horror movies.

Weaver, Richard. "Ultimate Terms in Contemporary Rhetoric." *Language Is Sermonic: Richard M. Weaver on the Nature of Rhetoric.* Baton Rouge: Louisiana State UP, 1970. A philosopher of language notes that ethics always lag behind science.

Whitman, Walt. "When I Heard the Learn'd Astronomer." *Complete Poetry and Collected Prose.* New York: Viking, 1982. A poet compares listening to a scientist to looking at the stars.

PART THREE

Who We Are

Gender:
Women . . . and Men

And the rib, which the LORD God had taken from man, made he a woman, and brought her unto the man.
Genesis, 2:21–22

If the first woman God ever made was strong enough to turn the world upside down all alone, these women together ought to be able to turn it back. . . .
SOJOURNER TRUTH, *Ain't I a Woman?*

The richest relationship many sane and highly creative men establish is with systems of ideas or with pieces of machinery.
LIAM HUDSON and BERNADINE JACOT, *The Way Men Think*

She obeyed him; she always did as she was told.
MAXINE HONG KINGSTON, *No Name Woman*

. . . we are in the presence here of nothing less than a brazen campaign to redefine seduction as a form of rape, and more slyly to identify practically all men as rapists.
NORMAN PODHORETZ, *Rape in Feminist Eyes*

Hill's performance convinced me of nothing save that if she told me the sun was shining, I should head straight for my umbrella and galoshes.
NAOMI MUNSON, *Harassment Blues*

Is there no way to interdict and terminate the traditional, abusive loneliness of black women in this savage country?
JUNE JORDAN, *Can I Get a Witness?*

Women can change the embryo to a boy, but only men can change the boy to a man.
ROBERT BLY, *Going Off on the Wild Man's Shoulders*

The Wild Man process involves five basic phases: Sweating, Yelling, Crying, Drum-beating, and Ripping Your Shirt Off Even if It's Expensive.
JOE BOB BRIGGS, *Get in Touch with Your Ancient Spear*

To every woman a happy ending.   MARGE PIERCY, *Barbie Doll*

6

287

Introduction

IN CHOOSING THE SELECTIONS for this chapter, we found ourselves talking about the old nursery rhyme:

> What are little girls made of?
> What are little girls made of?
> Sugar and spice and everything nice,
> That's what little girls are made of.

> What are little boys made of?
> What are little boys made of?
> Snips and snails and puppy dog tails,
> That's what little boys are made of.

The readings in this chapter ask you to give serious attention to the question this old rhyme asks. What *are* the differences between girls and boys, between men and women? Are such differences solely genetic/biological? Or are the differences due more to culture and to our life experiences? Are they some of both "nature" and "nurture"?

In thinking about these questions, you may want to consider a distinction many people make between sex and gender. Researchers often define "sex" as the chromosomal patterns that identify humans as male or female and "gender" as those psychological patterns that give humans a sense of being male or female. According to this distinction, we are born one sex or the other—but we develop gender identities through social and cultural practices. Another way to think about this distinction is to see sex as a bipolar set, either male or female, but gender as a range of roles people may adopt—from the intensely "feminine" at one extreme to the intensely "masculine" at the other, but with limitless degrees of variation in between.

We have realized during our discussion of readings in this chapter that though we have many things in common (we are about the same age, come from the same racial group, went to graduate school together, and even got our Ph.D.'s on the same day), we are also very different people. And we have puzzled and argued over how our differences may be related to our differing sexes. As you turn to the readings, you may wish to think about the ways in which being either male or female has affected your life—the choices you have made, the ways you have related to other people, and the way others have related to you. Each of the readings addresses this central concern or some of its implications. Following are some questions to start you thinking about gender:

1. List ten things—jokes, foods, sports, attitudes—you think of as characteristic of women and ten you consider characteristic of

men. Then compare the two lists. What do they reveal about your assumptions regarding gender?

2. Do men and/or women need to be liberated, and if so, from what? Why, or why not?

3. How have feminists improved—or failed to improve—the lot of women today?

4. Do you know of examples or have personal experience of sexual harassment on the job?

5. Can you remember a time when you were treated in a special way or treated unfairly because of your gender? You might want to meet with a group of classmates to exchange stories about these experiences.

• • •

Genesis 1–3

EVERY CULTURE WE KNOW OF has a story of creation, one that chronicles the origins of the world and, often enough, the making of the first man and/or woman. The ancient Greek culture, for example, told the story of Gaia, the Earth, who sprang out of chaos and created Uranus, the Heavens, with whom she then mated to produce the Titans. A Native American culture describes Raven, a powerful mythological creature, as discovering the first people in a large clamshell. One very familiar account of the creation appears in Chapters 1 through 3 of the book of Genesis in the Bible: God creates man in the image of God, gives man dominion over all things on earth, and then creates woman to be a helper to man. After she is tempted by the serpent, the couple fall out of a perfect existence and into self-consciousness and knowledge of evil.

This familiar story, of which the best-known English translation, the King James Version of 1611, is printed below, raises a number of questions about men and women. Are the two sexes equal creations of God—or is woman subordinate to man? Who is responsible for the temptation and fall? Most important for the discussion taking place in this chapter, how does this passage from Genesis represent the sexes—and how does this representation affirm or contradict your own views of the relationship between them? — A.L.

CHAPTER 1

26   And God said, Let us make man in our image, after our likeness: and let them have dominion over the fish of the sea, and over the fowl of the air, and over the cattle, and over all the earth, and over every creeping thing that creepeth upon the earth. . . .

CHAPTER 2

18   And the LORD God said, *It is* not good that the man should be alone; I will make him an help meet for him.
19   And out of the ground the LORD God formed every beast of the field, and every fowl of the air; and brought *them* unto Adam to see what he would call them: and whatsoever Adam called every living creature, that *was* the name thereof.

20   And Adam gave names to all cattle, and to the fowl of the air, and to every beast of the field; but for Adam there was not found an help meet for him.
21   And the LORD God caused a deep sleep to fall upon Adam, and he slept: and he took one of his ribs, and closed up the flesh instead thereof;
22   And the rib, which the LORD God had taken from man, made he a woman, and brought her unto the man.

CHAPTER 3

Now the serpent was more subtil than any beast of the field which the LORD God had made. And he said unto the woman, Yea, hath God said, Ye shall not eat of every tree of the garden?
2   And the woman said unto the serpent, We may eat of the fruit of the trees of the garden:
3   But of the fruit of the tree which *is* in the midst of the garden, God hath said, Ye shall not eat of it, neither shall ye touch it, lest ye shall die.
4   And the serpent said unto the woman, Ye shall not surely die:
5   For God doth know that in the day ye eat thereof, then your eyes shall be opened, and ye shall be as gods, knowing good and evil.*
6   And when the woman saw that the tree *was* good for food, and that it *was* pleasant to the eyes, and a tree to be desired to make *one* wise, she took of the fruit thereof, and did eat, and gave also unto her husband with her; and he did eat.
7   And the eyes of them both were opened, and they knew that they *were* naked; and they sewed fig leaves together, and made themselves aprons.

QUESTIONING THE TEXT

1. Look up *dominion* in the dictionary and find out its derivation—where the word comes from. What does it mean to have "dominion" over all things on earth? Write two or three sentences to explain this passage.
2. After eating the forbidden fruit, man and woman become suddenly aware of their nakedness. Why is this awareness a result of eating from the tree of knowledge of good and evil? Why were they unaware of their nakedness before?
3. Examine Genesis, Chapters 1–3 in their entirety. Then look at A.L.'s

---

ye shall be as gods . . . good and evil: For an exploration of the idea that modern science represents a human effort to "be as gods," see "The Hazards of Science," by Lewis Thomas, on p. 233.

excerpts from these chapters. Are there passages in those chapters you would have included? Why might A.L. have omitted them?

MAKING CONNECTIONS

4. In *The Way Men Think* (p. 296), Liam Hudson and Bernadine Jacot argue that males suffer from a primary "wound" of separation from their mothers. How might you relate their argument to the biblical account of the first man and woman? In what ways is a wound of separation implicit in this account?

5. In what ways might the serpent's interaction with the woman be interpreted as harassment? In thinking of this question, consider the arguments made by Norman Podhoretz (p. 331) and by June Jordan (p. 354).

JOINING THE CONVERSATION

6. Write your own version of the creation story, one that might come from your own culture or another culture you know about, keeping it fairly brief (a page or so). In it, put your own "spin" on how the first people were created.

7. Work with three or four classmates to conduct an informal survey of students or of some children you know, trying for a total of thirty to forty and for an equal number of males and females. Ask them to list the three most important differences between men and women and the three most important similarities. Then make a brief report to your class summing up your findings. Did men and women tend to answer your questions in different ways?

SOJOURNER TRUTH
Ain't I a Woman?

SOJOURNER TRUTH (1797–1883) took her name from mystical visions that urged her, after her escape from slavery, to sojourn and speak the truth. Though she never learned to write on paper, the words of her speeches often wrote on her listeners' souls. The following speech, one of her most famous, was originally written down by Elizabeth Cady Stanton, an early proponent of women's rights, and printed in The History of Woman Suffrage. *Truth delivered it at the Women's Rights Convention in Akron, Ohio, in 1851. On that occasion she spoke to an almost all-white audience, since African Americans were, ironically, not welcome at such events. In "Ain't I a Woman?" Truth speaks not just for women but for many who are oppressed, combining her devotion to abolitionism and to women's suffrage. With vigor and humor, she argues for basic human rights for "all God's children."*

This brief speech always reminds me of the power of the spoken word—and of the difference one voice can sometimes make. I love Truth's use of some of the colloquialisms I grew up with (like "out of kilter"), her familiar references to those in her audience as "honey" and "children," and other aspects of her speaking style that help me feel as though she is right here in front of me talking. I chose this speech for these reasons and because Truth counters perfectly all those voices down through the ages that have dismissed people such as her as "just" women. To hear her rebuttal, and to get at some of this speech's rhythmic power, try reading it aloud. – A.L.

Well, children, where there is so much racket there must be something out of kilter. I think that 'twixt the negroes of the South and the women of the North, all talking about rights, the white men will be in a fix pretty soon. But what's all this here talking about?

That man over there says that women need to be helped into carriages, and lifted over ditches, and to have the best place everywhere. Nobody ever helps me into carriages, or over mud-puddles, or gives me any best place! And ain't I a woman? Look at me! Look at my arm! I have ploughed and planted, and gathered into barns, and no man could head me! And ain't I a woman? I could work as much and eat as much as a man—when I could get it—and bear the lash as well! And ain't I a woman? I have borne thirteen children, and seen them most all sold off to slavery, and when I cried out with my mother's grief, none but Jesus heard me! And ain't I a woman?

Then they talk about this thing in the head; what's this they call it? [Intellect, someone whispers.] That's it, honey. What's that got to do with women's rights or negro's rights? If my cup won't hold but a pint, and yours holds a quart, wouldn't you be mean not to let me have my little half-measure full?

Then that little man in black there, he says women can't have as much rights as men, 'cause Christ wasn't a woman! Where did your Christ come from? Where did your Christ come from? From God and a woman! Man had nothing to do with Him.

If the first woman God ever made was strong enough to turn the   5
world upside down all alone, these women together ought to be able to turn it back, and get it right side up again! And now they is asking to do it, the men better let them.

Obliged to you for hearing me, and now old Sojourner ain't got nothing more to say.

QUESTIONING THE TEXT

1. Truth punctuates her speech with a rhetorical question—"And ain't I a woman?" What effect does the repetition of this question have on you as a reader? What answer does Truth invoke?

2. Make an attempt to write out Truth's speech in more formal language, following all the contemporary grammatical and usage conventions. What differences do you note in the two versions? Which is more powerful, and why?

3. Her introduction reveals that A.L. is obviously a fan of Sojourner Truth. What criticisms *could* she have leveled at Truth's argument?

MAKING CONNECTIONS

4. In the reading on p. 348, Naomi Munson says that women, having "finally been permitted to play with the big boys . . . found the game not to their liking." How might Truth respond to Munson? Write a brief (one-page) dialogue between them, and bring it to class for discussion.

5. Truth says that the first woman God made was "strong enough to turn the world upside down." Is this similar to the view of woman in the reading from Genesis—or not?

6. Truth sees her children sold into slavery, while the aunt in "No Name Woman" sees her child die at her own hand. What comparisons can you draw between the fates of Truth's and No Name Woman's children? What forces in society lead to these fates?

JOINING THE CONVERSATION

7. List as many reasons as you can to support the belief that men and women should or should not have the same rights and responsibilities. Explain from your own experiences *why* you believe as you do.
8. Working with two or three other members of your class, construct one or two arguments to add to Truth's speech, arguments that would support her thesis that women should have equal rights. Try putting each of your new arguments into language like hers, ending with her refrain of "And ain't I a woman?"

LIAM HUDSON and
BERNADINE JACOT
The Way Men Think

SINCE THE HISTORY *of the Western world could without much exaggeration be described as one gigantic men's movement, it seems more than a bit ironic that at the end of the twentieth century, a movement that claims to do for men what the women's movement has done for women is being hailed as something new under the sun. Whatever its origins, the men's movement is now in full swing in the United States, as evidenced by prominent articles in the media, by the popularity of recent books, tapes, and workshops on men's issues, by the appearance of men's studies programs in some universities, and by a growing and sophisticated literature exploring homosexual and heterosexual male experience. At issue is the question this chapter opened with: what, if any, are the qualities that make men unique? And what are the differences among men?*

In The Way Men Think: Intellect, Intimacy and the Erotic Imagination *(1991), Liam Hudson and Bernadine Jacot address these questions by considering the similarities and differences that both connect and separate men and women. The excerpt from their book that is reprinted here traces the differentiation of men from women and argues that this process of differentiation—of disidentification with the mother and counter-identification with the father—marks every male. Hudson (b. 1933), a former fellow of King's College of Cambridge University and professor at the Universities of Edinburgh and Brunel, is a member of the Institute for Advanced Study at Princeton, New Jersey. Jacot, a painter and research fellow in psychology, has worked with Hudson on a number of research projects, including the ones on which this book is based. Hudson and Jacot are married and have four children.*

Their discussion makes me acutely aware of my own relationships with a mother and father and leads me to try to remember my earliest awareness of being a female—and not *a male. Their book reminds me, further, of how complicated and complex is my sense of identity—of who "I" am. I chose this selection because my own reading on the subject of differences between men and women, and particularly between their styles and patterns of thinking, has left me genuinely perplexed, and because I want to understand not only my own characteristic ways of thinking but those of others as well.* — A.L.

STEP BY STEP, OUR PATHS DIVERGE

To begin with, in the earliest stages of the foetus's growth, only its chromosomes enable us to distinguish female from male. Although they will later develop either into testes or into ovaries, the male and female embryos' gonads are at this stage alike. The male's gonads grow more quickly than the female's, though; and, within a few weeks of conception, the male's are recognisable as testes. In another week or so, specialised cells make their appearance in the male's testes and, triggered by secretions from the placenta, these begin in turn to secrete the sex hormone testosterone. This causes the male's external genitalia to take shape as a penis and scrotum. From other specialised cells in the male's testes, there is also secreted a second hormone. This serves to atrophy the structures that, in the female, will later develop into the fallopian tubes. But it is the action of testosterone, it seems, that is crucial. Without it, the external genitalia of both sexes take the female form.

For the vast majority of mortals, this is the parting of the ways. Thereafter, we are each destined to live inside a body recognised as male or recognised as female. To the extent that our bodies are our fates, this is the point at which these are sealed.

This assertion strikes me as portentous and somewhat out of character, given the cautious tone of the article.
— J.R.

Although there have been dissenting voices, the orthodox view is that the female pattern is the basic one, and that the male pattern is a systematic, genetically programmed variation upon it, triggered by the action of the relevant sex hormones. This is certainly the view taken by Tanner.* 'The female', he says, 'is the "basic" sex into which embryos develop if not stimulated to do otherwise.' It is also the attitude expressed by Stoller:

I guess I'm one of those dissenting voices. Isn't "basic" a relative term? What if the "basic" pattern is production of testosterone, and suppression of testosterone is actually the deviation from the norm? — H.L.

> The biologic rules governing sexual behavior in mammals are simple. In all, including man, the 'resting state' of tissue—brain and

---

Tanner: Here Hudson and Jacot begin a review of scholarly books and articles on child development that are pertinent to their own thesis. As is customary in scholarly writing, the authors of these works are usually identified by just their last names.

peripheral—is female. We can now demonstrate without exception, in all experiments performed on animals, that if androgens in the proper amount and biochemical form are withheld during critical periods in fetal life, anatomy and behavior typical of that species' males do not occur, regardless of genetic sex. And if androgens in the proper amount and form are introduced during critical periods in fetal life, anatomy and behavior typical of that species' males do occur, regardless of genetic sex. We cannot experiment on humans, but no natural experiments (for example, chromosomal disorders) are reported that contradict the general mammalian rule.

It seems odd to me that this view has been accepted. Since it threatens notions of male supremacy, why wasn't it suppressed? – A.L.

For boys, but not for girls, a further surge of testosterone occurs in the six months after birth. Little work has yet been done on the psychological implications of this second surge, but it is a period in which important structures are taking shape in the brain, and in which differential effects on male and female could well arise. Evidence is still sketchy, but there are indications that visual perception in four-, five- and six-month-old girls is superior to that of boys, because, it has been suggested, testosterone inhibits the development of the appropriate cortical tissues in boys.

Our own argument begins with another such parting of the ways. This occurs in infancy, in the two or three years after birth rather than in the months before it; and instead of being anatomical and physiological, it is psychological—a question, that is to say, of individuals' perceptions of who they are and how they relate to the people who constitute their intimate world. Although impossible to locate neatly in time, this shift undoubtedly occurs; and it, too, moves the male away from a pattern which, until then, both sexes have shared. We are by no means the first to notice that this is so. We do seem to be the first, though, to realise how powerfully two-edged the implications of this developmental change are bound to be, and how comprehensively it undermines certain simple-

I wondered when they would get around to announcing their own agenda—here it comes! – A.L.

minded beliefs about the paths men and women are subsequently at liberty to follow.

The theoretical background is familiar and is at heart straightforward. As infants, both male and female usually draw primitive comfort and security from their mother or mother-substitute. It is on this intimate, symbiotic relationship with a caring and supportive maternal presence that the subsequent normality of an infant's development depends. As Greenacre says, the foetus 'moves about, kicks, turns around, reacts to some external stimuli by increased motion. It swallows, and traces of its own hair are found in the meconium. It excretes urine and sometimes passes stool.' Grunberger likens the uterus, accordingly, to a 'heavenly, radiant source of bliss and a chamberpot'. It is this pre-natal experience of wholly unqualified physical intimacy which is sustained in the symbiotic intimacy between mother and child. Where this bond is lacking, the individual's subsequent competence as an adult is disturbed—for chimpanzees no less than for human beings, as the Harlows' 'terry towelling mother' experiments show. In chimpanzees, mating and maternal behaviour are disrupted; in humans, it seems to be the capacity to form intimate relationships which is most seriously impaired. It is also in the context of this symbiotic bond with the mother, though, that the infant will first experience pain and frustration: milk that is not instantly forthcoming, griping pains in the stomach, the urge to explore thwarted. The mother, to put the same point in another way, becomes the butt not only of the infant's warmest pleasures but also of its fear and rage.

As well as establishing a position for itself *vis-à-vis* the emotionally charged features of its world, the infant must also establish a sense of its maleness or femaleness: its gender identity. For the little girl, it is easy to see what is at stake. She remains identified with her mother; the source of all her most potent emotions, positive and negative, pleasurable and painful. As a result, she perceives herself as the same sort of being as her mother, through and through. If, as she probably does, she

They seem to be discussing something beyond physical development. In that case, can "normal" really be defined? Doesn't it just mean "acceptable"? Is an inability to form intimate relationships necessarily bad? – H.L.

Why must an infant establish a gender identity? Won't this just reinforce stereotypes later on? – H.L.

Here is the distinction I like to make between sex and gender identity, but I note the authors' tendency to assume that the two are congruent with one another. What if the little girl doesn't

learns to perceive both her mother and herself as an amalgam of the pleasure-provoking and the pain-provoking, the 'good' and the 'bad', her sense of herself is to that extent internally fissured. Nevertheless, she remains all of a piece with the creature, her mother, on whom her sense of reality depends. When the little girl moves on to establish for herself an appropriate 'object' on whom to focus her desires, she again has her mother available to her as model. She can follow the line of her mother's gaze towards her father and towards other males.* The object of her desire is thus a creature inherently unfamiliar to her, even alien, but one whom she addresses from a psychologically coherent foundation.

follow the line of her mother's gaze toward her father and other males? What if her mother is a lesbian? The argument here doesn't seem to allow for differences among women. — A.L.

How does this theory account for homosexuality? — H.L.

The male infant's task is dissimilar. As the psychoanalyst Ralph Greenson seems to have been the first to point out, if the little boy is to identify with his father, he must first separate himself imaginatively from his mother—until then, the source of all comfort and security. Greenson describes this as 'a special vicissitude'. 'I am referring to the fact', he says, 'that the male child, in order to attain a healthy sense of maleness, must replace the primary object of his identification, the mother, and must identify instead with the father.' It is this additional step, he believes, that accounts for the special problems from which the adult male suffers and from which the adult female is exempt.

What does Greenson mean by "a healthy sense of male-ness"? Isn't that defined differently by each society and culture? — H.L.

Does this account of the male "wound" allow for differences among men? — A.L.

DIS-IDENTIFICATION AND COUNTER-IDENTIFICATION

This first step, the one that the little boy takes in order to free himself from his symbiotic connection to his mother, Greenson refers to as *dis-identification*. The subsequent step, independent of the first, and which enables him positively to identify with his father, Greenson calls *counter-identification*.

---

the little girl moves . . . towards other males: For the viewpoint of a little girl whose "mother's gaze" falls not on males but on females—and whose mother is a lesbian—see the reading by Serena, "Just Different, That's All," starting on p. 549.

The first establishes the boy's separateness; the second, his maleness. *It is these two developmental processes in combination which we call the male wound.*

With the benefit of hindsight, it is possible to see Greenson's account of the consequences of dis-identification and counter-identification as too limited, but there is no doubting the shrewdness of the insight itself. In order to align himself with his father, the little boy first creates within himself a dislocation; and in as much as he imitates his father's object choice—his desire for women—he must do so with this dislocation as its prior condition.

Initially, while symbiotically connected to their mother, both son and daughter perceive their father as 'other'. But then, as the male gender identity crystallises, the son sees that 'other' (his father) as 'same', and what was 'same' (his mother) as 'other'. That is to say, *the son experiences a reversal—one of similarity-in-difference and difference-in-similarity—which his sister does not.* The elements of this reversal carry a powerful emotional charge; and its form, we are going to argue, is one which will echo and reverberate throughout the male's subsequent experience. If we are right, it is in the light of this reversal that each of the male's later ventures will be cast, his choice of work and imaginative expression no less than the character of his sexual desire.

No one yet knows what causes the male infant to divert his attention from his mother, to dis-identify. It seems likely that, in some way as yet unestablished, he is biologically influenced to do so. For reasons eventually traceable to the intra-uterine environment, say, he may be more restless than his sisters, less tolerant of frustration, less attuned to the eye contact on which intimate traffic with his mother depends. Male and female infants, in other words, may be biologically programmed to respond differently to a given maternal regime.

An alternative line of explanation, on which there are several variants, is more transactional. It holds, again for reasons that may be largely biological in origin, that most mothers from the very outset treat their male infants in one way, their

These comparisons sound like stereotypes to me. I would like to know exactly how these are traceable to the womb. – H.L.

The fact that they offer several hypotheses here makes me think these writers are trying to be evenhanded and fair. – A.L.

female infants in another. There is evidence that mothers, while their babies are still new-born, are more likely to initiate interactions with their daughters than with their sons; and that in these interactions, it is the infant's physical movement which plays a central part in the case of the sons, whereas in the case of daughters it is mutuality of vocalisation and gaze. As Hinde and Stevenson-Hinde have stressed, quite small sex differences in biological propensity on the infant's part will in any case be quickly magnified by the mother, whose perception is bound to be influenced by cultural stereotypes of maleness and femaleness, and who is bound, too, to see her son as 'other' in a way that her daughter is not.

The child whom the mother sees as 'other', it is important to grasp, does actually differ in material ways from his sisters. While boys become larger and stronger than girls, girls mature more rapidly. Half way through pregnancy, the development of the skeleton is already three weeks more advanced in girls than in boys. At birth the difference in maturation corresponds to 4–6 weeks of normal growth, and by the time puberty is reached, to two years. This sex difference is common to many mammals and nearly all primates, and while the impact on the body is less than entirely uniform, the 'girls earlier' rule has few exceptions. Although both sexes acquire their milk teeth at the same time—one of those few exceptions—the permanent teeth erupt earlier in girls, and the canines by as much as eleven months. We know too that by the sixth or seventh month, girls are beginning to display greater powers of physical co-ordination than boys; and, more specifically, that they are more likely than boys to gain a measure of control over their urinary function. Girls are also quicker to acquire a control over language. At any given stage, their vocabulary is larger than that of boys and they are more articulate. Such differences are bound to be ones that are perceived, at least in part, as ones of *responsiveness;* of repaying the nurture the mother provides. However subliminally, the small boy will accordingly be perceived as the more in transigent

Could it simply be that in school and many homes, girls are pushed more toward English and language arts while boys are encouraged in math and the sciences? – H.L.

partner in the parent/child relationship, the small girl as the more rewarding (or biddable) one.

An adjacent train of thought expands on this differential perception on the mother's part. Long before her son is in a position to sit up—which he usually does at the age of 8 or 9 months—and to discover what his own genital apparatus looks like, his mother will be alert to this difference between his anatomy and her own. She may not simply see him as 'other', that is to say; she may become erotically invested in his 'otherness'. It could be this erotic preoccupation, sometimes physically expressed, which hastens her son's dis-identification. It does so, it might be argued, because he fears engulfment by his mother; because he is sensitive not just to his mother's erotic investment in him but also to her guilty ambivalence about that investment; or, as classical Freudian theory suggests, because he intuits that his mother's body differs anatomically from his own, and that this discovery creates in him intolerable anxiety.

I don't buy the speculations in this paragraph. I'd want to read the source(s) cited. – J.R.

We do not know which of these explanatory avenues will prove the most satisfactory. Whatever the predisposing circumstances turn out to be, it is clear that Greenson's insight permits three quite different patterns:

- The conventional one, in which the biological male dis-identifies with his mother and counter-identifies with his father;
- The biological male who neither dis-identifies nor counter-identifies; and
- The biological male who dis-identifies but fails to counter-identify.

At last—the possibility that men may differ in the ways in which they establish gender identity. But are their categories too rigid? – A.L.

Of these patterns, it is the first, we are arguing, that yields the 'male' male—the man who sees himself as male and acts as a male. The second leads to effeminacy, even in extreme cases to transsexuality—in adulthood, the man who, for all purposes of gender identity, is in substantially the same position as his sister, except that he will somehow have had to accommodate the fact that his own reproductive anatomy and secondary sexual characteristics are unlike his mother's and sister's, and like his father's and brother's. The third yields the male who in adulthood experiences a sense of androgyny or genderlessness.

Granted that no one knows how biology, psychology and culture interact in causing the wound, it would be an error to advance detailed qualifications. Nevertheless, it is easy to see how the effects of dis-identification and counter-identification might arise at later ages than the one we envisage—in adolescence, say, rather than at two or three. Appropriate scenarios can be conjured up. In one, a mother brings up her son alone. When her son is in his early teens, she marries and son and step-father subsequently establish a close bond. In such cases, the son's sense of himself as male could be real enough, but it may be less deeply rooted, less apparently instinctual, than it otherwise might. He may seem to belong to the first of the patterns just outlined, but in truth more nearly belongs to the second or third.

As one reflects on Greenson's distinction, it becomes clear, too, that other outcomes are possible. These are of special interest in that they help make explicit certain of the assumptions on which the theory of identification rests. Particularly, one can envisage:

- The male child who counter-identifies with his father without first having dis-identified with his mother.

At first sight implausible, such a pattern might arise in a household where the personalities of mother and father are somewhat similar, where both are emotionally distant in their dealings with their son, and where the responsibilities for his nurture are shared. The net effect, from the son's point of view, would be a personality in which the 'male' and 'female' are weakly etched and poorly differentiated. It is also a pattern, though, that could take a more extreme form. In this—as in Harry's personality*—both 'male' and 'female'

Isn't normalcy in the eye of the beholder? Is a sense of androgyny or genderlessness biologically abnormal or just socially unacceptable?
– H.L.

Would the authors have us believe then that it is in the best interests of a young

---

Harry's personality: a case study discussed earlier in *The Way Men Think*

characteristics are pronounced, coexisting on the strength of segregations and dissociations that, to the outside eye, are bound to seem arbitrary.

Such outcomes aside, one can also picture:

- The male child who dis-identifies with his mother, but counter-identifies with another woman.

The context for the emergence of such a pattern might be the community in which the care of children is the responsibility of women collectively. Likewise:

- The male child who dis-identifies with his mother, but counter-identifies, subsequently, not with a person but with an emotionally charged idea or symbol: the Fatherland, the Hero (Napoleon), the Leader (Stalin), the Genius (Beethoven or Freud).

Households in which the father is weak or absent form a likely setting for this configuration, likewise cultures where massive coercive pressures are brought to bear on children in the service of a civic ideal. As social psychologists point out, identifications with figures outside the family in any case become increasingly significant as a child grows older, developing both a social identity and the potential for extravagant commitments and loyalties.

The fifth and sixth of these patterns also raise an important issue of interpretation. The common-sense assumption is that the father or father-substitute must be present for counter-identification to occur. Such evidence as we have tends to bear this out. . . . Another train of thought is less literal. It assumes that the maleness at issue is abstract: a property not of individuals but of the disciplines inherent in child-raising and in the child's acquisition of impersonal symbolic skills. Either parent can be seen both as a source of physical and psychological comfort and as the embodiment of authority. On this argument, the male child counter-identifies not with his father, but with those aspects of his parents he intuitively perceives as impersonal (and in that sense 'male'). The role of the father,

boy to have his mother stay at home and raise him while his father works?
— H.L.

Are they making an argument for a traditional family structure, assuming that we want boys to identify with fathers and become "male" males? — J.R.

on this view, is essentially confirmatory. He consolidates developmental changes that can take place of their own accord within the confines of the mother/son relationship.

Without doubt, identity and identification are awkward notions, the modelling at issue concerning not just what one does but who one is; not just behavioural patterns and propensities, but states of being. These are precisely the sorts of questions with which philosophers, and especially Anglo-Saxon philosophers, have traditionally had difficulty. (In Exodus 3, God appears to Moses in a burning bush and says to him, 'I AM THAT I AM'. Moses's correct response, the Oxford philosophers of our youth* would insist, was 'You are that you are *what*?') Practically speaking, there is a distinction between the person's social identity—as a Catholic, or a member of the working class, or a Liverpool fan*—and the identifications implicit in the mother/infant relationship, the first being the province of the social psychologist, the second that of the developmental psychologist and psychoanalyst. In the latter, fundamental questions are at issue; ones about what it is that passes between any two people who are emotionally significant to one another. For our intimate relationships commit us not just to propinquity and rational dialogue, but to the non-rational; to a hazardous two-way traffic in unacknowledged desires and fears.

THE COSTS

One commentator's reassuring conclusion is that 'identity is a concept no one has defined with precision, but it seems we can move ahead anyway, because everyone roughly understands what is meant'. Our own policy, certainly, rather than

---

the Oxford philosophers of our youth: probably a reference to logical positivism, a philosophical movement concerned with the logic and structure of language

a Liverpool fan: a supporter of an athletic team, probably a soccer team, based in Liverpool

compounding difficulties of theory already dense, is to concentrate on consequences rather than causes.

In as much as he sees himself as male and acts as a male, the boy is cut off from the primitive comfort his mother could otherwise provide. It must follow, then—for lack of a better metaphor— that most males differ from most females in terms of what they have 'inside' them. Inside most males but not inside most females there must be a species of existential gulf. This, as Greenson and others have pointed out, will act to the male's disadvantage. The male's position is by no means entirely bleak, even so. It consists, in fact, of a pattern of strengths and shortcomings; and it is these we want to explore.

On the debit side, there are two shortcomings to which the adult male is particularly vulnerable:

- Personal insensitivity, and

- Misogyny

The small boy, Greenson's insight enables us to predict, will find it more difficult than his sister to reciprocate affection, and his capacity for empathy will be impaired. He will tend to see those aspects of the world that are unmistakably emotional in black and white terms, either as heaven-on-earth or as unspeakably distasteful. He will be slow, too, to make sense of emotions that conflict; to detect the many shades of grey that separate black from white, and to realise that greys are often blacks and whites intricately mixed. Whatever his strengths elsewhere, in the field of intimate relations the 'male' male is bound to be at a disadvantage; even something of a cripple. His ability to experience a relationship as 'intersubjective'—as a meeting of experiential worlds—will be curtailed.

In stepping clear of the warm, symbiotic presence of his mother, the small boy may also leave unresolved a sense of loss and resentment; and perhaps, too, the fear of punishment or revenge. A consequence is that there will often exist in the male mind subterranean currents of violently negative sentiment; and that while these will in some cases

I'm glad they resist making grand claims overtly— but do they sneak them in anyway? "Males certainly do differ," they seem to say, "but our theory shows that they're all insensitive!"
– A.L.

But why does a break with the mother lead a boy to see the world in either/or terms? Is it simply because the son must eventually see himself as different in some ways from his mother?
– J.R.

Sensitivity means different things to different people. Men and women may look at sensitivity in different ways. Perhaps this is just a case of living up to expectations, when people become what we already assume or think of them. Since we expect the small boy to have difficulty showing affection, he may not even make a full attempt.
– H.L.

work themselves out in symbolic form, remote from their source, in others they will focus directly on the female sex and on the female body. We would predict, then, that beneath the surface of his attitudes to the opposite sex the adult male will often betray potently misogynous attitudes and fantasies. Women may well be idealised, and the idea of sexual access to them idealised too. But, at the same time, there may circulate—perhaps just within the range of awareness, perhaps beyond it— the vision of women as pollutors, beheaders and castrators; creatures to be feared, and in whom, despite appearances, sinister powers reside.

These misogynous preoccupations are expressed stereotypically in Don Juan; the sexual athlete who perceives women as desirable objects, and who ravishes them, but who must make good his escape before the potentially engulfing dangers of sexual intimacy can wreak their havoc. They were also expressed with formidable accuracy during the Renaissance, in the northern, incipiently Protestant, tradition of painting and sculpting the female nude. Where the Italian tradition of Titian and Veronese depicted the nude in idealised terms, the draughtsmen and carvers working north of the Alps explored in minute detail precisely those ambivalences and reversals to which heterosexual desire renders the male subject. Naked rather than nude, the 'bulb-like' women and 'root-like' men of this northern art, as Kenneth Clark* remarks, seem dragged from the protective darkness of the previous thousand years. The alternative convention of the nude thus created is based on different bodily proportions from those established by the Greeks—broader in the hip, narrower in the shoulder, longer, more pear-like in the abdomen. It also dwells on puckers and wrinkles, not on the judicious arrangement of smoothed surfaces and coherent volumes. . . .

The causal analysis requires careful scrutiny. For example, if Hudson and Jacot are describing a common pattern of sexual development, why would the female nudes drawn or sculpted by Northern European males be more misogynous than those of Southern European males?
— J.R.

Having just completed a study of the status of women at my school, I must say that I've got a lot of firsthand evidence to support the picture they're painting. Though most men on my campus don't seem to recognize it, they are in many ways hostile to and fearful of women. This realization has made me sad— and mad.
— A.L.

Kenneth Clark (1903–83): art historian and author of *The Nude* (1960), the work Hudson and Jacot refer to here

Misogyny, then, is not a feature of the male mind which is simply a byproduct of a narrow-minded upbringing or of sexist biases in education. It is built into the male psyche. Stemming from fears which are a direct consequence of the wound, it lingers in a hinterland where notions of separation and engulfment, erotic excitement and dismay mingle. These fears, obviously, can express themselves in a variety of ways. In a generalised horror of women. In a specific revulsion from sexual intercourse with them, even though their presence is otherwise seen as pleasurable and a reassurance. Or in panic once sexual intercourse with them has been enjoyed. If they are not to be expressed destructively, these are sentiments which must somehow be contained or translated. . . .

THE BENEFITS

There are, however, more positive consequences in store. Three interest us particularly. These concern:

- The idea of agency—the individual's freedom, that is to say, to act on the world in the light of his own needs and intentions;
- The wound as a constantly replenishing source of psychic energy;
- The notion of abstract passions.

If his search for an alternative focus of identification is successful, the little boy has established for himself, as Greenson points out, a measure of separation. Even more tellingly, he has learnt a primitive lesson which he will not otherwise learn: that of *agency*. Where, in sustaining her gender identity with her mother, the female infant must somehow accommodate whatever frustration is inherent in the relation between them, the male infant discovers that you can reject a source of frustration, and, simultaneously, find a stance independent of it. This discovery will be made at the cost of anxiety, no doubt, and of anxiety's attendant suppressions and repressions; but it is a valuable one, even so. The more 'male' the male, the greater the imaginative gulf separating him from his sources of primitive comfort; and the greater that gulf, we would predict, the greater his underlying existential insecurity is bound to be. He is perfectly poised, nevertheless, to heal his wound at one symbolic remove; to use the anxiety his separation provokes in him to create systems of ideas which can stand in the place of lost intimacy, and within which he can strive for coherence and harmony.

Also, being rooted in a primitive separation, the male's energies are in principle inexhaustible. They will last as long as his wound lasts. With them at his command, he can go on for a lifetime searching for order in chaos. Alternatively, he can disrupt the forms of order that already exist—either for the pleasure of disrupting them, or with a view to replacing them with a form of order that is superior and identifiably his own. On this argument, the wound is not just an introduction to the experience of agency. It is an *energy source,* fuelling symbolically significant action—typically in fields distant from mothers and fathers, sex and gender. The defining characteristic of such activity is that it is pursued with passion; not for extraneous reasons like profit or status, but as an end in itself. As Anthony Storr has pointed out, conventional psychoanalytic theories tend to define good mental health by equating it with the ability to sustain rich human relationships. But in the 'male' male at least, the connections between creativeness, human relationships and mental health are not simple. The biographical evidence—and we shall rehearse what we hope are representative fragments of it later—

I'm sure some women form these same types of relationships.
– H.L.

suggests that the richest relationship many sane and highly creative men establish is with systems of ideas or with pieces of machinery.

From the moment an imagined space opens up between the small boy and his mother, we are suggesting, he is in principle primed to execute within it at least three separate but related sorts of manoeuvre. As he matures, he can pursue abstract ideas, which are, in a sense, surrogates for his

mother, in that they bear a complex symbolic relation to her. He can think about matters, personal
or inanimate, in ways that rehearse and celebrate
the distance from his mother he has created—he
can think, that is to say, in ways that appear objective and dispassionate. And, the possibility of most
immediate bearing on our own argument, he can
pursue ideas quite unrelated to his mother with the
kind of passion he had previously felt towards her.
(Notice, we are not saying that the thought processes of the 'male' male are distinctively objective.
What we are saying is that he has a driven need to
use his intelligence on impersonal problems; and
that in doing so he can display remorseless powers
of application.)

Psychologists' efforts to come to terms with
such phenomena have in the past had about them
an air of contrivance. They usually suggest either
that a biological energy—sex, aggression—has
somehow been diverted or 'sublimated' into a new
channel; or that the motive underlying abstract
thought cannot be what it seems: that, after all, it
must boil down to ambition, say, or territoriality,
or envy, or the desire for access to attractive members of the opposite sex. These explanatory enterprises, it has long been realised, sit uncomfortably
with the facts as we know them: the small boy
paying rapt attention to his collection of postage
stamps; Isaac Newton absorbed to the exclusion
of all other considerations by the laws of gravity.
In contrast, the idea of the male wound offers a
plausible account of just such absorption: that it
springs from a dissociative movement of the mind
in which the inanimate—things, systems of ideas—
acquires the intense emotional significance previously lodged in people, and in which people,
stripped of that significance, are treated as though
they were things.

It is the wound's capacity to engender fascination with the impersonal that immediately concerns us. For in doing so, it helps makes sense of
what, in evolutionary terms, is our species' most
conspicuous characteristic: *our capacity for abstract
passion*. It explains our ability not merely to think

*My many years
of teaching male
students adds
support to this
conclusion. So
my experi-
ences—as a
teacher and a
professional and
a woman—con-
firm the general
theory here. I still
worry, however,
that it treats men
as all essentially
the same in certain
ways. I'm in-
trigued by what
Hudson and Jacot
say but I'm not
convinced.*
– A.L.

analytically, nor even to think analytically with passionate intensity, but to think analytically and with passionate intensity about topics that have no detectable bearing on our ordinary biological appetites or needs. For the 'male' male—and, in explanatory terms, this is a crucial point—*such passions will be the more enduringly gratifying the more completely divorced from human relationships they are.* The more abstract their context, the more his enterprises take on a quality that is simultaneously impassioned and aesthetically pure. Nor is there any requirement that the operations the male performs within a framework of objectifying thought will themselves be disinterested in tone and inspiration. On the contrary, what is proposed is that the male can express within this framework—safely and at a distance—any of the impulses an intimate relationship might otherwise have inspired.

At the heart of our account of the psychology of the male imagination, then, is a two-part claim. That, in combination, dis-identification and counter-identification create in the 'male' male a sense of agency, allied to a constantly replenishing source of imaginative energy. And that these same processes draw him towards the inanimate—the world of things, mechanisms, abstract ideas and systems within which he operates with the commitment and fervour we might otherwise have expected him to display towards people.

PREDICTIONS AND CONJECTURES

If the theory discussed so far is substantially correct, we would expect that the wound's effects:

- Will be stable over broad stretches of the life-span, not evanescent byproducts of the individual's culture or the social roles he happens to occupy;

- Will express themselves in observable, quantifiable terms among samples of men, and between samples of men and women, as well as in the lives of individuals; and

- Will be resistant to changes in patterns of child-raising and family life.

We would expect, too, that:

- In the lives both of individuals and of groups, the wound's effects will often be characterised by apparently arbitrary inconsistencies and segregations.

The existence of the wound leads us to expect that character traits like misogyny or personal insensitivity will express themselves spontaneously among men whose gender identity is clearly 'male'. But we are dealing with a system within which migrations and dissociations are the norm. So misogyny could turn out to express itself in different ways, discipline by discipline: in womanising among poets, say, in celibacy among classical scholars, in high rates of divorce among radically innovative biologists, and in forthrightly sexist prejudice among engineers. Its expression could also alter within a discipline, decade by decade, as the nature of that discipline and recruitment to it changes. So while expecting a quality like misogyny to express itself in both the intellectual and the sexual spheres of an individual's life, we remain alert to the possibility that its expression can become localised, specialised. A man may be treacherous in his work, treacherous in his sex life, or treacherous in both alike. Over the years, his mendacious tendencies may spread from his working life to his sex life, or vice versa. They may also migrate. A previously blameless working life may be invaded by the tendency to lie and finagle at just the point when his private life, previously distorted by hostile impulses, at last achieves a more decorous balance.

Despite these propensities for translation and migration, we expect the evidence to reveal, both in its aggregate forms and in detail and nuance, the persistence of certain themes. We would expect the wound to be associated with:

- Segregations of the personal from the impersonal;

The term misogyny *can apparently encompass anything Hudson and Jacot want it to.*   — J.R.

Hudson and Jacot's use of a single concept to account for complex human behavior reminds me of earlier, similarly crude efforts to attribute human civilization to a "territorial imperative."   — J.R.

- A preoccupation with issues of intellectual control; and
- The conjunction of that control with partisan and aggressive sentiment.

More specifically, we would expect to find the wound associated with:

These characteristics of the male mind dovetail so conveniently with some radical feminists' views of men that I am now inclined to read this article more as a political tract than a scientific analysis. — J.R.

- Characteristic patterns of cost (misogyny, personal insensitivity) and benefit (agency, imaginative energy, abstract passion);
- Characteristic patterns of career choice; and
- Orderly relations between the first of these patterns and the second.

In terms of style, the 'male' cast of mind will:

- Be intolerant of 'messy' arguments—i.e., ones that lack formal structure and are, variously, intuitive, empathetic, indeterminate; and
- Emphasise the virtues of dispassion and objectivity (although what is displayed will usually be the exercise of intelligence in the service of enterprises which are partisan and combative, and in that sense impassioned and non-objective).

The existence of the wound also creates expectations of the evidence that are less clear-cut, and that have the status more of conjectures. Particularly, it leads us to expect the existence of 'male' formats of thought. These will differ, of course, from field to field, but, in essence, their features are those of the wound itself. The 'male' mind should typically show a taste for:

- Arguments cast in terms of dualities and dialectical oppositions (like male/female, conscious/unconscious, mind/body, theory/evidence)* and their reconciliations;
- Arguments that depend on the maintenance

Arguments . . . oppositions: For one perspective on dualistic thinking, see A.L.'s response to Shelby Steele on p. 121.

of conceptual boundaries and segregations (like that between natural sciences and the social ones), and on colonising forays across such boundaries;

- Arguments (e.g., about classification) that depend on a deep preoccupation with similarities and differences;

- Arguments that are reductive, especially ones that explain the subtly experiential in terms of the prosaic and literal; and

- Arguments centring on ideas—often highly technical—the truth of which is perceived as luminous.

There are also grounds for suspecting, as we have already said, that even the most stable solutions to the dilemmas of dis- and counter-identification contain hints of precariousness; and that, as a consequence, the work of maintaining the wound's dissociations is never quite done. As we shall see, even in the most austerely abstract of 'male' thought, traces of the wound's intimately human origin are often detectable, and are perhaps never finally expunged.

A f t e r w o r d s

My marginal comments reflect the doubts I have about Hudson and Jacot's concept of a male wound, so I won't belabor the issue. The idea just strikes me as too simple to account for the vagaries of human nature. Like A.L., I'm skeptical about even the simplest generalizations about male and female behavior. Yet like Hudson and Jacot, I sometimes can't help making my own.

For instance, I don't really see much difference between the sexes when it comes to general qualities like intelligence, ambition, sensitivity, courage, or common sense. Yet I also find these traits so entirely tied to gender that we sometimes don't recognize them in the opposite sex. Women, for example, usually show their sensitivity by opening up; men express their feelings by shutting down. Women often show courage through acts of endurance; men prefer to measure courage by action or rebellion. And so I'm not surprised that the sexes are eternally at odds, while at the same time remarkably compatible. When things are working right, we enlarge each other's worlds. — J.R.

I grew up with a father, a brother, and a whole passel of uncles and male cousins and playmates. I've worked in the company of many men, have taught thousands of men, have been married to men (two to date). I am a fond aunt of four nephews, ages one to twenty-seven, and adopted auntie to another score. I even like to think I have some pretty good friends who happen to be men, including my coeditor in this text. (And I know *I have some enemies who are men.) Yet until I was well into adulthood I thought reasonable people (and I included lots of men in this category) pretty much* THOUGHT LIKE I THOUGHT.

Writing this, I'm reminded of humorist Dave Barry saying something like "When I got married, I instantly made a shrewd deduction: WOMEN ARE WEIRD." *I wasn't as shrewd as Dave Barry, and learning to study the ways in which people think differently from me has been a painful as well as an enlightening process. Because my own study of "different" ways of thinking has revealed a dizzying range of differences, I'm resistant to any argument that starts out: "there are two kinds of people." In the case of this excerpt from Hudson and Jacot's book, I resist any easy assumption that those two kinds of people are (1) people that think like women and (2) people that think like men. I'm especially wary, as my annotations indicate, of equating sex with gender: in my experience women can and do take on masculine gender roles. So I came to this book prepared to encounter an overly simple argument and also prepared to disagree.*

I find I was partly wrong on both counts. In the end, I am not completely persuaded by Hudson and Jacot, but their work as well as the work of other biologists, neurobiologists, geneticists, and psychologists leads me at least to some cautious assent. In spite of the fact that I'm uneasy about making gross distinctions between men and women, I must admit that the evidence for some distinctions is mounting; and it is coming from numerous and varied quarters. More troubling perhaps, my own experience and my own study of "different" ways of thinking support some claim for distinctions between male and female ways of knowing. The men I know best, in short, do tend to exhibit the characteristics described by Hudson and Jacot. (Even as I write this response, I'm anticipating how I might see these characteristics in J.R.'s response.) And they don't *seem to "think" like I do. In both my personal and professional life, this insight has important consequences. It means, for instance, trying to* listen *harder and better—to myself as well as to others. It also means taking time to check on how and what others I care about are thinking—and talking about how that thinking differs from my own. And it means keeping a slice of humble pie always near. I can never go back to the old comfortable way of thinking that all reasonable people think like I do.* — A.L.

My initial impression of this piece is that it is just a bunch of excuses for men's behavior. The authors' points seem to be based on stereotypes of male and female roles. They give explanations for what is deemed traditional male behavior—insensitivity, fear of intimate relationships—in our society today. But I wonder if their arguments would be as plausible in other cultures, where male roles are differently defined.

My biggest criticism is that we do not grow up with our families in a vacuum, as the authors seem to want us to believe. Except for a few brief references, the authors ignore the influences of societal norms and mores. Also never mentioned is peer pressure, which I think is one of the biggest influences on gender identity. As a little girl, whether I played house or played soccer depended on whom I was playing with; I don't believe that I was genetically inclined to either activity. I think that during our formative years, we identify more with our friends than with our parents—most of us wish to remain part of the in crowd, and we wouldn't hesitate to rebel against our parents.

While I do not doubt there are genuine differences in the ways men and women think, I think that the authors give too much credit to biological factors. — H.L.

QUESTIONING THE TEXT

1. How do Hudson and Jacot define the "male wound"? How is the metaphor of a wound appropriate (or inappropriate) for the experiences they describe? What in your experience or the experiences of those you know confirms or disproves that such a wound exists?
2. What do Hudson and Jacot see as the major differences between men and women? What do they see as the similarities? How do they account for varying gender identities among males?
3. Look over J.R.'s commentary on this selection (and on other selections, if you wish) to see if you find evidence for any of Hudson and Jacot's assertions about "the way men think."
4. Spend some time rereading the annotations and responses to this excerpt from A.L., H.L., and J.R. Then write a brief response to these commentaries, explaining which set you identified with most closely, and why.

MAKING CONNECTIONS

5. Imagine Hudson and Jacot reading Robert Bly's account of the lack of male initiation rites in American culture (starting on p. 360). What might they have to say to Bly? Write a brief reader's response that you imagine they might make.
6. "Barbie Doll" (on p. 374) suggests that our society punishes or rejects

women who are not "perfect." How do Hudson and Jacot suggest that our society harms men?

JOINING THE CONVERSATION

7. Think for a few minutes about what in this reading you most agreed with, most disagreed with, or were most confused about. Then write a brief (one- or two-page) response that explains the reasons for your agreement, disagreement, or confusion.
8. Write a two-page description, based on your own experience as well as on what you have read, entitled "The Way Men (or Women) Think." Be prepared to bring your description to class and to compare it with those of two or three students. You may best begin by brainstorming with other students about questions such as "What do men (or women) think most about?" and "How do men (or women) I know most typically approach or solve a problem?"

MAXINE HONG KINGSTON
No Name Woman

THOUGH MAXINE HONG KINGSTON was born (in 1940) and raised in California, her roots grow deep in Chinese soil and culture, as is evidenced in two highly acclaimed books, The Woman Warrior *(1970) and* China Men *(1980). In these and other works, Kingston explores the effects of Chinese legend and custom on her own experiences as a woman and as a Chinese American.*

In "No Name Woman," an excerpt from The Woman Warrior, *Kingston examines one difference between women and men—the fact that women bear children—and she explores the consequences of that difference. Many readers of this text may be able to identify a shadowy relative in their own pasts—an absent parent, a grandparent much discussed but seldom seen, a mysterious uncle or aunt or cousin about whom older family members whispered. Few of us are likely to have written so powerfully about such a figure, however, or to have evoked in such a short space what it would be like to be "No Name Woman." I chose this selection precisely for its power. It is a passage that has stayed vividly with me ever since I first read it—so vividly, in fact, that "No Name Woman" seems like someone I know personally. To me, she tells not only her own story but the story of all those whose lives are destroyed by narrow and rigid beliefs.* — A.L.

"You must not tell anyone," my mother said, "what I am about to tell you. In China your father had a sister who killed herself. She jumped into the family well. We say that your father has all brothers because it is as if she had never been born.

"In 1924 just a few days after our village celebrated seventeen hurry-up weddings—to make sure that every young man who went 'out on the road' would responsibly come home—your father and his brothers and your grandfather and his brothers and your aunt's new husband sailed for America, the Gold Mountain. It was your grandfather's last trip. Those lucky enough to get contracts waved good-bye from the decks. They fed and guarded the stowaways and helped them off in Cuba, New York, Bali, Hawaii. 'We'll meet in California next year,' they said. All of them sent money home.

"I remember looking at your aunt one day when she and I were dressing; I had not noticed before that she had such a protruding melon of a stomach. But I did not think, 'She's pregnant,' until she began to look like other pregnant women, her shirt pulling and the white tops of her black pants showing. She could not have been pregnant, you see, because her husband had been gone for years. No one said anything. We did not discuss it. In early summer she was ready to have the child, long after the time when it could have been possible.

"The village had also been counting. On the night the baby was to be born the villagers raided our house. Some were crying. Like a great saw, teeth strung with lights, files of people walked zigzag across our land, tearing the rice. Their lanterns doubled in the disturbed black water, which drained away through the broken bunds. As the villagers closed in, we could see that some of them, probably men and women we knew well, wore white masks. The people with long hair hung it over their faces. Women with short hair made it stand up on end. Some had tied white bands around their foreheads, arms, and legs.

"At first they threw mud and rocks at the house. Then they threw   5 eggs and began slaughtering our stock. We could hear the animals scream their deaths—the roosters, the pigs, a last great roar from the ox. Familiar wild heads flared in our night windows; the villagers encircled us. Some of the faces stopped to peer at us, their eyes rushing like searchlights. The hands flattened against the panes, framed heads, and left red prints.

"The villagers broke in the front and the back doors at the same time, even though we had not locked the doors against them. Their knives dripped with the blood of our animals. They smeared blood on the doors and walls. One woman swung a chicken, whose throat she had slit, splattering blood in red arcs about her. We stood together in the middle of our house, in the family hall with the pictures and tables of the ancestors around us, and looked straight ahead.

"At that time the house had only two wings. When the men came back, we would build two more to enclose our courtyard and a third one to begin a second courtyard. The villagers pushed through both wings, even your grandparents' rooms, to find your aunt's, which was also mine until the men returned. From this room a new wing for one of the younger families would grow. They ripped up her clothes and shoes and broke her combs, grinding them underfoot. They tore her work from the loom. They scattered the cooking fire and rolled the new weaving in it. We could hear them in the kitchen breaking our bowls and banging the pots. They overturned the great waist-high earthenware jugs; duck eggs, pickled fruits, vegetables burst out and mixed in acrid torrents. The old woman from the next field swept a broom through the air and loosed the spirits-of-the-broom over our heads. 'Pig.' 'Ghost.' 'Pig,' they sobbed and scolded while they ruined our house.

"When they left, they took sugar and oranges to bless themselves. They cut pieces from the dead animals. Some of them took bowls that were not broken and clothes that were not torn. Afterward we swept up the rice and sewed it back up into sacks. But the smells from the spilled preserves lasted. Your aunt gave birth in the pigsty that night. The next morning when I went up for the water, I found her and the baby plugging up the family well.

"Don't let your father know that I told you. He denies her. Now that you have started to menstruate, what happened to her could happen to you. Don't humiliate us. You wouldn't like to be forgotten as if you had never been born. The villagers are watchful."

Whenever she had to warn us about life, my mother told stories that   10
ran like this one, a story to grow up on. She tested our strength to establish realities. Those in the emigrant generations who could not reassert brute survival died young and far from home. Those of us in the first American generations have had to figure out how the invisible world the emigrants built around our childhoods fit in solid America.

The emigrants confused the gods by diverting their curses, misleading them with crooked streets and false names. They must try to confuse their offspring as well, who, I suppose, threaten them in similar ways—always trying to get things straight, always trying to name the unspeakable. The Chinese I know hide their names; sojourners take new names when their lives change and guard their real names with silence.

Chinese-Americans, when you try to understand what things in you are Chinese, how do you separate what is peculiar to childhood, to poverty, insanities, one family, your mother who marked your growing with stories, from what is Chinese? What is Chinese tradition and what is the movies?

If I want to learn what clothes my aunt wore, whether flashy or ordinary, I would have to begin, "Remember Father's drowned–in–the–well sister?" I cannot ask that. My mother has told me once and for all the useful parts. She will add nothing unless powered by Necessity, a riverbank that guides her life. She plants vegetable gardens rather than lawns; she carries the odd-shaped tomatoes home from the fields and eats food left for the gods.

Whenever we did frivolous things, we used up energy; we flew high kites. We children came up off the ground over the melting cones our parents brought home from work and the American movie on New Year's Day—*Oh, You Beautiful Doll* with Betty Grable one year, and *She Wore a Yellow Ribbon* with John Wayne another year. After the one carnival ride each, we paid in guilt; our tired father counted his change on the dark walk home.

Adultery is extravagance. Could people who hatch their own chicks   15
and eat the embryos and the heads for delicacies and boil the feet in vinegar for party food, leaving only the gravel, eating even the gizzard lining—could such people engender a prodigal aunt? To be a woman, to have a daughter in starvation time was a waste enough. My aunt could not have been the lone romantic who gave up everything for sex. Women in the old

China did not choose. Some man had commanded her to lie with him and be his secret evil. I wonder whether he masked himself when he joined the raid on her family.

Perhaps she encountered him in the fields or on the mountain where the daughters-in-law collected fuel. Or perhaps he first noticed her in the marketplace. He was not a stranger because the village housed no strangers. She had to have dealings with him other than sex. Perhaps he worked an adjoining field, or he sold her the cloth for the dress she sewed and wore. His demand must have surprised, then terrified her. She obeyed him; she always did as she was told.

When the family found a young man in the next village to be her husband, she stood tractably beside the best rooster, his proxy, and promised before they met that she would be his forever. She was lucky that he was her age and she would be the first wife, an advantage secure now. The night she first saw him, he had sex with her. Then he left for America. She had almost forgotten what he looked like. When she tried to envision him, she only saw the black and white face in the group photograph the men had had taken before leaving.

The other man was not, after all, much different from her husband. They both gave orders: she followed. "If you tell your family, I'll beat you. I'll kill you. Be here again next week." No one talked sex, ever. And she might have separated the rapes from the rest of living if only she did not have to buy her oil from him or gather wood in the same forest. I want her fear to have lasted just as long as rape lasted so that the fear could have been contained. No drawn-out fear. But women at sex hazarded birth and hence lifetimes. The fear did not stop but permeated everywhere. She told the man, "I think I'm pregnant." He organized the raid against her.

On nights when my mother and father talked about their life back home, sometimes they mentioned an "outcast table" whose business they still seemed to be settling, their voices tight. In a commensal tradition, where food is precious, the powerful older people made wrongdoers eat alone. Instead of letting them start separate new lives like the Japanese, who could become samurais and geishas, the Chinese family, faces averted but eyes glowering sideways, hung on to the offenders and fed them leftovers. My aunt must have lived in the same house as my parents and eaten at an outcast table. My mother spoke about the raid as if she had seen it, when she and my aunt, a daughter-in-law to a different household, should not have been living together at all. Daughters-in-law lived with their husbands' parents, not their own; a synonym for marriage in Chinese is "taking a daughter-in-law." Her husband's parents could have sold her, mortgaged her, stoned her. But they had sent her back to her own mother and father, a mysterious act hinting at disgraces not told me. Perhaps they had thrown her out to deflect the avengers.

She was the only daughter; her four brothers went with her father,   20 husband, and uncles "out on the road" and for some years became western men. When the goods were divided among the family, three of the brothers took land, and the youngest, my father, chose an education. After my grandparents gave their daughter away to her husband's family, they had dispensed all the adventure and all the property. They expected her alone to keep the traditional ways, which her brothers, now among the barbarians, could fumble without detection. The heavy, deep-rooted women were to maintain the past against the flood, safe for returning. But the rare urge west had fixed upon our family, and so my aunt crossed boundaries not delineated in space.

The work of preservation demands that the feelings playing about in one's guts not be turned into action. Just watch their passing like cherry blossoms. But perhaps my aunt, my forerunner, caught in a slow life, let dreams grow and fade and after some months or years went toward what persisted. Fear at the enormities of the forbidden kept her desires delicate, wire and bone. She looked at a man because she liked the way the hair was tucked behind his ears, or she liked the question-mark line of a long torso curving at the shoulder and straight at the hip. For warm eyes or a soft voice or a slow walk—that's all—a few hairs, a line, a brightness, a sound, a pace, she gave up family. She offered us up for a charm that vanished with tiredness, a pigtail that didn't toss when the wind died. Why, the wrong lighting could erase the dearest thing about him.

It could very well have been, however, that my aunt did not take subtle enjoyment of her friend, but, a wild woman, kept rollicking company. Imagining her free with sex doesn't fit, though. I don't know any women like that, or men either. Unless I see her life branching into mine, she gives me no ancestral help.

To sustain her being in love, she often worked at herself in the mirror, guessing at the colors and shapes that would interest him, changing them frequently in order to hit on the right combination. She wanted him to look back.

On a farm near the sea, a woman who tended her appearance reaped a reputation for eccentricity. All the married women blunt-cut their hair in flaps about their ears or pulled it back in tight buns. No nonsense. Neither style blew easily into heart-catching tangles. And at their weddings they displayed themselves in their long hair for the last time. "It brushed the backs of my knees," my mother tells me. "It was braided, and even so, it brushed the backs of my knees."

At the mirror my aunt combed individuality into her bob. A bun 25 could have been contrived to escape into black streamers blowing in the wind or in quiet wisps about her face, but only the older women in our picture album wear buns. She brushed her hair back from her forehead, tucking the flaps behind her ears. She looped a piece of thread, knotted into a circle between her index fingers and thumbs, and ran the double strand across her forehead. When she closed her fingers as if she were making a pair of shadow geese bite, the string twisted together catching the little hairs. Then she pulled the thread away from her skin, ripping the hairs out neatly, her eyes watering from the needles of pain. Opening her fingers, she cleaned the thread, then rolled it along her hairline and the tops of her eyebrows. My mother did the same to me and my sisters and herself. I used to believe that the expression "caught by the short hairs" meant a captive held with a depilatory string. It especially hurt at the temples, but my mother said we were lucky we didn't have to have our feet bound when we were seven. Sisters used to sit on their beds and cry together, she said, as their mothers or their slave removed the bandages for a few minutes each night and let the blood gush back into their veins. I hope that the man my aunt loved appreciated a smooth brow, that he wasn't just a tits-and-ass man.

Once my aunt found a freckle on her chin, at a spot that the almanac said predestined her for unhappiness. She dug it out with a hot needle and washed the wound with peroxide.

More attention to her looks than these pullings of hairs and pickings at spots would have caused gossip among the villagers. They owned work clothes and good clothes, and they wore good clothes for feasting the new seasons. But since a woman combing her hair hexes beginnings, my aunt rarely found an occasion to look her best. Women looked like great sea snails—the corded wood, babies, and laundry they carried were the whorls on their backs. The Chinese did not admire a bent back; goddesses and warriors stood straight. Still there must have been a marvelous freeing of beauty when a worker laid down her burden and stretched and arched.

Such commonplace loveliness, however, was not enough for my aunt. She dreamed of a lover for the fifteen days of New Year's, the time for families to exchange visits, money, and food. She plied her secret comb. And sure enough she cursed the year, the family, the village, and herself.

Even as her hair lured her imminent lover, many other men looked at her. Uncles, cousins, nephews, brothers would have looked, too, had they been home between journeys. Perhaps they had already been restraining their curiosity, and they left, fearful that their glances, like a field of nesting birds, might be startled and caught. Poverty hurt, and that was their first reason for leaving. But another, final reason for leaving the crowded house was the never-said.

She may have been unusually beloved, the precious only daughter, 30 spoiled and mirror-gazing because of the affection the family lavished on her. When her husband left, they welcomed the chance to take her back from the in-laws; she could live like the little daughter for just a while longer. There are stories that my grandfather was different from other people, "crazy ever since the little Jap bayoneted him in the head." He used to put his naked penis on the dinner table, laughing. And one day he brought home a baby girl, wrapped up inside his brown western-style greatcoat. He had traded one of his sons, probably my father, the youngest, for her. My grandmother made him trade back. When he finally got a daughter of his own, he doted on her. They must have all loved her, except perhaps my father, the only brother who never went back to China, having once been traded for a girl.

Brothers and sisters, newly men and women, had to efface their sexual color and present plain miens. Disturbing hair and eyes, a smile like no other, threatened the ideal of five generations living under one roof. To focus blurs, people shouted face to face and yelled from room to room. The immigrants I know have loud voices, unmodulated to American tones even after years away from the village where they called their friendships out across the fields. I have not been able to stop my mother's screams in public libraries or over telephones. Walking erect (knees straight, toes pointed forward, not pigeon-toed, which is Chinese-feminine) and speaking in an inaudible voice, I have tried to turn myself American-feminine. Chinese communication was loud, public. Only sick people had to whisper. But at the dinner table, where the family members came nearest one another, no one could talk, not the outcasts nor any eaters. Every word that falls from the mouth is a coin lost. Silently they gave and accepted food with both hands. A preoccupied child who took his bowl with one hand got a sideways glare. A complete moment of total attention is due everyone alike. Children and lovers have no singularity here, but my aunt used a secret voice, a separate attentiveness.

She kept the man's name to herself throughout her labor and dying; she did not accuse him that he be punished with her. To save her inseminator's name she gave silent birth.

He may have been somebody in her own household, but intercourse with a man outside the family would have been no less abhorrent. All the village were kinsmen, and the titles shouted in loud country voices never let kinship be forgotten. Any man within visiting distance would have been neutralized as a lover—"brother," "younger brother," "older brother"—115 relationship titles. Parents researched birth charts probably not so much to assure good fortune as to circumvent incest in a population that has but one hundred surnames. Everybody has eight million relatives. How useless then sexual mannerisms, how dangerous.

As if it came from an atavism deeper than fear, I used to add "brother" silently to boys' names. It hexed the boys, who would or would not ask me to dance, and made them less scary and as familiar and deserving of benevolence as girls.

But, of course, I hexed myself also—no dates. I should have stood up, both arms waving, and shouted out across libraries, "Hey, you! Love me back." I had no idea, though, how to make attraction selective, how to control its direction and magnitude. If I made myself American-pretty so that the five or six Chinese boys in the class fell in love with me, everyone else—the Caucasian, Negro, and Japanese boys—would too. Sisterliness, dignified and honorable, made much more sense.

Attraction eludes control so stubbornly that whole societies designed to organize relationships among people cannot keep order, not even when they bind people to one another from childhood and raise them together. Among the very poor and the wealthy, brothers married their adopted sisters, like doves. Our family allowed some romance, paying adult brides' prices and providing dowries so that their sons and daughters could marry strangers. Marriage promises to turn strangers into friendly relatives—a nation of siblings.

In the village structure, spirits shimmered among the live creatures, balanced and held in equilibrium by time and land. But one human being flaring up into violence could open up a black hole, a maelstrom that pulled in the sky. The frightened villagers, who depended on one another to maintain the real, went to my aunt to show her a personal, physical representation of the break she made in the "roundness." Misallying couples snapped off the future, which was to be embodied in true offspring. The villagers punished her for acting as if she could have a private life, secret and apart from them.

If my aunt had betrayed the family at a time of large grain yields and peace, when many boys were born, and wings were being built on many houses, perhaps she might have escaped such severe punishment. But the men—hungry, greedy, tired of planting in dry soil, cuckolded—had been forced to leave the village in order to send food-money home. There were ghost plagues, bandit plagues, wars with the Japanese, floods. My Chinese brother and sister had died of an unknown sickness. Adultery, perhaps only a mistake during good times, became a crime when the village needed food.

The round moon cakes and round doorways, the round tables of graduated size that fit one roundness inside another, round windows and rice bowls—these talismans had lost their power to warn this family of the law: a family must be whole, faithfully keeping the descent line by having sons to feed the old and the dead who in turn look after the family. The villagers came to show my aunt and lover-in-hiding a broken house. The villagers were speeding up the circling of events because she was too shortsighted to see that her infidelity had already harmed the village, that waves of consequences would return unpredictably, sometimes in disguise, as now, to hurt her.* This roundness had to be made coin-sized so that she would see its circumference: punish her at the birth of her baby. Awaken her to the inexorable. People who

---

family must be whole . . . consequences: For another perspective on broken family structures, see Jay Overocker, "Ozzie and Harriet in Hell," p. 528.

refused fatalism because they could invent small resources insisted on culpability. Deny accidents and wrest fault from the stars.

After the villagers left, their lanterns now scattering in various directions toward home, the family broke their silence and cursed her. "Aiaa, we're going to die. Death is coming. Death is coming. Look what you've done. You've killed us. Ghost! Dead Ghost! Ghost! You've never been born." She ran out into the fields, far enough from the house so that she could no longer hear their voices, and pressed herself against the earth, her own land no more. When she felt the birth coming, she thought that she had been hurt. Her body seized together. "They've hurt me too much," she thought. "This is gall, and it will kill me." With forehead and knees against the earth, her body convulsed and then relaxed. She turned on her back, lay on the ground. The black well of sky and stars went out and out forever; her body and her complexity seemed to disappear. She was one of the stars, a bright dot in blackness, without home, without a companion, in eternal cold and silence. An agoraphobia rose in her, speeding higher and higher, bigger and bigger; she would not be able to contain it; there would be no end to fear.

Flayed, unprotected against space, she felt pain return, focusing her body. This pain chilled her—a cold, steady kind of surface pain. Inside, spasmodically, the other pain, the pain of the child, heated her. For hours she lay on the ground, alternately body and space. Sometimes a vision of normal comfort obliterated reality: she saw the family in the evening gambling at the dinner table, the young people massaging their elders' backs. She saw them congratulating one another, high joy on the mornings the rice shoots came up. When these pictures burst, the stars drew yet further apart. Black space opened.

She got to her feet to fight better and remembered that old-fashioned women gave birth in their pigsties to fool the jealous, pain-dealing gods, who do not snatch piglets. Before the next spasms could stop her, she ran to the pigsty, each step a rushing out into emptiness. She climbed over the fence and knelt in the dirt. It was good to have a fence enclosing her, a tribal person alone.

Laboring, this woman who had carried her child as a foreign growth that sickened her every day, expelled it at last. She reached down to touch the hot, wet, moving mass, surely smaller than anything human, and could feel that it was human after all—fingers, toes, nails, nose. She pulled it up on to her belly, and it lay curled there, butt in the air, feet precisely tucked one under the other. She opened her loose shirt and buttoned the child inside. After resting, it squirmed and thrashed and she pushed it up to her breast. It turned its head this way and that until it found her nipple. There, it made little snuffling noises. She clenched her teeth at its preciousness, lovely as a young calf, a piglet, a little dog.

She may have gone to the pigsty as a last act of responsibility: she would protect this child as she had protected its father. It would look after her soul, leaving supplies on her grave. But how would this tiny child without family find her grave when there would be no marker for her anywhere, neither in the earth nor the family hall? No one would give her a family hall name. She had taken the child with her into the wastes. At its birth the two of them had felt the same raw pain of separation, a wound that only the family pressing tight could close. A child with no descent line would not soften her life but only trail after her, ghostlike, begging her to give it purpose. At dawn the villagers on their way to the fields would stand around the fence and look.

Full of milk, the little ghost slept. When it awoke, she hardened her breasts against the milk that crying loosens. Toward morning she picked up the baby and walked to the well. 45

Carrying the baby to the well shows loving. Otherwise abandon it. Turn its face into the mud. Mothers who love their children take them along. It was probably a girl; there is some hope of forgiveness for boys.

"Don't tell anyone you had an aunt. Your father does not want to hear her name. She has never been born." I have believed that sex was unspeakable and words so strong and fathers so frail that "aunt" would do my father mysterious harm. I have thought that my family, having settled among immigrants who had also been their neighbors in the ancestral land, needed to clean their name, and a wrong word would incite the kinspeople even here. But there is more to this silence: they want me to participate in her punishment. And I have.

In the twenty years since I heard this story I have not asked for details nor said my aunt's name; I do not know it. People who comfort the dead can also chase after them to hurt them further—a reverse ancestor worship. The real punishment was not the raid swiftly inflicted by the villagers, but the family's deliberately forgetting her. Her betrayal so maddened them, they saw to it that she would suffer forever, even after death. Always hungry, always needing, she would have to beg food from other ghosts, snatch and steal it from those whose living descendants give them gifts. She would have to fight the ghosts massed at crossroads for the buns a few thoughtful citizens leave to decoy her away from village and home so that the ancestral spirits could feast unharassed. At peace, they could act like gods, not ghosts, their descent lines providing them with paper suits and dresses, spirit money, paper houses, paper automobiles, chicken, meat, and rice into eternity—essences delivered up in smoke and flames, steam and incense rising from each rice bowl. In an attempt to make the Chinese care for people outside the family, Chairman Mao encourages us now to give our paper replicas to the spirits of outstanding soldiers and workers, no matter whose ancestors they may be. My aunt remains forever hungry. Goods are not distributed evenly among the dead.

My aunt haunts me—her ghost drawn to me because now, after fifty years of neglect, I alone devote pages of paper to her, though not origamied into houses and clothes. I do not think she always means me well. I am telling on her, and she was a spite suicide, drowning herself in the drinking water. The Chinese are always very frightened of the drowned one, whose weeping ghost, wet hair hanging and skin bloated, waits silently by the water to pull down a substitute.

QUESTIONING THE TEXT

1. The narrator of "No Name Woman" tells several different versions of her aunt's life. Which do you find most likely to be accurate, and why?
2. What is the narrator's attitude toward the villagers? What in the text reveals her attitude—and how does it compare with your own attitude toward them?
3. In several places, this story juxtaposes an older Chinese culture with the more recent culture of the United States. Identify those passages and then write a very brief summary of the culture clash the narrator has experienced.
4. A.L.'s introduction sympathizes with No Name Woman. If one of the villagers had written the introduction, how might it differ from A.L.'s?

MAKING CONNECTIONS

5. The serpent in the Genesis reading (p. 291) tells the woman that eating the fruit will open her eyes so that thenceforth she will know good and evil. What of good and evil does No Name Woman learn after tasting her society's "forbidden fruit?"
6. June Jordan's description of Anita Hill's experiences (p. 354) seems on one level very different from Kingston's narrative of No Name Woman's. But in both accounts women are asked to keep a "dirty secret" and warned about what will happen if they "tell." After rereading these pieces, freewrite for 10 or 15 minutes on some "secrets" in our society that people are never supposed to tell.

JOINING THE CONVERSATION

7. Interview—or spend an hour or so talking with—one of your parents, grandparents, aunts or uncles, or an older person you know fairly well. Ask him or her to describe the attitudes that governed female

sexual behavior in his or her day. How were "good girls" supposed to act? What counted as *bad* behavior—and what were the subtle or overt social punishments for that behavior? Write a brief report of your findings, comparing the older person's description of attitudes at an earlier time with those you hold today.

8. Try your hand at rewriting one of Kingston's versions of No Name Woman's story from the point of view of the man. How might he see things differently? After you have written this man's version, go back and jot down a few things about him. What does he value? What does he think of women? What is his relationship to women? Finally, bring your version to class to compare with those of two other class-mates. After studying each of your versions, work together to make a list of the things the three versions have in common and the things that are different in the accounts.

NORMAN PODHORETZ
Rape in Feminist Eyes

MOST MEN AND WOMEN *agree that rape is a brutal crime deserving harsh, even retributive punishment. But what constitutes rape has become something more than just a legal question—as the public obsession with the rape trials of William Kennedy Smith and Mike Tyson demonstrated in recent years. Both of these men knew the women they were accused of raping, having met them in settings vastly different from the unlit back alleys where rapists in the popular imagination customarily lurk. Smith was acquitted, Tyson was convicted, and the public was educated about the concept of acquaintance rape.*

Most college students, however, were already familiar with that term or its synonym, date rape. Almost every campus now sponsors rape-awareness weeks and orientation seminars on responsible sexual conduct. Women's groups routinely draw attention to incidents of date rape to see that these crimes aren't swept under the rug. College administrations are being pressured by these groups and by parents into providing better security for women on campuses. And appalling statistics are bruited to keep the issue alive: almost a third of women, we are told, have been victims of some kind of sexual assault in their lives, if not of the stereotypically violent kind, then of a more subtle sort at the hands of men they knew and perhaps even trusted.

But has the definition of rape been extended so broadly that it now includes activities that many people consider acceptable sexual behavior? Norman Podhoretz (b. 1930) suggests that might be the case as he does some frank talking about the concept of date rape in the following reading. This is an essay likely to lead to heated arguments, but the points Podhoretz makes are not frivolous or without merit. The rhetorician Richard Weaver is credited the simple observation that "ideas have consequences." I think Podhoretz makes that point in a dozen different ways.

This essay originally appeared in 1991 in Commentary, *an influential journal of neoconservative thought edited by Podhoretz. He has also written a number of books, including* Why We Were in Vietnam *(1982) and* The Bloody Crossroads: Where Politics and Literature Meet *(1986). – J.R.*

1

If prostitution is the world's oldest profession, rape may well be the second oldest crime. But this ancient crime received, so to speak, a new lease on life about thirty-five years ago, when (as we learn from a scholarly paper written jointly by the "sexuality educator" Laurie Bechhofer and Professor Andrea Parrot of Cornell[1]) a sociologist at Purdue named Eugene Kanin "documented the existence of sexual aggression within courtship relationships. Of the women he sampled 30 percent had been victims of rape or attempted rape while on a date."

To be sure, Bechhofer and Parrot do not believe that this was a brand-new phenomenon. As they see it, "Forced sex between acquaintances has probably occurred as long as people have been involved in relationships with each other." This would seem to take us all the way to Adam and Eve, but Bechhofer and Parrot more modestly trace it only as far back as the rape of Tamar by her half-brother Amnon, the story of which in the biblical book of Samuel shows that its "dynamics . . . have not changed significantly over the past 2,000 years"[2]:

> Amnon forced Tamar to have sex despite her wishes. He got her into his bed through manipulation and then rejected her after the rape. Tamar was emotionally distraught by the rape, yet others simply trivialized her feelings.

"Despite its long history," however, it was not until Professor Kanin's pioneering research that this particular form of rape was "reported in the scholarly literature." Even then, according to the chronology supplied by Bechhofer and Parrot, another twenty-five years passed before it acquired a name. In September 1982, Karen Barett, a journalist, wrote an article for the feminist magazine *Ms.* in which (apparently ignorant of the book of Samuel) she drew attention to a "new and unusual" form of sexual aggression and called it "date rape."[3] The problem was that this name narrowed the field to couples actually going out together, and so a broader designation was needed to cover the many instances in which the aggressor was previously known to his victim but had not taken her to dinner or whatever. Out of this necessity the term "acquaintance rape" was born.

The "experts," as they are always described in newspaper stories on the subject, persist in referring to acquaintance or date rape as a "hidden crime." Well, hidden it may have been for several thousand years, but hidden it is no longer. In an amazingly short time, a vast literature has sprung up, much of it emanating from the women's-studies departments now enshrined on almost every campus in the country, but more and more of it also appearing in popular magazines and daily newspapers. Inevitably

---

[1] "What is Acquaintance Rape?," in *Acquaintance Rape: The Hidden Crime*, edited by Andrea Parrot and Laurie Bechhofer (New York: Wiley, 1991).

[2] Actually it is about 3,000 years, but let that pass.

[3] Actually the term "date rape" had already appeared in Susan Brownmiller's *Against Our Will: Men, Women, and Rape*, which was published in 1975, but let that pass, too.

Oprah and Geraldo have also chimed in, and by now there can hardly be anyone left in America who has not been alerted to the existence of a problem which, though supposedly coterminous with the human race itself, and though now said by the feminist journalist Robin Warshaw to be "more common than left-handedness or heart attacks, or alcoholism,"[4] was not even recognized as a problem until practically the day before yesterday.

It is reasonable to ask why such recognition should have been delayed until our own time. After all, rape is not only among the oldest of recorded crimes; as Susan Brownmiller, the Founding Mother of the antirape movement, documents in detail in *Against Our Will: Men, Women, and Rape*,[5] it has also and always inspired horror and been punished with the greatest ferocity.

For example, in the 10th century, during the reign of the Saxon king Athelstan, a rapist not only incurred "the loss of his life and members," as well as his property; it was even decreed that his horse be "put to shame upon its scrotum and tail." In the 13th century, the sentence was reduced to castration and blinding, under the following rationale:

> Let him lose his eyes which gave him sight of the virgin's beauty for which he coveted her. And let him lose as well the testicles which excited his hot lust.

Brownmiller is careful to emphasize that such gruesome punishments were restricted to rapists of virgins. Yet she acknowledges that commentators also spoke at the time of "severe" punishment for rapists of "matrons, nuns, widows, concubines, and even prostitutes." Furthermore, she herself hails as a great advance a late-13th-century English statute decreeing the death penalty for the rapist of "a married woman, dame or damsel." And she notes that the maximum penalty for rape is still life imprisonment.[6]

It is essential to Brownmiller's polemical purposes, and commanded by her quasi-Marxist ideology, that she attribute the seriousness with which rape has always been taken to the basest economic motive (males protecting their property). Nevertheless, the fact remains that the world did not need

5

---

[4]Warshaw's book, based on a survey done in 1985 for *Ms.* by Professor Mary P. Koss, now of the University of Arizona, is entitled *I Never Called It Rape: The* Ms. *Report on Recognizing, Fighting, and Surviving Date and Acquaintance Rape* (New York: Harper, 1988).

[5]A paperback edition came out in 1976 (Bantam).

[6]As an interesting measure of how seriously rape is taken by men today, just this past summer two men who were in a Connecticut jail on a charge of having raped a 19-year-old woman and videotaped the proceedings, were beaten up by other inmates. This is the kind of thing that used to happen in prison only to child molesters. (To complicate matters, the woman later denied that she had been raped.)

to wait upon the publication of her book or the birth of the modern feminist movement before learning to regard rape as a heinous crime. Nor, as the story of Tamar does indeed reveal, was the world oblivious to the possibility that rape could occur between acquaintances. Yet neither the Bible nor any other source found it necessary to distinguish between what today's "experts" designate as "stranger rape" on the one hand and "date rape" or "acquaintance rape" on the other. The rape of Tamar by Amnon is no different in the eyes of the Bible from the rape of Dinah by Shechem,* since in both instances the key element of physical force is present. And far from "trivializing" the episode, as Bechhofer and Parrot puzzlingly allege, the father of Tamar and Amnon, King David, is "very wroth," and her other brother Absalom is so distraught that he avenges her by contriving to have Amnon killed.

But if everyone has always understood that it was rape when a man used a weapon and/or physical violence or the threat of it to force a woman into sex, whether she had met him previously or not—and let me state here for the record that I myself consider life imprisonment none too harsh a penalty for any such man—why introduce the new category of date or acquaintance rape? The answer is that this is a way of applying the word "rape" to a multitude of situations in which, as Bechhofer and Parrot (and all other "experts") freely admit, "Assailants are more likely to use verbal or psychological coercion to overpower their victims than guns or knives."

Now, if we pause for a moment and remind ourselves that overcoming   10 a woman's resistance by "verbal and psychological" means has in the past been universally known as seduction, it will immediately become clear that we are in the presence here of nothing less than a brazen campaign to redefine seduction as a form of rape, and more slyly to identify practically all men as rapists. "Acquaintance-rape educator" Py Bateman, who once edited the *Journal of Sexual Assault and Coercion,* more or less lets the cat out of the bag when she declares:

> Rape is not some form of psychopathology that afflicts a very small number of men. In fact, rape is not that different from what we see as socially acceptable or socially laudable male behavior.

(Incidentally, the "we" who see rape as "socially laudable" are especially prevalent, it seems, in America: ". . . every man who grows up in

---

the rape of Dinah by Shechem: In Genesis 34, Dinah, the daughter of Jacob, is raped by Shechem, a stranger.

America and learns American English learns all too much to think like
a rapist. . . .")[7]

It is no wonder that the "experts," armed with the new category of
"non-violent sexual coercion,"[8] are able to estimate that at least one out of
four, and as many as one out of three, young American women are victims
of rape or attempted rape by a date or acquaintance.[9] The only wonder is
that they come up with so low an estimate. Why not 100 percent?

And indeed there are feminists who do not shrink even from that.
Brownmiller is sometimes seen as one of these, but she is not quite of their
company. True, she walks up to the edge in the most famous sentence of
her book—"[Rape] is nothing more or less than a conscious process of
intimidation by which *all men* keep *all women* in a state of fear" (the italics
are definitely her own). But she also denies believing that heterosexual
coupling is itself a species of rape. And she even gives her endorsement
(albeit, one might say, against her will) to this form of intercourse:

> Anatomically one might want to improve on the design of nature, but
> such speculation appears to my mind as unrealistic. The human sex act
> accomplishes its historic [*sic!*] purpose of generation of the species and
> it also affords some intimacy and pleasure. I have no basic quarrel with
> the procedure.

The radical feminist critic Andrea Dworkin, on the other hand, *does,*
to put it mildly, have a basic quarrel with the procedure. In her book
Intercourse (1987),[10] she denounces the "simple-minded prosex chauvinism
of Right and Left," and in effect extends Brownmiller's definition of rape
to the sex act itself:

> Without being what the society recognizes as rape, [intercourse] is what
> the society—when pushed to admit it—recognizes as dominance.

One of Dworkin's favorite metaphors for sex is "wartime invasion and
occupation," and she describes it as

---

[7]This lulu (quoted by Warshaw) comes from a man, Timothy Beneke, author of *Men
on Rape* (New York: St. Martin's, 1982).

[8]This phrase is the title of a paper by Professor Charlene L. Muehlenhard of the University of Kansas and one of her students, Jennifer L. Schrag, which is included in *Acquaintance
Rape: The Hidden Crime.*

[9]Professor Neil Gilbert of Berkeley—using the FBI's definitions of rape and attempted
rape, and basing himself on the FBI and Bureau of Justice Statistics data—shows in an excellent
piece in the Spring 1991 issue of the *Public Interest* that the actual figure for rape and attempted
rape of young women by dates and acquaintances is a tiny fraction of the figures thrown
around by the "experts," and has moreover been declining since 1980.

[10]A paperback edition was published in 1988 by the Free Press.

evil up against the skin—at the point of entry, just touching the slit; then it breaks in and at the same time it surrounds everything. . . .

In this nightmare inversion of D.H. Lawrence, even the element of coercion is irrelevant; the woman's consent only makes her a "collaborator" with her "rapist":

> Physically, the woman in intercourse is a space inhabited, a literal territory occupied literally; occupied even if there has been no resistance, no force; even if the occupied person said yes please, yes hurry, yes more.

But Dworkin, believe it or not, goes even further:

> . . . occupied women [are] more base in their collaboration than other collaborators have ever been: experiencing pleasure in their own inferiority, calling intercourse freedom. It is a tragedy beyond the power of language to convey when what has been imposed on women by force becomes a standard of freedom for women: and all the women say it is so.

2

At one point, Dworkin (in one of her gentler characterizations) describes intercourse as "the pure, sterile, formal expression of men's contempt for women." But however great men's contempt for women may be, it could hardly match the contempt for women exemplified in the above quotations and pervading the literature which has been spawned by the antirape subdivision of the contemporary feminist movement.

To read this stuff—not just outspoken radicals like Dworkin herself but mainstream academics like Andrea Parrot, who teaches not only at Cornell but also at SUNY,[11] and liberal journalists like Robin Warshaw—is to be presented with a picture of women as timorous, cowering, helpless creatures who are at the mercy of any male they may be unfortunate enough to run into. Those young women who still feel no fear upon meeting the boy next door are portrayed as naive and are sternly (but compassionately) lectured on their need to recognize that this clean-cut fellow, or any other "regular guy," is far more likely to rape them than (in Warshaw's words) the stereotypical "stranger (usually a black, Hispanic, or other minority) jumping out of the bushes . . . brandishing a weapon. . . ."

The women we meet here often blithely accompany their dates or

---

[11] In addition to editing the weighty academic tome *Acquaintance Rape: The Hidden Crime,* she is the author of a popular handbook aimed mainly at teenagers, *Coping with Date Rape & Acquaintance Rape* (New York: Rosen, 1988).

acquaintances into empty houses or apartments, proceed to engage in "certain behavior, like kissing or heavy petting," and are then shocked—shocked!—to discover "men assuming that [this] behavior . . . is an automatic precursor to intercourse."[12]

So widespread among the male sex is this outlandish "behavioral assumption" that a girl cannot even sleep in the same bed with a man without being pressured to go all the way. Here—direct from the pages of Robin Warshaw's *I Never Called It Rape*—is Carol, age 18, who attends a fraternity party with "some nice boy from the next suburb," where she does a little drinking. The next thing she knows,

> We went back to the guys' apartment and my friend Terri went too. It never occurred to me that anything was going to be going on. We were just going to be sleeping there.

But as Warshaw, in reporting on this case, comments ominously,

> just sleeping together is not what Carol's date had in mind. After they got into bed, he started kissing her, then escalated his sexual attention. Despite her repeated "No, no, no" and her physically pushing him away, he used the advantage of his six-foot-three body to overpower her five-foot frame.

Carol, incorrigibly innocent to the end, did not realize she had been raped. But thanks to the antirape movement, she realizes it now.

Thanks to the movement too, she also realizes that she bears no responsibility whatever for what happened to her. For from earliest childhood, writes Warshaw, Carol, like all girls, had been "taught directly and indirectly (by parents, teachers, playmates, and pop-culture role models) to be passive, weak, and opinionless." Even after she became a young adult, she was "expected to be fearful and inhibited" and was not "encouraged to develop independence and self-reliance." (This, in 1988!) Now, having had her consciousness raised by what is perhaps the most important precept of the movement, she understands that in no way and under no circumstances does any blame attach to the victim of a rape. According to an exquisitely delicate formulation of this precept, "It's his penis, and only he is responsible for where he puts it."

Admittedly, Carol might have been more careful, and from now on, some other, more fortunate, Carol, tutored by such books as Andrea Parrot's *Coping with Date Rape & Acquaintance Rape,* will adopt certain "strategies" the "experts" have developed to lessen the risk of being raped. She will try to "feel good" about herself, perhaps by getting professional counseling. She will lay off alcohol and drugs. She will even avoid "being isolated with a man." If by some unhappy chance, however, she should find herself alone

20

---

[12]New York *Times,* January 2, 1991.

with one of these brutes, she will send him a "clear message" both in words and in "body language." For instance, she might announce, "I don't go to bed on the first date," or "I want to wait until marriage." Also, she will not make the mistake of letting him unbutton her blouse while telling him that she just wants to be friends. If (or rather when) he refuses to get the message and forges ahead anyway, she will yell something like, "I don't want to have sex with you; if you force me, it is rape." In the, alas, almost inevitable event that even this fails to scare him off, she will (having already taken a self-defense course and done a lot of practicing) go after "the vulnerable target areas on [his] body (such as eyes, knees, ribs, neck, nose, instep)" with her most "effective weapons (such as fists, feet, elbows, head)."

3

"Sexual intercourse began/ In nineteen sixty-three/ (Which was rather late for me)—/ Between the end of the *Chatterley* ban*/ And the Beatles' first LP." For any man old enough to know at first hand what those famous lines by Philip Larkin mean (and, I suspect, even for many younger men who grew up under the auspices of the sexual revolution of the 60's), reading the literature on acquaintance and date rape is bound to be a bewildering experience.

There is, for one thing, that endless parade of helpless and stupid females who pass through this literature. Where, the male reader is likely to wonder, have such females been hiding all his life, and what has become of all the others—those swaggeringly self-assured women flaunting their sexual allure—he sees everywhere he goes? If these women are terrified of men, they give off not the slightest whiff of it. On the contrary, what they communicate, in their dress, in their bearing, in their carriage, is a serene confidence in the great power they have over men. And as almost any male reader can confirm, it is a confidence to which they are richly entitled. "Where do they all come from? What do they want from me?" cries a middle-aged character in a Paul Mazursky* movie as he sits ogling *this* parade from the table of an outdoor café in Los Angeles.

But if middle-aged men still feel this way, it is at least not as bad for them as it is for the adolescent male. An adolescent male is typically a creature in a state of perpetual sexual anguish. The sight of just about any girl at any time in any place can plunge him into a fever of lust, and what makes his plight even more maddening is the unfairness of it all. *He* may be in a state of endless turmoil over sex, but girls, the same girls who do

---

the Chatterley *ban:* the restriction on British publication of D.H. Lawrence's sexually explicit novel *Lady Chatterley's Lover* (1928), not lifted until 1960
Paul Mazursky (b. 1930): American screenwriter and director

this to him just by being there, seem able to take or leave sex at will. Though their very existence is a provocation even when they are not (or are they?) deliberately taunting and teasing him, neither he nor any other boy seems to have a comparable power over them. For them it is evidently as easy to say no to sex as it is impossible for him. From which he learns very early on that his only hope of ever breaking through this incomprehensible indifference is by not taking their no for an answer at any stage in the process of courtship—which, as he also learns very early on, is precisely what some (and probably most) of them want him to do.

Realities like these are not entirely absent from the literature on acquaintance rape, but they are presented in terms that are again bound to bewilder any normal male reader. According to Robin Warshaw, expressing the movement's party line on this matter, the whole thing is a "myth," a "dogma of what . . . it means to be male" into which boys are "indoctrinated" by "fathers, uncles, grandfathers, coaches, youth group leaders, friends, fraternity brothers, even pop stars." This, it appears, and not their bitter experience with girls, is why they come to "view their relationships with women as adversarial challenges," and why they end up believing

> that they must initiate sexual activity, that they may meet with reluctance from girls, but if they just persist, cajole, and refuse to let up, that ultimately they will get what they want.

So far as the feminist movement is concerned, any man who acts on this "myth" is on the road to becoming a rapist, if indeed he is not already there. For in the movement's eyes a woman's no always means no, her maybe always means no, and even—I do not exaggerate—her yes often means no: "Many feminists," writes Susan Estrich, late of the Dukakis campaign and now a professor at the Harvard Law School,[13] "would argue that so long as women are powerless relative to men, viewing 'yes' as a sign of true consent is misguided." Or as Muehlenhard and Schrag explain it in "Non-Violent Sexual Coercion":

> There could be many reasons why a woman might not resist a man's advances so that unwanted intercourse could occur without force. The woman may fear that resisting will make the man violent. She may be confused. Her socialization may make it difficult for her to resist.

Not only, then, is there never any justification for pressing ahead when the woman protests or resists, even mildly; if the "experts" get their way, any male who has intercourse with any female, including his wife or a girlfriend with whom he has been sleeping all along, without first practically

25

---

[13]*Real Rape: How the Legal System Victimizes Women Who Say No* (Cambridge: Harvard, 1987).

getting a signed and notarized consent form to cover that particular episode, will wind up in jail.

4

What on earth is going on here? Why should the feminist movement be promulgating a conception of rape that comes so close to turning seduction, and even heterosexual intercourse in itself, into a criminal act?

One possible explanation is that the influence of lesbian and other man-hating elements within the movement has grown so powerful as to have swept all before it. No doubt lesbians are only a small minority among feminists, but like other radicals in other political movements they tend to be more passionate, more energetic, and more ideologically coherent than the moderates, whose waverings and ambiguous feelings make them easy to manipulate. Once the moderates have been subjected to "consciousness raising," they begin to find more and more truth in the radical deconstruction or demystification.

Where sex is the issue, this takes the form of putting what is natural to male sexuality in the worst possible light. The ever restless masculine sex drive (so strange and frightening to so many young, and even not so young, women, ruled as they are by much more quiescent erotic impulses) gets to be seen as sheer aggression; its normally indiscriminate and promiscuous character (again very different from the much more focused erotic impulses natural to the female) becomes a deliberate insult to women; and the masculine need to conquer—a need obverse to and symbiotic with the natural motion of female sexuality from resistance to acquiescence—is interpreted as an expression of contempt for them.

To make things even easier for the lesbians and other man-haters, 30 there was the sexual revolution of the 1960's, which wound up giving women in general new reason to fear and resent men.

For men the sexual revolution meant that the war between the sexes had suddenly ended, and it had ended, moreover, on their terms. (Larkin: "Then all at once the quarrel sank:/ Everyone felt the same. . . .") Now, *mirabile dictu,* sex could be had exactly as men had always dreamed: promiscuously and with no conditions attached. Of course the reality turned out to be rather different from the dream, and once the novelty of meeting little or no resistance had worn off, the kick began to go out of the entire experience. (One hopes that Larkin, who lived just long enough to see this happen, derived some consolation from it.)

But for women it was worse, much worse. To the degree that they embraced the sexual revolution as a new dawn of equality which (in what Larkin mordantly described as "A brilliant breaking of the bank,/ A quite unlosable game") would make them as free as men had always been to jump happily into bed with anyone and everyone, they unilaterally disarmed themselves in the war between the sexes. No matter how ideologically committed they may have been to their new sexual freedom, and no matter how enthusiastic they may have thought they were about the abolition of the old double standard, it was soon borne in upon them that the game was not quite so unlosable as they had imagined, and that *they* were the losers. For the truth was that they did not feel the "same" as men, and there was no satisfaction to be had in striving to imitate the masculine sexual drive.

Nor, for all their emancipation from the puritanism of the past, did women who did this, or tried to do it, quite escape feeling cheap and even— though the word would never have been permitted to enter their minds— immoral. They also felt cheated and exploited and abused; and the fact that they themselves were the main authors of this predicament did not prevent them from blaming it on men.

About twenty years ago, Midge Decter[14] interpreted the rise of the women's liberation movement in the late 60's as (among other things) a covert revulsion against the sexual revolution. Wanting to say no again but having signed on to an ideology that deprived them of any reason or right to say it, women were desperately looking for a way back that would not seem regressive or reactionary, and they hit upon it in a counterrevolution which posed as a new and higher stage of revolutionary development.

This new stage arose out of the announcement that the sexual revolu- 35 tion had been no revolution at all but rather another in the long history of male conspiracies to degrade and dominate women. From here it was but a short and easy step to the conclusion that sex itself—heterosexual sex, that is—was the mother (or rather the father) of all these conspiracies. For some women the solution was to shun men altogether in favor either of abstinence (the "new chastity") or lesbianism. But this being too radical for most women, the movement adopted what appeared to be a more moderate objective: to work toward a wholesale change in the relation between the sexes.

As a delicious historical irony would have it, a prophet of the new sexual order envisaged by the movement was discovered in the formerly despised Victorian age in the person of one Victoria Woodhull, "the first publisher of the *Communist Manifesto* in the United States and the first woman stockbroker on Wall Street," as Andrea Dworkin, her leading disciple, informs us. It was not, however, in these capacities that Woodhull commended herself to contemporary feminist attention. It was, rather, in her role as, in Dworkin's words, "the greatest advocate of the female-first model

---

[14]In *The New Chastity and Other Arguments Against Women's Liberation* (New York: Coward, 1972).

of intercourse" (also known as the "female-supremacist model"). Woodhull insisted, Dworkin continues,

> that women had a *natural* right—a right that inhered in the nature of intercourse itself—to be entirely self-determining, the controlling and dominating partner, the one whose desire determined the event, the one who both initiates and is the final authority on what the sex is and will be.

Thus, having been bruised and disillusioned by their effort to end the war of the sexes through unconditional (if inadvertent and unconscious) surrender to the masculine principle, women would now move in the opposite direction and demand (this time in full consciousness) that the war be ended through unconditional surrender to the feminine way. Women would now have (again Dworkin, paraphrasing Woodhull)

> real and absolute control in each and every act of intercourse, which would be, each and every time, chosen by the woman.

It is here that we run smack into the main purpose of the campaign against date and acquaintance rape. To further the establishment of the new sexual dispensation, it becomes necessary to delegitimize any instance of heterosexual coupling that starts with male initiative and involves even the slightest degree of female resistance at any stage along the way. Hence almost the entire range of normal heterosexual intercourse must be stigmatized as criminal, and both women and men must be educated to recognize it as such. But to make sure that normal people are not put off by so weird a project, the new conception has to be framed in language that does not betray the antinomian radicalism behind it.

Here, then, is how Robin Warshaw translates the lunatic prescriptions of an antinomian radical like Dworkin into relatively bland "guidelines for change" that men are exhorted to follow if they are to avoid becoming rapists. Among these 11 guidelines are the following:

> 1. *Never force a woman to have sex*—even if she has "led" you on, even if she has slept with your friends, even if she at first said "yes" and then changed her mind before having sex, even if she had sex with you before. This includes *all* unwanted sexual contact—from kissing to "copping a feel." . . . When partners' desires conflict, the one who wants more activity has to yield to the one who wants less. . . .
> 2. *Don't pressure a woman to have sex.* Men often see their verbal pressuring as being less forceful than women do. Even when the words you use are not threatening, the woman may feel that she is in danger. . . .
> 6. *Do not confuse "scoring" with having a successful social encounter.* . . . You can have intercourse with 100 women and still not know anything

about good sex or what it means to be a "real" man. Ejaculating is no big deal; having a mutually agreed-upon and sustained relationship is. . . .

    8. *"No" means "no."* . . . When a woman says "no" that means "no." Stop. . . . Do not try to cajole her or argue with her. . . . If you think she's saying "no" to protect her "reputation" (even though you know she *really* wants to have sex with you), so what? When (and if) she's ready to have sex with you, let it be her choice to make. If a woman says "no" and really means "yes, but you have to convince me," then you don't want to be with her anyway. . . . Just walk away.

Fat chance.   40

5

    Which is to say (because "You can't fool Mother Nature") that the date-rape campaign has a very hard row to hoe. As the "experts" themselves are only too aware, what they with their usual elegance call "rape-supportive" attitudes remain almost as stubbornly in place as ever. In fact, they estimate that a whopping 84 percent of the men who are guilty of raping a date or acquaintance according to the new definition (that is, men who do not physically harm their "victims" but only ignore their protests and press on) refuse to regard themselves as rapists. As Warshaw informs us, some of the same "hyper-masculine" or macho "male zealots" even

> become oddly tender immediately afterward and try to dress the women or cover them. Some gallantly insist on walking or driving their victims home, telling the women that it's dangerous for them to be out alone. Others profess love and talk about having an ongoing relationship. Another type kisses their victims good-bye and says they will call them again soon.

    This is exactly what the "experts" would expect of the male sex after thousands of years of "socialization" by a "rape-supportive" culture. To their horror, however, women too are still resisting the new concept of rape.

    Thus, in a paper for *Acquaintance Rape: The Hidden Crime,* two professors at the University of North Carolina at Greensboro, Jacqueline W. White and her collaborator (in both senses of the word), John A. Humphrey, are appalled to report that adolescent girls (including Los Angeles teenagers, "a group that might be expected to hold egalitarian sex-role values") are still reluctant to attach the label rape to "nonconsensual sex" on a date unless a significant amount of force was used. Furthermore, a majority (56 percent) of girls (as compared with 76 percent of boys) believe that a boy has a right to ignore a girl's protests under certain circumstances—when, for instance, she has gotten him sexually excited.

As for adult women, they are even more retrograde than the teenagers, to the point where "women jurors are often especially harsh" in cases of alleged acquaintance rape. To Pauline B. Bart, co-author (with Patricia H. O'Brien) of *Stopping Rape: Successful Survival Strategies,*[15] this has nothing to do with understanding born of experience. It is all a matter of "denial":

> To live with the knowledge that not only are all women vulnerable to rape, but that frequently they are raped by men they know is difficult. If, however, women believe . . . that only bad women can be raped and only crazy men who are strangers are rapists, then they can feel safe.

The same mechanism of denial is hauled in to account for the fact that   45
the vast majority (73 percent) of women who in feminist eyes have been "victims" of "rape" by a date or an acquaintance persist in refusing to call it rape on the ground that, while they offered resistance of one kind or another, they were neither threatened by nor subjected to real physical force. Robin Warshaw, as usual providing a convenient summary of the movement's party line, is equally quick to dismiss as "typically self-blaming female explanations" such statements by these "victims" as "I must have misunderstood him," "I didn't make myself clear," or "I'm wrong for feeling bad about this." But neither the "rapists" nor their "victims" agree with the "experts." The much-cited survey done for *Ms.* by Mary P. Koss even showed that somewhere in the neighborhood of half of the women who were considered victims of rape by the "experts" were willing to have sex again with the dates or acquaintances who had "assaulted" them.

Of course, these surveys were conducted before the date-rape campaign really got rolling, with all its attendant publicity and with all the workshops and seminars and other "acquaintance-rape awareness" educational programs now being set up in high schools and colleges (they are especially necessary, says Warshaw, "during the most dangerous period—from the first day of classes to Thanksgiving break"). It is therefore safe to predict that future studies will yield results more heavily influenced by the new conception of rape. A larger percentage of men, and an even greater percentage of women, subjected to all this brainwashing, will no doubt apply the term rape to situations in which minimal or no physical force was used, or in which the only "coercion" consisted (as Neil Gilbert succinctly describes it) of the

---

[15]New York: Pergamon Press, 1985.

conventional script of nagging and pleading—"Everyone does it," "If you really loved me, you'd do it," "We did it last night," "You will like it." . . .

Yet if this will represent a triumph for the feminist movement, and most of all for its man-hating and lesbian sectors, it will only be another case of ashes in the mouth for the women to whom that movement, speaking in their name and presuming to act in their interest, has already done so much damage.

To the extent that men are bullied or persuaded into following, or at least trying to follow, the "guidelines" of the new sexual dispensation, the number of "wimps" about whom women have been complaining ever since women's lib was born (though without ever seeing any connection between the two phenomena) will multiply apace.* So—to the great joy of Andrea Dworkin and those "experts" like Muehlenhard and Schrag who believe that "discrimination against lesbians continues as a form of indirect sexual coercion," and constitutes "one more source of pressure for women to be in sexual relationships with men"—will the incidence of male impotence. The search for husbands, already so difficult that hordes of young women have taken to advertising in the personals columns, will in consequence grow even more desperate, and the already familiar female refrain, "Why are all the men I meet either wimps or married or gay?" will swell into an even mightier chorus. And yet, nature still being stronger after all than its antinomian enemies, most young men and most young women will not be repelled or frightened off and will play their naturally ordained parts in the unending and inescapable war between the sexes, suffering the usual wounds, exulting in the usual victories, and even eventually arriving at that armistice known as marriage.

Even these lucky ones, however, will have a harder time of it because of the lethal new poison which has been sprayed by the anti-date-rape brigades onto the battlefield of the war between the sexes in general and the struggles of courtship in particular. As for the unlucky ones, those young men and young women who will be too impressionable or too frightened or too weak to hold out against the imperatives of the new sexual dispensation, they will have its feminist authors to thank for a life of loneliness, frustration, resentment, and sterility.

"wimps" . . . multiply apace: For a satirical male view of the "wimps" issue, see the reading by Joe Bob Briggs, "Get in Touch with Your Ancient Spear," starting on p. 368.

QUESTIONING THE TEXT

1. According to Podhoretz, which historical periods provide evidence of society punishing rape as a crime? From what period does the concept of date or acquaintance rape originate? Why is it crucial to Podhoretz's argument that date rape be understood as a recent concept?
2. Podhoretz takes some care to differentiate among feminists. What adjectives does he apply to those he argues with in this essay, and what connotations do those terms have for you? What might his strategy be in so labeling his opponents? Record your response in your reading log, if you are keeping one.
3. According to Podhoretz, who has benefited most from the sexual revolution of the 1960s? Why?
4. Underline any words or phrases in J.R.'s introduction that you believe indicate a disposition in favor of or in opposition to Podhoretz's argument. Is the introduction disinterested and balanced, biased and blatant, interested and subtle? Explain your position.

MAKING CONNECTIONS

5. In Maxine Hong Kingston's "No Name Woman" (on p. 319) the aunt terrorized by the villagers' raid into killing her newborn child and herself is the victim of rape by a man she certainly knew. What similarities and differences do you see between this woman and the women victimized by acquaintances described in Podhoretz's essay?
6. Are there elements in Liam Hudson and Bernadine Jacot's argument in *The Way Men Think* (p. 296) that might support the position of feminists who regard all seduction as essentially hostile to women? Review the Hudson and Jacot essay with this question in mind, and then write a short paper exploring any connections between it and the Podhoretz article.

JOINING THE CONVERSATION

7. With a group that includes both men and women, discuss Podhoretz's assertion that "some (and probably most)" women do not want men to take initial indifference as a sign to abandon courtship entirely. After the discussion, each write a dialogue that reflects the range of opinions among the group. Then compare the dialogues to see whether members of the group interpreted comments in significantly different ways.

8. Read Podhoretz's conclusion two or three times, and then write an exploratory essay about the consequences of the campaign against date rape.

9. Working with a group that includes both men and women, write a definition of rape.

NAOMI MUNSON
Harassment Blues

IN THE FALL OF 1991, Anita Hill, a professor of law at the University of Oklahoma, testified before a committee of the United States Senate and a national television audience that Clarence Thomas, President George Bush's nominee for the Supreme Court, had sexually harassed her ten years earlier while she was working with him at the Equal Employment Opportunity Commission. In emotional testimony, Thomas rebutted Hill's charges, and when the hearings were finished, polls showed that a majority of Americans believed him and thought he should be confirmed. The Senate concurred, enabling him to take the seat formerly held by Thurgood Marshall.

Since the hearings, Hill has been celebrated by many in the media as a feminist heroine abused by an all-male committee. The drumbeat of media attention has shifted the polls in Hill's favor, with a majority of Americans now believing her *story. But the fact remains that on her own Hill had been unable to make a case convincing enough to derail the Thomas appointment—a point I believe to be worth remembering.*

In the following reading Naomi Munson, who has written for the American Spectator *and the* Wall Street Journal, *suggests why many people might not have believed Hill during the hearings themselves, before the intensive media massage of her image. Munson's piece appeared shortly after the hearings in* Commentary, *a journal of neoconservative thought.* – J.R.

When I was graduated from college in the early '70s, I had the good fortune to land a job at a weekly newsmagazine. It was a wonderful place to work, financially lucrative, intellectually demanding but not overwhelming, and, above all, fun.

There was, actually, a sort of hierarchy of fun at the office. Ranking lowest were the hard-news departments; although (or perhaps because) they offered the excitement of late-breaking news and fast-developing stories, both the national- and the foreign-affairs sections were socially rather staid. Next up the scale came the business section, where the people were lively enough but where the general tone nevertheless reflected the serious nature of the subject matter. Then there was the culture department, a barrel of laughs in its own way, though the staff did seem to spend a certain amount of time at the opera. At the top of the scale stood the department where I wound up, which included science, sports, education, religion, and the like. Though there might be the occasional breaking news, these sections generally called more for long thought and thorough research, which led to a very laid-back atmosphere and a lot of down time. Drinking at nearby bars, dining at the finest restaurants, and dancing at local discos occupied a great deal of that time. And sex played a major role in all of this. (It did throughout the magazine, of course, but nowhere so openly and unselfconsciously as here.)

The men were a randy lot, dedicated philanderers, and foul-mouthed to boot; the women, having vociferously demanded—and been granted—absolutely equal status, were considered fair game (though there were a couple of secretaries whose advancing age and delicate sensibilities consigned them to the sidelines).

Imagine my surprise, then, when one day a young woman who worked with me flounced into my office, cheeks flushed, eyes flashing, to announce that she had just been subjected to sexual harassment. (It was a fairly new concept back then, at the end of the '70s, but being in the vanguard of social trends, we had heard of it.) When she explained that the offense had occurred not in our own neck of the woods but in the national-affairs section, I was truly shocked. When she identified the offender, however—sexually, one of the least lively types on the premises—I began to be skeptical. And when she described his crime—which was having said something to the effect that he longed for the good old days of miniskirts when a fellow had a real chance to see great legs like hers—I scoffed. "Oh, come on," I said. "That's not sexual harassment; that's just D. trying to pay you a compliment." To myself, after she had calmed down and left, I said, "She's even dimmer than I thought. She thinks *that's* what they mean by sexual harassment."

If I was convinced that this woman's experience did not constitute   5
sexual harassment, I, like the vast majority of people at that time, had rather vague notions of what did. Whatever it was, however, it already seemed clear that the charge of sexual harassment would serve as a perfect instrument of revenge for disgruntled female employees. This was borne out by the story I came to know, years later, about a man at another office who had had several formal harassment charges brought against him by women who worked for him. The man was someone who would, as his co-workers saw it, "nail" anything that moved. He had, in fact, had longstanding affairs—which he had ended in order to move on to fresh conquests—with the women now accusing him of having offered financial inducements in exchange for sexual favors. The women claimed to have declined the offers and consequently suffered the loss of promotions.

Disgruntlement aside, however, it still seemed obvious to me that in a case of sexual harassment, something *sexual* might be supposed to have occurred. That quaint notion of mine was finally laid to rest during the Clarence Thomas–Anita Hill debacle. Professor Hill's performance convinced me of nothing save that if she told me the sun was shining, I should head straight for my umbrella and galoshes. The vast outpouring of feminist outrage that accompanied the event did, however, succeed in opening my eyes to the sad fact that it was I, way back when, who had been the dim one; my erstwhile colleague had merely been a bit ahead of her time. For, it now turns out, what she described is precisely what they *do* mean by sexual harassment.

During the course of the hearing, story after story appeared in the media supporting the claim that men out there are abusive to their female employees. It was declared, over and over, that virtually every woman in the country had either suffered sexual harassment herself or knew someone who had (I myself, I realize, figure in that assessment). This abuse, it appeared, had been going on since time immemorial and was so painful to some of the women involved that they had repressed it for decades.

It became clear amid all the hand-wringing that we were not talking here about bosses exacting sexual favors in exchange for promotions, raises, or the like. Even Professor Hill never claimed that Judge Thomas promised to promote her if she succumbed to his charms, or that he threatened to fire her if she failed to do so. What she said, as all the world now knows, was that he pestered her for dates; that he boasted of his natural endowments and of his sexual prowess; that he used obscene language in her presence; that he regaled her with the details of porno flicks; and that he discussed the joys of, as Miss Hill so expressively put it, "(gulp) oral sex." The closest anyone at the hearing came to revealing anything like direct action was a Washington woman who was horrified when a member of Congress played footsie with her under the table at an official function, and a friend of Anita Hill who announced that she had been "touched in the workplace."

What we—or, to be more precise, they—were talking about was sexual innuendo, ogling, obscenity, unwelcome importuning, nude pin-ups; about an "unpleasant atmosphere in the workplace"; about male "insensitivity." One columnist offered behavioral guidelines to men who had been reduced to "whining" that they no longer knew what was appropriate—something to the effect that though it is OK to say, "Gee, I bet you make the best blackened redfish in town," it is not OK to say, "Wow, I bet you're really hot between the sheets." Even Judge Thomas himself declared that if he *had* said the things the good professor was accusing him of, it *would* have constituted sexual harassment.

Yet in response to all of this it also emerged very plainly that the   10
American public just was not buying it. Single women were heard to worry that putting a lid on sex at the office might hurt their chances of finding a husband; one forthright woman was even quoted by a newspaper as saying that office sex was the spice of life. Rather more definitively, polls showed that most people, black and white, male and female, thought Judge Thomas should be confirmed, *even if the charges against him were true.*

How can it be that the majority of Americans were dismissing the significance of sexual harassment (as now defined) even as their elected representatives were declaring it just the most hideous, heinous, gosh–awful stuff they had ever heard of? How is it possible that, at the very moment newspapers and TV were proclaiming that American women were mad as hell and weren't going to take it anymore, most of these women themselves—and their husbands—were responding with a raised eyebrow and a small shrug of the shoulders?

For one thing, most Americans—unlike the ideologues who brought us sexual harassment in the first place, and who have worked a special magic on pundits and politicos for more than two decades now—have a keen understanding of life's realities. Having had no choice but to work, in order to feed and clothe and doctor and educate their children, they have always known that, while work has its rewards, financial and otherwise, "an unpleasant atmosphere in the workplace" is something they may well have to put up with. That, where women are concerned, the unpleasantness might take on sexual overtones gives it no more weight than the uncertainties, the frustrations, and the humiliations, petty and grand, encountered by men.

Most people, furthermore, have a healthy respect for the ability of women to hold their own in the battle of the sexes. They know that women have always managed to deal perfectly well with male lust: to evade it, to quash it, even to be flattered by it. The bepaunched and puffing boss, chasing his buxom secretary around the desk, is, after all, a figure of fun—because we realize that he will never catch her, and that even if he did, she would know very well how to put him in his place.

The women's movement and its fellow travelers, on the other hand, have never had any such understanding or any such respect. On the contrary, rage against life's imperfections, and a consequent revulsion against men, has been the bone and sinew of that movement.

The feminists came barreling into the workforce, some twenty years 15 ago, not out of necessity, but with the loud assertion that here was to be found something called fulfillment. Men, they claimed, had denied them access to this fulfillment out of sheer power-hungry selfishness. Women, they insisted, were no different from men in their talents or their dispositions; any apparent differences had simply been manufactured, as a device to deprive mothers, wives, and sisters of the excitement and pleasure to which men had had exclusive title for so long, and which they had come to view as their sole privilege.

No sooner had these liberated ladies taken their rightful place alongside men at work, however, than it began to dawn on them that the experience was not quite living up to their expectations. They quickly discovered, for example, what their fathers, husbands, and brothers had always known: that talent is not always appreciated, that promotions are not so easy to come by, that often those most meritorious are inexplicably passed over in favor of others. But rather than recognizing this as a universal experience, they descried a "glass ceiling," especially constructed to keep them in their place, and they called for the hammers.

Feminists had insisted that childbearing held no more allure for them than it did for men. That insistence quickly began to crumble in the face of a passionate desire for babies. But rather than recognizing that life had presented them with a choice, they demanded special treatment. They reserved the right to take leave from their work each time the urge to procreate came upon them. And they insisted that husbands, employers, and even the government take equal responsibility with them for the care and upbringing of the little bundles of joy resulting from that urge.

And as for sex in the workplace, well, that was pretty much what it had always been everywhere: an ongoing battle involving, on the one side, attentions both unwelcome and welcome, propositions both unappealing and appealing, and compliments both unpleasing and pleasing, and on the other, evasive action, outright rejection, or happy capitulation. Having long ago decided that the terms of this age-old battle were unacceptable to them, the women of the movement might have been expected to try to eliminate them. With the invention of sexual harassment, they have met that expectation, and with a vengeance. Laws have been made, cases have been tried and, in the Clarence Thomas affair, a decent man was pilloried.

Having, in other words, finally been permitted to play with the big boys, these women have found the game not to their liking. But rather than retiring from the field, they have called for a continuous and open-ended reformation of the rules. Indeed, like children in a temper, who respond to maternal placating with a rise in fury, they have met every accommodating act of the men in their lives with a further escalation of demands. The new insistence that traditional male expressions of sexual interest be declared taboo, besides being the purest revelation of feminist rage, is the latest arc in that vicious cycle.

QUESTIONING THE TEXT

1. Munson begins her article with a story about her past. Do you find this narrative an effective way of opening so serious an article? Why, or why not?
2. How is Munson's understanding of sexual harassment changed by Anita Hill's testimony?
3. Do you agree or disagree with Munson's assumptions about, and characterizations of, women in this piece? Why, or why not? Record your responses in your reading log, if you are keeping one.
4. Try your hand at writing your own introduction to "Harassment Blues." Then compare your introduction to J.R.'s, and note the differences. Compare, for example, the details you each cite from Munson

and the words you each use (to describe Hill as well as Munson's piece).

MAKING CONNECTIONS

5. How do you think Munson would reply to the next reading, June Jordan's "Can I Get a Witness?" What common ground, if any, do you find between the positions staked out by these writers?
6. Sojourner Truth describes herself (on p. 293) as a powerful and active woman, more than able to keep up with men. Who do you think she would have more sympathy with—Anita Hill or Naomi Munson? Explain your opinion in a short position paper that might serve as an opinion piece in a local newspaper.

JOINING THE CONVERSATION

7. Munson argues, in effect, that male "insensitivity" ("innuendo, ogling, obscenity, unwelcome importuning, nude pin-ups") ought not be considered criminal behavior. In a paper short enough to appear in the letters column of your daily newspaper, argue for or against Munson's contention.
8. Does Munson have more credibility in criticizing Anita Hill than a male writer would? Discuss this issue with a group of classmates.

JUNE JORDAN
Can I Get a Witness?

CURRENTLY PROFESSOR OF African American studies and women's studies at the University of California at Berkeley, June Jordan (b. 1936) is internationally known for her poetry, essays, and articles, which have appeared in Kikamo's Story *(1981),* On Call: Political Essays *(1985),* Naming Our Destiny: New and Selected Poems *(1989), and* Technical Difficulties *(1992). As a woman who grew up with the civil rights movement in the United States, she has seen firsthand that movement's triumphs and failures. Partially as a result of the urgency attending civil rights issues in the 1990s, the passionate voice that emerges from Jordan's work has no time for formal niceties, no time for hypocrisies of any kind. Jordan is a woman of very strong opinion, and she is also a speaker of great power. Listening to her describe the plight of the students in ramshackle inner-city schools and in run-down, overcrowded, and underfunded public community colleges a few years ago, I (and I dare say everyone else in that very large audience) was moved by Jordan's deep conviction, by her devotion to students, by her insistent calls for action, and by the haunting images and rhythms of her speech.*

In the essay that follows, originally published in The Progressive *in 1991, Jordan opens with a hypothetical letter to Anita Hill and uses the occasion to assail Clarence Thomas and the Senate panel that interrogated them, closing with a stern warning for the people and the government of "this savage country." These are more strong words from June Jordan. I chose this reading precisely because of the strong sense of anger and outrage it conveys, and because I wondered how many other people wanted to write a letter to Anita Hill and never did.* — A.L.

I wanted to write a letter to Anita Hill. I wanted to say thanks. I wanted to convey the sorrow and the bitterness I feel on her behalf. I wanted to explode the history that twisted itself around the innocence of her fate. I wanted to assail the brutal ironies, the cruel consistencies that left her—at the moment of her utmost vulnerability and public power—isolated, betrayed, abused, and not nearly as powerful as those who sought and who seek to besmirch, ridicule, and condemn the truth of her important and perishable human being. I wanted to reassure her of her rights, her sanity, and the African beauty of her ernest commitment to do right and to be a good woman: a good black woman in this America.

But tonight I am still too furious, I am still too hurt, I am still too astounded and nauseated by the enemies of Anita Hill. Tonight my heart pounds with shame.

Is there no way to interdict and terminate the traditional, abusive loneliness of black women in this savage country?*

From those slavery times when African men could not dare to defend their sisters, their mothers, their sweethearts, their wives, and their daughters—except at the risk of their lives—from those times until today: Has nothing changed?

How is it possible that only John Carr—a young black corporate   5
lawyer who maintained a friendship with Anita Hill ten years ago ("It didn't go but so far," he testified, with an engaging, handsome trace of a smile)— how is it possible that he, alone among black men, stood tall and strong and righteous as a witness for her defense?

What about spokesmen for the NAACP or the National Urban League?

What about spokesmen for the U.S. Congressional Black Caucus?

All of the organizational and elected black men who spoke aloud against a wrong black man, Clarence Thomas, for the sake of principles resting upon decency and concerns for fair play, equal protection, and affirmative action—where did they go when, suddenly, a good black woman arose among us, trying to tell the truth?

Where did they go? And why?

Is it conceivable that a young white woman could be tricked into   10
appearing before twelve black men of the U.S. Senate?

Is it conceivable that a young white woman could be tricked into appearing before a lineup of incredibly powerful and hypocritical and sneering and hellbent black men freely insinuating and freely hypothesizing whatever lurid scenario came into their heads?

Is it conceivable that such a young woman—such a flower of white womanhood—would, by herself, have to withstand the calumny and unabashed, unlawful bullying that was heaped upon Anita Hill?

Is it conceivable that this flower would not be swiftly surrounded by white knights rallying—with ropes, or guns, or whatever—to defend her honor and the honor, the legal and civilized rights, of white people, per se?

Anita Hill was tricked. She was set up. She had been minding her business at the University of Oklahoma Law School when the senators asked her to describe her relationship with Clarence Thomas. Anita Hill's dutiful answers disclosed that Thomas had violated the trust of his office as head of the Equal Employment Opportunity Commission. Sitting in that office of ultimate recourse for women suffering from sexual harassment,

---

no way . . . in this savage country: For highly charged language of a different sort entirely, see P. J. O'Rourke, "Among the Compassion Fascists," p. 556.

Thomas himself harassed Anita Hill, repeatedly, with unwanted sexual advances and remarks.

Although Anita Hill had not volunteered this information and only   15
supplied it in response to direct, specific inquiries from the FBI,

And although Anita Hill was promised the protection of confidentiality as regards her sworn statement of allegations,

And despite the fact that four witnesses—two men and two women, two black and two white distinguished Americans, including a federal judge and a professor of law—testified, under oath, that Anita Hill had told each of them about these sordid carryings on by Thomas at the time of their occurrence or in the years that followed,

And despite the fact that Anita Hill sustained a remarkably fastidious display of exact recall and never alleged, for example, that Thomas actually touched her,

And despite the unpardonable decision by the U.S. Senate Judiciary Committee to prohibit expert testimony on sexual harassment,

Anita Hill, a young black woman born and raised within a black farm   20
family of thirteen children, a graduate of an Oklahoma public high school who later earned honors and graduated from Yale Law School, a political conservative and, now, a professor of law,

Anita Hill, a young black woman who suffered sexual harassment once in ten years and, therefore, never reported sexual harassment to any of her friends except for that once in ten years,

Anita Hill, whose public calm and dispassionate sincerity refreshed America's eyes and ears with her persuasive example of what somebody looks like and sounds like when she's simply trying to tell the truth,

Anita Hill was subpoenaed by the U.S. Senate Judiciary Committee of fourteen white men and made to testify and to tolerate interrogation on national television.

1. Why didn't she "do something" when Thomas allegedly harassed her?

The senators didn't seem to notice or to care that Thomas occupied   25
the office of last recourse for victims of sexual harassment. And had the committee allowed any expert on the subject to testify, we would have learned that it is absolutely typical for victims to keep silent.

2. Wasn't it the case that she had/has fantasies and is delusional?

Remarkably, not a single psychiatrist or licensed psychologist was allowed to testify. These slanderous suppositions about the psychic functionings of Anita Hill were never more than malevolent speculations invited by one or another of the fourteen white senators as they sat above an assortment of character witnesses handpicked by White House staffers eager to protect the president's nominee.

One loathsomely memorable item: John Doggett, a self-infatuated black attorney and a friend of Clarence Thomas, declared that Thomas would not have jeopardized his career for Anita Hill because Doggett, a black man, explained to the Senate Committee of fourteen white men, "She is not worth it."

3. Why was she "lying"?

It should be noted that Anita Hill readily agreed to a lie-detector test and that, according to the test, she was telling the truth. It should also be noted that Clarence Thomas refused even to consider taking such a test and that, furthermore, he had already established himself as a liar when, earlier in the Senate hearings, he insisted that he had never discussed *Roe v. Wade,* and didn't know much about this paramount legal dispute.

Meanwhile, Clarence Thomas—who has nodded and grinned his way to glory and power by denying systemic American realities of racism, on the one hand, and by publicly castigating and lying about his own sister, a poor black woman, on the other—this Thomas, this Uncle Tom calamity of mediocre abilities, at best, this bootstrap miracle of egomaniacal myth and self-pity, this choice of the very same president who has vetoed two civil-rights bills and boasted about that, how did he respond to the testimony of Anita Hill?

Clarence Thomas thundered and he shook. Clarence Thomas glowered and he growled. "God is my judge!" he cried, at one especially disgusting low point in the Senate proceedings. "God is my judge, Senator. And not you!" This candidate for the Supreme Court evidently believes himself exempt from the judgments of mere men.

This Clarence Thomas—about whom an African-American young man in my freshman composition class exclaimed, "He's an Uncle Tom. He's a hypocritical Uncle Tom. And I don't care what happens to his punk ass"—this Thomas vilified the hearings as a "high-tech lynching."

When he got into hot water for the first time (on public record, at any rate), he attempted to identify himself as a regular black man. What a peculiar reaction to the charge of sexual harassment!

And where was the laughter that should have embarrassed him out of that chamber?

And where were the tears?

When and where was there ever a black man lynched because he was bothering a black woman?

When and where was there ever a white man jailed or tarred and feathered because he was bothering a black woman?

When a black woman is raped or beaten or mutilated by a black man or a white man, what happens?

To be a black woman in this savage country: is that to be nothing and no one beautiful and precious and exquisitely compelling?

To be a black woman in this savage country: is that to be nothing and no one revered and defended and given our help and our gratitude?

The only powerful man to utter and to level the appropriate word of revulsion as a charge against his peers—the word was "SHAME"—that man was U.S. Senator Ted Kennedy, a white man whose ongoing, successful career illuminates the unequal privileges of male gender, white race, and millionaire–class identity.

But Ted Kennedy was not on trial. He has never been on trial.

Clarence Thomas was supposed to be on trial but he was not: he is more powerful than Anita Hill. And his bedfellows, from Senator Strom Thurmond to President George Bush, persist—way more powerful than Clarence Thomas and Anita Hill combined.

And so, at the last, it was she, Anita Hill, who stood alone, trying to   45
tell the truth in an arena of snakes and hyenas and dinosaurs and power-mad dogs. And with this televised victimization of Anita Hill, the American war of violence against women moved from the streets, moved from hip-hop, moved from multimillion-dollar movies into the highest chambers of the U.S. government.

And what is anybody going to do about it?

I, for one, am going to write a letter to Anita Hill. I am going to tell her that, thank God, she is a black woman who is somebody and something beautiful and precious and exquisitely compelling.

And I am going to say that if this government will not protect and defend her, and all black women, and all women, period, in this savage country—if this government will not defend us from poverty and violence and contempt—then we will change the government. We have the numbers to deliver on this warning.

And, as for those brothers who disappeared when a black woman rose up to tell the truth, listen: It's getting to be payback time. I have been speaking on behalf of a good black woman. Can you hear me?

Can I get a witness?   50

QUESTIONING THE TEXT

1. Jordan uses powerful verbs, adjectives, and nouns to evoke images of Anita Hill and Clarence Thomas. Go through this essay, listing the major words she associates with each. Then look over your two lists and make some notes describing what effect these words have on your own characterization of Hill and Thomas. Bring the lists and notes to class for discussion.

2. Jordan says in paragraph 2 that she's "furious," that her "heart pounds with shame." Write a paragraph or two describing what she is furious about *or* why she feels shame. Then write another paragraph in which you describe how you think you would feel in June Jordan's position.

3. A.L.'s introduction to this reading presents a different point of view than that of J.R. in his introduction to the reading by Naomi Munson

(on p. 348). How would you characterize these two viewpoints? Are you more sympathetic to one than to the other? Why, or why not?

MAKING CONNECTIONS

4. Does Jordan provide any evidence that Anita Hill may become a legend—a Rosa Parks or an Eleanor Roosevelt (on pp. 460 and 474, respectively), for instance? What other evidence have you seen in the media to support the idea that Hill may become (or already be) a legend? Write a brief (no longer than one page) statement that argues for (or against) this title: "Anita Hill: A Legend in the Making."

5. List three or four points Jordan would likely make in response to Naomi Munson, the author of the preceding reading. Do you agree or disagree with those points, and why?

JOINING THE CONVERSATION

6. Write a letter to Anita Hill yourself, trying to sum up what you know of the conflict between her and Clarence Thomas, detailing what you wish she could tell you about that conflict, and concluding with your own point of view or perspective on this "case."

7. Working with three other class members, check out the transcript of the Senate Judiciary Committee's hearings into Hill's charges against Thomas (ask your reference librarian to help you locate them). Divide up the transcript among group members and examine it closely, looking for parts that either support or refute Jordan's portrayal of Hill, Thomas, and the members of the committee. Then meet together to pool your information and prepare a 20-minute presentation for class on "What a close look at the Hill-Thomas transcript reveals about their characters."

8. Jordon claims that Anita Hill is "a political conservative." Why is this claim significant? Use the library to research the claim and report your findings in a short paper.

ROBERT BLY
Going Off on the Wild Man's Shoulders

Until very recently, *Robert Bly (b. 1926) was best known as a poet, storyteller, and translator who had received many honors (including the prestigious National Book Award) for his poetry. Much of that poetry takes its inspiration from ancient myths and legends that are, Bly says, like ancient relationships: "Whenever a poet through imagination discovers a true analogy, he or she is bringing up into consciousness a relationship that has been forgotten for centuries; the object is then not only more seen, but the poet receives a permanent addition to his knowledge."*

Although Iron John: A Book About Men *is Bly's first full-length book of prose, this reinterpretation of a fairy tale from the collection of the Brothers Grimm is clearly related to his earlier interests in myth and legend and in "remembering relationships." Probably even Bly was unprepared for the unprecedented success this book has achieved since its publication in 1990. It appeared for weeks on best-seller lists, has been the subject of a television special, and has served as a major work in the burgeoning—and increasingly varied—men's movement.*

I found reading Iron John *an incredibly irritating experience; I wanted to argue with Bly on almost every page. Specifically, I object to the role of women in the world of* Iron John *and to Bly's depiction of men as inevitably in search of a "beast within." Yet clearly his tale struck a chord with many American men, enough to start a serious social movement, bring a host of imitators—and even garner a fair share of ridicule.*

For this chapter on men and women, I chose a section from Iron John *entitled "Going Off on the Wild Man's Shoulders," which interprets the moment in the Grimm story when a youthful prince allows Iron John to carry him into the forest to avoid a beating from his parents. According to Bly, the act marks for the boy a clean and permanent separation from his parents, especially his mother. Bly explains what this break means to the prince and then explores what happens in a society like our own when such ritual moments of male initiation are ignored.* — A.L.

The moment the boy leaves with Iron John is the moment in ancient Greek life when the priest of Dionysus accepted a young man as a student, or the moment in Eskimo life today when the shaman, sometimes entirely covered with the fur of wild animals, and wearing wolverine claws and snake vertebrae around his neck, and a bear-head cap, appears in the village and takes a boy away for spirit instruction.

In our culture there is no such moment. The boys in our culture have a continuing need for initiation into male spirit, but old men in general don't offer it. The priest sometimes tries, but he is too much a part of the corporate village these days.

Among the Hopis and other native Americans of the Southwest, the old men take the boy away at the age of twelve and bring him *down* into the all-male area of the kiva. He stays *down* there for six weeks, and does not see his mother again for a year and a half.

The fault of the nuclear family today isn't so much that it's crazy and full of double binds (that's true in communes and corporate offices too—in fact, in any group). The fault is that the old men outside the nuclear family no longer offer an effective way for the son to break his link with his parents without doing harm to himself.*

The ancient societies believed that a boy becomes a man only through   5
ritual and effort—only through the "active intervention of the older men."

It's becoming clear to us that manhood doesn't happen by itself; it doesn't happen just because we eat Wheaties. The active intervention of the older men means that older men welcome the younger man into the ancient, mythologized, instinctive male world.

One of the best stories I've heard about this kind of welcoming is one that takes place each year among the Kikuyu in Africa. When a boy is old enough for initiation, he is taken away from his mother and brought to a special place the men have set up some distance from the village. He fasts for three days. The third night he finds himself sitting in a circle around the fire with the older men. He is hungry, thirsty, alert, and terrified. One of the older men takes up a knife, opens a vein in his own arm, and lets a little of his blood flow into a gourd or bowl. Each older man in the circle opens his arm with the same knife, as the bowl goes around, and lets some blood flow in. When the bowl arrives at the young man, he is invited to take nourishment from it.

In this ritual the boy learns a number of things. He learns that nourishment does not come only from his mother, but also from men. And he learns that the knife can be used for many purposes besides wounding others. Can he have any doubt now that he is welcome among the other males?

Once that welcoming has been done, the older men teach him the myths, stories, and songs that embody distinctively male values: I mean not competitive values only, but spiritual values. Once these "moistening" myths are learned, the myths themselves lead the young male far beyond his personal father and into the moistness of the swampy fathers who stretch back century after century.

---

fault of the nuclear family . . . doing harm: For another look at the nuclear family, see Jay Overocker's "Ozzie and Harriet in Hell," p. 528.

In the absence of old men's labor consciously done, what happens?   10
Initiation of Western men has continued for some time in an altered form
even after fanatics destroyed the Greek initiatory schools. During the nineteenth century, grandfathers and uncles lived in the house, and older men
mingled a great deal. Through hunting parties, in work that men did together in farms and cottages, and through local sports, older men spent
much time with younger men and brought knowledge of male spirit and
soul to them.

Wordsworth, in the beginning of "The Excursion," describes the old
man who sat day after day under a tree and befriended Wordsworth when
he was a boy:

> He loved me; from a swarm of rosy boys
> Singled me out, as he in sport would say,
> For my grave looks, too thoughtful for my years.
> As I grew up, it was my best delight
> To be his chosen comrade. Many a time
> On holidays, we wandered through the woods . . .

Much of that chance or incidental mingling has ended. Men's clubs
and societies have steadily disappeared. Grandfathers live in Phoenix or the
old people's home, and many boys experience only the companionship of
other boys their age who, from the point of view of the old initiators, know
nothing at all.

During the sixties, some young men drew strength from women who
in turn had received some of their strength from the women's movement.
One could say that many young men in the sixties tried to accept initiation
from women. But only men can initiate men, as only women can initiate
women. Women can change the embryo to a boy, but only men can change
the boy to a man. Initiators say that boys need a second birth, this time a
birth from men.*

Keith Thompson, in one of his essays, described himself at twenty as
a typical young man "initiated" by women. His parents divorced when
Keith was about twelve, and he lived with his mother while his father
moved into an apartment nearby.

Throughout high school Keith was closer to women than to other   15
men, and that situation continued into college years, when his main friends
were feminists whom he described as marvelous, knowledgeable, and generous, and from whom he learned an enormous amount. He then took a job
in Ohio state politics, working with women and alert to the concerns of
women.

About that time he had a dream. He and a clan of she-wolves were

---

only men can initiate . . . men: Compare Bly's argument here to the one offered by Liam
Hudson and Bernadine Jacot in "The Way Men Think," p. 296.

running in the forest. Wolves suggested to him primarily independence and vigor. The clan of wolves moved fast through the forest, in formation, and eventually they all arrived at a riverbank. Each she-wolf looked into the water and saw her own face there. But when Keith looked in the water, he saw no face at all.

Dreams are subtle and complicated, and it is reckless to draw any rapid conclusion. The last image, however, suggests a disturbing idea. When women, even women with the best intentions, bring up a boy alone, he may in some way have no male face, or he may have no face at all.

The old men initiators, by contrast, conveyed to boys some assurance that is invisible and nonverbal; it helped the boys to see their genuine face or being.

So what can be done? Thousands and thousands of women, being single parents, are raising boys with no adult man in the house. The difficulties inherent in that situation came up one day in Evanston when I was giving a talk on initiation of men to a group made up mostly of women.

Women who were raising sons alone were extremely alert to the dangers of no male model. One woman declared that she realized about the time her son got to high-school age that he needed more hardness than she could naturally give. But, she said, if she made herself harder to meet that need, she would lose touch with her own femininity. I mentioned the classic solution in many traditional cultures, which is to send the boy to his father when he is twelve. Several women said flatly, "No, men aren't nurturing; they wouldn't take care of him." Many men, however—and I am one of them—have found inside an ability to nurture that didn't appear until it was called for.

Even when a father is living in the house there still may be a strong covert bond between mother and son to evict the father, which amounts to a conspiracy, and conspiracies are difficult to break. One woman with two sons had enjoyed going each year to a convention in San Francisco with her husband, the boys being left at home. But one spring, having just returned from a women's retreat, she felt like being private and said to her husband: "Why don't you take the boys this year?" So the father did.

The boys, around ten and twelve, had never, as it turned out, experienced their father's company without the mother's presence. After that experience, they asked for more time with their dad.

When the convention time rolled around the following spring, the mother once more decided on privacy, and the boys once more went off with their father. The moment they arrived back home, the mother happened to be standing in the kitchen with her back to the door, and the older of the two boys walked over and put his arms around her from the back. Without even intending it, her body reacted explosively, and the boy flew across the room and bounced off the wall. When he picked himself up, she said, their relationship had changed. Something irrevocable had happened. She was glad about the change, and the boy seemed surprised and a little relieved that he apparently wasn't needed by her in the old way.

This story suggests that the work of separation can be done even if the old man initiators do not create the break. The mother can make the break herself. We see that it requires a great deal of intensity, and we notice that it was the woman's body somehow, not her mind, that accomplished the labor.

Another woman told a story in which the mother-son conspiracy was   25
broken from the boy's side. She was the single parent of a son and two daughters, and the girls were doing well but the boy was not. At fourteen, the boy went to live with his father, but he stayed only a month or so and then came back. When he returned, the mother realized that three women in the house amounted to an overbalance of feminine energy for the son, but what could she do? A week or two went by. One night she said to her son, "John, it's time to come to dinner." She touched him on the arm and *he* exploded and *she* flew against the wall—the same sort of explosion as in the earlier story. We notice no intent of abuse either time, and no evidence that the event was repeated. In each case the psyche or body knew what the mind didn't. When the mother picked herself off the floor, she said, "It's time for you to go back to your father," and the boy said, "You're right."

The traditional initiation break clearly is preferable, and sidesteps the violence. But all over the country now one sees hulking sons acting ugly in the kitchen and talking rudely to their mothers, and I think it's an attempt to make themselves unattractive. If the old men haven't done their work to interrupt the mother-son unity, what else can the boys do to extricate themselves but to talk ugly? It's quite unconscious and there's no elegance in it at all.

A clean break from the mother is crucial, but it's simply not happening. This doesn't mean that the women are doing something wrong: I think the problem is more that the older men are not really doing their job.

The traditional way of raising sons, which lasted for thousands and thousands of years, amounted to fathers and sons living in close—murderously close—proximity, while the father taught the son a trade: perhaps farming or carpentry or blacksmithing or tailoring. As I've suggested elsewhere, the love unit most damaged by the Industrial Revolution has been the father-son bond.

There's no sense in idealizing preindustrial culture, yet we know that today many fathers now work thirty or fifty miles from the house, and by the time they return at night the children are often in bed, and they themselves are too tired to do active fathering.

The Industrial Revolution, in its need for office and factory workers,   30
pulled fathers away from their sons and, moreover, placed the sons in compulsory schools where the teachers are mostly women. D. H. Lawrence

described what this was like in his essay "Men Must Work and Women as Well." His generation in the coal-mining areas of Britain felt the full force of that change, and the new attitude centered on one idea: that physical labor is bad.

Lawrence recalls that his father, who had never heard this theory, worked daily in the mines, enjoyed the camaraderie with the other men, came home in good spirits, and took his bath in the kitchen. But around that time the new schoolteachers arrived from London to teach Lawrence and his classmates that physical labor is low and unworthy and that men and women should strive to move upward to a more "spiritual" level—higher work, mental work. The children of his generation deduced that their fathers had been doing something wrong all along, that men's physical work is wrong and that those sensitive mothers who prefer white curtains and an elevated life are right and always have been.

During Lawrence's teenage years, which he described in *Sons and Lovers,* he clearly believed the new teachers. He wanted the "higher" life, and took his mother's side. It wasn't until two years before he died, already ill with tuberculosis in Italy, that Lawrence began to notice the vitality of the Italian workingmen, and to feel a deep longing for his own father. He realized then that his mother's ascensionism had been wrong for him, and had encouraged him to separate from his father and from his body in an unfruitful way.

A single clear idea, well fed, moves like a contagious disease: "Physical work is wrong." Many people besides Lawrence took up that idea, and in the next generation that split between fathers and sons deepened. A man takes up desk work in an office, becomes a father himself, but has no work to share with his son and cannot explain to the son what he's doing. Lawrence's father was able to take his son down into the mines, just as my own father, who was a farmer, could take me out on the tractor, and show me around. I knew what he was doing all day and in all seasons of the year.

When the office work and the "information revolution" begin to dominate, the father-son bond disintegrates. If the father inhabits the house only for an hour or two in the evenings, then women's values, marvelous as they are, will be the only values in the house. One could say that the father now loses his son five minutes after birth.

When we walk into a contemporary house, it is often the mother who comes forward confidently. The father is somewhere else in the back, being inarticulate. This is a poem of mine called "Finding the Father":

> My friend, this body offers to carry us for nothing—as the ocean carries logs. So on some days the body wails with its great energy; it smashes up the boulders, lifting small crabs, that flow around the sides.
>
> Someone knocks on the door. We do not have time to dress. He

wants us to go with him through the blowing and rainy streets, to the dark house.

We will go there, the body says, and there find the father whom we have never met, who wandered out in a snowstorm the night we were born, and who then lost his memory, and has lived since longing for his child, whom he saw only once . . . while he worked as a shoe-maker, as a cattle herder in Australia, as a restaurant cook who painted at night.

When you light the lamp you will see him. He sits there behind the door . . . the eyebrows so heavy, the forehead so light . . . lonely in his whole body, waiting for you.

QUESTIONING THE TEXT

1. Do you agree with Bly that there are no moments of initiation for boys in American culture? What would such moments have to include? List contemporary activities that might meet your criteria.
2. A.L. announces in her headnote to this reading that she found it extremely irritating. What do you think J.R.'s reaction was? Read over his profile on p. xiii, study a couple of his headnotes and commentaries; and then try your hand at rewriting the third paragraph of A.L.'s headnote in J.R.'s style.

MAKING CONNECTIONS

3. Bly implicitly suggests that there are fundamental and irrevocable differences between men and women. How might Bly respond to Sojourner Truth's arguments (on p. 293) that men and women are "equal"?
4. In the next reading, Joe Bob Briggs parodies Bly's advice to men. Write a response from Bly to Briggs, taking either a serious or a humorous approach.

JOINING THE CONVERSATION

5. If you have read even three or four of the pieces in this chapter, you should have given some serious thought to the ways in which men and women are similar and different. Prepare a brief essay for your class (about three pages in length) explaining your thoughts on this matter. You might begin by brainstorming about a thesis such as "The major difference between men and women is X" or "Men and women have more in common than might at first be apparent."

6. Do you think there is a need for a men's movement? Argue your position in a letter that might appear on the editorial page of a school or local newspaper.
7. In a group that includes both men and women, discuss this question: To what extent do women really want men to be soft and sensitive? Then individually write short exploratory pieces on the subject. (You might want to try your hand here at humor.) Reassemble the original group and read the pieces out loud.

JOE BOB BRIGGS
Get in Touch with Your Ancient Spear

MEN NEED A MEN'S MOVEMENT about as much as women need chest hair. A brotherhood organized to counter feminists could be timely because—let's be honest—women are no more naturally inclined to equality and fairness than men are. They want power and dominion just as much as any group looking out for its own interests. Organizing to protect the welfare of males might make sense.

Unfortunately, the current men's movement does not. The only time I have ever doubted A.L.'s judgment was after she recommended that I read Robert Bly's Iron John, *the bible of New Age males and the book Joe Bob Briggs parodies in the following reading.* Iron John *is a fat target for abuse— a fairy tale that Bly would have us believe reveals a MAJOR TRUTH about the wound men suffer as a result of being male. Bly wants his brothers to rediscover a primitive Wild Man dwelling within their brutalized, industrialized souls— a beast who turns out to be (surprise! surprise!) a pretty sensitive nineties kind of guy, Bill Clinton with a tom-tom.*

Get real, I thought. You can't believe this, Andrea! And I am sure she doesn't.

But I imagine it wouldn't displease feminists if more men learned to parrot the "I'm oppressed, you're oppressed" mantra that propels so many progressive causes. Is it mere coincidence that leaders of the men's movement analyze the world in precisely the same terms so many trendy leftists do, railing passionately against patriarchy, hierarchy, and capitalism?

As it turns out, the current men's movement is just feminism with a spear, a parody of a more serious crusade. So I thought it appropriate to reply to Iron John *with a parody by Joe Bob Briggs, the pen name of John Bloom, an actor and comedian. The selection printed below is the introduction to his 1992 book* Iron Joe Bob *as adapted for and reprinted in* The New York Times Book Review. *Joe Bob may not be quite as funny as Bly, but to me he makes a lot more sense.* — J.R.

All right, guys, listen up.

It hasn't been our century, has it?

We kinda blew it, didn't we?

Even though you don't know exactly what I'm talking about, you kinda *know what I'm talking about,* don't you?

Haven't you had that morning where you wake up, look around and go, "Do I have to do this again?" And maybe you can't describe exactly what it is that's missing, but *something* is missing, right?

5

I'm here to tell you what's missing.

Your Ancient Spear is missing.

"Missing" is not quite the word. Maybe your Spear is broken, or maybe it's sagging in the middle, or maybe you just forgot how to use it. It doesn't matter. We'll get into the mythological aspects later, and you'll learn to Resurrect the Broken Spear, Mend the Sagging Ur-Spear, Launch the Warrior Spear and, of course, Spear the Psychic Fish. But right now it's enough to know that, well, let's put it this way: You're out of touch with your Spear.

Obviously I don't mean that you need to go out and buy a spear. If it was that easy, I'd be selling you a spear. Instead, I'm selling you a book.

No, what I'm talking about is something deeper, much deeper than   10
a plain wooden spear or one of those spears with a lot of feathers hanging off it like Cochise had. Yes, what I'm talking about is richer than that, *richer even than Michael Ansara's* spear.* I'm talking about the Golden Spear that lies at the bottom of the Soggy Gooey Lake.

Your true Spear is stuck in the mythic muck. All you have to do to get it back is start scooping the muck out of your psychic mind-swamp one bucket at a time. I'll never forget an experience I had one summer at a men's consciousness-raising sweat farm in western Nebraska. One Wednesday afternoon, a 38-year-old man from somewhere in the Midwest came up to me and he said: "Today I hated my father fully, and I remembered something he said to me once. He said, 'In or out! In or out! We can't air-condition the whole world!' And I realized for the first time how true that is. We *can't* air-condition the whole world, even though we try to do that every day of our adult male lives." We wept together for a moment. By the end of the summer, that man touched his Spear for the first time.

My point is that men don't know these things anymore. Men have lost touch with their Spears, their Maces, their Battering Rams, and what have they replaced them with? Weed Eaters.

We men fought an entire war in Europe so that a New Man could emerge in America, and what did we end up with?

Ward Cleaver.*

Gimme a break.   15

Let's face it, it's been all downhill since then, hasn't it?

We're weenies.

We've *been* weenies.

Women have known this for a long time.

It took us longer to figure it out. It normally takes us at least 20 years   20

Michael Ansara (b. 1922): an actor often cast in Native American roles; perhaps best known for the TV series "Broken Arrow" (1956–58)

Ward Cleaver: the father in the TV sitcom "Leave It to Beaver," who embodied traditional middle-class views and values

in a relationship just to admit that, when we were kids, we liked to get the empty toilet paper roll and play it like a trumpet. So when you get to anything more serious than that, it takes a major life-changing cataclysmic experience, like six weeks in alcohol rehab, before we'll even *begin* to say anything like "I am a weenie. I have never had a firm conviction, or even an opinion I cared about, in my entire life."

So lemme say it right here and get it over with:

WEENIES!

That's us.

Until you accept that, this advice will be of no use to you whatsoever. It's just like A.A. You've got to say that and *mean it* or we can't go on.

Here, I'll wait. . . .   25

I realize I'm dealing with a lot of 34-year-old fat guys still living at home, watching too much "Star Trek" and leaving Doritos crumbs on their pillow. So I'll wait a little longer. . . .

All right, have we all said it? Good.

Lesson No. 2: YOU DON'T HAVE TO BE A WEENIE!

I mean it. It's not too late.

Just because your dad spent his whole life building a toolshed, buying   30
tools, putting the tools in the toolshed, repairing the toolshed, enlarging the toolshed—you know what I'm talking about, don't you? this thing that dads do where they keep buying tools but they never *do anything* with the tools?—just because your dad did this doesn't mean *you* have to do it.

Think about it. How many times have you watched 37 college basketball games in a row on ESPN and then thought to yourself: "Who was that? Was it Villanova or Vanderbilt? Georgetown or George Washington?" You're disoriented. You're confused. You're starting to feel out of control. So what do you do? *Go to a basketball game!*

How many times have you gone to the Ace Hardware store and bought $340 worth of stuff for the yard, including mulch, a tiller, a wheelbarrow-load of sod and one of those automatic poison-spraying devices that hook onto your garden nozzle—and then realized, when you got home, that you still had all the same stuff from *last year,* stacked up in your garage? You're reeling. You're wasted. You're losing the battle with modern civilization.

How many times have you read about bizarre sexual practices and said to yourself, "I wonder if people really do that, or if they just make that stuff up to confuse people like me"?

All of these common ailments are part of being a weenie, but expressed in each one is the desire to *stop* being a weenie. But it's not enough just to finish the toolshed. It's not enough to start *using* the tools. It's not enough to remember the Vanderbilt score.

And, in fact, if you're reading all this and still thinking, "Wait a   35
minute, I'll ask my wife," then you're *not* getting it yet.

You can't just *decide* to stop being a weenie. The weenie lobe of the brain is buried deep in the cerebellum, where other people can't see it. And there's only one way to get rid of it.

Surgery.

Massive life-threatening surgery.

You've go to cut it out.

That's how I want you to think of this program. We're gonna be   40
cutting out that weenie lobe and replacing it with a new Mature Male nervous system. This is a shortened home-study version of my famous series of manliness seminars, which have been attended by thousands of weenies already. In fact, the first time I went on a Wild Man Weekend, it changed my life forever. You know what I'm talking about? One of those things where you go out in the woods with 20 other guys and put bandannas on your head and beat tom-toms together to prove you're not a wimp?

I'll never forget it. I sweated a lot. I cried. I sweated *while* I was crying. Of course, I was crying because they made me sweat so much. We had this one part of the weekend where we went in a giant sauna and turned it up to about, oh, 280, until everybody's skin turned the color of strawberry Jell-O and the veins in our foreheads started exploding, and it turned into this communal out-of-body *male* thing, where everybody was screaming, "I want *out* of my body!"

Are you starting to sense what I'm talking about here? Put that Dorito down and listen. It's the Masculine Movement, where we get back in touch with our cave man selves. *It's so powerful.* You really can't understand it unless you've been there.

The Wild Man process involves five basic phases: Sweating, Yelling, Crying, Drum-Beating and Ripping Your Shirt Off Even if It's Expensive.

You may wonder why we do this stuff. It's because the modern American male has lost touch with his primitive self. They used to have a ceremony called Separating From the Mother. (Of course, they still do. It's called the "Get a job!" ceremony.) But now most guys *never* separate from their mothers. They think *all* women are their mothers, and so they expect all their girlfriends to take care of their emotional needs.

Once I understood this, I called up my mother to tell her I was   45
separating from her.

"That's nice," she said. "I'm glad you have a hobby."

The other ceremony they used to have is called Initiation Into the Company of Men. Of course, we still have this one, too. It's called "beer." In primitive times they would ram crooked sticks through your breast, like in "A Man Called Horse,"* and then beat you with a Lincoln Log or

---

A Man Called Horse: a 1970 film about a European painfully initiated into a Native American tribe

something until you felt like a man. But the modern American man never does this, and so he spends his whole life feeling *uncomfortable* around other men, and never talking to them about anything except football.

I hope you're following this.

That's why we start off with the lobster-sauna Sweating Ceremony. Then we move on to the Yelling Like Banshees Ceremony. Then we sit in a circle, and whoever has the stick gets to talk, and he's supposed to say stuff from "A Chorus Line,"* like "I was always afraid I was a homosexual, and my father kicked my Tonka dump truck when I was 7 and I never got over it," until he starts bawling like a baby in front of everybody else.

Next comes Beating the Manly Tom-Tom. In order to get in touch   50
with our real Wild Man self, we whale away on these drums and slam-dance against trees until we lose control and *become the drum.* Sometimes guys get so carried away they start screaming out personal stuff, from the deepest part of the primitive brain lobe, like "She divorced me because I never could stand her sister!"

And, finally, we get to the Ceremony of the Ripping Shirt, where we cavort around like apes in the jungle, exposing our manly flesh to the elements, revealing our manliness to other men, becoming the true warrior-king-lover-gods that we always were, but Brenda Weatherby in 10th grade would never believe it. Then we make a conga line and dance out into the woods and plunge into the river and splash around until we feel manly enough to take off all our clothes and rip the guts out of a wild hog.

I felt so much better after doing this the first time. I went back to Grapevine, Tex., where I live, and I told my girlfriend, Wanda Bodine, everything I'd been through, and she said: "That sounds great. Did they teach you how to wear the same color sock on both feet?"

You ever feel like women don't *understand* just how manly we are?

It bugs me.

Anyhow, that's not the point. The point is that *you* could have all   55
these same Wild Man experiences that I had. And I know what you're thinking, right at this very moment. You're thinking, "I ain't getting nekkid in the woods."

Don't worry about it. Really. That'll come later.

All I want you to know right now is that, if you'll trust me, if you'll clear your head, get rid of your old weenie preconceptions, give me a little slack, then you'll feel a new male *power* rising inside you. You'll feel the whole course of manly civilization rushing through your manly veins. You'll know what it's like to Straighten the Broken Spear. You'll never feel like a wimp or a loser or a weakling again, for the rest of your life. We're gonna

---

A Chorus Line: a Broadway musical, later made into a film, in which the characters address personal revelations to the audience

do this together. We're gonna be men. And *how* are we gonna do it? By doing the most manly thing that men can do together:

I'll tell you a fairy tale.

It'll be fun, really.

It's a good one.   60

It has a beautiful princess in it.

You're not buying this, are you?

QUESTIONING THE TEXT

1. To whom is Iron Joe Bob supposedly speaking? To whom is he really speaking? How are you as a reader able to make that distinction?
2. What role do women play in "Get in Touch with Your Ancient Spear"? What is the tone of the women who speak? Do women come off well in this piece? Why, or why not?
3. How did J.R.'s introduction color your reading of this piece? Would a more traditional introduction have allowed you better to formulate your own opinion of the men's movement? What portion of the reading audience does the introduction seem willing to write off?

MAKING CONNECTIONS

4. Iron Joe Bob mocks the interest Robert Bly expresses in male initiation ceremonies, identifying "beer" as the modern version of such a ceremony. Freewrite for 10 minutes or so on the concept of male initiation. Is it as important as Bly thinks?
5. Can you imagine a dialogue between Iron Joe Bob and one of the women writers in this chapter—Maxine Hong Kingston, Sojourner Truth, June Jordan? (The selections by them start on pp. 319, 293, and 354, respectively.) Or maybe you'd like to imagine what happens when Iron Joe Bob meets Hillary Rodham Clinton, Barbara Walters, or Roseanne Arnold. Write the dialogue that might ensue.

JOINING THE CONVERSATION

6. Using the style of Iron Joe Bob, write a piece of several hundred words that parodies some aspect of male or female behavior.
7. With a group of classmates, discuss whether American men as a group face any problems today. Do some men face different challenges than others? What kind?

MARGE PIERCY
Barbie Doll

MARGE PIERCY (b. 1936) grew up in an area of Detroit in which, as one of only two Jews in her elementary school, she early encountered the effects of prejudice. An active worker for the rights of women and African Americans, Piercy has written poetry, novels, and essays. Many of her poems feature a dramatic, concrete image—of a person or of a phenomenon in nature—that sticks in the reader's mind. Certainly that is the case with the following poem, "Barbie Doll," whose protagonist society tries to create in the image of what it wishes to worship—pretty looks. This poem, from Piercy's book To Be of Use *(1973), asks us to think again about what makes a person "pretty" and about the ways in which we harm others by demanding that they fit into a mold that may not be right for them.* — A.L.

The girlchild was born as usual
and presented dolls that did pee-pee
and miniature GE stoves and irons
and wee lipsticks the color of cherry candy.
Then in the magic of puberty, a classmate said:
You have a great big nose and fat legs.
She was healthy, tested intelligent,
possessed strong legs and back,
abundant sexual drive and manual dexterity.
She went to and fro apologizing.
Everyone saw a fat nose on thick legs.

She was advised to play coy,
exhorted to come on hearty,
exercise, diet, smile and wheedle,
Her good nature wore out
like a fan belt.
So she cut off her nose and her legs
and offered them up.
In the casket displayed on satin she lay
with the undertaker's cosmetics painted on,
a turned-up putty nose,
dressed in a pink and white nightie.

Doesn't she look pretty? everyone said.
Consummation at last.
To every woman a happy ending.*

IN RESPONSE

1. This poem suggests that society expects certain things of every "girl-child." What are these things? How do you feel about such expectations? Record your responses to these questions in a reading log, if you are keeping one.
2. How did you learn what it means to be "pretty" or "handsome"? Where do such definitions come from? Do you agree with these definitions, or do you reject them? Write a page or two explaining your own definition of "attractive." How does it compare with the definition held by most people you know?
3. Try your hand at writing a male version of this poem, a piece that captures in concrete images the way society demands certain things of every "boychild."

So she cut off. . . . a happy ending: For another poem about a woman driven to destruction by society's relentless attention to her image, see "The Marilyn Monroe Poem" by Judy Grahn, starting on p. 511.

OTHER READINGS

Belenky, Mary Field, et al. *Women's Ways of Knowing: The Development of Self, Voice, and Mind*. New York: Basic, 1986. A study based on interviews with 135 women.

Brock, David. *The Real Anita Hill: The Untold Story*. New York: Free, 1993. Suggests that Hill invented her charges as part of a liberal conspiracy against the Thomas nomination.

Fausto-Sterling, Anne. *Myths of Gender: Biological Theories About Women and Men*. New York: Basic, 1985. Critiques theories of gender in biology.

Ferguson, Andrew. "America's New Man." *American Spectator* Jan. 1992: 26–33. Examines a men's movement convention in Texas.

Gaylin, Willard. *The Male Ego*. New York: Viking, 1992. Reviews psychological insights into this phenomenon.

Gilder, George. "Still Seeking a Glass Slipper." *National Review* 14 Dec. 1992: 38–41. Argues that the "glass ceiling" for women in American business is a myth.

Gilligan, Carol. *In a Different Voice: Psychological Theory and Women's Development*. Cambridge: Harvard UP, 1982. Considers the ways in which women's moral development differs from men's.

Konner, Melvin. "The Gender Option." *Why the Reckless Survive and Other Secrets of Human Nature*. New York: Viking, 1990. 169–80. Shows how societies manipulate the ratio of male to female children.

Leo, John. "Womenspeak vs. Mentalk." *How the Russians Invented Baseball*. New York: Delacorte-Bantam, 1989. 32–36. Examines comically the failings of men in speaking to women.

Likosky, Stephan, ed. *Coming Out: An Anthology of International Gay and Lesbian Writing*. New York: Pantheon, 1992. Challenges the dominant heterosexual assumptions in accounts of gender.

Morrison, Toni, ed. *Race-ing Justice, En-gendering Power: Essays on Anita Hill, Clarence Thomas, and the Construction of Social Reality*. New York: Pantheon, 1992. Explores the implications of the Hill-Thomas hearings in essays by a group of distinguished writers.

Difference: E Pluribus Unum?

7

*We have no princes, for whom we toil, starve, and bleed: we are the most
perfect society now existing in the world.*
HECTOR ST. JEAN DE CRÈVECOEUR, *What Is an American?*

*I have no separate feeling about being an American citizen and colored.
I am merely a fragment of the Great Soul that surges within the boundaries.
My country, right or wrong.*
ZORA NEALE HURSTON, *How It Feels to Be Colored Me*

*I did not remember ever having seen a real Indian, and my new awareness
that Piquette sprang from the people of Big Bear and Poundmaker, of Tecumseh, of the Iroquois who had eaten Father Brebeuf's heart—all this gave
her an instant attraction in my eyes.*
MARGARET LAURENCE, *The Loons*

*Say to the young man sitting by your brother's side,/"I'm his brother."/
Try not to be shocked when the young man says,/"I'm his lover. Thanks
for coming."*
MICHAEL LASSELL, *How to Watch Your Brother Die*

*What matters is not what you think, or what you stand for, but the color
of your skin, your gender, or your sexual tastes.*
DAVID RIEFF, *The Case Against Sensitivity*

*The son of a Mexican American doctor or lawyer is treated as if he suffered
the same disadvantage as the child of a Mexican farm worker; and both are
given preference over poor, non-Hispanic whites in admission to most
colleges or affirmative action employment programs.*
LINDA CHAVEZ, *Toward a New Politics of Hispanic Assimilation*

*I am what I am   I am Puerto Rican   I am U.S. American
I am New York Manhattan and the Bronx*
ROSARIO MORALES, *I Am What I Am*

*I guess being colored doesn't make me not like
the same things other folks like who are other races.
So will my page be colored that I write?
Being me, it will not be white.*
LANGSTON HUGHES, *Theme for English B*

Introduction

MORE THAN TWO CENTURIES AGO, Hector St. Jean De Crèvecoeur posed the daunting question "What Is an American?" Perhaps the query can never be answered fully, as the face of the nation will continue to evolve and change. Currently, however, many in the United States seem to be pledging allegiance not to a nation, which once celebrated its role as a melting pot of peoples, but to various interest groups. Citizens who trace their roots to Africa, Asia, or the North American continent itself routinely challenge the domination of U.S. history, literature, and political institutions by descendants of Europeans. While many citizens interpret the American saga as one of progress, development, growth, and inclusion, others read it as a story of oppression, alienation, violence, and betrayal. Indeed, the latter interpretation is often seen, albeit derisively, as the "politically correct" view.

Some would assert that racial, ethnic, sexual, and class fractures in our national unity have always been present, but deliberately hidden by those who stood to benefit from unequal distributions of wealth, power, or influence. Others invert the argument, claiming that interest groups today are exaggerating the ills they have suffered in order to gain a slice of the national pie. These issues are debated every day in the courts and legislatures, in businesses, and on college campuses.

To put these issues into more concrete terms, close your eyes and try to picture all the people in one of your classes. At a glance, in what ways are these people alike—and like you? In what ways do you differ? In this simple experiment lies a key question the readings in this chapter will address: how can we best honor and respect human commonalities while also honoring and respecting human differences? Can we in some sense be *both* together and separate from one another? In short, can we have at the center of our national life both "difference" and *"e pluribus unum"*?

Following are some questions that you may want to think about as you read this chapter:

1. In what ways is cultural diversity and public attention to it an advantage or a disadvantage to a society?

2. In what ways does prejudice show itself ?

3. Are the prejudices of the powerful and privileged more damaging than those of other groups? Why, or why not?

4. Is a fear of difference part of human nature?

5. Can you think of times when you judged someone on the basis of a stereotype that later turned out to be inaccurate or unfair?

Of times when you yourself were inaccurately or unfairly stereotyped? You may want to discuss these experiences with a group
of classmates.

•   •   •

HECTOR ST. JEAN DE CRÈVECOEUR
What Is an American?

HECTOR ST. JEAN DE CRÈVECOEUR'S letter "What Is an American?" is a classic statement of the virtues of integration and harmony, one of the defining documents of the American vision of the melting pot. Crèvecoeur (1735–1813) was himself something of an outsider when he wrote about life in the colonial United States. A native of France who worked for a time for the British government in Canada, he eventually became a farmer in New York until the American Revolution disrupted his peaceful life and his political loyalties. Fleeing to Europe, he spent his time there finishing an account of life in America, Letters from an American Farmer, *that would earn him fame and high regard after its publication in 1782.*

While aware of the plight of slaves and Native Americans, Crèvecoeur argued nonetheless that the spacious American territories were breeding a new and happier species of European. To him, the typical American was an immigrant free of aristocratic assumptions who had set aside the Old World's potent national and religious prejudices to construct new communities upon principles of liberty and individual merit.

"What Is an American?" may strike some readers today as a rustic fantasy or as testament to a dream betrayed. But we shouldn't be disappointed when a writer of an earlier era fails to anticipate our contemporary concerns. The pioneering Americans Crèvecoeur describes were more inclusive, democratic, and visionary than their forebears in Europe. Great changes were occurring in a green and pleasant land. Indeed, I'd be inclined to argue that the hardy farmers whose lives Crèvecoeur describes have proven to be more consequential revolutionaries than the sans-culottes of Paris, the Bolsheviks of Red Square, or the free-speechers of Berkeley. — J.R.

I wish I could be acquainted with the feelings and thoughts which must agitate the heart and present themselves to the mind of an enlightened Englishman, when he first lands on this continent. He must greatly rejoice that he lived at a time to see this fair country discovered and settled; he must necessarily feel a share of national pride, when he views the chain of settlements which embellishes these extended shores. When he says to himself, this is the work of my countrymen, who, when convulsed by factions, afflicted by a variety of miseries and wants, restless and impatient, took refuge here. They brought along with them their national genius, to which they principally owe what liberty they enjoy, and what substance they possess. Here he sees the industry of his native country displayed in a new manner, and traces in their works the embryos of all the arts, sciences, and ingenuity which flourish in Europe. Here he beholds fair cities, substantial villages, extensive fields, an immense country filled with decent houses, good roads, orchards, meadows, and bridges, where an hundred years ago all was wild, woody, and uncultivated! What a train of pleasing ideas this fair spectacle must suggest; it is a prospect which must inspire a good citizen with the most heartfelt pleasure. The difficulty consists in the manner of viewing so extensive a scene. He is arrived on a new continent; a modern society offers itself to his contemplation, different from what he had hitherto seen. It is not composed, as in Europe, of great lords who possess everything, and of a herd of people who have nothing. Here are no aristocratical families, no courts, no kings, no bishops, no ecclesiastical dominion, no invisible power giving to a few a very visible one; no great manufacturers employing thousands, no great refinements of luxury. The rich and the poor are not so far removed from each other as they are in Europe. Some few towns excepted, we are all tillers of the earth, from Nova Scotia to West Florida. We are a people of cultivators, scattered over an immense territory, communicating with each other by means of goods roads and navigable rivers, united by the silken bands of mild government, all respecting the laws, without dreading their power, because they are equitable. We are all animated with the spirit of an industry which is unfettered and unrestrained, because each person works for himself. If he travels through our rural districts he views not the hostile castle, and the haughty mansion, contrasted with the clay-built hut and miserable cabin, where cattle and men help to keep each other warm, and dwell in meanness, smoke, and indigence. A pleasing uniformity of decent competence appears throughout our habitations. The meanest of our log-houses is a dry and comfortable habitation. Lawyer or merchant are the fairest titles our towns afford; that of a farmer is the only appellation of the rural inhabitants of our country. It must take some time ere he can reconcile himself to our dictionary, which is but short in words of dignity, and names of honor. There, on a Sunday, he sees a congregation of respectable farmers and their wives, all clad in neat homespun, well mounted, or riding in their own humble wagons. There is not among them an esquire, saving the unlettered magistrate. There he sees a parson as simple as his flock, a farmer who does not riot on the labor of others. We have no princes, for whom we toil, starve, and bleed: we are the most perfect society now existing in the world. Here man is free as he ought to be; nor is this pleasing equality so transitory as many others are. Many ages will not see the shores of our great lakes replenished with inland nations, nor the unknown bounds of North America entirely peopled. Who can tell how far it extends? Who can tell the millions of men whom it will feed and contain? for no European foot has as yet traveled half the extent of this mighty continent!

The next wish of this traveler will be to know whence came all these people? They are a mixture of English, Scotch, Irish, French, Dutch, Germans, and Swedes. From this promiscuous breed, that race now called Americans have arisen. The eastern provinces* must indeed be excepted, as being the unmixed descendants of Englishmen. I have heard many wish that they had been more intermixed also: for my part, I am no wisher, and think it much better as it has happened. They exhibit a most conspicuous figure in this great and variegated picture; they too enter for a great share in the pleasing perspective displayed in these thirteen provinces. I know it is fashionable to reflect on them, but respect them for what they have done; for the accuracy and wisdom with which they have settled their territory; for the decency of their manners; for their early love of letters; their ancient college,* the first in this hemisphere; for their industry, which to me who am but a farmer is the criterion of everything. There never was a people, situated as they are, who with so ungrateful a soil have done more in so short a time. Do you think that the monarchical ingredients which are more prevalent in other governments have purged them from all foul stains? Their histories assert the contrary.

In this great American asylum, the poor of Europe have by some means met together, and in consequence of various causes; to what purpose should they ask one another what countrymen they are? Alas, two thirds of them had no country. Can a wretch who wanders about, who works and starves, whose life is a continual scene of sore affliction or pinching penury, can that man call England or any other kingdom his country? A country that had no bread for him, whose fields procured him no harvest, who met with nothing but the frowns of the rich, the severity of the laws, with jails and punishments; who owned not a single foot of the extensive surface of this planet? No! Urged by a variety of motives, here they came. Everything has tended to regenerate them; new laws, a new mode of living, a new social system; here they are become men: in Europe they were as so many useless plants, wanting vegetative mold and refreshing showers; they withered, and were mowed down by want, hunger, and war; but now by the power of transplantation, like all other plants they have taken root and flourished! Formerly they were not numbered in any civil lists of their country, except in those of the poor; here they rank as citizens. By what invisible power has this surprising metamorphosis been performed? By that of the laws and that of their industry. The laws, the indulgent laws, protect them as they arrive, stamping on them the symbol of adoption; they receive

---

eastern provinces: the area known as New England today
ancient college: Harvard, founded in 1636

ample rewards for their labors; these accumulated rewards procure them lands; those lands confer on them the title of freemen, and to that title every benefit is affixed which men can possibly require. This is the great operation daily performed by our laws. From whence proceed these laws? From our government. Whence the government? It is derived from the original genius and strong desire of the people ratified and confirmed by the crown. This is the great chain which links us all, this is the picture which every province exhibits, Nova Scotia excepted. There the crown has done all; either there were no people who had genius, or it was not much attended to: the consequence is that the province is very thinly inhabited indeed; the power of the crown in conjunction with the mosquitoes has prevented men from settling there. Yet some parts of it flourished once, and it contained a mild, harmless set of people. But for the fault of a few leaders, the whole were banished.* The greatest political error the crown ever committed in America was to cut off men from a country which wanted nothing but men!

What attachment can a poor European emigrant have for a country where he had nothing? The knowledge of the language, the love of a few kindred as poor as himself, were the only cords that tied him: his country is now that which gives him land, bread, protection, and consequence: *Ubi panis ibi patria** is the motto of all emigrants. What then is the American, this new man? He is either a European, or the descendant of a European, hence that strange mixture of blood, which you will find in no other country. I could point out to you a family whose grandfather was an Englishman, whose wife was Dutch, whose son married a French woman, and whose present four sons have now four wives of different nations. *He* is an American, who, leaving behind him all his ancient prejudices and manners, receives new ones from the new mode of life he has embraced, the new government he obeys, and the new rank he holds. He becomes an American by being received in the broad lap of our great *Alma Mater.** Here individuals of all nations are melted into a new race of men, whose labors and posterity will one day cause great changes in the world. Americans are the western pilgrims, who are carrying along with them that great mass of arts, sciences, vigor, and industry which began long since in the east; they will finish the great circle. The Americans were once scattered all over Europe; here they are incorporated into one of the finest systems of population which has ever appeared, and which will hereafter become distinct by the power of the different climates they inhabit. The American ought therefore to love this country much better than that wherein either he or his forefathers were

---

the whole were banished: The British government expelled the French-speaking Acadians from Nova Scotia during the French and Indian War (1755–63), when they were suspected of disloyalty.

Ubi panis ibi patria: Latin for "where one's bread is, there is one's native country"
Alma Mater: Latin for "Nourishing Mother"

born.* Here the rewards of his industry follow with equal steps the progress of his labor; his labor is founded on the basis of nature, *self-interest;* can it want a stronger allurement? Wives and children, who before in vain demanded of him a morsel of bread, now, fat and frolicsome, gladly help their father to clear those fields whence exuberant crops are to arise to feed and to clothe them all; without any part being claimed, either by a despotic prince, a rich abbot, or a mighty lord. Here religion demands but little of him; a small voluntary salary to the minister, and gratitude to God; can he refuse these? The American is a new man, who acts upon new principles; he must therefore entertain new ideas, and form new opinions. From involuntary idleness, servile dependence, penury, and useless labor, he has passed to toils of a very different nature, rewarded by ample subsistence.—This is an American.

QUESTIONING THE TEXT

1. What specific accomplishments does the Frenchman Crèvecoeur grant to the "unmixed descendants of Englishmen" who populate what is now New England? How are the descendants of these people sometimes regarded by other ethnic groups today?
2. According to Crèvecoeur, what do the poor gain in America that they never had in their native lands?
3. What is Crèvecoeur's attitude toward nature? Might he find contemporary attempts to preserve wilderness areas peculiar? Record your response in a reading log entry, if you are keeping one.
4. Do you agree or disagree with the assertion in J.R.'s introduction that pioneering American farmers were more important revolutionaries than those responsible for the French and Russian revolutions?

MAKING CONNECTIONS

5. Crèvecoeur considers it one of the blessings of America that "[t]he rich and the poor are not so far removed from each other as they are in Europe." With a group of other students, discuss whether this is a condition that still shapes the relationships among people of different economic classes in the United States. What other factors enter in? Read Rosario Morales's "I Am What I Am" (p. 436) before exploring this matter.
6. Crèvecoeur uses the image of "individuals of all nations" being

---

The American . . . born: For a longer argument in favor of assimilation rather than separatism on the part of immigrants, see the reading by Linda Chavez, "Toward a New Politics of Hispanic Assimilation," on p. 426.

"melted into a new race of men." Compare that image with the one of the "bag of miscellany" in the last paragraph of the next reading, "How It Feels to Be Colored Me," by Zora Neale Hurston. Which image of Americans appeals to you more—and why? Write an essay explaining your answer.

JOINING THE CONVERSATION

7. On the board, list all the national and ethnic ties represented by the people in your writing class. With that information fresh in mind, write a paragraph defining "American."
8. The America Crèvecoeur describes is "the most perfect society now existing in the world." Write an essay arguing that such is or is not the case today, either by the standards Crèvecoeur uses or by your own standards for a perfect society.

ZORA NEALE HURSTON
How It Feels to Be Colored Me

BORN AND RAISED *in the first all-black town in the United States to be incorporated and self-governing (Eatonville, Florida), Zora Neale Hurston (1891–1960) packed an astonishing number of jobs and careers into her sixty-nine years. She was a "wardrobe girl" for traveling entertainers, a manicurist, an anthropologist and folklorist, a college professor, a drama coach, an editor, and—above all—a writer of great distinction. Author of numerous articles, essays, and stories as well as folklore collections, plays, and an autobiography, Hurston is today probably best known for her novels:* Their Eyes Were Watching God, Jonah's Gourd Vine, *and* Moses, Man of the Mountain.

Hurston studied anthropology at Barnard College, where she was the only African American student, and gained a strong reputation for her academic work on folklore. But by the 1930s, she was being criticized for what were said to be caricatures of blacks, especially in her "minstrel" novels. Her growing conservatism led to further attacks from writers such as Richard Wright, and by 1950, her reputation gone, she was working in Florida as a maid. Evicted from her home in 1956, she suffered a stroke in 1959 and died, penniless, the next year. In recent years, Alice Walker sought out her unmarked grave in Fort Pierce, Florida, and erected a marker in memory of Hurston and her work, which is, today, widely read and influential.

The essay that follows, published in 1928, makes an intriguing companion piece to the passage from Crèvecoeur, particularly to his description of Americans as "united by the silken bands of mild government, all respecting the laws, without dreading their power, because they are equitable." His portrait of the "perfect society," where "man is free as he ought to be," would have come as a surprise to many African Americans in 1782. Hurston is deeply aware of such ironies and of the bitter struggles obscured by the happy image of the melting pot. But she is not cast down or resentful; she has no time to waste on negativity. I chose "How It Feels to Be Colored Me" for its irrepressible spirit in the face of what are clearly inequalities in America, for its forthright self-representation, and for the sheer delight it gives me to think that Hurston has triumphed after all. — A.L.

I am colored but I offer nothing in the way of extenuating circumstances except the fact that I am the only Negro in the United States whose grandfather on the mother's side was *not* an Indian chief.

I remember the very day that I became colored. Up to my thirteenth year I lived in the little Negro town of Eatonville, Florida. It is exclusively a colored town. The only white people I knew passed through the town going to or coming from Orlando. The native whites rode dusty horses, the Northern tourists chugged down the sandy village road in automobiles. The town knew the Southerners and never stopped cane chewing* when they passed. But the Northerners were something else again. They were peered at cautiously from behind curtains by the timid. The more venturesome would come out on the porch to watch them go past and got just as much pleasure out of the tourists as the tourists got out of the village.

The front porch might seem a daring place for the rest of the town, but it was a gallery seat for me. My favorite place was atop the gate-post. Proscenium box for a born first-nighter. Not only did I enjoy the show, but I didn't mind the actors knowing that I liked it. I usually spoke to them in passing. I'd wave at them and when they returned my salute, I would say something like this: "Howdy-do-well-I-thank-you-where-you-goin'?" Usually automobile or the horse paused at this, and after a queer exchange of compliments, I would probably "go a piece of the way" with them, as we say in farthest Florida. If one of my family happened to come to the front in time to see me, of course negotiations would be rudely broken off. But even so, it is clear that I was the first "welcome-to-our-state" Floridian, and I hope the Miami Chamber of Commerce will please take notice.

During this period, white people differed from colored to me only in that they rode through town and never lived there. They liked to hear me "speak pieces" and sing and wanted to see me dance the parse-me-la, and gave me generously of their small silver for doing these things, which seemed strange to me for I wanted to do them so much that I needed bribing to stop. Only they didn't know it. The colored people gave no dimes. They deplored any joyful tendencies in me, but I was their Zora nevertheless. I belonged to them, to the nearby hotels, to the county—everybody's Zora.

But changes came in the family when I was thirteen, and I was sent   5 to school in Jacksonville. I left Eatonville, the town of the oleanders, as Zora. When I disembarked from the river-boat at Jacksonville, she was no more. It seemed that I had suffered a sea change. I was not Zora of Orange County any more, I was now a little colored girl. I found it out in certain ways. In my heart as well as in the mirror, I became a fast brown—warranted not to rub nor run.

But I am not tragically colored. There is no great sorrow dammed up in my soul, nor lurking behind my eyes. I do not mind at all. I do not belong to the sobbing school of Negrohood who hold that nature somehow has given them a lowdown dirty deal and whose feelings are all hurt about it. Even in the helter-skelter skirmish that is my life, I have seen that the

---

cane chewing: chewing sugar-cane stalks

world is to the strong* regardless of a little pigmentation more or less. No, I do not weep at the world—I am too busy sharpening my oyster knife.*

Someone is always at my elbow reminding me that I am the grand-daughter of slaves. It fails to register depression with me. Slavery is sixty years in the past. The operation was successful and the patient is doing well, thank you. The terrible struggle* that made me an American out of a potential slave said "On the line!" The Reconstruction said "Get set!"; and the generation before said "Go!" I am off to a flying start and I must not halt in the stretch to look behind and weep. Slavery is the price I paid for civilization, and the choice was not with me. It is a bully adventure and worth all that I have paid through my ancestors for it. No one on earth ever had a greater chance for glory. The world to be won and nothing to be lost. It is thrilling to think—to know that for any act of mine, I shall get twice as much praise or twice as much blame. It is quite exciting to hold the center of the national stage, with the spectators not knowing whether to laugh or to weep.

The position of my white neighbor is much more difficult. No brown specter pulls up a chair beside me when I sit down to eat. No dark ghost thrusts its leg against mine in bed. The game of keeping what one has is never so exciting as the game of getting.

I do not always feel colored. Even now I often achieve the unconscious Zora of Eatonville before the Hegira. I feel most colored when I am thrown against a sharp white background.

For instance at Barnard. "Beside the waters of the Hudson"* I feel   10
my race. Among the thousand white persons, I am a dark rock surged upon, and overswept, but through it all, I remain myself. When covered by the waters, I am; and the ebb but reveals me again.

Sometimes it is the other way around. A white person is set down in our midst, but the contrast is just as sharp for me. For instance, when I sit in the drafty basement that is The New World Cabaret with a white person, my color comes. We enter chatting about any little nothing that we have in common and are seated by the jazz waiters. In the abrupt way that jazz orchestras have, this one plunges into a number. It loses no time in circumlocutions, but gets right down to business. It constricts the thorax

---

the world is to the strong: an allusion to the biblical passage (in Ecclesiastes 11) that reads "The race is not to the swift, nor the battle to the strong"

sharpening my oyster knife: an allusion to the saying "The world is my oyster," which appears in Shakespeare's *The Merry Wives of Windsor*

the terrible struggle: the Civil War

"Beside the waters of the Hudson": Barnard College is near the Hudson River in New York City. For another account of how it felt to be a black student at Columbia University in the early twentieth century, see the poem by Langston Hughes, "Theme for English B," on p. 439.

and splits the heart with its tempo and narcotic harmonies. This orchestra grows rambunctious, rears on its hind legs and attacks the tonal veil with primitive fury, rending it, clawing it until it breaks through to the jungle beyond. I follow those heathen—follow them exultingly. I dance wildly inside myself; I yell within, I whoop; I shake my assegai above my head, I hurl it true to the mark *yeeeeooww!* I am in the jungle and living in the jungle way. My face is painted red and yellow and my body is painted blue. My pulse is throbbing like a war drum. I want to slaughter something— give pain, give death to what, I do not know. But the piece ends. The men of the orchestra wipe their lips and rest their fingers. I creep back slowly to the veneer we call civilization with the last tone and find the white friend sitting motionless in his seat, smoking calmly.

"Good music they have here," he remarks, drumming the table with his fingertips.

Music. The great blobs of purple and red emotion have not touched him. He has only heard what I felt. He is far away and I see him but dimly across the ocean and the continent that have fallen between us. He is so pale with his whiteness then and I am *so* colored.*

At certain times I have no race, I am *me.* When I set my hat at a certain angle and saunter down Seventh Avenue, Harlem City, feeling as snooty as the lions in front of the Forty-Second Street Library,* for instance. So far as my feelings are concerned, Peggy Hopkins Joyce* on the Boule Mich* with her gorgeous raiment, stately carriage, knees knocking together in a most aristocratic manner, has nothing on me. The cosmic Zora emerges. I belong to no race nor time. I am the eternal feminine with its string of beads.

I have no separate feeling about being an American citizen and colored. 15 I am merely a fragment of the Great Soul that surges within the boundaries. My country, right or wrong.

Sometimes, I feel discriminated against, but it does not make me angry. It merely astonishes me. How *can* any deny themselves the pleasure of my company? It's beyond me.

But in the main, I feel like a brown bag of miscellany propped against a wall. Against a wall in company with other bags, white, red and yellow. Pour out the contents, and there is discovered a jumble of small things

---

I am so colored: For another perspective on this issue, see David Rieff's criticism of the slogan "It's a Black Thing. You Wouldn't Understand" in "The Case Against Sensitivity," p. 406.

the lions in front of the Forty-Second Street Library: two statues of lions that stand in front of the main building of the New York Public Library, on Fifth Avenue at 42nd Street

Peggy Hopkins Joyce: a famous beauty who set fashions in the 1920s

the Boule Mich: the Boulevard Saint-Michel, a street in Paris

priceless and worthless. A first-water diamond, an empty spool, bits of broken glass, lengths of string, a key to a door long since crumbled away, a rusty knife-blade, old shoes saved for a road that never was and never will be, a nail bent under the weight of things too heavy for any nail, a dried flower or two still a little fragrant. In your hand is the brown bag. On the ground before you is the jumble it held—so much like the jumble in the bags, could they be emptied, that all might be dumped in a single heap and the bags refilled without altering the content of any greatly. A bit of colored glass more or less would not matter. Perhaps that is how the Great Stuffer of Bags filled them in the first place—who knows?

QUESTIONING THE TEXT

1. Color is a central theme in this brief essay. Jot down as many of the ways color appears as you can remember. Then go back and check the text. Complete your list and compare it with the lists of others in your class. What are the different things color is attributed to?

2. In her introduction to this essay, A.L. makes absolutely clear how much she admires Hurston. How did her praise affect your evaluation of the essay?

3. Hurston exemplifies the *differences* among people in her vivid descriptions of her experience of jazz. First, try to describe your experience with the kind of music that most engages and moves you. What do you find in common with or different from Hurston's experience? Does what you have discovered lead you to see "sharp" contrasts, as Hurston does, or commonalities? What do such contrasts and commonalities have to do with your race?

MAKING CONNECTIONS

4. Read Hurston's piece along with Langston Hughes's "Theme for English B" (p. 439). Do these writers hold different—or similar—views on commonalities among all people? Explain your answer in an informal statement (about a page or two) addressed to your class.

5. Read David Rieff's "The Case Against Sensitivity" (p. 406). If Hurston had been in New York to greet Nelson Mandela, how might she have responded to the T-shirt slogan "It's a Black Thing. You Wouldn't Understand"?

6. What does *assimilate* mean to you? After jotting down your own definition, look up the word and compare your own and the dictionary definitions with the way Linda Chavez uses the word in "Toward

a New Politics of Hispanic Assimilation" (p. 426). Is Hurston an assimilationist? Why, or why not?

JOINING THE CONVERSATION

7. Hurston concludes this essay with a simile about bags. First, consider what simile or metaphor you might use to describe your own race or ethnicity and its relationship to others. Begin perhaps by completing the sentence "But in the main, I feel like . . . ." Then write an extended description of your simile or metaphor and bring it to class for discussion.
8. Working with two or three other members of your class, draft a composite description of the metaphors you came up with. What do these metaphors have in common? How do they differ?

MARGARET LAURENCE
The Loons

*A NATIVE OF THE SMALL TOWN of Neepawa, Manitoba, Margaret Laurence (b. 1926) lived for a number of years in Africa and England, learning about cultures very different from her own Canadian prairie traditions. She has published numerous books that reflect her sense of multiple cultures, including translations of African folk tales (*A Tree for Poverty*), novels (*This Side of Jordan, A Jest of God*), and stories (*A Bird in the House*). The following reading, "The Loons," comes from this 1970 volume of autobiographical stories and is, like a number of her other works (*The Stone Angel, The Fire Dwellers, The Diviners*), set in the make-believe Manitoba town of Manawaka.*

I chose this story because I came to admire Laurence's writing during the years that I taught at a Canadian university, and because she captures in this story, for me at least, both the yearning and the dread that often accompany our recognition of others as being different from ourselves. Finally, "The Loons" always makes me think of a difference I noted right away in Canada: while citizens of the United States for many years responded to an image of this country as a great melting pot, Canadians have traditionally spoken of their country as a cultural "mosaic." Does this image help to account for what happens in the story? You be the judge. – A.L.

Just below Manawaka, where the Wachakwa River ran brown and noisy over the pebbles, the scrub oak and grey-green willow and choke-cherry bushes grew in a dense thicket. In a clearing at the centre of the thicket stood the Tonnerre family's shack. The basis of this dwelling was a small square cabin made of poplar poles and chinked with mud, which had been built by Jules Tonnerre some fifty years before, when he came back from Batoche with a bullet in his thigh, the year that Riel* was hung and the voices of the Metis entered their long silence. Jules had only intended to stay the winter in the Wachakwa Valley, but the family was still there in the thirties, when I was a child. As the Tonnerres had increased, their settlement had been added to, until the clearing at the foot of the town hill was a chaos of lean-tos, wooden packing cases, warped lumber, discarded

---

Riel: Louis Riel (1844–85), who led two rebellions by Native Canadians and Metis (people of mixed European and Native Canadian descent) against Canadian governments. In 1885 his forces were defeated at their headquarters at Batoche, Saskatchewan, and Riel was convicted of treason and hanged.

car tyres, ramshackle chicken coops, tangled strands of barbed wire and rusty tin cans.

The Tonnerres were French halfbreeds, and among themselves they spoke a *patois* that was neither Cree nor French. Their English was broken and full of obscenities. They did not belong among the Cree of the Galloping Mountain reservation, further north, and they did not belong among the Scots-Irish and Ukrainians of Manawaka, either. They were, as my Grandmother MacLeod would have put it, neither flesh, fowl, nor good salt herring. When their men were not working at odd jobs or as section hands on the C.P.R.,* they lived on relief. In the summers, one of the Tonnerre youngsters, with a face that seemed totally unfamiliar with laughter, would knock at the doors of the town's brick houses and offer for sale a lard-pail full of bruised wild strawberries, and if he got as much as a quarter he would grab the coin and run before the customer had time to change her mind. Sometimes old Jules, or his son Lazarus, would get mixed up in a Saturday-night brawl, and would hit out at whoever was nearest, or howl drunkenly among the offended shoppers on Main Street, and then the Mountie would put them for the night in the barred cell underneath the Court House, and the next morning they would be quiet again.

Piquette Tonnerre, the daughter of Lazarus, was in my class at school. She was older than I, but she had failed several grades, perhaps because her attendance had always been sporadic and her interest in schoolwork negligible. Part of the reason she had missed a lot of school was that she had had tuberculosis of the bone, and had once spent many months in hospital. I knew this because my father was the doctor who had looked after her. Her sickness was almost the only thing I knew about her, however. Otherwise, she existed for me only as a vaguely embarrassing presence, with her hoarse voice and her clumsy limping walk and her grimy cotton dresses that were always miles too long. I was neither friendly nor unfriendly towards her. She dwelt and moved somewhere within my scope of vision, but I did not actually notice her very much until that peculiar summer when I was eleven.

"I don't know what to do about that kid," my father said at dinner one evening. "Piquette Tonnerre, I mean. The damn bone's flared up again. I've had her in hospital for quite a while now, and it's under control all right, but I hate like the dickens to send her home again."

"Couldn't you explain to her mother that she has to rest a lot?" my 5
mother said.

"The mother's not there," my father replied. "She took off a few years back. Can't say I blame her. Piquette cooks for them, and she says Lazarus would never do anything for himself as long as she's there. Anyway,

---

C.P.R.: Canadian Pacific Railway

I don't think she'd take much care of herself, once she got back. She's only thirteen, after all. Beth, I was thinking—what about taking her up to Diamond Lake with us this summer? A couple of months rest would give that bone a much better chance."

My mother looked stunned.

"But Ewen—what about Roddie and Vanessa?"

"She's not contagious," my father said. "And it would be company for Vanessa."

"Oh dear," my mother said in distress, "I'll bet anything she has nits   10
in her hair."

"For Pete's sake," my father said crossly, "do you think Matron would let her stay in the hospital for all this time like that? Don't be silly, Beth."

Grandmother MacLeod, her delicately featured face as rigid as a cameo, now brought her mauve-veined hands together as though she were about to begin a prayer.

"Ewen, if that half-breed youngster comes along to Diamond Lake, I'm not going," she announced. "I'll go to Morag's for the summer."

I had trouble in stifling my urge to laugh, for my mother brightened visibly and quickly tried to hide it. If it came to a choice between Grandmother MacLeod and Piquette, Piquette would win hands down, nits or not.

"It might be quite nice for you, at that," she mused. "You haven't   15
seen Morag for over a year, and you might enjoy being in the city for a while. Well, Ewen dear, you do what you think best. If you think it would do Piquette some good, then we'll be glad to have her, as long as she behaves herself."

So it happened that several weeks later, when we all piled into my father's old Nash, surrounded by suit-cases and boxes of provisions and toys for my ten-month-old brother, Piquette was with us and Grandmother MacLeod, miraculously, was not. My father would only be staying at the cottage for a couple of weeks, for he had to get back to his practice, but the rest of us would stay at Diamond Lake until the end of August.

Our cottage was not named, as many were, "Dew Drop Inn" or "Bide-a-Wee," or "Bonnie Doon." The sign on the roadway bore in austere letters only our name, MacLeod. It was not a large cottage, but it was on the lakefront. You could look out the windows and see, through the filigree of the spruce trees, the water glistening greenly as the sun caught it. All around the cottage were ferns, and sharp-branched raspberry bushes, and moss that had grown over fallen tree trunks. If you looked carefully among the weeds and grass, you could find wild strawberry plants which were in white flower now and in another month would bear fruit, the fragrant globes hanging like miniature scarlet lanterns on the thin hairy stems. The two grey squirrels were still there, gossiping at us from the tall spruce beside the cottage, and by the end of the summer they would again be tame enough to take pieces of crust from my hands. The broad moose antlers that hung above the back door were a little more bleached and fissured after the winter, but otherwise everything was the same. I raced joyfully around my kingdom, greeting all the places I had not seen for a year. My brother, Roderick, who had not been born when we were here last summer, sat on the car rug in the sunshine and examined a brown spruce cone, meticulously turning it round and round in his small and curious hands. My mother and father toted the luggage from car to cottage, exclaiming over how well the place had wintered, no broken windows, thank goodness, no apparent damage from storm-felled branches or snow.

Only after I had finished looking around did I notice Piquette. She was sitting on the swing, her lame leg held stiffly out, and her other foot scuffing the ground as she swung slowly back and forth. Her long hair hung black and straight around her shoulders, and her broad coarse-featured face bore no expression—it was blank, as though she no longer dwelt within her own skull, as though she had gone elsewhere. I approached her very hesitantly.

"Want to come and play?"

Piquette looked at me with a sudden flash of scorn. 20

"I ain't a kid," she said.

Wounded, I stamped angrily away, swearing I would not speak to her for the rest of the summer. In the days that followed, however, Piquette began to interest me, and I began to want to interest her. My reasons did not appear bizarre to me. Unlikely as it may seem, I had only just realised that the Tonnerre family, whom I had always heard called half-breeds, were actually Indians, or as near as made no difference. My acquaintance with Indians was not extensive. I did not remember ever having seen a real Indian, and my new awareness that Piquette sprang from the people of Big Bear and Poundmaker,* of Tecumseh,* of the Iroquois who had eaten Father Brebeuf's heart*—all this gave her an instant attraction in my eyes. I was a devoted reader of Pauline Johnson* at this age, and sometimes would orate aloud and in an exalted voice, *West Wind, blow from your prairie nest; Blow from the mountains, blow from the west*—and so on. It seemed to me that Piquette must be in some way a daughter of the forest, a kind of junior prophetess of the wilds, who might impart to me, if I took the right

---

Big Bear and Poundmaker (1842–86): Cree leaders

Tecumseh (1768?–1813): a Shawnee chief who organized and commanded a Native American military alliance against the U.S. government

Father Brebeuf: Saint Jean de Brébeuf (1593–1649), a French Catholic missionary killed by the Iroquois

Pauline Johnson (1861–1913): a Canadian poet whose father was Mohawk and whose mother was English; the quotation beginning *West Wind* is the first two lines of her *Song My Paddle Sings.*

approach, some of the secrets which she undoubtedly knew—where the whippoorwill made her nest, how the coyote reared her young, or whatever it was that it said in Hiawatha.

I set about gaining Piquette's trust. She was not allowed to go swimming, with her bad leg, but I managed to lure her down to the beach—or rather, she came because there was nothing else to do. The water was always icy, for the lake was fed by springs, but I swam like a dog, thrashing my arms and legs around at such speed and with such an output of energy that I never grew cold. Finally, when I had had enough, I came out and sat beside Piquette on the sand. When she saw me approaching, her hand squashed flat the sand castle she had been building, and she looked at me sullenly, without speaking.

"Do you like this place?" I asked, after a while, intending to lead on from there into the question of forest lore.

Piquette shrugged. "It's okay. Good as anywhere."   25

"I love it," I said. "We come here every summer."

"So what?" Her voice was distant, and I glanced at her uncertainly, wondering what I could have said wrong.

"Do you want to come for a walk?" I asked her. "We wouldn't need to go far. If you walk just around the point there, you come to a bay where great big reeds grow in the water, and all kinds of fish hang around there. Want to? Come on."

She shook her head.

"Your dad said I ain't supposed to do no more walking than I got   30 to."

I tried another line.

"I bet you know a lot about the woods and all that, eh?" I began respectfully.

Piquette looked at me from her large dark unsmiling eyes.

"I don't know what in hell you're talkin' about," she replied. "You nuts or somethin'? If you mean where my old man, and me, and all them live, you better shut up, by Jesus, you hear?"

I was startled and my feelings were hurt, but I had a kind of dogged   35 perseverance. I ignored her rebuff.

"You know something, Piquette? There's loons here, on this lake. You can see their nests just up the shore there, behind those logs. At night, you can hear them even from the cottage, but it's better to listen from the beach. My dad says we should listen and try to remember how they sound, because in a few years when more cottages are built at Diamond Lake and more people come in, the loons will go away."

Piquette was picking up stones and small shells and then dropping them again.

"Who gives a good goddamn?" she said.

It became increasingly obvious that, as an Indian, Piquette was a dead loss. That evening I went out by myself, scrambling through the bushes that overhung the steep path, my feet slipping on the fallen spruce needles that covered the ground. When I reached the shore, I walked along the firm damp sand to the small pier that my father had built, and sat down there. I heard someone else crashing through the undergrowth and the bracken, and for a moment I thought Piquette had changed her mind, but it turned out to be my father. He sat beside me on the pier and we waited, without speaking.

At night the lake was like black glass with a streak of amber which   40
was the path of the moon. All around, the spruce trees grew tall and close-set, branches blackly sharp against the sky, which was lightened by a cold flickering of stars. Then the loons began their calling. They rose like phantom birds from the nests on the shore, and flew out onto the dark still surface of the water.

No one can ever describe that ululating sound, the crying of the loons, and no one who has heard it can ever forget it. Plaintive, and yet with a quality of chilling mockery, those voices belonged to a world separated by aeons from our neat world of summer cottages and the lighted lamps of home.

"They must have sounded just like that," my father remarked, "before any person ever set foot here."

Then he laughed. "You could say the same, of course, about sparrows, or chipmunks, but somehow it only strikes you that way with the loons."

"I know," I said.

Neither of us suspected that this would be the last time we would   45
ever sit here together on the shore, listening. We stayed for perhaps half an hour, and then we went back to the cottage. My mother was reading beside the fireplace. Piquette was looking at the burning birch log, and not doing anything.

"You should have come along," I said, although in fact I was glad she had not.

"Not me," Piquette said. "You wouldn' catch me walkin' way down there jus' for a bunch of squawkin' birds."

Piquette and I remained ill at ease with one another. I felt I had somehow failed my father, but I did not know what was the matter, nor why she would not or could not respond when I suggested exploring the woods or playing house. I thought it was probably her slow and difficult walking that held her back. She stayed most of the time in the cottage with my mother, helping her with the dishes or with Roddie, but hardly ever talking. Then the Duncans arrived at their cottage, and I spent my days with Mavis, who was my best friend. I could not reach Piquette at all, and I soon lost interest in trying. But all that summer she remained as both a reproach and a mystery to me.

That winter my father died of pneumonia, after less than a week's illness. For some time I saw nothing around me, being completely immersed in my own pain and my mother's. When I looked outward once more, I scarcely noticed that Piquette Tonnerre was no longer at school. I do not remember seeing her at all until four years later, one Saturday night when Mavis and I were having Cokes in the Regal Café. The jukebox was booming like tuneful thunder, and beside it, leaning lightly on its chrome and its rainbow glass, was a girl.

Piquette must have been seventeen then, although she looked about   50
twenty. I stared at her, astounded that anyone could have changed so much. Her face, so stolid and expressionless before, was animated now with a gaiety that was almost violent. She laughed and talked very loudly with the boys around her. Her lipstick was bright carmine, and her hair was cut short and frizzily permed. She had not been pretty as a child, and she was not pretty now, for her features were still heavy and blunt. But her dark and slightly slanted eyes were beautiful, and her skin-tight skirt and orange sweater displayed to enviable advantage a soft and slender body.

She saw me, and walked over. She teetered a little, but it was not due to her once-tubercular leg, for her limp was almost gone.

"Hi, Vanessa." Her voice still had the same hoarseness. "Long time no see, eh?"

"Hi," I said. "Where've you been keeping yourself, Piquette?"

"Oh, I been around," she said. "I been away almost two years now. Been all over the place—Winnipeg, Regina, Saskatoon. Jesus, what I could tell you! I come back this summer, but I ain't stayin'. You kids goin' to the dance?"

"No," I said abruptly, for this was a sore point with me. I was fifteen,   55
and thought I was old enough to go to the Saturday-night dances at the Flamingo. My mother, however, thought otherwise.

"Y'oughta come," Piquette said. "I never miss one. It's just about the on'y thing in this jerkwater town that's any fun. Boy, you couldn' catch me stayin' here. I don' give a shit about this place. It stinks."

She sat down beside me, and I caught the harsh over-sweetness of her perfume.

"Listen, you wanna know something, Vanessa?" she confided, her voice only slightly blurred. "Your dad was the only person in Manawaka that ever done anything good to me."

I nodded speechlessly. I was certain she was speaking the truth. I knew a little more than I had that summer at Diamond Lake, but I could not reach her now any more than I had then. I was ashamed, ashamed of my own timidity, the frightened tendency to look the other way. Yet I felt no real warmth towards her—I only felt that I ought to, because of that distant summer and because my father had hoped she would be company for me, or perhaps that I would be for her, but it had not happened that way. At this moment, meeting her again, I had to admit that she repelled and embarrassed me, and I could not help despising the self-pity in her voice.

I wished she would go away. I did not want to see her. I did not know what to say to her. It seemed that we had nothing to say to one another.

"I'll tell you something else," Piquette went on. "All the old bitches an' biddies in this town will sure be surprised. I'm gettin' married this fall— my boyfriend, he's an English fella, works in the stockyards in the city there, a very tall guy, got blond wavy hair. Gee, is he ever handsome. Got this real classy name. Alvin Gerald Cummings—some handle, eh? They call him Al."

For the merest instant, then, I saw her. I really did see her, for the first and only time in all the years we had both lived in the same town. Her defiant face, momentarily, became unguarded and unmasked, and in her eyes there was a terrifying hope.

"Gee, Piquette—" I burst out awkwardly, "that's swell. That's really wonderful. Congratulations—good luck—I hope you'll be happy—"

As I mouthed the conventional phrases, I could only guess how great her need must have been, that she had been forced to seek the very things she so bitterly rejected.

When I was eighteen, I left Manawaka and went away to college. At the end of my first year, I came back home for the summer. I spent the first few days in talking non-stop with my mother, as we exchanged all the news that somehow had not found its way into letters—what had happened in my life and what had happened here in Manawaka while I was away. My mother searched her memory for events that concerned people I knew.

"Did I ever write you about Piquette Tonnerre, Vanessa?" she asked one morning.

"No, I don't think so," I replied. "Last I heard of her, she was going to marry some guy in the city. Is she still there?"

My mother looked perturbed, and it was a moment before she spoke, as though she did not know how to express what she had to tell and wished she did not need to try.

"She's dead," she said at last. Then, as I stared at her, "Oh, Vanessa, when it happened, I couldn't help thinking of her as she was that summer— so sullen and gauche and badly dressed. I couldn't help wondering if we could have done something more at that time—but what could we do? She used to be around in the cottage there with me all day, and honestly, it was all I could do to get a word out of her. She didn't even talk to your father very much, although I think she liked him, in her way."

"What happened?" I asked.

"Either her husband left her, or she left him," my mother said. "I don't know which. Anyway, she came back here with two youngsters, both only babies—they must have been born very close together. She kept house, I guess, for Lazarus and her brothers, down in the valley there, in the old Tonnerre place. I used to see her on the street sometimes, but she never spoke to me. She'd put on an awful lot of weight, and she looked a mess, to tell you the truth, a real slattern, dressed any old how. She was up in court a couple of times—drunk and disorderly, of course. One Saturday night last winter, during the coldest weather, Piquette was alone in the shack with the children. The Tonnerres made home brew all the time, so I've heard, and Lazarus said later she'd been drinking most of the day when he and the boys went out that evening. They had an old woodstove there— you know the kind, with exposed pipes. The shack caught fire. Piquette didn't get out, and neither did the children."

I did not say anything. As so often with Piquette, there did not seem to be anything to say. There was a kind of silence around the image in my mind of the fire and the snow, and I wished I could put from my memory the look that I had seen once in Piquette's eyes.

I went up to Diamond Lake for a few days that summer, with Mavis and her family. The MacLeod cottage had been sold after my father's death, and I did not even go to look at it, not wanting to witness my long-ago kingdom possessed now by strangers. But one evening I went down to the shore by myself.

The small pier which my father had built was gone, and in its place there was a large and solid pier built by the government, for Galloping Mountain was now a national park, and Diamond Lake had been renamed Lake Wapakata, for it was felt that an Indian name would have a greater appeal to tourists. The one store had become several dozen, and the settlement had all the attributes of a flourishing resort— hotels, a dance-hall, cafés with neon signs, the penetrating odours of potato chips and hot dogs.

I sat on the government pier and looked out across the water. At night the lake at least was the same as it had always been, darkly shining and bearing within its black glass the streak of amber that was the path of the moon. There was no wind that evening, and everything was quiet all around me. It seemed too quiet, and then I realized that the loons were no longer here. I listened for some time, to make sure, but never once did I hear that long-drawn call, half mocking and half plaintive, spearing through the stillness across the lake.

I did not know what had happened to the birds. Perhaps they had   75 gone away to some far place of belonging. Perhaps they had been unable to find such a place, and had simply died out, having ceased to care any longer whether they lived or not.

I remembered how Piquette had scorned to come along, when my father and I sat there and listened to the lake birds. It seemed to me now that in some unconscious and totally unrecognized way, Piquette might have been the only one, after all, who had heard the crying of the loons.

QUESTIONING THE TEXT

1. Think for a while about the role the loons play in the story. Are any of the characters like the loons in any way? How are the loons related to the physical landscape of the story? Brainstorm with several class members about these ideas, and then together come up with a paragraph explaining the significance of the story's last sentence.

2. What reasons might Piquette have had for being so silent during the summer at Diamond Lake? Why do you think she remains so unimpressed with the aspects of nature that interest Vanessa?

3. With which character(s) in the story do you most clearly identify or feel most empathy, and why? With which ones do you feel least empathy, and why?

MAKING CONNECTIONS

4. How is Vanessa's experience with Piquette similar to—or different from—the narrator's experience with his brother's lover in the next reading, Michael Lassell's "How to Watch Your Brother Die"? Write an essay exploring this question.

5. What does Vanessa most value? How do her values differ from Piquette's? From yours? How do her values differ from those David Rieff argues for in "The Case Against Sensitivity" (p. 406)?

JOINING THE CONVERSATION

6. Imagine that Vanessa or Piquette decides to write an essay for school called "What I Learned at Diamond Lake." Write that essay.

7. Have you ever reacted to someone who was different from you in a way similar to the way Vanessa reacts to Piquette—"she existed for me only as a vaguely embarrassing presence"? Freewrite for 15 to 20 minutes on this experience or on another kind of reaction you had in this situation.

8. Working with two or three other members of your class, do some research in the library about the native people who live either in the area where your college is or in the areas where each of you grew up. Who are these people? What can you find out about their history and their values? Prepare a brief report of your findings for the class.

MICHAEL LASSELL
How to Watch Your Brother Die

A FORMER EDITOR OF THE ADVOCATE, *a national gay and lesbian news magazine, Michael Lassell (b. 1947) is the author of several collections of poetry, including* Poems for Lost and Un-Lost Boys *(1985) and* Decade Dance *(1990).*

"How to Watch Your Brother Die," first published in 1985, is often reprinted, for it was one of the earliest poems attempting to respond to AIDS. In this brief and highly accessible work, the narrator evokes the confusing mass of emotions he feels during the death of a brother who happens to be gay. In doing so, he asks us to think about our own brothers, both literal siblings and all those for whom we feel brother- (or sister-)hood. In particular, the poem suggests to me that watching a brother die is in some ways also watching yourself die.

I chose this poem because human experience encompasses a diverse range of sexuality, in spite of our society's traditional and persistent focus only on heterosexuality. Lassell's poem challenges that focus and in doing so speaks for many, many gay people whose voices have been muted, ignored, or silenced. Finally, I chose this poem for a personal reason as well, for I watched my own brother, who lived with cancer for eight long years, die. — A.L.

When the call comes, be calm.
Say to your wife, "My brother is dying. I have to fly
to California."
Try not to be shocked that he already looks like
a cadaver.   5
Say to the young man sitting by your brother's side,
"I'm his brother."
Try not to be shocked when the young man says,
"I'm his lover. Thanks for coming."

Listen to the doctor with a steel face on.   10
Sign the necessary forms.
Tell the doctor you will take care of everything.
Wonder why doctors are so remote.

Watch the lover's eyes as they stare into
your brother's eyes as they stare into   15
space.
Wonder what they see there.

Remember the time he was jealous and
opened your eyebrow with a sharp stick.
Forgive him out loud   20
even if he can't
understand you.
Realize the scar will be
all that's left of him.

Over coffee in the hospital cafeteria   25
say to the lover, "You're an extremely good-looking
young man."
Hear him say,
"I never thought I was good enough looking to
deserve your brother."   30

Watch the tears well up in his eyes. Say,
"I'm sorry. I don't know what it means to be
the lover of another man."
Hear him say,
"It's just like a wife, only the commitment is   35
deeper because the odds against you are so much
greater."
Say nothing, but
take his hand like a brother's.

Drive to Mexico for unproven drugs that might   40
help him live longer.
Explain what they are to the border guard.
Fill with rage when he informs you,
"You can't bring those across."
Begin to grow loud.   45
Feel the lover's hand on your arm
restraining you. See in the guard's eye
how much a man can hate another man.
Say to the lover, "How can you stand it?"
Hear him say, "You get used to it."   50
Think of one of your children getting used to
another man's hatred.

Call your wife on the telephone. Tell her,
"He hasn't much time.
I'll be home soon." Before you hang up say,   55
"How could anyone's commitment be deeper than
a husband and wife?" Hear her say,
"Please. I don't want to know all the details."

When he slips into an irrevocable coma,
hold his lover in your arms while he sobs,
no longer strong. Wonder how much longer   60
you will be able to be strong.
Feel how it feels to hold a man in your arms
whose arms are used to holding men.
Offer God anything to bring your brother back.   65
Know you have nothing God could possibly want.
Curse God, but do not
abandon Him.

Stare at the face of the funeral director
when he tells you he will not   70
embalm the body for fear of
contamination. Let him see in your eyes
how much a man can hate another man.

Stand beside a casket covered in flowers,
white flowers. Say,   75
"Thank you for coming," to each of several hundred men
who file past in tears, some of them
holding hands. Know that your brother's life
was not what you imagined. Overhear two
mourners say, "I wonder who'll be next?" and   80
"I don't care anymore,
as long as it isn't you."

Arrange to take an early flight home.
His lover will drive you to the airport.
When your flight is announced say,   85
awkwardly, "If I can do anything, please
let me know." Do not flinch when he says,
"Forgive yourself for not wanting to know him
after he told you. He did."
Stop and let it soak in. Say,   90
"He forgave me, or he knew himself?"
"Both," the lover will say, not knowing what else
to do. Hold him like a brother while he
kisses you on the cheek. Think that
you haven't been kissed by a man since   95
your father died. Think,
"This is no moment not to be strong."

Fly first class and drink Scotch. Stroke
your split eyebrow with a finger and
think of your brother alive. Smile   100

at the memory and think
how your children will feel in your arms,
warm and friendly and without challenge.

IN RESPONSE

1. The word *forgive* appears a number of times in the poem. Who needs to forgive and/or to be forgiven, and why?
2. In "Theme for English B" (p. 439), the narrator says "I like to eat, sleep, drink, and be in love." What might the narrator of this poem list as his wishes—what he would most like?
3. What might the narrator say to David Rieff's argument *against* sensitivity in the next reading? Would he agree that "the alternative to sensitivity" is not "callousness" but "love"? Why, or why not? Record your answers to these questions in your reading log, if you are keeping one.
4. Write a page or two responding to this poem—how it made you feel, what it made you think of, ways in which it puzzled or troubled or comforted you.

DAVID RIEFF
The Case Against Sensitivity

"Politically correct" is an expression leftists once applied (some say ironically) to actions or beliefs that jibed with their political philosophy. Supporting Nelson Mandela, for example, was politically correct; drinking Coors beer was not. But in recent years the phrase and its abbreviation PC have acquired new connotations. The politically correct soul is now usually regarded as someone eager to impose a code of sensitivity on everyone else, a code that forbids saying anything nasty (or even negative) about groups and causes favored by the left— African Americans, Native Americans, homosexuals, women, environmentalism, homelessness. Inevitably, PC-ism has become a free-speech issue, with many conservatives and even some liberals seeing it as an effort to squelch political debate. But then, trying to silence one's political foes is an American tradition about as old as tarring and feathering—and just about as nasty.

The subtitle of David Rieff's exploration of ethnic and racial differences in the United States suggests just how tender our sensibilities have become: "Are we scrapping the First Amendment to spare people's feelings?" Rieff pulls no punches, nor does he leave any doubt about where he stands in his article, originally published in 1990 in Esquire, *a liberal men's magazine. What seems to separate the "thought police" he attacks from earlier censors is that they come, by and large, from groups that once stoutly defended the First Amendment. Now some of these same people want to save the rest of us from political sins by placing restraints on our language and behavior.*

Rieff is the author of several books, including portraits of contemporary Miami and Los Angeles. I think his opinion deserves attention, though it may ruffle a few feathers.

Is that tar I smell? — J.R.

Well before Nelson Mandela arrived in New York this past summer to begin a triumphal passage through the great cities of the United States, his impending visit had inspired entrepreneurs to manufacture a line of T-shirts bearing the likeness of the ANC deputy president and ornamented with maps of Africa and slogans affirming black unity. The biggest sellers carried a simple message: IT'S A BLACK THING. YOU WOULDN'T UNDERSTAND. Taken by itself, the sentiment expressed on the T-shirt, with its sad mixture of resignation and

My own strong conviction is that insensitivity is so rampant that we hardly need attacks on its opposite. I don't know anything about David Rieff or his work, so I have nothing to go on there. But I'm

Is this really a "sad mixture of resignation and defiance" or perhaps cultural self-awareness and pride? And how does Rieff know that Mandela would have repudiated such a slogan?
– T.M.

defiance, may not seem all that significant. Mandela, though he surely would have understood the message, would with equal certainty have repudiated such a slogan. But what the T-shirt says about blacks and Mandela is not as important as what it says about blacks and America and about Americans in general. For the phrase perfectly sums up the degree to which matters of ethics and allegiance—and even the most elementary questions of understanding—are now thought to be the exclusive intellectual and emotional property of those interest groups most affected by them.

For "It's a black thing," substitute "It's a [blank] thing," and you're in business. Mandela's visit may have made the sentiments of many New York blacks legible to everyone who cared to look, but as a way of thinking about the world it is by no means restricted to certain rancorously politicized segments of black America. For more than a decade, and far longer in some circles, a spirit of particularism has been setting in on college campuses, in the ongoing debate on pornography and free speech, and most pronouncedly, in the gay and feminist movements. Not only do people seem persuaded by the proposition that, when all is said and done, nobody can understand anybody outside one's own group, but by its corollary: For a member of one group—be it ethnic, sexual, or racial—to criticize the activities, the views, or the culture of someone in some other group is to be guilty, according to the current terms of art, of disrespect ("dissing") or insensitivity.

At first glance, it seems more than a little peculiar to worry about sensitivity in a country whose shameful crime statistics, faltering economy, increasingly illiterate and innumerate population, and frivolous political leadership are not getting a fraction of the attention they deserve. Nevertheless, sensitivity is now as important an issue for the Left, and for the educational establishment, both in the public schools and on university campuses, as the repeal of abortion rights has been for the Right. Increasingly, in a United States that becomes more racially diversified each year, every

expecting, because of the title, some attempt to set up freedom of speech and sensitivity as polar opposites.
– A.L.

While I understand Rieff's point and have seen evidence of it on my own campus, what seems equally obvious to me is something Rieff chooses to ignore: the increased emphasis on differences among members of any "group." Yet such an emphasis needn't mean that every individual is a "particularity."
– A.L.

group that views itself as oppressed or disenfranchised has chosen to construe its situation in the
language of the Civil Rights movement. Like the
Civil Rights movement, the battle has been partly
legal and partly linguistic. Gays, the disabled, and
women have all pressed for juridical redress, and
that demand is self-evidently just. But more and
more, the call has been for psychological and verbal
redress as well, and that demand may not only be
impossible to fulfill, but dangerous as well.

*I take it this is
Rieff's thesis. Is
this how he de-
fines "sensitiv-
ity" (a term that
still seems loose
and vague in this
article): "psy-
chological and
verbal redress"?
– A.L.*

The United States remains a puritan country in
which, despite everything that has happened during the past thirty years, the censor is never very
far below the surface. It is also a country where
people believe, as they always have, that there is
little about themselves, whether it be their phy-
siques or their beliefs, that they cannot alter if they
change their behavior radically enough. So it
should come as no surprise that Americans, finding
themselves in a society in which the tensions of
clashing interests, moralities, and ethnicities seem
to grow each year, would imagine that if they could
learn to think positively and respectfully about one
another everything would be okay.

*Is this unrealis-
tic? Doesn't this
trait make us
more liberal?
– T.M.*

The idea is peculiarly American. Certainly, it is
hard to imagine Europeans or Asians falling for
the illusion that if only they could learn to be sufficiently sensitive to other cultures, then age-old
conflicts would disappear. But then those cultures
believe in tragedy, in the continuing authority of
the past, whereas few Americans have ever really
believed that the past is anything except a prelude
to the future. The result has been that instead of
wanting to see differences aired in public, many
well-meaning Americans want to sweep them
under the rug. It sometimes seems as if the only
way you can get in trouble in the United States
these days is by *saying* something offensive; think
of the forced resignations of cabinet members Earl
Butz and James Watt. They were not hounded out
of office, as perhaps they should have been, for
the policies they carried out, but rather for making
offensive jokes.

*This section
makes me think
of the ethnic prob-
lems in Eastern
Europe, which
embody what
Americans
should fear
most—a society
divided by race
and nationality
into warring
camps.   – J.R.*

The examples are legion. The racist remarks of

a Jimmy Breslin or a Jimmy the Greek or an Al Campanis* find their echoes in the attitudes of rap group Public Enemy, whose anti-Semitism, however indirectly phrased, is clear enough. Indeed, which of us has not felt the painful sting of hate speech? What is different about the current climate is that whereas in the past most Americans assumed that the best way to combat hate speech was with other speech, today many are looking for ways to suppress it. Many decent people apparently have come to believe in a sort of affirmative-action equivalent of the genteel old small-town saw, "If you can't say something nice, don't say anything at all."

Rieff should note, perhaps, that not all groups are protected from offensive speech. On one campus, all males were branded by a women's group as "potential rapists." — J.R.

These well-intended thought police were neatly lampooned by Russell Baker, who recently wrote a column that imagined Wagner* receiving advice from an American well-wisher about how he might reconceive *The Ring* to make it better conform to contemporary American values. "Rewrite the opening," Baker's socially conscious bowdlerizer suggests helpfully, "to eliminate the insensitive treatment of dwarfs embodied in the character of the dwarf Alberich. The Rhine Maidens' calling him ugly and toadlike is offensive to dwarfs, as is the suggestion that a dwarf cannot be sexually interesting to mermaids. Having Alberich steal the Rhine Gold imputes criminal instincts to dwarfs and is an overt slur." Similar proposals to avoid offending the sensitivities of various oppressed groups are proffered concerning Wotan, Fricka, Siegmund, Brunhilde, and the rest. There is no Wagner left after this treatment, of course, but neither is there anything left in the opera that could remotely be interpreted as disrespectful toward anyone. Only the one group that the writer consid-

I'm uneasy with such a blanket statement. I am personally willing to state very strong opinions in debating principles or issues. I am much less willing to attack people on the basis of some personal characteristic. I was brought up not to not "say anything at all" but instead to say to others what I would have them say to me. — A.L.

Jimmy Breslin . . . Al Campanis: Breslin (b. 1929) is a newspaper columnist and novelist; Jimmy the Greek (b. 1919) is an oddsmaker and TV sports commentator; Campanis (b. 1916) is the vice-president of the Los Angeles Dodgers baseball team. All three were forced to apologize for making what were considered racially offensive remarks in public.

Wagner: Richard Wagner (1813–83), a German composer whose opera cycle *The Ring of the Nibelungs* (1853–74) is based on Germanic mythology and begins with the dwarf Alberich's theft of a hoard of gold from the Rhine River, where it is guarded by the Rhine Maidens

ers to be an oppressor, Episcopalians, is held up
as suitable for scorn and slander. Wagner is invited
to say anything he likes about them.

Baker's satire is actually a pretty faithful rendi-
tion of the views of an influential group of scholars,
activists, and writers for whom free speech, when
it offends those who can be called disempowered
by society, is by no means an absolute right. Make
fun of Episcopalians or real estate developers by
all means, they argue, but don't say anything even
passingly negative about members of oppressed
groups, because such remarks are less expressions
of opinion than harmful "speech acts" that have
the effect of perpetuating this disempowerment.

*Rieff has put his
finger on what
has caused seeth-
ing resentment on
many American
campuses—the
special privileges
of speech and ac-
tion accorded to
most-favored
groups by faculty
and
administrators.*
– J.R.

It was more or less on these grounds that Mari
Matsuda, a law professor at Stanford, wrote an
influential article in a 1989 issue of the *Michigan
Law Review* calling for universities to forbid hate
speech directed at minorities. Matsuda argued that
freedom of speech, properly understood, was a
guarantee really intended to protect the powerless.
By this she did not mean powerless individuals,
but members of outsider groups, like women or
racial minorities. Thus, a rich woman would presumably be protected by the First Amendment but
a poor white man (unless gay, or disabled, or otherwise "disenfranchised") would not.

Using logic similar to Matsuda's, 137 American
universities (including Stanford and the University
of Michigan) have in the last two years passed
proscriptions on hate speech. The Michigan code
was eventually struck down by the courts, but the
extent to which the principle of restricting speech
is gaining acceptance can be gauged by the divisive-

*Sadly, advocates
of unconstitutional
speech codes have
had to pay no
political price for
their assaults on
the First Amend-
ment. One even
made it—no sur-
prise really—
into the Clinton
cabinet.* – J.R.

ness the issue has provoked even within the American Civil Liberties Union, which until recently was
absolutist on all free-speech questions. True, the
national organization has hewed to its traditional
interpretation, but several of the largest affiliates,
most notably in northern and southern California,
have accepted the argument that speech is, at least
in certain instances, less an expression of personal
freedom than a form of power, and as such, is
subject to curtailment. The catalogue of what is

*Since I tend to see
words as sym-
bolic actions, ver-
bal abuse and
physical abuse
fall into a simi-
lar category.
Words* can
hurt. – A.L.

More recently, Ohio State proposed to punish "inappropriate reference to gender." Who determines what's "appropriate" speech? — J.R.

barred is broad. The University of Michigan policy prohibited "any behavior, verbal or physical, that stigmatizes or victimizes an individual on the basis of race, ethnicity, religion, sex, sexual orientation, creed, national origin, ancestry, age, marital status, handicap, or Vietnam-era-veteran status." Perhaps the "except Episcopalians" is implicit.

This kind of sensitivity used to be mainly the preserve of the Right. To cite an obvious example, the obscenity statutes have always been justified by the argument that most people in a given community are offended by pornography. The attacks that Senator Helms has been leading against the National Endowment for the Arts for underwriting exhibits of Robert Mapplethorpe's photos,* and the decision by a federal judge in Florida to ban the sale of rap group 2 Live Crew's record *As Nasty as They Wanna Be,* are only the most recent examples of this orthodox censorship. "It's a question," said the judge in the 2 Live Crew case, "between two ancient enemies—'anything goes' versus 'enough already.' " Not for nothing was the first major New Left group at the University of California at Berkeley in the early 1960s called the Free Speech Movement. Indeed, as recently as 1984, the ACLU could issue a report in which the threat to constitutional rights was presented as coming entirely from the Right. Ah, the good old days.

As the ongoing debate over federal funding of the arts has amply demonstrated, the danger from the Right has not receded. The neoconservatives* have even joined the fray (with the Cold War over, they must have so much . . . time). Samuel Lipman, the publisher of *New Criterion,** could be

---

Robert Mapplethorpe's photos: Jesse Helms, a Republican U.S. senator from North Carolina, attacked the funding of the Mapplethorpe exhibits by the National Endowment for the Arts, a federal agency, because the photos included explicit homosexual and sadomasochistic images.

neoconservatives: a group of prominent intellectuals, including Norman Podhoretz and Irving Kristol, who abandoned their earlier liberalism, especially in foreign policy, after the 1960s

New Criterion: a neoconservative journal of the arts

seen on a recent segment of the *MacNeil/Lehrer Newshour* arguing that the question of obscenity should really be decided by an ongoing process of popular referenda. Now, however, we are beginning to hear left-wing spins on the same argument, from what might be called the reform branch of the censorship movement. In place of "community standards," read "concern for the oppressed." A placard at a recent gay-rights march in Washington summed up this new mood nicely. BAN HOMO-PHOBIA, it said, NOT HOMOSEXUALITY.

I agree with Lip-man's idea. This goes back to the notion of majority rule. — T.M.

Among people on the Left, the conviction has taken root that disrespectful or offensive views can be blunted through the judicious application of what might be called linguistic martial law. Like all appeals for extreme measures, it has the force of righteous indignation and the limitations of both shortsightedness and wishful thinking. The demonstrator at the gay march probably never paused to wonder whether, if it came to *banning* anything, it might more likely be gays than gay bashing.

A familiar argu-mentative strat-egy, making his position seem like the sober middle ground between two more extreme views. — J.R.

Of course, it makes little sense to argue that banning any kind of speech, no matter how odious, will undermine the whole basis of freedom of speech in America, if you believe that insensitive speech is not simply offensive but harmful—an act, at the very least, of psychological violence. Some feminists go further, arguing that pornography ac-tually incites men to rape and brutalize women. For Catharine MacKinnon, the ACLU's decision to defend pornographers in effect deprives women of *their* civil liberties. MacKinnon has drafted statutes (one became law in Indianapolis before it was struck down by the Supreme Court) that ban por-nographic materials of all kinds. Not surprisingly, her arguments have been warmly endorsed by Fun-damentalist anti-pornography crusaders like the Reverend Donald Wildmon, with whom she can-not be imagined to have much else in common. For MacKinnon and Wildmon, as for so many utopian American reformers before them, symp-tom and cause have gotten mixed up. A copy of *Penthouse* found in the local 7-Eleven didn't cause the breakup of the family, although it may be a by-product of its onrushing dissolution. As for MacKinnon's notion that pornography causes violence against women, the truth is that violence against women is, alas, the bloody thread that unites almost all times and all cultures. What the censors are offering is nothing more than the old American fantasy of prohibition. Ban alcohol and no one will drink; ban racist speech and no one will be a racist; ban pornography and no one will ever have a perverse thought again. Implicit in such thinking is the curious assumption—one that belies all the populist pretensions of both Right and Left—that Americans are so gullible and childish that they will follow the lead of anything they see or hear. Show Mapplethorpe in Cincinnati and everyone will turn gay; sanction hate speech and soon it will drown out every other sound in the land.

Not surprisingly, pornography aside, conservatives and radicals have disagreed about exactly what should be banned. In Texas, parents' groups have campaigned for the removal of books that teach what they call "secular humanism" and what in fact is liberalism. In California, equally committed groups of parents, most but not all black, have sought to remove *Huckleberry Finn* from school library shelves on the grounds that it is racist. Now, if only Jim* could have been called "Episcopalian Jim." Reactions to all this tend to vary, depending on whose ox is being gored, although, if only because it originates on university campuses, the left-wing variant is usually described more respectfully in the media.

Amen. – J.R.

Still, what unites would-be censors of all political stripes is far greater, intellectually, than that which divides them, and what is abundantly clear is that in America today the idea of individual rights is steadily losing ground to the idea of group rights.

We have come a long way from the time when

Surely we can find some middle ground here, some way to protect individual rights within a doctrine of free speech. Rieff doesn't seem to be looking for any middle ground, however.
– A.L.

Jim: one of the central characters in *Huckleberry Finn,* an escaped slave who is often called Nigger Jim by other characters

I admire Rieff's deft linkage of the famous Skokie free speech case to the exchange from A Man for All Seasons. *He shows how protecting each person's freedom to speak protects us all.* — J.R.

the ACLU decided to go to court to defend the American Nazi party's right to hold a demonstration in Skokie, a suburban Chicago town densely peopled with Holocaust survivors. The martial-law definition of free speech proceeds apace. Given the rise in racial attacks on nonwhite students on college campuses, the argument goes, and the seemingly intractable problems of rape and the sexual harassment of women, what practical solution is there except to carve out a series of legal exemptions to the doctrine of free speech? This is, of course, exactly the same argument that people worried about crime make regarding the rights of criminal defendants. And, indeed, it is a difficult one to rebut. Most criminal defendants, for all the nonsense we all speak, are guilty—and that probably included a certain Arizona criminal by the name of Miranda,* he of the famous warning. Still, Aryeh Neier, the Jewish refugee from Nazi Germany who defended the Skokie fascists, had it right when he used in the introduction for his book on the affair an exchange from the play *A Man for All Seasons.** "What would you do? Cut a great road through the law to get after the devil?" Thomas More inquires of a pious disciple. And the man replies, "I'd cut down every law in England to do that." To which More retorts, "And when the last law was down, and the devil turned round on you—where would you hide, the laws all being flat?"

Not that the whole question can be defanged with a quotation, no matter how salient. If the MacKinnons of this world have never demonstrated to anyone's satisfaction but their own that pornography engenders violence against women, this does not make the problem of violence against women any less grave. And the Mari Matsudas of

---

Miranda: Ernesto Miranda, an accused robber whose case led to a landmark Supreme Court decision requiring that all arrested persons be informed of their rights

A Man for All Seasons: a play by Robert Bolt (b. 1924) about the life of Thomas More (1478–1535), the lord chancellor of England executed by King Henry VIII for opposing Henry's break with the Roman Catholic Church and proclamation of himself as the head of the Church of England

I'd like to see Rieff's figures on the number of hate crimes on campuses—and who collected them.   – J.R.

this world are right when they point out that hate crimes in universities *are* getting out of hand. Absolutist defenders of the First Amendment have to at least consider whether draconian legislation might have some positive effect, and not simply argue that the moral and political consequences are too severe. One has only to think back to Barry Goldwater's 1964 presidential campaign. "You can't legislate laws into the hearts of men," he intoned, denouncing the then-new Civil Rights law. But of course you can, up to a point anyway. When has force not ruled human affairs, whether in Little Rock or in Prague?* At the very least, change often occurs only when force is imposed, as in the South in the 1950s and 1960s, or when it is withdrawn, as in Eastern Europe in 1989.

Today, the extent to which blacks and whites do work together (if not live together) in cities like Richmond, Atlanta, and Mobile, and in reasonable amity at that, is partly due to the laws that were rammed down people's throats a generation ago. But when the federal government superseded more than one hundred years of Jim Crow legislation, it was risking no major legal side effects. We risk everything when we tamper with the First Amendment. Legal ramifications aside, we should be doing everything in our power to avoid imposing yet one more layer of conformity and blandness on a country where conformity and blandness in politics and thought are more and more the rule. Americans need to take stock, to argue, ridicule, and defame without worrying about hurting one another's feelings. If the country were in better shape, people could pretend they were better than they are. But the country is in lousy shape, and attempting to paper over the antagonisms that divide us with a juridical smile button is not going to help.

For the arts, certainly, this new sensitivity, if

I'd like to hear more on this comparison and more about what he means by "everything." – A.L.

A juridical smile button should be part of the answer. We have to start somewhere and the judiciary system is doing just that. – T.M.

---

    in Little Rock or in Prague: Federal troops were sent to Little Rock, Arkansas, in 1957 to enforce a school desegregation order. Troops from the USSR invaded Prague, Czechoslovakia, in 1968 to crush a growing democracy movement.

The perfect example to defuse his critics on the left—if they'll buy his argument that speech codes aren't much different from the Islamic attacks on Rushdie's novel.   — J.R.

it prevails, will be an unmitigated disaster. The Rushdie case* provides the perfect example of what is at risk. Whatever can be said about the orchestration of the campaign against *The Satanic Verses,* there can be no doubt that Rushdie's book did offend the sensibilities of many Moslems. Moreover, in England, in India, and in South Africa, where much of the controversy originated, Moslems are an oppressed and beleaguered minority. A Moslem Mari Matsuda might well have argued, as a few leftist critics (notably the novelist John Berger) have done, that Rushdie's right to say what he wants is far less important than the rights of the immigrant Moslem "outsiders" to be free of what radical literary critics (who, along with lawyers, are the theorists of the new sensitivity) would doubtless call "narratives" that prevent their full empowerment. If the jeers of white students on a college campus cause black and other minority students to fail, as these critics assert, what is one to make of a book whose promulgation has, say its detractors, perpetuated unfair stereotypes about the entire Moslem universe? If the argument for barring disrespectful speech is justified legally, at least in America, on the grounds of the Supreme Court's "fighting words" exemption* to the First Amendment, what is one to say about *The Satanic Verses?* Now *those* were fighting words.

At the University of Texas, one student's pro–gay rights art exhibit was taken down because it included images and phrases that might be offensive to gay students!   — J.R.

The kind of sensitivity that is being pushed on university campuses these days would make all serious art nearly impossible, for only a genius could make anything worthwhile in a context where only positive images are acceptable. Certainly artists will be among the first casualties if the case for sensitivity, which can never be anything else but a case for censorship, prevails. Art will exist, of course, but as a species of folklore, the product not of individuals but of groups. Those

I agree with much of Rieff's defense of the First Amendment. But I now see what's been worrying me about his use of the term "sensitivity." I'd rather call it "respect for others," even when their views differ from mine. We can disagree—and

---

The Rushdie case: Conservative Muslims called for the assassination of Salman Rushdie (b. 1947) because of what they considered his blasphemous ridicule of Mohammed in his novel *The Satanic Verses* (1989).

"fighting words" exemption: The Supreme Court has ruled that the First Amendment does not protect speech intended to provoke violence.

who argue for this kind of art almost always say that it enhances self-esteem, particularly among those who have felt denigrated by the dominant society. The fact that such a conception of art precludes a Rushdie does not seem to trouble its advocates. A feminist wall poster in SoHo* puts the argument succinctly: NO MORE MASTERPIECES, it reads.

This idea of self-esteem is even more central in American education. The examples are endless. In 1989 a New York State task force issued a report calling for a sweeping revision of the history curriculum taught in the public schools. Excessive emphasis on the Western (that is, the European) tradition, it was argued, had had a "terribly damaging effect on the psyches" of children of non-European origin. What was needed was a curriculum that would deemphasize Europe and "validate"—a word most often used in educational theory and in parking lots—African, Latino, Native American, and Asian contributions to the United States. That way, minority-group students would feel better about themselves and white students would become less "arrogant." A similar case is commonplace in the literature departments of many American universities, where there is a strong push for more women writers, black writers, gay writers, et cetera, and for fewer DWEMs (Dead White European Males)—perhaps Proust will wind up being taught only in gay literature courses.

In the case of the New York history curriculum, the report was accepted by the education commissioner. The Board of Regents agreed to form a panel that would recommend revisions in the curriculum, stipulating further that the drafters of this new multicultural master plan were to be chosen in such a way as to ensure that "among the active participants will be scholars and teachers who represent the ethnic and cultural groups under consideration." The author of the task-force report was none other than Lionel Jeffries, a black anthropolo-

The point about minority-group students feeling better about themselves and white students becoming less arrogant is not what I think the educational system is trying to push. Perhaps incorporating people of all races rather than simply Europeans just gives a more realistic view of American history! — T.M.

Rieff's right. Textbooks—including readers such as this one—are consciously edited to ensure that minority groups are proportionally represented. — J.R.

disagree powerfully—within the realm of human respect. — A.L.

The reform of history texts has been led not by wild-eyed members of some oppressed group, as Rieff here suggests, but by a Pulitzer Prize-winning white male middle-of-the-road historian who argues convincingly that an inclusive history has far greater veracity, just what Rieff seems to want. — A.L.

SoHo: a district in New York City that is a center for artists and art galleries

gist at the City University of New York, whose lifework it has been to argue that black people are *by nature* warm and generous, while whites are cold and greedy. (Inherited cultural traits! As the educator Diane Ravitch remarked at the time, there hasn't been anything so absurd since Lysenko.*) But that was less interesting than the Regents' sober decision that each ethnic group should have, in effect, the right to decide now what their history had been then. Gore Vidal, hardly the most lenient narrator of the American pageant, has called this "good citizenship history," in which people will be taught that "the Hispanics are warm and joyous and have brought such wonder into our lives, and before them the Jews, and before them the blacks. And the women."

Only in America could an educational reform be based more on its impact on the students' psyches than on its veracity. But the point isn't education (a piquant detail in New York is that the panel planning the revision of the *history* curriculum may wind up seating only one historian); it's just what Vidal says it is, feeling good; and for that, one needs facts less than good intentions, and rigor less than sensitivity and respect. It has always been like this in America, where the academic content of the curriculum has taken a backseat to the moral effect the schools were supposed to produce. "Little children," ran a third-grade reading commonplace in American schools in the 1880s, "you must seek to be good rather than wise." At the time, American public education emphasized vocational achievement, but educators were already evincing contempt for academic learning, at least when compared with sports, or with what in the 1950s were referred to as "life values." In retrospect, there is only a short distance between this view and the current cult of self-esteem.

Of course, once you have set up a system in

Recent studies show that American students typically know less than their foreign counterparts, but have higher self-esteem. – J.R.

Lysenko: Trofim Denisovich Lysenko (1898–1976), a Soviet biologist who promoted the theory, now discredited, that characteristics acquired by organisms from their environment can be inherited by their offspring

which the truth matters less than a sensitive or constructive narrative, all interactions, and for that matter, all institutions, are going to be judged on the basis of their contributions to people's sense of psychological well-being. The classroom radicals, however they may imagine themselves, are not so far removed from the aspirations of the larger, therapeutized culture that gave birth to them. Americans are obsessed with finding ways to think about themselves more positively. Whether it was Coué,* with his slogan, "Every day, in every way, I'm getting better and better," or "I'm okay, you're okay" and beyond, Americans are suckers for the idea that if they could learn to love themselves enough they could do anything.

If positive thinking has been a constant in American thinking since the days of Benjamin Franklin, and I think it has, it has been most influential in times of crisis and among communities at risk. Think of the widespread belief among cancer patients that they became sick because of negative self-image, or the conviction held by many gravely ill people—an attitude popularized by Norman Cousins—that if they reform their sense of self they may be able to induce remission. "Those of you who feel guilt because you believe you caused your own illnesses," instructs Dr. Bernie S. Siegel, author of the recent best seller *Peace, Love, & Healing,* "or who feel like failures if you cannot cure them, are giving your healing system a destructive message. You must let go of feelings of guilt and failure so that, unencumbered by these negative messages, you can utilize to the fullest your innate healing capacities."

Ironically, multicultural curricula often depend on the guilt of European-Americans too.
— J.R.

Black people, with their long and tragic history of enslavement and suffering, gay people in the midst of the AIDS pandemic, women, Native Americans—is it any surprise that these *Americans* have accepted the notion that positive thinking can relieve their oppression, and that negative think-

Coué: Émile Coué (1857–1926), a French psychotherapist whose theories became popular in the United States in the 1920s

ing, whether its source is stereotypes imposed by outsiders, or self-hatred, will perpetuate that oppression? For that is the force behind the demand for sensitivity, the belief that attitude is the key to everything. Thus, high black crime rates are increasingly explained by many blacks not in the socioeconomic language of liberalism, let alone in the religious language of sin, but as a by-product of internalized self-hatred. What is necessary, then, is less material improvement than pride. As a result, more effort is given to demonstrating in front of a Korean fruit stand in Brooklyn, where a shopkeeper is said to have treated a black customer disrespectfully, than to demonstrating in front of the New York office of the Small Business Administration for more loans for blacks who want to start fruit stands of their own.

Another enormous oversimplification. I can't think of anyone who would say that sensitivity or attitude is the "key to everything."
— A.L.

Is Rieff implying that blacks should weight one concern more heavily than the other? Should starting their own business be the answer to the problem of a denial of respect?
— T.M.

Similar attitudes are evident in the more materially privileged world of gay people, where the debate around outing has echoes of many of the same assumptions. Most gay people would probably still argue that they should be free to come out of the closet or to stay in as they choose. But others are saying that in fact the rights of the gay community must take precedence. If a famous gay, so the argument runs, were to come out, this would go a long way toward countering the negative self-images that many gays have, particularly if they live in small towns. If these gay role models were available, the suicide rate among gay teenagers might even drop. So the decision to come out, far from being a private matter, comes to be construed as a matter of life and death. Moreover, gayness is also viewed by many activists as an inherited cultural trait. A recent book called *Gay Men and Women Who Enriched the World,* on sale at my local bookstore, offers potted biographies of forty famous gay men and women, ranging rather improbably from Alexander the Great to Gertrude Stein. Though it would be hard to conjure up two human beings more different, the author insists that they are bound by their "gay sensibilities."

In the end, it seems, Americans are so haunted by the division of the world according to special-interest groups that all other forms of differentiation have become unimportant. The gay activists who heaped scorn on Malcolm Forbes for concealing his alleged homosexuality were, for the most part, fierce critics of the capitalist system. And yet they saw no inconsistency, so much had the racial or ethnic model of gayness won their allegiance, in demanding that this excoriated plutocrat come out so that he could serve as a model for other gays. Far from being an interesting or subtle way of understanding the world, this tribal conception robs the world of its complexity and its depth.

Though couched in the rhetoric of enlightenment, the politics of race and ethnicity are in fact a form of Know-Nothingism—the ultimate denial of politics. What matters is not what you think, or what you stand for, but the color of your skin, your gender, or your sexual tastes. This is cultural nationalism in the truest sense of the term, a romantic idea of identity in which there are no contradictions between individuals, only between groups. And since these groups, by definition, cannot understand one another, the only solution is deference, respect, sensitivity. "It's a [blank] thing. You wouldn't understand." There used to be a name for that in America: It was called separate but equal. A lot of people died to get rid of it, but now, with a new wardrobe, it's back.

In the past, ambitious people had the idea that their role models could come from anywhere, not just from among members of their own ethnic group, or for that matter, from people they actually knew. The idea was to transcend the situation into which they were born. Today, many would agree with the admonition of the black playwright August Wilson, who told an interviewer: "Never transcend who you are." And, indeed, if one's identity is, by definition, both good and immutable, then to be anything other than sensitive is to perform a spiritual mugging. The problem is that identity is not fixed, it's fluid, and that a "pure" culture is as preposterous an idea as a "pure" race. Because cultures, like races, are hybrids, it makes no more sense to see nothing wrong in a culture,

This is an important paragraph, summing up Rieff's argument with a gut-wrenching reminder of an earlier era's "separate but equal" mendacities. — J.R.

At last I can assent to something. I agree that identity politics is dangerous— though perhaps for reasons different from Rieff's. — A.L.

except the ways in which it has been deformed by oppression, than it does to see nothing wrong in a person. When the defenders of 2 Live Crew argue that the band is an expression of black culture, they are probably right, but they are begging the question. Cultures are mixtures of good and bad, and the greatest problem of the new sensitivity is that it makes condemning anything, or even thinking critically about anything, an impermissible act of bad faith.

Real respect comes not from restrictions on hate speech, or empty slogans promoting group pride, but from the acknowledgment of complexity. "What have I in common with the Jews?" Franz Kafka* once wrote. "I have nothing in common with myself." Throughout history, all spiritual understanding has been based on the willingness to embrace these sorts of contradictions, and in doing so, to accept that human imperfection is not derived from the machinations of strangers but stems from the human condition itself. All the sensitivity training in the world, whether psychological or political, will not change this. For despite what August Wilson says, the only hope for humanity *is* transcendence, not the polite fictions of sensitivity and respect, which are really invitations—"It's a [blank] thing. You wouldn't understand"—to mutual incomprehension. Far from being a time when we should be saying less, as the advocates of the new sensitivity keep insisting, we should be saying more. We need a hundred novels as offensive as *The Satanic Verses*. We need to let the tragedy in, not pretend we can legislate it away. In an age of slogans and mind-numbing hype, we do not need pabulum, no matter how well intended.

People often argue that the alternative to sensitivity is callousness. It isn't. The alternative is love, which is an emotion that does not come entailed with lies, or the reductive fictions of political activism and ethnic solidarity, or the exaggerated punctilio of a society that can no longer cope with the

Ah, here is the word I've been looking for. — A.L.

The constant repetition of "It's a [blank] thing. You wouldn't understand," makes the words seem sinister. — J.R.

Franz Kafka (1883–1924): a Czech-born German novelist who was Jewish

crisis of belief and community in which it finds itself becalmed. There is no point in pretending, as Americans so often try to do, that the world is not a tragic place. And there is no need to pretend that all cultures—or for that matter, all people— are good at the same things any more than sane parents would make such claims about their children. It is only necessary to love human beings— as individuals, not as groups or factions—in the same way that parents love their children, imperfections, weaknesses, and all. That, and, however insensitive the message may at first appear, to tell the truth.

These last 2 paragraphs are very different from the preceding 30. I wish he had begun here—and that he hadn't felt the need to attack so many other people in his defense of values like respect and love. – A.L.

A f t e r w o r d s

I am considerably more critical of Rieff's arguments than J.R. is. Most of all, I am uncomfortable with the binary opposition Rieff sets up between free speech and speaking your mind (the good guys) and attempts to be sensitive to others (the bad, politically correct guys). It's an easy opposition that doesn't, in my experience, hold up under any kind of close scrutiny or examination. Nevertheless, I do not disagree with everything Rieff says. Far from it. I agree, for instance, that "Americans need to take stock, to argue," and so forth, and I agree that "attempting to paper over the antagonisms that divide us with a juridical smile button is not going to help." What I can't go along with is Rieff's implicit conclusion that the only way to address our differences and our antagonisms is in some kind of big, ugly national fight. He gives no evidence that convinces me that such a fight will do any good. In fact, a smile button might actually do more good than any such all-out antagonisms would.

So I'm not against sensitivity, but neither am I against freedom of speech or the First Amendment. Pitting them against one another is a trap for the unwary thinker. Rather, I want to look for a way to address our very great differences, to get at the antagonisms that divide (and conquer?) us, and generally to try to do so by invoking and acting on the principles outlined only very sketchily in Rieff's final paragraphs. Still, I can't accept all of what Rieff says even here. Finding a way to generate what he calls "real respect" or "love" for one another, I agree, does seem necessary. But it will not be as simple as he makes it seem in the closing of this essay. Not as long as people like him are writing mean-spirited and antagonistic articles—all in the name of respect and love. – A.L.

Among the first pieces I selected for this chapter, David Rieff's "The Case Against Sensitivity" survived many subsequent reviews and cuts. That's because, despite some dated allusions to events in 1989–90, the article remains one of the most lucid discussions yet of politically correct speech—an issue that has subsequently provided grist for many writers' mills. Having tackled the issue less successfully myself, I admire not only Rieff's arguments, but how powerfully he shapes them.

To be sure, the editors of Esquire *wouldn't tolerate a dry-as-dust defense of the First Amendment; so Rieff examines the legal questions surrounding "sensitivity" by taking readers on an impassioned tour of the American political scene. He wraps his argument around one key phrase—"It's a [blank] thing. You wouldn't understand"—and populates his essay with a memorable cast, everyone from Nelson Mandela, Russell Baker, 2 Live Crew, and Catharine MacKinnon to Salman Rushdie, Malcolm Forbes, Gore Vidal, and even Benjamin Franklin. As a result, the essay speaks in a human voice, one that really seems to care more about people than ideology. I admire how passionately and convincingly Rieff reaches for the heart of the American body politic.* – J.R.

Rieff's overall intention seems to be to argue that people should be allowed to think and express themselves freely and, as a result, that they should be allowed to step on others' feelings if the point they're trying to get across is the truth. This idea reminds me of Malcolm X's notion of "By any means necessary."

I have several questions for Rieff: If people follow your advice by reacting in any way they feel to anything they may not agree with, in what direction is this going to lead society? Don't we need some type of social order to prevent mass confusion? If a judiciary system would help prevent this, isn't it a start? And don't we have to start somewhere to progress? – T.M.

QUESTIONING THE TEXT

1. What does Rieff mean when he suggests that "[t]he United States remains a puritan country"? Can you cite evidence that supports or contradicts this assertion?

2. What are the connotations of "thought police" as Rieff uses the term in this article? If you keep a reading log, record your response there.

3. Why would Rieff want to associate the current "politics of race and ethnicity" with the earlier expression "separate but equal"? Is this an effective argumentative strategy? Why, or why not?

4. J.R.'s introduction mentions "tarring and feathering." Is this just a colorful expression? Do a little library research to find out. What effect does his use of this expression have on your reading of Rieff?

MAKING CONNECTIONS

5. In the reading that starts on p. 436, Rosario Morales proclaims that

"I am what I am and you can't take it away with all the words and sneers at your command." Does Morales's proud assertion of self conflict with Rieff's argument that enhanced self-esteem won't solve anybody's problems?

6. How easy is it to be offended? Annotate any essay in this collection that upset you, focusing on the words, expressions, or stereotypes that provoked your anger. Then write a brief response to the essay.

7. In a short essay, contrast the United States Rieff describes, full of conflicting groups, with that portrayed by Hector St. Jean De Crèvecoeur in "What Is an American?" (p. 380).

JOINING THE CONVERSATION

8. Write an editorial for your school or local paper arguing for or against Rieff's assertion that "[w]e risk everything when we tamper with the First Amendment." Is the statement true or does Rieff overstate his point?

9. Rieff cites Gore Vidal's satiric term "good citizenship history" to challenge those groups that pressure publishers to rewrite history texts so that minorities and women appear in a uniformly favorable light. Drawing upon your own experiences, write an essay exploring to what extent and in what ways history courses and textbooks shape students' attitudes toward such groups.

10. The courts have generally ruled against speech codes such as that at the University of Michigan described in this article. In your class, discuss whether there is any kind of speech you would ban on your campus. Let those who believe bans are useful come up with specific rules or guidelines. Then let those who disagree with speech codes prepare written challenges to those rules.

LINDA CHAVEZ
Toward a New Politics of Hispanic Assimilation

"Hispanic" is a term adopted by federal bureaucrats to describe people in the United States who speak Spanish, but who often have little else in common. Falling under the Hispanic rubric are Puerto Ricans, heavily concentrated in the Northeast; Cuban-Americans, predominantly in Florida; immigrant Mexicans in Texas and California; people of Mexican and Spanish ancestry native to all portions of the Southwest; refugees from El Salvador and Nicaragua; and immigrants from other Latin American countries. Although it obscures significant cultural and political differences, the Hispanic (some prefer "Latino") label confers political clout on this group as a sizable minority in the United States, second in number only to African Americans.

In "Toward a New Politics of Hispanic Assimilation," the last chapter of her book Out of the Barrio *(1991), Linda Chavez describes the reluctance of various Hispanic leaders to champion the path of assimilation followed by immigrants to the United States from Germany, Ireland, Poland, China, and elsewhere. Unlike their leaders, however, most Hispanics are eager to enter the American mainstream, Chavez claims, and they are succeeding in great numbers.*

Chavez (b. 1947) is a senior fellow of the Manhattan Institute for Policy Research and a former member of the U.S. Commission on Civil Rights. In 1986, she ran as a Republican for a U.S. Senate seat from Maryland. I chose to include this reading because Chavez provides an alternative to the mainstream view of minorities as people struggling without hope within a hostile system. She suggests that the political and social destinies of Hispanics are, like those of other minority groups who shaped this country, in their own hands—an empowering and radical notion these days. — J.R.

Assimilation has become a dirty word in American politics. It invokes images of people, cultures, and traditions forged into a colorless alloy in an indifferent melting pot. But, in fact, assimilation, as it has taken place in the United States, is a far more gentle process, by which people from outside the community gradually become part of the community itself. Descendants of the German, Irish, Italian, Polish, Greek, and other immigrants who came to the United States bear little resemblance to the descendants of the countrymen their forebears left behind. America changed its immigrant groups—and was changed by them. Some groups were accepted more reluctantly than others—the Chinese, for example—and some with great struggle. Blacks, whose ancestors were forced to come here, have only lately won their legal right to full participation in this society; and even then civil rights gains have not been sufficiently translated into economic gains. Until quite recently, however, there was no question but that each group desired admittance to the mainstream. No more. Now ethnic leaders demand that their groups remain separate, that their native culture and language be preserved intact, and that whatever accommodation takes place be on the part of the receiving society.

Hispanic leaders have been among the most demanding, insisting that Hispanic children be taught in Spanish; that Hispanic adults be allowed to cast ballots in their native language and that they have the right to vote in districts in which Hispanics make up the majority of voters; that their ethnicity entitle them to a certain percentage of jobs and college admissions; that immigrants from Latin America be granted many of these same benefits, even if they are in the country illegally. But while Hispanic leaders have been pressing these claims, the rank and file have been moving quietly and steadily into the American mainstream. Like the children and grandchildren of millions of ethnic immigrants before them, virtually all native-born Hispanics speak English—many speak only English. The great majority finish high school, and growing numbers attend college. Their earnings and occupational status have been rising along with their education. But evidence of the success of native-born Hispanics is drowned in the flood of new Latin immigrants—more than five million—who have come in the last two decades, hoping to climb the ladder as well. For all of these people, assimilation represents the opportunity to succeed in America. Whatever the sacrifices it entails—and there are some—most believe that the payoff is worth it. Yet the elites who create and influence public policy seem convinced that the process must be stopped or, where this has already occurred, reversed.

From 1820 to 1924 the United States successfully incorporated a population more ethnically diverse and varied than any other in the world. We could not have done so if today's politics of ethnicity had been the prevailing ethos. Once again, we are experiencing record immigration, principally from Latin America and Asia. The millions of Latin immigrants who are joining the already large native-born Hispanic population will severely strain our capacity to absorb them, unless we can revive a consensus for assimilation. But the new politics of Hispanic assimilation need not include the worst features of the Americanization era. Children should not be forced to sink or swim in classes in which they don't understand the language of instruction. The model of Anglo conformity would seem ridiculous today in a country in which 150 million persons are descended from people who did not come here from the British Isles. We should not be tempted to shut our doors because we fear the newcomers are too different from us ever to become truly "American." Nonetheless, Hispanics will be obliged to make some adjustments if they are to accomplish what other ethnic groups have.

LANGUAGE AND CULTURE

Most Hispanics accept the fact that the United States is an English-speaking country; they even embrace the idea. A *Houston Chronicle* poll in 1990 found that 87 percent of all Hispanics believed that it was their "duty to learn English" and that a majority believed English should be adopted as an official language.[1] Similar results have been obtained in polls taken in California, Colorado, and elsewhere. But Hispanics, especially more recent arrivals, also feel it is important to preserve their own language. Nearly half the Hispanics in the *Houston Chronicle* poll thought that people coming from other countries should preserve their language and teach it to their children. There is nothing inconsistent in these findings, nor are the sentiments expressed unique to Hispanics. Every immigrant group has struggled to retain its language, customs, traditions. Some groups have been more successful than others. A majority of Greek Americans, for example, still speak Greek in their homes at least occasionally.[2] The debate is not about whether Hispanics, or any other group, have the right to retain their native language but about whose responsibility it is to ensure that they do so.

The government should not be obliged to preserve any group's distinctive language or culture. Public schools should make sure that all children can speak, read, and write English well. When teaching children from non–English-speaking backgrounds, they should use methods that will achieve English proficiency quickly and should not allow political pressure to interfere with meeting the academic needs of students. No children in an American school are helped by being held back in their native language when they could be learning the language that will enable them to get a decent job or pursue higher education. More than twenty years of experience with native-language instruction fails to show that children in these programs learn English more quickly or perform better academically than children in programs that emphasize English acquisition.

If Hispanic parents want their children to be able to speak Spanish and know about their distinctive culture, they must take the responsibility to teach their children these things. Government simply cannot—and should not—be charged with this responsibility. Government bureaucracies given the authority to create bicultural teaching materials homogenize the myths,

5

---

[1]Jo Ann Zuniga, "87% in Poll See Duty to Learn English," *Houston Chronicle,* July 12, 1990.

[2]Commission on Civil Rights, *The Economic Status of Americans of Southern and Eastern European Ancestry* (Washington, D.C.: GPO, 1986), 45.

customs, and history of the Hispanic peoples of this hemisphere, who, after all, are not a single group but many groups. It is only in the United States that "Hispanics" exist; a Cakchiquel Indian in Guatemala would find it remarkable that anyone could consider his culture to be the same as a Spanish Argentinean's. The best way for Hispanics to learn about their native culture is in their own communities. Chinese, Jewish, Greek, and other ethnic communities have long established after-school and weekend programs to teach language and culture to children from these groups. Nothing stops Hispanic organizations from doing the same things. And, indeed, many Hispanic community groups around the country promote cultural programs. In Washington, D.C., groups from El Salvador, Guatemala, Colombia, and elsewhere sponsor soccer teams, fiestas, parades throughout the year, and a two-day celebration in a Latin neighborhood that draws crowds in the hundreds of thousands.[3] The Washington Spanish Festival is a lively, vibrant affair that makes the federal government's effort to enforce Hispanic Heritage Month in all of its agencies and departments each September seem pathetic by comparison. The sight and sound of mariachis strolling through the cavernous halls of the Department of Labor as indifferent federal workers try to work above the din is not only ridiculous; it will not do anything to preserve Mexican culture in the United States.

Hispanics should be interested not just in maintaining their own, distinctive culture but in helping Latin immigrants adjust to their American environment and culture as well. Too few Hispanic organizations promote English or civics classes, although the number has increased dramatically since the federal government began dispensing funds for such programs under the provisions of the Immigration Reform and Control Act, which gives amnesty to illegal aliens on the condition that they take English and civics classes.[4] But why shouldn't the Hispanic community itself take some responsibility to help new immigrants learn the language and history of

---

[3]In May 1991, a riot broke out in a Latino neighborhood in Washington, D.C., where many new immigrants live (many of them illegal aliens). Both the local and national media described the two nights of arson and looting in political terms, as an expression of the alienation of the Hispanic community. In fact, fewer than half of the people arrested during the incident were Hispanic; most were young black males from a nearby neighborhood. There were few injuries and no deaths, and much criticism was directed at the police by local residents for standing by while young men looted stores, many of which were owned by Latinos. The Washington, D.C., metropolitan area is home to nearly a quarter of a million Hispanics, more than 80 percent of whom live in the suburbs of the city, far from the neighborhood where this incident occurred. Nonetheless, national Hispanic leaders, including members of the Hispanic Congressional delegation, flocked to the scene of the violence to portray as typical of the area's Latino population the problems which occurred in the few blocks of this urban settlement of recent immigrants.

[4]For fiscal year 1989 the federal government distributed nearly $200 million in grants to state and local governments to assist in providing English and civics classes for adults and other services for those eligible for amnesty.

their new country, even without government assistance? The settlement houses of the early century thrived without government funds. The project by the National Association of Latino Elected and Appointed Officials (NALEO) to encourage Latin immigrants to become U.S. citizens is the exception among Hispanic organizations; it should become the rule.

POLITICAL PARTICIPATION

The real barriers to Hispanic political power are apathy and alienage. Too few native-born Hispanics register and vote; too few Hispanic immigrants become citizens. The way to increase real political power is not to gerrymander districts to create safe seats for Hispanic elected officials or treat illegal aliens and other immigrants as if their status were unimportant to their political representation; yet those are precisely the tactics Hispanic organizations have urged lately. Ethnic politics is an old and honored tradition in the United States. No one should be surprised that Hispanics are playing the game now, but the rules have been changed significantly since the early century. One analyst has noted, "In the past, ethnic leaders were obliged to translate raw numbers into organizational muscle in the factories or at the polls. . . . In the affirmative-action state, Hispanic leaders do not require voters, or even protestors—only bodies."[5] This is not healthy, for Hispanics or the country.

Politics has traditionally been a great equalizer. One person's vote was as good as another's, regardless of whether the one was rich and the other poor. But politics requires that people participate. The great civil rights struggles of the 1960s were fought in large part to guarantee the right to vote. Hispanic leaders demand representation but do not insist that individual Hispanics participate in the process. The emphasis is always on rights, never on obligations. Hispanic voter organizations devote most of their efforts toward making the process easier—election law reform, postcard registration, election materials in Spanish—to little avail; voter turnout is still lower among Hispanics than among blacks or whites. Spanish posters urge Hispanics to vote because it will mean more and better jobs and social programs, but I've never seen one that mentions good citizenship. Hispanics (and others) need to be reminded that if they want the freedom and opportunity democracy offers, the least they can do is take the time to register and vote. These are the lessons with which earlier immigrants were imbued, and they bear reviving.

Ethnic politics was for many groups a stepping-stone into the main-   10

---

[5]Peter Skerry, "Keeping Immigrants in the Political Sweatshops," *Wall Street Journal,* Nov. 6, 1989.

stream. Irish, Italian, and Jewish politicians established political machines that drew their support from ethnic neighborhoods; and the machines, in turn, provided jobs and other forms of political patronage to those who helped elect them. But eventually, candidates from these ethnic groups went beyond ethnic politics. Governor Mario Cuomo (D) and Senator Alfonse D'Amato (R) are both Italian American politicians from New York, but they represent quite different political constituencies, neither of which is primarily ethnically based. Candidates for statewide office—at least success-ful ones—cannot afford to be seen merely as ethnic representatives. Ethnic politics may be useful at the local level, but if Hispanic candidates wish to gain major political offices, they will have to appeal beyond their ethnic base. Those Hispanics who have already been elected as governors and U.S. senators (eight, so far) have managed to do so.

EDUCATION

Education has been chiefly responsible for the remarkable advance-ments most immigrant groups have made in this society. European immi-grants from the early century came at a time when the education levels of the entire population were rising rapidly, and they benefited even more than the population of native stock, because they started from a much lower base. More than one-quarter of the immigrants who came during the years from 1899 to 1910 could neither read nor write.[6] Yet the grandchildren of those immigrants today are indistinguishable from other Americans in educational attainment; about one-quarter have obtained college degrees. Second- and third-generation Hispanics, especially those who entered high school after 1960, have begun to close the education gap as well. But the proportion of those who go on to college is smaller among native-born Hispanics than among other Americans, and this percentage has remained relatively constant across generations, at about 10–13 percent for Mexican Americans. If Hispanics hope to repeat the successful experience of genera-tions of previous immigrant groups, they must continue to increase their educational attainment, and they are not doing so fast enough. Italians, Jews, Greeks, and others took dramatic strides in this realm, with the biggest gains in college enrollment made after World War II.[7] Despite more than

---

[6]Richard A. Easterlin, "Immigration: Economic and Social Characteristics," in Stephan Thernstrom, ed., *Harvard Encyclopedia of American Ethnic Groups* (Cambridge: Harvard Univer-sity Press, 1981), 478.

[7]See Richard Alba, *Ethnic Identity: The Transformation of White America* (New Haven: Yale University Press, 1990), 7. Both men and women born after 1930 showed large gains, although the gains were higher for men, probably reflecting the increase in college attendance by veterans under the G.I. Bill.

two decades of affirmative action programs and federal student aid, college graduation rates among native-born Hispanics, not to mention immigrants, remain significantly below those among non-Hispanics.

The government can do only so much in promoting higher education for Hispanics or any group. It is substantially easier today for a Hispanic student to go to college than it was even twenty or thirty years ago, yet the proportion of Mexican Americans who are graduating from college today is unchanged from what it was forty years ago. When the former secretary of education Lauro Cavazos, the first Hispanic ever to serve in the Cabinet, criticized Hispanic parents for the low educational attainment of their children, he was roundly attacked for blaming the victim. But Cavazos's point was that Hispanic parents must encourage their children's educational aspirations and that, too often, they don't. Those groups that have made the most spectacular socioeconomic gains—Jews and Chinese, for example—have done so because their families placed great emphasis on education.

Hispanics cannot have it both ways. If they want to earn as much as non-Hispanic whites, they have to invest the same number of years in schooling as these do. The earnings gap will not close until the education gap does. Native-born Hispanics are already enjoying earnings comparable to those of non-Hispanic whites, once educational differences are factored in. If they want to earn more, they must become better educated. But education requires sacrifices, especially for persons from lower-income families. Poverty, which was both more pervasive and severe earlier in this century, did not prevent Jews or Chinese from helping their children get a better education. These families were willing to forgo immediate pleasures, even necessities, in order to send their children to school. Hispanics must be willing to do the same—or else be satisfied with lower socioeconomic status. The status of second- and third-generation Hispanics will probably continue to rise even without big gains in college graduation; but the rise will be slow. Only a substantial commitment to the education of their children on the part of this generation of Hispanic parents will increase the speed with which Hispanics improve their social and economic status.

ENTITLEMENTS

The idea of personal sacrifice is an anomaly in this age of entitlements. The rhetoric is all about rights. And the rights being demanded go far beyond the right to equality under the law. Hispanics have been trained in the politics of affirmative action, believing that jobs, advancement, and even political power should be apportioned on the basis of ethnicity. But the rationale for treating all Hispanics like a permanently disadvantaged group is fast disappearing. What's more, there is no ground for giving preference in jobs or promotions to persons who have endured no history of discrimination in this country—namely, recent immigrants. Even within Hispanic groups, there are great differences between the historical discrimination faced by Mexican Americans and Puerto Ricans and that faced by, say, Cubans. Most Hispanic leaders, though, are willing to have everyone included in order to increase the population eligible for the programs and, therefore, the proportion of jobs and academic placements that can be claimed. But these alliances are beginning to fray at the edges. Recently, a group of Mexican American firemen in San Francisco challenged the right of two Spanish Americans to participate in a department affirmative action program, claiming that the latter's European roots made them unlikely to have suffered discrimination comparable to that of other Hispanics. The group recommended establishing a panel of twelve Hispanics to certify who is and who is not Hispanic.[8] But that is hardly the answer.

Affirmative action politics treats race and ethnicity as if they were   15 synonymous with disadvantage. The son of a Mexican American doctor or lawyer is treated as if he suffered the same disadvantage as the child of a Mexican farm worker; and both are given preference over poor, non-Hispanic whites in admission to most colleges or affirmative action employment programs. Most people think this is unfair, especially white ethnics whose own parents and grandparents also faced discrimination in this society but never became eligible for the entitlements of the civil rights era. It is inherently patronizing to assume that all Hispanics are deprived and grossly unjust to give those who aren't preference on the basis of disadvantages they don't experience. Whether stated or not, the essence of affirmative action is the belief that Hispanics—or any of the other eligible groups—are not capable of measuring up to the standards applied to whites. This is a pernicious idea.

Ultimately, entitlements based on their status as "victims" rob Hispanics of real power. The history of American ethnic groups is one of overcoming disadvantage, of competing with those who were already here and proving themselves as competent as any who came before. Their fight was always to be treated the same as other Americans, never to be treated as special, certainly not to turn the temporary disadvantages they suffered into the basis for permanent entitlement. Anyone who thinks this fight was easier in the early part of this century when it was waged by other ethnic groups does not know history. Hispanics have not always had an easy time of it in the United States. Even though discrimination against Mexican Americans and Puerto Ricans was not as severe as it was against blacks, acceptance has come only with struggle, and some prejudices still exist.

---

[8]"Spanish Progeny Are Not Hispanic, S.F. Group Insists," *San Diego Union,* Nov. 24, 1990. Ironically, both Spanish American firemen would have been promoted in the department even without benefit of affirmative action; they received the third- and sixth-highest scores on exams administered to sixty-eight persons for twenty promotion slots.

Discrimination against Hispanics, or any other group, should be fought, and there are laws and a massive administrative apparatus to do so. But the way to eliminate such discrimination is not to classify all Hispanics as victims and treat them as if they could not succeed by their own efforts. Hispanics can and will prosper in the United States by following the example of the millions before them.

QUESTIONING THE TEXT

1. According to Chavez, what process statistically obscures the success of Hispanic assimilation into the United States?
2. What in Chavez's views might have made her so controversial that she was "disinvited" from speaking on several college campuses during the years (1983–85) she served on the U.S. Commission on Civil Rights? Who might have a vested interest in silencing her political views?
3. Does the introduction provide you with sufficient information about Chavez? What other information might you have liked to have?

MAKING CONNECTIONS

4. Compare the attitudes toward immigrant assimilation described or implied in Crèvecoeur's "What Is an American?" (p. 380) and Chavez's piece.
5. Explore the difference in style between Chavez's writing and Rosario Morales's "I Am What I Am" (p. 436). Why does each writer create the tone and mood she does? In what ways do the styles of these writers support their messages?
6. Read Langston Hughes's poem on p. 439, "Theme for English B." How does the poem speak to Chavez's comments about education for Hispanics? Record your answer in your reading log, if you are keeping one.

JOINING THE CONVERSATION

7. Chavez argues that real economic progress for Hispanics will be stifled until their families place a greater emphasis on education. Is she just reciting a pious platitude, or can education make a difference? Write a narrative about the role education has played in your own life or that of your family. Then form a group with two or three classmates and compare your stories.

8. Chavez claims that Hispanic leaders place greater emphasis on citizens' rights than on their obligations: "Spanish posters urge Hispanics to vote because it will mean more and better jobs and social programs, but I've never seen one that mentions good citizenship." Is this a tendency limited to minority politics, or has Chavez identified a more general problem with contemporary leaders? What are the consequences of such attitudes?
9. In class, discuss the implications of Chavez's assertion that "[t]he government should not be obliged to preserve any group's distinctive language or culture." Then write a short position paper on the issue.
10. Write a proposal paper in which you suggest how parents of any group might place a greater emphasis than they now do on the importance of education. Be sure to begin this proposal paper by defining a problem—in this case, it might be a high dropout rate in high school, or low enrollments in college.

ROSARIO MORALES
I Am What I Am

ROSARIO MORALES (b. 1930) describes herself as a "New York Puerto Rican living in Cambridge, Massachusetts—a feminist independentist and communist since 1949." A native of Manhattan, she farmed and raised a family with her husband in Puerto Rico before moving back to the mainland, where she says she broke "a lifetime of silence" to write. She has produced a number of essays and in 1986 she and her daughter, Aurora Levins Morales, published Getting Home Alive, *a collection of vignettes, memoirs, stories, and poems. In 1990 Morales received the Boston Contemporary Writers Award, as a result of which her poem "The Dinner" was emblazoned on a wall of a Boston train station.*

The essay reprinted here appeared in what has become a classic text of feminism by and for women of color, Cherríe Moraga and Gloria Anzaldúa's This Bridge Called My Back. *So influential was this 1981 collection that it was published in a second edition in 1983 and is widely used in college courses. For a chapter on cultural diversity in this book, I naturally turned to it, and indeed I could have chosen any of its contents for inclusion here. I chose this particular essay because, like Morales, I am a lover of accents and dialects; I love the sounds of speech. I also like the questions that she implicitly raises about what it means to be an American, for her experiences in many ways clearly fall outside those described by Crèvecoeur, whose treatment of "the American" as a male implicitly excludes Morales and other women.*   – A.L.

I am what I am and I am U.S. American   I haven't wanted to say it because if I did you'd take away the Puerto Rican but now I say go to hell   I am what I am and you can't take it away with all the words and sneers at your command   I am what I am   I am Puerto Rican   I am U.S. American   I am New York Manhattan and the Bronx   I am what I am I'm not hiding under no stoop   behind no curtain   I am what I am   I am Boricua as boricuas come from the isle of Manhattan and I croon Carlos Gardel tangoes in my sleep and Afro-Cuban beats in my blood and Xavier Cugat's lukewarm latin is so familiar and dear   sneer dear but he's familiar and dear   but not Carmen Miranda   who's a joke because I never was a joke   I was a bit of a sensation   See! here's a real true honest-to-god Puerto Rican girl and she's in college   Hey! Mary   come here and look she's from right here   a South Bronx girl and she's honest-to-god in college now   Ain't that something   who would believed it Ain't science wonderful or some such thing a wonder a

436   wonder

And someone who did languages for a living stopped me in the subway because how I spoke was a linguist's treat   I mean there it was yiddish and spanish and fine refined college educated english and irish which I mainly keep in my prayers   It's dirty now   I haven't said my prayers in decades but try my Hail Marrrry full of grrrace with the nun's burr with the nun's disdain   its all true and its all me   do you know I got an English accent from the BBC I always say   For years in the mountains of Puerto Rico when I was 22 and 24 and 26   all those young years   I listened to the BBC and Radio Moscow's English   english announcers announce and denounce and then I read Dickens all the way thru three or four times at least and then later I read Dickens aloud in voices and when I came back to the U.S. I spoke mockdickens and mockBritish especially when I want to be crisp efficient I know what I am doing and you can't scare me   tough   that's why I am what I am and I'm a bit of a snob too   Shit! why am I calling myself names   I really really dig the funny way the British speak   and it's real it's true   and I love too the singing of yiddish sentences that go with shrugs and hands and arms doing melancholy or lively dances   I love the sound and look of yiddish in the air   in the body   in the streets   in the English language   nooo   so what's new   so go by the grocer and buy some fruit   oye vey   gevalt gefilte fish   raisele   oh and those words hundreds of them dotting the english language like raisins in the bread shnook and schlemiel   suftik   tush schmata   all those soft sweet sounds saying sharp sharp things   I am what I am and I'm naturalized Jewish-American   wasp is foreign and new but Jewish-American is old show familiar   schmata familiar and its me dears its me   bagels blintzes and all   I am what I am   Take it or leave me alone.

QUESTIONING THE TEXT

1. Go through this brief text and note every word or phrase that is unfamiliar to you. Then, working with three or four classmates, make a list of terms unfamiliar to any of you, divide up the list, and look up the terms. Have the group member who looked up each term provide a brief definition of it and one or two sentences explaining what it means in the context of Morales's piece. Then reread the entire text.

2. With several classmates, take turns reading this piece aloud. Then freewrite individually for 10 to 15 minutes on differences you noted in the readings, particularly on any of Morales's points that struck you during a certain reading and that hadn't occurred to you before. Finally, have each member of the group write in one or two sentences what Morales's major point is. Compare your sentences and see in

what ways you agree or disagree on the major point. Bring these sentences to class for discussion.

3. A.L. tells us directly why she admires Morales's essay; she tells us somewhat less directly why *we* should value it. Find information and language in her headnote to this essay that "argues" for our favorable reaction.

MAKING CONNECTIONS

4. Try to write a very brief definition of "American" that Morales might accept. Then compare it with the definition offered implicitly by Linda Chavez (p. 426) or by Hector St. Jean De Crèvecoeur (p. 380).
5. Would Morales agree with Chavez that "Hispanics should be interested . . . in helping Latin immigrants adjust to their American environment and culture"? Why, or why not?

JOINING THE CONVERSATION

6. What is your ethnic background? Do some investigation if necessary and then write a passage, about as long as Morales's but in whatever style you prefer, entitled "I Am What I Am."
7. What accent or dialect or language is particularly appealing or intriguing to you? Do a bit of research by listening carefully to speakers with that accent or of that dialect or language and noting down what you like to listen to, as Morales says she loves "the singing of yiddish sentences." Then write a paragraph or two in support of your thesis that "I really _____ the _____ way the _____ speak."
8. Write a paragraph of response to Morales's last sentence.

LANGSTON HUGHES
Theme for English B

AS A YOUNG MAN in Joplin, Missouri, Langston Hughes (1902–67) worked as an assistant cook, a launderer, and a busboy—jobs similar to ones you may have held—before leaving to attend Columbia University in New York City. (He eventually graduated in 1929 from Lincoln University in Pennsylvania.) A prolific writer and part of the great artistic movement of the 1920s and 1930s known as the Harlem Renaissance, Hughes worked in many genres—novels, short stories, plays, essays, and poems. From his early collection of poems, The Weary Blues *(1926), to his posthumous volume of essays,* Black Misery *(1969), he explored numerous themes touching on the lives of African Americans, including that of higher education.*

The poem that follows, from 1926, describes one event in the speaker's college career and raises questions about relationships between instructors and students, between those "inside" the university and those "outside." It is one of my favorite poems, one of the few special ones I carry around with me and, in fact, now find that I know "by heart." With every new class I teach, I think of Hughes's "Theme for English B," for it speaks volumes to me about the necessity of respecting individual differences while at the same time valuing those bonds that link us to one another. – A.L.

The instructor said,

> Go home and write
> a page tonight.
> And let that page come out of you—
> Then, it will be true. 5

I wonder if it's that simple?

I am twenty-two, colored, born in Winston-Salem.
I went to school there, then Durham, then here
to this college on the hill above Harlem.
I am the only colored student in my class. 10
The steps from the hill lead down to Harlem,
through a park, then I cross St. Nicholas,
Eighth Avenue, Seventh, and I come to the Y,
the Harlem Branch Y, where I take the elevator
up to my room, sit down, and write this page: 15

It's not easy to know what is true for you or me
at twenty-two, my age. But I guess I'm what

I feel and see and hear. Harlem, I hear you:
hear you, hear me—we two—you, me talk on this page.
(I hear New York, too.) Me—who?   20

Well, I like to eat, sleep, drink, and be in love.
I like to work, read, learn, and understand life.
I like a pipe for a Christmas present,
or records—Bessie,* bop, or Bach.

I guess being colored doesn't make me not like   25
the same things other folks like who are other races.
So will my page be colored that I write?
Being me, it will not be white.
But it will be
a part of you, instructor.   30
You are white—
yet a part of me, as I am a part of you.
That's American.

Sometimes perhaps you don't want to be a part of me.
Nor do I often want to be a part of you.   35
But we are, that's true!
As I learn from you,
I guess you learn from me—
although you're older—and white—
and somewhat more free.   40

This is my page for English B.

IN RESPONSE

1. Near the end of the poem, the speaker says, addressing his instructor,
   "You are white—/yet a part of me, as I am a part of you./That's
   American." What do you think Hughes means by "American"?
2. The speaker of this poem notes that given who he is, his theme will
   not be "white," but he goes on to say that it will still be "a part of
   you, instructor." What do you think he means? Can you describe a
   time when you've had a similar experience?
3. Shelby Steele writes at length (in the reading starting on p. 102) of
   the myth of inferiority among African American youths. What (if any)
   evidence of a myth of inferiority do you find in Hughes's poem? How
   might Hughes respond to Steele's essay?

Bessie: Bessie Smith (1898?–1937), a famous blues singer

4. Would Hughes—or his teacher—be likely to be found in John Henry Newman's ideal university, as described in the reading starting on p. 34? Why, or why not?
5. Consider what effects your own gender, race, class, or family background has had on your success in school. Then write a brief (one- or two-page) essay explaining those effects.
6. Brainstorm with two or three classmates about whether it is important for students to identify with their teachers, to have a number of things in common with them. Come to an agreement among yourselves on how to answer this question, and then write one page explaining why you answered it as you did.

OTHER READINGS

Hacker, Andrew. "The Myths of Racial Division." *New Republic* 23 Mar. 1992: 21–25. Examines what statistics say about racial division in the United States.

Hill, Patrick J. "Multi-Culturalism: The Crucial Philosophical and Organizational Issues." *Change* July–Aug. 1991: 38–47. Examines the debates about multiculturalism in higher education.

Hughes, Robert. "The Fraying of America." *Time* 3 Feb. 1992: 44–49. Examines the controversy over political correctness.

Jordan, June. "Toward a Manifest New Destiny." *Progressive* Feb. 1992: 19–23. Engages with the PC controversy and argues for expanding the so-called canon in education.

Katz, Jacob. "Accounting for Anti-Semitism." *Commentary* June 1991: 52–54. Traces historical roots of anti-Semitism.

Konner, Melvin. "The Stranger." *Why the Reckless Survive . . . and Other Secrets of Human Nature*. New York: Viking, 1990. 65–74. Suggests that human beings may be biologically programmed to fear difference.

Lee, Alice. "Spinsterhood and the Chinese Lesbian Group: A Visit to My Aunts." *Out the Other Side: Contemporary Lesbian Writing*. Ed. Christian McEwen and Sue O'Sullivan. Freedom, CA: The Crossing P, 1989. 4–7. Looks at "Spinsterhood as a way of life."

Leo, John. "Why All Villains Are Thin, Middle-Aged WASPS." *How the Russians Invented Baseball*. New York: Delacorte, 1989. 110–16. Pokes fun at sensitivity.

Mura, David. "Strangers in the Village." *The Graywolf Annual Five: Multi-Cultural Literacy*. Ed. Rick Simonson and Scott Walker. St. Paul, MN: Graywolf P, 1988. Explores the sometimes inability of white colleagues and neighbors of the author, a Japanese American, to "come to terms with the differences between us" and the role that anger can play in confronting such inabilities.

Porter, Rosalie Pedalino. *Forked Tongue: The Politics of Bilingual Education*. New York: Basic, 1991. Suggests that bilingual programs in our schools don't work.

Walker, Scott, ed. *The Graywolf Annual Seven: Stories from the American Mosaic*. St. Paul, MN: Graywolf P, 1990. Illustrates interactions between minority and mainstream cultures.

Yamato, Gloria. "Something About the Subject Makes It Hard to Name." *Making Face, Making Soul = Haciendo Caras: Creative and Critical Perspectives by Women of Color*. Ed. Gloria Anzaldúa. San Francisco: Aunt Lute Foundation Books, 1990. Analyzes racism.

Legends: I Want a Hero

8

*"The winnah, and still heavyweight champeen of the world
. . . Joe Louis."*
MAYA ANGELOU, *Champion of the World*

*Why would the state of New Mexico . . . advertise the doings of a
century-old murderer, a gang member, a buck-toothed rube with a hot temper
and no morals, no compunction about taking human life?*
JAKE PAGE, *The Life—and Legend—of Billy the Kid*

*At this point I felt that, if I did stand up, it meant that I approved of the
way I was being treated, and I did not approve.*
MARCIA McADOO GREENLEE, *An Interview with Rosa Parks*

Now it is Eleanor Roosevelt's turn to have her private life exhumed.
ELLEN GOODMAN, Knowing *Eleanor Roosevelt*

*It is a sure sign that a culture has reached a dead end when it is no longer
intrigued by its myths . . . .*
GREIL MARCUS, *Elvis: Presliad*

Madonna is the future of feminism.
CAMILLE PAGLIA, *Madonna—Finally, a Real Feminist*

"A man. A legend. A way of life."
TERRY EASTLAND, *Rush Limbaugh: Talking Back*

*[Malcolm] would make you angry as hell, but he would also
make you proud.*
OSSIE DAVIS, *Why I Eulogized Malcolm X*

*As an example of charity, Live Aid couldn't be worse. Charity entails
sacrifice. Yet the Live Aid performers are sacrificing nothing. Indeed,
they're gaining public adulation and a thoroughly unmerited good opinion
of themselves.*
P. J. O'ROURKE, *Fiddling While Africa Starves*

I have come to claim/Marilyn Monroe's body/for the sake of my own.
JUDY GRAHN, *The Marilyn Monroe Poem*

Introduction

"I WANT A HERO," says the English poet Lord Byron (1788–1824) in the introduction to *Don Juan*, his satiric epic about the legendary lover. In fact, every country, every culture, every people that we know of shares at least one thing in common: they all tell stories, stories that are often about the legends and heroes and heroines who reflect a society's deepest values and goals. In the United States, many legends tell varying narratives of America and Americans—legends based on real people like George Washington, Pocahontas, or Malcolm X or on mythical figures like Paul Bunyan, Br'er Rabbit, or White Buffalo Woman. In addition to these cultural legends, many smaller, more intimate groups (such as families) tell legends that pass on traditions from generation to generation. You may indeed have such legends in your family or in some other group you belong to.

Where do such legends come from? How are heroes and heroines created? Who in our own society, for instance, can become "hero material"—and who cannot? What values and attitudes do we find reflected in the legends and heroes characteristic of American cultures? And finally, in what ways may such values clash with one another? In short, under what circumstances may one person's hero be another person's villain, one person's powerful legend another person's meaningless tale? These are questions central to this chapter's conversation, for each of the readings in it treats a legend or hero and, in doing so, implicitly explores what it means to be "a legend" as well as what functions legends fulfill in our personal and public lives.

As we made the difficult choices necessary to come up with final selections for this chapter, we have been interested to note that one of us has tended to choose legends and heroes from public political life—Rosa Parks, Eleanor Roosevelt, Malcolm X—while the other has tended to choose from popular culture—Billy the Kid, Madonna, Elvis. Why not begin this chapter by making your own list of your most significant legends and heroes? As you do so, you may benefit from considering any or all of the following questions:

1. How would you define a legend? A hero/heroine?

2. Make a list of the legends or heroes that have been or are most important in your own life. What do such legends represent to you? Get together with two or three classmates to compare your lists, noting the differences in your choices.

3. How do you think heroes/heroines get made? What characteristics are necessary for someone (or something) to become a legend or hero?

4. Does your family have any legends or stories that are passed down from generation to generation? What are they?

5. Are your heroes the same as those of your parents? Why, or why not?

• • •

MAYA ANGELOU
Champion of the World

Bᴏʀɴ ɪɴ Sᴛ. Lᴏᴜɪs ɪɴ 1928, *Maya Angelou spent her youth in Arkansas and California, a period described evocatively in her autobiographical* I Know Why the Caged Bird Sings *(1970), the volume from which the following excerpt is taken. She has written four more books about her eventful life, which among other things has included jobs as a Creole cook, a cocktail waitress, a dancer, a singer, a streetcar conductor, and a coordinator for the Southern Christian Leadership Conference. She has also published six volumes of poetry and was invited by Bill Clinton to compose a poem to read during his inauguration as president of the United States. Currently a professor of American studies at Wake Forest University, Angelou says that she quite simply loves writing, loves "the sense of achievement" when she's "almost got the sentence right."*

In the chapter that appears below, Angelou has gotten many such sentences right. In them, she tells about her childhood memories of her grandmother and uncle's store, a center of activity for the black people in their small Arkansas community, on the night that Joe Louis, the boxer who symbolized the ideals and hopes of African Americans, was to defend his title as world heavyweight champion against a white contender. This brief chapter exemplifies the way in which a sport and a particular athlete can take on the symbolic hopes and fears of an entire group. For the people gathered around the radio on this evening in the 1930s, Joe Louis was a hero fighting not only for the title but also for dignity and justice for black people everywhere.

I chose this chapter from Angelou's book because she is herself a hero and legend to me, even as she writes about another legend, Joe Louis. In addition, I have always particularly liked this chapter because I too can remember sitting around a radio as a very small child, feeling warm and happy in the circle of my grandmother and other family members and friends. — A.L.

The last inch of space was filled, yet people continued to wedge themselves along the walls of the Store. Uncle Willie had turned the radio up to its last notch so that youngsters on the porch wouldn't miss a word. Women sat on kitchen chairs, dining-room chairs, stools, and upturned wooden boxes. Small children and babies perched on every lap available and men leaned on the shelves or on each other.

The apprehensive mood was shot through with shafts of gaiety, as a black sky is streaked with lightning.

"I ain't worried 'bout this fight. Joe's gonna whip that cracker like it's open season."

"He gone whip him till that white boy call him Momma."

At last the talking finished and the string-along songs about razor   5
blades were over and the fight began.

"A quick jab to the head." In the Store the crowd grunted. "A left
to the head and a right and another left." One of the listeners cackled like
a hen and was quieted.

"They're in a clinch, Louis is trying to fight his way out."

Some bitter comedian on the porch said, "That white man don't mind
hugging that niggah now, I betcha."

"The referee is moving in to break them up, but Louis finally pushed
the contender away and it's an uppercut to the chin. The contender is
hanging on, now he's backing away. Louis catches him with a short left to
the jaw."

A tide of murmuring assent poured out the door and into the yard.   10

"Another left and another left. Louis is saving that mighty right . . ."
The mutter in the Store had grown into a baby roar and it was pierced by
the clang of a bell and the announcer's "That's the bell for round three,
ladies and gentlemen."

As I pushed my way into the Store I wondered if the announcer gave
any thought to the fact that he was addressing as "ladies and gentlemen"
all the Negroes around the world who sat sweating and praying, glued to
their "master's voice."*

There were only a few calls for RC Colas, Dr Peppers, and Hires root
beer. The real festivities would begin after the fight. Then even the old
Christian ladies who taught their children and tried themselves to practice
turning the other cheek would buy soft drinks, and if the Brown Bomber's
victory was a particularly bloody one they would order peanut patties and
Baby Ruths also.

Bailey and I laid the coins on top of the cash register. Uncle Willie
didn't allow us to ring up sales during a fight. It was too noisy and might
shake up the atmosphere. When the gong rang for the next round we pushed
through the near-sacred quiet to the herd of children outside.

"He's got Louis against the ropes and now it's a left to the body and   15
a right to the ribs. Another right to the body, it looks like it was low . . .
Yes, ladies and gentlemen, the referee is signaling but the contender keeps
raining the blows on Louis. It's another to the body, and it looks like Louis
is going down."

My race groaned. It was our people falling. It was another lynching,
yet another Black man hanging on a tree. One more woman ambushed and

---

their "master's voice": a reference to a long-standing symbol of RCA Victor recordings,
which features a dog apparently listening to an old-fashioned phonograph with the caption
"His Master's Voice"

raped. A Black boy whipped and maimed. It was hounds on the trail of a man running through slimy swamps. It was a white woman slapping her maid for being forgetful.

The men in the Store stood away from the walls and at attention. Women greedily clutched the babes on their laps while on the porch the shufflings and smiles, flirtings and pinching of a few minutes before were gone. This might be the end of the world. If Joe lost we were back in slavery and beyond help. It would all be true, the accusations that we were lower types of human beings. Only a little higher than apes. True that we were stupid and ugly and lazy and dirty and, unlucky and worst of all, that God Himself hated us and ordained us to be hewers of wood and drawers of water,* forever and ever, world without end.

We didn't breathe. We didn't hope. We waited.

"He's off the ropes, ladies and gentlemen. He's moving towards the center of the ring." There was no time to be relieved. The worst might still happen.

"And now it looks like Joe is mad. He's caught Carnera* with a left   20
hook to the head and a right to the head. It's a left jab to the body and another left to the head. There's a left cross and a right to the head. The contender's right eye is bleeding and he can't seem to keep his block up. Louis is penetrating every block. The referee is moving in, but Louis sends a left to the body and it's an uppercut to the chin and the contender is dropping. He's on the canvas, ladies and gentlemen."

Babies slid to the floor as women stood up and men leaned toward the radio.

"Here's the referee. He's young. One, two, three, four, five, six, seven . . . Is the contender trying to get up again?"

All the men in the store shouted, "NO."

"—eight, nine, ten." There were a few sounds from the audience, but they seemed to be holding themselves in against tremendous pressure.

"The fight is all over, ladies and gentlemen. Let's get the microphone   25
over to the referee . . . Here he is. He's got the Brown Bomber's hand, he's holding it up . . . Here he is . . ."

Then the voice, husky and familiar, came to wash over us—"The winnah, and still heavyweight champeen of the world . . . Joe Louis."

---

hewers . . . water: a reference to the biblical verse Joshua 9:23, which in the King James Version reads "Let them live; but let them be hewers of wood and drawers of water unto all the congregation." The verse, referring to the Gibeonites after their surrender to Joshua's forces, was often cited by those arguing that blacks were naturally or divinely destined to perform menial physical labor.

Carnera: an apparent error by Angelou. Primo Carnera fought Louis only once, in 1935, two years before Louis became world heavyweight champion, so the fight she recalls must have involved a different contender.

Champion of the world. A Black boy. Some Black mother's son. He was the strongest man in the world. People drank Coca-Colas like ambrosia and ate candy bars like Christmas. Some of the men went behind the Store and poured white lightning in their soft-drink bottles, and a few of the bigger boys followed them. Those who were not chased away came back blowing their breath in front of themselves like proud smokers.

It would take an hour or more before the people would leave the Store and head for home. Those who lived too far had made arrangements to stay in town. It wouldn't do for a Black man and his family to be caught on a lonely country road on a night when Joe Louis had proved that we were the strongest people in the world.

QUESTIONING THE TEXT

1. What is the attitude toward Louis of the crowd gathered at the store? Point out places in the text that allow you to identify this attitude. Is Angelou's attitude the same as that of the other listeners she describes? What supports your answer to this question?
2. Why does Angelou put quotation marks around "master's voice"? List all the reasons you can think of.
3. Read this story aloud, noting those places where the language sounds "spoken" instead of "written." What effect does the use of the sounds and rhythms of spoken English have on the story?
4. Why do you think A.L., as she says in her introduction to the reading, sees Angelou herself as a hero and a legend?

MAKING CONNECTIONS

5. In his essay on Elvis Presley (p. 478), Greil Marcus touches on those elements that made Elvis a legend. What elements does Angelou draw on to establish Joe Louis's legendary status? How do they compare with those cited by Marcus? If you are keeping a reading log, record your answers to these questions there.
6. Angelou might have called Louis "Our Shining Black Prince." What does Louis have in common with the Malcolm X described by Ossie Davis (p. 500)? In what ways do the two legends differ? Write a paragraph or two comparing and contrasting them.

JOINING THE CONVERSATION

7. Jot down what you know or have heard about Joe Louis. Then do a little research about him and prepare a brief summary of his career

for your class. In what ways does what you find out about Louis agree or disagree with what Angelou says about him?

8. Working with two other classmates, devise a new "national game" that would be the "perfect" game for America. Give it a name, decide on its rules, and create a "legend" who would epitomize its appeal and its characteristics. Come to class ready to describe the game and its legendary hero to your classmates.

JAKE PAGE
The Life—and Legend—of Billy the Kid

THE UNITED STATES ISN'T OLD ENOUGH for its legends to have petrified. We are still in the process of shaping them. Billy the Kid, for instance, died barely a century ago in New Mexico, a click of the snooze alarm by Egyptian or Chinese standards. So diligent researchers can pry into the records, read old newspaper accounts, roam Billy's haunts in New Mexico, and debunk the best parts of this gunslinger's fable.

But that's not exactly what Jake Page does in the following article, "The Life—and Legend—of Billy the Kid." As it turns out, the making of Billy's legend is at least as interesting as the buck-toothed twenty-one-year-old behind it.

In his own day, Billy seems to have caught the public's attention for his combination of youth, intelligence, and daring. He was also in the right place at the right time, a New Mexico Territory still rugged enough to shelter desperadoes, but civilized enough to have journalists eager to describe them. Today, we'd probably call Billy a punk or make him a veejay on MTV.

Page's article originally appeared in Smithsonian *in 1991. I picked it because it makes a readable point about the way legends get made. —* J.R.

What do Paul Newman, Aaron Copland, Gore Vidal, Kris Kristofferson and the University of Illinois Department of Biomedical Visualization have in common? Along with a host of other actors (including Robert Taylor and the memorable Lash LaRue), novelists (like Zane Grey and Larry McMurtry), poets, historians, composers and folklorists, a choreographer and plain cranks, they have participated in the ongoing ballyhoo, now more than a century old, that arose even before a young man born in New York City became a corpse in New Mexico—a young man named Henry McCarty, then Henry Antrim, then William Bonney and finally Billy the Kid.

Billy the Kid, the monster who shot 40 men, or maybe it was 21 (one for each year of his short life), or maybe . . . 4? Billy the Kid, "a little, small-sized cow-and-horse-thief who lived grubbily," according to one account; and by others "courteous," "a gentleman," "generous," the Robin Hood of the American frontier, a young man surrounded by corruption and greed who had to follow his own moral code, a kind of Jeffersonian egalitarian caught up in the empire-building rape of the West, a tragic hero, a romantic hero, an antihero, a juvenile delinquent, a brilliant marksman, a terrible shot, a practiced dancer, a lady's man, a slob, a short-tempered rube, left-handed, right-handed, shot dead by a sheriff named Pat Garrett sometime around midnight in the town of Fort Sumner on July 14, 1881, or . . . the shooting was a hoax and Billy escaped and ran off to Texas, taking the name of Ollie (Brushy Bill) Roberts or, no, he ran off to western New Mexico and died there, a reclusive old rancher, in 1937.

According to Janean Grissom, a handsome blonde woman who looks like the proprietor of the sort of ranch you can see in the movie *Giant,* these impostors are "just senile old men having a dream." Janean is president of what has recently erupted as the Billy the Kid Outlaw Gang, which issues a license plate and an infrequent bulletin to its 800 members. The Gang hosts a grand fete in the summer in Lincoln County, New Mexico, where many of Billy's exploits took place (Janean and her husband own the property near Fort Sumner where Billy the Kid surrendered to Pat Garrett—of which more later). The Gang is looked upon with great favor by New Mexico's tourist department.

Why would the state of New Mexico decide that one of the best ways to get people to come and spend money within its borders is to advertise the doings of a century-old murderer, a gang member, a buck-toothed rube with a hot temper and no morals, no compunction about taking human life? The reason is that Billy the Kid sells. He resonates, even today during the active academic debunking of the Old West.

Historians today—the few that worry about such things—are bent on 5 demythologizing the West, the Frederick Jackson Turner idea of the frontier as a formative feature of the American character. Charles Russell's* cowboys are out. The men of the West were often inward, uncommunicative chauvinists like the folks in Larry McMurtry's *Lonesome Dove.* They destroyed Indian cultures, the land and everything else, including most of themselves— a bunch of drunks with the sense of boys and the weapons of men. Their influence in the West has been blown out of all proportion, these historians say, compared with the role of women, Indians, Hispanics and blacks, and with the importance of, well, anything: economics, transportation, the Civil War, trade unionism, whatever. Billy the Kid? A nasty little nobody, yes, but with no effect on Western history or even on the outcome of the Lincoln County War, itself a degrading squabble between two greedy merchants.

Billy, nevertheless, is apt to remain with us. An authentic if violent folk hero, or a two-bit delinquent, the problem is getting to the truth about him—the facts. This has been made difficult by the process of myth making that had already set in a few months before the Kid's death, thanks to a ravenous hunger east of the 100th meridian for gory news of the rawboned West, and thanks to the florid prose and imaginations of the Western news-

---

Charles Russell (1864–1926): an American painter and sculptor whose work often depicts cowboys

paper editors, all of whom would have felt at home in the offices of the *National Enquirer*. The Las Vegas, New Mexico, *Optic* called him a "young demon" and "urged by a spirit hideous as hell."

In Silver City, New Mexico, in 1875, Billy, age 15, had his first real brush with the law. His mother, Catherine McCarty, had died of tuberculosis. He was caught with some clothes stolen from a Chinese laundry, was jailed and escaped by climbing up and out through the chimney. After only two years, following a stint in Arizona where he learned the use of horses and guns, engaged in some relatively harmless horse thievery, and shot and killed a man who had bullied him relentlessly, he emerged in southeastern New Mexico with the name William Bonney. Not till later did he become known as Billy the Kid.

Then as now, celebrity distorts, and historians have had a run for their money trying to find the real Billy amid all the accretions that have built up like a series of coral reefs.

Why did this foreshortened life, one played out quite sordidly, capture the American imagination to the point of producing the premier outlaw figure in the vast panoply of outlaws who spattered the frontier with lead and derring-do?

Apparently, if you want to be a hero of mythic proportion, it helps   10
to have origins that are a bit mysterious. The records show two Henry McCartys born in New York City in 1859, a few months apart. No one knows or probably will ever know which one became Billy the Kid. There is no record of a father. There is only one known real photograph of William Bonney, a tintype by an itinerant photographer in Fort Sumner in 1879. According to the Kid's most distinguished biographer, Robert Utley, former chief historian for the National Park Service, there were four tintypes of Billy. (Some tintype cameras had four lenses and so made four images simultaneously.) Because tintype images are reversed, a lot of people were led to believe that Billy had been a southpaw (there was even a movie made about the Kid called *The Left-Handed Gun*). Three of the tintypes are missing, and the picture of Billy seen in books is a reproduction of a reproduction of the remaining one, showing what appears to have been a slope-shouldered, dopey-looking youth wearing a stupid hat and a silly grin—a hillbilly. It pays to look at the original image, located in the Lincoln County Heritage Trust Museum in the largely restored town of Lincoln, which shows a more chiseled face of challenging intelligence.

In 1936, a former shepherd named José García y Trujillo was interviewed about the Kid by a researcher for the New Mexico Federal Works Project and spoke of his extraordinary quickness of mind. Speaking of the Kid, García y Trujillo "pointed to his forehead and then with a quick motion to the sky. '*Un función eléctrica,*' he said. Something that worked like lightning." The Kid was too smart to have been trapped by Pat Garrett, the old man ventured. " 'You think Billy the Keed let himself be shot in the dark like that? No, *señora*—Billy the Keed?—never. I see Billy the Keed with these eyes. Many times, with these eyes.' ''

Many of the Kid's Hispanic friends in New Mexico died convinced that Billy escaped death at the hands of Garrett. Such frail beliefs are fed by the fact that, while there is a coroner's report, there is no death certificate. The Kid is still not legally dead, and in spite of a marker in Fort Sumner, no one is certain where he is buried. In 1950 a man called "Brushy Bill" Roberts from Hico, Texas, aided by a lawyer, claimed to be Billy and was so convincing that arrangements were made to have New Mexico's governor award Brushy Bill the pardon the Kid had always wanted. But Brushy Bill was illiterate, and Billy the Kid, when he was Henry McCarty, had fed his fantasies by reading the *Police Gazette.** And it was unlikely that Brushy Bill could speak or understand Spanish, in which Billy was fluent. At a time when the Hispanics and the Anglos in New Mexico got along uneasily at best, the Hispanics loved Billy—in particular the women. Said a Texas belle: "He was the best-natured kid and had the most pleasant smile I most ever saw in a young man."

In any event, we have at least three basic Billy the Kids: the one who was shot and killed at age 21; the one who escaped and lived a long life as a recluse or a braggart, far from Lincoln; and the totally malleable Billy who lived on in the mind of America, unkillable like Elvis, and who has since been sinner and saint.

We know a lot about Billy, thanks to historian Utley and his recent book *Billy the Kid: A Short and Violent Life.* The first professional historian to have taken a serious whack at the Kid, Utley told me that this distinction put him in a difficult position: right beween the pros who scoff at wasting time on such trivia, and the amateurs for whom the Kid is paramount, nearly sacrosanct, and who "will not want to hear the historical truth. They'll keep him left-handed, if that's the way they've seen him up to now."

All right, then: the *true* Kid, according to Utley.   15

He reemerged in New Mexico at age 17, in 1877, at a time when an ugly situation was building up in that territory's southeastern quadrant, which comprised Lincoln County. A group led by James Dolan in Lincoln held a monopoly on buying cattle and produce from nearby ranchers to sell to the government as rations for Indians and the Army installation at Fort Stanton. The monopoly was being challenged by a newly arrived young Englishman, John Tunstall, who wanted to get rich quick just like everybody else at the time.

This was a period, according to Utley, when a frontier ethic ruled in

---

Police Gazette: The National Police Gazette: New York, a lurid illustrated tabloid of news, sports, and sensational events established in 1845

those parts: you didn't allow an insult to go unchallenged; you didn't put much value on a human life; you probably had more than one gun with you at all times; and you were probably tipsy, if not downright drunk, all day long.

The young William Bonney evidently did not drink, but like many other impressionable youths whose older peer group subscribed to a pretty exciting ethic, he had surely bought the rest of the concept. In Lincoln he found himself allied with the Tunstall forces, a loose, posselike group called the Regulators, and almost immediately became embroiled in a lethal and sloppy "war." Each side consisted of true believers who claimed the law was on their side. The Regulators ambushed the Lincoln County sheriff and shot several other men.

Meanwhile, they had been surrounded in the house of Tunstall's lawyer. The siege lasted several days before the clever and resourceful Bonney, who proved to be something of an escape artist, worked out and implemented an escape plan.

By the time the Lincoln County War ran out of gas in 1880, with the   20 principals of both sides either dead or bankrupt, the adolescent Bonney had participated in the group-shooting of five men and had singlehandedly killed one, the bully in Arizona. There were warrants out all over Lincoln County for his arrest as a murderer, along with the other Regulators. Except for Billy, virtually everyone involved got pardoned or let off one way or another.

After the Lincoln County War, Billy drifted around the territory as a fugitive. He hooked up with one or another bunch of cronies to rustle some Texas cattle over to New Mexico, made money beating people at cards in saloons (he was very good at the game of monte) and went to dances, which he loved. He was also fond of singing, his favorite tune being "Turkey in the Straw." During this period he shot another bully in a barroom, a Texan named Joe Grant, who was drunk and making generalized challenges to the world. Complimenting Grant on his ivory-handled revolver, Billy took the gun from Grant's holster, looked at it admiringly, spun the cylinder deftly and handed it back. As Grant got more menacing, Billy challenged him and then turned his back. When Grant fired, his gun's pin fell on an empty chamber in the cylinder—where Billy had set it. Billy spun around and blew Grant away.

Self-defense? Entrapment? Anyway, it was the "second killing with which the Kid can be solely and incontestably credited," according to Utley.

By then, locals were getting upset at all the violence. Pat Garrett, a former buffalo hunter, was elected sheriff of Lincoln County with the express task of cleaning up the likes of Billy the Kid. In due course, Billy and a small group of rustler friends were trapped by Garrett and a large posse in a stone house at Stinking Springs (now a ruin on Janean Grissom's spread). After a long shoot-out one of Billy's friends was killed, as was a horse that died in the doorway, blocking Billy from making a dramatic escape on his own horse. The desperadoes surrendered and Billy was stashed in jail.

"The laugh's on me this time," Billy told a reporter, who later described him: ". . . there was nothing very mannish about him in appearance. . . . He is about five feet eight or nine inches tall, slightly built and lithe, weighing about 140; a frank open countenance, looking like a school boy, with the traditional silky fuzz on his upper lip; clear blue eyes, with a roguish snap about them; light hair and complexion. He is, in all, quite a handsome looking fellow, the only imperfection being two prominent front teeth slightly protruding like a squirrel's teeth, and he has agreeable and winning ways."

Perhaps the most famous (true) event in the Kid's life (aside from his death) was his escape from the courthouse jail in the town of Lincoln. In handcuffs and leg-irons, he nonetheless managed to get hold of a guard's gun and shoot him dead, then shoot another guard dead with a shotgun. Freeing himself of his shackles, he escaped on horseback before an awed crowd on Lincoln's single street.   25

Instead of lighting out for Mexico or some other remote and safe place, Billy returned to the salubrious haunts of Fort Sumner, where he had friends. In a house there, on July 14, 1881—perhaps after a nocturnal tryst with a young Hispanic woman—he wandered out of his room into that of the house's owner, Pete Maxwell. Noting another presence in the gloom, Billy asked in Spanish, *"Quien es?"* ("Who is it?") Pat Garrett's reply was a bullet that conclusively dispatched Billy.

And that was that.

The Kid's death was noted as far away as England. The New York *Daily Graphic* said he "had built up a criminal organization worthy of the underworld of any of the European capitals. He defied the law to stop him and he stole, robbed, raped and pillaged . . . he became, in the short span of his twenty-one years, the master criminal of the American southwest."

This understated obituary proved predictive. About 12 dime novels published between 1881 and 1906 all portrayed Billy the Kid as Satan's lieutenant on Earth, an utterly ruthless, bloodthirsty killer whose death at the hands of Pat Garrett symbolized the welcome end of savagery and lawlessness in the West. With a ghostwriter, Garrett produced his own version of history, *The Authentic Life of Billy the Kid, Noted Desperado of the Southwest, Whose Deeds of Daring and Blood have Made His Name a Terror in New Mexico, Arizona & Northern Mexico,* in which he attempted to show a few good features in the Kid's makeup, but pointed out forcefully that, with the Kid no longer around, Lincoln County was now a peaceful place.

After a two-decade lapse of interest, as cultural historian Stephen Tatum has pointed out, after 1925 the public rediscovered Billy "as a quix-otic, romantic idealist who symbolized a lost pastoral world." He became at best a Robin Hood figure, at worst a misguided youth caught up in a   30 difficult world. His first killing, it was said (in the initial Book-of-the-Month Club selection, *The Saga of Billy the Kid*), was to avenge an insult to his mother; the others, to avenge the death of his employer Tunstall. This was the view that informed Johnny Mack Brown's 1930 movie *Billy the Kid:* the good outlaw, increasingly isolated, serving the cause of justice, if not the law. By 1938, though, the boy had become a relentless, amoral killer in the popular ballet *Billy the Kid,* by Eugene Loring and Aaron Copland.

In the 1940s, a string of B movies with the likes of Buster Crabbe presented Billy as a populist hero protecting the countryside in the manner of the Lone Ranger. In the 1950s, Paul Newman played the Kid twice—in a Gore Vidal television drama and in a movie—both times as a James Dean–like rebel without a cause.

From that point on, Billy pops up all over the place. He was a romantic hero who warded off Count Dracula, of all things, in 1966. He was a doomed avenger in John Wayne's macho *Chisum*; a symbol of the loss of individual freedom in Sam Peckinpah's dreary *Pat Garrett and Billy the Kid.* After these films of the 1970s he dropped from national view, to reemerge in the late '80s.

Larry McMurtry followed his highly successful novel *Lonesome Dove* with the eerie, aberrant tale *Anything for Billy*, in which a Billy the Kid figure (called Billy Bone) goes through a long series of adventures that have no relation whatsoever to any historical aspects of Billy the Kid. McMurtry's Billy emerges as a rather petulant and needy youth, a terrible marksman, impetuous and often lethal, but vague. In the company of a beautiful female scientist named Cecily Snow, he reminds the narrator "of one of the nearly transparent fish Cecily had shown me. . . . An outline was visible, but the fish—as you ordinarily think of it, with guts and fins and scales—didn't seem to be there."

Then two movies, *Young Guns* and a sequel, evidently made for a youthful audience, actually portrayed Billy as a kid—an attractive-looking but troubled and short-tempered adolescent. Their message, after much violence, is, in essence: say no to violence. In all, there have been more than 40 movies about the Kid.

Meanwhile, an Albuquerque publisher, Helen Airy, turned up evi-   35
dence of what she is convinced is an escaped and retired Billy the Kid: a man named John Miller, who lived on a ranch near Ramah, New Mexico, until his death in 1937. A mysterious man with a hidden stash of money, and a penchant for guns, he evidently told several people he was the Kid. They included an adopted son and a Canadian lawman to whom he gave a pistol. The gun wound up in the hands of another Canadian, who discovered that it is an 1880 Army revolver and could have been the Kid's.

Helen Airy supplied the Lincoln County Heritage Trust with two photographs of John Miller. They have been sent to the University of Illinois in Chicago, where a computer-enhanced study of 25 facial characteristics in the "Billy tintype" has already been checked against photographs of Brushy Bill and 150 convicted Chicago felons of both sexes. Forensic anthropologist Clyde Snow has declared that 40 convicts bear more resemblance to Billy than does Brushy. Now John Miller's and a dozen other photographs are to be examined.

"There isn't a shred of evidence, not a single credible piece of paper, that suggests that Billy the Kid didn't die on July 14, 1881, or that these other guys were the Kid," says Robert Utley. No expert takes those claims seriously, but people cherish the legend, and a few just need Billy to have lived on.

"On the other hand," Utley continues, "behind the legend is a truly interesting human being." There were, it seems, two Billy the Kids: an outer one of sunshine and merriment, banter and laughter, and an inner, calculating Billy, steely and dangerous. "When he was rough," said somebody who knew him, "he was as rough as men ever get to be. . . ."

"The main thing to remember about Billy the Kid," according to Utley, "is that he was just that—a kid among men. Most 21-year-olds are rebellious, and Billy was consistently rebellious. And when others realized it was time to stop using violence as a form of persuasion, Billy simply wouldn't conform. That was his undoing."

And, of course, that is why he continues to ride across the landscape   40
of the American consciousness—elusive, irrepressible, lethal, an insouciant reminder that in matters of conformity and rebellion, violence and civility, justice and corruption, we Americans can't make up our minds.

QUESTIONING THE TEXT

1. According to Page, the legend of Billy the Kid is a gold mine for tourism in the state of New Mexico. Why do you think that's so?
2. Page briefly mentions revisionist historians of the American West who minimize the role of cowboys and gunslingers to focus on the influence of Native Americans, women, Hispanics, and blacks. Are such historians likely to tell a more complete or accurate story than earlier ones? Why, or why not? Is Page's essay a revisionist version of the life of Billy the Kid?
3. What did you find the most surprising information in Page's retelling of Robert Utley's account of Billy?
4. What does J.R.'s introduction to this reading assume that readers already know about Billy? Is that a safe assumption? Should the introduction have paid more attention to historical details?

MAKING CONNECTIONS

5. Elsewhere in this chapter, Maya Angelou describes Joe Louis (p. 446) and Camille Paglia discusses Madonna (p. 486). How useful might these articles be a hundred years from now for a writer like Jake Page writing a magazine piece about Louis or Madonna? Are the pieces factual enough to provide dependable information? Do they convey some sense of why Louis and Madonna became conspicuous figures in the twentieth century?

6. Ellen Goodman suggests in "*Knowing* Eleanor Roosevelt" (p. 474) that "every generation writes its own history." In what ways has that been true of Billy the Kid's legend? In a paragraph, explain what we might see in him now that earlier decades missed.

JOINING THE CONVERSATION

7. Working with a group of two or three classmates, try to define the essential features of the Billy the Kid legend—what most people know about him, what aspects of his personality make him attractive, what accomplishments make him famous. Then make a list of other American figures or fictional characters (in novels, television, or movies) who share similar traits. Write a paragraph summarizing your findings.

8. The most recent major films about Billy the Kid are probably *Young Guns* and *Young Guns II*. But there have been many others. *Halliwell's Filmgoer's and Video Viewer's Companion* lists more than ten, including *Pat Garrett and Billy the Kid* (1974), *Billy the Kid Meets Dracula* (1966), *The Left-Handed Gun* (1958), and *The Kid from Texas* (1949). Rent any film on Billy the Kid and write a comparison between the film's version of him and Page's.

9. Write an exploratory essay about the ideas raised in the last paragraph of Page's essay. Is what he asserts about the American character especially evident today: "in matters of conformity and rebellion, violence and civility, justice and corruption, we Americans can't make up our minds"?

MARCIA McADOO GREENLEE
An Interview with Rosa Parks

ON DECEMBER 1, 1955, *Rosa Parks (b. 1913) boarded a bus in Montgomery, Alabama. She ended her ride by making history, becoming surely and swiftly a legend in her own time by refusing to give up her seat to a white passenger. This act may seem a simple and uncontroversial one now, but it was not so in 1955. At that time, schools and other institutions in the South were still largely segregated by race, as were public facilities such as buses, where African Americans were expected to "step to the back of the bus." Rosa Parks chose to resist this system, and although she was jailed for her transgression, it led to a massive boycott of the Montgomery bus system under the leadership of a young clergyman named Martin Luther King, Jr., a boycott that ended segregation on the city's buses and launched King's career as a civil rights leader.*

In the following transcript of a 1978 interview (part of the Black Women Oral History Project*), Parks speaks of her childhood, her responsibilities, her schooling, her marriage to another civil rights worker, and her lifetime of working for human dignity and freedom. Reading these understated and very modest responses to the interview questions, you may have a hard time telling that Parks is honored throughout the world for her steadfast commitment to such ideals, that she was awarded the Martin Luther King, Jr. Nonviolent Peace Prize in 1980 and an honorary degree from Mt. Holyoke College in 1981. She seems unconcerned with such honors, returning repeatedly to her central concerns—to care for her family and those around her and to make "whatever contribution I can make."*

Rosa Parks has long been one of my own personal heroines, a woman who managed to stand up for her people—by quietly and persistently keeping her seat on that bus. To me, she represents the difference that just one person can make. — A.L.

MARCIA M. GREENLEE: Could you tell me something about your family background?

ROSA PARKS: My mother was a teacher in the rural schools in Alabama, and my father was a carpenter. When they married, they moved to Tuskegee and started keeping house, and that's where I was born. Shortly after I was about, maybe not quite two years old, my father wanted to go to the North to live and work and he . . . they broke up housekeeping. My mother came back to the rural part of Montgomery County, Pine Level, Alabama, to live with her parents, my grandmother and grandfather. This was when my brother was born.

MMG: This was Pine Level?

RP: Yes, Pine Level, Alabama. It was in Montgomery County, about thirty miles south of Montgomery, the capital of Alabama. I can remember when I was quite small my mother was teaching in a one-teacher rural school . . . various places in the county. Sometimes they would be the church buildings where she would hold classes, with one, two . . . It was through the sixth grade, I believe it was. . . .

MMG: So then you stayed in Alabama in the Pine Level area until you   5 married? Is that right or did you move?

RP: No, I attended school in Montgomery, the city of Montgomery, from the time I was eleven years old until I finished—well, I didn't finish high school—until I had to leave high school.

MMG: Did you live with relatives then, or board or . . .

RP: I lived with my mother's sister most of the time, and sometimes other people. I stayed once in a while with one of my mother's girlfriends. But most of the time I spent was with my mother's sister.

MMG: What are your memories of that early schooling?

RP: Well, it's hard for me to recall. The school that I was attending was an   10 all girls school with white women teachers and principal, women who came from various parts of the North to teach, and they were all unmarried women. I suppose they must have had dedication, because at that time, being white and teaching black children, they were separated from the white community. They lived in a building next to the school building—that was their dormitory where they lived. We were taught, aside from just the regular reading, writing and arithmetic, we were taught home economics and sewing—I guess home economics would be the same thing—cooking and sewing. It's a little difficult for me to express any special interest, because I know Miss White, the principal, was a very strict disciplinarian, and she always saw to it that the girls were not liars, or that they dressed neatly, wore no jewelry. She frowned on— we called it bobbed hair, at that time—cutting of the hair, and so on. . . .

MMG: . . . What do you remember about leisure activities when you were a girl?

RP: I didn't have too much leisure. Well, first of all, when I was going to Miss White's school, it was a private school, and there was a tuition fee. I can't remember what the amount was, but my mother obtained what was called a scholarship, where I could clean two classrooms after school and sweep the floor and dust the desks and tidy it up for the evening. But it really meant that I didn't have to . . . that she didn't have to pay tuition for me. At that time, I lived quite a long way from school, so I was walking home from school. Then, going to where I lived, there would be general chores around the house, getting my uniform washed and cleaning it for the next day, and doing other things around the house. I lived with my aunt, she was quite ailing in health, she worked at that time at the Jewish country club. Because she was so ill she would take me along with her children to the place where she worked, and you know, help her do some of the work that she couldn't do, cleaning and doing dishes, and so on. And we did a great deal of work under her supervision, it was a job. And there were times when we would go just walking along the roadside through the woods, because this was not right downtown, this was out on the edge of the city, and pick berries. And occasionally we would, if enough of us children could get together and we'd have a little time, we might play a little ball. But I never had a whole lot of leisure time just to play. There was always duties and things to do. When we were in Pine Level, however, I used to go fishing with my grandmother a great deal and I rather enjoyed that, because we'd catch the fish and then we'd have some fish for supper when we got home. . . .

MMG: When you were young, were you ever thinking about what you might do when you grew up?

RP: There wasn't a great deal to think about when I . . . There were not too many opportunities. My mother had hoped, I think, that I would be a teacher, but life as a teacher in a rural community seemed so very hard that it didn't appeal to me at that time that much. I was concerned with trying to get an education and be prepared to have a career. I thought very strongly of nursing when I was real young. I suppose with so many ill members of the family, I felt a sympathy for ill people. Of course, I myself was not too strong. I had suffered tonsillitis when I was still a baby, about two years old. I think my tonsils were removed at the age of eleven, just before my mother put me to school in Montgomery. After that I didn't get into any nurse training, I had a lot of experience with the family and friends . . .

MMG: You had been doing that.   15

RP: . . . I sewed quite a bit, although I didn't feel like I wanted to sew for a living. I found myself doing quite a bit of that for myself and my cousins and others. I remember I did sewing for the family of a friend, and I often remember that she was very economical with material, and she could have a piece of material and make a dress for myself out of one, she made for herself and some of the neighbors.

MMG: What was the role of the church in your life during that period? Were you much involved with church activities?

RP: Yes, church, and Sunday school also, all the time in Montgomery. It was one of the events that I could look forward to. I have always liked to attend church . . . all the people in the church would be singing and praying. I can remember enjoying hymns, singing hymns, say the Lord's Prayer, you know, even when I was a child—it was just a part of my life. And we are members of the A.M.E. church—that is the African Methodist Episcopal church—and we had a group called the Allen Christian Endeavor League, that would meet on Sundays, just before the night prayers. . . .

MMG: Were there, apart from your family and your church, any other persons or events in those early years that you would say were important influences on you?

RP: Do you mean racially, or just as a person in any way . . . 20

MMG: Well, of any nature. Of any nature, including racially.

RP: I believe . . . well, my mother was my teacher while . . . part of the time when I was in rural school. I think about three years . . . I remember my mother's teaching very well, that she was very sincere . . . She didn't just put the work before the youngsters. If they needed any help, she would take time out to make sure that they were learning what she was teaching. One of the things that I always appreciated about her was if there was anything that came up of a racial nature, she never impressed upon me, that even with segregation and going through a schoolhouse that was just a little shack—you might call it a shack, a building with no glass windows—that it was the way it was supposed to be. And sometimes my grandfather and grandmother, also—these are my mother's parents—I learned what it was like for them as small children during slavery and before Emancipation. In our family, that's how we referred to the time of Emancipation as when the Yankees came through . . . The hardships, the struggles, before the Yankees came through, to let the people know, the slaves know, that they were free. I felt that I was fortunate not to have been a child during that time, and that there was such a person as Abraham Lincoln who signed the Emancipation Proclamation. But I couldn't understand why, if we were free people, that we had to be deprived of the better things, like a building. . . .

MMG: In 1933 you married Raymond Parks. Is this in Tuskegee?

RP: No, I didn't marry him in Tuskegee. And we married in 1932.

MMG: Oh, 1932. 25

RP: It was in Pine Level, my mother's home.

MMG: Oh, I see. Would you tell me a little about your husband?

RP: Well, he was a barber in Montgomery, Alabama. I was eighteen, he was maybe twenty-two at the time. He was also an orphan, he didn't have a living mother or father. He was living in Montgomery, working in a barber shop, the Atlas barber shop. One of the things that interested me most [about him was] the fact that he was very neat, very thin, very serious behavior. His interest was with the Scottsboro case,* working

---

the Scottsboro case: a famous case in which nine African American youths were charged with raping two young white women in Alabama in 1931. They were twice tried and convicted, but the convictions were overturned on various grounds (including the recantation of her testimony by one of the women), and the case became a leading cause among liberals and leftists nationwide, who mounted a campaign for the defense. Eventually charges against five

to free them, so he would tell me about the trial, what was going on, what was happening. And he would tell me some of the things that happened to him as a child. He had been deprived of an education and yet in appearance you would never believe that he was an illiterate person. In fact, I don't think he was illiterate, because he taught himself to read when he was in school. He would tell me about his grandmother, his grandfather. His father and his mother did not remain together—they had separated. He never knew him. His mother was dead. Some of the tragic things that he . . . Well, he came from Randolph County, Alabama, the little place that he was born was called . . . where he lived in Roanoke, Alabama, some of the experiences that he had. He was from a community where there were very few black people. One of the reasons that he didn't attend school until later . . . There were no schools at all where he could go unless he could go to a white school, but the nearest what we called, colored school, was too far away for him to get there. So at that time, he was about ten years old, his grandfather and grandmother both were ill and he had to do what he could, try to work to help them, cook for them. I think they'd have wished that he spent . . . About 1913, when he was ten, and I was just a baby—and he didn't have shoes, didn't have food much of the time, [didn't] get enough food, he had a rough time of it. When he left Roanoke and went to Tuskegee, and he went . . . I think he said he started school—that was after his mother, she had another child . . . At her death, he moved in with a cousin and he started going to school when he was twenty-one years old.

MMG: And he was starting out then at the beginning?

RP: Yes, going to school, I think he advanced to the seventh grade of school.   30
He went to Tuskegee Institute, he got to go to school there—not that that . . . Somewhere, either at Roanoke or somewhere he tried to pick up a trade as a barber. But [he did] other work: farming, mill work, janitor—what we called a sexton down South—of a white church. Tuskegee for a while, then he decided to go to Montgomery but he had planned to attend school somewhere in the vicinity of Montgomery, but didn't have the time. However, he went to Montgomery and became a barber there. . . .

MMG: So the two of you shared the commonality of early hard experiences, hard work. Even though you were young people, you had heavy responsibilities, both of you, and interest in the racial situation. Did you have other interests in common?

---

of the defendants were dropped, three others who had been convicted in a third trial were paroled, and the ninth escaped to Michigan, where the government refused to return him to Alabama.

RP: I think we did. I'm sure we must have, because I enjoyed, I just enjoyed listening to him. I didn't talk a great deal. I was rather quiet, and he, I enjoyed listening to him talk about whatever he wanted to talk about. One of the things that . . . He was a very gentle person, very polite. I didn't know exactly what to say, I guess, because I hadn't been, I hadn't . . . The few boys—not too many—that I had been in the company of were of a different disposition and they were all right, I guess, but I suppose it didn't matter.

MMG: Well, you and your husband moved to Detroit in—what was it—1957?

RP: Yes.

MMG: How did you make a living together in the South before you came 35 to Detroit?

RP: Well, he was a barber, and some of the time I stayed home and did sewing at home, very little money because living expenses were high. And then I did some work for [insurance]. Finally in about . . . well, during the war time, I started working at night. Sometimes I'd do some sewing and I left that and started doing insurance work, so I worked for the [Metro Life] Insurance Company, had a small [position]; then I gave that up, and started working for an office as a clerk. . . .

MMG: You were active in the Montgomery chapter of the NAACP. When did you begin work . . .

RP: That was the early 1940's. I think it was 1943. I found myself secretary before I even . . . I had read about it, the Scottsboro case. My husband was active before I was. People considered the registering to vote . . .

MMG: Well, what were some of the projects that the NAACP was involved in once you began work with them?

RP: When I first started as secretary, at the early date, we were not doing 40 that much. Well, mostly having meetings, I remember discussing the segregation issue, but it doesn't seem like we were actually doing anything special. I think the very first things I remember working on was a rape case involving a young black serviceman in Georgia whose father lived in Montgomery, and a white woman whose brother had been . . . from childhood. We didn't have any legal representation in Montgomery, and if we could get a person who had been violated in any way to sign an affidavit, they would have to apply to the Department of Justice in Washington.

MMG: There were no black attorneys to represent them.

RP: No, and no white attorneys in the early years, except there was one that I remember. In other words, if one would take a case for a person, the white community ostracized [them] . . .

MMG: On the first of December 1955, you refused to give up your seat to a white passenger on a Montgomery bus. Your action and the subsequent developments from that action resulted in a Montgomery bus boycott, which in turn launched a new phase in the civil rights struggle. Other black passengers could have refused to give up their seats. The person next to you on the bus could have remained seated beside you. But everyone else dutifully acquiesced to the white bus driver's demand that they move. Only you stayed in your seat. Why?

RP: I think it was because I was so involved with the attempt to bring about freedom from this kind of thing. I had seen so much within reach on the basis of the Whitney Young* experience under the same situation that I felt that there was nothing else I could do to show that I was not pleased with. . . . People have said that I was a great democrat, people say things like that, but I was not conscious of being . . . I felt just resigned to give what I could to protest against the way I was being treated, and I felt that all of our meetings, trying to negotiate, bring about petitions before the authorities, that is the city officials, really hadn't done any good at all. And as long as we continued to give them our patronage . . . I recall Mr. Eddie Mitchell saying that he had a committee that had gone before the bus company for the extension of the bus line to the same area and the community where most of our people lived, instead of them having to walk an hour, or whatever length of time it was . . . And then came the [time] to propose it, and they were told that as long as they thought . . . was there any need of them extending the line? This wasn't conscious in my mind at that moment, but so many incidences where I think that always make it appear that if a few of us form a committee, which [try to] have this thing remedied . . . make it appear that that was what we wanted. And they were pleased that they didn't have to extend it, as long as we accepted it to be that way. At this point I felt that, if I did stand up, it meant that I approved of the way I was being treated, and I did not approve.

MMG: Had you ever broken any segregation laws or practices previously?   45

RP: I had not, to a great extent, but I hadn't . . . I started to think about some of the times . . . I, this to me . . . First of all, I wanted to say that at this point on the bus ride, I didn't consider myself breaking any segregation laws that I wanted . . . because he was extending what we considered our section in the bus. I had refused on any number of occasions to give my fare at the front of the bus, and then go around to the back to get in. That was another thing that some of the bus drivers would do. See, all of the bus drivers did not practice the same . . . it was not uniform. There were just certain bus drivers that would insist on you going to the back after you give him the fare. You would step up in the bus, get in the bus, and then step back off the bus and go around to the

---

Whitney Young (1921–71): the leader of the National Urban League, a leading civil rights organization, during the height of the civil rights movement in the 1950s and 1960s

rear to enter. And neither did all of them ask you to stand up if there was white people standing. So it seemed like each driver was at his own discretion.

MMG: And this was a zealous one that you encountered that night.

RP: It seemed to be.

MMG: What was the reaction of the other black people on the bus when this happened?

RP: They didn't any of them say anything to me. Some few did get off the bus, and I know some of them asked for a transfer, and then some just got off by [the] main door. But during the time when I was there, all remained the same exactly where they were.

MMG: Nobody tried to interfere with what was going on between you and the white driver?

RP: No.

MMG: Did you resent that in any way?

RP: No.

MMG: Did you expect some support?

RP: No, I didn't. It didn't even enter my mind. Because I knew the attitude of people. It was pretty rough to go against the system to the extent that you might not . . . There was one man who was on the bus, he lived next door to where we lived, and he could have if he'd wanted to, gotten off the bus to let my husband know that I was arrested. My husband thinks kind of hard of him for not at least telling him what had happened on the bus. Because he knew him very well. And then there was another man who got on the bus, and he got on just after me, 'cause I spoke to him as he was stepping on the bus. He asked me a few days later if I had needed him as a witness, and I said I didn't even remember . . .

MMG: Did you ever find out the name of that bus driver? Was there ever any direct reference to him in the legal matters that developed later?

RP: Oh, yes. I remember his name very shortly. His last name was Blake. I can't remember his initial.

MMG: What does he think about the incident in retrospect? Do you remember what he said?

RP: I can't remember exactly what he said. As far as he was concerned, it was all in his duty.

MMG: What was your family's reaction? Your mother and brother and husband?

RP: Well, my mother was pretty upset when I called her. She answered the telephone, and I told her I was in jail. And I don't remember exactly what my brother said to me, he was here, in Detroit, not Montgomery. I'll have to find out, better than I, if she can remember anything special. I know he was . . . I don't know if he was so surprised or not, but he was pretty upset, too, I'm sure. He didn't want us to . . .

MMG: During any of this time, just after the incident occurred, and you were taken off and arrested, and broken arrest, yet did you ever feel fearful?

RP: Well, it was a strange feeling because you always feel that something could . . . even before the incident of my arrest, I could leave home feeling that anything could happen at any time . . . harassment. I think the hardest days I had were when I was still working in the department store. I would see some of the people who worked in the store, and I don't know whether there was anything personal to it, I could see their attitude, the attitude they had. Some of them were very . . . well, they didn't say anything to me, but they were just, they'd ignore me as though I wasn't there.

MMG: Were you ever involved with the Montgomery Improvement Association, or the boycott that followed, in a policy making capacity?

RP: I was on the board—I'm trying to think, board of directors—and I sat in on some meetings, but I didn't have too much time to be in the actual planning. But I did for a short while. But at that time, while so much of this was being fought, and so many plans were being made, I was being invited away from Montgomery quite a bit. I don't remember—it's hard to remember now, except that I did as many as I could, if I could, and if they called on me, if they had any marching or anything, if I could.

MMG: How did you come to Detroit?

RP: You mean, how did I travel?

MMG: Well, no, not that so much as what made you decide to go ahead and come?

RP: Because my brother was living here.

MMG: And you and your husband felt that conditions just weren't going to get better immediately where they were?

RP: Well, they were not any too good. Of course, it was quiet before there was any disturbance or any harassment at that time. And my mother wanted to spend as much time as she could with the two of us and she couldn't spend time with him if she remained with me there. And if she left me there, then she felt uneasy, I think. Part of our . . . , she and my brother got together more so than I did, and found a place for us to move, for us to live, and we came.

MMG: What was life like for you and your husband after you moved to Detroit?

RP: Well, it was not any too easy. Well, shortly after I moved to Detroit, I was offered a job and accepted one in Hampton, Virginia, at Hampton Institute. I earned a little money, and he was working in a barber school. He didn't have a Michigan license or anything, so he had to pass the examination, be officially [licensed]. He was working in a barber school for a man of our [race], teaching some apprentice barbers the work and training them.

MMG: Did you get any, ever get any specific support from civil rights groups   75
during this time when you first went to Detroit? Did they try and offer
you employment or see that you were taken care of or anything?

RP: I didn't get any work, but I went to a lot of meetings, and sometimes
when they would take up contributions, but that was never high.

MMG: Ten years after you came to Detroit, there were race riots here in the
city. What were your feelings about the progress of the civil rights
movement at that point?

RP: I actually . . . I mean, I would see that . . . I would associate the
activity of the burning and looting, and so on, with what I had done
and would have done. And yet, on the other hand, if you looked beneath
the surface, we could see the frustration of some of these people, they
could see the deprivation. I guess for whatever reasons it came about, I
felt that something had to be wrong with the system.

MMG: So you could understand it, although it might not have been the way
you would have gone about it.

RP: That's true. But it did . . . it was a very, very severe blow to my   80
husband, who wasn't well at the time. It was just something he just
couldn't deal with at all, especially right near us, because we were within
a half a block, a short block from where quite a bit of that was going
on, and this particular grocery store that was looted so very much by
some of the people right around us, and then some we knew and some
that we didn't know. It upset him very much because when he was
working, these people had given him quite a bit of work, and had been
his customers. And that upset him a great deal, he just couldn't, it was
such a severe thing to him, that he couldn't eat or sleep. They had a
curfew, and he wouldn't stay inside, and he was threatened by some of
the officers, I think the National Guard, because he didn't stay inside the
house. All the time, he would be outside looking, seeing what was going
on. Took him to the doctor, he had to have a sedative to quiet his nerves,
and it was hard on all of us.

MMG: Do you have any preference among the terms "Negro," "colored,"
and "black"?

RP: Well, I've gotten into using "black" quite a bit, and I never really cared
for the particular word "colored." Years ago, "Negro" was considered
proper. But I actually would prefer it if I didn't have to use any kind of
racial terms . . . more concerned with humanity, and not be so much
involved that every person has to be labeled racially.

MMG: I wanted to ask you a couple of questions about integration. Do you
see integration as open access to institutions, or does it also involve social
contact with white people? You know, being with them, or just being
where they are, in their schools, or also in their homes, at parties, in
their churches, that kind of thing.

RP: I haven't given it too much thought, other than the fact that I feel that people should be free to associate with any person that they choose, without having to think in terms of their race, if that's what they want to do. I don't think anyone should be ostracized or circumscribed or denied association or contact with another person as long as they're part of the world.

MMG: Do you think that there's any danger to black institutions such as   85
churches and schools and some clubs from integration?

RP: I hadn't thought of any.

MMG: Is there any reason that all-black institutions, some of them, should be preserved if they want?

RP: I hadn't actually thought of that either. Well, it would be good to be able to appreciate their heritage. I don't know whether that could be done if there were finally complete integration or not. I hadn't gone into that in my mind too much.

MMG: Well, just a couple of last questions about the women's movement— is that all right. It's 11:30. I just wanted to ask you what you thought of the women's movement.

RP: In the past few years, it's been so popular. That's another thing that I   90
hadn't searched my mind too closely on. I have been involved so much in kind of family matters, illness and death of my husband, my mother's illness.

MMG: When you hear talk about liberated women, does that mean anything particular to you, or do you feel you've been pretty well liberated all your life?

RP: Well, I feel to some extent in my mind that I have been liberated, not physically always, but at least my thinking.

MMG: There was a film on television recently on King. Did you see that?

RP: Yes, I did.

MMG: And what did you think of the depictions?   95

RP: You mean, the actors?

MMG: Yes, and the way that the movement was represented.

RP: I felt that the representation stressed more violence and conflict than the actual peace and harmony and love that Dr. King would have wanted it to be. And the person who portrayed him, a good actor, to my mind, did not capture Dr. King's manner as I remember it, his position, actions, the way he spoke.

MMG: How about the way that you were represented?

RP: She did quite good. As I remember it, she spoke the words that I   100
did. When she got up and left the bus, she didn't look around at anybody to see . . . I remember doing that. I remember just walking right off the bus, with the officers when they told me I was arrested, not looking at anybody or noticing what anybody was thinking. For her part, she was good. Very quiet, she didn't get excited or use any extra words.

MMG: You have become a symbol of the civil rights movement. There are great demands made on your time, such as this interview. You're asked to visit and to speak all over the country, all the time. Has this created problems for you in the private life that you must lead?

RP: Yes, it has. To a great extent, I feel that there are many other things I would like to do and need to do, that I can't get to. I don't feel like I really have a private life. There are many other things that need my attention. But on the other hand, I always have to refer to something Dr. King once said, in the early days in Montgomery when his first child was very young, demands were made on him, and he was thinking in terms of his not being able to be the father and husband he would like to, he would like to spend more time with his family. But at the same time, he would have to speak about this, and he was called on, and he never had any time at home, or when he was home, he was always being called there. Then, of course . . . community with people, and how they were working together towards freedom and what they were doing, contribution. He asked the question, "Why should I expect personal happiness when so much depends on any contribution that I can make?" But I find myself asking myself, "Why should I expect personal happiness, if people want to find out what, who I am or what I am or what I have done . . . ?"

MMG: So you've really been, you've given yourself.

RP: Yes. Somewhat resigned to whatever contribution I can make, if I'm making any contributions to, especially with young people, where I go to schools to see if I can do them any . . . There are times when I feel I can hardly get up and go, and once I get there and I see their reaction, I feel somewhat rewarded.

MMG: What kind of advice do you give young people today? 105

RP: I try to get them to look within themselves to find out what they're trying to do in any given situation, and to look around them and see the opportunities that they have, and do whatever they can to make the best of the opportunities, to develop their potential, as they grow up, to get the very best they can in education, get the very best they can as human beings, and to above all have respect in God's eyes, for themselves and other people.

MMG: How do you see the racial situation today? Do you think it's better than when you were working in Alabama?

RP: I would have to say it is better, even with all the problems that they have. Because if you go back to the days of old, the incident of my arrest in Montgomery and shortly after the Supreme Court decision on racial segregation in schools and . . . many things. I'd have to say, with all the problems they have now, that there's still much racism and reactionary attitudes among people, but you'd have to say it's better, and it should be even better still.

MMG: What gives you the most satisfaction now, as you look back over your life and your accomplishments, all that's happened to you? What pleases you?

RP: The fact that we have acquired enough freedom to be able to be vocal and   110
to say what we wish, act as human beings, and to make . . . politically to see many of our people in top positions in the government, all the way from Washington to local government.

QUESTIONING THE TEXT

1. What effect does the format of this selection—an almost unedited transcript of an interview—have on your reading of it? How does Parks "come across" to you in the interview?
2. In commenting on the person who portrayed her in a recent film, Parks says, "For her part, she was good. Very quiet, she didn't get excited or use any extra words." In what ways does this description characterize Parks's interview?
3. How does Parks describe the reactions of other black people on the bus that day? Does anything about their reaction puzzle or surprise you? Why, or why not?
4. What is Parks's attitude toward the rioting that took place in Detroit in 1967? Does it differ from that of her husband? From the stance you believe you would have taken? Do Parks's comments remind you of anything you felt or learned during the 1992 Los Angeles riots?
5. Look at the words and phrases A.L. uses in her introduction to describe Parks and her actions. How do they lead readers to see Parks?

MAKING CONNECTIONS

6. Parks says that she is most satisfied or proud of "[t]he fact that we have acquired enough freedom to be able to be vocal and to . . . act as human beings . . ."—that this has been her ambition and her contribution. Judging from the previous reading, what do you think were Billy the Kid's ambitions and contributions? What does each of these legendary figures represent about American culture? In what ways do they conflict with or confirm each other? Record your responses to these questions in a paragraph or two, and bring them to class for discussion.
7. In his eulogy of Malcolm X (starting on p. 500), Ossie Davis says Malcolm represented "our black manhood." Could Rosa Parks be said to represent "our black womanhood"? How would you compare these two figures?

JOINING THE CONVERSATION

8. Parks says that "there's still much racism and reactionary attitudes among people, but you'd have to say it's better, and it should be even better still." Do your knowledge and experience confirm Parks's conclusion? Write about a page of response to this statement—and address your response to Rosa Parks.

9. This interview originally appeared in a collection of oral histories of black women. You could begin conducting an oral history of your own, focusing perhaps on an important older person in your life—a parent or grandparent, another relative, a teacher, or some other role model. Using the Parks interview to get some ideas, devise a set of questions about the person's early memories, schooling, work—whatever you are particularly interested in knowing about. With your subject's permission, tape-record your interview. Afterward, prepare a transcript of four or five pages and bring it to class for discussion.

10. Working with two or three other class members, conduct some additional research on Rosa Parks and the Montgomery bus boycott. One person may check out the *New York Times* stories about this event; another might look up contemporary reports in *Time* or *Newsweek* or *Life*—or in his or her local newspaper. Still another might look up a Montgomery newspaper to see what it had to say. In addition, consider interviewing people who remember this event well and asking them to share those memories with you. On the basis of the information you gather, prepare a presentation for your class on "Contemporary Responses to Rosa Parks and the Montgomery Bus Boycott."

ELLEN GOODMAN
Knowing *Eleanor Roosevelt*

ELLEN GOODMAN (b. 1941) has worked as a researcher for Newsweek, *a reporter for the* Detroit Free Press *and the* Boston Globe, *and a syndicated columnist. The author of four collections (*Turning Points, Close to Home, At Large, *and* Making Sense*), Goodman has won numerous awards, including the Pulitzer Prize for distinguished commentary in 1980.*

In the brief column that follows, written in 1979, Goodman focuses on Eleanor Roosevelt (1884–1962), subject of numerous biographies, and on the values she and her life represent. The wife of Franklin Delano Roosevelt, thirty-second president of the United States, Eleanor Roosevelt constructed a life out of which legends seemed naturally to spring. As Goodman notes, she was an "ugly duckling" who turned many crises in her life into opportunities for growth.

In the year following her husband's partial paralysis from poliomyelitis, Roosevelt worked for legislation favoring women's rights, founded a furniture factory to benefit the unemployed, and taught history and literature to high school students in New York. After her husband was elected president in 1932, she worked for legislation benefiting young people, the poor, and minority groups and wrote a syndicated column, "My Day," all the profits of which went to charity. After President Roosevelt's death in 1945, she served as a delegate to the United Nations, where she worked on the writing and passage of the Declaration of Human Rights. The mother of six children and author of five books, she remained socially and politically active until her death in 1962.

I have been particularly struck by the differing treatments of Eleanor Roosevelt in recent films and by the way in which such media interpretations tend to confer the status of legend on some people while withholding it from others. I also continue to wonder what any person who becomes a legend makes of this experience. I wonder if it is what Eleanor Roosevelt would have wanted. Something tells me I wouldn't want to be a legend. What about you? — A.L.

Now it is Eleanor Roosevelt's turn to have her private life exhumed. Someone has said that the woman we buried was not who we thought she was, and so they have disinterred her letters, dissected their vital organs and sent them to the cruelest coroner of all, the public.*

Those who think her prose was purple are arguing with those who

---

Now it is . . . the public: For another perspective on "digging up" cultural heroes, see Judy Grahn's "The Marilyn Monroe Poem," p. 511.

think her life was tinged with lavender. Across the tabletops and country, people are talking about her "sexual preference" as if it were hair color: Did she or didn't she? Only her friend knew for sure.

Well, they say that every generation writes its own history. Ours, it appears, is sexual. We thrust our own obsessions back into time and come up with JFK's promiscuity, Thomas Jefferson's black mistress and, now, Eleanor's friend Lorena Hickok.

It seems, moreover, that we have greater taste for suspicions than for facts, for the unknown than for the known. We continually want to unmask our heroes as if there were more to be learned from their nakedness than from their choice of clothing.

It is odd in this case, especially, because what we do know about   5
Eleanor Roosevelt is so much more vital than what we don't know. A tall woman with a voice that begged caricaturing, she grew up in an era when form dictated feelings—when, as she said, "you dressed, not according to the weather but the date."

We know that by all accounts, including her own, she had a miserable childhood. Regarded coolly by her mother, who called her "Granny," she was told that, "In a family that had great beauty, you are the ugly duckling of that family."

We know, too, that she worshiped—and struggled to please—her father long after that attractive, self-destructive and unreliable man was gone.

At forty-three years of age she could still write, "I knew a child once who adored her father. She was an ugly little thing, keenly conscious of her deficiencies, and her father, the only person who really cared for her, was away much of the time . . . (but) he wrote her letters and stories telling her . . . she must be truthful, loyal, brave, well-educated. . . . She made herself as the years went on into a fairly good copy of the picture he had painted."

From the time she was ten and an orphan, she spent a neglected childhood with her grandmother in a dark, gloomy house where, as a cousin recalled, "We ate our suppers silently."

At a very young age, then, Eleanor knew too much about life's blows.   10
As a young wife, she learned more. After ten years of marriage and six children, her husband fell in love with Lucy Mercer, and: "The bottom dropped out of my particular life, and I faced myself, my surroundings, my world, honestly for the first time. I really grew up that year."

Even when her husband died, Eleanor knew, ". . . he might have been happier with a wife who was completely uncritical. That, I was never able to be. . . . Nevertheless, I think I sometimes acted as a spur even though spurring was not always wanted or welcome. I was one of those who served his purposes."

She became a great lady, then, not because she was a first lady, but because she was able through enormous will to turn her pain into strength, to turn disappointment into purpose. It was as if her backbone had been permanently strengthened by the brace she wore in childhood.

The facts, just the facts, of her life might have defeated any of us. Add to that list a dead child and a husband stricken with polio. But she used them, the way she used her rigorous disciplines of calisthenics and ice-cold showers, to make herself stronger.

With this gutsiness, she cared about the poor even when the press accused her of interfering, and supported civil rights in the days when an antilynch law was highly controversial with southern Democrats. She promoted women in government when others disparaged them and, as a widow, worked for human rights in the world and the United Nations when others grew resigned.

And, yes, she was also effusive and loving in letters to women friends.   15
She was as intimate as her husband was remote. As James Roosevelt once wrote: "Of what was inside him, of what really drove him, Father talked with no one."

All this, the important facts, the fundamental truths, are known, not suspected. As Arthur Schlesinger once added them up: "Her life was both ordeal and fulfillment. It combined vulnerability and stoicism, pathos and pride, frustration and accomplishment, sadness and happiness."

That is still the best epitaph.

QUESTIONING THE TEXT

1. Do you agree with Goodman that we want to "unmask our heroes"? What are your reasons for agreeing or disagreeing?
2. In her headnote to this essay, A.L. provides some details about Eleanor Roosevelt's life. How does her selection of details affect your understanding of Roosevelt? What other information might she have included?

MAKING CONNECTIONS

3. Given her discussion of Madonna (p. 486), do you think Camille Paglia would view Eleanor Roosevelt as a "real feminist"? Give your reasons for the answer you choose.
4. A.L.'s introduction and Goodman's text give some idea of why during her husband's presidency Eleanor Roosevelt was referred to by conservatives simply as "that woman." In his introduction to the reading "Rush Limbaugh: Talking Back" (on p. 492), J.R. refers to the wife of President Bill Clinton as "that Rodham woman." On the basis of

what A.L. and Goodman say about Eleanor Roosevelt and what you know about Hillary Rodham Clinton, why do you think these two first ladies stir up such strong feelings among conservatives? What points of similarity and difference do you see between them?

JOINING THE CONVERSATION

5. The last few years have seen an increasing debate over how much information about the private lives of public figures (or legends) the public is appropriately entitled to. Some argue that matters of home—and especially the bedroom—have nothing to do with how well a person does a job or holds an office. Others argue that such personal matters reflect the person's deepest values and hence provide important clues to character and ethics. Where do you stand on this issue? Write a two- or three-page position paper explaining and justifying your views on this question.

6. Working with two other members of your class, do some research on Eleanor Roosevelt. Perhaps have one person check out a film or video about her, another look up newspaper and magazine articles that appeared shortly after her death, and a third interview a person on campus (in the history or women's studies department, for example) who is knowledgeable about her. Give yourselves a week to come up with information you can pool. Then together create a handout for class entitled "Things Ellen Goodman Didn't Tell Us about Eleanor Roosevelt."

GREIL MARCUS
Elvis: Presliad

L*IKE EVERYONE ELSE WHO GREW UP in the fifties, I remember the controversy Elvis's early music stirred. Girls screamed, guys slicked back their hair, and Ed Sullivan finally televised the dark-eyed, gyrating southerner on his variety show one Sunday night—but only from the waist up. It bothered a lot of people that a white boy was singing "colored music," but both that music and the man soon gained acceptance, even in Ohio, where I grew up.*

But I never realized how seriously people took Elvis until I moved to Texas in the late seventies. Shortly after his death in 1977, I made a snide remark about the bloated self-caricature that Elvis had become to a racquetball partner from Missouri. Looking at me as if I had just cut someone's throat in church, he explained with surprising solemnity how much he respected and admired Elvis. Clearly, I'd struck a nerve.

It prepared me for the remarkable and still growing reaction of Americans to Elvis's demise. It mattered little to a public anxious to believe in something that the King of Rock 'n' Roll had died (like the Emperor Vespasian) on the throne, his body and talent ravaged by drugs. It was enough that in life Elvis had transcended ordinary human limitations, raising himself from backwoods obscurity to international fame. He had acquired boundless wealth, met Richard Nixon, conferred Cadillacs on his friends. What more could be expected?

*Greil Marcus (b. 1943), a commentator on American music and popular culture, has been writing about Elvis for years and has recently published a collection of materials documenting the transfiguration of the singer since his death—*Dead Elvis: A Chronicle of a Cultural Obsession. *But for this anthology, I've selected an essay about the living Elvis that Marcus published in 1975 in* Mystery Train: Images of America in Rock 'n' Roll Music. *As you'll see, it contains elements of prophecy.* – J.R.

FANFARE

Elvis Presley is a supreme figure in American life, one whose presence, no matter how banal or predictable, brooks no real comparisons. He is honored equally by long-haired rock critics, middle-aged women, the City of Memphis (they finally found something to name after him: a highway), and even a president.* Beside Elvis, the other heroes of this book seem a

---

*Richard Nixon had Elvis over to the White House once, and made him an honorary narcotics agent. Nixon got his picture taken with the King. An odd story, though, from rock

little small-time. If they define different versions of America, Presley's career almost has the scope to take America in. The cultural range of his music has expanded to the point where it includes not only the hits of the day, but also patriotic recitals, pure country gospel, and really dirty blues; reviews of his concerts, by usually credible writers, sometimes resemble biblical accounts of heavenly miracles. Elvis has emerged as a great *artist,* a great *rocker,* a great *purveyor of schlock,* a great *heart throb,* a great *bore,* a great *symbol of potency,* a great *ham,* a great *nice person,* and, yes, a great American.

Twenty years ago Elvis made his first records with Sam Phillips, on the little Sun label in Memphis, Tennessee; then a pact was signed with Col. Tom Parker, shrewd country hustler. Elvis took off for RCA Victor, New York, and Hollywood. America has not been the same since. Elvis disappeared into an oblivion of respectability and security in the sixties, lost in interchangeable movies and dull music; he staged a remarkable comeback as that decade ended, and now performs as the transcendental Sun King that Ralph Waldo Emerson only dreamed about—and as a giant contradiction. His audience expands every year, but Elvis transcends his talent to the point of dispensing with it altogether. Performing a kind of enormous victory rather than winning it, Elvis strides the boards with such glamour, such magnetism, that he allows his audience to transcend their desire for his talent. Action is irrelevant when one can simply delight in the presence of a man who has made history, and who has triumphed over it.

Mark now, the supreme Elvis gesture. He takes the stage with a retinue of bodyguards, servants, singers, a band, an orchestra; he applies himself vaguely to the hits of his past, prostrates himself before songs of awesome ickiness; he acknowledges the applause and the gasps that greet his every movement (applause that comes thundering with such force you might think the audience merely suffers the music as an excuse for its ovations); he closes with an act of show-biz love that still warms the heart; but above all, he throws away the entire performance.

How could he take it seriously? How could anyone create when all one has to do is appear? "He *looks* like Elvis Presley!" cried a friend, when the Big E stormed forth in an explosion of flashbulbs and cheers, "What a burden to live up to!" It is as if there is nothing Elvis could do to overshadow

---

critic Stu Werbin: "It seems that the good German who arranges the White House concerts for the President and his guests managed to travel the many channels that lead only in rare instances to Col. Tom Parker's phone line. Once connected, he delivered what he considered the most privileged invitation. The President requests Mr. Presley to perform. The Colonel did a little quick figuring and then told the man that Elvis would consider it an honor. For the President, Elvis's fee, beyond traveling expenses and accommodations for his back-up group, would be $25,000. The good German gasped.

'Col. Parker, nobody gets paid for playing for the President!'

'Well, I don't know about that, son,' the Colonel responded abruptly, 'but there's one thing I do know. Nobody asks Elvis Presley to play for nothing.' " (*Creem*, March, 1972).

a performance of his myth. And so he performs from a distance, laughing at his myth, throwing it away only to see it roar back and trap him once again.

He will sing, as if suffering to his very soul, a song called "This Time, You [God, that is] Gave Me a Mountain," which sums up his divorce and his separation from his little girl. Having confessed his sins, he will stand aside, head bowed, as the Special Elvis Presley Gospel Group sings "Sweet, Sweet Feeling (In This Place)." Apparently cleansed of his sins, he will rock straight into the rhythm and blues of "Lawdy, Miss Clawdy" and celebrate his new-found freedom with a lazy grin. But this little melodrama of casual triumph will itself be a throwaway. As with the well-planned sets, the first-class musicians, the brilliant costumes, there will be little life behind the orchestration; the whole performance will be flaccid, the timing careless, all emotions finally shallow, the distance from his myth necessitating an even greater distance from the musical power on which that myth is based.

Elvis gives us a massive road-show musical of opulent American mastery; his version of the winner-take-all fantasies that have kept the world lined up outside the theaters that show American movies ever since the movies began. And of course we respond: a self-made man is rather boring, but a self-made king is something else. Dressed in blue, red, white, ultimately gold, with a superman cape and covered with jewels no one can be sure are fake, Elvis might epitomize the worst of our culture—he is bragging, selfish, narcissistic, condescending, materialistic to the point of insanity. But there is no need to take that seriously, no need to take anything seriously. "Aw, shucks," says the country boy; it is all a joke to him; his distance is in his humor, and he can exit from this America unmarked, unimpressed, and uninteresting.

"From the moment he comes out of the wings," writes Nik Cohn, "all the pop that has followed him is made to seem as nothing, to be blown away like chaff." That is *exactly* what that first moment feels like, but from that point on, Elvis will go with the rest of it, singing as if there are no dangers or delights in the world grand enough to challenge him. There is great satisfaction in his performance, and great emptiness.

It is an ending. It is a sure sign that a culture has reached a dead end when it is no longer intrigued by its myths (when they lose their power to excite, amuse, and renew all who are a part of those myths—when those myths just bore the hell out of everyone); but Elvis has dissolved into a presentation of his myth, and so has his music. The emotion of the best music is open, liberating in its commitment and intangibility; Elvis's presentation is fixed. The glorious oppression of that presentation parallels the all-but-complete assimilation of a revolutionary musical style into the mainstream of American culture, where no one is challenged and no one is threatened.

History without myth is surely a wasteland; but myths are compelling only when they are at odds with history. When they replace the need to make history, they too are a dead end, and merely smug. Elvis's performance of his myth is so satisfying to his audience that he is left with no musical identity whatsoever, and thus he has no way to define himself, or his audience—except to expand himself, and his audience. Elvis is a man whose task it is to dramatize the fact of his existence; he does not have to create something new (or try, and fail), and thus test the worth of his existence, or the worth of his audience.

Complete assimilation really means complete acceptance. The immi-   10 grant who is completely assimilated into America has lost the faculty of adding whatever is special about himself to his country; for any artist, complete assimilation means the adoption of an aesthetic where no lines are drawn and no choices are made. That quality of selection, which is what is at stake when an artist comes across with his version of anything, is missing. When an artist gives an all-encompassing Yes to his audience (and Elvis's Yes implicitly includes everyone, not just those who say Yes to *him*), there is nothing more he can tell his audience, nothing he can really do for them, except maybe throw them a kiss.

Only the man who says No is free, Melville once wrote. We don't expect such a stance in popular culture, and anyone who does might best be advised to take his trade somewhere else. But the refusal that lurks on the margins of the affirmation of American popular culture—the margins where Sly Stone* and Randy Newman* have done their best work—is what gives the Yes of our culture its vitality and its kick. Elvis's Yes is the grandest of all, his presentation of mastery the grandest fantasy of freedom, but it is finally a counterfeit of freedom: it takes place in a world that for all its openness (Everybody Welcome!) is aesthetically closed, where nothing is left to be mastered, where there is only more to accept. For all its irresistible excitement and enthusiasm, this freedom is complacent, and so the music that it produces is empty of real emotion—there is nothing this freedom could be for, nothing to be won or lost.

At best, when the fans gather around—old men and women who might see their own struggles and failures ennobled in the splendor of one who came from the bottom; middle-aged couples attending to the most glamorous nightclub act there is; those in their twenties and thirties who have grown with Elvis ever since he and they created each other years ago (and who might have a feeling he and they will make their trip through history together, reading their history in each other)—at best, Elvis will

Sly Stone: stage name of Sylvester Stewart (b. 1944), leader of the psychedelic-soul group Sly and the Family Stone
Randy Newman (b. 1943): singer and songwriter whose first album appeared in 1968

confirm all who are there *as* an audience. Such an event, repeated over and over all across the land, implies an America that is as nearly complete as any can be. But what is it worth?

When Elvis sings "American Trilogy" (a combination of "Dixie," "The Battle Hymn of the Republic," and "All My Trials," a slave song), he signifies that his persona, and the culture he has made out of blues, Las Vegas, gospel music, Hollywood, schmaltz, Mississippi, and rock 'n' roll, can contain any America you might want to conjure up. It is rather Lincoln-esque; Elvis recognizes that the Civil War has never ended, and so he will perform The Union.

Well, for a moment, staring at that man on the stage, you can almost believe it. For if Elvis were to bring it off—and it is easy to think that only he could—one would leave the hall with a new feeling for the country; whatever that feeling might be, one's sense of place would be broadened, and enriched.

But it is an illusion. A man or woman equal to the song's pretension   15
would have to present each part of the song as if it were the whole story, setting one against each other, proving that one American really could make the South live, the Union hold, and slavery real. But on the surface and beneath it, Elvis transcends any real America by evading it. There is no John Brown* in his "Battle Hymn," no romance in his "Dixie," no blood in his slave song. He sings with such a complete absence of musical personal-ity that none of the old songs matter at all, because has has not committed himself to them; it could be anyone singing, or no one. It is in this sense, finally, that an audience is confirmed, that an America comes into being; lacking any real fear or joy, it is a throwaway America where nothing is at stake. The divisions America shares are simply smoothed away.

But there is no chance anyone who wants to join will be excluded. Elvis's fantasy of freedom, the audience's fantasy, takes on such reality that there is nothing left in the real world that can inspire the fantasy, or threaten it. What *is* left is for the fantasy to replace the world; and that, night after night, is what Elvis and his audience make happen. The version of the American dream that is Elvis's performance is blown up again and again, to contain more history, more people, more music, more hopes; the air gets thin but the bubble does not burst, nor will it ever. This is America when it has outstripped itself, in all of its extravagance, and its emptiness is Elvis's ultimate throwaway.

There is a sense in which virtually his whole career has been a throw-away, straight from that time when he knew he had it made and that the

---

John Brown (1800–59): an abolitionist who was executed after leading a raid on the federal arsenal at Harpers Ferry, (West) Virginia, in 1859. "The Battle Hymn of the Republic" was set to music that had been popularized in a song called "John Brown's Body Lies A-Moulderin' in the Grave," which had become an anthem of the abolitionist cause.

future was his. You can hear that distance, that refusal to really commit himself, in his best music and his worst; if the throwaway is the source of most of what is pointless about Elvis, it is also at the heart of much of what is exciting and charismatic. It may be that he never took *any* of it seriously, just did his job and did it well, trying to enjoy himself and stay sane—save for those first Tennessee records, and that night, late in 1968, when his comeback was uncertain and he put a searing, desperate kind of life into a few songs that cannot be found in any of his other music.

It was a staggering moment. A Christmas TV special had been decided on; a final dispute between Colonel Parker (he wanted twenty Christmas songs and a tuxedo) and producer Steve Binder (he wanted a tough, fast, sexy show) had been settled; with Elvis's help, Binder won. So there Elvis was, standing in an auditorium, facing television cameras and a live audience for the first time in nearly a decade, finally stepping out from behind the wall of retainers and sycophants he had paid to hide him. And everyone was watching.

In the months preceding Elvis had begun to turn away from the seamless boredom of the movies and the hackneyed music of the soundtrack albums, staking out a style on a few half-successful singles, presenting the new persona of a man whose natural toughness was tempered by experience. The records—"Big Boss Man," "Guitar Man," "U.S. Male"—had been careful, respectable efforts, but now he was putting everything on the line, risking his comforts and his ease for the chance to start over. He had been a bad joke for a long time; if this show died, little more would be heard from Elvis Presley. Did he still have an audience? Did he still have anything to offer them? He had raised the stakes himself, but he probably had no idea.

Sitting on the stage in black leather, surrounded by friends and a rough   20
little combo, the crowd buzzing, he sang and talked and joked, and all the resentments he had hidden over the years began to pour out. He had always said yes, but this time, he was saying no—not without humor, but almost with a wry bit of guilt, as if he had betrayed his talent and himself. "Been a long time, baby." He told the audience about a time back in 1955, when cops in Florida had forced him to sing without moving; the story was hilarious, but there was something in his voice that made very clear how much it had hurt. He jibed at the Beatles, denying that the heroes who had replaced him had produced anything he could not match, and then he proved it. After all this time he wanted more than safety; he and the men around him were nervous, full of adventure.

"I'd like to do my favorite Christmas song," Elvis drawls—squeals of familiarity from the crowd, the girls in the front rows doing their job, imitating themselves or their images of the past, fading into an undertone of giggles as the music begins. Elvis sings "Blue Christmas," a classically styled rhythm and blues, very even, all its tension implied: a good choice.

He sings it low and throaty, snapping the strings on his guitar until one of his pals cries, "Play it dirty! Play it dirty!"—on a Christmas song! All right! But this is re-creation, the past in the present, an attempt to see if Elvis can go as far as he once did. Within those limits it works, it is beautiful. The song ends with appropriate, and calculated, screams.

"Ah think Ah'll put a strap around this and stand up," Presley says. AHAHAHAHAHAHAHAAHAHA! God, what's that? Nervous laughter from a friend. Slow and steady, still looking around for the strap no one has bothered to hook onto the guitar, Elvis rocks into "One Night." In Smiley Lewis's original, it was about an orgy, called "One Night of Sin" (with the great line, "The things I did and I saw/ Would make the earth stand still"); Elvis cleaned it up into a love story in 1958. But he has forgotten— or remembered. He is singing Lewis's version, as he must have always wanted to. He has slipped his role, and laughing, grinning, something is happening.

> . . . *The things I did and I saw, could make* . . . these dreams—*Where's the strap?*

Where's the strap, indeed. He falls in and out of the two songs, and suddenly the band rams hard at the music and Elvis lunges and eats it alive. No one has ever heard him sing like this; not even his best records suggest the depth of passion in this music. One line from Howlin' Wolf tells the tale: "When you see me runnin', you know my life is at stake." That's what it sounds like.

Shouting, crying, growling, lusting, Elvis takes his stand and the crowd takes theirs with him, no longer reaching for the past they had been brought to the studio to reenact, but responding to something completely new. The crowd is cheering for what they had only hoped for: Elvis has gone beyond all their expectations, and his, and they don't believe it. The guitar cuts in high and slams down and Elvis is roaring. Every line is a thunderbolt. *AW, YEAH!,* screams a pal—he has waited years for this moment.

> *UNNNNNNH! WHEW!* When . . . I ain't nevah did no wrong!

And Elvis floats like the master he is back into "One night, with you,"   25 even allowing himself a little "Hot dog!", singing softly to himself.

It was the finest music of his life. If ever there was music that bleeds, this was it. Nothing came easy that night, and he gave everything he had— more than anyone knew was there.

QUESTIONING THE TEXT

1. If the last sentence of the first paragraph of "Elvis: Presliad" is its thesis, how would you describe Marcus's attitude toward Elvis Presley

as a cultural phenomenon? If you are keeping a reading log, respond in an entry.

2. According to Marcus, good popular music is challenging, threatening, and unassimilated. Does any current artistic form (or do any current artists) meet Marcus's criteria? (You need not limit yourself to music or musicians.)

3. What is J.R.'s attitude about Elvis? What words and facts in his introduction to this essay allow you to identify those attitudes?

MAKING CONNECTIONS

4. Compare Marcus's assessment of Elvis with Camille Paglia's treatment of Madonna in the next reading, annotating the margins of both essays with your comments. Which of the artists strikes you as more important? Or are both overrated? Write a short paper comparing and/ or contrasting these pop legends.

5. How does one compare the achievements of a performer like Elvis with those of an Eleanor Roosevelt, as described by Ellen Goodman in the previous reading? Is this an apples and oranges comparison, not worth making? Does our society pay too much attention to people who are lumped together as celebrities?

6. In some respects, both Elvis and Malcolm X (see Ossie Davis's eulogy starting on p. 500) transcend faults attached to them in their lifetimes. Is this selective forgetting part of the public's process of legend-making? Write an essay examining what we may not want to know about our heroes.

JOINING THE CONVERSATION

7. In a group, discuss who profits from the Elvis myth. How much of that myth do you feel is manufactured? How much is genuine? (And how would you define a "genuine" myth?)

8. Marcus describes Elvis as trapped by his own fame: "It is as if there is nothing Elvis could do to overshadow a performance of his myth." Illustrate what Marcus may mean by listing other examples of celebrities unable to meet the expectations of the public. (Don't limit your analysis to performers.)

9. In a short article, describe a concert (rock or otherwise) you have attended, using for a model Marcus's lively account of Elvis's comeback Christmas TV special.

CAMILLE PAGLIA
Madonna—Finally, a Real Feminist

*M*ADONNA HERSELF ADMITS *that she is not a great singer, dancer, or actor. Yet she is one of the best-known performers in the world, a Kmart Marilyn with more incarnations than Shirley MacLaine. One might argue that Madonna has made herself legendary by pursuing celebrity, that is, doing things just to attract attention, thereby making herself even better known and thus capable of grabbing still more tabloid renown. It may be that Madonna's real talent is accumulating fame.*

Fame brings influence, and Madonna has wielded her power in the service of AIDS *research and for various political causes. She rattled some feminists when she sang a song about choosing to have a baby. Then she battled local authorities and even the Vatican over issues of "artistic freedom"—which in her case can mean the right to grab her crotch in public or to wear Watts Tower–like bras onstage. Yet she didn't take kindly to Sinéad O'Connor's "Saturday Night Live" denunciation of Pope John Paul II.*

What does one do with a phenomenon of this importance? In America, we make it rich.

But is Madonna something more than a clever pop icon? Camille Paglia clearly thinks so. Shortly after the following eye-opening, take-no-prisoners piece was published in The New York Times *in 1990, an amazed colleague of mine brought it to an English department committee meeting and disrupted our sober deliberations by reading choice sentences aloud. Reactions ran from applause to suppressed rage—just about the reaction Madonna gets from the general public.*

Indeed, Paglia's full frontal assaults on orthodox feminism have made her a celebrity in her own right. Spin *magazine describes her as the "Johnny Rotten of academia." Naomi Wolf, author of* The Beauty Myth *and a target of Paglia's criticism, blasts her as "the nipple-pierced person's Phyllis Schlafly." Obviously, she could not be omitted from this chapter.*

Paglia teaches at the College of the Arts in Philadelphia and is the author of Sexual Personae: Art and Decadence from Nefertiti to Emily Dickinson *and* Sex, Art, and American Culture. *– J.R.*

Madonna, don't preach.

Defending her controversial new video "Justify My Love" on "Nightline" last week, Madonna stumbled, rambled and ended up seeming far less intelligent than she really is.

Of course, what "Nightline"

Madonna, 'fess up.

The video is pornographic. It's decadent. And it's fabulous. MTV was right to ban it, a corporate resolve long overdue. Parents cannot possibly control television, with its titanic omnipresence.

Prodded by correspondent Forrest Sawyer for evidence of her responsibility as an artist, Madonna hotly proclaimed her love of children, her social activism and her condom endorsements. Wrong answer. As Baudelaire and Oscar Wilde knew, neither art nor the artist has a moral responsibility to liberal social causes.

"Justify My Love" is truly avant-garde, at a time when that word has lost its meaning in the flabby art world. It represents a sophisticated European sexuality of a kind we have not seen since the great foreign films of the 1950's and 1960's. But it does not belong on a mainstream music channel watched around the clock by children.

On "Nightline," Madonna bizarrely called the video a "celebration of sex." She imagined happy educational scenes where curious children would ask their parents about the video. Oh, sure! Picture it: "Mommy, please tell me about the tired, tied-up man in the leather harness and the mean, bare-chested lady in the Nazi cap." O.K., dear, right after the milk and cookies.

Mr. Sawyer asked for Madonna's reaction to feminist charges that, in the neck manacle and floor-crawling of an earlier video, "Express Yourself," she condoned the "degradation" and "humiliation" of women. Madonna waffled: "But I chained myself! I'm in charge." Well, no. Madonna the producer may have chosen the chain, but Madonna the sexual persona in the video is alternately a cross-dressing dominatrix and a slave of male desire.

But who cares what the feminists say anyhow? They have been outrageously negative about Madonna from the start. In 1985, *Ms.* magazine pointedly feted quirky, cuddly singer Cyndi Lauper as its woman of the year. Great judgment: gimmicky Lauper went nowhere, while Madonna grew, flourished, metamorphosed and became an international star of staggering dimensions. She is also a shrewd business tycoon, a modern woman of all-around talent.

Madonna is the true feminist. She exposes the puritanism and suffocating ideology of American feminism, which is stuck in an adolescent whining mode. Madonna has taught young women to be fully female and sexual while still exercising total control over their lives. She shows girls how to be attractive, sensual, energetic, ambitious, aggressive and funny—all at the same time.

American feminism has a man problem. The beaming Betty Crockers, hangdog dowdies and parochial prudes who call themselves feminists want men to be like women. They fear and despise the masculine. The academic feminists think their nerdy bookworm husbands are the ideal model of human manhood.

But Madonna loves real men. She sees the beauty of masculinity, in all its rough vigor and sweaty athletic perfection. She also admires the men who are actually like women: transsexuals and flamboyant drag queens, the heroes of the 1969 Stonewall rebellion, which started the gay liberation movement.

"Justify My Love" in an eerie, sultry tableau of jaded androgynous creatures, trapped in a decadent sexual underground. Its hypnotic images are drawn from such sado-masochistic films as Lililana Cazani's "The Night Porter" and Luchino Visconti's "The Damned." It's the perverse and knowing world of the photographers Helmut Newton and Robert Mapplethorpe.

Contemporary American feminism, which began by rejecting Freud because of his alleged sexism has shut itself off from his ideas of ambiguity, contradiction, conflict, ambivalence. Its simplistic psychology is illustrated by the new cliché of the date-rape furor: " 'No' always means 'no'. " Will we ever graduate from the Girl Scouts? "No" has always been, and always will be, part of the dangerous, alluring courtship ritual of sex and seduction, observable even in the animal kingdom.

Madonna has a far profounder vision of sex than

When I interviewed Paglia, she said the same about Sharon Stone. — G.H.

The English teacher in me says "name-calling"; the man says "right on." — J.R.

When you listen to Madonna's "Justify My Love," do you really think of it as a Freudian examination of androgyny, or just as kinky sex? — G.H.

Does no always mean no? Some college males have to figure this out every Saturday night. — G.H.

What is a "true" feminist? Paglia tends to argue from assertion rather than from good reasons. — A.L.

Academe is fraught with weak and whiny men. — G.H.

For all of her criticism of feminists, Paglia is no conservative. It's unlikely that Barbara Bush or Margaret Thatcher would ever promote drag queens. — G.H.

This sketch of feminism is exaggerated, a caricature probably intended for effect more than for substance. — A.L.

Tell that to Anita Hill. — A.L.

do the feminists. She sees both the animality and the artifice. Changing her costume style and hair color virtually every month, Madonna embodies the eternal values of beauty and pleasure. Feminism says "No more masks." Madonna says we are nothing but masks.

This is less a conclusion than a declaration. — J.R.

Is any mask as good or valuable as any other? I don't think all masks are created equal. — A.L.

Through her enormous impact on young women around the world, Madonna is the future of feminism.

A f t e r w o r d s

Paglia's style is superficially amusing to me (I particularly remember reading a very funny dialogue between Paglia and Neil Postman in which the speeches were punctuated by a description of the food being served up to these two quarrelsome folks at a posh restaurant), but it doesn't wear well at all. It seems somehow sophomoric or juvenile, all flash and glitter and machine-gun rhythms, but little if any substance.

I can, however, see why Paglia would admire Madonna: both are terrific self-promoters, salesmen of themselves. And both value (perhaps idolize?) shock value for its own sake. Maybe they can make a movie—or a rock video—together. I'd watch it—at least once. — A.L.

Molly Ivins Can't Say That, Can She? *is the title of a book by Ivins, a Texas political pundit with a national following. I think Camille Paglia might stake her own claim on a portion of Ivins's title, as this short piece proves. Yet saying outrageous things isn't enough to win plaudits; one's notions have to ring true.*

And that's what I credit Paglia with—saying clearly and forcefully what many people have thought, but few have had the guts to put into print. Just consider three statements from this essay, all of them simple and declarative: "Madonna is the true feminist . . . American feminism has a man problem . . . Madonna is the future of feminism." A column in The New York Times *is not the place to argue the quiddities of these positions, and Paglia doesn't. It is enough that she shoves them—sixties style—in the face of monolithic feminism and makes the tenured establishment quiver.*

I like Paglia's style. (Can I say that?) — J.R.

In rapid-fire prose, Paglia skillfully shoots down the feminist opposition. Regrettably, though, Paglia makes the mistake made by many in academia: she gives popular culture undeserved attention.

Academics can learn from pop culture and its icons. But the basis for high intellectual praise of Madonna's dirty dance songs is questionable. I enjoy

Madonna's music precisely because it is so simplistic that you can thoughtlessly wiggle to its beat. It's doubtful Madonna's general audience finds much depth in the MTV *sensation. Madonna has made some inroads toward women's liberation, but Paglia gives her too much credit.* – G.H.

As you might expect, Paglia's article drew a quick response from readers, almost all of whom begged, in one way or another, to disagree. One of those readers was Susan Suleiman (b. 1939), professor of Romance and comparative literatures at Harvard University and author or editor of several influential works, including *The Female Body in Western Culture: Contemporary Perspectives* (1986) and *Subversive Intent: Gender, Politics and the Avant-Garde* (1990). To add yet another "reading" of Paglia's article, I include Suleiman's letter to the editor here. – A.L

Does Suleiman represent feminism's "tenured establishment"? Note the techniques she employs to discredit Paglia. Are they fair? – J.R

To the Editor:
I agree with Camille Paglia ("Madonna—Finally, a Real Feminist," Op-Ed, Dec. 14) that Madonna's influence on today's young women has in many ways been positive, showing them that a woman can be "attractive, sensual, engergetic, ambitious, aggressive and funny—all at the same time." I am puzzled, however, by the all-out war that Ms. Paglia feels compelled to declare against American feminists and feminism in making this argument.

As she certainly knows, American feminism has many strands, in and out of academia—the diversity of theoretical positions is what has made feminist criticism and theory a dynamic force in American intellectual life. One can only smile in disbelief, therefore, to see American feminists reduced to the caricature of "beaming Betty Crockers, hangdog dowdies and parochial prudes." As alliterative invective, that's not bad—but really, do we need this kind of cheap stereotyping? Besides, it's not even original. It's simply a reinvention, 20 years later, of the old caricature of the bra-burning man-hater.

Ms. Paglia excoriates feminists for "simplistic psychology" and avoidance of complexity or ambiguity, but her own version of feminism is nothing if not simple-minded. As for her contribution to the discussion of date-rape ("'No' has always been, and will always be, part of the dangerous, alluring courtship ritual of sex and seduction"), it is irrelevant to the issue of rape, which is the antithesis of seduction. To claim otherwise is unconscionable and simple-minded.

This variety of feminist-bashing, which would like to see itself as truly avant-garde, might be dismissed as mere publicity-seeking wordplay, not worth responding to, were it not for the spate of right-wing attacks on women's studies and other curricular innovations of the last two decades at American colleges and universities. The right wingers who attack feminists on campus at least know who their enemies are. One can only wonder whether or not Camille Paglia does.

Susan Rubin Suleiman
Cambridge, Mass., Dec. 14, 1990

QUESTIONING THE TEXT

1. Are you engaged or put off by Paglia's sharp criticism of "academic feminists" and their "nerdy bookworm husbands"? Do you find such bluntness (and stereotyping) refreshing or unfair?
2. What do you think Paglia means when she asks, "Will we ever graduate from the Girl Scouts?"
3. Who are the Baudelaire and Oscar Wilde Paglia alludes to and what are they doing in this essay? Use an encyclopedia or dictionary of biography to find out.
4. Underline or list all the allusions, names, or expressions in J.R.'s introduction that require a knowledge beyond what is available in the text itself (such as "Kmart Marilyn" or "Shirley MacLaine"). What assumptions is J.R. making about his readers?

MAKING CONNECTIONS

5. How would you describe the purpose of Paglia's essay? Is it an argument, a satire, a diatribe? Does it convince you? With which other selections in this chapter do you think it has most in common?
6. In an appropriate style, write what you think might be Paglia's response to Ellen Goodman's "*Knowing* Eleanor Roosevelt" (p. 474). Would Paglia be as dismissive as Goodman of those suggesting that the former first lady had a lesbian relationship?

JOINING THE CONVERSATION

7. With a group of five or six classmates, evaluate Paglia's description of a "true feminist." What does a true feminist do? See if you can agree as a group on your own definition of the term.
8. Write a letter to *The New York Times* responding to Paglia's piece.
9. Write a full essay exploring Paglia's concluding assertion: Madonna is the future of feminism. Or, if you prefer, substitute another name for Madonna's—Margaret Thatcher, Camille Paglia, Hillary Rodham Clinton.

TERRY EASTLAND
Rush Limbaugh: Talking Back*

DITTOHEADS WILL APPRECIATE THIS. *I'm on the phone with my co-editor in 1992.*

A.L.: Who's Rush Limbaugh?
J.R.: You've never heard of Rush Limbaugh?
A.L.: No. But let me ask my research assistant.
[Overheard] Have you ever heard of Rush Limbaugh?
J.R.: So?
A.L.: He made a face and said Limbaugh's a fascist.

I'm on the phone with my editor at St. Martin's Press in 1993.

MARILYN: I don't think we want Rush Limbaugh in the legends chapter. He doesn't fit.
J.R.: Millions of people tune him in every day. He's going to have more influence in the next four years than any political figure except Clinton and maybe that Rodham woman. Besides, the chapter is as much about "Pop Icons" now as about "Legends."
MARILYN: Isn't he just a modern-day Arthur Godfrey? Arthur Godfrey's no legend. And I've been thinking of legends as people who are dead.
J.R.: Rosa Parks isn't dead. Neither is Madonna. They're in the chapter.
MARILYN: Well, we'll have to talk more about this.

No doubt about it, Limbaugh makes people squirm. You either hate him or love him . . . or you never heard of him. But try as you might, you can't ignore the man William Bennett describes (with appropriately Limbaughian hyperbole) as "our greatest living American."

It's tough to imagine a more unlikely pop hero than Limbaugh—a portly, conservative, forty-somethingish Missourian who's gotten rich bashing feminists, environmentalists, and liberals on the radio. Yet his first book drove Madonna's Sex *off the top of the best-seller lists and his television talk show poses a ratings threat even to "The Tonight Show." Apparently, for conservatives and Republicans, Limbaugh's satire serves as a balm for the daily roasting they get from Hollywood and the liberal news media.*

Talking Back: For a provocative contrast to Eastland's use of the phrase "talking back," see the selection by bell hooks (p. 124) from her book by the same name.

The somewhat edited portrait below appeared just prior to the 1992 presiden-tial election in The American Spectator, *a magazine sympathetic to Lim-baugh's politics. Its author is Terry Eastland, a columnist for* The American Spectator *and editor of* Forbes MediaGuide Quarterly.

So liberals beware. With Rush on the teeter-totter, don't expect balance. − J.R.

The Dollar Rent-A-Car shuttle is carrying me and my family across the non-fruited plain of the Dallas–Fort Worth Airport. The driver spends much of his day in this bus, which of course comes with a radio, and in Dallas you can get the show on KUII 1190. It's on three hours a day, five days a week, on over five hundred stations coast to coast, and my driver is one of the 12 million who listen to him daily.

"Yes, I listen to Rush," he says. "And the scary thing is, I agree with him."

Scary? Perhaps my driver has been intimidated by what Rush Lim-baugh calls the "dominant media culture," for only a hidebound liberal could be afraid of what Limbaugh has to say. Limbaugh is a political conser-vative for whom no hyphen is necessary: neither neo- nor paleo- nor any-thing else. In this he is much like his hero, Ronald Reagan. What's more, he has a rock-'n'-roll energy that busts the conventional image of the conser-vative as unfunny and out of it. Or maybe it's Limbaugh's shameless bragga-docio, his apologetic admission that he is right only "97.9 percent of the time." Or maybe it's the weird, even tasteless stuff that sometimes finds its way onto the show—such as Limbaugh's recent discussion with several callers about lamb and pig castration.

Four years after it started, "The Rush Limbaugh Show" enjoys the largest audience of any radio talk show since the advent of television. No longer is it possible to say, as Limbaugh does, that he is just "a radio guy." When ABC's "Nightline" did a program last February on environmen-talism's declining appeal, it chose to pit against Sen. Al Gore not another politician but Rush H. Limbaugh III. "What I intended by [having him on]," Ted Koppel, a frequent Limbaugh listener, told *Vanity Fair,* "was an acceptance of what he clearly has become over the last two or three years, and that is something of an icon to millions of conservative listeners around the country."

Likewise, last July, when William Bennett made his first appearance   5
as a Heritage Foundation fellow in that institution's *Policy Review,* he did so not as an interviewee, but as an interviewer . . . of Rush Limbaugh. The questions included: "What accounts for Ross Perot's popularity?" "What are the most important issues for the elections this year?" "How would you cut the $400-billion deficit?" "Are you worried about our third century . . . about the balkanization of American life . . . about radical feminism?"

It's rare that a radio personality gets to answer such substantive questions—especially a college dropout like Limbaugh.

"He's very smart," Koppel says. "He does his homework. He is well informed." And he is a star. Bennett tells the story of eating dinner in a restaurant with Limbaugh, when all of a sudden people started coming over to get his—Limbaugh's—autograph. "I became security, organizing the line," says Bennett. Of Limbaugh, never short of superlatives to describe himself, Bennett says, as though he were on the show, "He is possibly our greatest living American."

Limbaugh is pursued by media of every stripe, and by conservatives eager to hitch their wagons to his rising star in an age of ostensible conservative decline. This fall Limbaugh invades television, with a nationally syndicated half-hour show produced by Roger Ailes; his first book, *The Way Things Ought to Be,* is due out soon from Pocket Books; a newsletter is also in the works. All these projects have temporarily taken Limbaugh off the speaking circuit, where his fee was $25,000. Nonetheless, it's expected that he'll gross more than $2 million this year, up from $500,000 in 1989 and not bad for a guy who not too long ago had trouble paying the mortgage.

Born in 1951 in Cape Girardeau, Missouri, Limbaugh went to work as a disc jockey for a station in his hometown at age 16, later moving on to Pittsburgh and Kansas City. Tired of spinning platters, he joined the Kansas City Royals in 1979 as director of group sales, but he couldn't stay away from the mike. By 1984 he was hosting a daytime talk show on KFBK in Sacramento. There Limbaugh developed parts of the show that since 1988 he has syndicated from New York—a show that many credit with raising AM radio from the dead.

Limbaugh's career path did not please his father, who died in 1990. Descended from a line of lawyers and Republicans (his grandfather served as Eisenhower's ambassador to India, and his uncle is a Reagan-appointed judge), Limbaugh chucked college after only one year. He did retain his father's political conservatism, however, and he remains an autodidact, confessing on air in May, for example, that, although coming to them late in life, he recently had been reading the *Federalist Papers.*

Radio is where Limbaugh can be himself—which formula, he says, is   10
the key to his success. Being Limbaugh is something only Limbaugh can do. By his hearty voice you might suspect he shops at big men's stores, which, weighing 317 pounds, he does. There is nothing shy about his performance, as he variously describes himself as "serving humanity," being "on the cutting edge of societal evolution," "redefining greatness on the radio," and "saying more in five seconds than most talk show hosts say in a whole show." Limbaugh's mother did well by following family precedent in naming him Rush; imagine a refrigerator of a fullback stomping across the North American continent, gleefully stiff-arming every liberal in his

path. Limbaugh takes some getting used to, but he says you're wrong if you think he's arrogant—he's just self-confident. Limbaugh's self-descrip-tions are a sort of trademark: in selling himself he's really selling his show, carving his own identity indelibly in the American mind. And it doesn't hurt that he pokes fun at himself, too.

So it is that, when the news at noon is over and 12:06 p.m. has arrived, Limbaugh begins:

> Greetings, conversationalists across the fruited plain, this is Rush Lim-baugh, the most dangerous man in America, with the largest hypothala-mus in North America, serving humanity simply by opening my mouth, destined for my own wing in the Museum of Broadcasting, executing everything I do flawlessly with zero mistakes, doing this show with half my brain tied behind my back just to make it fair because I have talent on loan from . . . God. Rush Limbaugh. A man. A legend. A way of life.

I have entered Two Penn Plaza here in Manhattan and taken the elevator high above Madison Square Garden to a floor that is home to WABC 770, where the scourge of liberals holds forth weekdays from noon to three. I wait in the small reception room, but not long. The door opens and before me appears a red-haired guy in khaki shorts and a T-shirt. My eyes are drawn to his footwear, a pair of Chuck Taylor's Converse, black low-tops. Immediately I know I am nowhere near the straight-faced solemnity of the "dominant media culture." Kit Carson, chief of (a very small) staff for the show—and whose real name *is* Kit, just as his brother's is Johnny—leads me to the control room from which I can observe the world's most danger-ous man.

I see a large face framed by a headset that covers the ears as thoroughly as a pair of earmuffs. Whatever else may be happening in America, this man is having a rollicking good time. Whenever music rolls, he drums his fingers on the table before him, as though he were still a DJ. At eye level is the microphone, and at arm's length, on a stand, are various papers. Limbaugh pulls at this bit of paper and then that, commenting in a Midwest-ern accent that has a touch of Harry Caray* in it on what's in the news or in the faxes that pour into his office. The voice *must* be listened to, for not only is there no telling what will be said next, there is not even any figuring how it might be said, and all the while an experienced (even for a day) listener has the expectation that a huge laugh, in which he can join, is about to break out. Throughout his commentary Limbaugh snaps his sheets of paper between his thumbs and forefingers, as loudly as he can. The sound zips through the mike: it is background music of sorts for the "Excellence in Broadcasting Network," which has one and only one show.

Harry Caray (b. 1919): the longtime radio announcer for the Chicago Cubs

"I see stuff," Limbaugh later tells me, "and say 'Wow! What a good show I'm going to have today!' " He had seen some good stuff that morning, just days after Bill Clinton took on Sister Souljah. Limbaugh expresses his strong agreement with Clinton and excoriates black leaders, like Jesse Jackson, who want him to apologize. What she said "can't stand the test of reason or morality," says Limbaugh. "I'm appalled by it." Today, as always, Limbaugh does with Jesse Jackson what cannot be done in print and what would not come across so effectively on television. He refers to him as The Reverend Jackson, pausing between "The" and "Reverend," and "Reverend" and "Jackson," drawing out the first syllable of "Reverend," and pronouncing the three words in a near whisper because, as Limbaugh explains, this is a man no one dares reproach. Limbaugh draws a cartoon, in effect. The Clinton-Souljah-Jackson topic leads Limbaugh on to urban matters: he goes after Ice-T's "Cop Killer" album, deplores the rioting in Chicago that occurred the night the Bulls won their NBA Championship, and speaks his mind (as he has since late April) about the rioting in Los Angeles and the apologetic political responses to it.

Limbaugh has occasion to praise Oliver North and Dan Quayle, to   15
laud talk shows ("You people in the dominant media culture don't understand why candidates go on talk shows. . . . This is a wonderful development"), to knock the *New York Times* for an anti-Quayle story, and to criticize Ross Perot's bid for the presidency. Every mention of Perot's name triggers a playing of "When Johnny Comes Marching Home Again."

Today, as on other days, there is an "Animal Rights Update" and, per usual, a few calls: one about racial hatred, another about a First Amendment case, another about Oliver North's appearance on CNBC (Limbaugh: "He's very cool, he's mastered the medium"), another from a woman who identifies herself as a "feminazi liberal" but nonetheless tells "Rush" (every caller calls him that), "I love you anyway." Limbaugh exits to commercials with "bump" music, usually rock 'n' roll. Today, at one point, Limbaugh signals his crew to use the "Cultural Bump." A while ago some Limbaugh fan wrote and sung lyrics to a Puccini tune; the operatic composition includes a description of Limbaugh as "the conservative voice of freedom heard throughout all America." It is a stitch to hear this sung, and Carson and company, who have heard it many times before, are laughing along with Limbaugh.

Limbaugh focuses on three causes in particular—environmentalism, animal rights activism, and feminism—because he believes that underlying all three are anti-capitalism, secular humanism, and socialism. He does make distinctions: for example, the environmentalist wackos, whom he excoriates, are not to be confused with serious "ecology-minded people," whom he applauds. But Limbaugh paints with a broad brush, and his targets are in ready supply: all those who seek to eliminate natural differences between man and nature, between men and women, and even between man and God.

Limbaugh may seem an unlikely conservative warrior. Twice divorced with no children, he is now single, and though he believes in God, he does not go to church. But Limbaugh disdains the "lifestyle liberalism" of many in the media (and Hollywood and politics), who live on the basis of the proposition that there is no higher authority than the individual, no higher end for man (which is to say for the human person) than his constant self-creation. Limbaugh has come to his cultural conservatism not through intellection but naturally, having been formed by a Missouri culture much sterner than what prevails in many places today. It's no wonder that Limbaugh has gone to bat repeatedly on behalf of Dan Quayle in his war against Murphy Brown and others, even suspending his no-guests-in-the-studio rule to allow Quayle to share his microphone for half an hour one afternoon in July.

Limbaugh battles the absurd by *being* absurd, as he puts it. Because he thinks it absurd that public schools now distribute condoms, Limbaugh produces his mock commercials about "bungee condoms." He thus does not avoid the word "condoms," as might those cultural conservatives who are put off by Limbaugh's occasional crudity and not always PG language. Limbaugh opposes the excrescences of modernity by being excrescently modern—another irony.

What Limbaugh's impact upon the nation will be is unclear. Limbaugh [20] believes liberalism is dying. I'm not so sure. Some of the more extreme aspects of *political* liberalism have died. But cultural liberalism has deep roots in ideologies dating from the last century, is difficult to address through most of the ordinary instruments of our politics, and will need exposure to something much stronger than EIB* if it is to be constrained. And bear in mind James Q. Wilson's observation (made in his seminal 1980 *Commentary* piece, "Reagan and the Republican Revival") that in periods of broad cultural change, such as we have been witnessing since the 1960s, "the forces of tradition have ultimately lost." The battle over the nation's future will continue to take place in the classroom, from kindergarten through graduate school, and conservatives have yet to mount an effective takeover of a major university. Still, Limbaugh has become a major point of resistance to liberalism in the popular culture, and the ultimate effect of his daily cartooning may be to delegitimize for a huge segment of Americans those whom the dominant media have lionized. Whether this subversive work will lead to a more sensible national discourse is an open question. . . .

EIB: the Excellence in Broadcasting Network (see paragraph 13)

Might the card-carrying Republican eventually cross over into politics? Limbaugh says he's not interested in becoming a politician, that he knows and respects the enormous difference between politics and talk radio. Harder to accept is his contention that he does not seek political influence. "I have no cause, no political agenda," he says. "I just want to be the best radio guy I can be. If I succeed, it will be because I do a good show." But his show will not be a good show unless Limbaugh is being himself, and that means he will be talking politics, and who ever seriously talked about politics without hoping to win the argument?

Perhaps Limbaugh's most important impact will be on his fellow conservatives. Evans and Novak* reported in May that "a longtime Bush backer" had advised the President that "to save himself" this election year, he would do well "to imitate the style of Rush Limbaugh." It's not so much that Bush and others should emulate Limbaugh's style as partake of his hearty optimism. There's nothing wrong with being right at least 97.9 percent of the time.

QUESTIONING THE TEXT

1. Early in this article, Eastland mentions a "dominant media culture." Do you believe that such a culture exists? If so, how would you characterize it? If not, why might Limbaugh and Eastland believe in it?

2. How would you characterize Eastland's attitude toward Limbaugh? What specific strategies does he use to portray him?

3. According to "Nightline" host Ted Koppel, Limbaugh has become "something of an icon to millions of conservative listeners." Look up the various meanings of *icon* in the dictionary and then write an extended definition of the word as you believe Koppel is employing it. Be sure your definition names other people regarded as icons by our culture.

4. Notice J.R.'s use of dialogue in the introduction to this essay. Why do you think he brings in other voices here? What are the advantages and disadvantages of this strategy?

MAKING CONNECTIONS

5. Eastland makes much of the fact that Limbaugh is a college dropout

---

Evans and Novak: Rowland Evans, Jr. (b. 1921), and Robert Novak (b. 1931), syndicated columnists and television commentators

and an autodidact. Which of the other legends cited in this chapter would you guess didn't attend or finish college? Can you draw any conclusions from this limited sample?

6. Describing himself as "A man. A legend. A way of life," Limbaugh promotes himself agressively. Do (did) other icons in this chapter have similar control over their images? To what extent is self-promotion necessary for fame? Think about this question and then see if you can write a paragraph about yourself in the mode that Limbaugh uses on p. 495 to greet his audience.

JOINING THE CONVERSATION

7. Write two or three paragraphs describing a person at work that are modeled after Eastland's description of Limbaugh in his radio studio. Be attentive to sights, sounds, and dialogue.

8. During the 1992 presidential campaign, much was made of Bill Clinton's and Ross Perot's effective use of talk show appearances to reach the public. Since then, the role talk shows (both radio and TV) should play in democratic politics has been the subject of considerable debate. Do people like Larry King, Phil Donahue, Oprah Winfrey, and Rush Limbaugh focus debate or distort it? Defend your opinion in a guest editorial for your school or local paper.

9. Limbaugh claims that his highly political radio and TV shows are primarily just entertainment. In class, discuss the relationship between entertainment, entertainers, and politics in the United States. Then write an exploratory essay on the subject, examining whether the two realms are or ought to be separate.

OSSIE DAVIS
Our Shining Black Prince
and
Why I Eulogized Malcolm X

ACTOR, AUTHOR, PLAYWRIGHT, PRODUCER, DIRECTOR, *television host and commentator, social activist, community leader, longtime husband of Ruby Dee, father of three—Ossie Davis (b. 1917) is all these things and more. He has spent much of his distinguished career documenting and celebrating African American experiences, particularly in his dramatic fable* Purlie Victorious *and its musical adaptation,* Purlie, *about which Davis has said, "Purlie told me I would never find my manhood by asking the white man to define it for me, that I would never become a man until I stopped measuring my black self by white standards." It seems particularly appropriate, then, that Davis deliver a eulogy for Malcolm X, whom he sees as "our living, black manhood."*

Davis also acknowledges that Malcolm X (1925–65) was an extraordinarily complex and controversial person. His swift rise to power in the Nation of Islam (known to many as Black Muslims) linked his name with militant black separatism, but after being suddenly rejected by that movement and undertaking a pilgrimage to the holy Muslim cities of Mecca and Medina, he was inspired by a new vision of equality and freedom among people of all races. His autobiography (1965) reveals his feeling that he might not see the book's publication, and, indeed, early that year in Harlem he was assassinated. Three Black Muslims were later convicted for his murder.

Malcolm X provides us with an extraordinary example of a person who was a legend—in both positive and negative ways—during his own lifetime. Since his death, a number of forces have competed in constructing the legend of Malcolm that will, perhaps, go down in history. You may have seen Spike Lee's recent film or television specials that are part of the effort to codify Malcolm's legendary status. If so, reading the following eulogy (delivered at Malcolm's funeral) and retrospective essay explaining the reasons for the eulogy will be especially interesting, because doing so will allow you to compare the interpretations of Malcolm in each treatment of him.

I chose these pieces because I have been strongly affected by Malcolm's autobiography and because in my lifetime I have seen him portrayed in a startling number of diverse ways. Will the "real" Malcolm X ever emerge? Only in the minds and imaginations of readers and viewers like you and me. – A.L.

500

OUR SHINING BLACK PRINCE

Here—at this final hour, in this quiet place—Harlem* has come to bid farewell to one of its brightest hopes—extinguished now, and gone from us forever.

For Harlem is where he worked and where he struggled and fought—his home of homes, where his heart was, and where his people are—and it is, therefore, most fitting that we meet once again—in Harlem—to share these last moments with him.

For Harlem has ever been gracious to those who have loved her, have fought for her, and have defended her honor even to the death. It is not in the memory of man that this beleaguered, unfortunate but nonetheless proud community has found a braver, more gallant young champion than this Afro-American who lies before us—unconquered still.

I say the word again, as he would want me to: Afro-American—Afro-American Malcolm, who was a master, was most meticulous in his use of words. Nobody knew better than he the power words have over the minds of men. Malcolm had stopped being a "Negro"* years ago.

It had become too small, too puny, too weak a word for him. Malcolm   5
was bigger than that. Malcolm had become an Afro-American and he wanted—so desperately—that we, that all his people, would become Afro-Americans too.

There are those who will consider it their duty, as friends of the Negro people, to tell us to revile him, to flee, even from the presence of his memory, to save ourselves by writing him out of the history of our turbulent times.

Many will ask what Harlem finds to honor in this stormy, controversial and bold young captain—and we will smile.

Many will say turn away—away from this man, for he is not a man but a demon, a monster, a subverter and an enemy of the black man—and we will smile.

They will say that he is of hate—a fanatic, a racist—who can only bring evil to the cause for which you struggle!

And we will answer and say unto them: Did you ever talk to Brother   10
Malcolm? Did you ever touch him, or have him smile at you? Did you ever really listen to him? Did he ever do a mean thing? Was he ever himself associated with violence or any public disturbance? For if you did you would know him. And if you knew him you would know why we must honor him: Malcolm was our manhood, our living, black manhood! This was

---

Harlem: For another writer's assessment of his own relationship to Harlem, see Langston Hughes's poem "Theme for English B," on p. 439.

"Negro": For another reaction to the use of this term and alternatives to it, see the interview with Rosa Parks on p. 460.

his meaning to his people. And, in honoring him, we honor the best in ourselves.

Last year, from Africa, he wrote these words to a friend: "My journey," he says, "is almost ended, and I have a much broader scope than when I started out, which I believe will add new life and dimension to our struggle for freedom and honor and dignity in the States. I am writing these things so that you will know for a fact the tremendous sympathy and support we have among the African States for our Human Rights struggle. The main thing is that we keep a United Front wherein our most valuable time and energy will not be wasted fighting each other."

However much we may have differed with him—or with each other about him and his value as a man—let his going from us serve only to bring us together, now. Consigning these mortal remains to earth, the common mother of all, secure in the knowledge that what we place in the ground is no more now a man—but a seed—which, after the winter of our discontent, will come forth again to meet us. And we will know him then for what he was and is—a Prince—our own black shining Prince!—who didn't hesitate to die, because he loved us so.

WHY I EULOGIZED MALCOLM X

You are not the only person curious to know why I would eulogize a man like Malcolm X. Many who know and respect me have written letters. Of these letters I am proudest of those from a sixth-grade class of young white boys and girls who asked me to explain. I appreciate your giving me this chance to do so.

You may anticipate my defense somewhat by considering the following fact: no Negro has yet asked me that question. (My pastor, Reverend Samuel Austin, of Grace Baptist Church where I teach Sunday school, preached a sermon about Malcolm in which he called him a "giant in a sick world.") Every one of the many letters I got from my own people lauded Malcolm as a man, and commended me for having spoken at his funeral.

At the same time—and that is important—most all of them took special pains to disagree with much or all of what Malcolm said and what he stood for. That is, with one singing exception, they all, every last, black, glory-hugging one of them, knew that Malcolm—whatever else he was or was not—Malcolm was a man!

White folks do not need anybody to remind them that they are men. We do! This was his one incontrovertible benefit to his people.

We used to think that protocol and common sense required that Negroes stand back and let the white man speak up for us, defend us, and lead us from behind the scene in our fight. This was the essence of Negro politics. But Malcolm said to hell with that! Get up off your knees and fight your

5

own battles. That's the way to win back your self-respect. That's the way to make the white man respect you. And if he won't let you live like a man, he certainly can't keep you from dying like one!

Malcolm, as you can see, was refreshing excitement; he scared hell out of the rest of us, bred as we are to caution, to hypocrisy in the presence of white folks, to the smile that never fades. Malcolm knew that every white man in America profits directly or indirectly from his position vis-à-vis Negroes, profits from racism even though he does not practice it or believe in it.

He also knew that every Negro who did not challenge on the spot every instance of racism, overt or covert, committed against him and his people, who chose instead to swallow his spit and go on smiling, was an Uncle Tom and a traitor, without balls or guts, or any other commonly accepted aspects of manhood!

Now, we knew all these things as well as Malcolm did, but we also knew what happened to people who stick their necks out and say them. And if all the lies we tell ourselves by way of extenuation were put into print, it would constitute one of the great chapters in the history of man's justifiable cowardice in the face of other men.

But Malcolm kept snatching our lies away. He kept shouting the painful truth we whites and blacks did not want to hear from all the house-tops. And he wouldn't stop for love nor money.

You can imagine what a howling, shocking nuisance this man was to   10
both Negroes and whites. Once Malcolm fastened on you, you could not escape. He was one of the most fascinating and charming men I have ever met, and never hesitated to take his attractiveness and beat you to death with it. Yet his irritation, though painful to us, was most salutary. He would make you angry as hell, but he would also make you proud. It was impossible to remain defensive and apologetic about being a Negro in his presence. He wouldn't let you. And you always left his presence with the sneaky suspicion that maybe, after all, you *were* a man!

But in explaining Malcolm, let me take care not to explain him away. He had been a criminal, an addict, a pimp, and a prisoner: a racist, and a hater, he had really believed the white man was a devil. But all this had changed. Two days before his death, in commenting to Gordon Parks about his past life, he said: "That was a mad scene. The sickness and madness of those days! I'm glad to be free of them."

And Malcolm was free. No one who knew him before and after his trip to Mecca could doubt that he had completely abandoned racism, separatism, and hatred. But he had not abandoned his shock-effect statements, his bristling agitation for immediate freedom in this country not only for blacks, but for everybody.

And most of all, in the area of race relations, he still delighted in twisting the white man's tail, and in making Uncle Toms, compromisers, and accommodationists—I deliberately include myself—thoroughly ashamed of the urbane and smiling hypocrisy we practice merely to exist in a world whose values we both envy and despise.

But even had Malcolm not changed, he would still have been a relevant figure on the American scene, standing in relation as he does, to the "responsible" civil rights leaders, just about where John Brown stood in relation to the "responsible" abolitionist in the fight against slavery. Many disagreed with Brown's mad and fanatical tactics which led him to attack a Federal arsenal at Harpers Ferry, to lose two sons there, and later to be hanged for treason.

Yet today the world, and especially the Negro people, proclaim Brown   15
not a traitor, but a hero and a martyr in a noble cause. So in future, I will not be surprised if men come to see that Malcolm X was, within his own limitations, and in his own inimitable style, also a martyr in that cause.

But there is much controversy still about this most controversial American, and I am content to wait for history to make the final decision.

But in personal judgment, there is no appeal from instinct. I knew the man personally, and however much I might have disagreed with him from time to time, I never doubted that Malcolm X, even when he was wrong, was always that rarest thing in the world among us Negroes: a true man.

And if, to protect my relations with the many good white folks who make it possible for me to earn a fairly good living in the entertainment industry, I was too chicken, too cautious, to admit that fact when he was alive, I thought at least that now, when all the white folks are safe from him at last, I could be honest with myself enough to lift my hat for one final salute to that brave, black, ironic gallantry, which was his style and hallmark, the shocking *zing* of fire-and-be-damned-to-you, so absolutely absent in every other Negro man I know, which brought him, too soon, to his death.

QUESTIONING THE TEXT

1. In the final line of his eulogy for Malcolm, Davis invokes a Christian comparison, for Jesus is another important figure who "didn't hesitate to die, because he loved us so." What other implicit or explicit comparisons can you find in Davis's texts between Malcolm and other people, events, or types (such as champions)? How do such comparisons lead readers to build an interpretation of Malcolm?
2. Does Davis feel any ambivalence toward Malcolm? What in his eulogy or his defense of it leads you to answer the question as you do?
3. What is A.L.'s own attitude toward Malcolm? What words and phrases in her headnote reveal her attitude?

MAKING CONNECTIONS

4. Ellen Goodman argues (p. 475) that we want to "unmask our heroes." Does anything in Ossie Davis's eulogy or defense suggest an "unmasking"?
5. Greil Marcus says that the legends described in his book *Mystery Train* "define different versions of America." What version of America does Malcolm X define, and how does it compare with the version defined by Elvis Presley—or by Billy the Kid or Madonna or Eleanor Roosevelt or Rosa Parks? (The readings about these figures start on pp. 478, 451, 486, 474, and 460, respectively.)

JOINING THE CONVERSATION

6. Choose a person, either living or dead, you very much admire and respect (even if you sometimes, like Ossie Davis, do not agree with the person). Then try your hand at writing a eulogy for this person, using Davis's as a guide to format, length, or even tone.
7. Working with two or three classmates, either interview several people (on or off campus) who are particularly knowledgeable about Malcolm X or gather three sources on Malcolm that take differing stands toward him. In addition, one group member should read Malcolm's autobiography. Then pool your information, looking for competing versions of or responses to Malcolm. Finally, working together, prepare a 10-minute class presentation on "Varying Versions of Malcolm X."

P. J. O'ROURKE
Fiddling While Africa Starves

STAGE A "PROCHOICE" RALLY, an antiwar buffet, or an environmental protest these days and Hollywood stars gather like politicians around a pork barrel. No director, actor, screenwriter, or personality, *it seems, can afford to be without his or her cause-of-the-moment.*

But frankly, I'm skeptical when celebrities who can barely read a Tele-PrompTer pontificate about global warming or genetic engineering. I generally ignore lectures about homelessness from superstars with thousand-acre ranches in Bozeman, Montana.

A few notables support causes with admirable grace, like Elizabeth Taylor for AIDS and Jerry Lewis for muscular dystrophy. But I'm afraid Madonna is more typical, making videos to promote voter registration but rarely straying into a voting booth herself. I guess cameras aren't allowed there.

If one sanctimonious star is insufferable, a chorus of do-gooders is enough to make the Archangel Gabriel defect. Just such a choir is the subject of P. J. O'Rourke's hilarious meditation on the rich and fatuous, "Fiddling While Africa Starves." O'Rourke (b. 1947) charges after a target that, at first glance, seems unassailable: concerts and records intended to raise money for starving people. But who really benefits the most from these extravaganzas? Guess.

"Fiddling While Africa Starves" appears in a collection of O'Rourke's essays entitled Give War a Chance *(1993). O'Rourke also writes for* The American Spectator *and* Rolling Stone. *– J.R.*

When the "We Are the World" video first slithered into public view, I was sitting around with a friend who himself happens to be in show business. The thing gave him the willies. Me too. But neither of us could figure exactly why. "Whenever you see people that pleased with themselves on a stage," said my friend, "you know you're in for a bad show."* And the USA for Africa performers did have that self-satisfied look of toddlers on a pot. But in this world of behemoth evils, such a minor lapse of taste shouldn't have upset us. We changed the channel.

Half a year later, in the middle of the Live Aid broadcast, my friend called me. "Turn on your television," he said. "This is horrible. They're in a frenzy."

"a bad show": For an account of a show that the writer apparently felt suffered from such complacency on the part of the performer, see Greil Marcus, "Elvis: Presliad," p. 478.

"Well," I said, "at least it's a frenzy of charity."

"Oh, no," he said, "it could be *anything*. Next time it might be 'Kill the Jews.'"

A mob, even an eleemosynary mob, is an ugly thing to see. No good ever came of mass emotion. The audience that's easily moved to tears is as easily moved to sadistic dementia. People are not thinking under such circumstances. And poor, dreadful Africa is something which surely needs thought.

The Band Aid, Live Aid, USA for Africa concerts and records (and videos, posters, T-shirts, lunch buckets, thermos bottles, bath toys, etc.) are supposed to illuminate the plight of the Africans. Note the insights provided by these lyrics:

> *We are the world* [solipsism], *we are the children* [average age near
> forty]
> *We are the ones to make a brighter day* [unproven]
> *So let's start giving* [logical inference supplied without argument]
> *There's a choice we're making* [true as far as it goes]
> *We're saving our own lives* [absurd]
> *It's true we'll make a better day* [see line 2 above]
> *Just you and me* [statistically unlikely]

That's three palpable untruths, two dubious assertions, nine uses of a first-person pronoun, not a single reference to trouble or anybody in it and no facts. The verse contains, literally, neither rhyme nor reason.

And these musical riots of philanthropy address themselves to the wrong problems. There is, of course, a shortage of food among Africans, but that doesn't mean there's a shortage of food *in* Africa. "A huge backlog of emergency grain has built up at the Red Sea port of Assab," says the *Christian Science Monitor*. "Food sits rotting in Ethiopia," reads a headline in the *St. Louis Post-Dispatch*. And according to hunger maven William Shawcross, 200,000 tons of food aid delivered to Ethiopia is being held in storage by the country's government.

There's also, of course, a lack of transport for that food. But that's not the real problem either. The authorities in Addis Ababa have plenty of trucks for their military operations against the Eritrean rebels, and much of the rest of Ethiopia's haulage is being used for forcibly resettling people instead of feeding them. Western governments are reluctant to send more trucks, for fear they'll be used the same way. And similar behavior can be seen in the rest of miserable Africa.

The African relief fad serves to distract attention from the real issues. There is famine in Ethiopia, Chad, Sudan and areas of Mozambique. All these countries are involved in pointless civil wars. There are pockets of famine in Mauritania, Niger and Mali—the result of desertification caused mostly by idiot agricultural policies. African famine is not a visitation of fate. It is largely man-made, and the men who made it are largely Africans.

Enormous irrigation projects have been put onto lands that cannot support them and into cultures that cannot use them. Feeble-witted nationalism puts borders in the way of nomadic peoples who used to pick up and move when things got dry. Rural poverty drives populations to African cities where governments keep food prices artificially low, thus increasing rural poverty. Bumbling and corrupt central planning stymies farm production. And the hideous regimes use hunger as a weapon to suppress rebellion. People are not just starving. They are *being* starved.

"Socialist" ideals infest Africa like malaria or dengue fever. African leaders, lost in the frippery of centrist thinking, fail to deal with market forces or any other natural phenomena. Leave it to a Marxist to see the world as the world is not. It's not unusual for African intellectuals to receive their education at such august bodies of learning as Patrice Lumumba U. in Moscow. That is, they are trained by a nation which intentionally starved millions of its citizens in order to collectivize farming.

Death is the result of bad politics. And the Aid concerts are examples of the bad logic that leads to bad politics. It's probably not going too far to say that Africa's problems have been produced by the same kind of dim, ignorant thinking found among American pop artists. "If we take, say, six months and not spend any money on nuclear weapons, and just spend it on food, I think we could make a big dent," says Waylon Jennings in the USA for Africa publicity packet. In fact, a small nuclear weapon placed directly under Haile Mariam Mengistu* and his pals would probably make a more beneficial dent than a whole U.S. defense budget worth of canned goods.

Anyway, money is not going to solve the problem. Yet the concert nonsense is all put strictly in terms of cash. Perhaps it is the only thing the idiot famous understand.

Getting people to give vast amounts of money when there's no firm   15
idea what that money will do is like throwing maidens down a well. It's an appeal to magic. And the results are likely to be as stupid and disappointing as the results of magic usually are.

But, say some, Live Aid sets a good example for today's selfish youth, reminding them to be socially concerned. Nonsense. The circus atmosphere of the Live Aid concerts makes the world's problems seem easy and fun to solve and implies that the solutions are naturally uncontroversial. As an example of charity, Live Aid couldn't be worse. Charity entails sacrifice. Yet the Live Aid performers are sacrificing nothing. Indeed, they're gaining public adulation and a thoroughly unmerited good opinion of themselves. Plus it's free advertising. These LPs, performances and multiform by-products have nothing in common with charity. Instead they levy a sort of

---

Haile Mariam Mengistu (b. 1937): former Marxist head of state of Ethiopia

regressive alms tax on the befuddled millions. The performers donate their time, which is wholly worthless. Big corporations donate their services, which are worth little enough. Then the poor audience pledges all the contributions and buys all the trash with money it can ill afford. The worst nineteenth-century robber barons wouldn't have had the cheek to put forward such a bunco scheme. They may have given away tainted money, but at least they didn't ask you to give away yours.

One more thing, the music's lousy. If we must save the world with a song, what's the matter with the Metropolitan Opera Company?

Rock and roll's dopey crusade against African hunger has, I posit, added to the stock of human misery. And not just audibly. Any religious person—whether he worships at a pile of gazelle bones or in the Cathedral of St. Paul—will tell you egotism is the source of sin. The lust for power that destroys the benighted Ethiope has the same fountainhead as the lust for fame that propels the lousy pop band. "Not every one that saith unto me, Lord, Lord, shall enter into the kingdom of heaven."* Let alone everyone that saith sha la la la la and doobie doobie do.

QUESTIONING THE TEXT

1. Underline any words and phrases that convey O'Rourke's particular disdain for the "We-Are-the-Worlders." Is he engaging in name-calling, or is the technique more effective than that?
2. Have you seen any of the concerts or videos O'Rourke criticizes? Do you find his comments about them fair? Has he changed your point of view about them?
3. How is your reading of "Fiddling While Africa Starves" influenced by the tone of J.R.'s introduction? Does an introduction that so clearly takes sides intrude upon your independent judgment of O'Rourke's piece?

MAKING CONNECTIONS

4. To what good ends might fame be put? Survey the people described throughout this chapter (Joe Louis, Billy the Kid, Rosa Parks, Rush Limbaugh, Eleanor Roosevelt, Elvis Presley, Madonna, and Malcolm X) and then, in a paragraph or so, praise one whose notoriety has served useful purposes.

"Not every . . . heaven": a biblical quotation (Matthew 7:21 in the King James Version) in which the speaker is Jesus

JOINING THE CONVERSATION

5. Write a brief summary of O'Rourke's article, leaving out the humor and satire but retaining his basic arguments. With a group of several classmates, review your abstracts. Are O'Rourke's arguments coherent? What do they lose when reduced to a summary?

6. Choose a subject that you think deserves to be shown in a different light from the one in which it is usually seen, the way O'Rourke overhauls his readers' perceptions of charity concerts. Then write a paper on that subject for an audience of college students.

JUDY GRAHN
The Marilyn Monroe Poem

Even a generation after her death, you needn't use the last name: everyone knows her as Marilyn. She was Hollywood's greatest production, bigger than Cinerama, Gone With the Wind, *or* The Ten Commandments. *Until she died mysteriously in her bed from an overdose of sleeping pills (the official account, not much believed anymore), Marilyn seemed to embody the American dream, catapulting in a few luminous years from calendar girl to superstar, even before that word was coined.*

She was as garishly American as a '59 Cadillac, outrageous and innocent in the same breathless breath. The original "material girl," she created an image that starlets today still parody, dreaming of success. She married at least two American icons, Arthur Miller and Joe DiMaggio, mind and batter. She made some terrible films—and just enough good ones to give substance to her legend. She wanted to be a serious actress, but her real genius was for comedy. She wanted to be loved, but had to settle for idolatry.

Everyone, it seems, now has a version of Marilyn. The following is poet Judy Grahn's. Grahn (b. 1940) writes poetry that addresses political, social, and sexual issues, particularly those affecting working-class women. Her poems have been collected in The Work of a Common Woman *(1978). "The Marilyn Monroe Poem" was first published in 1971.* — J.R.

I have come to claim
Marilyn Monroe's body
for the sake of my own.
dig it up, hand it over,
cram it in this paper sack. 5
hubba. hubba. hubba.
look at those luscious
long brown bones, that wide and crusty
pelvis. ha Ha, oh she wanted so much to be serious
but she never stops smiling now. 10
Has she lost her mind?

Marilyn, be serious—they're taking
your picture, and they're taking the pictures
of eight young women in New York City

who murdered themselves for being pretty   15
by the same method as you, the very
next day, after you!
I have claimed their bodies, too,
they smile up out of my paper sack
like brainless cinderellas.   20

the reporters are furious, they're asking
me questions
what right does a woman have
to Marilyn Monroe's body? and what
am I doing for lunch? They think I   25
mean to eat you. Their teeth are lurid
and they want to pose me, leaning
on the shovel, nude. Don't squint.
But when one of the reporters comes too close
I beat him, bust his camera   30
with your long, smooth thigh
and with your lovely knucklebone
I break his eye.

Long ago you wanted to write poems;
Be serious, Marilyn   35
I am going to take you in this paper sack
around the world, and
write on it:—the poems of Marilyn Monroe—
Dedicated to all princes,
the male poets who were so sorry to see you go,   40
before they had a crack at you.
They wept for you, and also
they wanted to stuff you
while you still had a little meat left
in useful places;   45
but they were too slow.

Now I shall take them my paper sack
and we shall act out a poem together:
"How would you like to see Marilyn Monroe,
in action, smiling, and without her clothes?"   50
We shall wait long enough to see them make familiar faces
and then I shall beat them with your skull.
hubba. hubba. hubba. hubba. hubba.
Marilyn, be serious
Today I have come to claim your body for my own.   55

IN RESPONSE

1. Describe your feelings after reading "The Marilyn Monroe Poem." What surprises or shocks you?
2. Why do you think the speaker in the poem digs Marilyn up?
3. Write a page of response to the last line of the poem: "Today I have come to claim your body for my own."
4. Write a poem about one of the legends or authors featured in this chapter, calling it "The Joe Louis Poem," "The Maya Angelou Poem," "The Billy the Kid Poem," and so on.

OTHER READINGS

Farber, Celia. "Antihero." *Spin* Sept. 1991: 86–104; Oct. 1991: 84–88. Introduces Hurricane Camille. Paglia, that is.

Fire Lame Deer, John. "The White Buffalo Woman." *American Indian Myths and Legends*. Ed. Richard Erdoes and Alfonso Ortiz. New York: Pantheon, 1984. 47–52. Tells the story of perhaps the predominant figure in Sioux legend.

Himmelfarb, Gertrude. "Of Heroes, Villains, and Valets." *Commentary* June 1991: 20–26. Analyzes heroism and history.

Marcus, Greil. *Dead Elvis: A Chronicle of a Cultural Obsession*. New York: Doubleday, 1991. Explores the Elvis myth.

Morgan, Kathryn L. "Caddy Buffers: Legends of a Middle Class Black Family in Philadelphia." *Talk That Talk: An Anthology of African-American Storytelling*. Ed. Linda Goss and Marian E. Barnes. New York: Simon/Touchstone, 1989. 295–98. Tells the story of a legendary ancestor who was like a talisman family members could use to "buffer" themselves from hurtful racism.

Murphy, Cullen. "The 40th Parallel." *Atlantic* May 1990: 18–24. Argues that every town has its hero.

"The Power of Talk." *Newsweek* 8 Feb. 1993: 24–28. Explores why people are turning to radio talkmeisters for political enlightenment.

Quindlen, Anna. "Nowadays, Being a Princess Has Lost Its Romantic Appeal." *Columbus Dispatch* 1 June 1993: 5A. Argues that the dream of being a princess is no longer a popular one.

Tompkins, Jane P. *West of Everything: The Inner Life of Westerns*. New York: Oxford UP, 1992. Explores the power of Western heroes and the relation of Westerns to gender from a feminist perspective.

Ward, Geoffrey C. *American Originals: The Private Worlds of Some Singular Men and Women*. New York: HarperCollins, 1991. Includes politicians, entertainers, writers, artists, and "bad men and liars."

Wolf, Naomi. "Feminist Fatale." *New Republic* 16 Mar. 1992: 23–25. Suggests that Camille Paglia is the anti-Christ.

PART FOUR

How We Live

I would like to promise [my daughter] that she will grow up with a sense of her cousins and of rivers and of her great-grandmother's teacups. . . .
JOAN DIDION, *On Going Home*

My children are strangers/My family is back "home"
KAREN COOPER, *A Native Woman—1982*

". . . a poignant rejoinder to the caricatures of 'prolifers' . . . ."
NATIONAL REVIEW, *Another Pro-life Extremist*

The nuclear family's death has been greatly exaggerated, usually by those who have a stake in its demise.
JAY OVEROCKER, *Ozzie and Harriet in Hell*

Those who think of themselves as progressive . . . don't mind, in principle, the idea of interracial unions, but the prospect of children clouds the issue. . . .
DAVID UPDIKE, *The Colorings of Childhood*

Sometimes I feel strange having a lesbian mom. Sometimes it's hard, and sometimes it's just different.
SERENA, *Just Different, That's All*

"Good morning, ladies. It's 5 a.m. Time to get up."
COLLETTE H. RUSSELL, *A Day in the Homeless Life*

"I've got five kids! We live in one room! We're homeless!" No, ma'am, you're not. Your housing may be as bad as your family planning, but you're not homeless.
P. J. O'ROURKE, *Among the Compassion Fascists*

The long-term-care facility . . . I work for is owned by a corporation that owns nursing homes throughout the country. Giving corporations like this control over the quality of medical care is handing over control to the fox.
JILL FRAWLEY, *Inside the Home*

Grandpa's flowers are scattered/down the line of tombstones, decorating the graves of his wife, his children
ED MADDEN, *Family Cemetery, near Hickory Ridge, Arkansas*

Introduction

CONSIDER FOR A MOMENT some well-known phrases that feature the word *home*: "Home is where the heart is," for example, or "there's no place like home"; "home, sweet home"; "the home of the brave"; "you can't go home again." These phrases suggest that "home" is a place of comfort or solace, or at least "where the heart is." They capture what might be described as an American ideal of "home": a place where you can be safe and secure and living among those who care unconditionally for you.

In one of the most famous opening passages in literature, however, Leo Tolstoy complicates such an ideal vision of home: "All happy families resemble one another," he says, but "every unhappy family is unhappy in its own fashion" *(Anna Karenina)*. Tolstoy's sentence suggests what most of us know already in our bones: homes can be sites not only of comfort and solace but of pain and bitter unhappiness as well. In addition, one person's happy home is another person's disaster; what may look like a peaceful, loving home from one perspective may look just the opposite from another.

As this chapter will illustrate, in fact, what is "home" to one person may well be a "shelter" or a "long-term-care facility" or a place that exists only in the imagination to another. And whatever your own individual experience has been, you have certainly had some experience with the concept of "home." In fact, you have probably had multiple experiences with homes of various kinds, and some of these experiences may contradict or conflict with one another. This chapter may provide a timely opportunity, then, to consider the various places, people, or concepts you have known as "home" and to explore your own thinking about them. Before beginning it, you might want to consider these questions:

1. What places could be categorized as "home" for you?

2. What are some of the positive and/or negative qualities you associate with "home"?

3. What kind of home would you most like to be part of? What problems might keep you from having the home and family you desire?

4. How is "home" represented in the media? How is the word used in music and in the titles of films and TV and radio shows? You may want to brainstorm these questions with two or three classmates and bring your list to class for discussion.

• • •

JOAN DIDION
On Going Home

JOAN DIDION (b. 1934) has been writing for most of her life, from her days in high school and college in California through her years as copywriter and feature editor at Vogue *magazine to her ensuing highly successful career as a novelist and essayist. The essay on home and family that opens this chapter's conversation was written in 1966 and included in one of Didion's best-known collections,* Slouching Towards Bethlehem *(1969). The collection's title alludes to W. B. Yeats's poem "The Second Coming," which ends with the haunting question "And what rough beast, his hour come round at last, slouches towards Bethlehem to be born?"*

In "On Going Home," Didion says that for her "home" is not the place where she lives with her husband and baby daughter, but the one where the family in which she grew up lives. In that home, Didion locates the tension that comes from having had a "happy" home life that in adulthood routinely reduced her to tears after a phone conversation with family members. As she contemplates her baby daughter's birthday, she is certain that her daughter will receive the "ambushes" of family life in her own time. But Didion hopes for more for her daughter, more of a sense of home and family that will endure and sustain her.

This essay seems to me to capture the ambivalence many people feel about home and family. Certainly I can recall ambushes, pains, and fears associated with family life as I knew it, as well as deeply felt connections—particularly with my sisters—that have brought great happiness to me. And I am aware that although I live alone now, I have a very strong sense of the home I have made and the extended family I count as part of that home. I chose this essay, then, to prompt my own reassessment of what home and family mean to me. I hope they will prompt yours as well. — A.L.

I am home for my daughter's first birthday. By "home" I do not mean the house in Los Angeles where my husband and I and the baby live, but the place where my family is, in the Central Valley of California. It is a vital although troublesome distinction. My husband likes my family but is uneasy in their house, because once there I fall into their ways, which are difficult, oblique, deliberately inarticulate, not my husband's ways. We live in dusty houses ("D-U-S-T," he once wrote with his finger on surfaces all over the house, but no one noticed it) filled with mementos quite without value to him (what could the Canton dessert plates mean to him? how could he have known about the assay scales, why should he care if he did know?), and we appear to talk exclusively about people we know who have been committed to mental hospitals, about people we know who have been booked on drunk-driving charges, and about property, particularly about property, land, price per acre and C-2 zoning and assessments and freeway access. My brother does not understand my husband's inability to perceive the advantage in the rather common real-estate transaction known as "sale-leaseback," and my husband in turn does not understand why so many of the people he hears about in my father's house have recently been committed to mental hospitals or booked on drunk-driving charges. Nor does he understand that when we talk about sale-leasebacks and right-of-way condemnations we are talking in code about the things we like best, the yellow fields and the cottonwoods and the rivers rising and falling and the mountain roads closing when the heavy snow comes in. We miss each other's points, have another drink and regard the fire. My brother refers to my husband, in his presence, as "Joan's husband." Marriage is the classic betrayal.

Or perhaps it is not any more. Sometimes I think that those of us who are now in our thirties were born into the last generation to carry the burden of "home," to find in family life the source of all tension and drama. I had by all objective accounts a "normal" and a "happy" family situation, and yet I was almost thirty years old before I could talk to my family on the telephone without crying after I had hung up. We did not fight. Nothing was wrong. And yet some nameless anxiety colored the emotional charges between me and the place that I came from. The question of whether or not you could go home again was a very real part of the sentimental and largely literary baggage with which we left home in the fifties; I suspect that it is irrelevant to the children born of the fragmentation after World War II. A few weeks ago in a San Francisco bar I saw a pretty young girl on crystal* take off her clothes and dance for the cash prize in an "amateur-topless" contest. There was no particular sense of moment about this, none of the effect of romantic degradation, of "dark journey," for which my generation strived so assiduously. What sense could that girl possibly make of, say, *Long Day's Journey into Night?** Who is beside the point?

That I am trapped in this particular irrelevancy is never more apparent to me than when I am home. Paralyzed by the neurotic lassitude engendered by meeting one's past at every turn, around every corner, inside every cupboard, I go aimlessly from room to room. I decide to meet it head-on and clean out a drawer, and I spread the contents on the bed. A bathing suit I wore the summer I was seventeen. A letter of rejection from *The*

---

crystal: a stimulant drug
Long Day's Journey into Night: an autobiographical play by Eugene O'Neill (1888–1953) focusing on his early family life

*Nation,** an aerial photograph of the site for a shopping center my father did not build in 1954. Three teacups hand-painted with cabbage roses and signed "E.M.," my grandmother's initials. There is no final solution for letters of rejection from *The Nation* and teacups hand-painted in 1900. Nor is there any answer to snapshots of one's grandfather as a young man on skis, surveying around Donner Pass in the year 1910. I smooth out the snapshot and look into his face, and do and do not see my own. I close the drawer, and have another cup of coffee with my mother. We get along very well, veterans of a guerrilla war we never understood.

Days pass. I see no one. I come to dread my husband's evening call, not only because he is full of news of what by now seems to me our remote life in Los Angeles, people he has seen, letters which require attention, but because he asks what I have been doing, suggests uneasily that I get out, drive to San Francisco or Berkeley. Instead I drive across the river to a family graveyard. It has been vandalized since my last visit and the monuments are broken, overturned in the dry grass. Because I once saw a rattlesnake in the grass I stay in the car and listen to a country-and-Western station. Later I drive with my father to a ranch he has in the foothills. The man who runs his cattle on it asks us to the roundup, a week from Sunday, and although I know that I will be in Los Angeles I say, in the oblique way my family talks, that I will come. Once home I mention the broken monuments in the graveyard. My mother shrugs.

I go to visit my great-aunts. A few of them think now that I am my   5
cousin, or their daughter who died young. We recall an anecdote about a relative last seen in 1948, and they ask if I still like living in New York City. I have lived in Los Angeles for three years, but I say that I do. The baby is offered a horehound drop, and I am slipped a dollar bill "to buy a treat." Questions trail off, answers are abandoned, the baby plays with the dust motes in a shaft of afternoon sun.

It is time for the baby's birthday party: a white cake, strawberry-marshmallow ice cream, a bottle of champagne saved from another party. In the evening, after she has gone to sleep, I kneel beside the crib and touch her face, where it is pressed against the slats, with mine. She is an open and trusting child, unprepared for and unaccustomed to the ambushes of family life, and perhaps it is just as well that I can offer her little of that life. I would like to give her more. I would like to promise her that she will grow up with a sense of her cousins and of rivers and of her great-grandmother's teacups, would like to pledge her a picnic on a river with fried chicken and her hair uncombed, would like to give her *home* for her birthday, but we live differently now and I can promise her nothing like that. I give her a

---

The Nation: a long-standing liberal weekly magazine

xylophone and a sundress from Madeira, and promise to tell her a funny story.

QUESTIONING THE TEXT

1. What does Didion mean by saying that she and her mother are veterans of a "guerrilla war"? Do the details she gives us in this essay support this statement? Explain.
2. Didion says she thinks that perhaps people in their thirties when this essay was written (1966) are the "last generation to carry the burden of 'home,' to find in family life the source of all tension and drama." Do you think her hunch is accurate? Why, or why not?
3. What, finally, is Didion's attitude toward "home"? What in the text helps you identify her attitude? Summarize this attitude in your own words, and bring your summary to class for discussion.

MAKING CONNECTIONS

4. How do you think Didion would respond to Jay Overocker's essay (on p. 528)? Is his definition of "home" similar to or different from the one she offers? Explain these differences or similarities in a paragraph or two.
5. What might Serena's mother (see p. 549) wish for her daughter on her birthday? How does this wish compare with Didion's wish for her young daughter? Finally, what would you wish for your own daughter or son, and why?

JOINING THE CONVERSATION

6. Take one of the following quotations from Didion's essay and write a response to it, detailing what the sentence(s) makes you think of and feel, whether you identify with it, and providing examples from your own experience to back up your identification or lack of it. (a) "Marriage is the classic betrayal." (b) "We did not fight. Nothing was wrong. And yet some nameless anxiety colored the emotional charges between me and the place that I came from." (c) "I smooth out the snapshot and look into [my grandfather's] face, and do and do not see my own."
7. Working with two classmates, compose a letter to Didion, telling her how you responded to this essay and explaining your reasons. Be sure to include differences of opinion, if you have them, in your letter.

KAREN COOPER
A Native Woman—1982

IN NATIVE AMERICAN CULTURES, the concepts of the earth as the mother of us all and of the land as a home we inhabit but can never "own" are everywhere apparent. To litter and pollute the earth is literally to throw trash upon our mother's face; to divide the land among owners who can mistreat it is to leave all of us "landless"; to think of time as the ticking minutes of a clock rather than as the natural cycles of the moon and the rhythms of our own blood is to be a stranger, a doer of unnatural things.

    In "A Native Woman—1982," published in A Gathering of Spirit: A Collection by North American Indian Women, *Karen Cooper makes a bold statement of those things she values. In the final stanza she identifies herself as a "Native Woman," saying that knowing herself in that way is more than most people have by way of identity. As a Native Woman, she says, she "know[s] what life should be." I was struck by this poem because it raised questions for me about the way in which Joan Didion talks about home as a place where her family is. Cooper asks us to consider a broader definition of home: as the earth we live upon and that we, in her eyes, defile and "trash." Her poem also recalled for me Alice Walker's claim in Chapter 4 that "Everything Is a Human Being" and her identification of Native Americans as those who can most profoundly teach us what that means. Thus in the brief span of twenty-three lines, Cooper led me to consider my own relationship to Mother Earth, my ultimate home during those years I have to live.*   – A.L.

Living in the air
Landless
I pretend the floor
Is ground.

The only earth I visit   5
Is the dump
Asking Mother to forgive
My trash upon her face.

Time in its metered regularity is irregular
I do nothing that is natural   10
I have even taken the moon's control from my blood
My children are strangers
My family is back "home."

I am alone—
Landless   15
9 to 5
driven by bills to pay,
and a car to feed.

I am a Native Woman
I have that much   20
It's more than most
I am not ignorant
I know what life should be.

IN RESPONSE

1. Read Cooper's poem over several times. Then take 15 minutes or so to discuss it with a classmate or friend. Following your reading and discussion, "translate" this poem into a paragraph, trying to capture Cooper's ideas and sentiments in your own words. Bring your paragraph to class for presentation and discussion.

2. Working with one or two other members of your class, brainstorm about which writer in this chapter Cooper would have most in common with, would share the values of most closely. Then brainstorm about which writer she would have least in common with, would disagree with most. Finally, write up a brief (one-page) summary explaining the reasons for your choices.

3. How would Cooper define "home" and "family"? Write brief definitions that capture what you take to be her understanding of these terms.

4. By what right does one claim to be "native" to a place? Discuss this issue as it relates to struggles among different peoples in the human family.

NATIONAL REVIEW
Another Pro-life Extremist

IT IS MILDLY COMFORTING *that perhaps the only woman more internationally famous than Madonna is Mother Teresa (b. 1910), a tiny Catholic nun who has dedicated her life to serving the poor in India. Winner of the Nobel Peace Prize (1979), Mother Teresa reminds us—as Alice Walker does in an essay earlier in this book—that we are all part of one earthly family.*

But families have arguments, and none in the United States has been more painful or sustained than that over abortion. The Supreme Court's 1973 decision in Roe v. Wade *legalized abortions nationwide, even in the last three months of pregnancy unless individual states acted specifically to prohibit the aborting of fetuses after "viability." While many people hailed* Roe *as a triumph for women's rights, others saw it as a sanction for infanticide.*

I need not recap here the story of opposition to Roe v. Wade, *nor can I even comment on the legal status of abortion, since it is likely to change by the time this book is published. What I do wish to suggest is that opponents of abortion have had no easy time getting their message across in the popular media (though they have been successful in other ways). One would be very hard pressed, for example, to recall a single sympathetic treatment of a prolife position on television or in films in the last decade. TV sitcom characters have elected to continue unwanted pregnancies in difficult circumstances, but their decisions— as in the case of Murphy Brown—have brought almost ritual endorsements of a woman's right to choose abortion. Given the bias of Hollywood's opinion makers, it seems unlikely that a high-profile TV or film character would speak in defense of an unborn child; news programs, too, have depicted most prolife advocates as religious fanatics.*

And that is a context for the December 22, 1989, cover of National Review, *a conservative journal of political thought. I think the photograph of Mother Teresa embracing a child serves as a poignant rejoinder to the caricatures of "prolifers" found on too many other magazine covers.*   – J.R.

Special Christmas Books Issue

NATIONAL REVIEW

ANOTHER PRO-LIFE EXTREMIST

DECEMBER 22, 1989 $1.95

Wm. F. Buckley Jr., Ernest van den Haag, and William McGurn
on the Morality, Legality, and Politics
...bortion

...e: The Bloc Votes

IN RESPONSE

1. Describe what you see in the photograph and how you react to it. Can you separate your reaction to the photograph from the headline immediately above it? Why, or why not?
2. Does it make a difference that Mother Teresa appears on the December 22 issue of *National Review*? Why, or why not?
3. Can you think of any photographs or scenes that have had a powerful political impact either on you personally or upon the nation as a whole? In a position paper, describe the strengths and weaknesses of using images such as this one for political persuasion. Who is likely to be convinced?
4. After pondering the photograph of Mother Teresa, write an exploratory piece (perhaps even a poem) about the concept of family.

JAY OVEROCKER
Ozzie and Harriet in Hell

When Former Vice President Dan Quayle addressed the issue of family values in a speech delivered to the Commonwealth Club of California on May 19, 1992, the national press—with its penchant for the sound bite—sensationalized the lone sentence in the address criticizing Murphy Brown, a TV character played by Candice Bergen. "It doesn't help matters," Quayle noted, "when prime time TV has Murphy Brown—a character who supposedly epitomizes today's intelligent, highly paid professional woman—mocking the importance of fathers by bearing a child alone, and calling it just another 'life style choice.' "

Quayle did not have to contrive a sudden concern for family values. The deteriorating condition of the American family has been under scrutiny for some time and will surely be one of the hot-button political issues of the 1990s. Even up for debate is the definition of "family" itself. That's the subject of the following piece, which finds reports of the demise of the two-parent family greatly exaggerated. Jay Overocker's essay appeared in November 1992 in Heterodoxy, *a conservative journal of popular culture edited by former 1960s radicals Peter Collier and David Horowitz. — J.R.*

Back in 1989, *Fortune* writer Daniel Seligman got so fed up with reading yet another *Washington Post* story about the demise of the traditional "Ozzie and Harriet" nuclear family he did a computer search on the phrase "Ozzie and Harriet" and turned up some 80 stories just in the previous six month period. What was the context in which these two names were typically invoked? "A politician was on stage," Seligman found, "reciting the news that the traditional nuclear family—the kind symbolized by the Nelsons during their marathon stint on black-and-white TV—was dead or dying. Usual moral of the recitation: we need a government program to help the new nontraditional family—the kind where mom is a cop, the kids are on dope, and dad is nonexistent or worse."

In the three years since Seligman did his little survey, announcements of the death of the nuclear family have gotten much more intense, especially since Dan Quayle spoke out on its behalf, leading countless reporters, essayists and commentators to attack him for his regressive patriarchy.

"The white middle class family is a fairy tale," sniffed Ellen Snortland in the *Los Angeles Times*.

The Reagan/Bush administrations were trying to recreate the "June Cleaver nuclear family," charged Tammy Bruce, president of the Los

Angeles Chapter of NOW. "The nuclear family doesn't exist anymore. The majority of families are headed by women. The economy is based on something that doesn't exist."

"The number of kids who will grow up [in a traditional family] is   5
minuscule," said Robert Turner in the *Boston Globe*.

"Only 26% of U.S. households with children under 18 are headed by a married couple," said the *Daily News* in the most misleading of all the statistics slung at Quayle and at America, "[and this is] down from 31% in 1980."

What these people (and all the intellectuals whose scholarship, argumentation and revisionism stand behind them) are telling us is that the nuclear family is dead and we had best get on to the next phase of civilization by focusing on *families* rather than *the family*. This would be tragic if true, a development worthy of deep mourning rather than mere nostalgia. But the fact is that the nuclear family's death has been greatly exaggerated, usually by those who have a stake in its demise.

According to 1990 Bureau of the Census figures, 72.5% of children in the country under the age of 18 live in a home headed by a married couple. Another 21.6% live with their mothers only. The remaining 6% live with their fathers, grandparents or other guardians.

In Los Angeles County, for instance, allegedly a bellwether of breakdown, the figures are even more dramatic with the percentage of children living with two parents ranging from 89% in white middle class areas, to 47% in impoverished and chaotic Compton. For Los Angeles County as a whole, the figure is 64%.

So why do so many people think the nuclear family has disappeared?   10
One reason, suggests William Mattox, Director of Policy Analysis for the Family Research Council, is that many middle-class, well-educated feminists erroneously assume that "everyone lives the same way they do." That is to say, in fast-track urban enclaves with disproportionately high rates of alienation, anomie, divorce and single parenthood.

Another, larger reason is most reporters' lack of patience with (and insight into) statistics. The *Daily News* reporter cited above, for example, thought that only 26% of children under 18 lived with their parents. What the Census actually shows, says Census Bureau information specialist Larry Hugg, is that 27% of all households consist of two parents and their children.

Well, you might say—that's still a tragic number. But attempt actually to understand the statistic. The percentage of households made up of nuclear families has certainly declined, but the reason isn't because most kids nowadays are being raised by single moms or strangers. The reason is that there are so many more households made up of widows, college students, childless married couples, empty nest couples, and gay households. If you confine your inquiry to what Mattox calls "the universe of children" (which is what you must do if your goal is to discover who is raising the children), then you discover, he says, that "70% to 75% of all kids are being raised in a nuclear family."

Then where, you might well wonder, do people like Connecticut Senator Christopher Dodd get off saying that only "one in ten American families" fit the fifties mold of dad at work and mom at home with the kids? Or how can Colorado Congressperson Pat Schroeder preach from her bully pulpit as chairman of the House Select Committee on Children, Youth and Families that "the traditional Ozzie and Harriet" family represents a mere 7.1% of all American families?

The short answer is that Schroeder uses statistics the same way the Queen of Hearts* uses words—"They mean whatever I want them to mean." In order to make the percentage of traditional families (a breadwinner father, and a mother at home with children) look vanishingly small, Schroeder includes in her calculations both families with children and those without any at all. (This alone makes the problem of the nuclear family look 50% worse than it would otherwise.) Further, she defines "traditional" to mean only those families where the mother does no work whatsoever outside the home. (Under the government classification, says William Mattox, even an hour's work a week outside the home is enough to cause a woman to be considered a working mother.)

But the most deceitful aspect of Schroeder's semantics is to use the   15
phrase "traditional Ozzie and Harriet family" not according to general usage (a mother and father and some kids) but quite literally as a family *exactly like the Nelsons* with a mother and father and precisely two children (David and Ricky). Under Schroeder's definition, a family with one child isn't a "traditional Ozzie and Harriet family" and neither is a family with three or more children.

Demeaning nuclear families and the fathers who play a pivotal role in them has a history that stretches back at least to the 1960s when feminists first started constructing the cliches which held that marriage is a "comfortable concentration camp." This was Betty Friedan's groundbreaking phrase which Hillary Clinton plagiarized in a now famous 1974 article in the *Harvard Educational Review* when she described marriage as "a dependence relationship" not unlike "slavery and the Indian reservation system."

The anti-male part of this attack was a contempt that stretched even to children of women's own wombs. Thus, in a famous 1974 article in *Ms.*, a feminist related the disgust she felt when her obstetrician held up her

---

the *Queen of Hearts:* a character in Lewis Carroll's *Alice's Adventures in Wonderland* (1865). However, it is Humpty Dumpty in Carroll's *Through the Looking Glass* (1872) who says "When *I* use a word . . . it means just what I choose it to mean."

newborn and it turned out to be a member of the oppressor class: "All I could see was cock!" The family was patriarchal and therefore a bastion of a conservative social structure.

The rantings of the radical feminist left had an impact. As University of Southern California sociologist Carlfred Broderick points out, a spate of books soon began to appear confidently predicting the death of the nuclear family or at least asserting that it would have [to] give way to more "flexible institutions."

Not surprisingly, says Broderick, the people hurt most by the derogation of fatherhood and the attack on the much maligned "traditional" family were the people least able to defend themselves—the children. "The hippies had this notion of the free human child, who didn't belong to his parents but was everyone's child, who had no sexual hangups and didn't have to learn the alphabet or any hard thing and why should they be encumbered with the crust of the ages. It turned out that the kids couldn't read or write or add or hold jobs. It turned out that the kids who had multiple parents didn't have any parents. They tended to be abandoned and sexually abused and drug abused. They turned out to be the saddest children of all because their parents didn't take adult responsibility for them."

Despite all the predictions about the need for more "flexible" family structures in the '60s and '70s, the family didn't disappear, not even when, in the '80s, the gay and lesbian movement lent its voice to the attack. ("You can't erase a million years of human evolution in a ten year period," says Broderick.) And by the mid-eighties a widespread if fragile consensus was attempting to form around the notion that all things being equal a two-parent home was better for children than one.   20

But then Dan Quayle gave a speech blaming the L.A. riots on the disintegrating family structure in the inner city. Suddenly there were hundreds of intellectuals and critics—who had previously been forced to hold their tongues because of the evidence showing the salutary nature of the traditional family—who emerged from the closet to bash the nuclear family because it had once again been identified as a fortress of conservatism.

The most egregious example of such ideological attacks was an astonishing front page article in the *Washington Post*, which argued among other things that fathers were much less important than had previously been believed, new research having indicated that the education of the mother was now the most important factor in a child's prospects, and, at least for black girls, having both parents was worse than being raised by a single mom.

In the post–Quayle furor the view that the family was the fountainhead of racism and sexism once again was proposed. Family values was a code phrase for hate. "Family values and the cult of the nuclear family," wrote Katha Pollitt in a particularly obnoxious piece in *The Nation*, "is at bottom just another way to bash women, especially poor women."

As for the father, under the new dispensation, he is at best irrelevant and at worst dangerous. ". . . Nothing is more unsuitable to the needs of the young than 'suitable role models,' " New York writer Leonard Kriegal asserted in the *Los Angeles Times*. "The idea that role models can make substantial contributions to the prospects of the young . . . is nonsense."

It's no mystery why so many poor women rely on welfare checks,   25
argued feminist social critic Barbara Ehrenreich: they're a lot less trouble than relying on a man. "I disagree that a father's influence is positive," snapped Tammy Bruce, President of the Los Angeles chapter of NOW. "I think it is absurd to say that a boy needs a father." Abuse, she sputtered in an interview in the aftermath of the Quayle speech, "skyrockets" when a father is present in the home. The only way to keep men from passing their violent "male mind set" to their sons was to get the man out of the family entirely and give the mother a chance to raise a generation of feminist boys "who love women."

Bruce later modified her remarks somewhat, but even so, just for a second we had an uncommonly clear insight into the kind of radical feminist soul that has contempt for men, dismisses fathers, and sees the state as a husband of first resort providing the money, the childcare and whatever other social services are necessary for a woman to raise children without the benefit of either a husband or a job.

Despite these savage attacks on the usefulness of fathers, in the sociological literature evidence of the need for fathers is incontestable, says Randall Blankenhorn, President of the Institute for American Values. Boys with fathers are more mature, more outgoing, more independent, warmer, more self-confident and have better self-esteem.* Girls who grow up without fathers are simultaneously more suspicious of men and more dependent on them. The most reliable indicator or whether a girl gets pregnant or a boy [joins] a gang isn't income or race—it's whether or not the child has a father at home.

"The data is overwhelming," says author Warren Farrell [. Without fathers at home,] both sexes are more likely to become drug addicts, do worse in school on every single subject from math to literature, more likely to become delinquent, join gangs, go to prison, commit suicide and commit homicide. Children of unmarried mothers are twice as likely to end up in juvenile hall, three times as likely to be expelled from school and six times as likely to live in poverty.

As for the radical feminist notion that the easy way to make boys love women is to remove them from their father's influence, Farrell says, "We

---

Boys with fathers . . . better self-esteem: For another argument for the importance of adult male involvement in the development of boys, see the reading by Robert Bly, "Going Off on the Wild Man's Shoulders," starting on p. 360.

have been raising boys without fathers for 20 years in the black community, and the result is not gentle black men. The result is a society in which black men are [as] likely to be in prison as college."

In the inner city, teenage mothers do not get married; and almost half   30
of the young men are arrested before they reach 18. "The black community is being destroyed by this," says UC Long Beach psychologist Kevin Mac-Donald. "Anyone who says single-parent families are good for black people is nuts."

Even so, every time someone tries to address the issue of the family, the media elite responds not so much with an analysis of the problem as an attack on the messenger. When Dan Quayle came to Los Angeles late last May to tour a public school, a *Los Angeles Times* editorial characterized his remarks as "simplistic put downs of the evils of single motherhood." And the *Times* gleefully described a 14-year-old girl's fatuous challenge to the vice-president: "What would you prefer? A single mom, or a dad who gets drunk and beats your mom?" As if there were no other alternative.

For over 20 years now certain radical feminists have been making the case that men are wife-beaters, rapists, child abusers, murderers and plunderers of the planet—all for the purpose of delegitimizing marriage, destabilizing family, and marginalizing men. So when someone comes along and says, "Hey, wait a minute, children need fathers," it generates "real anger," says *Playboy*'s men's columnist Asa Baber.

Baber got a firsthand lesson in just how deep that anger really was when he took part in a debate last Mother's Day with feminist author Susan (*Backlash*) Faludi at the 92nd Street Y in New York City. During his opening remarks to an audience of 1,000 feminists, Baber noted that on Mother's Day the phone circuits are usually jammed with people calling home. But on Father's Day, finding a free line is no problem. He noted, "We have to ask why there is so much less interest in fathers."

"It brought down the house," Baber says of his comment. "At first, I didn't get it. I thought my fly was open. I said, 'If you think this is funny, you are going to think this is a laugh riot: I think the fact that our fathers are so much out of the loop is a major tragedy in our culture.'"

At this point, said Baber, the audience stopped laughing and started   35
hissing. Why, I asked him, because they thought men were useless, irrelevant and potentially dangerous?

"You got it," Baber said.

QUESTIONING THE TEXT

1. What to you is the most surprising information in Overocker's article? Record your response in an entry in your reading log, if you are keeping one.

2. Working in a group, list all the traditional nuclear families (a mother and father and at least one child) and then all the nontraditional families you can think of among the current crop of prime-time television sitcom families. Then identify those traditional families that would fit Pat Schroeder's definition of a "traditional Ozzie and Harriet family" (a father, a mother who does not work outside the home, and *precisely* two children). Write a paragraph summarizing your observations.

3. Underline or note in the margins of "Ozzie and Harriet in Hell" any words or phrases that strike you as "loaded"—that is, that stack the argument in the author's favor. Do such phrases make the argument livelier or diminish its appeal for you?

4. Does J.R.'s introduction influence your reading of "Ozzie and Harriet in Hell"? If so, how?

MAKING CONNECTIONS

5. According to Overocker, overwhelming scientific evidence suggests that children are more likely to develop into healthy, emotionally secure adults if they have two parents, one a male. How might he react to the homosexual parenting Serena describes in "Just Different, That's All" (p. 549)? Considering these different points of view, try to write a definition of "family" that both Overocker and Serena might agree on. Can you do it?

6. Overocker uses statistics to argue that the nuclear family is not endangered. Joan Didion, in her essay on p. 519, uses personal reminiscences to suggest that family life is changing. Write an exploratory essay about family, drawing on both authors.

JOINING THE CONVERSATION

7. "Ozzie and Harriet in Hell" appeared in a conservative journal. In the margins, annotate some of the places where it might need to be altered if it were to be published for a readership less inclined to agree with Overocker. Identify one such specific audience and then revise two or three paragraphs of the article for this different readership.

8. Interview someone older than fifty about how American attitudes toward families have changed in his or her lifetime. Prepare a list of specific questions before the interview, and then report your findings in class.

9. With a group of four or five classmates, make a list of the kinds of family arrangements that group members have experienced or observed. Working from that data base, write a group report about the nature of the American family as it is represented by your class.

DAVID UPDIKE
The Colorings of Childhood

THE AUTHOR OF A COLLECTION of short stories (Out on the Marsh) *and several books for children and a teacher of writing at Middlesex Community College in Bedford, Massachusetts, David Updike offers in the following essay his reflections on what has been a most important choice in his life: to marry an African and to have a multi-racial child. As a result of his choice, Updike had to confront what he calls a "suppressed, looming understanding": that "the country at large will perceive the child as 'black,' and, consequently, this son or daughter . . . will grow up on the opposite side of the color line from us [white Americans] and, as such, will be privy to a whole new realm of the American Experience, which we, by virtue of our skin color, have previously avoided." This, he says, for the "vast majority of white Americans," is a "new and not altogether comforting experience."*

Nevertheless, Updike made his choice, and he now clearly revels in it, in his home and in the family he has been a part of creating. Though he recognizes the pressures of the implicit and explicit racism he and his wife and son will face, he feels cautiously optimistic about the larger results of his choice. Perhaps, he concludes, his son will enjoy some advantages in being a child of two cultures. More important, he wonders, may the layers of identity that his son will inhabit provide—when multiplied among many multi-racial children—a means of expanding the world, of dissolving boundaries and "obstacles that hold us all in a kind of skittish, social obeisance"? If so, these children will inhabit a wider and more complicated but also more tolerant world in which they are not "multi-racial" but rather "American."

I chose this article, which appeared in Harper's *magazine in 1992, because it connects not only to a number of other readings in this chapter that attempt to explore and expand our notions of what "home" and "family" are but also because it speaks to many pieces in Chapter 7, on difference within American society. In addition, I want to believe that the United States has at least a slim chance of becoming the more expansive, generous, and tolerant world evoked toward the end of Updike's article. A lot depends on this possibility, for your family and for mine. — A.L.*

Five or six years ago, when my older sister revealed to the rest of our family her intention of marrying her boyfriend, from Ghana, I remember that my reaction, as a nervous and somewhat protective younger brother, was something like "Well, that's fine for them—I just wonder about

It's interesting that he doesn't tell us he's white; I just assumed it. — A.L.

535

the children." I'm not sure what I was wondering, exactly, but it no doubt had to do with the thorny questions of race and identity, of having parents of different complexions, and a child, presumably, of some intermediate shade, and what that would mean for a child growing up here, in the United States of America.

I had no idea, at the time, that I, too, would one day marry an African, or that soon thereafter we would have a child, or that I would hear my own apprehensions of several years before echoed in the words of one of my wife's friends. She was a white American of a classic liberal mold—wearer of Guatemalan shawls, befriender of Africans, espouser of worthy causes—but she was made uneasy by the thought of Njoki, her friend from Kenya, marrying me, a white person. She first asked Njoki what my "politics" were and, having been assured that they were okay, went on to say, "Well, I'm sure he's a very nice person, but before you get married I just hope you'll think about the children."

The question about politics strikes me as odd. Updike just breezes by it. What sort of politics would be considered wrong in an interracial marriage? — J.R.

I recognized in her remarks the shadow of my own, but when it is one's own marriage that is being worried about, one's children, not yet conceived, one tends to ponder such comments more closely. By this time, too, I was the uncle of two handsome, happy boys, Ghanian-American, who, as far as I could tell, were suffering no side effects for having parents of different colors. Njoki, too, was displeased.

Is Updike suggesting that children are more important than parents? Shouldn't the feelings of each person in the family unit be considered equally? — T.M.

"What is she trying to say, exactly—that *my* child will be disadvantaged because he looks like me?" my wife asked. "So what does she think about me? Does she think *I'm* disadvantaged because I'm African?"

In a society that caters more to whites, unfortunately it may be true that on some occasions the child may be disadvantaged. — T.M.

I responded that our liberal friend was trying to get at the complicated question of identity, knowing, as she did, that the child, in a country that simplifies complicated, racial equations to either "black" or "white," wouldn't know to which group he "belonged."

"To both of them," Njoki answered, "or to neither. He will be Kenyan-American. The ridiculous part is that if I was marrying an African she wouldn't mind at all—she wouldn't say, 'Think of the children,' because the child would just be black, like me, and it wouldn't be her problem. She wouldn't have to worry about it. Honestly," she finally said, her head bowed into her hand in resignation, "this country is so complicated."

But her friend's reaction is not, I suspect, an uncommon one, even among those who think of themselves as progressive and ideologically unfettered: They don't mind, in principle, the idea of interracial unions, but the prospect of children clouds the issue, so to speak, and raises the identity issue—if not for the child, the *beheld*, then for us, the beholders. For as I slowly pondered the woman's remarks, it occurred to me that she was not saying, "He won't know who he is" but something closer to, "*I* won't know who he is—I won't know to which group this child belongs, the black people or the white." Added to this is the suppressed, looming understanding that, however the child sees himself, however we see the child, the country at large will perceive the child as "black," and, consequently, this son or daughter of a friend, this child to whom we might actually be an aunt or uncle, parent or grandparent, cousin or friend, this person whom we love and wish the best for in life, will grow up on the opposite side of the color line from us and, as such, will be privy to a whole new realm of the American Experience, which we, by virtue of our skin color, have previously avoided; and this—for the vast majority of white Americans—is a new and not altogether comforting experience.

Harlem, Anacostia, Roxbury, Watts: In every major city in America, and most minor ones, there is a neighborhood that most whites have never been to, will never go to, and regard, from a distance, with an almost primordial fear, akin to the child's apprehension of the bogeyman. They have read about this place in the paper and heard on the nightly news of the crime and violence there, but the thought of actually going there for a visit is

Yet, curiously, isn't it so-called "progressives" who have abandoned the notion of a colorblind society to advance a politics of race and ethnicity?
– J.R.

This seems just right to me. It's my own identity I may be worrying about when I question others.
– A.L.

almost unthinkable; if they ever found themselves there, they imagine—got off at the wrong subway stop or took an ill-fated wrong turn—they would be set upon by hordes of angry, dark people with nothing better to do than sit around waiting for hapless white people to amble into their lair. Most white Americans, I suspect, would be more comfortable walking through the streets of Lagos, or Nairobi, or Kingston, than they would be walking through any predominantly black neighborhood in America.

I'd guess Updike, wealthy and well-connected, would have little in common with blue-collar urban whites either. That's my background.
— J.R.

I agree.   — A.L.

For a couple of years Njoki lived in Harlem, on Riverside Drive and 145th Street, and was visited there one evening by a couple of our friends and their one-year-old child. When it came time to leave, after dark, the woman asked Njoki if she would walk them to the corner, to hail a cab—as if the presence of a black person would grant them free passage and protect them from the perils of the neighborhood. Njoki explained that it was okay, that the neighborhood was quite safe and they wouldn't be singled out for special attention because they were white.

I wonder how people of color feel walking in all-white areas? Is there any useful comparison?
— A.L.

"It's okay for us," the friend explained. "I just wouldn't want anything to happen to the baby."

Njoki relented and walked them over to Broadway, but as they went she wondered what made her friends think the residents of Harlem wanted to attack a couple with a baby, or why she, an African and a stranger to this country, was called upon to somehow protect her American friends from their own countrymen. At the corner they hailed a cab, and they were whisked off to some safer corner of the city, leaving Njoki to walk back alone to her apartment, at far greater risk, as a single woman, than any group of people, white or black, would ever be.

Njoki should have been offended and then helped to enlighten her friends by sticking to her original response and not walking along with them.
— T.M.

Which is not to say that I myself felt at perfect ease walking through the streets of Harlem, but simply that the more time I spent there the more I realized that no one was particularly interested, or concerned, that a pale man in collegiate tweeds was walking through the neighborhood. During the two years that my wife lived there, I walked

I wondered if he would say this. But is the uneasiness related more to fears of crime or drug-related activities than to race?   — A.L.

often from her apartment down to City College, where I taught, and from there to Columbia University, and I was never bothered or heckled by anyone. As a friend of mine, a resident of Harlem, said to me once, "Black people are around white people all the time."

But as a child growing up in a small New England town, I was almost never around black people. My impressions of the world beyond, or of African-Americans, were mostly gleaned from television and magazines and movies, from which, it seems to me, it is nearly impossible not to acquire certain racist assumptions about people, however slight and subtle; and even when one has become aware of them they are nearly impossible to shed entirely. Like astronomers who can hear the "background radiation" that marks the beginning of the universe, so can one hear, in the background of one's own thoughts, the persistent, static hiss of American history.

By the time my second nephew was born I had written two children's books, both about a boy and his dog and their various adventures in the small New England town where they lived. As I began to think about a third book in this series it occurred to me that the boy could now have a friend, and if he was to have a friend it might be nice if his complexion was somewhat closer to that of my two nephews, so that when they read the book they would find a character who, in this regard, looked somewhat like themselves. I wrote such a book and sent in the manuscript with a letter explaining that, although there was no reference to race in the book, I would like the second boy to appear darker than his friend in the illustrations.

A few weeks later I received the editor's response: He liked the plot and story line, he said, but was confused by this new character, which seemed underdeveloped and vague. The editor didn't understand what this character was doing in a small New England town. I ran the risk, too, of being accused of "tokenism" by some of the

There shouldn't be any reference to race in the book! Being of a color other than white is natural. Therefore, naturally the book should include more than the white race because this is how society is. If Updike expected some type of applause for being a

Is the implication that there are still no African Americans in small New England towns? This can't be true. — A.L.

"nice guy" by incorporating people of color into his story, applause denied.
— T.M.

My experience has been different. Most textbook publishers insist on racial balance these days—almost to the point of setting quotas.
— J.R.

Racial differences mean little to Njoki and David because their cultures rarely have direct contact and don't share much recent history. Ironically, a European American and an African American living side by side would have vastly more in common but also more grounds for enmity. — J.R.

members of the library associations—black women especially, he pointed out—who were on the lookout for such things.

I wrote back and, among other things, suggested that children are less encumbered by problems of race and ethnicity than their parents or teachers, and I thought it unlikely they would worry what he was doing in a small New England town. I was willing to run the risk of being accused of tokenism either by reviewers or watchdogs of the children's-book world. In the end, we agreed on a few small editorial changes, and when the book came out the character in question was indeed of brown skin, and I never heard another word about it either from teachers or reviewers or disgruntled children. But this editorial skirmish gave me a taste of the children's-book world I had not quite imagined, and I've since had dealings with several other publishers, most of whom, it seemed to me, exhibited a kind of heightened vigilance when it came to books about "children of color," so wrought were editors with anxieties about tokenism and marketing and whatever other obstacles lie between them and a slightly broader vision of what constitutes suitable subject matter for children.

Njoki is often asked what my family thinks of my being married to an African woman, a black woman, but she is almost never asked what her family thinks of her being married to a "mzungu"—a white person. Her interviewers are surprised to learn that my parents don't mind and that hers don't either, and that her parents regret much more that neither she nor I is a practicing Catholic. They are also surprised to learn that there would be much more apprehension and mutual suspicion had she married a Kenyan of another ethnic group, or an African of another country. And I am married to an African, not an African-American, and in my case, too, the suspicions and animosities of history are diffused by the absence of a common and adversarial past. And, similarly, for Njoki, the thought of her being married to a white Kenyan—the descendants of Karen Blixen

An accurate comment? — A.L.

This paragraph reminds me how often I tend to lump all people of one group together (all Africans, for instance, or all women) when I know the enormous range of differences among members of any group. — A.L.

(more commonly known as Isak Dinesen) and her ilk—is almost laughable.

Several summers ago we spent six weeks in Kenya and passed much of our time there in a middle-class suburb of Nairobi called "Karen," named after this same Karen Blixen, who once lived here in the shadow of the Ngong Hills. One night we were invited to dinner at the house of a neighbor—a couple in the tourist industry who had invited a group of traveling Americans over to their house for dinner. Their home was in the typically grand style of the Kenyan middle class, the "grounds" surrounded by a tall barbed-wire and electrified fence, and further protected by an all-night watchman and several roaming dogs. But inside the floors were polished wood parquet, the furniture was tasteful, and, aside from a few African prints, we could have been in an upper-middle-class dwelling in Los Angeles, or Buenos Aires, or Rome. The other guests had already arrived, and sat on couches eating and drinking and talking with their hosts. As it turned out, all of the guests were African-American, mostly from New Jersey and New York; we were introduced, and joined them, but it became clear that some were not very happy to find me, a white American, here in the home of an African, 8,000 miles from the country they and I so uneasily shared. When I tried to speak to one of the African-American women she would answer in clipped monosyllables and stare into distant corners of the room; another woman had brought a tape recorder, with which to record some of the conversations, but whenever I spoke, it was observed, she would turn off the machine and wait for my polluting commentary to pass. I did find one woman who was not, outwardly, troubled by my presence, and spent much of the evening talking with her, but my otherwise chilly reception had not been lost on Njoki's sister and brother-in-law and niece, who were both mystified and amused. On the car ride home we tried to explain—about the history of the United States, and slavery, and about African-Americans' identification with Africa as the place from which their

Is he experiencing racism in the same way most African Americans have experienced it? Almost certainly not. — A.L.

Racism takes many forms. No group has a monopoly on prejudice. — J.R.

ancestors were taken, stolen, for hundreds of years. Njoki tried to explain how their visit here was a kind of homecoming, a return to the continent they probably would have never left, were it not for the unpleasant fact of slavery.

"Yes, but that was West Africa—it has nothing to do with here. And besides, they're Americans now—and you're American, too."

"Yes, but . . ."

"And you're a guest. You have as much right to be here as they do."

"Yes, but . . ."

It is difficult to accurately convey the complexities of race in America to someone who has never been here, and they remained unconvinced. Our American dinner companions, I suspect, would have been saddened, if not maddened, by our sour postmortem of the evening, and I was sorry to have been, as far as they were concerned, in the wrong place at the wrong time, was sorry to have diminished their enjoyment of their visit. But I still felt that I had more in common with my fellow African-American guests than either of us did with our Kenyan hosts—an idea to which they might have heartily objected. They shared with our hosts a genetic and, to some extent, cultural "Africanness," and the experience of being mistreated by peoples of European ancestry; I shared with my hosts the experience of growing up in a place where people of one's own ethnicity, or color, were in the majority; but with my fellow guests I shared the more immediate experience of having grown up in America, where our experiences have been rather different, where we also live, as uneasy acquaintances, on opposing sides of the same, American coin.

I am asked, sometimes, either directly or by implication, how it is that both my sister and I— New Englanders of northern European extraction—came to marry Africans, people of another culture and color and continent. I have never had much of an answer for these people, except to say that both my sister and I are compatible with our

Updike and the African Americans also share basic political and cultural ties—assumptions about law, government, and human nature— that make them more alike than different. Curiously, the Africans understand that commonality better than the Americans do.
— J.R.

This makes me think of Steele's argument in Chapter 3 that we should honor commonalities more than differences. I wonder if Updike would agree? — A.L.

respective spouses in ways neither of us had been with previous companions, all of whom were far closer to our own complexions. When I was five or so, and my sister seven, my family lived for two months on a small island in the Caribbean, and it is my mother's rather whimsical theory that it was from impressions gleaned during this trip—for my sister from the somewhat older boys she played with in an old, rusty model T that sat beside our house, and for me from the long-limbed, beautiful baby-sitters who used to take care of us—that led us both, thirty years later, to marry Africans. Nor do I think that it was any strain of "jungle fever" that caused us to marry who we did. More likely, my sister and I both married Africans because, as children, we were not conditioned not to, were not told that this was not one of life's options, and so, when the opportunity arose, there were no barriers—neither our own nor our parents'. And in the "white liberal" world in which I grew up, it would have been uncouth to make any outward show of disapproval—though I suspect some amused speculation went on behind closed doors about my sister's and my choice of mates, and I believe some of my parents' friends expressed quiet concern, but I have never personally received any negative commentary, neither from friends nor passersby. It had been more of an issue for Njoki, who has some friends who believe marrying a white man is a "sellout" of some kind, a "betrayal" of the race, and that with it comes the loss of some strain of political correctness. But such friends either tend to adjust or to fade away into a world more cleanly divided between black and white, where they will be irritated and confused no more.

By some unexpected confluence of genes our son Wesley's hair is, to our surprise, relatively straight—long, looping curls that tighten slightly when it rains—and this, too, will mean something in America, means something already to the elderly neighborhood women who tell us, with a smile, that he has "good" hair, and to other people,

Yet one wonders whether the Updikes would have had barriers against marrying African Americans. If anything, this essay demonstrates that prejudice is often a matter less of color than of community.

— J.R.

This seems to contradict what he says about taking racist assumptions from the mass media. — A.L.

The "white liberal" world Updike grew up in sounds wonderful, but extremely different from the stories he wrote about children growing up in New England, which hadn't thus far included children of color.
— T.M.

I'm thinking here of a great video montage artist Walter Bing Davis has made—it's a celebration of hair. — A.L.

friends and strangers both, who tell us he looks like he is from Central America, or India, or the Middle East, implicitly meaning *rather than black.* Children, however, are less circumspect in their observations, and I have no doubt my son will be called a few names while growing up, both by white children and by brown; he may be told that he is really "black," and he may be told that he thinks he's "white"; in Kenya, I have been assured, he will be considered "half-caste"—an unpleasant linguistic relic from colonial days. He may also be treated badly by teachers prone to impatience, or a lack of empathy, with students of lighter, or darker, complexions than their own. He may be embarrassed by the sound of his mother's language; he may be embarrassed by my whiteness. He may go through a time when he is, indeed, confused about his "identity," but in this respect I don't think he will be much different from other children, or teenagers, or adults. There is no way of my knowing, really, what his experience as a multi-racial child will be, or, for that matter, how helpful I or his mother will be to him along the way. We can only tell him what we think and know, and hope, as all parents do, that our words will be of some use.

What in life can ever be secure or predictable for any child? Wesley also bears a very famous last name, one that will color his future. Will it open doors for him or place him under a microscope?
— J.R.

We are not bothered by mothers in the park who seem to get a little nervous, overly vigilant, when their children begin to commiserate with other, darker children, as if their children are in some sort of subtle, ineffable danger—too close for comfort. Their fears seem laughable, absurd, and one comes to almost pity the children who will grow up in the shadow of such fearful, narrow people, from whom they will inherit the same nervous bundle of apprehensions and pathologies. Many of them will be sent to private schools, not because the public schools in our city are not very good but because of the subconscious assumption that schools with so many children of other races *can't* be that good: Such schools and students will hold their own children back somehow. But in the end, these people tend to recede, not disappear, exactly, but shrink before the simple, overwhelm-

"Fearful" and "narrow" seem very good words to describe these people. He makes me want to save all children from such people.   — A.L.

ing presence of your child, who shrieks with joy at something as simple as the sound of your key turning in the door.

Wesley will visit Africa and live there for a time, and will know the Kenyan half of his family there and the American half here, and into the bargain will know his Ghanian uncle and his Ghanian-American cousins and a whole West African branch of his extended family. And it may just be that, contrary to the assumptions of concerned friends, this child of a "mixed" marriage will suffer no great disadvantages at all, but rather will enjoy advantages denied the rest of us; for as the child of two cultures he will "belong" to neither of them exclusively but both of them collectively, will be a part of my Americanness and Njoki's Africanness, and will be something neither she nor I ever will be—African-American—and as such will be a part of a rich and varied culture that will always hold me at arm's length. And in these layers of identity lies an opportunity for a kind of expansion of the world, a dissolution of the boundaries and obstacles that hold us all in a kind of skittish, social obeisance, and he thus may be spared the suspicions and apprehensions that plague those of us who have grown up with an exclusive, clearly defined sense of belonging. In the end, my son will be, simply, an American child, an American adult. His will be a wider, more complicated world than mine was, and to him will fall the privilege and burden, as it falls to us all, of making of it what he will.

> *It may just be that this child of a "mixed" marriage will suffer no great disadvantages at all. Being a product of two different ethnicities can actually be a beautiful and educational experience.*
> – T.M.

Afterwords

David Updike's "The Colorings of Childhood" is the only piece both A.L. and I independently chose for this anthology. Yet now I find myself straining to respond to it, unable to identify powerfully with the author's experience or, curiously, to find engaging points of difference. Updike's observations about racial and ethnic identity strike me as true, thoughtful, and ultimately hopeful. But they also feel remote, safe, and slightly bland.

I remember reading an article many years ago that claimed that people prejudiced against members of particular ethnic, racial, or religious groups often harbor no ill will against individual members of those groups, differentiating their black, Jewish, or Italian acquaintances from blacks, Jews, and Italians in general. Archie Bunker is the archetypal bigot of this type, but we've all met people like Archie. We may even spot him in our own mirrors sometimes. When we lump people into categories—even useful ones like Americans, or Japanese, or balding men—we tend to note the features that make them different from us. When we meet people one-on-one, perhaps we're more inclined to see a human being. We may still not like the individual, but at least we're dealing with a person.

But how do we get to the point nationally where we learn to deal with ethnic groups as humanely as we usually do with individuals? Perhaps that's the question that "The Colorings of Childhood" poses. Is it a beginning to regard Wesley Updike, as his father ultimately does, as "simply, an American child, an American adult"? That might entail learning, once again, what it would mean to be an American family, two hundred fifty million strong. — J.R.

In an undergraduate class recently, we spent some time talking about whether or not the "self" as our culture has known it for roughly three hundred years may "exist" anymore or whether we are beginning to experience "self" in varying ways. One of the students remembered a Monty Python sketch of the knight who keeps fighting after losing one limb after another and wondered aloud where in our physical bodies, if anywhere, the "self" resides. We talked about this problem in personal terms and in political and professional terms, asking questions about how we acquire a sense of self and how systems in our society seem to value some versions of "self" more than others. Finally, we wrote for a few minutes about how we identified our "self."

In light of Updike's very interesting and moving essay, I found it particularly noteworthy that no one in the class identified "self" in terms of his or her color or race. In other words, when we listed words that we thought of as related to our "selves," we didn't think first (if at all) of race. The situation changed, however, when we spoke of other people. With others, race often surfaced early, especially but not exclusively if the person in question belonged to a race other than ours. This classroom discussion perhaps makes Updike's point in an indirect way. Race or color is something people, and especially white people, attribute to others, just as the people in Updike's article worried about the "race" or "color" of his multi-racial child rather than about their own. Now I'm looking forward to reading Updike's article with my class. I'm anxious to get their thinking on the issues he raises. What will they have to say about Updike's "self"—or that of his son? And what will they say about his hope that his multi-racial son may be "simply, an American child"? Will they see this as a desirable goal—or as one more way to suppress diversity? Whatever they say, I bet I will come away with some new thinking of my own. That's one of the reasons I like my teaching job so much and why, when I listed words to describe my "self," I included "teacher" and "learner" among them. — A.L.

Generally, if parents aren't happy, neither will their children be. This works both ways. So is it better for you to marry within your own race solely because you think your children will have an easier life, or is it better to marry who you are truly happy with and as a result perhaps enable your children to grow up with a happier family life? The child of an interracial couple may have some advantages, such as receiving something closer to the total *American experience.*

Why doesn't society (and let's not forget one of its subdivisions, the media) make a fuss over Poles and Italians who decide to wed? Or over Japanese and Greeks? How far have we come as a nation that is supposed to be the land of the free? Should races other than blacks or whites be offended or relieved that society doesn't feel their choice of a marriage partner is important enough to worry over the way Updike's friends worried over his?

Unfortunately, most people today (including Updike?) fail to realize that the majority of the human race is a combination of more than one ethnicity. The problem people have with interracial couples seems to result from the struggle between blacks and whites that has been going on for centuries. Couples of these two ethnicities who decide to marry raise bitter feelings that have not yet been completely buried. This article leaves me with the same question that no one has been able to answer for years: "Why can't we all *just get along?"* — T.M.

QUESTIONING THE TEXT

1. Why was Updike told he might be accused of "tokenism"? What is his attitude toward that accusation? How does he answer it?

2. Updike sketches in some of what he calls the "burdens and privileges" facing his multi-racial son. Summarize these burdens and privileges. Then consider whether or not you agree with him about which are burdens and which are privileges. Jot down the reasons you have for agreeing or disagreeing with him on these categories. Finally, add several other burdens and privileges that Updike has failed to consider, and bring the list to class for discussion.

3. In their responses, both A.L. and J.R. comment on Updike's ending and his evocation of a child who is "simply . . . American." Compare their responses to this conclusion. What is your own response to it?

MAKING CONNECTIONS

4. In "On Going Home" (p. 519), Joan Didion makes a special wish for her daughter. What wish or wishes do you think Updike would make for his son? Write out a sentence capturing such wishes and then compare it with the final paragraph of Didion's essay. Note differences and similarities in these wishes, and bring yours to class for discussion.

5. Do you think Updike would agree with Jay Overocker's characteriza-

tion (p. 528) of the ideal American home and family? Why, or why not?

JOINING THE CONVERSATION

6. Take some time to explore your own attitudes toward marrying someone of another race—and thus, if you have children, having "multi-racial" ones. In a two- or three-page journal entry, record your thoughts by freewriting or jotting notes or brainstorming on paper. Then write a paragraph in which you sum up your position on this question.

7. Working with another member of your class, identify one or two people on your campus who have multi-racial families and who are willing to give you an hour of their time for an interview about their experiences in such a family. Then prepare a summary of Updike's article to give them in advance and a series of ten or so questions you would like to ask them. At the interview(s), take careful notes. Then meet together to go over your notes and decide on the most important points the interviewee(s) made. Finally, prepare a class presentation in which you can summarize what you learned in the interview(s).

SERENA
Just Different, That's All

SERENA'S MOTHER IS A LESBIAN—"*just different, that's all.*" *In this brief article, Serena talks about living in a lesbian home, about her realization of what that means for her, and about her complicated and very thoughtful responses to her home and family life. Along the way she considers different kinds of families, what it might be like to have a father or brothers and sisters, what might be good about such a life and what is good about her own life. Serena was seven when she wrote this article, just going into second grade. When she grows up, she says, she knows she wants to live with someone, but she doesn't know if she wants to get married and/or have children. She does know she likes to tell stories and that she likes her mom.*

The issues Serena raises are particularly timely today, as gay and lesbian activists call for recognizing same-sex marriages, extending spousal benefits to same-sex partners, and barring discrimination against homosexuals in the workplace, the military, and elsewhere. Serena brings these often abstract arguments down to earth, makes them concrete and people-centered. That's one of the reasons I chose this article, published in a 1990 volume called Different Mothers. *In addition, I was simply captivated by Serena's voice, by her directness and candor. Her comments challenge all of us to examine our own definitions of what a home is or can or should be. I think Serena does us all a favor in making that challenge. I hope you think so too.* — A.L.

I'm seven and a half and I live in Albany, California. I'm about to go into second grade. I live with my mother now, but other times I've lived with lots of women. My mom's a nurse. I take kung-fu and want to be a therapist when I get older. I enjoy telling stories.

I started knowing my mother was different when I was five and I started school. A lot of people there were straight, and my mother started to talk to me about how she was different. But it wasn't until I started first grade that I really realized things. Nothing was really different, but my mom started to ask me what I felt about her being a lesbian mother, because a lot of people weren't lesbian mothers. I asked my mom what a lesbian was, and she said it was like, instead of a man and woman being together, it was two women that were in love. Then I knew what a lesbian was.

I knew it was different to be a lesbian, but it's really hard to think about. I brought this book to first grade for my sharing day. It's called *Many Mommies*. My teacher had this whole big talk about it. She talked

549

about all different kinds of families. Then she read the book to everyone and told me it was a really great book. A couple kids said it was a good book, but no one said anything else.

Now I know a few other kids who have lesbian moms, and this makes me feel better. I know a lot of lesbian women, but not a lot of lesbian moms. Lesbian moms seem different than married women. It seems like married women get a lot more help; they don't have to work so much. Their husbands go to work and so they get to stay home with the kids. When I go to kids' houses who have a mom and a dad, it seems like they're really rich, like they have a lot of money.

Maybe it seems easier to be married, but then that might be hard   5
because maybe straight women get in fights with their husbands a lot. My mom works all the time, and I wonder if maybe she had a husband she could stay home with me in the summer and I wouldn't have to go away to my grandparents'.

When I go to my grandparents' for the summer I get spoiled. We have ice cream all the time. But it's hard because we can't really . . . you see, my grandma and grandpa are kind of mad that my mom is not with a man and that everybody else is married. They don't even like saying the word lesbian. They don't talk about it, but my mom talks about it and she told me they didn't like it. I don't like the way they feel about her.

They feel that women should be with men. So do most of my aunts and uncles. They don't tell me this stuff, but grownups keep quiet about things like that. They don't think children should hear that kind of stuff, or maybe they don't think kids should know about different types of families. Maybe they think their family is the way all families are supposed to be. Or maybe they're embarrassed. Maybe I should send this book to the whole family!

But you know, when I was visiting my uncle, he would sit there at the dinner table and talk about business. Business, business, business. I got kind of bored talking about business at dinner. When I go out with my mom for dinner we talk about kung-fu, or sometimes we talk about my mom being a lesbian mother. It's more interesting.

I like having lots of friends who are lesbians; they take care of me and take me places. When I lived with a bunch of lesbian women, I liked coming home because there was always someone there. I have a couple of men friends who are really nice guys. Sometimes I feel like I kind of miss out on some stuff, but I like having a lesbian mother. Sometimes I like being different. Sometimes I feel special being different. Other times I wish my mom was married and that I had a dad. It depends.

It seems like everyone who has a dad also has a brother or a sister. It   10
seems like lesbian mothers usually have one kid. But maybe it's better they only have one kid; it's less to handle. Sometimes when I want somebody to play with, I wish I had a brother or sister. Other times I'm glad I'm an

only kid. There's nobody to step on my sandcastles when I make them! Maybe if I had a brother we'd fight a lot. My mom is happy she didn't have seven kids like her mom did.

I don't tell other kids about my mom. At school it kind of bothers me because when we play or tell stories, there's always a mom and a dad. There's never a mom and a mom or a dad and a dad—always just a mom and a dad. Some kids ask me who is my dad, and why I don't live with him. I don't really know how to explain it to them. I say I don't really have a dad, but then they say that's impossible. So see, it's like they don't believe me or I have to pretend I have a dad because I feel like I have to have one.

What really bothers me is when my friends come over and then they get into this whole divorce thing. They ask if my parents are divorced or what. I say yes, but then they ask me if I know my dad. So I tell them no, not really. Then they ask who he is, and what does he do, and I hate that. I really don't like it. But then they only talk about it for a couple seconds and then they want to play something. They don't want to talk about dad stuff for very long.

Sometimes I ask my mom about my dad but . . . you see, I wonder about him. I don't know where he is. I don't think my mom knows either. It's just hard to know that other kids have dads. Everybody else has a dad.*

My mom has had a couple relationships with other women, but I didn't realize it at the very time. I just thought that we were sleeping over at their house, or they were sleeping over. It's really okay with me, but sometimes I like just being with her and nobody else. I like spending alone time with my mom. I like living with just my mom, but I wish it was in a house, not an apartment. In this apartment I have to be really quiet, and I don't enjoy being quiet.

When I grow up I want to live with someone; I don't know if I want to get married and I don't know if I want to have kids. It seems like you need a lot of money to have kids. Sometimes I feel strange having a lesbian mom; sometimes it's hard, and sometimes it's just different. It's good to have all kinds of families. My mom is the best mom in the world and I want that to be in this book.

15

QUESTIONING THE TEXT

1. Serena sees both advantages and disadvantages to her life in a lesbian family. Summarize her thoughts on these issues. In the final analysis,

---

Everybody else has a dad: For a commentary on the absence of fathers in contemporary families, see Jay Overocker's "Ozzie and Harriet in Hell," p. 528.

what is Serena's attitude toward her family? What in her article lets you know her attitude?

2. Why are Serena's grandparents "kind of mad" at her mother? In what ways are their values different from those of Serena and her mother?

3. A.L.'s introduction to this essay tells us clearly what she likes about it. Does the introduction also carry a message about what *we* should think about the essay? Cite examples in your response.

MAKING CONNECTIONS

4. In the previous article, David Updike describes a number of the pressures his multi-racial son will have to face. What are some pressures Serena will have to face that are different from those Updike names?

5. In her essay on p. 519, Joan Didion refers to marriage as "the classic betrayal." Review Didion's essay, determining what it is she thinks that marriage betrays. Then return to Serena's discussion and consider what she might say in response. Would she agree with Didion? Why, or why not?

JOINING THE CONVERSATION

6. Suppose you were Serena's aunt or uncle—or big sister or brother. What advice would you give her—and why? Write this advice in a letter for Serena to open when she is several years older.

7. Working with one or two classmates, brainstorm about what questions the person(s) who talked with Serena might have asked to elicit her thoughts. (The book is subtitled *Sons and Daughters of Lesbians Talk About Their Lives.*) Then devise a brief list of simple questions you would like to ask some children about how they see their families, how they feel about their parents, how they define "home," and so on. If possible, have each member of your group interview two children. Pool the information you gather and prepare a brief presentation for your class on "Kids' Talk: What They Say About Home and Family."

COLLETTE H. RUSSELL
A Day in the Homeless Life

O*RIGINALLY PUBLISHED IN* S*TREET* M*AGAZINE in 1989, this very brief essay takes readers through one day in one homeless woman's life. It is not a happy day, a safe day, a productive day. Not, in fact, a day much worth living. On the verge of madness, the author is "rescued" by her son and finds a job. Yet the glimpse she has given us of the homeless life suggests that even the best job she can get will not be enough to sustain life. And so it goes: a little over two years after writing this article, Collette Russell died alone in a motel room. Her brief article could have predicted that death, and it serves well as her epitaph.*

I chose this essay because it seems to me to be brutally honest, simply and clearly evoking one woman's experience of homelessness. The picture it paints will remain with me for many years to come, reminding me of my own position of privilege and safety. I will hear Collette Russell's voice every time I am tempted to make easy generalizations about people for whom "home" is a shelter or a street corner or when I may be tempted to laugh at the cynical, holier-than-thou posturing of a P. J. O'Rourke (the author of the next reading) and the spiteful stereotypes he creates. Thanks to Collette Russell, "homelessness" means more than a concept, an idea, or a problem to me now. So also does "home." — A.L.

"Good morning, ladies. It's 5 a.m. Time to get up." Ceiling lights were suddenly ablaze. This message boomed repeatedly until nearly everyone was out of bed.

Two toilets and three sinks for 50 women; no toilet paper in the morning, invariably. Three tables with benches bordered by beds on two sides were our day room, dining room, and lounge.

Breakfast usually arrived at 5:45 a.m., too late for those who were in the day-labor van pools. They went to work on empty stomachs, and they were the ones needing food the most.

Breakfast generally consisted of rolls and sausage and juice until it ran out. The coffee was unique: It didn't taste like coffee, but that's what we had to drink.

At 6:30 a.m. we were ordered to go down to the lobby, where we joined 50 other women either standing or sitting on wooden benches awaiting the light of day. Some talked to themselves. Some shouted angrily. Some sat motionless. Some slept sitting up. Some jumped up and down, walking away and then returning. Some chain-smoked. 5

All of us had our belongings with us. Carrying everything every step of the way every day was hard on the arms, and I felt it was a dead giveaway that I was homeless.

At 7:30 a.m. the clothing room opened. It was shocking to be told "Throw away what you're wearing after you get a new outfit." No laundry, just toss out yesterday's garments. We were allotted five minutes to paw through racks looking for articles that fit.

I was always happy to see 8:30 a.m. roll around. Grabbing my bags, I headed down Berkeley Street away from the jam-packed, smoke-filled "holding cell." Always I felt guilty at not going to work like everyone else who hurried by as I approached the business district.

The main library was my daily stop. I positioned myself at a table where I could watch the clock: We had to return to the shelter before 4 p.m. to get in line for a bed, otherwise we might miss out.

Reading was the high point of the day. Escape into a book. There   10 was relative privacy at a library table. It was heavenly. I hated to leave.

The clock signaled the task of trudging back, at 3:45 p.m., with even heavier bags. The bags, of course, were no heavier; they just seemed heavier.

Back in the "yard" I joined the group already assembled. Some women never left the grounds, staying all day in the small yard by the building. God forbid. With the appearance of a staff member we would form a line as the staffer prepared a list of our names and bed requests.

I was always glad when the lights went out at 9 p.m. and I could climb into bed (a bottom sheet and a blanket—no top sheet) and close my eyes and pretend I wasn't there but back in my apartment on the West Coast.

Twice I was robbed. Once a bag was taken. Another time my new blue underpants disappeared out of one of my bags. Who knew they were there?

Even if I were to do day labor at $4 per hour and clear $28 or so a   15 day, how many weeks would it take to save enough for first and last months' rent on an apartment plus deposit and enough to pay for initial utilities? I was too depressed to even try to work and took frequent breaks to sit down while doing kitchen volunteer work. I was tired all the time.

The true stories I heard were heartbreaking. Which was the sadder?

One young woman with no skills and no job training had been OK financially until her CETA* job ended—the program was abolished—and the YWCA raised its weekly room rate. She couldn't afford a room and couldn't find a job. She'd been in shelters for three or four years. I marveled that she was still sane. She did crossword puzzles while waiting everywhere.

Another older lady had held the same job for 10 years and would still have been working had not the corporation, without notice, closed up shop.

CETA: the Comprehensive Employment and Training Act, a federal jobs program

She was 59 years old and out of a job, with a little severance pay and no help to find new work. She tried but was unsuccessful in finding a new job. She exhausted her savings after her unemployment ran out. One June day in 1987 she found herself homeless. No money for rent.

Both of these women are intelligent, honest, pleasant, clean, and neatly dressed. And both are penniless and homeless. How will they escape the shelters? Will they?

I got by, all right, by keeping my mouth shut around the staff and   20
talking only with two or three women whom I knew to be sane and sociable. I was lucky. Two and a half months after I'd first gone into a shelter my son rescued me. I was on the verge of madness, so hungry for a little privacy and peace that I was afraid I'd start screaming in my sleep and be shunted off to a mental ward.*

Now I've got a job paying more than I've ever earned. But I remember those days and nights.

No one should have to live like that. Too many do. And will, I fear, unless and until we who do have homes and jobs help them end their eternal, living nightmare.

Eighteen months after writing this article, Collette H. Russell was back living in the streets. Nine months later she died alone in a motel room in Las Vegas.

IN RESPONSE

1. What questions would you like to ask Collette Russell? What more would you like to know about her life and her situation? How do you suppose she would have responded to your questions?
2. How do you feel after reading Russell's essay? Jot down two or three words that describe your feelings. Then freewrite for 10 or 15 minutes about why you think you feel the way you do.
3. In the concluding paragraphs of the next essay, P. J. O'Rourke likens giving attention to the plight of the homeless to "feeding the dog at the table." How might Collette Russell respond to O'Rourke's implicit suggestion that the homeless are subhuman? Think for a while about his essay and Russell's and then try your hand at writing a letter from Russell to O'Rourke.

I was on the verge . . . a mental ward: For another perspective on the relationship between homelessness and mental illness, see the next reading, "Among the Compassion Fascists," by P. J. O'Rourke.

P. J. O'ROURKE
Among the Compassion Fascists

LIKE FEMINISTS ON THE LEFT, the political right is sometimes accused of lacking a sense of humor. P. J. O'Rourke (b. 1947) disproves that charge almost single-handedly. Take, for example, his Parliament of Whores *(1991), which he glosses rather grandly: "A Lone Humorist Attempts to Explain the Entire U.S. Government." While O'Rourke cannot resist barn-sized targets like white-shoed Republican conventioneers and former President George Bush, his best shots are aimed squarely at liberalism's sacred cows, which he gleefully sets out to topple.*

O'Rourke is a reformed product of the sixties, a time when, he confesses, he "believed Yoko Ono was an artist." He's written for National Lampoon *and is still a correspondent for* Rolling Stone. *O'Rourke's bad-boy wit comes across especially well in the following piece from* Parliament of Whores, *a truly nasty exposé of homeless advocates. If O'Rourke seems a trifle insensitive (consigning activist Mitch Snyder to hell, for example), I'll trade sensitivity for plain speaking in the political arena any day.* — J.R.

On October, 7, 1989, I went to see the National March for Housing Now! on the Mall in Washington. The demonstrators seemed sincere in their desire to solve the various habitation-cost and dwelling-availability problems we have in the United States. The organized-labor contingent carried banners calling for a uniform national building code, increased factory mass production of modular homes, stricter Taft-Hartley anti-featherbedding regulations and a federal right-to-work law. Homeless advocates, community activists and welfare-rights organizers led the crowd in chants of

> Apartments, yes!
> Shelters, no!
> Rent control has got to go!

> Quit your whining,
> Stop your dithers,
> Sell public housing to the highest bidders!

> We're sick of living in a ditch,
> Give real estate tax breaks back to the rich!

while thousands of homeless men and women waved signs reading "JAIL US, WE'RE DRUNK" and "WE ARE CRAZY. PUT US IN MENTAL INSTITUTIONS, PLEASE."

The actual National March for Housing Now! didn't have thousands of homeless men and women or even hundreds, as far as I could see. At the pre-march rally beside the Washington Monument I did hear one woman say she was homeless. She was a big, resentful woman—the kind who's always behind the counter at the Department of Motor Vehicles when you go to renew your car registration. She was co-chairhuman of something or other, and she was declaiming from the podium: "I've got five kids! We live in one room! We're homeless!" No, ma'am, you're not. Your housing may be as bad as your family planning, but you're not homeless.

We usually think of "special interests" as being something out of a Thomas Nast cartoon—big men with cigars conspiring over a biscuit trust. But in fact, a special interest is any person or group that wants to be treated differently from the rest of us by the government. Every charity is a special interest. So is the League of Women Voters, the Episcopalian church, *Consumer Reports* magazine and anybody who threatens to write to his congressman. A special interest may be humble. It may be (this happens) worthy. It may even be morally correct about its need for special treatment.

Politics would not exist if it weren't for special interests. If the effect of government were always the same on everyone and if no one stood to lose or gain anything from government except what his fellows did, there would be little need for debate and no need for coalitions, parties or intrigue. Indeed, when some great national item appears on the governmental agenda, something that involves every person in the country—World War II or the interstate highway system—government turns apolitical (at least until the defense and paving contracts begin to be handed out).

Traditionally American special interests have been frank about their   5 political goals: They want money and privileges that other Americans don't get. The agriculture lobby . . . is a good example. Farmers argue that they, as a special interest, should receive special treatment because they're special—they feed us (or did until we started importing all our fast food burger meat from Argentina). Veterans make the same kind of claim—they risked their lives to protect the rest of us, so they should get funny hats to wear on Memorial Day and some cash. But recently special interest groups have begun dressing themselves in the clothes of altruism. And some of these groups have become so well costumed that it's hard to tell what their special interest is, let alone what's so special about it.

Aside from the big, resentful woman with the five kids, the rest of the Housing Now! demonstrators seemed to come from normal homes, that is, the kinds of homes that demonstrators normally come from—homes where they had sufficient resources to become half-educated and adequate leisure to hate their parents. They were all present and accounted for:

World Council of Churches* sensible-shoe types who have self-
righteousness the way some people have bad breath

Angry black poverty pests making a life and a living off the
misfortunes of others

Even angrier feminists doing their best to feminize poverty before
the blacks use it all up

Earnest neophyte Marxists, eyes glazed from dialectical epiphanies
and hands grubby from littering the Mall with ill-Xeroxed
tracts

College bohos dressed in black to show how gloomy the world is
when you're a nineteen-year-old rich kid

Young would-be hippies dressed exactly like old hippies used to
dress (remarkable how behind the times the avant-garde has
gotten)

And some of those old hippies themselves, faded jeans straining
beneath increasing paunches, hair still tied into a ponytail in
the back but gone forever on the top

Together these people constitute America's loudest special interest (and only
true, permanent underclass)—the Perennially Indignant. As always these
days, they were joined by greedy celebrities who aren't contented with fame
and money and want a reputation for moral goodness, too.

The labor unions were also on hand, but their members stood away
to one side in well-pressed sport clothes and snappy nylon windbreakers
embossed with the names of their locals. The United Auto Workers; American Federation of State, County and Municipal Employees; Steelworkers
and various building trades each had neat stacks of professionally made
picket signs. The International Brotherhood of Electrical Workers even
brought along its kilted bagpipe band. The plump, scrubbed union folk,
enjoying a subsidized bus trip with their softball buddies, were as out of
place as yarmulkes on a motorcycle gang. And more power to them. If
government is going to fling money at homelessness, I'd like at least some
of the money to land on people who hold jobs.

That morning as I was going out the door of my own housing—
which is handsome, spacious and frankly underpriced due to the District
of Columbia Housing Act of 1985, which in the name of keeping DC homes
"affordable," instituted rent ceilings that have led to the destruction of rental
stock in the less affluent sections of the city while providing a cost-of-living
subsidy to rich, unfeeling conservatives like myself. But I digress. . . . As
I was going out the door, my wife said, "Will there be lots of people from
South Carolina at the housing march?"

World Council of Churches: a worldwide fellowship of Protestant and Orthodox Christian
denominations that generally supports liberal social causes

I said, "Huh?"

"You know," she said, "where Hurricane Hugo just destroyed every-   10
body's house." My wife, like many wives, is under the impression that
mankind is as rational and pragmatic as wives are. I had to explain that
there wouldn't be any people from South Carolina in the march demanding
houses from the government because the people from South Carolina were
too busy building houses for themselves.

The big, resentful woman I mentioned earlier went on to extol a
group of what appeared to be just plain street bums called the New Exodus
Marchers who had walked to DC from New York. When the New Exodus
people arrived in Washington, they promptly got into a fistfight at the
Center for Creative Non-Violence. The fight had to do with the disposition
of royalty proceeds from the sale of HOMELESS T-shirts. (I am not making
this up.) Ms. Big Resentful said, "Five babies died on the walk from New
York City! The mothers miscarried but they kept on walking! This was
amazing! This was supernatural!"

This was grounds for arrest.

Over on the other side of the crowd I heard somebody shouting
through a bullhorn that they were from Alliance, Ohio. "And you may
not believe this," they shouted, "but even in little Alliance, Ohio, we have
two hundred people in our shelter." I didn't believe this. I'm from Ohio.
Alliance is a pleasant, semirural town in the northeast of the state. On
Monday I called the Alliance town office and was put right through to
Mayor Carr, who sounded puzzled. "The figure is new to me," he said.
"I'd never heard the two-hundred figure. Our shelter was put up for people
whose houses burn down, things like that. We haven't thought of it in
terms of the homeless."

Around noon the demonstrators traipsed down Constitution Avenue
and came to a halt, standing dully before a large sound stage near the
Reflecting Pool. It was a crowd numbering—as NBC News, with TV's
keen eye for hard facts, put it—"between 40,000 and 250,000 people." The
marchers packed themselves into the Mall between Third and Fourth Streets
(packed themselves very tightly, if we accept the 250,000 figure). They
were then regaled by the moderately famous: Richie Havens, Martin Sheen,
Dick Gregory, Olatunji, Mary Wilson. There was a fenced-off area beside
the stage, a sort of celebrity pen, where additional fairly well-known people
were being kept. Demonstrators pressed in to catch a glimpse of Casey
Kasem, Susan Dey, Rita Coolidge, Jon Voight and to try to figure out
which one of them was which.

The crowd was addressed with much bruiting of homelessness num-   15
bers, three million being the favorite. Since this is 500 percent more than
any serious estimate, housing advocates seem, rather than ameliorating
homelessness, to have created 2.4 million cases of it. A lot of equivalency

was in the air. "For the price of one B-2 bomber . . ." began most if not all the speeches. (As if there were a redemption center someplace where you could make a straight up trade of social progress for national defense.) The savings-and-loan bailout has replaced the moon shot as the Perennially Indignants' pet if-then theorem. "If the government can find $500 billion to . . ." But, of course, the government *couldn't* find $500 billion and ended up taking it from you and me.

The only break in the day's smug outrage and furious self-congratulation was a round of catcalls for Washington Mayor Marion Barry. I don't know why these people were mad at Barry. He advocated more federal money for housing and everything else. But Mayor Barry had been accused of taking drugs, and I guess the homeless wanted those drugs back.

Coolly considered over lunch (a pheasant-under-glass-and-caviar sandwich with a six-pack of Dom Perignon, because I mean to spend this money before it all goes to build flophouses), the most prominent feature of the Housing Now! march was its beggary. The march organizers weren't even pretending that the members of their special interest were deserving or that spending tax dollars on them would be useful, wise or fair. Nor were any definite programs proposed. The message of the Housing Now! demonstration was simply and entirely "give me some money."

The Perennially Indignant have, of course, good reasons for not putting forth definite programs. First, the homeless problem isn't what they say it is. Homelessness is not the result of a lack of warm, dry abodes in the United States. It's the result of mental-patient deinstitutionalization, de facto legalization of drug use, elimination of vagrancy laws, destruction of urban neighborhoods through infringement on property rights and a lot of other things that the Perennially Indignant themselves hold dear. Listening to people advocate programs to solve a problem caused by the programs those people advocated—this would be as absurd as, oh, I don't know, letting lawyers make laws.

Second, the Perennially Indignant don't want homelessness to go away (though I'll give them the benefit of the doubt and say that they aren't conscious of this). In our prosperous, peaceful and happy era, homelessness is one of the few undeniable (and telegenic!) social injustices left. No matter what somebody has done to himself or others, he doesn't deserve to freeze in the gutter is the Indignants' almost reasonable argument.

For the Perennially Indignant homelessness is a fine rallying flag where   20
they can all gather and show off how much they care. Homelessness is also a splendid way to indict the American system and, while they're at it, all of Western civilization and its individualism and freedom. Of Thomas Paine's "natural and imprescriptible rights of man . . . liberty, property, security and resistance to oppression," the Indignants believe only in security. They

would replace the democratic paradigm of government as a free association of equals with the totalitarian paradigm of the state as family.

Fortunately, few people in government take the Housing Now! kind of special interest lobbying seriously. Actual policymakers (we're not talking about liberal Democrats here) are familiar with the real homeless-population estimates generated by Dr. Martha Burt for the Food and Nutrition Service of the U.S. Department of Agriculture—the only nationwide probability-based study that's been done on the subject. Policymakers know about Thomas J. Main's and Dr. E. Fuller Torrey's investigations of the psychiatric and behavioral problems of the homeless. They have seen or at last heard about William Tucker's regression analysis showing the causal relationship of rent control to housing shortages. Et cetera. Et cetera.

The facts are simple. A government house-building orgy won't work because one third of the homeless are crazy and will jump out the windows and one third are screwed up on drink and drugs and will sell the plumbing. The rest have primarily economic problems, but we can keep giving them free housing forever, and it won't help. The law of supply and demand tells us that when the price of something is artificially set below market level there will soon be none of that thing left—as you may have noticed the last time you tried to buy something for nothing.

But the Perennially Indignant don't care if a policy works. In many ways it's better for them when a policy fails. What's a family for?

I went back to have another look at the demonstration, passing a number of homeless on the way. Despite a sizable protest on their behalf just around the corner, they remained at their posts, cadging change. One fellow was sitting athwart the sidewalk on Twelfth Street near the Old Post Office Building. He had an overnight bag with him and a pile of newspapers and magazines. He'd set out a paper cup primed with a few quarters and was listening to his Sony Walkman while he read the *Washington Post*. I went into a store to get my own copy of the *Post*. There was an Asian man, about fifty, behind the counter. He spotted my press tags and said, in compassionate if barely comprehensible English, "Oh, is Saturday, beautiful day—you must work?"

I told him yes, I was covering the housing march. "But you're working   25 on Saturday, too," I said.

"Oh, yes!" He smiled widely. "Seven days!"

I hesitate to even mention these two encounters. Some things are too amazing for fiction. But the Asian and the sidewalk squatter were too real for reportage.

In certain ways the Housing Now! march was a success. Turnout was a heartening 40 percent of the organizers' advance estimates. Press coverage was slavering yet perfunctory. The march got thirty-three column inches in the next day's *Washington Post*, but in the Section-D metro pages, not with the real news. The network news broadcasters made sympathetic noises but mostly en passant on the way to the day's meatier stories.

It's hard to imagine anyone who got a close look at the Housing Now! demonstration ever voting for a social program again. It was as though we as a nation had made the mistake of feeding the dog at the table. Now Spot won't leave us alone and is going to have to be tied out in the yard.

A few mainstream politicians paid lip service to the aims of the march, but they kept an arm's length between themselves and the chief Housing Now! organizers, who were Donna Brazile, the former Dukakis campaign aide who accused George Bush of having a girlfriend, and Mitch Snyder, the perennial homeless advocate and incessant protest-faster who would commit suicide a few months later, thereby obtaining an eternal home, and a warm one at that.   30

Best of all, there were hardly any beautiful women at the rally. I saw a journalist friend of mine on the Mall, and he and I pursued this line of inquiry as assiduously as our happy private lives allow. Practically every female at the march was a bowser. "We're not being sexist here," my friend insisted. "It's not that looks matter per se. It's just that beautiful women are always on the cutting edge of social trends. Remember how many beautiful women were in the anti-war movement twenty years ago? In the yoga classes fifteen years ago? At the discos ten years ago? On Wall Street five years ago? Where the beautiful women are is where the country is headed," said my friend. "And this," he looked around him, "isn't it."

"By the way," I said, "where *are* the beautiful women?"

"Well, we know where two of them are," said my friend. "One is married to you, and one is married to me, and they're *home*."

QUESTIONING THE TEXT

1. Works of satire often offer solutions to the problems they expose and mock. Does O'Rourke furnish any solutions to America's problem of homelessness?
2. How does O'Rourke define "special interest"? Is his definition valid?
3. What hard evidence does O'Rourke offer to undermine the credibility of his targets and enhance his own? What point does he make by calling the mayor of Alliance, Ohio?
4. Do you agree with J.R. that O'Rourke is "a trifle insensitive"? Cite examples from O'Rourke's essay in support of your answer.

MAKING CONNECTIONS

5. Which readings in this chapter (or from other chapters in this book) do you think O'Rourke might regard as expressions of "compassion fascism"? Write a short report describing the characteristics of this mentality, using examples from these or other readings. Or use your report to challenge this characterization of liberal activists.
6. Can you imagine any of the other issues in this chapter argued satirically? Describe how you might write such a piece. For example, can you imagine a humorous version of Serena's "Just Different, That's All" (starting on p. 549)? Why, or why not?

JOINING THE CONVERSATION

7. Try your hand at a piece of satire or parody. Poke fun—O'Rourke style—at any target ripe for skewering.
8. In class, discuss the effectiveness of humor in making a point. Where in this essay do you think O'Rourke is most convincing in his ridicule of homeless activists? Are there any subjects that should be off-limits to such humor?

JILL FRAWLEY
Inside the Home

A REGISTERED NURSE AND ADVOCATE for patients, Jill Frawley—as you may quickly guess—left the employment of the nursing home described in this article. Originally published in Mother Jones *magazine in 1991, this article demonstrates in graphic detail why she left and, in so doing, exposes the "big lie" told by institutions such as the one she worked for: "long-term care facilities" owned by big corporations care little or nothing for the patients whose money supports them or for the employees who do their bidding.*

I chose this essay because—in spite of the designation "nursing home"— I had never considered the word home *to include such institutions. In fact, asked to list dozens of places that might count as "home," I would have failed to include facilities such as the one Frawley describes. And yet I have friends whose parents are even now in such homes. How, then, to explain my omission? Perhaps, I have reflected since reading Frawley's essay, because my silent neglect of such "homes" is part of the big lie she speaks of. Perhaps by ignoring them I bear some responsibility for the many nursing homes that are insufferable and insupportable.*

Perhaps I should think more carefully about what is and is not designated as a "home." And perhaps I should think more carefully when big corporations call themselves "families." Are they families I want to support or belong to? Are the homes they provide ones I'd want to inhabit? Now read "Inside the Home."   — A.L.

I'm just one little nurse, in one little "care facility." Each shift I work, I carry in my soul a very big lie. I leave my job, and there aren't enough showers in the world to wash away my rage, my frustration, my impotence.

The long-term-care facility (nursing home) I work for is owned by a corporation that owns nursing homes throughout the country. Giving corporations like this control over the quality of medical care is handing over control to the fox. Every chicken in the coop knows there is no hope—only the ticking away of a life devoid of dignity or even minimal respect.

I watch the videos they show to new employees during "orientation." Smiling people spout corporate policy and speak of "guest relations." They tell us we are special; we are going to participate in a rewarding job. Elderly people in the video are dressed nicely; they are coherent and grateful for the help the staff member has time to give.

We sign the attendance sheet: We saw it; now we know what "guest relations" means. It means to act in front of the families so that they think everything is okay.

The truth is ugly; I confess it in a burst of desperation. The elderly lie in feces and urine because there is only one aide for thirty patients. Eventually, they get changed abruptly—too fast, too harshly. They cry out in confused terror. Doors are closed to "protect their privacy"—but really so no one will see. The covers get flung back. It's evening bed check. The old person is shoved from one side of the bed to the other. He tries to protest; he thinks something bad is happening. Whip out the soiled underpad, wipe him, throw the covers over him . . . on to the next body.

No time for mouth care; sometimes no time for showers; never time   5 to hold someone's hand even for a moment. Aides feed the helpless two spoonfuls of pureed stuff, dripping down chins; no time to wait for them to swallow. It gets charted: "Resident didn't eat much tonight." She loses weight; she gets more frail as each day passes. The food is so bad I can't begin to describe it. The cook is young and doesn't care much; if I complain, he gets mad. One resident asks me for a cup of hot water so she can use the instant soup in her drawer. She can't eat the cold, badly cooked stuff that is on her tray. Slow starvation is hard to get used to.

Why is there only one aide on these halls night after night? Most employees don't stay. They can't stand being flung into jobs that are too hard, too horrid, for too little money. The ones that do stay have given up complaining. They shut their eyes and ears and do the best they can. They have children to support, no education, are caught by life in such a way that quitting would intensify their own suffering and not alleviate anyone else's.

We're always short-staffed. We know it's to save money. One tired aide does a double shift, straining to do a job it takes two people to do correctly. I guess when you make four dollars and something an hour, it takes working double shifts (that's sixteen hours) to make enough to live on. Tired people get impatient, make mistakes, take shortcuts. A nurse calls in sick. That means one nurse does three halls. One nurse to pass out medicines for eighty residents.

Patients are dropped or fall. My coworkers agree that it's a widespread practice to chart this to avoid problems. Every incident report I have ever seen states that the patient or resident was "found on the floor" or appeared to have bruises or skin tears of "unknown" origin. When there's no time to turn the bedridden every two hours, skin breaks down and ulcers develop. The elderly get skin tears and bruises because they are fragile, but also because there is no time to handle them gently. Again, we chart carefully so there is no blame. We let our old ones die for many reasons. Sometimes it is because of sickness; sometimes it is from neglect.

The admissions director is a nice lady. She lives uneasily with her task. She tells anxious families not to worry, that the facility will be like a second home to their relative. She tells them what they want to hear. The families go away determined to believe everything will be fine. Secretly, they are relieved that they won't have to deal with dementia, incontinence, or the total dependency of a senile elder.

The silence is ominous in the evening. Nothing to do; no place to go.   10 The residents sit and wait for death. The staff is ground down in despair and hopelessness. The guys at corporate headquarters must be patting each other on the back about the profits they're making.

It got bad at the place I work. Too many unhappy people; too much barely controlled anger always close to erupting. A corporate spokesperson was sent from headquarters to listen to grievances. He listened, this quiet, intelligent man who had been to our facility before. I asked some of my fellow workers why they weren't going to speak out. "It doesn't do any good," was the response. "He's been coming for three or four years. Nothing changes." I went; I spoke out; they were right. Nothing changes.

The elderly suffer quietly. They are afraid they will be punished if they speak up for themselves. Most of them can't speak for themselves. They just want to escape this hell. I do too. They need a place to stay; I need a job. We're trapped.

I am one little nurse, in one little care facility, living with this terrible secret. If they knew I was telling on them, I wouldn't have a job. What about my rent? What about my needs? But I need to tell. I confess to my participation in these crimes. I can't keep this secret any longer.

If you have an elderly relative in a facility:

1. Visit at odd hours.
2. Visit at mealtime.
3. Don't believe what the staff tells you.
4. Ask questions.
5. Don't worry if small items are missing. Petty theft is not serious. Abuse is.
6. Make sure your relative is clean.
7. Notice if your relative is losing weight.
8. Check your relative's skin for bruises.
9. Let "them" know you are watching.
10. Be polite to staff, but raise hell with the administrator or the director of nursing. Though they are just employees and will tell you what you want to hear, it's worth a try.
11. Contact local ombudsmen if you can't get results. If that doesn't work, contact the state regulatory agency.
12. Complain to headquarters or whoever owns the facility.
13. Don't allow yourself to be blackmailed by veiled threats of being forced to move your relative.
14. Don't give up; wear them down.

QUESTIONING THE TEXT

1. What does Frawley mean by the "big lie"? Write out a brief definition of this "big lie."
2. What is Frawley's attitude toward her employers? Toward her patients? Toward herself? Point to places in the essay that reveal these attitudes to you.
3. Are the questions A.L. poses at the end of her introduction to this reading rhetorical ones, or does she intend for you to answer them? How do you know?

MAKING CONNECTIONS

4. Review the essays, poems, and illustration in this chapter and then list all the places in them that fall under the category of "home." What do all these places have in common? Try to write a definition of "home" that would accommodate all these places.
5. Imagine a dialogue between Frawley and P. J. O'Rourke, the author of the previous reading, on the definition and importance of home. Write out a page or so of that dialogue.

JOINING THE CONVERSATION

6. Think for a while about the work you now do or have done. What about that work made you feel good about what you were doing? Did anything about it seem like a "big lie"? What, if anything, filled you with frustration? Based on your exploration of these questions, write a brief position paper on "how I feel about the work I do (or have done)."
7. Working with several members of your class, do some research on nursing homes in your area. How are they regulated? Who owns them? How much does it cost to stay in them? Who works there, and how are such people licensed or certified? Have each member of your group visit one nursing home, taking notes on the facilities and the atmosphere and talking, if possible, to people who work there, as well as to people who live there. Pool your notes and prepare a report for your class on whether your research does or does not support Frawley's picture of nursing homes.

ED MADDEN
Family Cemetery, near Hickory Ridge, Arkansas

We feel the touch of our extended families at important moments of transition: birth, graduation, marriage, death. Anyone with a large clan knows, however, that such occasions can bring out the worst in people. Cousins grown a lanky foot taller in the last year may trade blows (or gossip) at a wedding; at a baptism, aunts from different sides of the family will quarrel over the choice of godparents; and otherwise dutiful children will spend a holiday reunion silently tallying Grandpa's power tools, wondering who will inherit them when the old man finally crosses the bar.

Yet at such thresholds, we need our families too and look for support from these people who knew us from our birth, who share our rambling gait, conspicuous nose, and deepest memories.

In the following poem Ed Madden writes about one such family time. Madden (b. 1963) is a poet and teacher, completing a Ph.D. at the University of Texas at Austin. He grew up on a rice and soybean farm in northeast Arkansas. His interests range from theology and feminist theory to pop culture and Elvis Presley, and his poems have appeared in College English, Christianity and Literature, *and elsewhere.* – J.R.

I

Redwing blackbirds shout
themselves hoarse from the oaks
of the cemetery. A crop-duster drones
above a nearby ricefield. The long

caravan of cars that left the church   5
is still arriving, the dust drifting
in waves that coat the dull green rows
of grain sorghum and soybeans, dust

still hanging in air hot
with the smell of Arkansas honeysuckle   10
and vetch and the sweet maroon
ferment of funeral roses.

II

I breathe deeply: the summer
grass rich at the verge of brown,
freshly mown, the musty, almost acrid   15
earth of this sandy hillside,

piled by the grave. These things
must be remembered, like the daffodils
in solemn yellow spurts that marked
my grandma's death, standing in silent   20

clusters of mourning at the cemetery,
dotting her yard like relatives, nodding,
touching, like cousins laughing, flaring
their bright lives against the grey spring wind.

III

Grandpa's flowers are scattered   25
down the line of tombstones, decorating
the graves of his wife, his children;
it seems the office of aunts to gather

the blooms, to drape these odd dots
and splashes against brown earth, grey stone.   30
We the men, the sons and grandsons,
take the shovels in groups of three,

marking our ties with the thuds that fill
the grave: it is love, it is something
of God. And there must be a word   35
to fill the hole it creates.

IN RESPONSE

1. Read "Family Cemetery" along with Karen Cooper's "A Native
   Woman—1982" (on p. 523), and respond with an entry in your reading
   log, if you are keeping one.
2. Examine the role that nature plays in "Family Cemetery." In a short
   analysis, explain your reaction to the sights, sounds, and smells in this
   poem.
3. In a group, share your experience of a family moment that you might
   turn into a poem.

OTHER READINGS

Ferguson, Sarah. "Us Versus Them: America's Growing Frustration with the Homeless." *Utne Reader* Sept.–Oct. 1990: 50–55. Presents conflicting views on how to deal with homeless people.

Goodman, Ellen. "Boy's 'Divorce' from Neglectful Mother Advances Rights of Children Everywhere." *Columbus Dispatch* 2 Oct. 1992: 7A. Relates a 12-year-old's struggle to create a family for himself.

Hochschild, Arlie. *The Second Shift: Working Parents and the Revolution at Home.* New York: Viking, 1989. Gives case studies of the home life of working couples.

Monahan, John. "When the Cold Wind Blows." *Newsweek* 17 Feb. 1992: 10. Expresses the author's emptiness after divorce.

Okin, Susan Moller. "Change the Family; Change the World." *Utne Reader* Mar.–Apr. 1990: 74–79. Argues that changes in traditional family structure could result in positive changes in society. Excerpted from Okin's *Justice, Gender & the Family* (New York: Basic, 1989).

Raspberry, William. "Teaching Boys to Become Men." *Washington Post* 20 Jan. 1992: A25. Argues that boys raised by traditional fathers become good men.

Rector, Robert. "Fourteen Myths About Families and Child Care." *Harvard Journal on Legislation* 26: 517–47. Presents a conservative perspective on the family.

Rhodes, Richard. *Farm: A Year in the Life of an American Farmer.* New York: Simon, 1989. Examines in detail the life of a farm family.

Washington, Mary Helen, ed. *Memories of Kin: Stories About Family by Black Writers.* New York: Anchor, 1991. Includes stories by June Jordan, Alice Walker, Charles Chesnutt, Audre Lorde, James Baldwin, and others.

Wattenberg, Ben J. "Wedded to Intermarriage." *The First Universal Nation.* New York: Free, 1990. Argues that ethnic intermarriage is reshaping America.

Whitehead, Barbara Dafoe. "Dan Quayle Was Right." *Atlantic* Apr. 1993: 47–84. Argues that American children have been hurt by disruptions of the nuclear family.

Wright, Patricia. "Triple Jeopardy." *Sojourner: The Women's Forum* June 1992: 6P. Depicts the lesbian community as family.

A Car Culture: On the Road 10

I could feel the road some twenty inches beneath me, unfurling and flying and hissing at incredible speeds. . . .
JACK KEROUAC, *On the Road*

This turn has killed runaway trucks
WALTER McDONALD, *The Hairpin Curve at Durango*

The VW bus . . . has been the vehicle of choice for those . . . who have wished to make personal statements about their values via their mode of transport.
STEVEN SPENCE, *The Van of Aquarius*

Before she fell in love with a machine, Carol was a more or less conventional middle-aged woman.
MARILYN MURPHY, *Roam Sweet Home*

Magazines . . . are full of allusions to the erotic potential of motoring.
PETER MARSH and PETER COLLETT, *The Love Affair*

A man doesn't care about staying alive in a car: a man cares about feeling alive in a car.
TONY KORNHEISER, *Radio Daze*

The windshield wipers said "Gracie Allen Gracie Allen Gracie Allen."
BAILEY WHITE, *Someday the Old Junker Will Be a Neat Car Again*

I have seen and admired "Thunderbird" as a Ford designation. It would be hard to match. . . .
MARIANNE MOORE, *Correspondence with the Ford Motor Company*

. . . the car kept coming up, the car in motion. . . .
STEPHEN DUNN, *The Sacred*

Introduction

IF THERE IS A DEPENDABLE BAROMETER of economic prosperity in the United States, it is the automotive industry. If Americans share one rite of passage into adulthood, it is attaining a driver's license. If one object embodies the strengths and weaknesses of the American dream, it is the private automobile, truck, or van. For many people, General Motors' advertising slogan rings true: "It's not just your car, it's your freedom." In many ways, American popular culture in the twentieth century is a *car culture*—understanding "car" in a broad sense to include all the pickups, motorcycles, minivans, maxivans, eighteen-wheelers, lowriders, hot rods, limousines, and recreational vehicles that ply American highways today.

Yet as a subject for serious cultural analysis, we pay far more attention to music, television, even minor poets, than we do to the motorized objects that have reshaped our landscapes, dominated our economy, altered the structures of our families, and embodied our dreams.

Given the near–continental size of the United States, the love of Americans for their vehicles might seem inevitable. But distances alone do not explain why the car or pickup truck is one of life's necessities for Americans. Other nations of similar size have not developed comparable obsessions with their vehicles. But then the United States is a country perhaps uniquely defined by ceaseless motion, both geographical and economic. We have never stopped believing in Manifest Destiny.

We also use our vehicles to express who we are and what we believe. We sing about them, decorate them for weddings, put our opinions on their bumpers, even live in them. Henry Ford put Americans behind the wheel, but it was William C. Durant, the founder of General Motors, who made motor vehicles conspicuous symbols of success by offering products to mark the progress of a career, from low-ball Chevys and Pontiacs to sober Oldsmobiles and Buicks and, finally, on to the pinnacle of American achievement, the Cadillac—"Standard of the World."

A lot has changed since the 1950s when Jack Kerouac wrote *On the Road,* the key text for this chapter. We still have more cars per capita than any major nation on earth; if we all got in our cars at the same time, the entire population could ride in the front seats. The United States reigns as the only military superpower, and its political values dominate the world. But economically, its rivals have begun to usurp portions of the American dream. The standards of the world, in automobiles at least, are now often built in Germany and Japan, and youthful Americans dream of Z-cars and Beamers as much as of

Corvettes and Vipers. What that will mean in time we can only guess.

While you consider this prospect, you might also want to think about some of the following questions:

1. What roles do automobiles and trucks play in American popular culture—on television and in films, books, music?

2. How has your life been shaped or defined by the presence of the automobile in American culture?

3. If it is true that many Americans are obsessed with the automobile, is such an obsession troubling or problematic?

4. How may the private automobile be affected by growing concerns for the environment?

5. Do cars seem to have personalities? What might a Ross Perot of cars be? An Oprah Winfrey? A Michael Jordan? You might enjoy discussing this issue with a few classmates.

•   •   •

JACK KEROUAC
On the Road

JACK KEROUAC'S ON THE ROAD has often been called the novel that defined the "beat generation," those young Americans who reached adulthood after World War II disillusioned and discontented with their lives despite prosperity and opportunities. Kerouac (1922–69) in fact coined the term "beat generation" and, along with Allen Ginsberg, William Burroughs, Gary Snyder, Gregory Corso, and Lawrence Ferlinghetti, gave a new, rougher, and more colloquial idiom to American literature.

Not everyone regarded On the Road *as literature, however. Drafted in a three-week burst of energy in 1951, the novel was rejected (and revised) time and again before Viking finally published it in 1957. The work was different and puzzling, even troubling, less a novel than a memoir of Kerouac's adventures crossing and recrossing the United States and Mexico in the late 1940s, usually in the company of his friend Neal Cassady. The characters in* On the Road *spend their time blasting up and down American highways, casing cities, making love (often leaving wives and children behind), smoking marijuana, thieving, and digging black jazz. Indeed, it's in seedy jazz clubs that Kerouac (as Sal Paradise) and Cassady (as the charismatic near-criminal Dean Moriarity) come closest to finding the mysterious "it" they are seeking—there and, of course, on the road.*

Dean Moriarity himself is a bigger-than-life antihero, a dizzyingly amoral conniver constantly searching for adventure and for his father (also a bum, riding the rails). With his eloquent chatter and his relentless inquiries into the details of life, this reform-school graduate dominates and eventually antagonizes just about everyone in On the Road. *In love with America as well as profoundly disappointed by it, he is cut from the same cloth as other heroes of what was to become a youth-oriented counterculture, one that idolized the young Marlon Brando, identified with James Dean, and gave ear to Bob Dylan.*

The chapter from the novel reprinted here shows Dean, Sal, and two college boys barreling from Denver to Chicago in a 1947 Cadillac provided by a travel bureau—an agency that delivers cars to people who for one reason or another have left them behind on trips. At the wheel of the limousine, Dean storms across the middle of the American continent at 110 miles an hour while Sal ponders what it all means. – J.R.

In no time at all we were back on the main highway and that night I saw the entire state of Nebraska unroll before my eyes. A hundred and ten miles an hour straight through, an arrow road, sleeping towns, no traffic, and the Union Pacific streamliner* falling behind us in the moonlight. I wasn't frightened at all that night; it was perfectly legitimate to go 110 and talk and have all the Nebraska towns—Ogallala, Gothenburg, Kearney, Grand Island, Columbus—unreel with dreamlike rapidity as we roared ahead and talked. It was a magnificent car; it could hold the road like a boat holds on water. Gradual curves were its singing ease. "Ah, man, what a dreamboat," sighed Dean. "Think if you and I had a car like this what we could do. Do you know there's a road that goes down Mexico and all the way to Panama?—and maybe all the way to the bottom of South America where the Indians are seven feet tall and eat cocaine on the mountainside? Yes! You and I, Sal, we'd dig the whole world with a car like this because, man, the road must eventually lead to the whole world. Ain't nowhere else it can go—right? Oh, and are we going to cut around old Chi with this thing! Think of it, Sal, I've never been to Chicago in all my life, never stopped."

"We'll come in there like gangsters in this Cadillac!"

"Yes! And girls! We can pick up girls, in fact, Sal, I've decided to make extra-special fast time so we can have an entire evening to cut around in this thing. Now you just relax and I'll ball the jack all the way."

"Well, how fast are you going now?"

"A steady one-ten I figure—you wouldn't notice it. We've still got   5 all Iowa in the daytime and then I'll make that old Illinois in nothing flat." The boys fell asleep and we talked and talked all night.

It was remarkable how Dean could go mad and then suddenly continue with his soul—which I think is wrapped up in a fast car, a coast to reach, and a woman at the end of the road—calmly and sanely as though nothing had happened. "I get like that every time in Denver now—I can't make that town any more. Gookly, gooky, Dean's a spooky. Zoom!" I told him I had been over this Nebraska road before in '47. He had too. "Sal, when I was working for the New Era Laundry in Los Angeles, nineteen forty-four, falsifying my age, I made a trip to Indianapolis Speedway for the express purpose of seeing the Memorial Day classic hitch, hiking by day and stealing cars by night to make time. Also I had a twenty-dollar Buick back in LA, my first car, it couldn't pass the brake and light inspection so I decided I needed an out-of-state license to operate the car without arrest so went through here to get the license. As I was hitchhiking through one of these very towns, with the plates concealed under my coat, a nosy sheriff who thought I was pretty young to be hitchhiking accosted me on the main drag. He found the plates and threw me in the two-cell jail with a county delinquent who should have been in the home for the old since he couldn't feed himself (the sheriff's wife fed him) and sat through the day drooling

---

the Union Pacific streamliner: a passenger train

and slobbering. After investigation, which included corny things like a fatherly quiz, then an abrupt turnabout to frighten me with threats, a comparison of my handwriting, et cetera, and after I made the most magnificent speech of my life to get out of it, concluding with the confession that I was lying about my car-stealing past and was only looking for my paw who was a farmhand hereabouts, he let me go. Of course I missed the races. The following fall I did the same thing again to see the Notre Dame–California game in South Bend, Indiana—trouble none this time and, Sal, I had just the money for the ticket and not an extra cent and didn't eat anything all up and back except for what I could panhandle from all kinds of crazy cats I met on the road and at the same time gun gals. Only guy in the United States of America that ever went to so much trouble to see a ballgame."

I asked him the circumstances of his being in LA in 1944. "I was arrested in Arizona, the joint absolutely the worst joint I've ever been in. I had to escape and pulled the greatest escape in my life, speaking of escapes, you see, in a general way. In the woods, you know, and crawling, and swamps—up around that mountain country. Rubber hoses and the works and accidental so-called death facing me I had to cut out of those woods along the ridge so as to keep away from trails and paths and roads. Had to get rid of my joint clothes and sneaked the neatest theft of a shirt and pants from a gas station outside Flagstaff, arriving LA two days later clad as gas attendant and walked to the first station I saw and got hired and got myself a room and changed name (Lee Buliay) and spent an exciting year in LA, including a whole gang of new friends and some really great girls, that season ending when we were all driving on Hollywood Boulevard one night and I told my buddy to steer the car while I kissed my girl—I was at the wheel, see—and *he didn't hear me* and we ran smack into a post but only going twenty and I broke my nose. You've seen before my nose—the crooked Grecian curve up here. After that I went to Denver and met Marylou in a soda fountain that spring. Oh, man, she was only fifteen and wearing jeans and just waiting for someone to pick her up. Three days three nights of talk in the Ace Hotel, third floor, southeast corner room, holy memento room and sacred scene of my days—she was so sweet then, so *young,* hmm, ahh! But hey, look down there in the night thar, hup, hup, a buncha old bums by a fire by the rail, damn me." He almost slowed down. "You see, I never know whether my father's there or not." There were some figures by the tracks, reeling in front of a woodfire. "I never know whether to ask. He might be anywhere." We drove on. Somewhere behind us or in front of us in the huge night his father lay drunk under a bush, and no doubt about it—spittle on his chin, water on his pants, molasses in his ears, scabs on his nose, maybe blood in his hair and the moon shining down on him.

I took Dean's arm. "Ah, man, we're sure going home now." New York was going to be his permanent home for the first time. He jiggled all over; he couldn't wait.

"And think, Sal, when we get to Pennsy we'll start hearing that gone Eastern bop on the disk jockeys. Geeyah, roll, old boat, roll!" The magnificent car made the wind roar; it made the plains unfold like a roll of paper; it cast hot tar from itself with deference—an imperial boat. I opened my eyes to a fanning dawn; we were hurling up to it. Dean's rocky dogged face as ever bent over the dashlight with a bony purpose of its own.

"What are you thinking, Pops?"   10

"Ah-ha, ah-ha, same old thing, y'know—gurls gurls gurls."

I went to sleep and woke up to the dry, hot atmosphere of July Sunday morning in Iowa, and still Dean was driving and driving and had not slackened his speed; he took the curvy corndales of Iowa at a minimum of eighty and the straightaway 110 as usual, unless both-ways traffic forced him to fall in line at a crawling and miserable sixty. When there was a chance he shot ahead and passed cars by the half-dozen and left them behind in a cloud of dust. A mad guy in a brand-new Buick* saw all this on the road and decided to race us. When Dean was just about to pass a passel the guy shot by us without warning and howled and tooted his horn and flashed the tail lights for challenge. We took off after him like a big bird. "Now wait," laughed Dean, "I'm going to tease that sonofabitch for a dozen miles or so. Watch." He let the Buick go way ahead and then accelerated and caught up with it most impolitely. Mad Buick went out of his mind; he gunned up to a hundred. We had a chance to see who he was. He seemed to be some kind of Chicago hipster traveling with a woman old enough to be—and probably actually was—his mother. God knows if she was complaining, but he raced. His hair was dark and wild, an Italian from old Chi; he wore a sports shirt. Maybe there was an idea in his mind that we were a new gang from LA invading Chicago, maybe some of Mickey Cohen's men,* because the limousine looked every bit the part and the license plates were California. Mainly it was just road kicks. He took terrible chances to stay ahead of us; he passed cars on curves and barely got back in line as a truck wobbled into view and loomed up huge. Eighty miles of Iowa we unreeled in this fashion, and the race was so interesting that I had no opportunity to be frightened. Then the mad guy gave up, pulled up at a gas station, probably on orders from the old lady, and as we roared by he waved gleefully. On we sped, Dean barechested, I with my feet on the dashboard, and the college boys sleeping in the back. We stopped to eat breakfast at a diner run by a white-haired lady who gave us extra-large portions of potatoes as church-bells rang in the nearby town. Then off again.

---

a brand-new Buick: For a love poem to a Buick, see the reading by Peter Marsh and Peter Collett, "The Love Affair," starting on p. 599.

Mickey Cohen's men: Cohen (1912–76) was a mobster.

"Dean, don't drive so fast in the daytime."

"Don't worry, man, I know what I'm doing." I began to flinch. Dean came up on lines of cars like the Angel of Terror. He almost rammed them along as he looked for an opening. He teased their bumpers, he eased and pushed and craned around to see the curve, then the huge car leaped to his touch and passed, and always by a hair we made it back to our side as other lines filed by in the opposite direction and I shuddered. I couldn't take it any more. It is only seldom that you find a long Nebraskan straightaway in Iowa, and when we finally hit one Dean made his usual 110 and I saw flashing by outside several scenes that I remembered from 1947—a long stretch where Eddie and I had been stranded two hours. All that old road of the past unreeling dizzily as if the cup of life had been overturned and everything gone mad. My eyes ached in nightmare day.

"Ah hell, Dean, I'm going in the back seat, I can't stand it any more,   15 I can't look."

"Hee-hee-hee!" tittered Dean and he passed a car on a narrow bridge and swerved in dust and roared on. I jumped in the back seat and curled up to sleep. One of the boys jumped in front for the fun. Great horrors that we were going to crash this very morning took hold of me and I got down on the floor and closed my eyes and tried to go to sleep. As a seaman I used to think of the waves rushing beneath the shell of the ship and the bottomless deeps thereunder—now I could feel the road some twenty inches beneath me, unfurling and flying and hissing at incredible speeds across the groaning continent with that mad Ahab at the wheel. When I closed my eyes all I could see was the road unwinding into me. When I opened them I saw flashing shadows of trees vibrating on the floor of the car. There was no escaping it. I resigned myself to all. And still Dean drove, he had no thought of sleeping till we got to Chicago. In the afternoon we crossed old Des Moines again. Here of course we got snarled in traffic and had to go slow and I got back in the front seat. A strange pathetic accident took place. A fat colored man was driving with his entire family in a sedan in front of us; on the rear bumper hung one of those canvas desert waterbags they sell tourists in the desert. He pulled up sharp, Dean was talking to the boys in the back and didn't notice, and we rammed him at five miles an hour smack on the waterbag, which burst like a boil and squirted water in the air. No other damage except a bent bumper. Dean and I got out to talk to him. The upshot of it was an exchange of addresses and some talk, and Dean not taking his eyes off the man's wife whose beautiful brown breasts were barely concealed inside a floppy cotton blouse. "Yass, yass." We gave him the address of our Chicago baron and went on.

The other side of Des Moines a cruising car came after us with the siren growling, with orders to pull over. "Now what?"

The cop came out. "Were you in an accident coming in?"

"Accident? We broke a guy's waterbag at the junction."

"He says he was hit and run by a bunch in a stolen car." This was   20
one of the few instances Dean and I knew of a Negro's acting like a suspicious
old fool. It so surprised us we laughed. We had to follow the patrolman to
the station and there spent an hour waiting in the grass while they telephoned
Chicago to get the owner of the Cadillac and verify our position as hired
drivers. Mr. Baron said, according to the cop, "Yes, that is my car but I
can't vouch for anything else those boys might have done."

"They were in a minor accident here in Des Moines."

"Yes, you've already told me that—what I meant was, I can't vouch
for anything they might have done in the past."

Everything was straightened out and we roared on. Newton, Iowa,
it was, where I'd taken that dawn walk in 1947. In the afternoon we crossed
drowsy old Davenport again and the low-lying Mississippi in her sawdust
bed; then Rock Island, a few minutes of traffic, the sun reddening, and
sudden sights of lovely little tributary rivers flowing softly among the magic
trees and greeneries of mid-American Illinois. It was beginning to look like
the soft sweet East again; the great dry West was accomplished and done.
The state of Illinois unfolded before my eyes in one vast movement that
lasted a matter of hours as Dean balled straight across at the same speed.
In his tiredness he was taking greater chances than ever. At a narrow bridge
that crossed one of these lovely little rivers he shot precipitately into an
almost impossible situation. Two slow cars ahead of us were bumping over
the bridge; coming the other way was a huge truck-trailer with a driver
who was making a close estimate of how long it would take the slow cars
to negotiate the bridge, and his estimate was that by the time he got there
they'd be over. There was absolutely no room on the bridge for the truck
and any cars going the other direction. Behind the truck cars pulled out
and peeked for a chance to get by it. In front of the slow cars other slow
cars were pushing along. The road was crowded and everyone exploding
to pass. Dean came down on all this at 110 miles an hour and never hesitated.
He passed the slow cars, swerved, and almost hit the left rail of the bridge,
went head-on into the shadow of the unslowing truck, cut right sharply,
just missed the truck's left front wheel, almost hit the first slow car, pulled
out to pass, and then had to cut back in line when another car came out
from behind the truck to look, all in a matter of two seconds, flashing by
and leaving nothing more than a cloud of dust instead of a horrible five-
way crash with cars lurching in every direction and the great truck humping
its back in the fatal red afternoon of Illinois with its dreaming fields. I
couldn't get it out of my mind, also, that a famous bop clarinetist had died
in an Illinois car-crash recently, probably on a day like this. I went to the
back seat again.

The boys stayed in the back too now. Dean was bent on Chicago before nightfall. At a road-rail junction we picked up two hobos who rounded up a half-buck between them for gas. A moment before sitting around piles of railroad ties, polishing off the last of some wine, now they found themselves in a muddy but unbowed and splendid Cadillac limousine headed for Chicago in precipitous haste. In fact the old boy up front who sat next to Dean never took his eyes off the road and prayed his poor bum prayers, I tell you. "Well," they said, "we never knew we'd get to Chicaga sa fast." As we passed drowsy Illinois towns where the people are so conscious of Chicago gangs that pass like this in limousines every day, we were a strange sight: all of us unshaven, the driver barechested, two bums, myself in the back seat, holding on to a strap and my head leaned back on the cushion looking at the countryside with an imperious eye—just like a new California gang come to contest the spoils of Chicago, a band of desperados escaped from the prisons of the Utah moon. When we stopped for Cokes and gas at a small-town station people came out to stare at us but they never said a word and I think made mental notes of our descriptions and heights in case of future need.* To transact business with the girl who ran the gas-pump Dean merely threw on his T-shirt like a scarf and was curt and abrupt as usual and got back in the car and off we roared again. Pretty soon the redness turned purple, the last of the enchanted rivers flashed by, and we saw distant smokes of Chicago beyond the drive. We had come from Denver to Chicago via Ed Wall's ranch, 1180 miles, in exactly seventeen hours, not counting the two hours in the ditch and three at the ranch and two with the police in Newton, Iowa, for a mean average of seventy miles per hour across the land, with one driver. Which is a kind of crazy record.

QUESTIONING THE TEXT

1. Do you think Sal, the narrator of *On the Road*, shares all of Dean's values and attitudes? Does he admire Dean? If you keep a reading log, record your answers there.
2. How would you characterize the style of *On the Road*? Point out sentences or paragraphs you find particularly noteworthy. Does Dean's way of talking strike you as unusual? How would you describe it?
3. Shortly after it was published in 1957, *On the Road* made the *New York Times* best-seller list. How might you explain the popularity of such a book in the supposedly conservative 1950s? Do you think the book would have a similar appeal today? Freewrite on that issue.

---

we stopped for Cokes and gas: For another person's perspective on travellers passing through a small town, see Zora Neale Hurston's "How It Feels to Be Colored Me," p. 386.

MAKING CONNECTIONS

4. In a position paper, explore what Sal might mean when he observes that Dean's soul "is wrapped up in a fast car, a coast to reach, and a woman at the end of the road." Before you write, read "The Love Affair" (starting on p. 599).

5. Note in the margins all the references to the car Dean is driving. What role does the Cadillac play in this selection? What does it represent to Dean, Sal, and the people who see it on the road? Write an analysis comparing the cultural role of the Cadillac to that of the Volkswagen vans described in "The Van of Aquarius" (starting on p. 584) or the recreational vehicles in "Roam Sweet Home" (starting on p. 592).

6. Keep a travel journal for some trip you take, long or short. Try writing in the bold and dramatic style Kerouac uses in *On the Road*. Or employ the more controlled style of Bailey White in "Someday the Old Junker Will Be a Neat Car Again" (starting on p. 618).

JOINING THE CONVERSATION

7. In the library, explore the "beat generation" and the so-called beatniks of the late 1950s. Write a brief report explaining how *On the Road* represents some of the values of the beats.

8. Write a dialogue between the Buick driver and his passenger—whom Sal assumes is his mother—during the road duel with Dean.

9. *On the Road* inspired a generation of hitchhiking, backpacking Americans. In a group, discuss why people travel. What do people—especially younger people—expect to find at the end of their journeys? Then write an exploratory paper about being on the road.

WALTER McDONALD
The Hairpin Curve at Durango

*T*RUCKERS *PILOTING EIGHTEEN-WHEELERS cut a glamorous figure in our car culture, an image reinforced by movies and country songs. If you believe Hollywood or Nashville, the trucker is one part road warrior and two parts vagabond—a lawless, fearless good ol' boy who nonetheless respects God, country, Elvis, and the girl back home. Most of the time. And not necessarily in that order.*

The truth is it's no easy life, running mile after mile of featureless interstate, dodging radar traps, squeezing past RVs always in the wrong lane, hoping that the freezing slush won't fix to glare ice or that the idiot in the Subaru doesn't slam on his brakes down the grade. Even so, it is truckers Garth Brooks writes ballads about, not clerks at the A&P. Perched high above the road, powerful diesels rumbling beneath them, truckers seem more in control of their destinies than most of us—even when they aren't.

Walt McDonald (b. 1934) explores this contradiction in "The Hairpin Curve at Durango," a poem my students in a writing course called "The Automobile in American Culture" loved. Named Texas Professor of the Year in 1992, the year this poem was published, McDonald is a former U.S. Air Force pilot, the Horn Professor of English at Texas Tech University, and one of the most respected poets in the Southwest. His poems have appeared in The Atlantic, The Kenyon Review, Prairie Schooner, *and* The New York Review of Books. — J.R.

Where the road dips back on itself
downhill, I slow the rig so I won't
jackknife, or sail off into space.

This turn has killed runaway trucks
smashed on the stones below,   5
convertibles and fast sports cars

careening smartly out
and tumbling. Truckers I know
don't dread crashing head-on

with drivers who fall asleep   10
on the straightaway,
don't mind running sassy pickups

off the road, the devil
and bar ditch take them.
But icy roads that curve   15

and slide us helpless into air
are trouble. Dieseling downhill
I bluff oncoming traffic

to the rails, no way
I'll risk the edge   20
for courtesy. Climbing home,

groaning with a load of wood
or pigs for market, I grind uphill,
no sweat, my right wheels safe

on asphalt, letting the poor guys   25
creeping downhill hug the centerline.
Knowing the gray sky twists

and disappears inches away
below them, I glance at their eyes
wide to all possibilities, both hands   30

knuckled on their wheels.
I see their tight lips yelling
at their kids, *Shut up. Shut up.*

IN RESPONSE

1. What does the open road represent to Americans? Freewrite on this question.
2. What elements make a profession the subject of songs, movies, or stories? Why do we sing about truckers and not, say, taxidermists or dental hygienists?
3. Write a prose response to Walt McDonald's poem, perhaps as an entry in your reading log, if you keep one. What ideas does the poem inspire? What emotions does it provoke, especially in its concluding line?
4. Write the kind of poem about driving that you imagine Dean Moriarity from *On the Road* might compose.

STEVEN SPENCE
The Van of Aquarius

*P*LAYING ON A LYRIC *from "Aquarius," a popular song from the rock opera* Hair, *Steven Spence suggests in the following reading that the ubiquitous Volkswagen van was the perfect vehicle for the wanderlust of the free-spirited "aquarians," the generation that reached adulthood in the late 1960s. "Plain as a brick, simple as a lawnmower, slow as glue, cheap to buy, cheap to run, and cheap to fix," the VW "bus" made a style out of ignoring style. Although its sales have fallen sharply since its days as the vehicle of choice for the sixties counterculture (65,069 were sold in 1969 alone), the bus lingers on—as Spence's article makes clear—in its association with Deadheads, that enormous horde of tie-dyed-T-shirt-and-Birkenstock groupies who move around the country with their namesake, The Grateful Dead.*

A few years ago, The Grateful Dead performed in an enormous pasture near the city I live in. Out of curiosity and a bit of nostalgia, I rounded up some friends and headed for the concert. The 20-some miles I drove on the interstate (in my tiny Toyota Tercel) proved to me that the VW bus is alive and well in 1990s America: I counted 263 such vehicles, most erupting with children, laden with supplies of goodies to sell at the concert, and sporting (as Spence says) stickers and signs of every description. By the time we reached the performance site, my car was afloat in a sea of VWs, moving along in rhythm, snaking our way into parking lots already populated by more vans than I'd ever seen in one place. Back to the future, I thought, or forward to the past. The van in front of me read "I love my bus" and "Deadheads to the Death."

To be perfectly frank, I have been hard-pressed to get involved in this chapter, with its none-too-subtle adulation of the car. I chose this article, originally published in the popular automotive magazine Car and Driver, *because there's something lighthearted and irreverent about the Deadhead vehicle of choice, not to mention something very inexpensive. It's my guess that lots of people today are looking for a safe, serviceable, environmentally friendly means of transport— sort of like the VW.* – A.L.

A palpable buzz of electricity was in the air of the pretty, clapboard towns surrounding Richfield Coliseum south of Cleveland, even though the excitement—a three-night stand by the cosmic old fogeys, the Grateful Dead—was still two days away.

The buzz began with the first wave of wiggy old Volkswagen buses that began appearing on the suburban landscape. Soon the local folks could be seen leaning forward over the steering wheels of their cars, squinting out at all the strange messages decorating the buses. Look at that bumper sticker, Glenda!

"WE ALL LIVE DOWNSTREAM."

"I NEED A MIRACLE."

"MEAT STINKS."   5

The "Deadheads" had arrived, the camp followers of the middle-aged rock group who will travel any distance to attend these mini-Woodstock gatherings of their musical tribe. They pulled their buses and vans off roads near busy intersections and set up shop, hanging up tie-dyes—sheets, shirts, hippie-style dresses, T-shirts, Grateful Dead posters and paraphernalia, rastafarian hair-wraps—on clotheslines. Overnight, the landscape was transformed. It was as if a traveling sixties roadshow of gypsy hippies had come to town.

One supposes the locals appreciated the atmosphere of festival. There was a lot of grinning and shaking of their heads in local coffeeshops, but it was all good-natured. (In the sixties, there would have been a local brick-throwing contingent, for those gypsies brought with them strange ideas and mind-expanding chemicals.)

The night before the Cleveland concert, some Deadheads, suited up in their tie-dyed finery and sporting serious big hair and T-shirts with messages like "Eat, Drink and See Jerry,"* appeared to drink beer and eat among the locals at the nearby Winking Lizard Tavern, one of those places that employ clean-cut college kids who have the exuberant look of having experienced farm work. You could feel the excitement, you could even smell the perfume of patchouli in the barroom.

The bartender, a strapping college-age youth, was asked if he was going to the concert. He grinned widely. "I was thinking of going," he said, "but I'm kind of afraid it'd change my life." A waitress his age heard that, and laughed somewhat uneasily. She understood what he meant; strange ideas still have their allure, and there was always the possibility of moral defection, the temptation to dump tired old values. Who among these nineties kids had not heard stories of the wicked sixties, the sexual revolution, the Age of Aquarius?

So while the bartender laughed it off, maybe he considered the vague   10
possibility of being overcome by a strange emotion to drop out, to buy a beat-up VW bus for $500, to toss in a mattress, a hot plate, and a portable fridge, and to head off after the Grateful Dead. What a trip! Thousands of Deadheads do just that, and they manage to make a living in the process.

VW buses and other provocative forms of weird transport were everywhere: lined up behind filling stations, parked in vacant lots and behind motels, and, most of all, jammed into a nearby state-park campground. Down in that park, the Age of Aquarius had returned.

Jerry: Jerry Garcia (b. 1942), leader of the Grateful Dead

The VW bus has gone by many names*—Microbus, Panel Van, Kombi, Crew Cab, Camper, Station Wagon, Vanagon—but it is the simplest van, the bus, built between 1949 and '79, that has been the vehicle of choice for those who have turned their backs on convention, or those who have wished to make personal statements about their values via their mode of transport.*

The VW bus, like the Beetle, has been "a negative status symbol" for most of its 42 years—plain as a brick, simple as a lawnmower, slow as glue, cheap to buy, cheap to run, and cheap to fix, it has hauled a lot of people (and surfboards) around in a style that *disdains* style. If you're a Deadhead, it's not just a vehicle—it's home.*

Something on the order of 6.7 million VW buses have been built since 1949. Oddly enough, the idea for this simple "hauler" was not hatched in VW's Wolfsburg plant in Germany, but in the head of an ambitious Dutchman named Ben Pon, who saw the potential of VW after the war and was to become an early exporter of its products (he personally brought the first Beetle to America).

Pon thought VW needed to offer more than just the Beetle, and with   15
a simple sketch in a spiral notebook that is now a museum artifact at Wolfsburg, he drew a rendering of what he had in mind.

Pon's idea so captivated Heinz Nordhoff, the late head man at VW, that to launch the bus in 1950 he had to cut back on production of the Beetle at a time when Volkswagen could not keep up with orders for its inexpensive car. It was called the "Type 2" (Type 1 being the Beetle). Nordhoff and Pon had guessed correctly—by the mid-fifties, VW had to build a plant in Hanover just to build the Type 2s. Eventually the homely hauler would be sold in 140 countries.

Imagine a 2300-pound van that promised to carry as many as nine people but was propelled—hardly the right word—by a 25-horsepower engine! By 1962, when the one-millionth "Bully" (named for its bulldog, workhorse stance) came off the line, its output had been increased to 34 hp and it finally got a synchronized transmission.

VW offered its bus in countless configurations, with varying interior heights and bed plans and door arrangements. American buyers, who had to get up to speed on freeways, soon got a model with a 1.5-liter, 42-

---

The VW bus . . . many names: For a dialogue on naming cars, see Marianne Moore's "Correspondence with the Ford Motor Company," starting on p. 622.

make personal statements . . . mode of transport: For another perspective on this issue, by someone who *doesn't* want a van, see the reading by Tony Kornheiser, "Radio Daze," starting on p. 612.

it's home: For another account of being "at home on the road," see the next reading, "Roam Sweet Home," by Marilyn Murphy.

horsepower engine. (Still, it was an adventure to be hit by a gust of wind in a VW bus while crossing the Golden Gate Bridge.) The first major facelift came in 1967; the two-piece windshield was replaced by a single pane, its nose was flattened, and the doors, which had opened like those on a barn, were now sliding. The VW bus craze in this country reached its peak in 1969, with a record 65,069 sold that year. More minor facelifts continued, and in 1972, a bus arrived with a Porsche 914 engine. The following year, an automatic transmission was offered. In 1974, the Hanover plant was able to build an astounding 1200 buses in a single day, and sales went over the four-million mark.

The modern-day bus, the Vanagon, appeared in 1979. It now had an all-wheel-drive model and a squared-off, all-business front. It was the best bus ever made, but it had lost its goofy charm. Sales that had begun to slide in the seventies slipped even further in the eighties (5147 in 1989). The heyday of the VW bus was over.

John Hollander, who goes by the name Emmett and is just 23,   20
had parked his '77 VW bus behind a truck stop among a crazy quilt of Deadhead vehicles, including a couple of converted yellow school buses reminiscent of Ken Kesey's Merry Pranksters' bus of sixties psychedelic fame* ("Positive Vibrations," it announced). Kids roamed through the area, girls in muslin tie-dyes, and Jerry Garcia's voice boomed forth from the open doors of cars. Hollander had driven all the way from Seattle, and he was digging around inside looking for something; the inside of his bus looked like a twister had visited it recently. His hair was wild in rastafarian fashion, and he was slight of build, looking as if he hadn't spent much time eating.

The bus was painted a flat white, as if he'd done it with a paintbrush. The entire bus was covered with hand prints in various bright colors.

Emmett is a budding entrepreneur learning the tie-dye ropes. It has not been all gravy. At a Denver concert of the Dead, "the cops busted me for vending without a license. They took twenty shirts off me. I went home with $4." It's not easy being a Deadhead, although Emmett did not want to be described as one.

"What's the deal with the hand prints?" he was asked.

"Well, I had a stencil of a hand, so . . ." He thinks for a moment. What was his purpose? ". . . so, I figured I'd put a black hand on one side, and, well, it just went from there."

Like a lot of the independent thinking Deadheads, he gave me an   25

---

a couple . . . sixties psychedelic fame: a reference to the legendary 1964 cross-country bus trip chronicled in Paul Perry and Ken Babbs's *On the Bus*. Ken Kesey (b. 1935) is the author of *One Flew Over the Cuckoo's Nest* (1962) and *The Further Inquiry* (1990), a twenty-fifth-anniversary reflection on the bus trip.

answer that had the ring of Zen when I ask what it is he likes about his bus, which has a rebuilt engine and cost him $2000.

"Uh, I kind of liked the idea of an air-cooled engine, you know?"

We wished him luck, and headed off for the park campground. A long gravel road led finally to a gated checkpoint, where we paid a $10 fee to get in. "Are there any Deadheads down there?" we asked a young woman wearing a khaki uniform and a Smokey the Bear hat. She rolled her eyes around in her head, like it was a question not worth answering.

Coming down the hill's incline to a meadow where the tribe of Deadheads suddenly came into view, where Grateful Dead music filled the air, I was somehow reminded of Custer, and how he must have felt so momentarily strange coming upon the sight of an entire nation of Sioux camped at the Little Big Horn. It is reflexive upon seeing a sight like this to utter Christ's first name, though not in vain. "Jesus."

The first VW bus that caught my eye belonged to Anthony Vanderford of Casper, Wyoming. Vanderford, who was 20, had been following the Dead since high-school graduation two and a half years ago. He had set up a table with all sorts of things for sale, and tie-dyed sheets were pinned to trees forming a canopy above his bus.

The cheerful Vanderford invited me to look inside the bus. Poking   30
out from under a pile of bedding and clothing was a sleeping woman's head. There was a sink and a stove and a refrigerator and running water, and a series of bunk beds.

"It's a little home. It's got everything you need," he said proudly. Meanwhile, some potential customers poked over his goods. But these were Deadhead camp followers like himself, and I wondered out loud if it was possible to sell stuff to other Deadheads, who were in the same business.

He gave me a cosmic grin, like the whole thing was a mystery to him, too. "I know what you're saying, but I've only been here a couple of hours and I've already made two hundred dollars!"

I came upon Conrad and Dan Neil, brothers from Manitoba, Canada. Conrad was selling exotic posters for $10 each. This was Dan's third concert, but his brother has traveled to 30 of them.

Asked what it is about the Dead's music that he found so alluring, Conrad had to think a moment. Finally he said, "The feel, man. It talks to you. It's a natural high, and everybody's calm. I like the calmness of it."

An upholsterer by trade, Conrad had a fine '78 bus loaded with ameni-   35
ties. He summed up his affection for it: "It can sleep six and it's great on gas. What else can I say? The guy I bought it from wanted $5000, but I got it for $3600. You can't beat that."

But in fact Jeff Johns of Pottstown, Pennsylvania, who was parked fifty feet away, beat that. His '73 bus cost him $475 just five months earlier. Okay, it wasn't as nice as Conrad's. Johns, 20, a cycle mechanic "on and off," said he bought the bus from a Czech who "buys them, fixes them up and sells them." The Czech, it turned out, wasn't setting any entrepreneurial records. "He bought this van for $400, and he was asking $550 for it. We told him our situation, which basically was we don't have any money. So he sold it to us for $475."

Intrigued by an old '72 bus with a humorous protective vinyl bra strapped over its nose, I came around the back and ran into Angie Padgett, who would be, hands down, *The Prettiest Freckled Girl in the World* were there such a contest. She was posing for a picture when her boyfriend, Steve Yatson, showed up. They are both in their early twenties, and he'd given up the yuppie lifestyle to follow the Dead for awhile, learning tie-dying.

"I went from a Porsche 944 to this," he said laughing, amused by his own change of lifestyle. "I paid $400 for this bus, but I did tons of work on it."

Angie said, "At some places, if you've got problems with your bus, there are mechanics around who will work for beer."

Yatson said, "I used to sell construction materials, and did very well.   40 But you can make money here, too." Pointing to a tie-dyed sheet he'd made that was draped over his van, he said, "That sheet cost about $2 to make, and we sell it for $35." It was clear that for Angie and Steve, this was a temporary lark. "I'm going to have to do the real-life thing again pretty soon." Sometime soon he will be headed for college in San Jose, California.

We wandered around, and I was reminded of a conversation I had with Blair Jackson, a Dead historian from Berkeley, California, who puts out a periodical of Grateful Dead lore called *The Golden Road*. "The Volkswagen bus is the cheap warhorse vehicle of the seventies.

"There's a whole iconography of the Dead and the VW." I had to look that up. It means the images and pictures that become the symbols that describe a culture.

"The Dead has a tradition of taking traditional items from the culture and then twisting them—in a friendly way. Like [a depiction of] Calvin and Hobbes, only they're smoking a bong or doing nitrous oxide." Just then I saw a Charlie Brown T-shirt, with Charlie's head ballooned to watermelon size, making him "Cosmic Charlie." Another shirt declared, "Bo Knows Jerry." A Disney-like theme park reads, "Deadheadland."

No one, including the Grateful Dead, now in their 26th year, can quite explain their popularity. Says leader Jerry Garcia: "Here we are, we're getting into our fifties, and where are these people who keep coming to our shows coming from? What do they find fascinating about these middle-aged bastards playing basically the same thing we've always played? I mean, what do 17-year-olds find fascinating about this? . . . So what is it about the 1990s in America? There must be a dearth of fun out there in America.

Or adventure. Maybe that's it: maybe we're just one of the last adventures in America. I don't know."

Blair Jackson says there's a "sense of adventure" to it. "It's rock 'n' roll   45 with a bit of country-western. And blues. Actually, it's like a jazz band—they never play the same set twice. They have such a large body of music—probably 110 to 120 songs at any given time. They played six shows in the Bay Area, and during all that, they repeated just one song—'Promised Land.' "

Whatever the case, in the first half of 1991, Dead concerts grossed $20 million. Their average take per show, according to Pollstar, a firm that reports on the music industry, was more than $1.1 million, or nearly twice that of the summer's second biggest touring act, Guns n' Roses. The Dead played nine nights in New York's Madison Square Garden, three in Cleveland, and six at Boston Garden—and all of them were sold-out performances.

"We didn't invent the Grateful Dead," says Garcia. "The crowd invented the Grateful Dead. We were just in line to see what was going to happen."

Like the popularity of the VW bus, it defies explanation.

QUESTIONING THE TEXT

1. What distinctions, if any, does Spence draw between the 1990s Deadheads and those of the 1960s? Does he have the same attitude toward the two groups? How do you know?
2. What does Jerry Garcia mean when he says, "The crowd invented the Grateful Dead"? Do you agree? Why, or why not?
3. What questions did this article leave you with? That is, what in it do you wish you knew more about? Jot down some notes, including ways you could go about answering your own questions.
4. In her introduction to this reading, A.L. says she will be "perfectly frank" and admit she had trouble getting involved in this chapter. What effect does her saying she is "perfectly frank" have on you as a reader? What effect do you think A.L. intended?

MAKING CONNECTIONS

5. If Grateful Dead music seems an appropriate accompaniment for the VW bus, what music goes with the "old junker" Bailey White describes starting on p. 618 or with the Cadillac described by Jack Kerouac in *On the Road* (p. 574)? Explain the reasons for your choices.
6. Look carefully at the language Spence uses to describe the VW bus. How do you think the bus supports—or doesn't support—the argu-

ment Peter Marsh and Peter Collett make (p. 599) about the relationship between cars and sexuality? Turn your answers into a one-page informal report to your class.

JOINING THE CONVERSATION

7. Decide on a contemporary musical group or artist—your own personal favorite—and then imagine the perfect car to symbolize that group. Write a brief position paper explaining you choice. (You may want to try for a humorous theme or for the kind of exaggeration that characterizes parody.)
8. Working with three classmates, survey several members of each of the four following groups of people, asking them what they remember or know about the VW bus and what they associate with it: (a) men in Jerry Garcia's age group, (b) women in Garcia's age group, (c) men in their early to middle twenties, (d) women in their early to middle twenties. Pool the results of your research and prepare a 15-minute report on your findings for class.

MARILYN MURPHY
Roam Sweet Home

*P*OPULAR CULTURE, *particularly of the sort evoked by Kerouac's* On the Road, *typically represents cross-country exploration by automobile as a decidedly masculine sport. Man and machine, in fact, often seem synonymous, at least symbolically—as Peter Marsh and Peter Collett argue in the next reading. Enter Marilyn Murphy and the RVing Women, a large and growing group who have taken to the road in recreational vehicles (RVs) in search of independence, sisterhood, and peace. Now numbering over 2,500, they are linked by a newsletter, a directory of members, phone-line services, and frequent gatherings.*

Although I travel a great deal, often two or three times a month, I do not associate that travel with peace or sisterhood, for most of the travel I do is work-related. Moreover, I have always associated RVs with huge, gas-guzzling, polluting machines; tacky plastic lanterns; and Muzak squawking through places with names like Kamper Kountry Kampgrounds. So reading Murphy's article in Ms. *magazine in 1992 gave me much food for thought. I'm now interested in finding out more about this particular automotive subculture, perhaps by reading Murphy's 1991 volume* Are You Girls Traveling Alone? Adventures in Lesbianic Logic. *Or perhaps I'll try out a subscription to* RVing Women, c/o P.O. Box 82606, Kenmore, Washington 98028. *If RVing Women are here, can RVing Men be far behind?* — A.L.

Before she fell in love with a machine, Carol was a more or less conventional middle-aged woman. She was an Oregon high school teacher, whose youngest of three children, a daughter, still lived at home and whose husband, while amiable enough, was dull, dull, dull. She had a few interesting women friends, time for reading and gardening. Her life was pleasant and comfortable. She thought she was content.

Carol took a new route home from work one afternoon, and there "it" was, on the corner, in a sales lot for recreational vehicles. The RV was small, no longer than a big car. Later, Carol was unable to clearly articulate what it was about the RV that captivated her. All she remembers is her intake of breath and pounding heart. In a moment, she was parked and in the lot admiring the tiny treasure.

Inside, the micro-mini motor home was even more adorable than Carol had imagined. A bed was built over the cab of the small truck chassis, and in the seven-foot-wide, nine-foot-long, six-foot-high body of the unit were tucked a stove, a sink, a refrigerator that ran on gas or electricity, a table with two upholstered swivel chairs, an enclosed flush toilet, a closet, a pantry, a gas heater, and an electric air conditioner. Across the back stretched a six-foot-long, narrow couch, just right for Carol's spare, five-foot nine-inch frame. There were skylights over the bed and table, and windows at the side and back. The salesperson told Carol the RV was "self-contained," with holding tanks for fresh water and for sewage and sink water, and a second battery to power lights and the water pump. "Being 'self-contained' means you can go to wilderness areas, to bird-watch or something, and not need to hook up to water and electricity for up to a week, if you're careful." That said, he exited the RV and left Carol alone to imagine birding in the wilderness with her new love.

Carol's husband was uninterested* in the little RV. He didn't care that one could see the stars while lying in bed, that it got 15 miles to a gallon of gas. He did not want an RV, did not need an RV, and furthermore, neither did she! No, he would *not* go out to look at it, *not* tonight or tomorrow or anytime. And he didn't want to hear about getting close to nature. What on earth was the matter with her? Had she *lost her mind*?

Carol, of course, had not lost her mind. She had lost her heart. She   5
began driving past the RV lot on her way home from work. She took her daughter and her friends to see it. She wrote for information on Oregon's parks and wilderness areas. She did not discuss these activities with her husband.

One afternoon, the RV was gone from its corner location. Carol rushed into the sales lot and breathed a sigh of relief when she saw it in the service area being washed. The next day, she withdrew some of her retirement money from the credit union and bought the RV. That purchase was the first independent act of her 26-year marriage. Others followed. She began exploring her home state on weekends, sometimes with her daughter or friends. Often, she went alone, cherishing her solitude. Meanwhile, her husband waited for her to return to "normal," to get over what he described as "menopausal" acting out. He was shocked when she told him she wanted a divorce—and when she got one.

When her daughter left for college, Carol spent a six-month sabbatical traveling. On her return, she quit her job, sold her house, and banked the money. She now lives on the interest plus her reduced pension. She's been traveling full-time for seven years now. She enjoys her brief visits with family and friends, attends cultural and educational events wherever on the continent they occur, and renews her spirit with weeks of "self-contained" solitude* in North America's wilderness areas. She is pleased to be 60 and eligible for Elderhostel programs. Her first Elderhostel course was a great

---

Carol's husband was uninterested . . . . : For a wife's reaction to her husband's obsession with a vehicle, see the reading by Tony Kornheiser, "Radio Daze," starting on p. 612.

renews her spirit . . . solitude: For another expression of how a vehicle can provide a "spiritual" place for solitude, see the poem by Stephen Dunn, "The Sacred," on p. 630.

adventure, snorkeling in the Florida Keys. Carol loves her life. She is a happy, independent traveling woman.

Carol's response to her RV is not unusual. Irene and I fell in love with our first RV, one that was a sister to Carol's. We also fell in love with RVing, though we didn't realize it at first. It was early spring in 1983. We were living in Los Angeles and realized that work, plus our lesbian and feminist political activities, kept us too busy. We needed to get away once in a while. A friend offered us her truck camper (a small RV that slides into the bed of a pickup truck). We went to the Anza-Borrego Desert State Park. We took long walks, watched the desert flowers bloom, and sat in lawn chairs, reading by the side of a stream. When it rained, we were cozy in Bev's little house. Except for the sound of the park ranger's truck as he made his daily rounds, the only noises we heard were natural ones: birds, wind, rain, the stream, critters rustling in the thickets. Both of us had always lived in cities and had not "communed with nature" before. We were surprisingly content.

Home again, we were restless and discontent. We *wanted* a truck camper. Irene's (early) retirement money and what I earned teaching part-time could not stretch for payments on a truck and camper. Then luck intervened. A friend repaid a $7,000 loan we had given up as lost. Quick, before we could do something "serious" with the money, we began looking for a used truck camper. We found our tiny, used motor home instead. It was love at first sight.

But we were still too busy to get away. We started saying, "It would   10
be easier to leave for three months than for three days." Then we talked about six months, then a year. A friend put us to the test. Her sister was coming to L.A. for postgraduate work and would rent our house for a year. Were we interested? *Hah!* By August 24, we had settled our affairs, had wills, living wills, and medical powers of attorney drawn up, and were on our way.

That year was probably the happiest either of us have ever lived. We stayed mostly in national, state, provincial, county, and town campgrounds. We found used bookstores and read for as long as we wished, *without interruption.* We bought a bird book and identified 234 birds during our year. We fished, but never caught anything. We learned to net crabs. We camped on the shores of all the Great Lakes and many lesser ones, and on the banks of countless rivers and streams. We visited friends and family, staying a day or two in their driveways, then moving on. We never, ever wished we were home.

Three years earlier, Irene and I had gone to Britain for six weeks. We loved the traveling, and could have continued indefinitely, but we were exhausted. We said, over and over again, "If only we could have our own bed and things about, if we could cook for ourselves, and take naps when we wanted to, we could travel for years!" When we discovered RVing, we remembered those longings. We *were* home in our RV, with our things around us—our own bed, our favorite coffee cups and soup bowls—eating food we cooked ourselves and following our own schedule. This is the lure of RVing, especially for women. With an RV, we can be "at home" anywhere—on a spit of land off the coast of Newfoundland or sleeping overnight in a Safeway parking lot.

When we returned from our trip, we no longer felt "at home" in Los Angeles. We pined for our traveling life. Somewhere, during our year away, we had lost the insulation that enabled us to live comfortably in cities. We waited for our "at home" feeling to return. After six months, we traded the little RV for a bigger one, rented out (and eventually sold) our house, and lived happily on the road for almost four years. We own a small beach cottage on the Atlantic in north Florida now, and travel whenever we feel like it. We are planning to travel around Europe again, this time in an RV.

Not all RVers have such dramatic beginnings. Some women have traveled in RVs since they were children. Others started when their children were young and continued to travel "alone" after divorce or their husband's death. Some tent camped, gradually moving to RVing when they could afford it or as their joints began creaking when they got up off the ground in the middle of the night. Others backed into RVing. Jean wanted a convenient way to bring her dogs with her when she visited friends, so she outfitted a van all by herself. Nancy and Lois bought a used RV so they could have separate space while caring for Nancy's dying mother, and to transport her comfortably to and from the hospital. Jo Ann and Sharon borrowed their brother's 35-foot trailer for a sabbatical year, so they could get away to write their book. They are all avid RVers now, and are dues-paying members of a group called RVing Women.

Irene and I were so excited to learn of the group that we mailed our application for membership, with the $29 yearly fee per household, the day we received it from a friend. RVing Women, a support network for women RVers, is the brainchild of Lovern King and Zoe Swanagon. Four years ago, they began living full-time on the road in a 24-foot, Class C RV (an eight-cylinder, larger version of Carol's RV). They thought it would be fun to rendezvous with other women occasionally, to swap stories and make new friends. To find them, they conducted seminars for women at RV club rallies. The women, overjoyed to be talking RV with other women, wished for opportunities to meet again.

Before they retired, Lovern was a college professor and Zoe was a business consultant. They figured they had the expertise to develop a network to meet the needs of the 50 or so women they expected to sign up. They launched RVing Women with a newsletter, sent to their small mailing list in January 1991. Sixteen months later, the newsletter goes to 2,500 women's households, and every week Zoe and Lovern receive 50 to 80 letters from women interested in joining. Since almost all of us heard of

RVing Women from a woman friend, its quick success is the result of "tell-a-woman" advertising at its best.

RVing Women's rapid growth created a dilemma for its founding mothers. They could either quit traveling and rent an office, or get a bigger RV. So they traded in the Class C for a 34-foot fifth wheel (a trailer that is hitched to the bed of a pickup truck). Now, Lovern and Zoe have an office equipped with two computers, two printers, and a copy machine in their rig, where they handle the mail and newsletter comfortably. They also publish a directory and maintain a Phonelink service so members can find each other on the road, organize caravans, and plan excursions and outings. In addition, with help from members, they have organized eight gatherings around the country, with 16 more planned for the rest of 1992. It's beginning to look as if Zoe and Lovern's new pastime is turning into their second careers.

Women are very enthusiastic about these gatherings. Some drive hundreds of miles to attend. We all *knew* there must be other women RVers, so meeting a crowd of them at one time is a new and exhilarating experience for us. We talk about our adventures, about the sweet place in which we camped for almost no money at all, about the conflict of family attachments and wanderlust, all the while enjoying potluck dinners, bonfires, hikes. We share our experiences during the technical RV maintenance workshops and during workshops conducted by attendees: women's spirituality, women's health, "full-timing," money, safety, and working on the road.

Physical safety is a serious issue for women. Irene and I think RVing is the safest, as well as the most enjoyable, mode of travel for women. At the safety workshops, we were pleased to discover our belief well founded. Many women have CB radios, cellular phones, alarms, baseball bats, tire irons, mace, their dogs, stun guns, and even regular guns with them for protection. However, none of us, and none of the women RVers we know or know of, have ever had any "male violence" trouble at all. We did learn, however, that we were not the only ones to leave a remote camp in a hurry, "just to be on the safe side," after being disquieted by a lone male circling the campground in a car.

As for money, there's no upper limit to how much one can spend on   20
the road, but frugal women, staying mostly in national and state parks and wilderness areas, can travel for $400 to $500 monthly. As for RVs, there is no spending limit, either. I suggest women begin with campers and trailers. A new, 16-foot trailer or truck camper, fully equipped, costs about $7,000, much less if used. Instead of falling for an RV, one could fall for an adorable, and much less expensive, camper or trailer and drive it home with a pickup truck or minivan.

When Irene and I attended our first RVing Women gathering, the handouts included a humorous article I had written about the responses of women and men to women RVers. Learning that the article was the title piece of my new book, one woman, a librarian, asked if I would do a reading that evening. I told her my book has a lesbian perspective, something that is not obvious from the piece I sent RVing Women. She said she was straight, but a lesbian perspective didn't upset her. She'd check it out with other women and get back to me.

Twenty women, ages 33 to 78, gathered to hear me read a few essays from my book. I have seldom met a group so alive to, and interested in, discussing the difficult topics—the topics that, until recently, women were afraid or ashamed to talk about. It was as if a dam had broken, the way the words tumbled out of their mouths. We were re-creating one of those magical 1970s consciousness-raising groups. The discussion lasted three hours. For most of the women, this was the first time they had ever talked, in a circle of women, about their "secrets"—their incest, molestation, rape, battering, humiliation, terrorization. Then they talked about their present happiness, the joys of being single and traveling "alone," women-only space, and lesbianism, too. The spirit of openness and acceptance demonstrated by the women at this gathering created a space where women who are lesbians and women who are not lesbians were able to be ourselves, known to each other and respected. It was a rare and affirming experience for us all.

I shouldn't have been surprised by the openness of the women. Women RVers *must* have an unconventional streak, or else they wouldn't be meandering down the roads of North America in a house on wheels, accompanied "only" by dogs, cats, or other women—in other words, traveling "alone."

Take Sarah, for example. She is a farm woman, the mother of six grown children, with hordes of grandchildren. After her husband died, she spent the life-insurance money on a camper for the pickup he had bought shortly before his death. The first place she drove it to was the RVing Women gathering I attended. She and her dog were on their way to Texas to join a caravan of RVers touring Mexico. Her kids were questioning her sanity. They didn't see any reason for "Granny" to take off, though she told them she had always wanted to travel and to see Mexico. She was scared and looking for encouragement. She got plenty of it, especially from the women who had recently caravaned through Mexico. She's in Mexico now, and, I suspect, getting more independent by the minute. Like Sarah and Carol, most women RVers I've met are, or are becoming, independent women, living their own lives, doing what pleases and nurtures them, and for some, claiming for themselves the last decades of their lives.

QUESTIONING THE TEXT

1. Is it RVs that the women Murphy writes about seem to love, or is it something else that RVs represent or allow for? What in this article supports your answer?
2. Murphy reports that the RVing woman Sarah has children who are

"questioning her sanity." What reasons might they give for their questioning? What, on the other hand, might Sarah say in defense of her sanity?

3. What does the author of this article seem to value? That is, what values seem most dear to her? How do you know?

4. A.L. says in her introduction that she has always associated RVs with things she finds unpleasant, such as pollution, "tacky plastic lanterns," and Muzak. What associations, if any, do RVs have for you? What do these associations suggest about A.L.'s values—and yours?

MAKING CONNECTIONS

5. What does the lifestyle represented in "Roam Sweet Home" have in common with that of *On the Road*? In what ways do the lifestyles most dramatically differ? If you had to say in one or two words what *On the Road* celebrates, what would your response be? What does "Roam Sweet Home" celebrate?

6. What names might Marianne Moore (see p. 622) come up with for an RVing woman's vehicle? Why?

7. What response might Murphy make to Peter Marsh and Peter Collett's discussion of cars and sexuality in the next reading? Freewrite briefly on this question and bring the results to class for discussion.

JOINING THE CONVERSATION

8. What group might you like to meet up with at RV gatherings around the country? Give your group a name (like RVing Women) and then write a brief invitation to others to join your group.

9. Working with one or two classmates, do some research on the types of RVs currently available, gathering information on price range, fuel consumption, safety records, and so on. Prepare a report for classmates on "If You Want to Buy an RV, Think First About . . ."

PETER MARSH
and PETER COLLETT
The Love Affair

*T*HE AUTOMOBILE HAD BEEN *in production for almost a generation before General Motors established the first styling studio. Up until the creation of this "Art and Color Section" in the late 1920s, the appearance of automobiles had been left to the talents of engineers and private coach builders. They had produced many enduring designs that stirred the imaginations and hearts of would-be owners. But it had never occurred to automotive pioneers such as Henry Ford that the styling of a vehicle itself might become a reason to own it.*

That miscalculation cost Ford his dominance of the U.S. automobile industry. In 1927, handsomely designed Chevrolets available in many styles and colors outsold Fords for the first time. Looks began to displace reliability and engineering as the chief concern of buyers purchasing a vehicle. The shift was probably inevitable, given the way automobiles had quickly become symbols of power, status, and freedom in the United States. For young people in particular, the car represents an escape from parental control, moving the rituals of courtship from the parlor and porch swing to lovers' lane and back seat. So the romance of the road is more than just a metaphor and the vehicles themselves—two tons of metal, plastic, and rubber—are sexy in ways no other industrial products can be.

It is the relationship between sexuality and the automobile that Peter Marsh and Peter Collett explore rather frankly in "The Love Affair." Be forewarned that the authors are sometimes comically naughty in a British manner—leering and giggling while keeping straight faces. The selection is from Driving Passion: The Psychology of the Car *(1986); Marsh and Collett, together and separately, have written books about various aspects of human behavior, including gestures and football hooliganism.* – J.R.

The relationship between cars and sexuality has always been reflected in popular culture. In the early days it was the song sheets of tin-pan alley which highlighted the association most clearly. 'In My Merry Oldsmobile' was one of the all-time best sellers back in 1905 and is still known today. Written by Vincent Bryan and Gus Edwards, the song, while extolling the virtues of marriage, hinted at other less conformist pastimes with lines

Cars suggest a macho attitude to me rather than a sexual one. – A.L.

such as: 'You can go as far as you like with me in our merry Oldsmobile.' Such naughty intimations may perhaps have led other songwriters of the time such as Irving Berlin to warn innocent young ladies of the Edwardian era to 'Beware of the Man in the Automobile'.

Such kill-joy lyrics, however, were in a distinct minority. There was a rather dull tune called 'I'd Rather Go Walking With The Man I Love Than Ride in Your Automobile', but songs mostly celebrated the new-found opportunities for lovemaking. 'On the Back Seat of the Henry Ford' and a later song, 'Tumble in a Rumble Seat', hinted at some rather uncomfortable contortions. 'When He Wanted to Love Her He Put up the Cover' was a similarly honest reflection of what went on in the early days of motoring. Songs like 'I'm Going to Park Myself in Your Arms', 'Fifteen Kisses to a Gallon of Gas', and 'In Our Little Lovemobile', seem rather coy in comparison. 'Take a Little Ride With Me Baby', though, does have a ring of *double entendre* about it.

The problem with double entendres in songs is in not knowing who has the more fertile imagination, the lyricist or the interpreter. Do Marsh and Collett read too much into these songs? — J.R.

Such songs reflected the sensual novelty of the car. It was different from the horse and buggy, even though in the pre-motorized age such vehicles were regularly used by courting couples for activities which, when discovered, aroused considerable censure. As the novelty of the car wore off, popular songs made fewer references to love on the back seat. But the general theme has remained in other artifacts of popular culture. Magazines such as *Playboy* and *Penthouse,* for example, are full of allusions to the erotic potential of motoring. The letters pages of these magazines are particularly interesting. Some, purportedly from driving instructors and RAC* patrolmen, tell of quite exceptional good fortune that has come their way while they were pursuing their otherwise dull and routine jobs. Although many of these letters, one suspects, are made up by the magazines' staff, they clearly

---

RAC: Royal Automobile Club, the British counterpart of the American Automobile Association

reflect what people would like to do in their automobiles, and usually the cars referred to are of the more potent and glamorous variety. A recent letter in *Penthouse* is fairly typical of this fantasy genre. It tells how the driver of a Jaguar XJS came to lose his license after meeting a forward young girl called Fiona and engaging in acts which are certainly not mentioned in the Highway Code. It was his car that initially attracted this adventurous young lady. ' "Oh, I love fast cars", she murmured as she ran her hands over the hood of my XJS in such a sensual way as to leave me feeling jealous of my own car. "They're a real aphrodisiac I find, don't you?" '. The aphrodisiac qualities of this particular car must have been quite exceptional given the graphic explanation of what happened while driving along in the fast lane before the police called a halt to the whole escapade.

I bet most of these "potent" fantasy letters are written in by men. – A.L.

Such letters must be treated as projections of sexual fantasy rather than accurate accounts. But the fact that cars figure so prominently in them is an interesting reflection of the role that automobiles play in people's sex lives, real or imaginary. Cartoons in this type of publication serve as similar mirrors on the world of automotive sexuality. One features a man trying to find a parking place who asks the clearly preoccupied occupant of a stationary vehicle if he is 'pulling out soon'. In Britain, the advent of seat-belt legislation provided *Mayfair* with the opportunity to devote three pages to cartoons dealing with the sexual potential of this relatively trivial feature of the car. . . .

I certainly hope *so.* – A.L.

Some *people, no* doubt, but surely *not people in general.* – A.L.

Though they pass judgments on the smut, one wonders why they take such enthusiasm in explicating the puns. – G.H.

Smutty picture postcards and Valentines are also among the ephemera of popular culture that reflect the erotic aspects of cars. Particular parts of automobiles lend themselves to risqué puns and innuendo—crankshafts, pistons and clutches all conjure up sexual imagery. This particular theme, however, is best explored in the more serious medium of poetry, and the classic example of the erotic car poem comes from the work of e.e.cummings, the celebrated American poet with a disdain of upper case. *she being Brand* is a clever exploration of the similarities between driving and the sexual act. Consider these few stanzas:

she being Brand

-new;and you
know consequently a
little stiff i was
careful of her and(having

thoroughly oiled the universal
joint tested my gas felt of
her radiator made sure her springs were O.
K.)i went right to it flooded-the-carburetor
   cranked her
up, slipped the
clutch . . .

. . . (it
was the first ride and believe i we was
happy to see how nice she acted right up to
the last minute coming back down by the Public
Gardens i slammed on
the

internalexpanding
&
externalcont racting
brakes Bothatonce and

brought allofher tremB
-ling
to a:dead.

stand-
;Still)

Cummings's poem is a classic—a tribute to those deep metaphors which shape our relationship with the automobile. In another perhaps less well known poem by Karl Shapiro called 'Buick', the car appears not as a symbol of the sexual act but as a goddess—a tempting, coquettish dream of nubility. Listen to the affection and sense of excitement expressed in just a few lines:

As my foot suggests that you leap in the air
   with hips of a girl,
My finger that praises your wheel and
   announces your voices of song,
Flouncing your skirts, you blueness of joy, you

The authors stretch things when they say this poem is a "tribute to those deep metaphors which shape our relationship. . . ." The poem is marvelously humorous but says nothing at all about my relationship to cars. — A.L.

flirt of politeness,
You leap, you intelligence, essence of
      wheelness with silvery nose,
And your platinum clocks of excitement stir like
      the hairs of a fern

Shapiro was thought by some people to be making a satire, an ironic statement about the symbolism of Buicks. This is not the case. In a letter to Laurence Goldstein, Professor of English at the University of Michigan, he says quite plainly, 'It's absolutely straight; a love poem to a Buick! A big fat Buick.' It is the Buick, of course, which has one of the most blatantly erotic insignia which, until very recently, was displayed as a hood ornament. A silver ring pierced by a projectile—a symbol recognized throughout the world for the sexual act.

In line with the poets' vision of sex and the automobile, visual artists have similarly explored not only the phallic aspects of automobiles but also the act of back-seat lovemaking. A drawing by John Held Junior from the 1920s, for example, is a witty illustration of a 'flapper' with her legs wide apart, thighs revealed, being kissed by her consort whose attention has strayed from the task of driving. A much more contemporary painting by Kenneth Price titled 'Don't Think About Her When You Drive' echoes the same theme, although in this illustration the car is careering over the edge of a mountain road. Even the salaciousness of the spark plug receives treatment by Mel Ramos in his oil on canvas 'Kar Kween', where a naked girl presses herself close to a tall, phallic version of this usually taken-for-granted mechanical object made by AC. The American artist James Rosenquist portrays, in comparison, rather more enigmatic reflections of cars and sexuality. Crashes and the sex act are fused into a single metaphor in 'Ultra Violet Car Touch'. 'I Love You With My Ford', while making a fairly simple statement about the opportunities for sexual behavior that a car provides, simultaneously hints at the awesome lethality of the automobile.

It is, however, the three-dimensional work by Edward Kienholz that is the most explicit and celebrated of work in this genre. *Back Seat Dodge '38* aroused a storm of controversy when it was first shown in Los Angeles in 1964. The work was so evocative of what really happens in cars, and what everybody *knows* happens in cars, that there were serious attempts to have the show closed down. Warren Dorn, who was running for Governor of California at the time, seized the opportunity to demonstrate his own moral rectitude by leading the campaign against this apparently unacceptable reflection of the car's function. In the end a bizarre compromise was reached. The door of the Dodge was closed so that the activities inside could only be viewed voyeuristically through the window.

Here's a case where censorship may actually enhance the power of a work of art. Back Seat Dodge '38 should be examined furtively.
– J.R.

The erotic symbolism of the car has been recognized by novelists as well as artists. In Stephen King's *Christine,* the car, a Plymouth, is portrayed as a jealous, volitional and feminine machine which came to life under the attention of its owner, Arnie. The metaphor pervades the entire story and the relationship between Arnie and Christine, the car, is loaded with sexual symbolism. Arnie's girl-friend, Leigh, resents the time he spends tinkering with Christine. She wants his hands on her own body, not in the deeper recesses of the engine compartment. 'Cars are girls, she had said. She hadn't been thinking about what she was saying; it had just popped out of her mouth.' Such was the strength of her feeling that being in the car was like being in the body of another woman, so much so that she was unable to make love to Arnie in the car. '. . . Leigh did not feel that she *rode* in Christine; when she got in to go somewhere with Arnie she felt *swallowed* in Christine. And the act of kissing him, making love to him, seemed a perversion worse than voyeurism or exhibition-ism—it was like making love in the body of her rival.'

This just seems ridiculous to me. – A.L.

While *Christine* extends the theme of car–as–sex-object beyond reasonable bounds of fantasy, the erotic symbolism of the car has featured promi-nently in the advertising and marketing of automo-biles since the 1920s. Even the early posters for Michelin Tires showed no tires at all. Instead they featured women with revealed breasts floating above winged circles. The style was Classical, the message distinctly sexual. Similarly, the frontispiece to Filson Young's book *The Complete Motorist,* published in 1904, shows nymphs and satyrs in various stages of undress, cavorting on the roadside as a car approaches. European manufacturers at the turn of the century vied with each other to associate their products with the most elegant and sensual female forms that the poster artists could conjure up. While modern representations of the automobile may be somewhat more cautious, the messages conveyed are substantially the same. They pay attention to the same subtle anatomical comparisons which, due to the evolution of the shape and style of cars, are inescapable.

These messages which essentially glorify males and put women in subservient positions are not unique to car ads. – A.L.

Everybody knows of course that a long hood is really a phallic symbol. So commonplace is this comparison that there are untold jokes about it. The Germans, for example, will tell you that a man who drives a Porsche is a man with his fly undone. Psychoanalysts seize upon such imagery in dreams as decisively as Freud would have become excited at the mention of trains entering dark tunnels. The Id is revealed by the most significant metaphors of the historical era, and for us, most powerfully by projections of the car. But to see the car as little more than a motorized penis is to overlook the whole catalogue of symbolic features that have earned it a secure niche in the social history of sexual fantasy and behavior.

This is news to me. – A.L.

They push their thesis a bit far here. What's the evidence that long hoods are phallic? – J.R.

The shape of a car is not dictated by its function. There are limitless ways of attaching three or four wheels and an engine to a chassis which will accommodate up to five people. In fact, for true functionalism, Buckminster Fuller's Dymaxion came close to the ideal but, partly because it was built on functionalist principles, it looked terrible. It had neither hood nor fenders, and a pointed rear cowling which contained the engine and transmission. It certainly looked aerodynamic, but it was neither sexy nor aesthetic. The Dymaxion, built as a prototype in the early 1930s, shows up very clearly all those features of 'normal' cars which are built-in, not to serve a specific function, but to endow them with sexual imagery.

Sources of sexual imagery change over time as fashions and the idealization of the female form also vary. In the 1950s, for example, even fairly modest cars were equipped with a pair of pointed bumper overriders. These resembled bosoms so closely that they were known as 'Dagmars', after the over-endowed starlet of that name. They were, however, modelled on bosoms of the 1950s, forced into a pert, aggressive shape by tough and padded bras. Today's ideal breasts are gently enclosed, if at all, by light stretchy fabric which allows their natural shape to be evident. Thus, overriders, which don't have much real function, are now less clearly accentuated and are certainly less reminiscent of wire and whale bone.

What this demonstrates to me is that cars have always been designed for men. That's all. – A.L.

Cowls over the top of headlights are another good example of changing tastes in erotic symbols. Originally they gave the impression of mascara-laden lashes—coquettish but otherwise quite useless embellishments. Heavy mascara went out with the swinging Sixties, and so did cowls. The female beauty of today is slim and lithesome, curved but without bulges, with an understated but clearly communicated sexuality. Exaggerated decoration has given way to a quieter glamour, and while zany hair and make-up may figure in the glossy magazines, it is no longer there expressly to appeal to men. In fact it has become the hallmark of liberation. In the same way, the bulging protuberances of the 'fat fender' cars have been ousted by the new aerodynamic and decorum—an athletic, healthy beauty raised on aerobics and Jane Fonda.

One can hardly imagine GM executives rummaging through the pages of Vogue *to catch up on the latest trends in women's cosmetics.* – G.H.

It has to be said, of course, that some cars are distinctly lacking in sexuality. The 1970s were particularly lean years in this respect, due mainly to Detroit's commitment to the 'three box' design. Cars were rectangular and masculine—square-shouldered and reminiscent of three-piece suits. Nobody liked them much, which is why European manufacturers were able to gain a toehold in both the British and the American markets. The Europeans were making sexy cars—curvaceous

When did a '72 Mustang remind anyone, except the authors, of a 3-piece suit? – G.H.

Citroëns with their evocative hydraulic suspension, and upmarket *femmes fatales* in the guise of Porsche and Mercedes Sports cars—cars which simultaneously created images of beautiful women and embodied the virility and anatomy of the dominant male.

Ford in America has largely been responsible for turning mass-produced car styling back toward evocative imagery. However much they may deny it, they are beginning to build sexy cars again. They push technical excellence because they know that the public has a poor opinion of Ford's achievements in this area. But it is the new shape, rather than what lies underneath it, which will influence more powerfully and more subtly the decision to buy. There is, however, a warning to be made. As in all things to do with sex, an overly explicit invitation or display can become not an attraction but an offence, and Ford built just such a car in the late 1950s. It was called the Edsel and it was a disaster. The name (one of Henry Ford's sons) did not help,* but it was the radiator which killed it. Shaped so uncannily like a female vulva, its labial explicitness would have been more at home in a gynecology textbook. It evoked images not of sensuality but of reproduction. Somehow threat and predation, not beauty, were the messages it communicated.

The ability of the automobile to convey both masculine and feminine imagery makes it a unique object. It is a modern hermaphrodite and thus appeals equally to men and women. For men the car can be both a phallic extension of their manhood and a mistress to covet. For women, the car serves both as an object of adoration and a reflection of their own sexuality. The female attachment to cars is nicely observed in Thomas Pynchon's novel *V*. Here Rachel Owlglass mutters lovingly to her MG: ' "You beautiful stud",* she said, "I love you. Do

Brawny, square-shouldered pickups are the most popular vehicles in America today. What would Marsh and Collett say about them?
— J.R.

This car was a dog. But the radiator couldn't have affected the car's marketability nearly as much as its dysfunctional features, like the pushbutton gearshift.
— G.H.

The name . . . did not help: For some other names that were proposed for what became the Edsel, see Marianne Moore's "Correspondence with the Ford Motor Company," p. 622.

"You beautiful stud": For the perspective of a woman who addresses her car in masculine—but not sexual—terms, see the reading by Bailey White, "Someday the Old Junker Will Be a Neat Car Again," p. 618.

you know what I feel when we're on the road? alone, just us?'' She was running her hands caressingly over the front bumper. "Your funny responses, darling, that I know so well. The way your brakes pull a little to the left, the way you start to shudder around 5,000 rpms when you're excited. And you burn oil when you're mad at me, don't you?''.'

Pynchon's perception of how females relate to their automobiles is an accurate one. The car works as a metaphor of the most basic aspect of human behavior for both males and females past the point of puberty. The symbolism evoked by its shape is fused with inevitable connotations of its mechanical functions. In the internal combustion engine pistons pump reciprocatingly in lubricated cylinders. So close are the parallels that they arouse embarrassment. To point out the details is to invite accusations of smuttiness, and so we avoid them in polite conversation. But the combination of evocative shape and symbolic mechanics can hardly be suppressed by mere etiquette. They, more than elementary considerations of privacy and concealment, are at the root of a particular aspect of the relationship with the automobile and our continuing desire to use it as a vehicle for sexual acts.

The variety and intensity of peak experiences that the automobile is capable of providing ensures it a continuing niche in the collective psyche of motorized societies. Some people, like Toad,* are turned on by the sense of power and speed that comes through driving. Others may see the car as both a sexy machine and an environment for sexual pleasures. Few people are indifferent to the sexual potential of the automobile or to its sexual symbolism. They may suppress their feelings, but behind the wheel of a car they are different people with different emotions and unique experiences. They are in enclosed worlds which, from the very early days of motoring history, have been associated

Is it? Could most men, let alone women, give such detailed analyses of their cars' functions? — G.H.

Symbolic mechanics? Marsh and Collett strain credulity here. Half the drivers in America don't even know what goes on inside an internal combustion engine. I know of no one, however, who thinks of electric cars as sexy. Hmmm. — J.R.

This is Pynchon's view—not a woman's view. How do they know it's accurate? — A.L.

How about seeing the car as a way to get around efficiently and, one hopes, safely? — A.L.

Toad: Mr. Toad, a character in Kenneth Grahame's *The Wind in the Willows* (1908) who is "the Terror of the Highways"

with pleasure and escape from the ties of the conformist world. For both men and women the car
has given, and will continue to give, both the stim-
ulus and the opportunity for thrills. Cars, speed,
mastery and sex are all ingredients of a recipe that
will ensure the survival of automobiles long after
their ostensible utility as efficient forms of transportation has completely vanished. When automobiles can no longer compete with other rapid public
transportation systems, perhaps then we will admit
its real function. When people have no excuse for
having a car, perhaps then we will own up to
the real passions and emotions that the 'insolent
chariots' instil. Gone then will be the techno-
babble of the manufacturers and their advertising
agents. Gone will be the contorted rationalizations
that people use in order to justify owning and driving a car. When the guilt and dishonesty have finally been driven out, perhaps then we might
confess that we knew all along what the Italians
mean by 'donne e motori—gioe e dolori'—'women
and cars—joys and tribulations'.

*I do like cars, but
I am not part of
the audience this
essay addresses,
one that essen-
tially equates
women and cars
as objects for
male pleasure.*
– A.L.

Afterwords

Are these guys serious?

*I'm afraid they are. And I must say I came away from this article about
cars and sex almost tempted to join in the game they are playing: find the sexual
symbolism and* WIN A PRIZE. UNCOVER HIDDEN MEANINGS EVERYWHERE.
BE AS SMART AS WE ARE! *But only "almost." Though Marsh and Collett get
carried away (to say the very least) here, they make one important point—but
miss an equally important one. Yes, cars as we know them carry sexual freight;
the nuances and the suggestions of sexuality are there and they are for the most
part intentional (marketing, marketing). But sexual imagery is part of many
other technologies—look at "plugs" and "receptacles," for instance, or the names
for other electrical apparatus or for the working parts of a printing press or a
typewriter—as well as many, many other things in our society. More important,
note how such imagery is used in our society, how it relates to an economy that
values and gives preference to certain attributes (almost always masculine) and
commodifies or sees as services other attributes (almost always feminine). Here
is the point Marsh and Collett miss, and probably on purpose, for it and the
serious questions it raises about how people treat one another in our society might*

spoil some of their fun. Guess I'll go get in my car, take a long drive in the country, and think that one over.   – A.L.

If you've never vectored a mountain curve in a topless roadster, downshifting into third, bringing up the revs to 4200, keeping off the brakes, snaking past lumbering Cutlass Cieras piloted by Walter Mittys, you can't begin to understand the pleasures of a fine automobile. Marsh and Collett insist that such kicks are ultimately sexual. I'm not convinced. I must confess that before I read "The Love Affair," it had never occurred to me that "In My Merry Oldsmobile" might be an R-rated tune. And no doubt, a car does increase the opportunities for sexual adventure and can sometimes serve for sexual display—the hot metal equivalent of a peacock's fan.

    But not every automotive pleasure is a sexual one. The guy who buys a Camaro to cruise the Dairy Queen misses five-eighths of his car's allure; the young woman who hopes an RX-7 will snare her a Tom Cruise had better expect a bumpy ride (and big payments). It is just possible that many people buy and even cherish their vehicles for something other than their sex appeal.   – J.R.

One hopes the authors did not receive a government grant to write this piece. Marsh and Collett go out of their way to attribute everything relating to automotives to sexual motives. But they have failed to address a significant point: many cars have zero sex appeal. As I screech to a stop two or three yards into an intersection—because the brakes on my '79 burnt orange Malibu don't work—I am not impelled to ponder the erotic.   – G.H.

QUESTIONING THE TEXT

1. What influences what kind of car you desire or buy? Is sexiness a factor? Explain in a paragraph or two.
2. Are people different when they get behind the wheel, as Marsh and Collett suggest? Do cars, indeed, make people more open to "peak experiences"? Better confine your response to your reading log.
3. Notice the words A.L. emphasizes using "regular" roman type (rather than italics) in her annotations of this reading. What do they convey about her reaction to the essay? Do they make her comments more— or less—convincing to you? Why?

MAKING CONNECTIONS

4. Does the selection from *On the Road* (p. 574) confirm or complicate the relationship between cars and sexuality sketched out by Marsh and Collett? Write a page explaining your answer.

5. Compare the stanzas from e.e.cummings's "she being Brand" that were quoted in this essay with Stephen Dunn's poem "The Sacred" (on p. 630). Write a short essay comparing the ways the two poems deal with car culture.

6. From the perspective on automobiles offered by Marsh and Collett, read the correspondence starting on p. 622 between the poet Marianne Moore and the Ford Motor Company. Then write a parody of their correspondence—imagine, for example, the names Marsh and Collett might have suggested to Ford.

JOINING THE CONVERSATION

7. Marsh and Collett assert that automobiles are symbols of masculinity. Do you regard that as an oversimplification? How might you construct a contrary argument—that automobiles have traits or qualities associated with women?

8. By focusing so much on the sexual character of the automobile, do Marsh and Collett in effect exaggerate it? Do most people really see their vehicles in sexual terms? Is the automobile inherently a sexual object, or is it just that songwriters, poets, painters, and novelists find sex in everything? Explore the subject in a short essay.

9. Marsh and Collett argue that automotive designs change to reflect "changing tastes in erotic symbols." Discuss this argument in class and then write a paper supporting or opposing it.

TONY KORNHEISER
Radio Daze

*J*ACK KEROUAC'S FAVORED MUSIC *in the early 1950s was bop, so in* On the Road *Dean Moriarity and Sal Paradise drive America in search of soulful black musicians. Less than a decade later, young Americans were all listening to rock and roll while cruising in low-riding Hudsons, customized Chevys, or T-bird convertibles. Tony Kornheiser's essay relives that era, brought to life most memorably, perhaps, in George Lucas's film* American Graffiti *(1973).*

Tony Kornheiser (b. 1948) is an award-winning journalist who has written for Sports Illustrated, Esquire, *and* The New York Times. *(He also appears on* ESPN.*) I chose this 1990 piece from* Life *magazine because it summarizes many themes introduced in this chapter, especially those that explain how the American car culture became the youth culture. I also feel a connection to the author; his writing helps me to recall my own coming of age in the sixties, right down to the details—our family car for a while was a white 1960 Ford Fairlane just like the one Kornheiser learned to back up in.*

And, psst, I'm one of those guys in wire-rims he describes driving a Miata today. No bow tie, however, and barely any hair. — J.R.

My father taught me to drive in our family car, a white 1960 Ford Fairlane as big and bulky as an offensive tackle. The first time he took me out, he had me ride shotgun while he drove to a junior high school parking lot. Just before he handed me the wheel, he told me his two inviolate rules of driving.

One: I would first learn to drive in reverse. He felt once I mastered going backward, going forward would be easy. So for hours at a time and for weeks at a stretch, I rolled backward around the lot. Only one person ever spent more time with a swiveled neck than me—the girl in *The Exorcist.*

Two: No radio. "I hate the stuff you listen to," my father said. "It's not music. It's garbage. You can't understand the words." So I sang him all the words. And he hated them.

When I finally got my own car, I told my father I had only one rule: He wasn't allowed in it.

We are the freest nation in the world but not the most liberated— 128 years after the Bill of Rights we still hadn't given women the vote. The American popular culture in the 1700s was about men and revolution. In the 1800s it was about men and six-guns. Now it's about men and cars. If you want to see ground zero of American pop culture, go outside any sunny weekend day and look at the men proudly washing and waxing their cars. What wine is to France, what electronics are to Japan, cars are to America.

What do you drive, and how fast does it go? Men believe the kind of car they drive influences how others perceive them: their cars are extensions of their selves, says Michael Marsden, professor of popular culture at Bowling Green State University. As a symbol the car represents freedom, vitality and masculinity. For a man, the sensual pleasure of getting in and driving a car—controlling the thrust of the car—is unmistakably similar to seducing a woman. It's no coincidence that men commonly refer to their cars as "she."

Postwar America was unquestionably the richest and most powerful nation on earth. Our men were the strongest. Our cars were the biggest, the longest, the best. Their big fins and never-ending chrome—Detroit's Freudian version of the big cigar and the diamond pinkie ring—were symbols of our global supremacy. So what if they guzzled gas? We had money enough to buy all the gas we needed. To the victors belonged the spoils.

America's perceived decline in the late 1970s and '80s parallels the sudden rejection of American cars by American consumers. We still loved cars, we just stopped loving *our* cars. They were too big and cluttered, too profligate, unresponsive to an ecoconscious, downsize environment. Our entrepreneurs switched from Caddys and Lincolns to Mercedes and BMWs. Our insurance agents switched from Oldsmobiles and Buicks to Volvos and Mazdas. Our workers switched from Fords and Chevys to Toyotas and Hondas. The sad truth was, we didn't make the best cars anymore. Europe and Japan did. Reagan tried to jolly us out of our inferiority complex, but there weren't enough Grenadas to sweeten the bitter taste that we had to go elsewhere for the most important single symbol of American pop culture, the automobile.

It could be worse—they could make 'em without radios. At least the foreign manufacturers have been briefed to appreciate the critical relationship between the radio and the American male driver.* If having a car was the most important thing in life, playing the radio loud was the signature act of having a car.

The car gave you mobility, and therefore freedom.   10

The radio gave you identity.

It was rock and roll that cemented the car to the pop culture. Prior to the 1950s the car was still a luxury, inaccessible to many Americans. But as the postwar economy prospered, more families could afford cars. Through a serendipitous coincidence, cars became common at the same time rock and roll developed—teen music for teen drivers.

---

the critical relationship . . . driver: For another expression of this relationship, see the poem by Stephen Dunn, "The Sacred," on p. 630.

Because he lived at home, under his parents' roof and rules, the only sense of independence a teenager felt was in his car. A car was his apartment and his sanctuary. One of the earliest rock stars, Chuck Berry, understood it. In "Maybellene," Berry breathlessly describes finally overtaking his randy girlfriend's Cadillac Coupe de Ville in his V-8 Ford, leaving little doubt what the conquest symbolized. Berry's notorious double entendre was never sharper than in "No Particular Place to Go" when he whined, "Can you imagine the way I felt? I couldn't unfasten her safety belt."

Although teenagers have long had to contend with bucket seats—the introduction of the Ford Mustang in 1964 firmly relocated prone sex to the rear bench seat—trysting in the car is eternally celebrated in rock lyrics. In "Taxi," Harry Chapin brags, "We learned about love in the back of a Dodge." Bob Seger practiced his night moves "out in the back seat of my '60 Chevy." Bruce Springsteen pants, "Honey, I just wonder what it feels like in the back of your pink Cadillac, pink Cadillac." Perhaps the most articulated vision of teenage lust in a car is Meat Loaf's beatific "Paradise by the Dashboard Light."

Cars carried such universal stature in teenage culture that many early rock groups named themselves after what they drove—or wished to drive: the Impalas, the Fleetwoods, the Cadillacs, the El Dorados. (More recently we have the Cars, whose best-known lyric is ironically self-serving: "Who's gonna drive you home tonight?") In the 1960s, following on the heels of the southern California Surf Sound, a distinct car music became the vogue. The Surf Sound often mentioned cars as the means to get to the ocean: Jan and Dean owned "a '34 wagon, and we call it a woody" in "Surf City," and the Trade Winds bemoaned, "My woody's outside, covered with snow, nowhere to go now. New York's a lonely town, when you're the only surfer boy around." Car music was dominated by the quintessential American band, the Beach Boys, with songs such as "Little Deuce Coupe," "409," "Shut Down," "Fun, Fun, Fun" and their haunting boy-loves-car-and-girl chordal, "Don't Worry Baby."

A darker side of the '60s Car Sound surfaced in the splinter group of tunes devoted to a car crash sound. The fascination with speed and danger that had defined teen car culture since *Rebel Without a Cause* went hurtling headlong over the cliff with such necrophiliac hits as "Dead Man's Curve," "Teen Angel," "Leader of the Pack" and "Last Kiss." I remember feeling eerie behind the wheel singing along with these songs. But I still drove as fast as I could because I felt I owed it to my times. What was the worst that could happen? That I'd explode in a flaming fireball with my girl's ring around my neck and the sweet aftertaste of her kiss still fresh on my lips? What a romantic, glorious way to go, speeding into a hot summer night. They'd write songs about me, like the Beach Boys' "Spirit of America." I'd live in their hearts forever.

On the first real day of spring, that day when for the first time in months you go outside in the early morning to pick up the paper and you feel the unfamiliar warmth of the sun on your bare arms and instinctively begin humming, "Little darlin', it's been a long, cold, lonely winter,"* on that day, I announced to my wife of 19 years that I wanted to drive to the beach.

"By yourself?" she asked.

"Unless you and the kids want to go."

"I have work to do, and the kids have school," she said.   20

"So we'll take them out of school for the day."

She gave me a look like I was hopeless. "You're 40 years old," she scolded. "You can't drive to the beach whenever you feel like it."

"Why not?" I said. I thought back to high school on Long Island, how on the first warm day we'd pile into cars at lunchtime, seven or eight of us to a car, throw the tops down and head out to the beach. I rode in my pal Matt's Bonneville 305. Matt was on an Andy Granatelli* scholarship; the only people who burned more rubber than Matt worked for Union Carbide. It was a 25-minute shot to the Atlantic Ocean. Matt made it in 15. "Help Me, Rhonda" was on the radio. It's 25 years, and I can't drive along a shoreline without hearing "Help Me, Rhonda" in my head.

"Look, I need to be riding in a convertible with the top down and the Beach Boys cranked up," I told my wife. "I need to go to the beach. I'm renting a car."

"This is Washington, D.C.," she said. "The closest beach is four hours   25 away. In four hours it could be winter again."

"I'll take the chance."

"Fine," she said. "Be a madman. But if you actually do rent a convertible, wear a hat. The doctor warned you about getting sun on your head."

"I wasn't bald in high school," I informed her.

"You didn't own a convertible either," she said.

O.K., so this is a crisis, right? This is the point where I feel my   30 youth falling away, disappearing into some terrifying black hole, and I have nothing to look forward to but the gulag of arthritic bones and small ducklike steps, so I begin this last-chance frantic search for some connection to youth. It's not the experiences I want to trade, it's only the years. If there really was a fountain of youth, how many of us wouldn't sign up with Ponce de León for the cruise?

I'm a typical American male entering middle age. I have a wife and two kids, own my own home. I drive a safe, dependable car with four

---

"Little darlin', . . . winter": a lyric from the Beatles' song "Here Comes the Sun," from the album *Abbey Road.*

Andy Granatelli (b. 1923): American entrepreneur and automotive enthusiast

doors. I would like to push my safe, dependable four-door car over a cliff and watch it explode.

I don't want a Volvo station wagon. No man does. Women buy that car. A man doesn't care about staying alive in a car: a man cares about feeling alive in a car. I don't want a van. I would rather eat poison than drive a Little League team to the Pizza Hut. I don't want a Honda Accord for the same reason I don't want a Ford Taurus or an Olds Cutlass—deliver me from the ordinary. I don't want a BMW or a Mercedes, either, particularly that idiotic baby Mercedes people buy so others will assume they're rich when what others really assume is that you are a goat.

I want a Miata.

I want a convertible. I don't care about the color—red is fine, blue is fine, white is fine. I want to take it out on an open road, put the top down, turn the radio up to blast-off and go just as fast as I can.

I see men driving to work in their Miatas. I see them in their bow   35
ties and their wire-rimmed glasses, with their hair deftly parted down the middle. I close my eyes and see them in '57 T-birds and '64 Mustangs. They are forever young. The sky is blue, the air is clean, and whoever drives such a car will stay young forever. I will do what it takes. I will buy glasses and bow ties. I will get a hair transplant.

I need this car.

QUESTIONING THE TEXT

1. Is Kornheiser being sexist in suggesting that American popular culture today is about "men and cars"? Why, or why not?
2. Does this essay have a thesis? If so, what do you think it is?
3. Kornheiser wants a Miata. What kind of car do you want, and what does your choice suggest about your personality—if anything? Make an entry in your reading log, if you are keeping one.
4. J.R. writes his introduction from the perspective of someone from the "baby boom" generation. How might the introduction differ if it had been written by someone born after 1970?

MAKING CONNECTIONS

5. Do middle-aged and older Americans look back so fondly to the 1950s and 1960s because of problems today, or is nostalgia just inevitable? Use the Kornheiser piece as a springboard for your thinking on this subject, reflecting, too, on the nostalgic role the VW van plays in Steven Spence's "The Van of Aquarius" (p. 584).
6. Kornheiser's essay repeats many of the themes in the previous reading,

Peter Marsh and Peter Collett's "The Love Affair," but these pieces are clearly written for different reasons and different audiences. In a brief paper, explain the nature of these differences.

7. Does the selection from Jack Kerouac's *On the Road* (p. 574) give you a different perspective on the past than does Kornheiser's piece? Write a short paper explaining any differences.

JOINING THE CONVERSATION

8. If you are younger than thirty, write a reaction to the last part of "Radio Daze," in which Kornheiser describes how a convertible might bring back his youth. Can you imagine writing such a piece ten or twenty years from now? What objects from contemporary popular culture might you recall as fondly as Kornheiser remembers Bonnevilles, T-birds, and Mustangs?

9. Interview two people from a generation other than your own. Ask them what they recall most vividly about their youth and what made (or makes) their growing up distinctive. Use the answers to write a short paper describing that generation.

10. Working with one or two classmates, spend half an hour in a video store making a list of all the films you can find with cars either mentioned in their titles or featured on the cassette boxes. When you've completed your survey, try drawing some conclusions about the role the automobile plays in American popular culture. Report your findings jointly in a short informal essay.

BAILEY WHITE
Someday the Old Junker Will Be a Neat Car Again

NOT EVERYONE REGARDS THE AUTOMOBILE as a dream machine or the open road as a mythic path to Oz. People like Bailey White, the author of the following article, drive cars to get places and do things. They treat their cars like appliances and don't ask much more than that they run. Henry Ford would have understood.

Yet even White cherishes her old car. She couldn't write about it in such affectionate detail if she didn't. I especially like it when she mentions driving the car to the funeral of an uncle who ten years earlier had advised her against buying it. That's poetic justice.

Many of us think that we can't write well unless we have an abstract or serious issue to address. But watch how effortlessly White finds a story in her small subject. She makes her point just by paying attention to the textures of life—the sound of a windshield wiper, the remarks of her friends, the smell of brake fluid.

White (b. 1950) is a first-grade teacher in southern Georgia, where she lives in the house where she was born. Her essays and stories have appeared in a number of magazines, and she is a regular commentator on National Public Radio's show All Things Considered. *Her writing has been collected in* Mama Makes Up Her Mind *(1993).*

Smithsonian *magazine is one of my favorite periodicals, and the place I always turn to first is the last page, where each issue wraps up with a short, personal essay. I was delighted in 1991 to find this funny and thoughtful article there, and I offer it here as a tribute to all the normal people, my co-editor included, for whom a car is just a car. — J.R.*

It really makes you feel your age when you get a letter from your insurance agent telling you that the car you bought, only slightly used, the year you got out of college is now an antique. "Beginning with your next payment, your premiums will reflect this change in classification," the letter said.

I went out and looked at the car. I thought back over the years. I could almost hear my uncle's disapproving voice. "You should never buy a used car," he had told me the day I brought it home. Ten years later I drove that used car to his funeral. I drove my sister to the hospital in that car to have her first baby, and I drove to Atlanta in that car when the baby graduated from Georgia Tech with a degree in physics.

"When are you going to get a new car?" my friends asked me.
"I don't need a new car," I said. "This car runs fine."

I changed the oil often, and I kept good tires on it. It always got me   5
where I wanted to go. But the stuffing came out of the backseat and the
springs poked through, and the dashboard disintegrated. At 300,000 miles
the odometer quit turning, but I didn't really care to know how far I had
driven. A hole wore in the floor where my heel rested in front of the
accelerator, and the insulation all peeled off the fire wall. "Old piece of
junk," my friends whispered. The seat-belt catch finally wore out, and I
tied on a huge bronze hook with a fireman's knot.

Then one day on my way to work, the car coughed, sputtered and
stopped. "This is it," I thought, and I gave it a pat. "It's been a good car."

The mechanic laughed at me. "You know what's wrong with that
car?" he asked. "That car is out of gas." So I slopped some gas in the tank
and drove ten more years.

The fuel gauge never worked again after that, but I got to where I
could tell when the gas was low by the smell. I think it was the smell of
the bottom of the tank. There was also a little smell of brake fluid, a little
smell of exhaust, a little smell of oil and, after all the years, a little smell
of me. Car smells.

And sounds. The wonderful sound when the engine finally catches
on a cold day, and an ominous *tick tick* in July when the radiator is working
too hard. The windshield wipers said "Gracie Allen Gracie Allen Gracie
Allen." I didn't like a lot of conversation in the car, because I had to keep
listening for a little skip that meant I needed to jump out and adjust the
carburetor. I kept a screwdriver close at hand, and a pint of brake fluid and
a new rotor, just in case. "She's strange," my friends whispered. "And she
drives so slow."

I don't know how fast I drove. The speedometer had quit working   10
years ago. But when I would look down* through the hole in the floor and
see the pavement, a gray blur, whizzing by just inches away from my feet,
and feel the tremendous heat from the internal-combustion engine pouring
back through the fire wall into my lap, and hear each barely contained
explosion, just as a heart attack victim is able to hear her own heartbeat, it
didn't feel like slow to me. A whiff of brake fluid would remind me just
what a tiny thing I was relying on to stop myself from hurtling along the
surface of the Earth at an unnatural speed. When I arrived at my destination,
I would slump back, unfasten the seat-belt hook with trembling hands and

---

But when I would look down . . . .: Compare the description of the sensation of riding
in a fast car in this paragraph with the one in *On the Road* (starting on p. 574).

stagger out. I would gather up my things and give the car a last look. "Thank you, sir," I would say. "We got here one more time."

But after I received that letter I began thinking about buying a new car. I read the newspaper every night. Finally I found one that sounded good. It was the same make as my car, but almost new. "Call Steve," the ad said. I went to see the car. It was parked in Steve's driveway. It was a fashionable wheat color. There was carpet on the floor and the seats were covered with soft, velvety-feeling stuff. It smelled like acrylic, and vinyl, and Steve. I turned a knob. Mozart's Concerto for Flute and Harp poured out of four speakers. "But how can you listen to the engine with music playing?" I asked Steve.

I turned the key. The car started instantly. I fastened my seat belt. Nothing but a click. Steve got in the passenger seat, and we went for a test drive. We floated down the road. I couldn't hear a sound, but I decided it must be time to shift gears. I stomped around on the floor and grabbed Steve's knee before I remembered the car had automatic transmission.

"You mean you just put it in 'Drive' and drive?" I asked. Steve scrunched himself against his door and clamped his knees together. He tested his seat belt. "Have you ever driven before?" he asked.

I bought it. I rolled all the windows up by mashing a button beside my elbow, set the air-conditioning on "Recirc" and listened to Vivaldi all the way home.

So now I have two cars. I call them my new car and my real car.   15 Most of the time I drive my new car. But on some days I go out to the barn and get in my real car. I shoo the rats out of the backseat and crank up the engine. Even without daily practice my hands and feet know just what to do. My ears perk up, and I sniff the air. I add a little brake fluid, a little water. I sniff again. It'll need gas next week, and an oil change. I back it out and we roll down the road. People stop and look. They smile. "Neat car!" they say.

QUESTIONING THE TEXT

1. Mark all the places where White uses dialogue in her essay. What functions does it serve? Do you find her use of dialogue effective?
2. Does any single sentence in the essay summarize the point you believe White wants to make? If so, which sentence? If not, why not?
3. White seems charmingly eccentric in this piece because she controls the narrative and that's how she portrays herself. Can you imagine the story of this particular car and driver told from other perspectives? What might they be?

4. J.R. mentions in his introduction that *Smithsonian* is one of his favorite magazines. What are some of yours? What can you tell about a person from the magazines he or she reads? Speculate in your reading log, if you are keeping one.

MAKING CONNECTIONS

5. Imagine a dialogue on driving among Jack Kerouac, Marianne Moore (the author of the next reading), and Bailey White. Would they have much to say to one another? Do they live in different cultures? Write a portion of that dialogue.
6. This essay is as much about the driver as the car. What do you learn about the author from the way she treats her old car and the people who comment upon it? Are any other readings in this chapter also about drivers as much as vehicles?

JOINING THE CONVERSATION

7. Using White's essay as a model, tell the story of a vehicle you have owned or driven.
8. Would it be fair to suggest that White's essay represents a woman's view of the automobile? Discuss that suggestion with two or three classmates, and then write individual position papers about one page long on the subject.

MARIANNE MOORE
Correspondence with the Ford Motor Company

IN HER ELEGANT POETRY, Marianne Moore (1887–1972) always makes every word count. In one of her best-known poems, for instance, Moore identifies poetry as the kind of verse that presents "imaginary gardens with real toads in them."

In the series of letters that follows, Moore's words were directed at an unusual audience—the Ford Motor Company. Invited by Ford's Special Products Division in 1955 to contribute a name for a new car that would capture "some visceral feeling of elegance, fleetness, advanced features and design," Moore put her considerable imaginative powers to the task, offering such possibilities as the Ford Silver Sword or the Anticipator. According to a major advertising trade publication, Ford spent over $350 million in creating and promoting the product for which Moore contributed potential names. What an irony to realize that the car turned out to be the Edsel—one of the most spectacular marketing failures in the history of American business.

I chose this correspondence because it points up "what's in a name," because it suggests that behind the leisure-time driving habits of America lies a vast money-making empire, and because I simply like imagining Marianne Moore, one of my favorite poets, writing these witty letters and thinking up these zany names! In my interpretation, Moore's letters have a mischievous tongue-in-cheek quality to them. What do you think? — A.L.

October 19, 1955

Miss Marianne Moore,
Cumberland Street,
Brooklyn 5, New York

Dear Miss Moore:

This is a morning we find ourselves with a problem which, strangely enough, is more in the field of words and the fragile meaning of words than in car-making. And we just wonder whether you might be intrigued with it sufficiently to lend us a hand.

Our dilemma is a name for a rather important new series of cars.

We should like this name to be more than a label. Specifically, we should like it to have a compelling quality in itself and by itself. To convey, through association or other conjuration, some visceral feeling of elegance, fleetness, advanced features and design. A name, in short, that flashes a dramatically desirable picture in people's minds. (Another "Thunderbird" would be fine.)

Over the past few weeks this office has confected a list of three hundred–odd candidates, which, it pains me to relate, are characterized by an embarrassing pedestrianism. We are miles short of our ambition. And so we are seeking the help of one who knows more about this sort of magic than we.

As to how we might go about this matter, I have no idea. But, in any event, all would depend on whether you find this overture of some challenge and interest.

Should we be so fortunate as to have piqued your fancy, we will be pleased to write more fully. And, of course, it is expected that our relations will be on a fee basis of an impeccably dignified kind.

> Respectfully,
>
> David Wallace
> *Special Products Division*

October 21, 1955

Let me take it under advisement, Mr. Wallace. I am complimented to be recruited in this high matter.

I have seen and admired "Thunderbird" as a Ford designation. It would be hard to match; but let me, the coming week, talk with my brother, who would bring ardor and imagination to bear on the quest.

> Sincerely yours,
>
> Marianne Moore

October 27, 1955

Dear Mr. Wallace:

My brother thought most of the names I had considered suggesting to you for your new series too learned or too labored, but thinks I might ask if any of the following approximate the requirements:

THE FORD SILVER SWORD

This plant, of which the flower is a silver sword, I believe grows only on the Hawaiian Island Maui, on Mount Haleakala (House of the Sun); found at an altitude of from 9,500 to 10,000 feet. (The leaves—silver-white—surrounding the individual blossoms—have a pebbled texture that feels like Italian-twist backstitch allover embroidery.)

My first thought was of a bird series—the swallow species—Hirundo, or, phonetically, Aerundo. Malvina Hoffman is designing a device for the radiator of a made-to-order Cadillac, and said in her opinion the only term surpassing Thunderbird would be hurricane; and I then thought Hurricane Hirundo might be the first of a series such as Hurricane Aquila (eagle), Hurricane Accipiter (hawk), and so on. A species that takes its dinner on the wing ("swifts").

If these suggestions are not in character with the car, perhaps you could give me a sketch of its general appearance, or hint as to some of its exciting potentialities—though my brother reminds me that such information is highly confidential.

Sincerely yours,

Marianne Moore

November 4, 1955

Dear Miss Moore:

I'm delighted that your note implies that you are interested in helping us in our naming problem.

This being so, procedures in this rigorous business world dictate that we on this end at least document a formal arrangement with provision for a suitable fee or honorarium before pursuing the problem further.

One way might be for you to suggest a figure which could be considered for mutual acceptance. Once this is squared away, we will look forward to having you join us in the continuation of our fascinating search.

Sincerely,

David Wallace
Special Products Division

November 7, 1955

Dear Mr. Wallace:

It is handsome of you to consider remuneration for service merely enlisted. My fancy would be inhibited, however, by acknowledgment in advance of performance. If I could be of specific assistance, we could no doubt agree on some kind of honorarium for the service rendered.

I seem to exact participation; but if you could tell me how the suggestions submitted strayed—if obviously—from the ideal, I could then perhaps proceed more nearly in keeping with the Company's objective.

Sincerely yours,

Marianne Moore

November 11, 1955

Dear Miss Moore:

Our office philodendron has just benefitted from an extra measure of water as, pacing about, I have sought words to respond to your recent generous note. Let me state my quandary thus. It is unspeakably contrary to procedure to accept counsel—even needed counsel—without a firm prior agreement of conditions (and, indeed, to follow the letter of things, without a Purchase Notice in quadruplicate and three Competitive Bids). But then, seldom has the auto business had occasion to indulge in so ethereal a matter as this. So, if you will risk a mutually satisfactory outcome with us, we should like to honor your wish for a fancy unencumbered.

As to wherein your earlier suggestions may have "strayed," as you put it—they did not at all. Shipment No. 1 was fine, and we would like to luxuriate in more of same—even those your brother regarded as overlearned or labored. For us to impose an ideal on your efforts would, I fear, merely defeat our purpose. We have sought your help to get an approach quite different from our own. In short, we should like suggestions that we ourselves would not have arrived at. And, in sober fact, have not.

Now we on this end must help you by sending some tangible representation of what we are talking about. Perhaps the enclosed sketches will serve the purpose. They are not IT, but they convey the feeling. At the very least, they may give you a sense of participation should your friend Malvina Hoffman break into brisk conversation on radiator caps.

> Sincerely yours,
>
> David Wallace
> *Special Products Division*

November 13, 1955

Dear Mr. Wallace:

The sketches. They are indeed exciting; they have quality, and the toucan tones lend tremendous allure—confirmed by the wheels. Half the magic—sustaining effects of this kind. Looked at upside down, furthermore, there is a sense of fish buoyancy. Immediately your word "impeccable" sprang to mind. Might it be a possibility? The Impeccable. In any case, the baguette lapidary glamour you have achieved certainly spurs the imagination. Car-innovation is like launching a ship—"drama."

I am by no means sure that I can help you to the right thing, but performance with elegance casts a spell. Let me do some thinking in the direction of impeccable, symmechromatic, thunderblender. . . . (The exotics, if I can shape them a little.) Dearborn might come into one.

If the sketches should be returned at once, let me know. Otherwise, let me dwell on them for a time. I am, may I say, a trusty confidante.

I thank you for realizing that under contract esprit could not flower. You owe me nothing, specific or moral.

> Sincerely,
>
> Marianne Moore

November 19, 1955

Some other suggestions, Mr. Wallace, for the phenomenon:

THE RESILIENT BULLET
or Intelligent Bullet
or Bullet Cloisonné or Bullet Lavolta

(I have always had a fancy for THE INTELLIGENT WHALE—the little first Navy submarine, shaped like a sweet potato; on view in our Brooklyn Yard.)

THE FORD FABERGE

(That there is also a perfume Fabergé seems to me to do no harm, for here allusion is to the original silversmith.)

THE ARC-en-CIEL (the rainbow) ARCENCIEL?

Please do not feel that memoranda from me need acknowledgment. I am not working day and night for you; I feel that etymological hits are partially accidental.

The bullet idea has possibilities, it seems to me, in connection with Mercury (with Hermes and Hermes Trismegistus) and magic (white magic).

Sincerely,

Marianne Moore

November 28, 1955

Dear Mr. Wallace:

MONGOOSE CIVIQUE

ANTICIPATOR

REGNA RACER (couronne à couronne) sovereign to sovereign

AEROTERRE

Fée Rapide (Aérofée, Aéro Faire, Fée Aiglette, Magi-faire) Comme Il Faire

Tonnerre Alifère (winged thunder)

Aliforme Alifère (wing-slender, a-wing)

TURBOTORC (used as an adjective by Plymouth)

THUNDERBIRD Allié (Cousin Thunderbird)

THUNDER CRESTER

DEARBORN Diamante

MAGIGRAVURE

PASTELOGRAM

I shall be returning the sketches very soon.

M.M.

December 6, 1955

Dear Mr. Wallace:

Regina-rex

Taper Racer   Taper Acer

Varsity Stroke

Angelastro

Astranaut

Chaparral

Tir à l'arc (bull's eye)

Cresta Lark

Triskelion (three legs running)

Pluma Piluma (hairfine, feather-foot)

Andante con Moto (description of a good motor?)

My findings thin, so I terminate them and am returning the sketches. Two principles I have not been able to capture: 1, the topknot of the peacock and topnotcher of speed. 2, the swivel-axis (emphasized elsewhere), like the Captain's bed on the whaleship, Charles Morgan—balanced so that it levelled whatever the slant of the ship.

If I stumble on a hit, you shall have it. Anything so far has been pastime. Do not ponder appreciation, Mr. Wallace. That was embodied in the sketches.

M.M.

I cannot resist the temptation to disobey my brother and submit

TURCOTINGA (turquoise cotinga—the cotinga being a South-American finch or sparrow) solid indigo.

(I have a three-volume treatise on flowers that might produce something but the impression given should certainly be unlabored.)

December 8, 1955

Mr. Wallace:

May I submit UTOPIAN TURTLE-TOP? Do not trouble to answer unless you like it.

Marianne Moore

December 23, 1955

MERRY CHRISTMAS TO OUR FAVORITE TURTLETOPPER.

David Wallace

December 26, 1955

Dear Mr. Wallace:

An aspiring turtle is certain to glory in spiral eucalyptus, white pine straight from the forest, and innumerable scarlet roses almost too tall for close inspection. Of a temperament susceptible to shock though one may be, to be treated like royalty could not but induce sensations unprecedented august.

Please know that a carfancyer's allegiance to the Ford automotive turtle—extending from the Model T Dynasty to the Wallace Utopian Dynasty—can never waver; impersonal gratitude surely becoming infinite when made personal. Gratitude to unmiserly Mr. Wallace and his idealistic associates.

Marianne Moore

November 8, 1956

Dear Miss Moore:

Because you were so kind to us in our early days of looking for a suitable name, I feel a deep obligation to report on events that have ensued.

And I feel I must do so before the public announcement of same come Monday, November 19.

We have chosen a name out of the more than six thousand–odd candidates that we gathered. It fails somewhat of the resonance, gaiety, and zest we were seeking. But it has a personal dignity and meaning to many of us here. Our name, dear Miss Moore, is—Edsel.

I hope you will understand.

Cordially,

David Wallace
Special Products Division

QUESTIONING THE TEXT

1. Make a list of four or five words Moore uses that are unfamiliar to you. Look up their meanings and bring your list to class for discussion.
2. What do you think David Wallace's attitude toward Moore is? How do you know?
3. A.L.'s introduction says that she reads Moore's letters as having a "tongue-in-cheek" tone. Do you agree? How would you describe their tone? What parts of the letters best reveal that tone?

MAKING CONNECTIONS

4. Would any of the names Moore suggests be appropriate for the RV described by Marilyn Murphy at the beginning of "Roam Sweet Home" (p. 592) or for the Cadillac in *On the Road* (p. 574)? What would be particularly appropriate about the name(s)? What other names might you suggest, and why?
5. Do any of the names Moore suggests carry sexual connotations or overtures? Which ones, and why? What support, if any, do these names provide for the claims made by Peter Marsh and Peter Collett in "The Love Affair" (starting on p. 599)? Jot down some notes in response to these questions, and bring them to class for discussion.

JOINING THE CONVERSATION

6. Reread David Wallace's last letter to Moore. Then consider ways to revise it, making it perhaps more appreciative. Or imagine that Wallace had written to Moore after the spectacular failure of the Edsel. Revise the letter accordingly.

7. Working with two or three classmates, gather all the names you can of cars currently on the American market. (Check *Consumer Reports*'s annual automobile edition and other magazines devoted to cars and/or driving.) Are any names Moore suggested—or any similar ones— now in use? Pool your information and see if you can find ways to categorize the names of cars (planets or stars, for instance, as opposed to numbers and animals). Then brainstorm about what these patterns symbolize and prepare a 15-minute report to your class on "What's in a Name—in Contemporary Cars."

STEPHEN DUNN
The Sacred

ED MADDEN, WHOSE OWN POEM concludes Chapter 9, suggested "The Sacred" as an appropriate work to summarize what the car culture can mean today. I think it is an excellent choice. Elsewhere in this book, we include a selection from Virginia Woolf's "A Room of One's Own." For some people, many of them young, that necessary private place is the car.

To me, a car is most mysterious and wonderful when one is driving just before dawn, with the instruments on the dash still aglow, the radio silent, and the horizon slowly brightening with the promise of an endless highway. There is something sacred in that prospect.

"The Sacred" appears in Stephen Dunn's volume of poetry Between Angels *(1989). Dunn (b. 1939) writes and teaches poetry. His most recent work, however, is the book of essays* Walking Light *(1993).* — J.R.

After the teacher asked if anyone had
   a sacred place
and the students fidgeted and shrank

in their chairs, the most serious of them all
   said it was his car,   5
being in it alone, his tape deck playing

things he'd chosen, and others knew the truth
   had been spoken
and begin speaking about their rooms,

their hiding places, but the car kept coming up,   10
   the car in motion,
music filling it, and sometimes one other person

who understood the bright altar of the dashboard
   and how far away
a car could take him from the need   15

to speak, or to answer, the key
   in having a key
and putting it in, and going.

IN RESPONSE

1. Does "The Sacred," though published in 1989, in any way help explain *On the Road* to you? To which work do you feel closer?
2. Why do you think the students are reluctant at first to answer their teacher's question? If you are keeping a reading log, record the answer you would have given the teacher and explain why.
3. Why do the students insist that the car, as their hiding place, be moving and its radio playing?
4. What may Dunn be suggesting about the role now played by religion in our culture? Write an essay defining what we seem to mean now by the term "sacred." Would any earlier period have applied it to a material object like the automobile?
5. A.L. suggested that in contrast to this poem, the essay by Peter Marsh and Peter Collett (p. 599) might be titled "The Profane." How do the attitudes toward cars expressed in the two readings differ? Are there any points of similarity between seeing cars as religious spaces or objects and seeing them as sexual or romantic ones?

OTHER READINGS

Bryson, Bill. "Road Scholars." *Esquire* June 1990: 118–27. Describes the people and philosophy behind the Morgan, a British car virtually unchanged since 1936.

Collier, Peter, and David Horowitz. *The Fords: An American Epic*. New York: Summit, 1987. Chronicles one of the most important American families of the twentieth century.

Hazleton, Lesley. *Confessions of a Fast Woman*. Reading, MA: Addison-Wesley, 1992. Tells a story about "transcending gender boundaries in search of experience."

Iacocca, Lee. *Iacocca: An Autobiography*. Toronto: Bantam, 1984. Explains how Iacocca invented the Mustang, created the Pinto, was fired from Ford, and then saved Chrysler. Whew!

King, Stephen. *Christine*. New York: Signet, 1983. Proves that a boy's best friend probably isn't his red 1958 Plymouth Fury.

Least Heat Moon, William. *Blue Highways: A Journey into America*. Boston: Little, 1982. Presents the United States as seen from its back roads.

Lewis, David L., and Laurence Goldstein. *The Automobile and American Culture*. Ann Arbor: U of Michigan P, 1983. Presents a wide range of views about the American car.

Thelma and Louise. Dir. Ridley Scott. MGM, 1991. Portrays two women on the road from an arguably feminist perspective.

Tignor, Samuel, and Davey Warren. "Driver Speed Behavior on US Streets and Highways." *Car and Driver* May 1991: 93. Seeks to prove scientifically that speed limits on most American highways are set too low.

Williams, Heathcote. *Autogeddon*. London: Jonathan Cape, 1991. Severely criticizes car culture as seen through the eyes of an alien who comes to Earth every few centuries to see what has changed.

Wolkomir, Richard. "Big Boys, Big Toys, and the Perfect Hot Rod." *Smithsonian* July 1993: 50–58. Evokes "a time when cars were cars and men were, to put it mildly, nuts about them."

Yates, Brock. *The Decline & Fall of the American Automobile Industry*. New York: Random-Vintage, 1983. Provides an accurate reading of problems that later almost kayoed Detroit in the late 1980s.

Acknowledgments (continued from page iv)

Allan Bloom. "The Student and the University" from *The Closing of the American Mind* by Allan Bloom. Copyright © 1987 by Allan Bloom. Reprinted by permission of Simon & Schuster, Inc.

Robert Bly. From *Iron John*, © 1990 by Addison-Wesley Publishing Company, Inc. Reprinted with permission of the publisher.

Anthony Brandt. "Do Kids Need Religion?" Originally appeared in *Parenting* magazine, December 1987. Reprinted by permission of the author.

Joe Bob Briggs. From *Iron Joe Bob* by Joe Bob Briggs. Copyright © 1992 by John Bloom. Used by permission of the Atlantic Monthly Press.

Gwendolyn Brooks. "We Real Cool" by Gwendolyn Brooks © 1991. Published in *Blacks,* Third World Press, Chicago.

Linda Chavez. Excerpt from *Out of the Barrio* by Linda Chavez. Copyright © 1991 by BasicBooks, A Division of HarperCollins Publishers Inc. Reprinted by permission of HarperCollins Publishers Inc.

Karen Cooper. "A Native Woman—1982" from *A Gathering of Spirit, A Collection by North American Indian Women,* edited by Beth Brant. Copyright © 1984 by Karen Cooper. Used by permission of Firebrand Books, Ithaca, New York.

Ossie Davis. "Our Shining Black Prince" and "Why I Eulogized Malcolm X." From *Malcolm X—The Man and His Times*. Reprinted by permission of The Artists Agency.

Joan Didion. "On Going Home" from *Slouching Towards Bethlehem* by Joan Didion. Copyright © 1967, 1968 by Joan Didion. Reprinted by permission of Farrar, Straus & Giroux, Inc.

Stephen Dunn. "The Sacred" is reprinted from *Between Angels, Poems by Stephen Dunn,* by permission of W.W. Norton & Company, Inc. Copyright © 1989 by Stephen Dunn.

Freeman J. Dyson. "Engineers' Dreams" from *Infinite in All Directions* by Freeman Dyson. Copyright © 1988 by Freeman Dyson. Reprinted by permission of HarperCollins Publishers.

Terry Eastland. "Rush Limbaugh: Talking Back" from *The American Spectator,* September 1992. Reprinted by permission.

Jill Frawley. "Inside the Home." Reprinted from *Mother Jones* magazine, © 1991, Foundation for National Progress.

George Gallup, Jr., and Jim Castelli. Reprinted with the permission of Macmillan Publishing Company from *The People's Religion: American Faith in the 90's* by George Gallup, Jr., and Jim Castelli. Copyright © 1989 by George Gallup, Jr., and Jim Castelli.

Ellen Goodman. From *At Large* by Ellen Goodman. Copyright © 1981 by The Washington Post Company. Reprinted by permission of Summit Books, a division of Simon & Schuster, Inc.

Judy Grahn. "The Marilyn Monroe Poem" from *The Work of a Common Woman: Collected Poetry (1964–1977)*. Copyright © 1978 by Judy Grahn. Reprinted by permission of The Crossing Press, publisher.

Daniel Grossman. "Neo-Luddites: Don't Just Say Yes to Technology." Copyright 1990 by Daniel Grossman. Reprinted by permission of the author.

Will Herberg. From *Protestant Catholic Jew* by Will Herberg. Copyright © 1955 by Will Herberg. Used by permission of Doubleday, a division of Bantam Doubleday Dell Publishing Group, Inc.

bell hooks. "Keeping Close to Home" from *Talking Back: Thinking Feminist, Think-*

Index

637